DAT* LESSON BOOK

Special thanks to the team that contributed to this book:

Mike Aebly, Khal Albaba, Matt Belinkie, Kim Bowers, Josh Brooks, Matt Burke, Boris Dvorkin, Kay Christensen, Mike Costa, Tim Eich, Ali El Husseiny, Samantha Fallon, Tyler Fara, Joanna Graham, Adi Hanash, Allison Harm, Beth Hoffberg, Liz Laub, Tami Miller, Chris Murphy, Matt Rasmussen, Larry Rudman, Teresa Rupp, Amjed Saffarini, Tom Sargent, Eli Schwartz, J. Ethan Sterling, Rebecca Stover, Stephen Sylwestrak, Chris Thipphavong, Lee Weiss, Mike Welch

Published by Kaplan Publishing, a division of Kaplan, Inc.
750 Third Avenue
New York, NY 10017

Printed in the United States of America

10 9 8 7 6 5 4 3

ISBN: 978-1-62523-897-9

TABLE OF CONTENTS

STRATEGY 1

TOPICS COVERED

- The Kaplan DAT Course
- The DAT
- Kaplan DAT Strategies
- Your DAT Study Plan

After this session you will be able to:

- Describe the sections of the DAT and their scoring systems
- Formulate a personal study calendar that includes all the necessary actions from now until Test Day
- Recall the steps of Kaplan's question, answer choice, and CBT strategies

The Kaplan DAT Course

Goal: Earn a higher score on your DAT and get the results you want.

What will this course include?

- Content
- Strategies
- Study Planning
- Crisis Prevention

The DAT

Scoring

Score	Basis
Biology	performance on questions 1–40 of the Survey of the Natural Sciences section
General Chemistry	performance on questions 41–70 of the Survey of the Natural Sciences section
Organic Chemistry	performance on questions 71–100 of the Survey of the Natural Sciences section
Total Science	performance on all questions (1–100) in the Survey of the Natural Sciences section; not simply an average of the three subsection scores
Reading Comprehension	performance on all questions in the Reading Comprehension section
Quantitative Reasoning	performance on all questions in the Quantitative Reasoning section
Academic Average	the simple arithmetic average of the following five standard scores, rounded to the nearest whole number: Biology, General Chemistry, Organic Chemistry, Reading Comprehension, and Quantitative Reasoning
Perceptual Ability	performance on all questions in the Perceptual Ability section; does not constitute any component of any other reported score

Distribution of Scores by Percentile

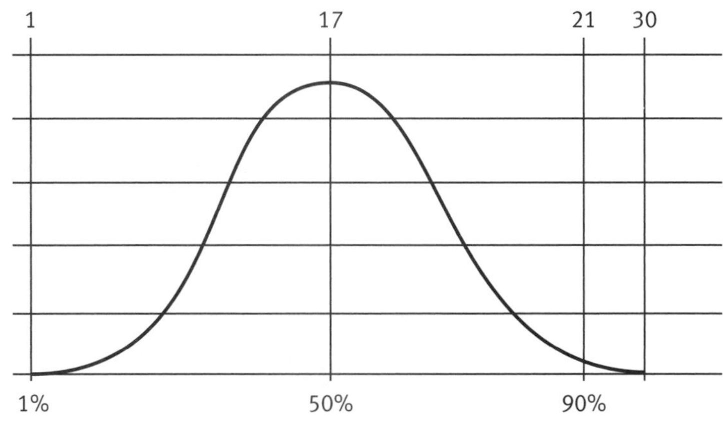

Setting Expectations

Student	Diagnostic	FL 1	FL 2	FL 3	FL 4	FL 5	Δ
A	15	16	17	17	17	17	2
B	16	17	19	19	19	19	3
C	19	18	21	20	19	25	6
D	11	16	17	17	16	18	7
E	13	16	17	18	17	20	7
F	16	20	23	22	22	23	7

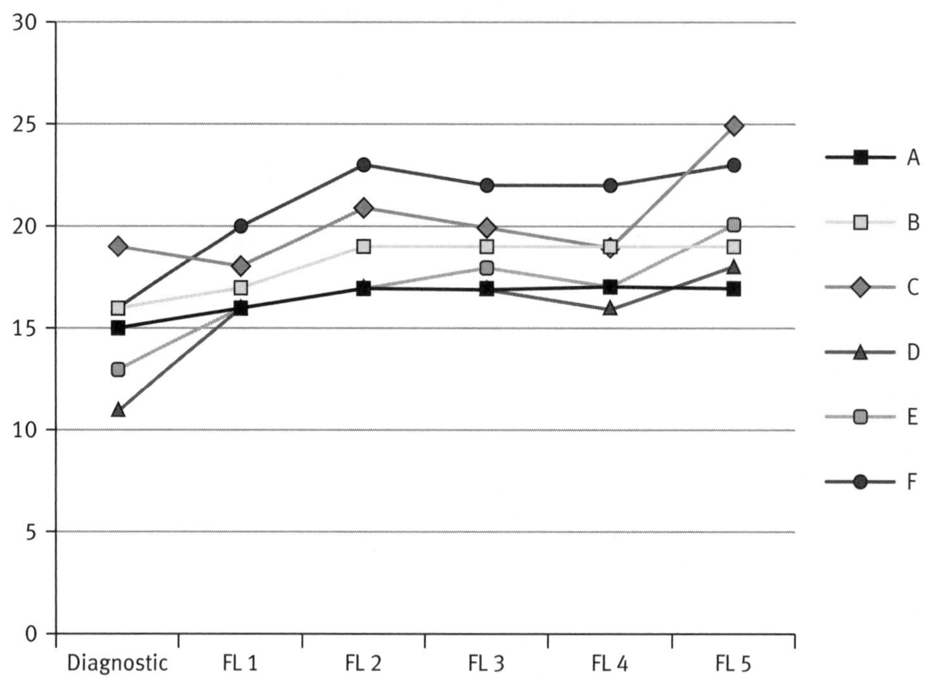

Your Goal Score

My target score is ____

The reason this is my target score is because ______________________________

The three biggest obstacles to me achieving this score are:

1. ____

2. ____

3. ____

I can overcome these obstacles by:

1. ____

2. ____

3. ____

The Kaplan Question Strategy

STOP

- Triage: Should you do this question now, later, or never?

THINK

- What is the question really asking?

PREDICT

- Formulate a framework or prediction for your answer.

MATCH

- Select the answer that truly meets the requirements of the prediction.

A Worked Example

1. Fifteen movie theaters average 600 customers per day. If 6 are shut down, but the same number of people still attend the movies, what is the new average attendance for the movie theaters that remain open?

   A. 100
   B. 500
   C. 900
   D. 1,000
   E. 1,500

Expert Thinking

STOP

Answers are numbers that are far apart. This question requires rough calculation where estimation could be sufficient.

THINK

The question is asking for the new average attendance given a smaller number of open theaters but the same number of customers.

PREDICT

First, find the total number of customers. Before any closures, there were 15 theaters with 600 customers each. When multiplied, this comes to 9,000 customers. Now there are only 9 theaters open. 9,000 divided by 9 gives an average of 1,000 customers per day for each theater.

MATCH

The final answer should be 1,000 customers, which matches answer choice (D).

Kaplan Answer Choice Strategy

Wrong Answer Choice Pathologies

Pathology	Why It's Wrong	Why It's Seductive
Faulty Use of Detail		
Opposite		
Distortion		
Out of Scope		
Miscalculation		

Kaplan Computer-Based Test Strategy

Overview

Scratch Work Strategy

Marking and Skipping Strategy

- Non-Reading Comprehension
- Reading Comprehension

Maximizing Area for Scratch Work

Non-Writing Hand and the Mouse

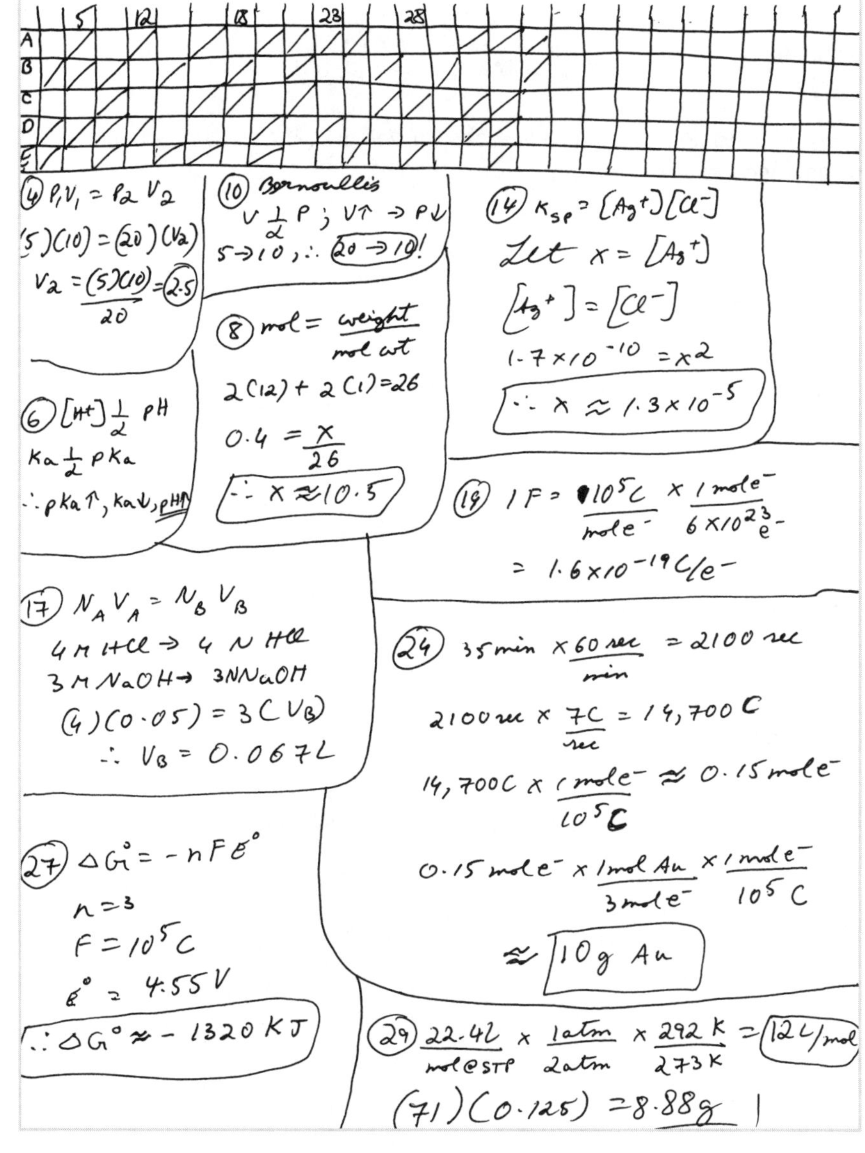

Your DAT Study Plan

Using Your Kaplan Resources Effectively

Diagnostic

Your Diagnostic is critical to establish a baseline and guide your prep.

Preview Homework

Complete the assigned Preview Homework prior to each session.

Class Sessions

Attend all required sessions or view as Lessons On Demand. Have your Lesson Book on hand for every class and use it to take notes.

Review Homework

Complete your Review Homework within 24 hours of your lesson if at all possible.

Full-Length Exams

Use full-length practice tests to mimic Test Day.

Additional Resources

Several additional resources are available on your Online Syllabus and in your Home Study Kit to help you maximize your DAT score.

Building a Study Plan

Register for Your DAT

Create a Study Calendar

The Dirty Dozen

#12: Doing the same thing as everybody else.

#11: Letting stress get in the way.

#10: Timing yourself in the beginning.

#9: Focusing on difficulty levels.

#8: Testing under nontest conditions.

#7: Not committing to your study schedule.

#6: Listening now but studying later.

#5: Only studying the right answers.

#4: Ignoring your strengths.

#3: Forgoing explanations and mistakes.

#2: Making it about the number, not the process.

#1: Taking test after test after test after test.

READING COMPREHENSION 1

TOPICS COVERED

- The Reading Comprehension Section
- Kaplan Method for Reading Comprehension
- Reading Strategically
- The Kaplan Question Strategy
- Question Types

After this session you will be able to:

- Recall Kaplan's strategies for reading strategically and classifying Reading Comprehension question types

The Reading Comprehension Section

Overview

- 50 questions across 3 passages in 60 minutes
    - Each passage is 9–14 paragraphs long
    - Each passage has 16–18 questions
- Familiarity with the subject matter is not required
    - Subject areas: natural and medical sciences
- Every operational question within Reading Comprehension counts equally toward your score

Pacing

- Spend approximately 20 minutes per passage.
    - Use 7–8 minutes reading and mapping the passage.
    - Save 12–13 minutes for the questions, giving yourself about 45 seconds per question.

Kaplan Method for Reading Comprehension

READ STRATEGICALLY

- → Preview the passage for Topic.
- → Anticipate while reading using Keywords.
- → Map each paragraph's Scope.
- → Determine the author's Tone.
- → Identify the author's overall Purpose.

Reading Strategically

Preview the Passage for Topic

Topic is the author's basic subject matter.

The passages on the test will be titled according to the Topic.

Telescopes: Refractors Versus Reflectors

(1). The earliest telescopes were refractors, in that they used lenses to bend incoming light. By using refractive lenses, early astronomers were able to gather light and view images with greater resolution and magnification than possible with the naked eye. But because pioneer telescope makers knew relatively little about optics, their lenses exhibited two serious defects. The first problem, spherical aberration, is a distortion that occurs when a lens with round surfaces fails to focus light from a point object to a point image. The second problem, chromatic aberration, stems from the fact that an ordinary lens refracts different wavelengths of light to slightly different degrees, resulting in a different focal length for each color and, therefore, an out-of-focus image with a colorful halo.

(2). A number of scientists, among them Johannes Kepler, realized that spherical aberration could be corrected simply by using a differently shaped lens. A solution to chromatic aberration, however, proved more difficult. When Sir Isaac Newton announced that it seemed impossible to correct chromatic aberration, scientists turned their attention to reflecting telescopes. Like refractors, these telescopes also increased light, resolution, and magnification of an image, but reflectors use curved mirrors in lieu of clear lenses in order to avoid the chromatic distortion of refraction. However, early reflecting telescopes had their problems too: the mirrors they utilized were made of metal alloys, which absorbed light and thus obscured images. One solution to this problem was to build larger telescopes, since bigger mirrors mean greater light reception and brighter images. Unfortunately, the opticians and foundries of the day were not yet up to the challenge. Mirror technology progressed slowly, as did the development of better reflector telescopes.

(3). Chromatic aberration remained a problem in refractors until Englishman Peter Hall discovered that a compound lens (i.e., one that combined different surfaces) could compensate for the dispersion of different colors by focusing them back together. Unfortunately, his findings were little known. Later, mathematician Leonhard Euler hit upon a similar solution using two lenses with water between them. Soon after, noted optician John Dolland followed Euler's lead and sandwiched a piece of flint glass between two pieces of crown glass, an arrangement that corrected both chromatic and spherical aberration. As a result of this advancement and subsequent modifications, the refractor once again became the telescopic instrument of choice and remained so for about 100 years.

(4). But the refractor continued to have one inescapable limitation—a constraint on the maximum effective lens diameter, which limits the light-gathering property of the telescope. For this reason, as well as because of technical advances in mirror making, the reflector would once again assume prominence. At the Great Exposition of 1851, Varnish and Mellish presented the first chemical technique for layering silver onto glass. The mirrors that ultimately resulted from this breakthrough were silvered on the front and represented a double advantage. First, the silver surface (financially feasible because of the small amount of silver required) increased reflectivity of mirrors some 50 percent. Second, using glass in place of metal eliminated problems of shrinkage and cracking.

(5). The refractor never again surpassed the reflector. With further advances in the development of heat-resistant glass and casting techniques, larger and larger mirrors became possible, and astronomers saw farther and farther into the universe.

Anticipate While Reading Using Keywords

Keywords are structural clues that every author uses to organize and shape the text.

The best critical readers pick up on these structural clues and are thus able to anticipate while reading.

Keywords in Context

Astronomers noted more than 150 years ago that sunspots wax and wane in number in an 11-year cycle. Ever since, people have speculated that the solar cycle might exert some influence on the earth's weather. In the 20th century, for example, workers linked the solar cycle to droughts in the American Midwest. Until recently, however, none of these correlations has held up under closer scrutiny.

Types of Keywords

1. Continuation

Continuation keywords indicate that more of the same idea or argument will follow. A subtype of Continuation keywords is Illustration keywords, which introduce examples the author uses to elaborate on a point.

Examples: ____________________

____

2. Sequence

Sequence keywords denote an order of ideas, points, or events.

Examples: ____________________

____

3. Evidence

Evidence keywords are clues that the author is about to provide support for a point.

Examples: ____________________

____

4. Contrast

Contrast keywords indicate that something different is coming next or that the author is making a shift in focus.

Examples: ____

____

5. Emphasis

Emphasis keywords highlight the elements of the passage that the author finds most important.

Examples: ____

____

6. Conclusion

Conclusion keywords signal the sum of an argument.

Examples: ____

____

TAKEAWAY

Identifying Keywords on Test Day can help you to not only anticipate what will come next in the passage, but also to anticipate what the DAT will ask about in the questions.

Map Each Paragraph's Scope

Scope is the specific aspect of the Topic on which the author focuses.

e.g., chromatic aberration problems

Practice

Genetic engineering may offer the best hope of improving yields of *Oryza sativa* (cultivated rice) and perhaps, in time, other important U.S. crops. The insertion of foreign genetic material into the DNA of cultivars appears to confer an herbicidal protection on the resultant plants, enabling them to compete successfully for nutrients with uncultivated grasses.

Topic: ____

Scope: ____

Media coverage of Alzheimer's disease, an ultimately fatal form of dementia that primarily afflicts the elderly, generally focuses on the disease itself: the difficulty of establishing a diagnosis and the lack of any effective treatment. Far less attention is paid to the tremendous physical, psychological, and financial toll that the disease takes on family members who live with and care for Alzheimer's patients 24 hours a day.

Topic: ____

Scope: ____

Creating a Roadmap

The key to success on the Reading Comprehension section is structured, targeted mapping.

The Roadmap is a diagram of the passage noting the Scope of each paragraph. A good Roadmap helps you find information in the passage quickly.

Sample Roadmap

P1 Q1–16

¶1 *1st telescopes = refractors; 2 probs*

¶2 *try reflectors; also probs*

¶3 *fix refractor chromatic aberration prob*

¶4 *refractor still limited*
mirrors ↑ reflectors

¶5 *reflector › refractor*

Using Your Roadmap

1. Of the following, the author is most interested in discussing

   A. how different shapes of lenses influence resolution and magnification in telescopes.
   B. why refractors have become more popular than reflectors.
   C. how two basic telescope designs alternately succeeded each other in importance and popularity.
   D. the ways in which technological constraints have shaped the course of science.
   E. the ways dispersion impacts the resolution in telescopes.

2. The author mentions the views of Sir Isaac Newton (paragraph 2) in order to

   A. explain why scientists initially turned toward reflecting telescopes.
   B. emphasize the severity of the problem of spherical aberration.
   C. show that early scientists often reached erroneous conclusions.
   D. tacitly challenge the view that Sir Isaac Newton was a brilliant scientist.
   E. give the history of the first refractor telescopes used.

3. According to the passage, chromatic aberration can be corrected by

   A. a lens with rounded surfaces.
   B. using glass in place of metal alloys.
   C. building larger telescopes for greater light reception.
   D. an arrangement of two lenses separated by water.
   E. rotating the lenses between 15° and 30°.

Determine the Author's Tone

Tone is the author's attitude.

Positive, Negative, Neutral

Practice

Animal behavior was formerly thought to consist of simple responses, some of them innate and some of them learned, to incoming stimuli. Complex behavior, if it was considered at all, was assumed to be the result of complex stimuli. However, a group of ethologists, notably Konrad Lorenz, Nikolaas Tinbergen, and Karl von Frisch, established a new view of animal behavior.

Tone: ____

Astronomers and astrophysicists who believe that intelligence exists only on Earth base their claim on an argument taken from the field of evolutionary biology. Intelligent life does not exist anywhere else in the galaxy, they contend, because the process that culminated in the development of life on Earth was so complex and so dependent on chance events (e.g., the extinction of the dinosaurs) that it could not have occurred twice. What this argument fails to take into account, however, is a crucial distinction made by evolutionary biologists: the distinction between the evolution of a specific species and the evolution of a specific trait. According to evolutionary biologists, it is indeed extremely unlikely that a species similar to *Homo sapiens* exists elsewhere; the probability of the same sequence of events occurring under the same environmental conditions is so small that it can be discounted. However, this does not imply that intelligent life very different in form from *Homo sapiens* could not have developed on other planets.

Tone: ____

Identify the Author's Overall Purpose

Purpose is why the author is writing. Identifying the Purpose will help you to understand the passage as a whole. All of the details in the passage are meant to support the author's overall Purpose.

The Purpose should always be given in verb form.

Explain, Evaluate, Argue, Compare

Before moving on to the questions, you should create a Purpose sentence in your mind to solidify your understanding of the passage.

Crisis Prevention

What if I don't know what to map?

What if I am running out of time?

What if I don't know the meaning of a word?

TAKEAWAY

Reading strategically can help you not only to anticipate what will come next in a passage but also to anticipate what the DAT will ask about in the questions.

Passage 1

The Harbor Seal

(1). The harbor seal, *Phoca vitulina*, is a member of the order Pinnepedia and lives amphibiously along the northern Atlantic and Pacific coasts. This extraordinary mammal, which does most of its fishing at night when visibility is low and where noise levels are high, has developed several unique adaptations that have sharpened its visual and acoustic acuity. The need for such adaptations has been compounded by the varying behavior of sound and light in each of the two habitats of the harbor seal—land and water.

(2). While the seal is on land, its ear operates much like that of a human, with sound waves traveling through air and entering the inner ear through the auditory canal. The directions from which sounds originate are distinguishable because the sound waves arrive at each inner ear at different times. In water, however, where sound waves travel faster than they do in air, the ability of the brain to differentiate arrival times between each ear is severely reduced. Yet it is crucial for the seal to be able to pinpoint the exact origins of sound in order to locate both its offspring and prey. Therefore, through processes of adaptation to the demands of its environment, the seal has developed an extremely sensitive quadraphonic hearing system, composed of a specialized band of tissue that extends down from the outer ear to the inner ear. In water, sound is conducted to the seal's inner ear by this special band of tissue, making it possible for the seal to identify the exact origins of sounds.

Scratch Work

Paragraph 1

Paragraph 2

(3). The eye of the seal is also uniquely adapted to operate in both air and water. The human eye, adapted to function primarily in air, is equipped with a cornea, which aids in the refraction and focusing of light onto the retina. As a result, when a human eye is submerged in water, light rays are further refracted and the image is blurry. The seal's cornea, however, has a refractive index similar to that of water. Therefore, in water, light rays are transmitted by the cornea without distortion and are clearly focused on the retina. In air, however, the cornea is astigmatic. The result is a distortion of incoming light rays. The seal compensates for this by having a stenopaic pupil, which constricts into a vertical slit. Since the astigmatism is most pronounced in the horizontal plane of the eye, the vertical nature of the pupil serves to minimize its effect on the seal's vision.

(4). Since the harbor seal procures its food under conditions of low visibility, some scientists hypothesize that harbor seals have an echolocation system akin to the sensory capabilities of bats, porpoises, and dolphins. This kind of natural and instinctual radar involves the emission of high frequency sound pulses that reflect off of obstacles such as predators, prey, or natural barriers. The reflections are received as sensory signals by the brain, which interprets them and processes them into an image. The animal, blinded by unfavorable surroundings or lighting conditions, is thus able to perceive its surroundings. Scientists believe that echolocation in the harbor seal is suggested by the fact that these seals emit "clicks," i.e., high-frequency sounds produced in short, fast bursts that occur mostly at night, when visual acuity is low.

Scratch Work

Paragraph 3

Paragraph 4

(5). Finally, there is speculation that the seal's vibrissae, or whiskers, act as sensory receptors. Evidence for this is found in the fact that vibrissae are unusually well developed in Pinnepedia and are highly sensitive to movement. Scientists hypothesize that the vibrissae may be instrumental in catching prey and, because they are sensitive to vibrations, may sense wave disturbances produced by nearby moving fish, allowing the seal to home in on and capture prey.

(6). Having met the sensory demands of dual habitats, the harbor seal is one of the most interesting animals on earth. Its amphibious existence has demanded a sensory acuity and flexibility matched by few other mammals.

Scratch Work

Paragraph 5

Paragraph 6

Purpose

The Kaplan Question Strategy

STOP

→ Characterize the question type.

THINK

→ What is the question really asking?

→ Where is the relevant information you need?

PREDICT

→ Formulate a framework or prediction for your answer.

MATCH

→ Select the answer that truly meets the requirements of the prediction.

Question Types

There are seven main question types on the DAT.

If you understand how to approach each question type, you can more easily attack questions on Test Day.

Global Questions

Global questions ask for the general purpose or main idea of the passage. Predict the answer using your Purpose sentence.

Examples of question stems:

- *The main purpose of the passage is to . . .*
- *Which one of the following best states the main idea of the passage?*
- *Which one of the following best describes the organization of the passage?*
- *The passage can best be described as . . .*

Practice

4. The main purpose of the passage is to

   A. discuss how the harbor seal fishes at night.
   B. explain the adaptations of the harbor seal in its two habitats.
   C. evaluate the effectiveness of the harbor seal's hearing on land.
   D. compare the way a harbor seal uses echolocation on land and in water.
   E. argue that the harbor seal is the mammal with the best night vision.

Detail Questions

Detail questions are the most common question type on the DAT. The answer to a Detail question can be found directly in the passage. Refer back to the passage to see what was stated in order to formulate your prediction.

Examples of question stems:

- *According to the passage . . .*
- *As stated in the passage . . .*

Practice

5. According to the passage, the sensitivity of the harbor seal's whiskers to vibrations is most beneficial for

   A. triggering fish in surrounding areas to move about.
   B. improving the seal's ability to smell nearby predators.
   C. enhancing the seal's balance on land.
   D. perceiving wave disturbances produced by prey.
   E. sensing echolocation waves produced by other seals.

Detail EXCEPT Questions

These questions are similar to Detail questions, but they will use words like *EXCEPT* or *NOT*. More research in the passage will be required to get these questions right. The questions are not necessarily difficult, but can be more time-consuming.

Examples of question stems:

- *Each of the following statements is used as evidence in the passage EXCEPT one. Which one is the EXCEPTION?*
- *According to the passage, which of the following is NOT true ...*

Practice

6. According to the passage, all of the following are true about the harbor seal's quadraphonic hearing system EXCEPT one. Which is the EXCEPTION?

   A. It is composed of a specialized band of tissue.
   B. It extends from the outer ear to the inner ear.
   C. It is used to conduct sound in water to the seal's inner ear.
   D. It is used mostly on land, where sound waves travel more slowly.
   E. It helps the seal to pinpoint the exact origins of sounds originating from its offspring.

Tone Questions

By tracking the author's attitude while you make your Roadmap, you will be able to answer Tone questions, which ask how the author feels about something. Check to see if the author is positive, negative, or neutral.

Examples of question stems:

- *The tone of this passage is . . .*
- *Which phrase from the fifth paragraph reflects a negative bias?*

Practice

7. The author's tone is one of

   A. astonishment that the seal has developed capabilities to live in dual habitats.
   B. accusation toward skeptics of the theory of evolution.
   C. ambivalence regarding the seal's amphibious adaptations.
   D. condemnation of the seal's predators.
   E. admiration of the harbor seal's sensory acuity and flexibility.

Function Questions

Function questions will ask you why or how the author used certain tools to build the argument. These questions may also ask you about the purpose of an individual paragraph. Use your Roadmap and refer back to the passage to find the answer.

Examples of question stems:

- *The author of the passage refers to X in order to . . .*
- *In the second paragraph, the author of the passage is primarily concerned with . . .*

Practice

8. The author mentions other mammals such as bats, porpoises, and dolphins in paragraph 4 in order to

   A. provide examples of other animals that use echolocation.
   B. substantiate the claim that seals use a stenopaic pupil.
   C. explain a type of instinctual radar used by seals.
   D. contrast the harbor seal's "clicks" with the high-frequency sounds of other animals.
   E. support the scientific hypothesis that adaptations are most important at night.

Inference Questions

To answer an Inference question correctly, you must make a small logical leap from the passage. Be careful—the correct answer will be extremely similar to what you actually read. Only the answer that must be true based on the passage is correct.

Examples of question stems:

- *It can be inferred from the passage that the author would be most likely to agree with which one of the following?*
- *The passage suggests which one of the following about . . . ?*
- *Based on the passage . . .*
- *The passage implies that . . .*

Practice

9. Based on the passage, it can be inferred that

A. humans also have a stenopaic pupil.
B. bats, porpoises, and dolphins have an astigmatic cornea.
C. the refractive index of a seal's cornea differs from that of a human's.
D. light rays are distorted when a seal is in water.
E. the seal's retina is more effective than a human's retina.

Strengthen/Weaken Questions

Strengthen/Weaken questions, though rare, can appear on the DAT. They will ask you to apply new information to what you've read and determine what effect the new information has on the passage. Your job is to consider the argument made in the passage and how the new information either makes it more likely (strengthen) or less likely (weaken) to be true.

Examples of question stems:

- *Which of the following statements, if true, would most strengthen the theory put forth in paragraph 3?*
- *Suppose that [new information] is found to be true. What effect would this have on the author's conclusion?*

Practice

10. Suppose that the walrus, *Odobenus rosmarus*, also from the order Pinnepedia, is found to use its vibrissae to sense differences in shapes while grazing along the seafloor, thereby enabling it to detect mollusks and other organisms that comprise the walrus's diet. How would this new information impact the author's argument about the harbor seal?

    A. This would provide evidence against the author's claims about the way the harbor seals use their vibrissae for sensory receptors in water.

    B. This would support the author's theory that the walrus developed before the harbor seal.

    C. This would conflict with the author's claim that the vibrissae in harbor seals are unusually well developed.

    D. This would offer a supporting illustration of how other pinnepeds use vibrissae to home in on prey.

    E. This would present a case substantiating the author's hypothesis that pinnepeds are the only animals to use their whiskers as sensory receptors.

TAKEAWAY

Determining what type of question is being asked helps you to think only about the most relevant material and to make an informed prediction.

Passage 2

Dental Caries

(1). The development of dental caries is characterized by bacteria-induced destruction of the mineral and organic components of the tooth's enamel and underlying dentin. It is a progressive process. The initial lesion can, if untreated, expand to involve the tooth's pulp, which consists of connective tissue supplied with nerve fibers and blood vessels. Pulpal involvement can lead to inflammation and a variety of symptoms, including pain after the consumption of sugar and a throbbing sensation associated with thermal hypersensitivity. If still untreated, the oral infection eventually can affect systemic health. The initiation of dental caries is highly dependent on the microenvironment of the host's oral cavity and involves complex interactions between the host, bacteria and their metabolic products, and the calcified tissues of the teeth.

(2). In the 19th century, Louis Pasteur showed that certain microorganisms convert sugars to lactic acid and that a resulting acidic environment can cause the dissolution of tooth surfaces. In experiments conducted with three groups of young rats in the 1950s, researchers fed one group a cariogenic diet under germfree conditions; no caries developed. A second group, which included the first group's littermates, was also fed a cariogenic diet but was infected with a specific bacterial strain; caries developed. A control group was raised in a normal environment and fed a cariogenic diet; caries also developed in this group.

(3). Experts generally now agree that dental caries is caused by specific bacteria indigenous to the human oral cavity, such as *Streptococcus mutans*. The preliminary event in the development of caries is deposition on the tooth's surface of plaque, a complex aggregation of salivary proteins, bacteria, dietary nutrients, and minerals. Such deposition is initiated by a thin film of salivary proteins that coats a tooth's surface. The proteins attach to the tooth by ionic interactions between their polar sulfate and ammonium groups and the calcium ions contained in the organic matrix of the tooth's enamel. In turn, the sticky dextrans that are part of the bacteria's extracellular coats enable the microorganisms to attach to the salivary proteins.

(4). The bacteria, which thrive in acidic conditions, convert carbohydrates to organic acids, such as lactic acid, and produce proteolytic enzymes. The organic acids lower the pH at the plaque-enamel interface, and calcium salts in the enamel are slowly dissolved due to the acidic conditions. Once the salts in the tooth's enamel have dissolved, proteolytic enzymes can attack and digest the organic matrix of the enamel. Nevertheless, enamel is the primary barrier to the development of dental caries and is far more resistant to demineralization than is the underlying dentin.

(5). The replication and degree of metabolic activity of oral bacteria are strongly dependent on the availability of carbohydrates. The diets of many people in industrialized nations—high in sucrose and other sugars—supply the bacteria with a preferential metabolic substrate, strongly activating their metabolic systems and facilitating the carious process. Other host factors that affect the incidence of dental caries are salivary composition and flow rate, the physiochemical nature of the tooth's surface, and the type and form of teeth. Individuals with xerostomia (a failure to form saliva) often exhibit rampant dental caries. In most people, however, a flow of saliva bathes tooth surfaces and clears carbohydrates from the oral cavity.

(6). The chemical nature of the tooth's surface also plays a key role in determining susceptibility to dental caries and the ultimate course of the disease. Surface application of fluoride, for example, can reduce the solubility of the enamel. The fluoride ion inhibits the progress of caries by replacing hydroxyl ions in the hydroxylapatite to form fluorapatite, aiding in the remineralization of the carious lesion by promoting the deposition of calcium phosphate.

(7). The frequency of dental caries varies with the different types and positions of teeth. Interproximal surfaces (the tooth's surfaces that oppose neighboring teeth) are prime sites for the initiation of caries, especially in the contact areas. The teeth that are least susceptible to dental caries are the mandibular central and lateral incisors.

11. The main point of this passage is that

    A. a dietary intake high in refined carbohydrates causes dental caries.
    B. the mouth represents a complex microenvironment affected by a variety of physiochemical processes.
    C. the development of dental caries is a complex process involving bacteria and the host's oral cavity and teeth.
    D. dental caries should be clinically recognized during early biochemical stages.
    E. there are mechanisms by which dental caries can be prevented.

12. The initial event leading to the development of dental caries is

    A. invasion of the oral cavity by pathogenic bacteria.
    B. the direct adherence of bacterial dextrans to the tooth's enamel.
    C. the dissolution of inorganic ions.
    D. the formation of plaque on enamel.
    E. the production of proteolytic enzymes.

13. Dental caries is least likely to occur in

    A. interproximal surfaces.
    B. areas in which teeth contact each other.
    C. lateral incisors.
    D. individuals with no salivary flow.
    E. between the bicuspids.

14. A throbbing pain associated with the eating of ice cream most likely indicates that a carious lesion has begun to

    A. involve a tooth's pulp.
    B. affect the individual's systemic health.
    C. inflame a tooth's dentin.
    D. dissolve the inorganic structure of a tooth's enamel.
    E. destroy the minerals in tooth enamel.

15. A recent immigrant from a third-world country visits the dentist. Based on the information in the passage, the dentist would most likely NOT see

    A. damage to enamel caused by carbohydrate consumption.
    B. a high incidence of dental caries.
    C. a failure to form saliva.
    D. tooth damage caused by lack of fluoride in the diet.
    E. mandibular central incisors particularly susceptible to dental caries.

16. The author of the passage refers to Louis Pasteur (paragraph 2) primarily in order to

    A. give historical perspective to a scientific study.
    B. give an example of an opposing argument.
    C. give historical context to dental caries experiments.
    D. explain how bacteria form dental caries.
    E. explain how scientific research may be inconclusive.

17. The author clearly believes that

    A. scientific experiments involving dental caries largely have been unsuccessful.
    B. patients with poor hygiene deserve to have dental caries.
    C. national fluoridation programs have largely been successful.
    D. a number of complex factors influence the frequency and course of dental caries.
    E. understanding dental caries helps patients to prevent them from forming.

18. The author describes the "diets of many people in industrialized nations" as being "high in sucrose and other sugars" (paragraph 5) in order to

    A. suggest that people in industrialized nations eat more calories than people in underdeveloped nations.
    B. provide evidence for the smaller percentage of cases of dental caries in industrialized nations as compared to other nations.
    C. present a case for the correlation between the incidence of dental caries and diabetes.
    D. explain why these diets cultivate ideal conditions for the formation of dental caries.
    E. indicate that factors such as diet are irrelevant to salivary composition.

Study Plan

After Class: Reading Comprehension 1		
Complete Remaining *Lesson Book* Practice Questions	30m	
Reading Comprehension Test A	1h 0m	

Before Class: Biology 1		
Read *Review Notes* Chapters 4–9, 19–21	4h 30m	
Generalized Eukaryotic Cell Workshop	45m	
Molecular Genetics Workshop	45m	

BIOLOGY 1

TOPICS COVERED

- The Survey of Natural Sciences Section
- The Biology Subsection
- Diversity of Life
- Cell and Molecular Biology
- Genetics
- Evolution, Ecology, and Behavior

After this session you will be able to:

- Differentiate between the taxonomy kingdoms
- Describe the parts of a cell, including their origins and functions
- Explain the processes of replication, transcription, and translation
- Calculate individual and population genetics
- Describe relationships among different organisms and environments

The Survey of Natural Sciences Section

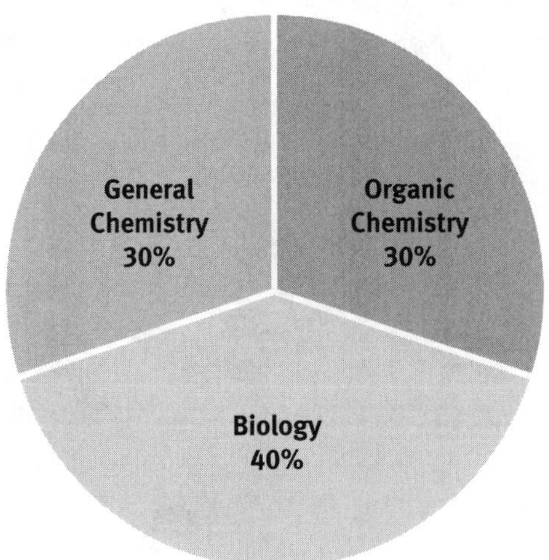

The distribution of Survey of Natural Sciences questions

Overview

- 100 questions in 90 minutes
- Consists of 40 Biology questions, 30 General Chemistry questions, and 30 Organic Chemistry questions
- Allows for use of a Periodic Table of the Elements, accessible by clicking the "Exhibit" button
- No calculator will be available during any part of the Survey of Natural Sciences

The Biology Subsection

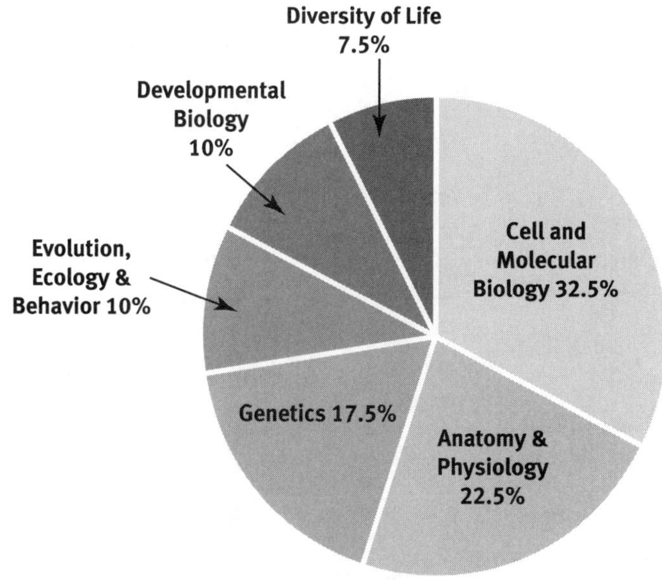

The distribution of Biology questions

Overview

- 40 questions (40% of the Survey of Natural Sciences section)

Topics

Cell and Molecular Biology (13)

- Cellular Structure and Processes
- Organelle Structure and Function
- Cell Metabolism
- Thermodynamics
- Photosynthesis
- Mitosis and Meiosis
- Origin of Life
- Experimental Cell Biology

Developmental Biology (4)

- Fertilization
- Descriptive Embryology
- Developmental Mechanisms

Genetics (7)

- Molecular Genetics
- Human Genetics
- Classical Genetics
- Chromosomal Genetics
- Genetic Technology

Evolution, Ecology, and Behavior (4)

- Natural Selection
- Speciation
- Population and Community Ecology
- Ecosystems
- Animal Behavior

Diversity of Life (3)

- Eubacteria
- Archaea
- Plantae
- Animalia
- Protista
- Fungi
- Relationships

Anatomy and Physiology (9)

- Integumentary
- Skeletal
- Muscular
- Circulatory
- Immunological
- Digestive
- Respiratory
- Urinary
- Nervous
- Endocrine
- Reproductive

The Kaplan Question Strategy

STOP

- ➜ Characterize the answer choices.

THINK

- ➜ What is the question really asking?
- ➜ What relevant information do you need?

PREDICT

- ➜ Formulate a framework or prediction for your answer.

MATCH

- ➜ Select the answer that truly meets the requirements of the prediction.

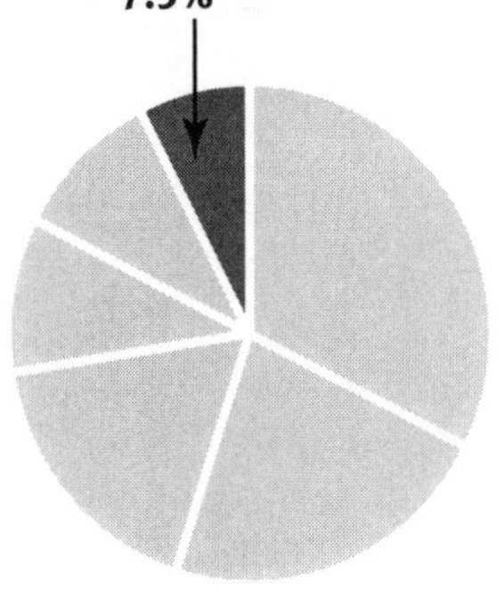

Diversity of Life

Six-Kingdom, Three-Domain System

Bacteria Domain

Eubacteria Kingdom

Archaea Domain

Archaea Kingdom

Eukarya Domain

Protista Kingdom

Fungi Kingdom

Plantae Kingdom

Animalia Kingdom

Cell and Molecular Biology

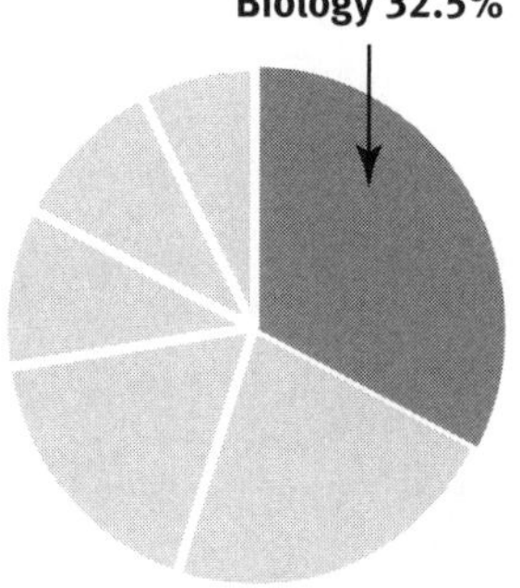

Origin of Life

Early Conditions

Primordial Soup

First Biological Molecules

Coacervate Droplets

Chemoautotrophs

Aerobes

Practice Questions

1. Suppose you find a previously unidentified, multicellular species with cells containing a nucleus, membrane-bound organelles, and a rigid cell wall but no cellulose. Based on this information alone, which kingdom is the best fit for this species?

   A. Monera
   B. Plantae
   C. Animalia
   D. Protista
   E. Fungi

2. Platyhelminthes are members of the kingdom

   A. Monera.
   B. Plantae.
   C. Animalia.
   D. Protista.
   E. Fungi.

3. Which of the following free elements was likely most essential to the first life on Earth?

   A. Sulfur
   B. Iron
   C. Oxygen
   D. Phosphorus
   E. Calcium

Cell Structure

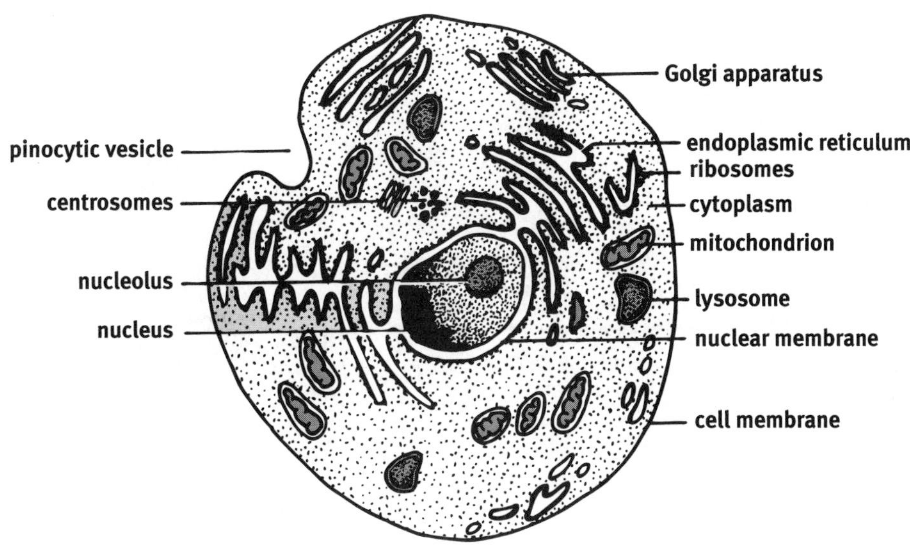

Components

Nucleus

Endoplasmic Reticulum

Ribosome

Golgi Apparatus

Mitochondrion

Lysosome

Cell Processes

Plasma Membrane

Cellular Transport

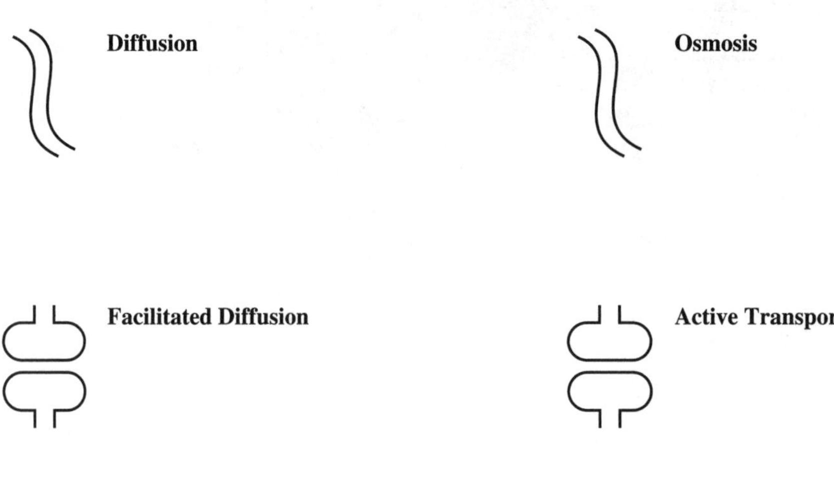

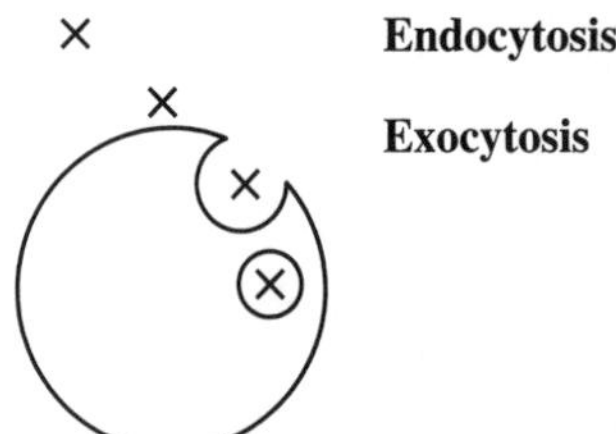

Practice Questions

4. Autophagy, the degradation of unnecessary cellular components, is most likely dependent on which organelle?

   A. Ribosome
   B. Chloroplast
   C. Lysosome
   D. Golgi apparatus
   E. Rough endoplasmic reticulum

5. All of the following statements describe a mitochondrion EXCEPT one. Which statement is the EXCEPTION?

   A. It contains double-stranded, circular DNA.
   B. It contains its own ribosomes.
   C. It is a two-membrane structure.
   D. It is directly involved in carbohydrate synthesis.
   E. It replicates by binary fission.

6. Which one of the following statements most accurately describes a process of membrane traffic?

   A. Active transport requires energy in the form of NADPH.
   B. Facilitated diffusion requires a carbohydrate carrier.
   C. Osmosis is the passive transport of nonpolar molecules.
   D. Endocytosis is an active transport process that moves large volumes of substances into the cell.
   E. Diffusion is the movement of molecules from lower to higher concentration.

Practice Questions

7. What happens to an ocean (saltwater) fish after it moves into a river (fresh water)?

   A. Water flows into the fish, causing its cells to lyse.
   B. Water flows out of the fish, causing its cells to become flaccid.
   C. Ions flow into the fish, causing the fish to become hypertonic relative to its environment.
   D. Ions flow out of the fish, causing the fish to become hypertonic relative to its environment.
   E. No change occurs.

8. You set up a container separated into two compartments by a membrane permeable to water but not ions and then add 1.5 M NaCl to the left compartment and 2.0 M glucose to the right compartment, causing

   A. water to flow into the left compartment.
   B. water to flow into the right compartment.
   C. Na^+ and Cl^- to flow into the left compartment.
   D. Na^+ and Cl^- to flow into the right compartment.
   E. Na^+ but not Cl^- to flow into the right compartment.

9. The sodium potassium pump is an ATPase that pumps 3 Na^+ out of the cell and 2 K^+ into the cell for each ATP hydrolyzed. Cells can use the pump to help maintain cell volume. Which of the following would most likely happen to the rate of ATP consumption immediately after a cell is moved to a hypotonic environment?

   A. It would increase.
   B. It would decrease.
   C. It would increase and then decrease.
   D. It would decrease and then increase.
   E. It would remain the same.

Cell Metabolism

ATP

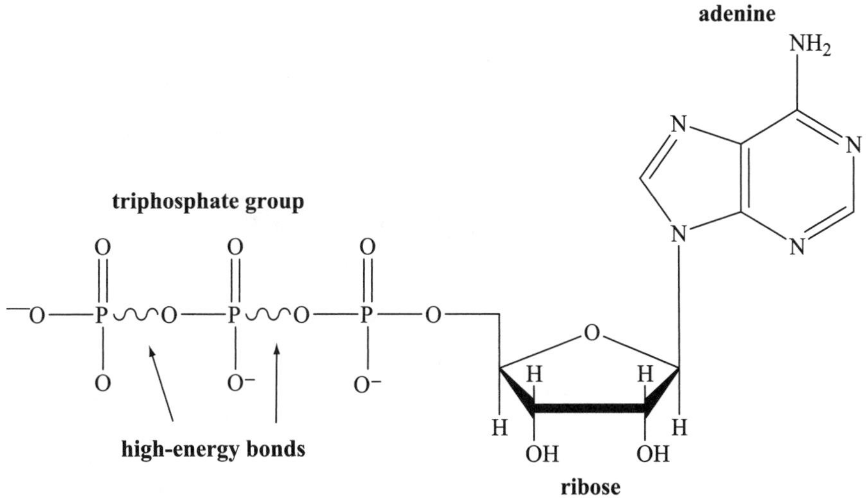

adenine

NH_2

triphosphate group

high-energy bonds

ribose

Glycolysis

Anaerobic Metabolism

Fermentation

Aerobic Metabolism

Pyruvate Decarboxylation

Krebs Cycle (Citric Acid Cycle)

Electron Transport Chain/Oxidative Phosphorylation

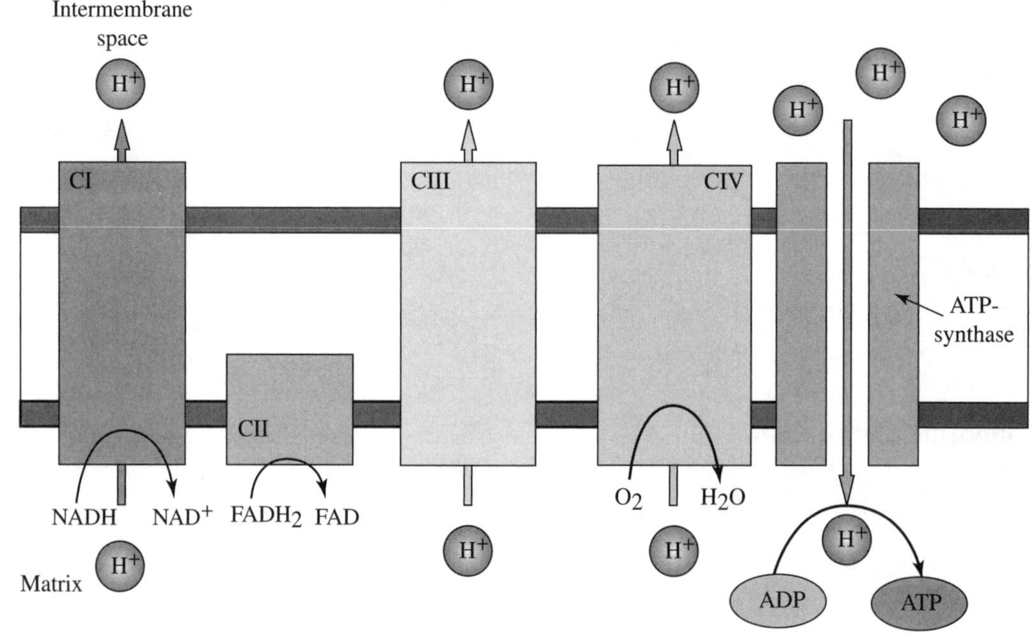

Thermodynamics

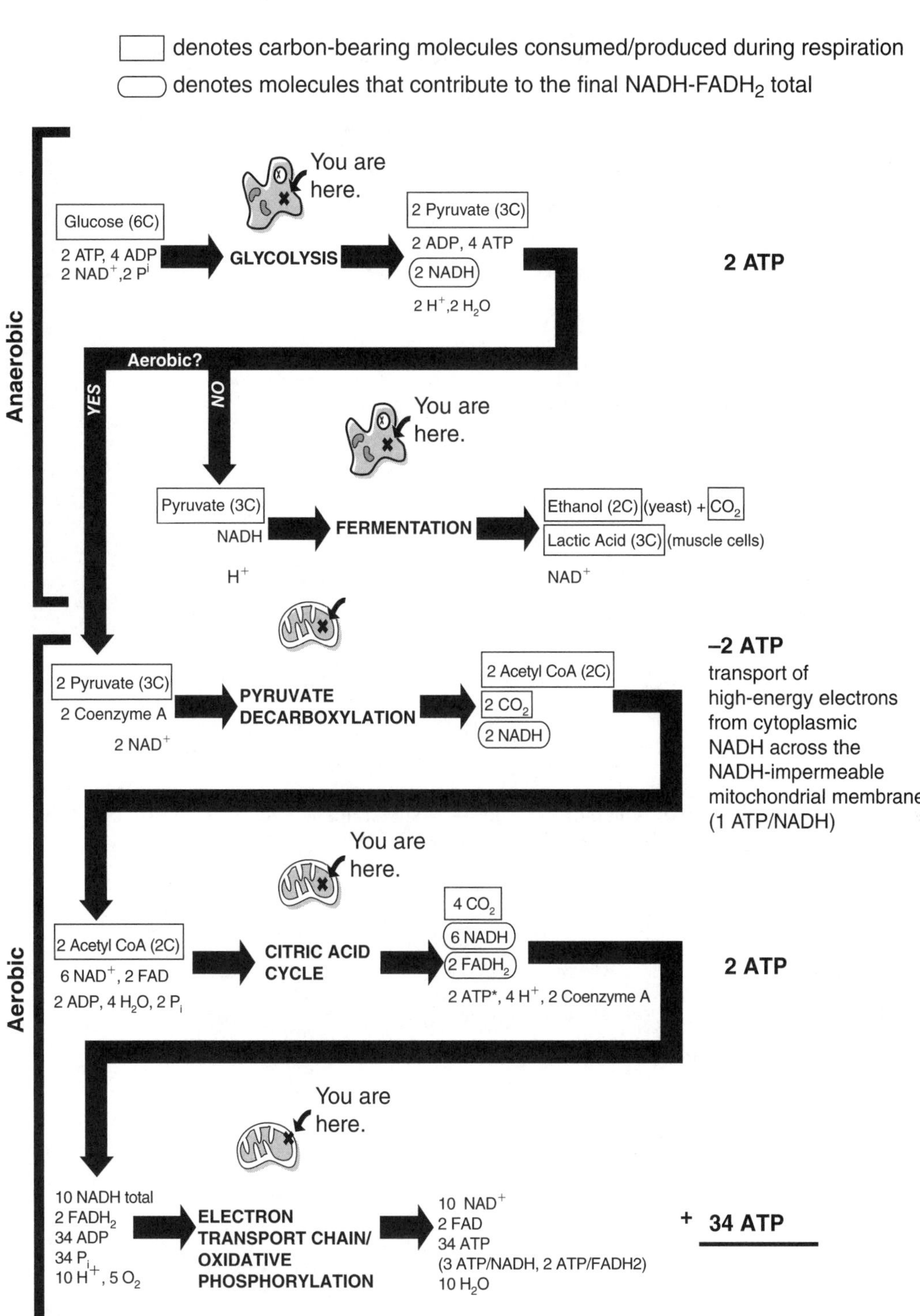

*2 GTP are the direct products of the citric acid cycle. The 2 GTP subsequently donate their phosphate to 2 ADP to form 2 ATP and regenerate the original 2 GDP.

Practice Questions

10. Which one of the following statements accurately describes cellular metabolism?

    A. Alcohol produced during fermentation undergoes glycolysis to produce 2 ATP.
    B. $FADH_2$ molecules yield three ATP each during oxidative phosphorylation.
    C. Pyruvate decarboxylation directly produces 2 net ATP.
    D. Glycolysis cannot occur in the absence of oxygen.
    E. Oxidative phosphorylation takes place across the inner mitochondrial membrane.

11. What is the last enzyme used during cellular respiration?

    A. Hexokinase
    B. Pyruvate decarboxylase
    C. Alcohol dehydrogenase
    D. Cytochrome C oxidase
    E. Phosphoglucose isomerase

12. The complete absence of which of the following substrates would NOT be expected to limit the rate of oxidative phosphorylation?

    A. NAD^+
    B. H^+
    C. O_2
    D. $FADH_2$
    E. Inorganic phosphate

Photosynthesis

Leaf Anatomy

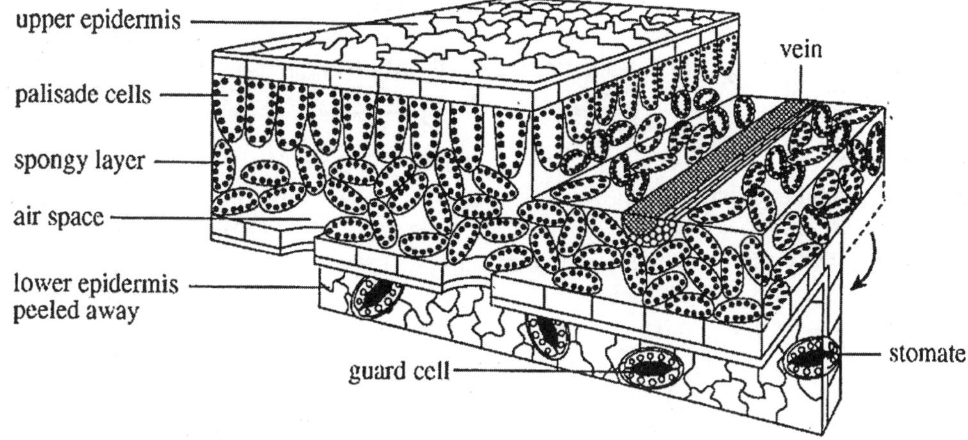

Upper Epidermis

Cuticle

Mesophyll

Chloroplasts

Thylakoids

Stroma

Lower Epidermis

Stomata

Guard cells

Veins

Xylem

Phloem

Reactions

$3\ CO_2 + 3\ H_2O + \text{light energy} \rightarrow C_3H_6O_3 + 3\ O_2$

Light Reaction

Chlorophyll captures light energy from the sun to generate high-energy molecules.

$6\ H_2O + 6\ NADP^+ + 9\ ADP + 9\ P_i + \text{light energy} \rightarrow 6\ NADPH + 6\ H^+ + 9\ ATP + 3\ O_2$

Calvin Cycle (Dark Reaction)

RuBisCO captures CO_2 from the environment to generate PGAL.

$3\ CO_2 + 9\ ATP + 6\ NADPH + 6\ H^+ \rightarrow C_3H_6O_3 + 3\ H_2O + 6\ NADP^+ + 9\ ADP + 8\ P_i$

Practice Questions

13. In plants, the Calvin cycle of photosynthesis takes place within the

A. cuticle.
B. grana.
C. stroma.
D. stomata.
E. xylem.

14. How many total PGAL must be produced for a plant to create one sucrose molecule ($C_{12}H_{22}O_{11}$)?

A. 4
B. 6
C. 12
D. 24
E. 30

15. During a drought, a plant may adapt in all of the following ways EXCEPT one. Which is the EXCEPTION?

A. Allowing its leaves and stems to turn brown
B. Expanding its root system
C. Changing concentrations of solutes within its phloem
D. Slowing or halting its rate of photosynthesis
E. Opening additional stomata within its leaves

Enzymology

Enzyme Properties

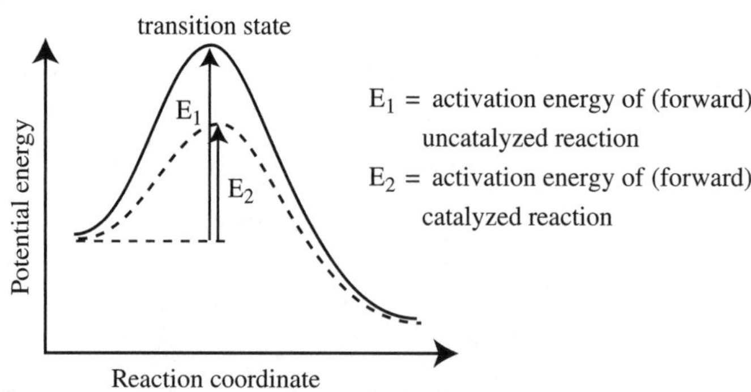

Factors that Affect Enzymes

Temperature

pH

Cofactors/Coenzymes

Concentrations of Substrate and Enzyme

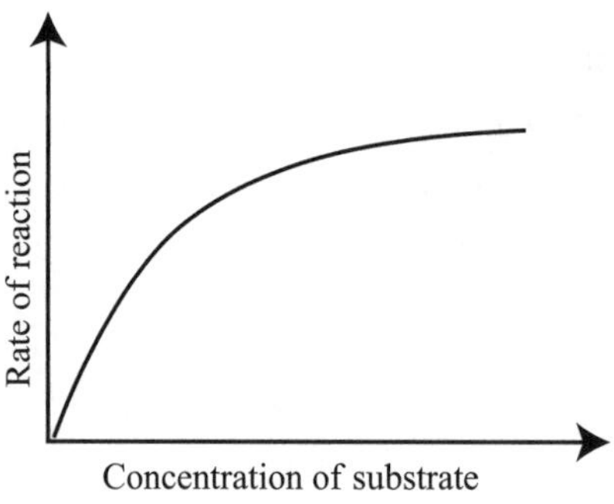

Inhibition

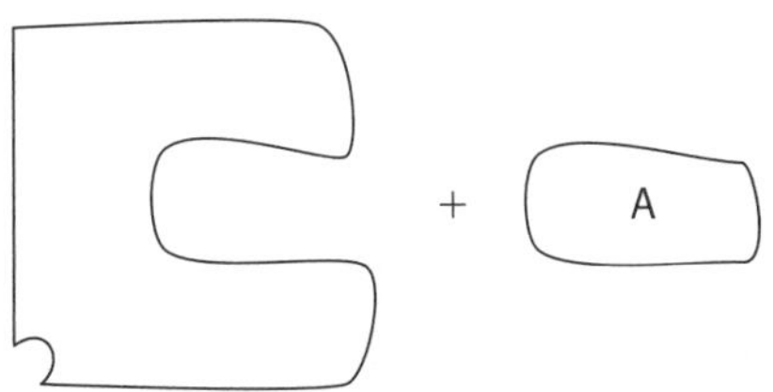

Competitive

Noncompetitive

Negative Feedback

STUDY TIP

Cell and molecular biology have many facts to memorize. Use your flashcards regularly to commit these topics to memory and earn fast points on Test Day.

Practice Questions

16. Which set of graphs best depicts the optimal temperature and pH range for pepsin activity?

A.

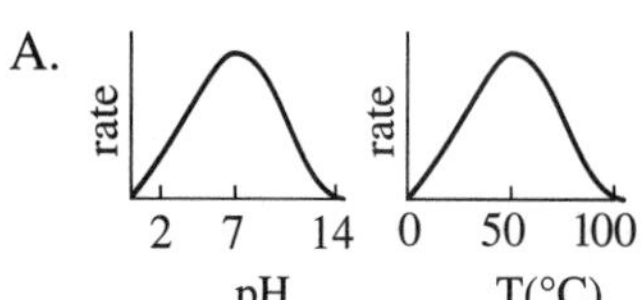

B.

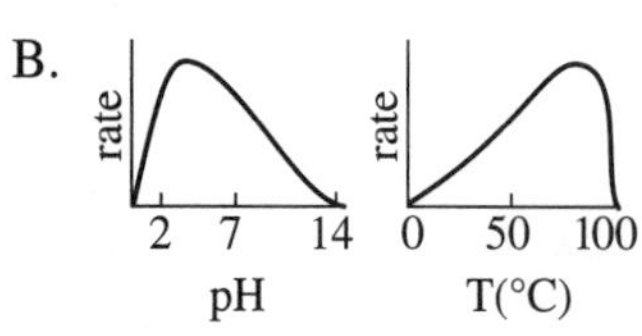

C.

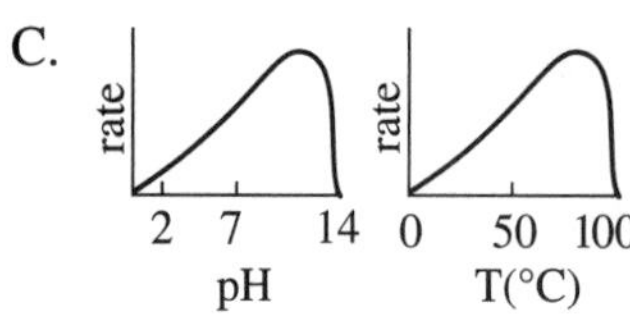

D.

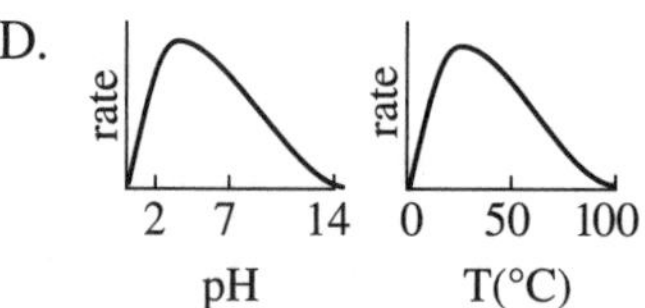

E.

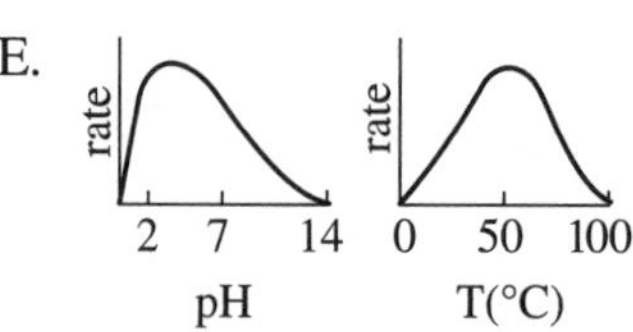

17. In the diagram below, what role does thyroxine play?

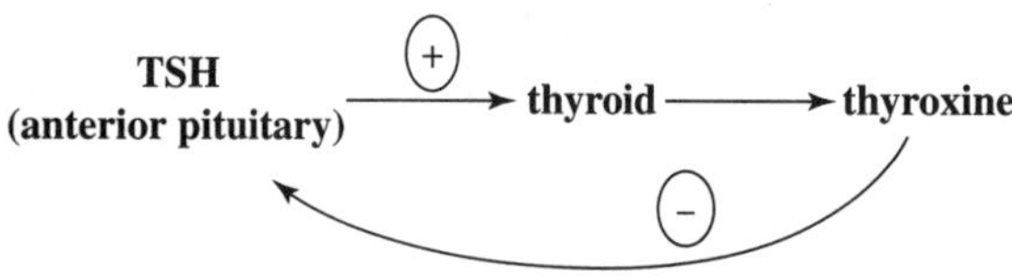

A. It reduces enzyme specificity.
B. It triggers a positive feedback loop.
C. It stimulates catalyst production.
D. It triggers a negative feedback loop.
E. It serves as a substrate for further reaction.

18. An enzyme is introduced into a reaction for which the reactants are substrates to that enzyme. Which of the following occurs?

A. The rate at which the equilibrium is reached is increased.
B. The equilibrium point is shifted forward.
C. The activation energy is increased.
D. The free energy of the reaction is increased.
E. The equilibrium point is shifted backward.

Genetics

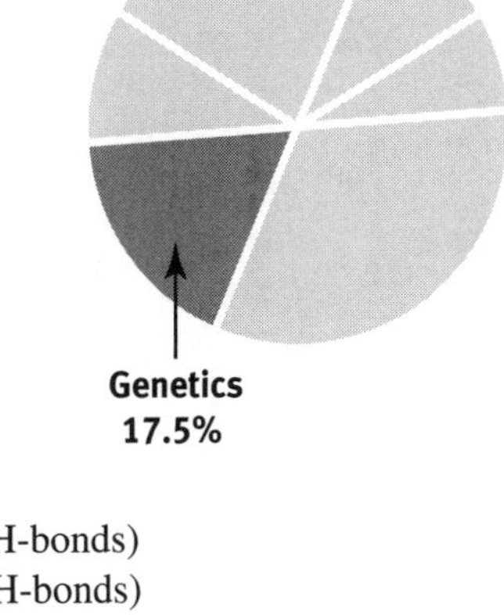

Molecular Genetics

DNA Structure

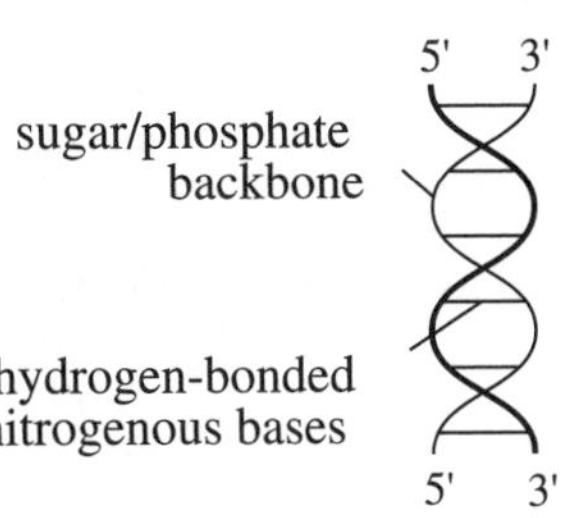

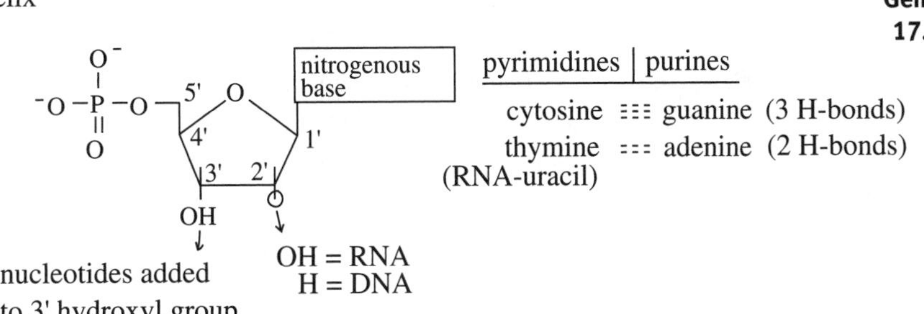

DNA Replication

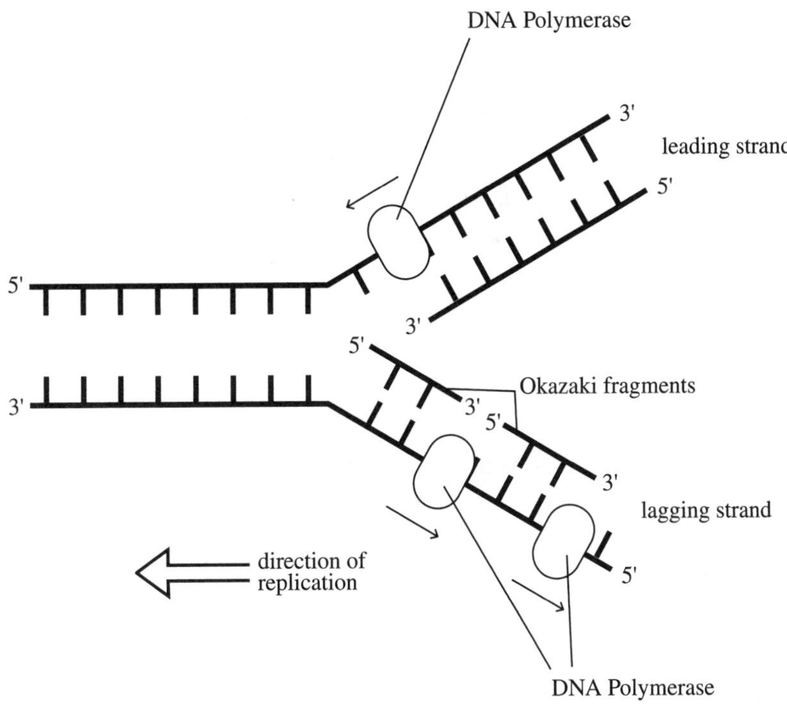

Practice Questions

19. Which daughter strand is more likely to have a mutation?

    A. The leading strand; more molecules dock and exit during the creation of this strand as compared to the lagging strand.
    B. The lagging strand; more molecules dock and exit during the creation of this strand as compared to the leading strand.
    C. The leading strand; fewer molecules dock and exit during the creation of this strand as compared to the lagging strand.
    D. The lagging strand; fewer molecules dock and exit during the creation of this strand as compared to the leading strand.
    E. Neither strand; the same number of molecules dock and exit during the creation of both strands.

20. You have two fragments of DNA: Fragment A melts (comes apart) at 97°C, and fragment B melts at 65°C. What can you conclude about the two fragments with respect to their nucleotide composition?

    A. Fragment A contains more guanine than fragment B.
    B. Fragment B contains more cytosine than fragment A.
    C. Fragment A contains more thymine than fragment B.
    D. Fragment B contains less adenine than fragment A.
    E. Fragment A contains less uracil than fragment B.

21. What gives a molecule of DNA its negative charge?

    A. The nitrogenous bases
    B. The ribose sugar
    C. The presence of cytosine or thymine
    D. The hydroxyl group
    E. The phosphate group

Transcription

Differences between DNA and RNA in Humans

	DNA	RNA
Base pairs		
Single- or double-stranded		
Functions		

Three Types of RNA

mRNA: messenger RNA; codes for amino acids

tRNA: transfer RNA; brings amino acids to ribosome

rRNA: ribosomal RNA; component of ribosome

Process of Transcription

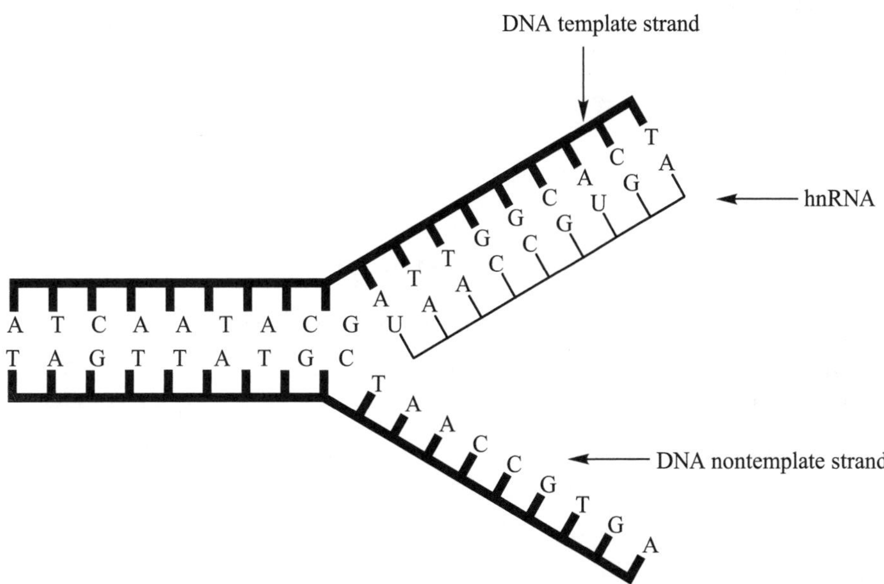

Post-Transcriptional RNA Processing

Practice Questions

22. A segment of a DNA strand has the base sequence 5'—GTTCATTG—3'. What would be the base sequence of the mRNA strand transcribed from this DNA?

    A. 5'—CAATGAAC—3'
    B. 5'—GTTCATTG—3'
    C. 5'—CAAUGAAC—3'
    D. 5'—ACCGUCCA—3'
    E. 5'—CAAGUAAC—3'

23. A person has a mutation in the promoter site of the gene for the lactase enzyme, rendering the promoter site nonfunctional. What symptom(s) will occur?

    I. Less digestion of lactose by the person
    II. More digestion of lactose by the person's symbiotic gut bacteria
    III. Malnutrition due to glucose deficiency

    A. I
    B. II
    C. I and II
    D. I and III
    E. I, II, and III

24. Researchers measure the concentration of RNA found in a set of cells for a particular gene and find it to be elevated. What must be occurring in the cells?

    A. The cells are erythrocytes responding to an oxygen deficit.
    B. The cells are leukocytes responding to an infection.
    C. A signal has been received by these cells to upregulate the translation of the gene.
    D. A signal has been received by these cells to downregulate the replication of the gene.
    E. A signal has been received by these cells to upregulate the transcription of the gene.

Translation

Three Stages

- Initiation
- Elongation
- Termination

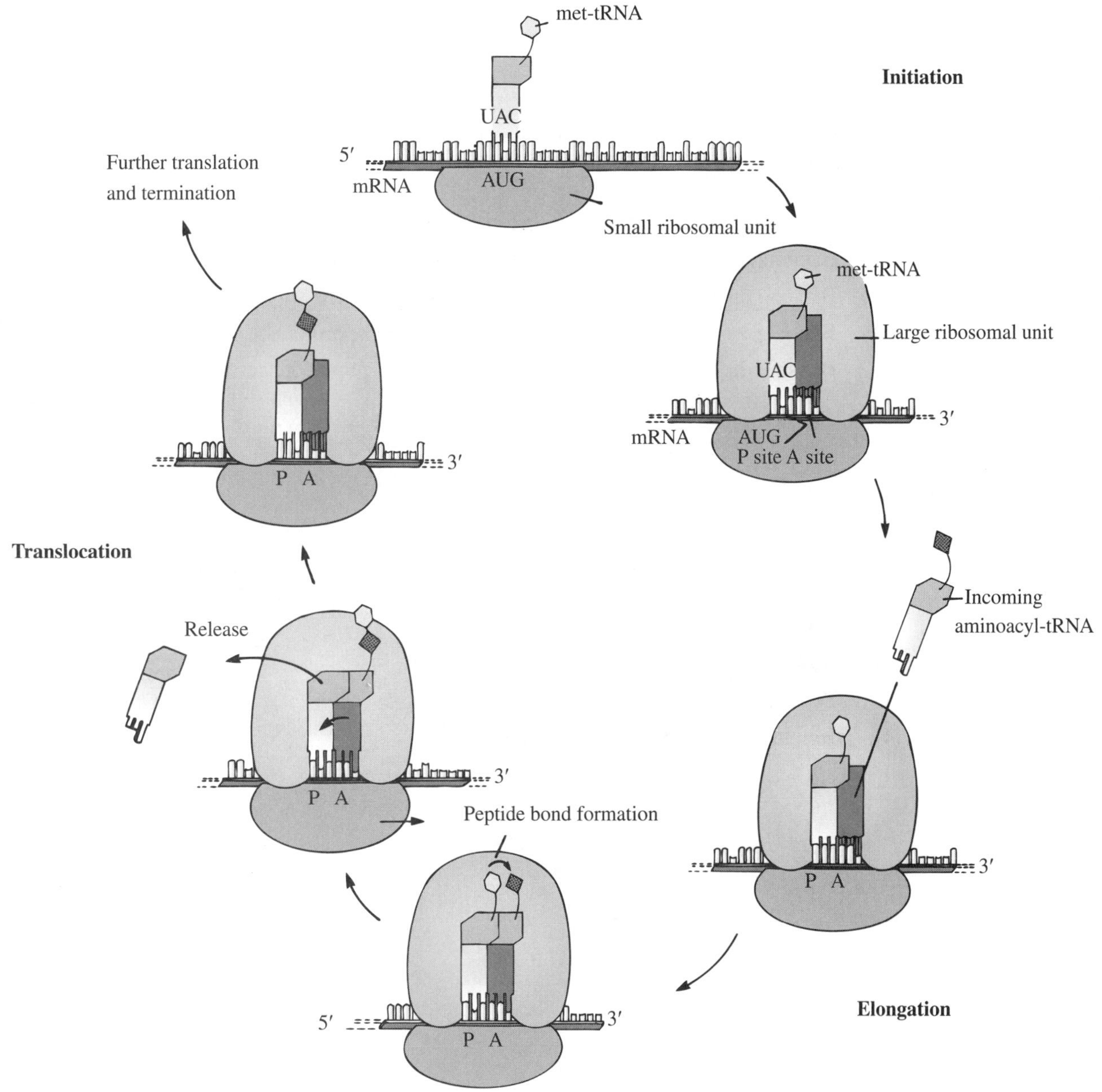

Practice Questions

25. What would happen if a tRNA with an anti-codon for alanine was actually carrying the amino acid valine?

    A. An alanine would be added where a valine was coded for during translation.
    B. A valine would be added where an alanine was coded for during translation.
    C. No amino acid would be added for that codon during translation.
    D. Both an alanine and a valine would be added at that codon during translation.
    E. Translation would immediately stop if the tRNA was to bind to the ribosome complex.

26. A new type of antibiotic targets and destroys bacterial ribosomes. How does this antibiotic work?

    A. Bacteria die because they can no longer synthesize plasmids.
    B. Bacteria die because they can no longer synthesize lipids.
    C. Bacteria die because they can no longer synthesize carbohydrates.
    D. Bacteria die because they can no longer synthesize proteins.
    E. Bacteria die because they can no longer synthesize nucleic acids.

27. A mutation causes peptidyl transferase to be nonfunctional. What process would this halt?

    A. Ribosome assembly
    B. tRNA anticodons recognizing mRNA codons
    C. Peptide bond formation
    D. Binding between rRNA and mRNA
    E. None of the above

Mutations

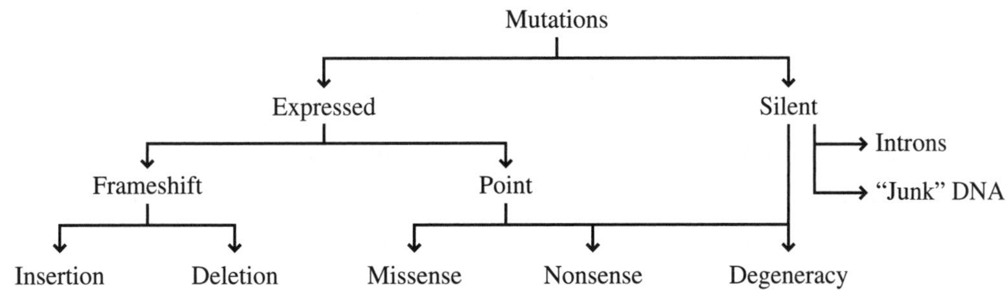

Point Mutation

Silent Mutation

Missense Mutation

Nonsense Mutation

Frameshift Mutation

Chromosomal Mutation

Turner Syndrome

Klinefelter Syndrome

Down Syndrome

Practice Questions

28. What must happen for a mutation to be noticeable in a human?

    A. The mutation is a point mutation.
    B. The mutation changes one amino acid to another.
    C. The mutation is in a region of DNA that is transcribed often.
    D. The mutation is not on a somatic chromosome.
    E. The mutation causes a change in function of a protein.

29. Which of the following mutations is most likely to cause a fetus to be nonviable?

    A. Nonsense
    B. Frameshift
    C. Point
    D. Silent
    E. Chromosomal

30. What causes some point mutations NOT to be expressed?

    I. The degeneracy of the amino acid codon code
    II. If the point mutation is in the second position of the codon
    III. The concept of "wobble" in the codon code

    A. I
    B. II
    C. I and III
    D. II and III
    E. I, II, and III

Classical Genetics

Punnett Square

Phenotypic and Genotypic Ratios

Monohybrid Cross

Dihybrid Cross

Human Genetics

Autosomal Recessive Pedigree

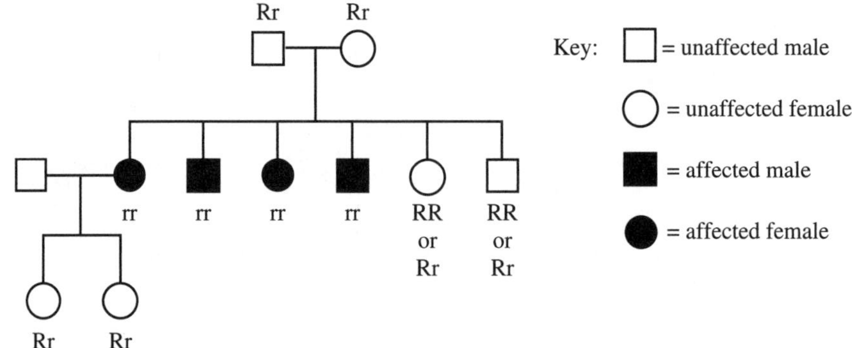

Autosomal Dominant Pedigree

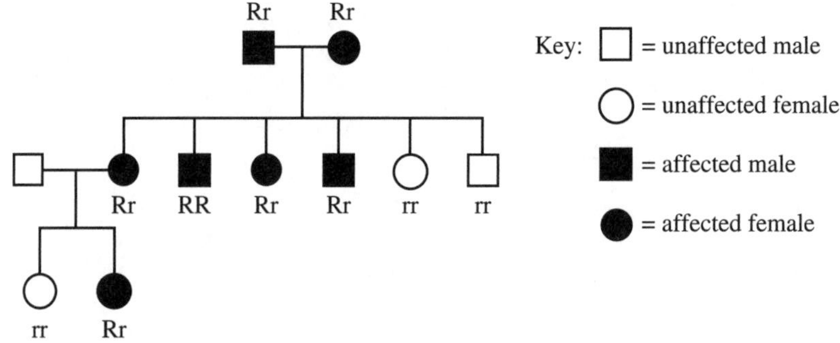

X-Linked Recessive Pedigree

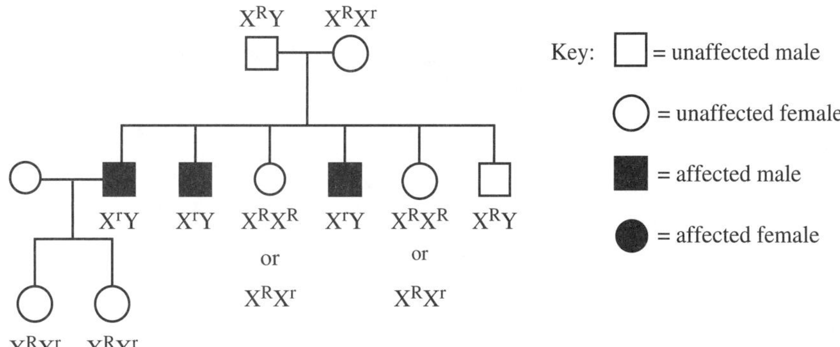

> **TAKEAWAY**
> When tackling pedigree questions, focus on the specific patterns rather than wasting time by mapping all of the genotypes.

Practice Questions

31. Given the pedigree below, what is the likelihood the offspring is a carrier?

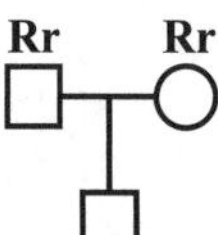

A. 25%
B. 50%
C. 66%
D. 75%
E. 100%

32. What is the inheritance pattern of the observed trait indicated by the pedigree below?

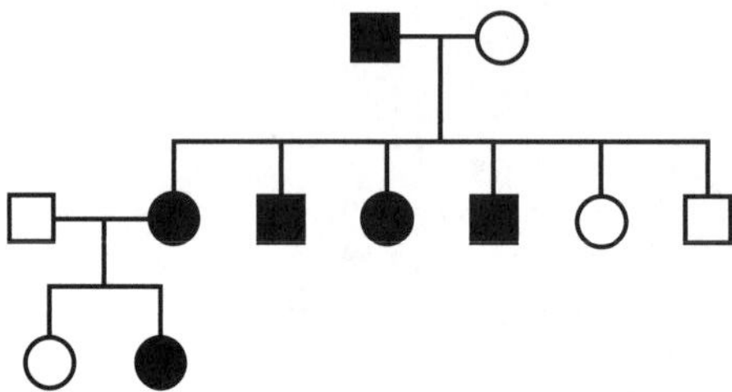

A. Autosomal recessive
B. Autosomal dominant
C. X-linked recessive
D. Y-linked
E. Cannot be determined

33. What is the inheritance pattern of the observed trait indicated by the pedigree below?

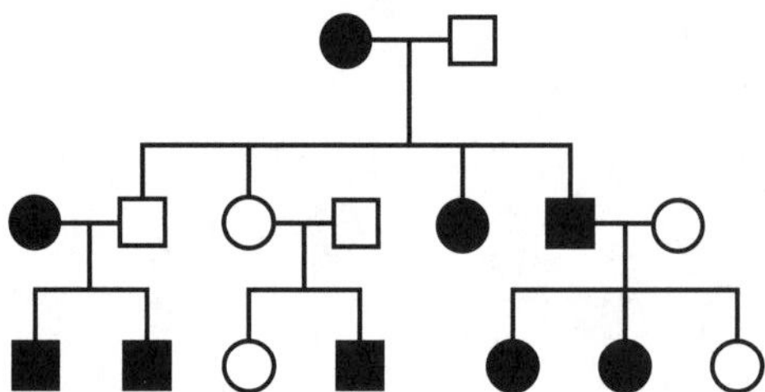

A. Autosomal recessive
B. Autosomal dominant
C. X-linked recessive
D. X-linked dominant
E. Cannot be determined

Evolution, Ecology, and Behavior

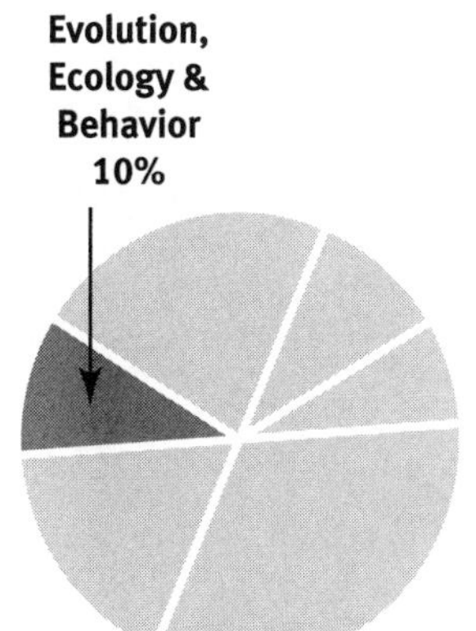

Evolution

Natural Selection

Patterns of Evolution

Divergent

Convergent

Parallel

Coevolution

Population Genetics

Hardy-Weinberg Conditions

1. Random Mating
2. No Natural Selection
3. No Migration or Emigration
4. Large Population
5. No Mutations

Hardy-Weinberg Equations

$(p + q)^n = 1$

$p + q = 1$

$p^2 + 2pq + q^2 = 1$

Practice Questions

34. If 84% of the population has Rh^+ blood, which is coded for by a dominant allele, then what is the frequency of the recessive allele, assuming Hardy-Weinberg equilibrium?

    A. 8.3%
    B. 16%
    C. 40%
    D. 60%
    E. 92%

35. Red hair, a recessive trait, appears in only 1% of the world's population. Assuming no source of evolution is occurring, what is the frequency of the allele for red hair?

    A. 0.1%
    B. 1%
    C. 2%
    D. 10%
    E. 20%

36. Some plants, such as cotton and potatoes, are tetraploid ($4n$). If a recessive allele q has a frequency of 0.20 for a certain population of tetraploid plants in equilibrium, what is the frequency of the homozygous recessive genotype of qqqq?

    A. 0.16%
    B. 0.80%
    C. 4.0%
    D. 8.0%
    E. 16%

Practice Questions

37. Sharks, which are a type of fish, and dolphins, which are a type of mammal, share similar, torpedo-shaped body plans with fins. This is most likely due to

 A. divergent evolution.
 B. convergent evolution.
 C. the founder effect.
 D. speciation.
 E. vestigial structures.

38. On a certain island, one bird species faces heavy competition for a sole food source. If a mutation is introduced that leads to exploitation of a new food source and eventually speciation, what type of evolution occurred?

 A. Divergent evolution
 B. Convergent evolution
 C. Coevolution
 D. Sexual selection
 E. Parallel evolution

39. The wings of bats and the wings of birds can be considered

 A. vestigial structures.
 B. homologous traits.
 C. analogous traits.
 D. comparative embryology evidence for evolution.
 E. comparative biochemistry evidence for evolution.

Ecosystems

Terrestrial Biomes

Freshwater Biomes

Marine Biomes

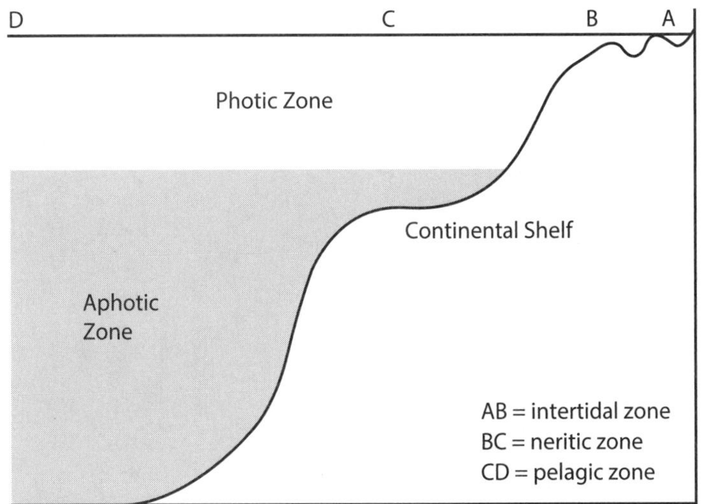

Ecological Succession

Pioneer Organisms

Climax Community

Community Ecology

Commensalism

Mutualism

Parasitism

Predation

Animal Behavior

Classical Conditioning

Operant Conditioning

Behavioral Displays

Pecking Order

Territoriality

Pheromones

STUDY TIP

Don't neglect studying plants, animals, and the relationships between them. The DAT tests more than just human biology!

Practice Questions

40. A biome with thin soil and that contains significant populations of pines, spruces, bison, and beaver is best characterized as

    A. coniferous forest.
    B. grassland.
    C. rainforest.
    D. taiga.
    E. tundra.

41. Which of the following species is most likely to be found as a permanent resident of the intertidal zone?

    A. Hammerhead shark
    B. Stingray
    C. Seagull
    D. Tuna
    E. Mussel

42. After a lichen has settled a barren rock, the next species to settle is most likely to be a

    A. pine tree.
    B. blueberry shrub.
    C. mountain moss.
    D. scrub hare.
    E. buffalo grass.

43. The human digestive tract is home to hundreds of species of bacteria. The bacteria are provided with a relatively stable environment, while the host benefits from increased immune function and vitamins as a byproduct of the bacteria. This is an example of

    A. commensalism.
    B. mutualism.
    C. brood parasitism.
    D. obligate parasitism.
    E. predation.

Study Plan

After Class: Biology 1		
Complete Remaining *Lesson Book* Practice Questions	30m	
Practice with Tests and Quizzes		

Before Class: Perceptual Ability 1		
Read *Review Notes* Chapter 63	30m	

PERCEPTUAL ABILITY 1

TOPICS COVERED

- The PAT
- Keyholes
- Top-Front-End
- Angle Ranking
- Hole Punching
- Cube Counting
- Pattern Folding

After this session you will be able to:

- Recall the rules for each PAT subsection
- Apply specific Kaplan strategies to each subsection

The PAT

What does this section test?

How does this section test its content?

Timing

60 minutes, 90 questions

The Subsections

15 questions per subsection

Keyholes (12.5 minutes recommended)

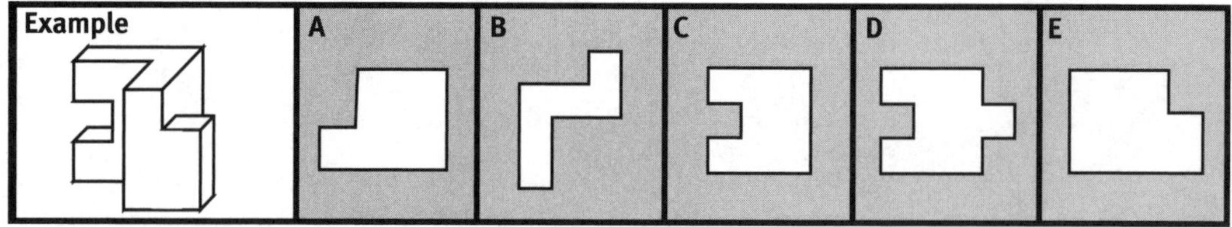

Top-Front-End (12.5 minutes recommended)

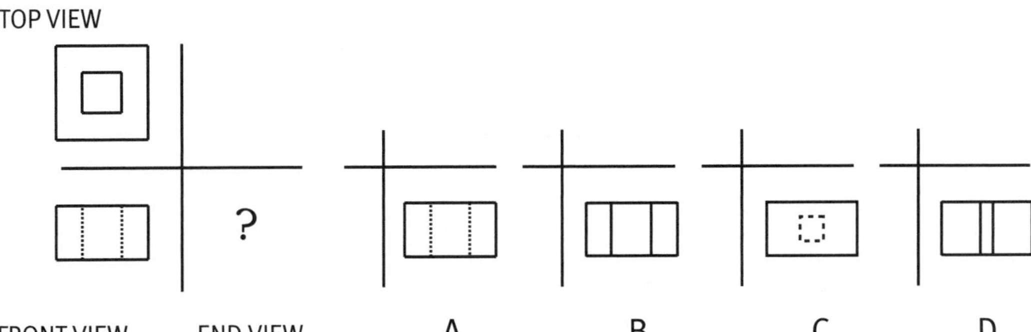

Angle Ranking (5 minutes recommended)

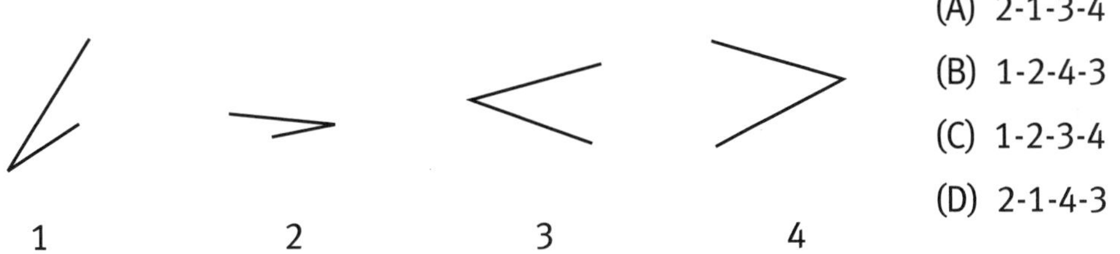

(A) 2-1-3-4

(B) 1-2-4-3

(C) 1-2-3-4

(D) 2-1-4-3

Hole Punching (5 minutes recommended)

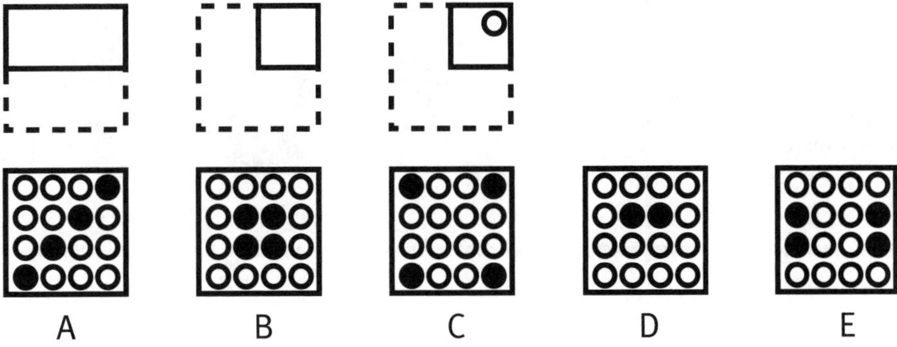

Cube Counting (10 minutes recommended)

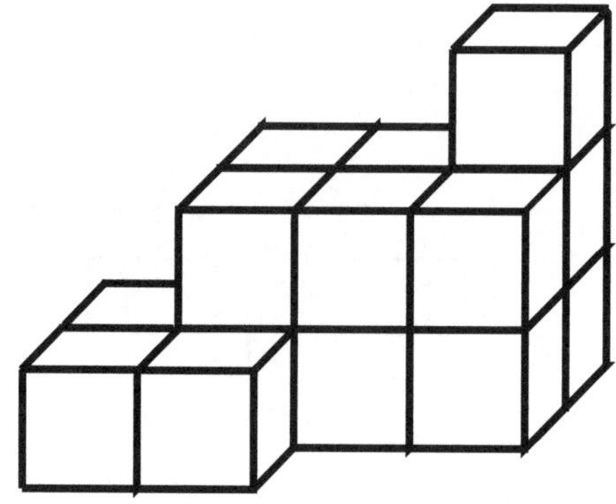

How many cubes have one of their sides painted?

A. 1 cube
B. 2 cubes
C. 3 cubes
D. 4 cubes
E. 5 cubes

Pattern Folding (15 minutes recommended)

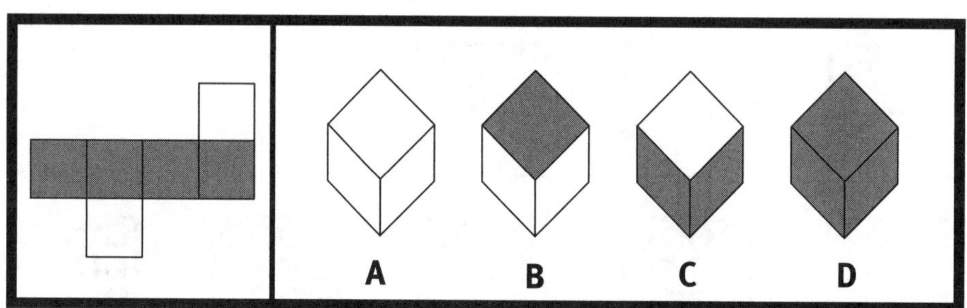

Keyholes

PART 1

For each question, a three-dimensional object is displayed at left. This figure is followed by outlines of five openings or apertures.

The assignment is the same for each question. Imagine how the object at left looks from all directions, not just the one shown. Choose one of the five openings presented that would allow the object to pass through if the proper sides were inserted first.

Basic Rules:

1) The irregular object at left may be rotated in any manner. It may be inserted through the aperture starting with a side not shown.

2) Once the irregular object has started through the aperture, it may not be rotated or turned in any way. The object must pass completely through the aperture. The aperture is always the exact shape of the external outline of the object.

3) Both the irregular object and openings are drawn to the same scale. It is possible that a correct opening may be too small for the object even though it is the proper shape.

4) There are no irregularities in any hidden part of the object. If a figure has symmetric indentations, hidden portions are symmetric with visible parts.

5) There is only one correct answer choice for each object.

Example

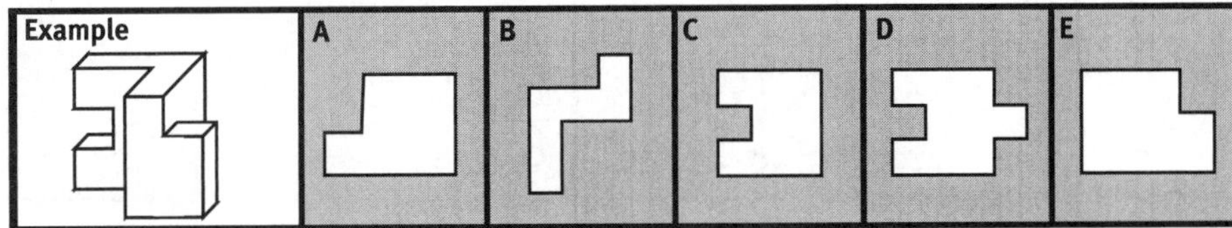

The correct answer is choice (B) since the object would pass through this aperture if the bottom were inserted first.

Proceed to Questions

Overview

Keyholes are the first section of the PAT. A 3D object is presented, and you must determine through which of five openings this object can pass.

The Rules

The object can pass through the opening in any orientation.

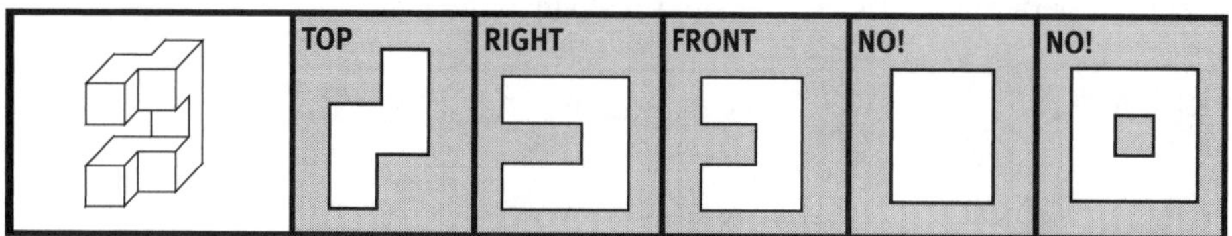

The object cannot be rotated once it has started through the opening. The external outline of the object is the exact shape of the opening.

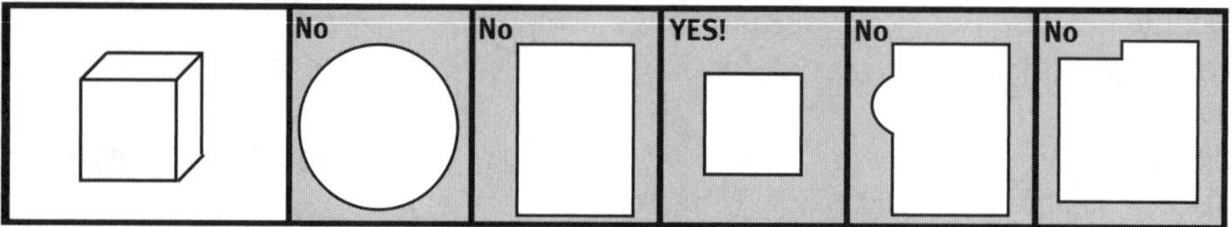

The object and opening are drawn to the same scale.

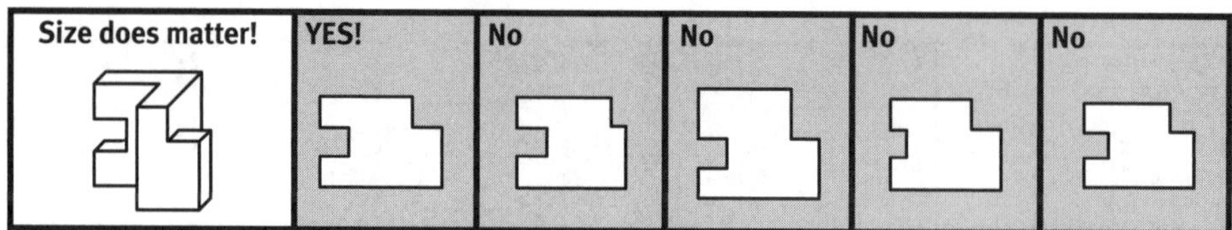

There are no irregularities in any hidden part of the object.

Here is the front of the object . . .

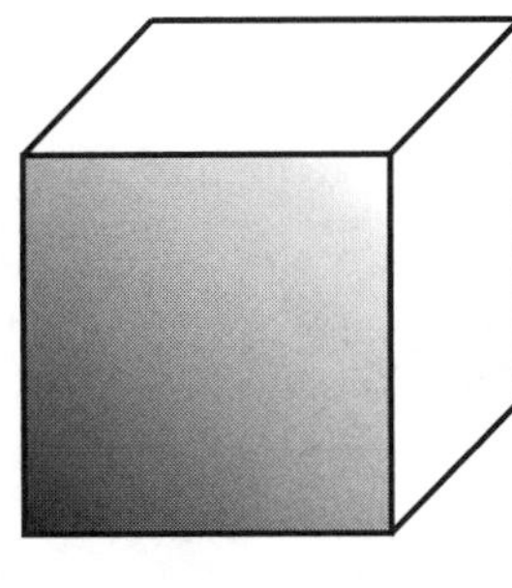

Could this be the back?

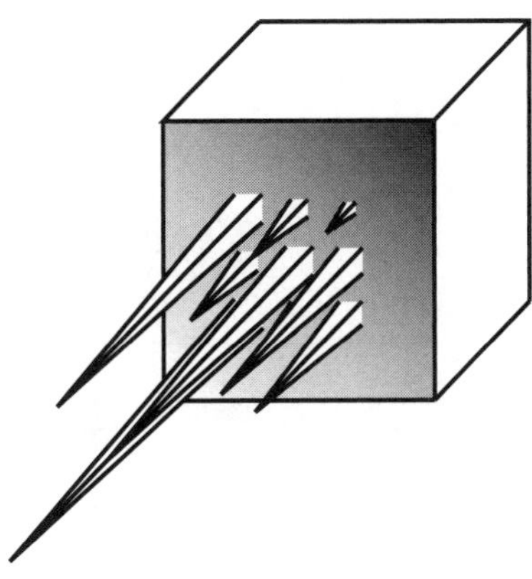

There is only one correct answer.

Strategies

Projections

- Back
- Bottom
- Right

Crushing the Object

Projections

A projection is a two-dimensional "shadow" of a three-dimensional object.

Examples

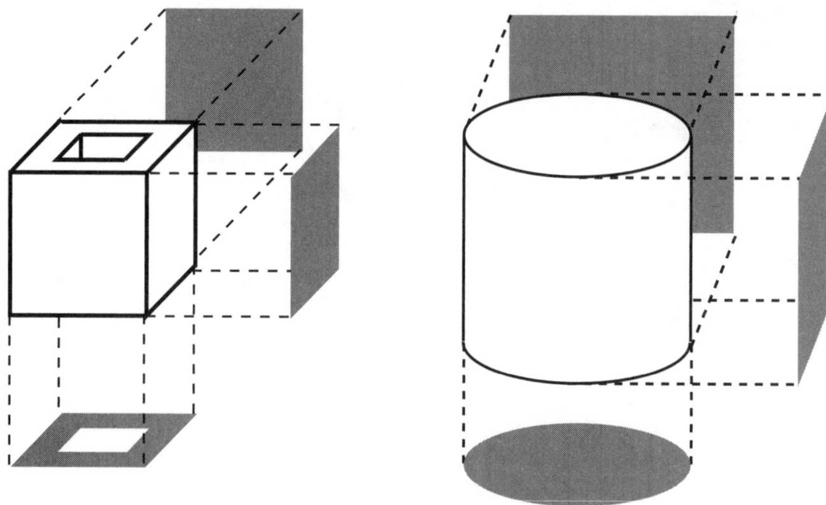

What will a sphere fit through?

What will a pyramid fit through?

Practice with Projections

a. 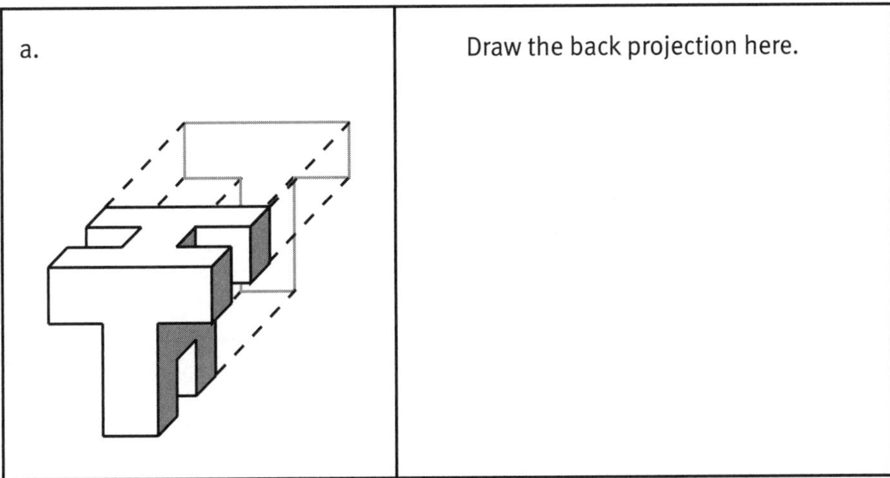	Draw the back projection here.
b. 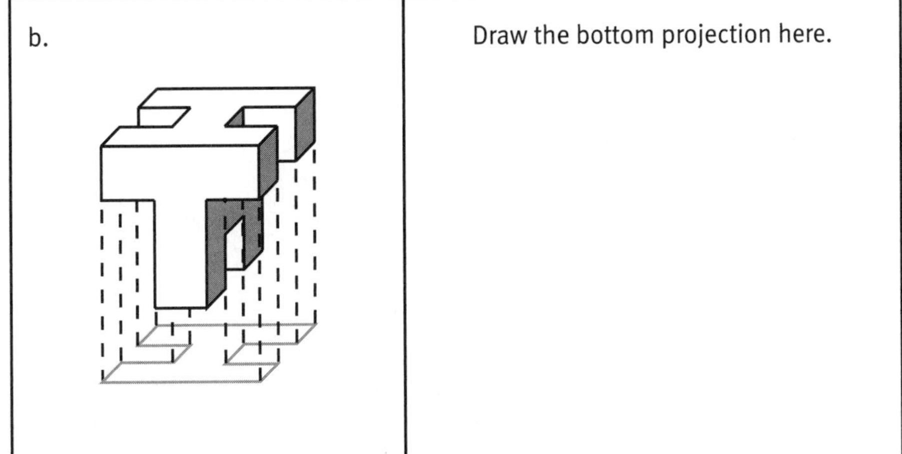	Draw the bottom projection here.
c. 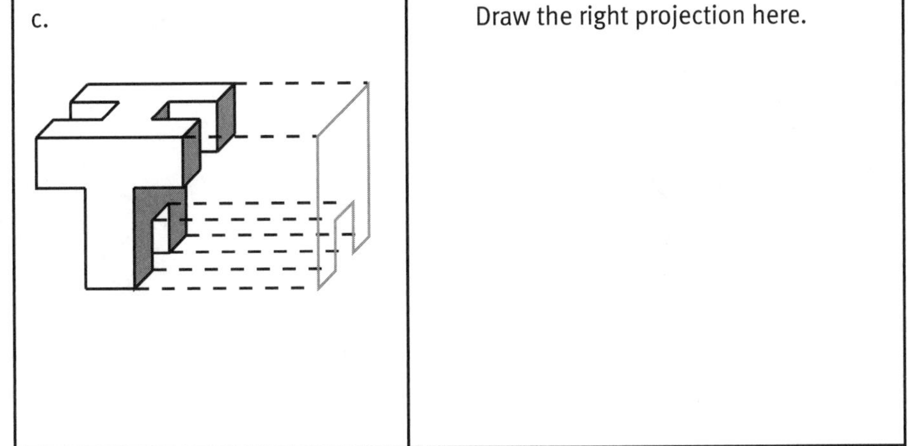	Draw the right projection here.

d.

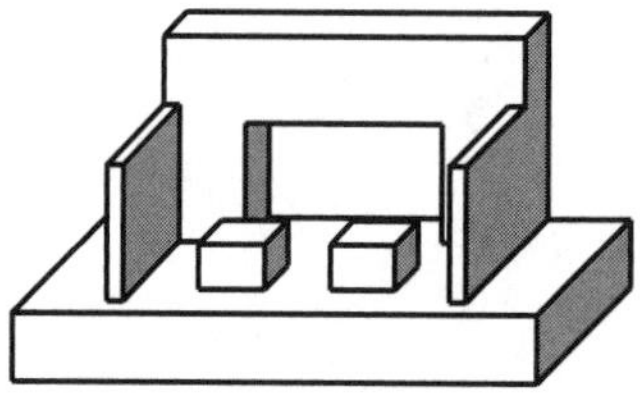

Draw the back projection here.

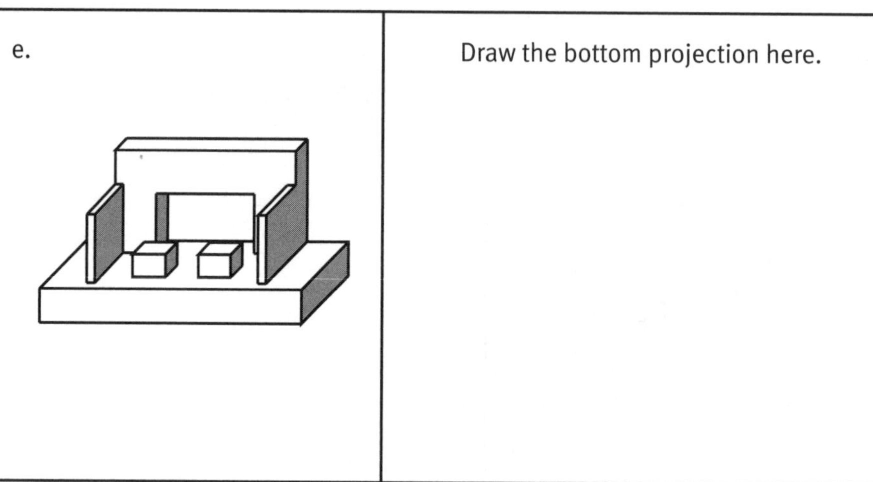

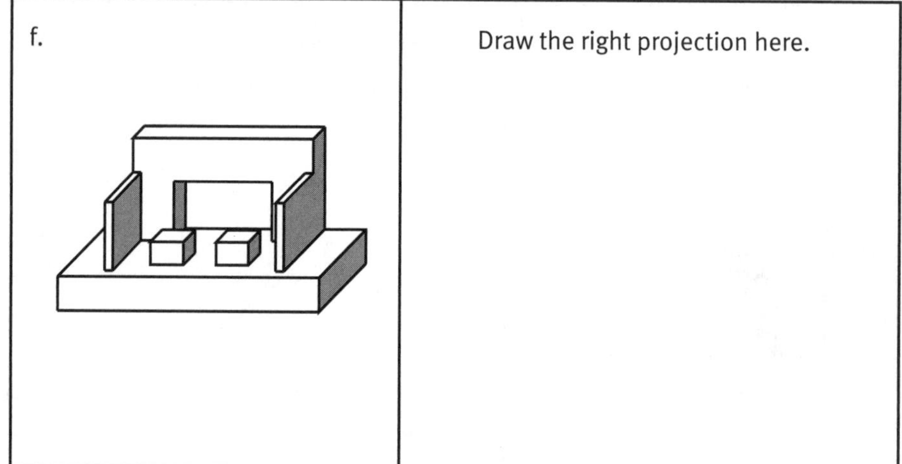

g.

Draw the back projection here.

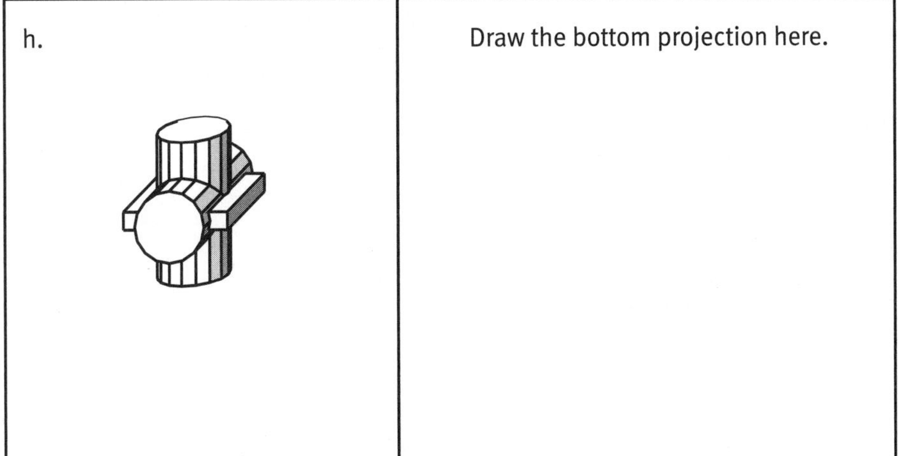

h.

Draw the bottom projection here.

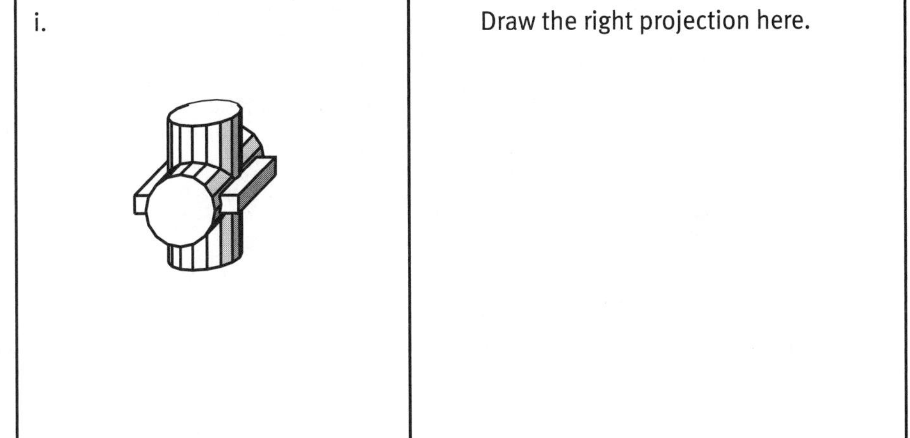

i.

Draw the right projection here.

j.

Draw the back projection here.

k.

Draw the bottom projection here.

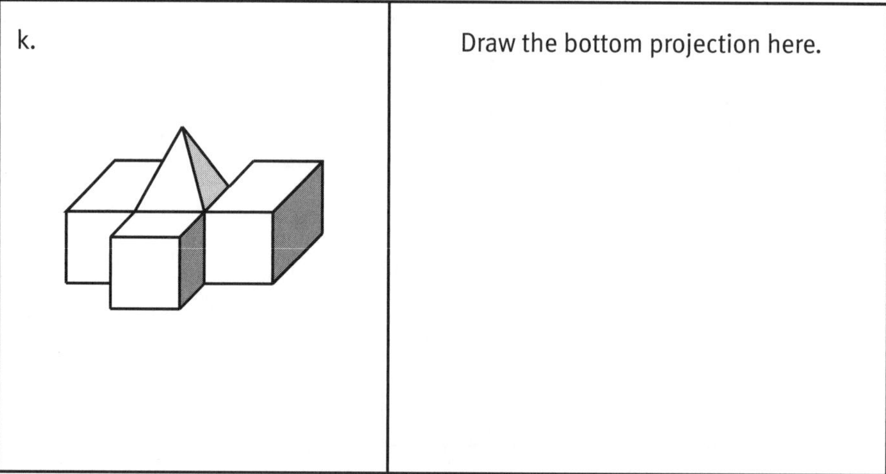

l.

Draw the right projection here.

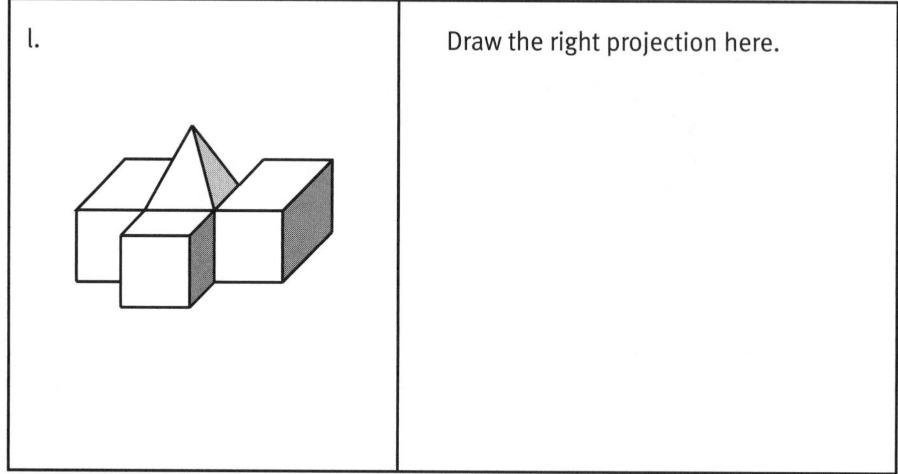

Left vs. Right Projections

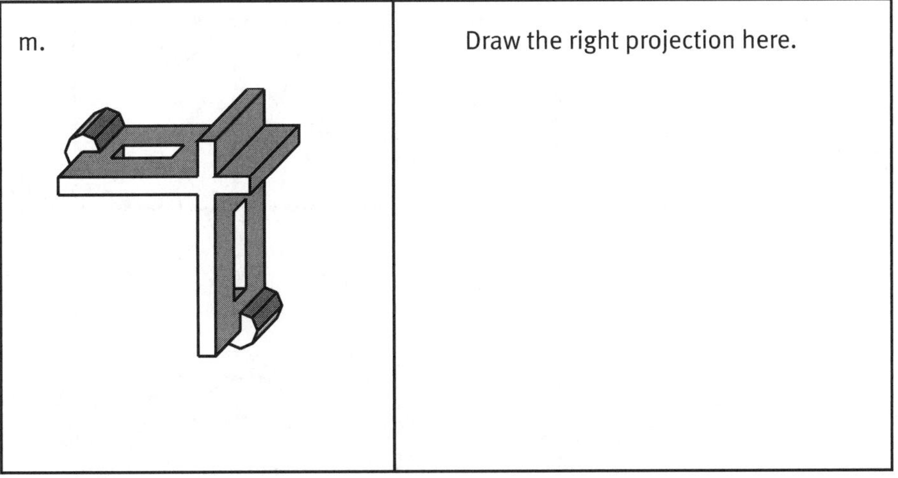

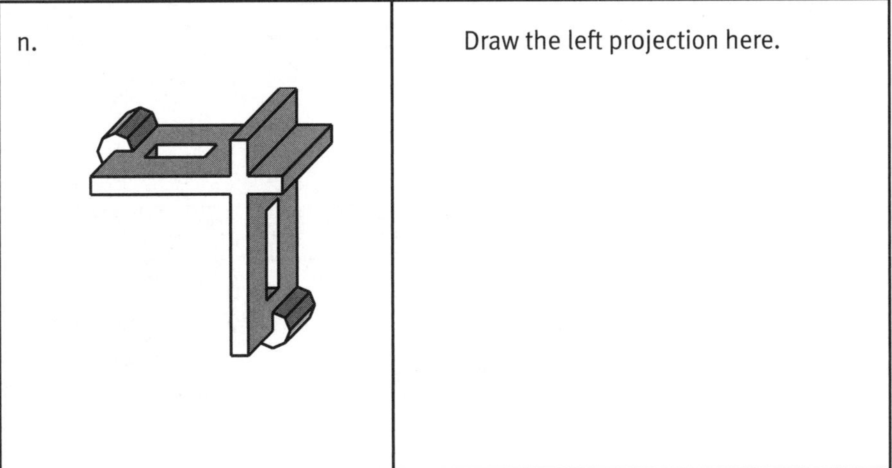

Judging Distance in 3D

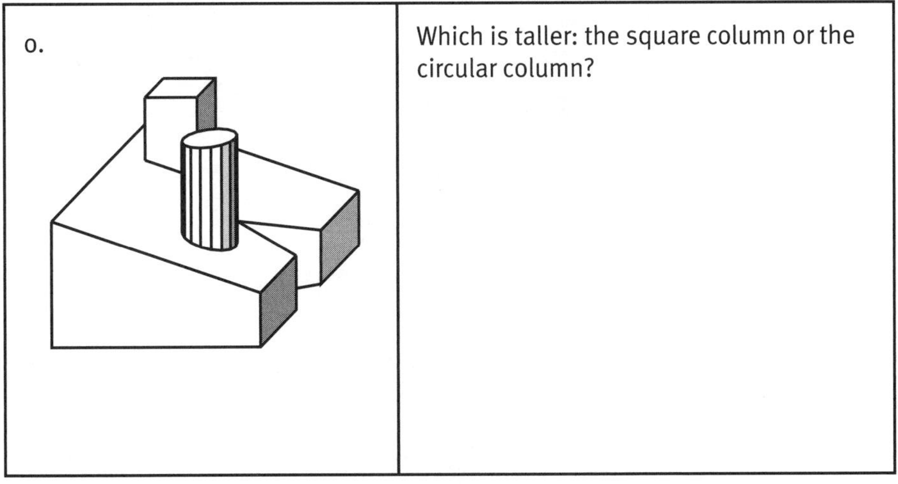

Practice Questions

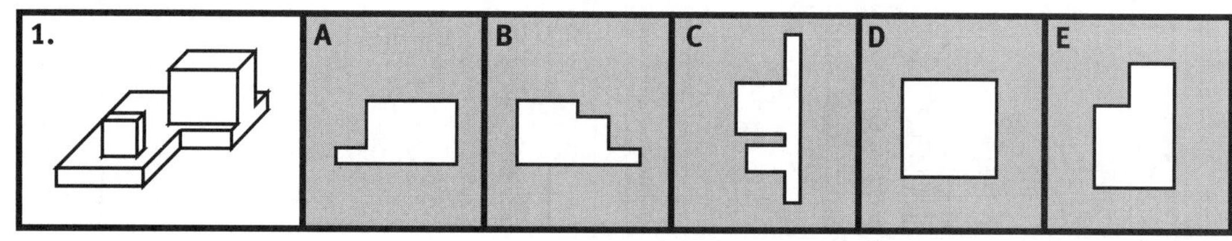

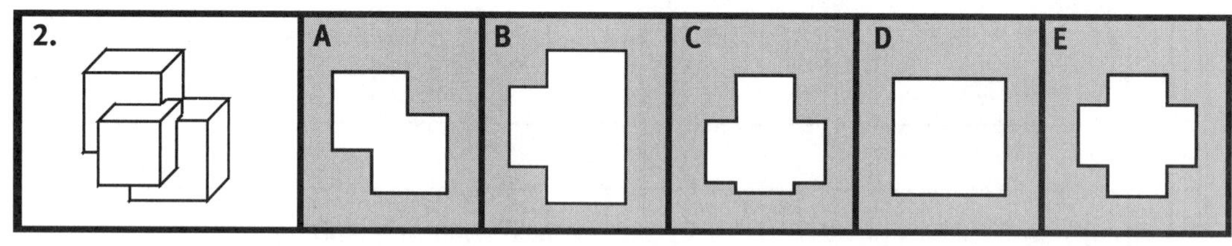

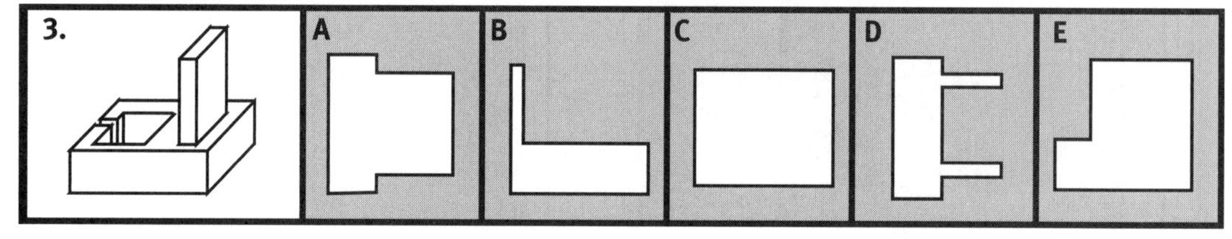

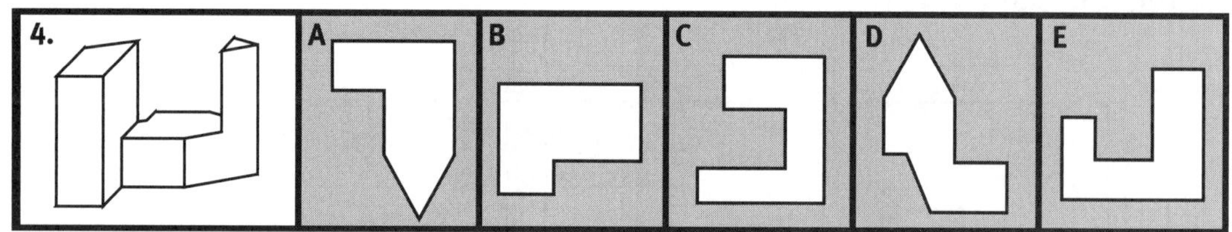

Practice Questions

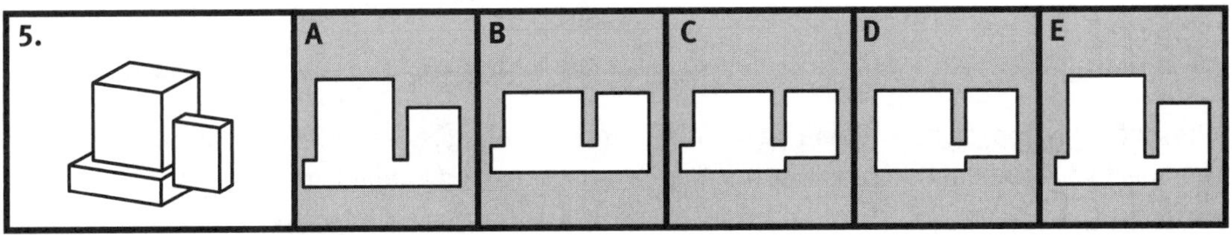

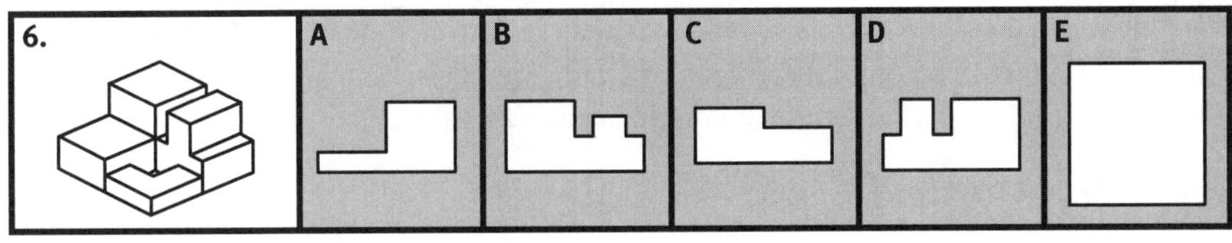

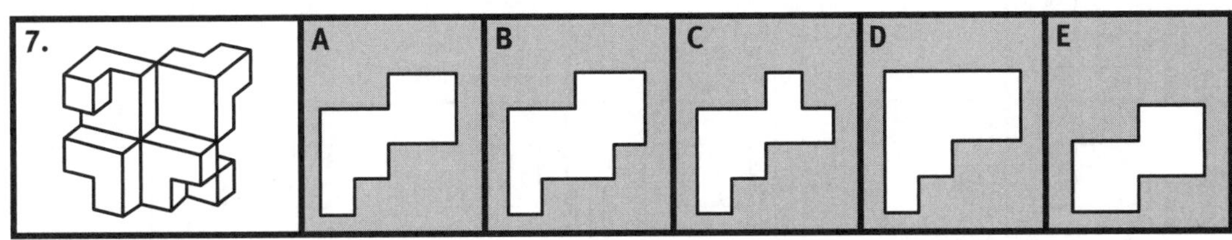

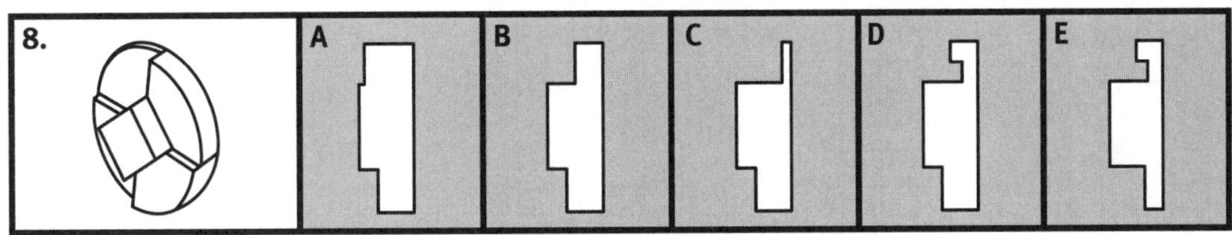

Top-Front-End

PART 2

Presented are top, front, and end views of various solid objects. All views are presented without perspective. Points in the viewed surface are presented along parallel lines of sight.

The TOP VIEW image of the object presents the projection of looking down on the object. The FRONT VIEW image presents a view of the object from the front. The END VIEW illustrates a lateral view of the object from the right. These views are always in the same position.

Lines that cannot be seen in some perspectives are represented by DOTTED lines.

The problems that follow present two views of a particular object. Four alternatives are shown to complete the set. Select the correct alternative. Try the following example:

Example Choose the correct END VIEW.

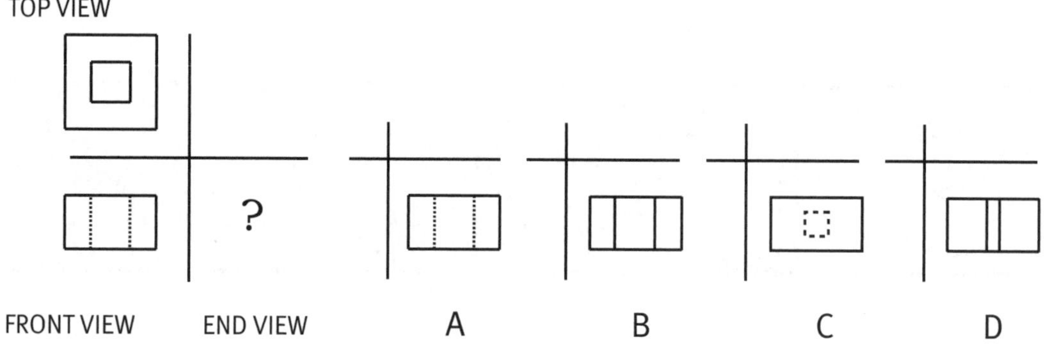

The correct answer is choice (A). The following views are shown:

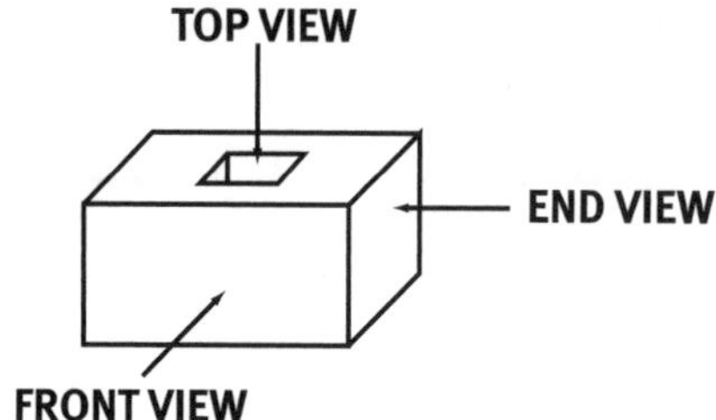

Proceed to Questions

Overview

Two views of an object are presented and you must extrapolate the third.

The Rules

Presented are top, front, and end views of various solid objects.

This means that you will never encounter a hollow object, like a box, with another shape hidden within.

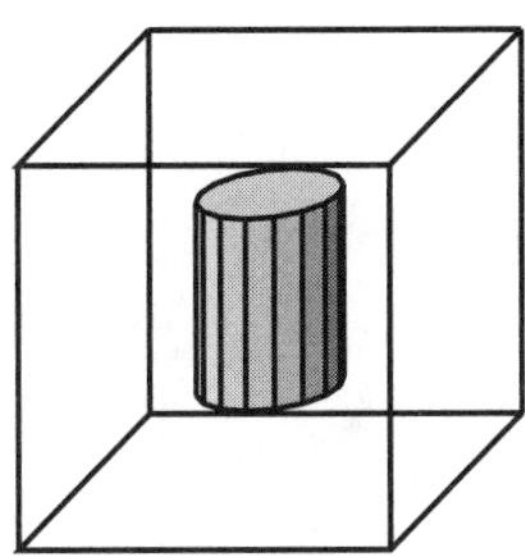

You will never see an object like this cube with a cylinder hidden inside. All objects will be solid.

All views are presented without perspective. Points in the viewed surface are presented along parallel lines of sight.

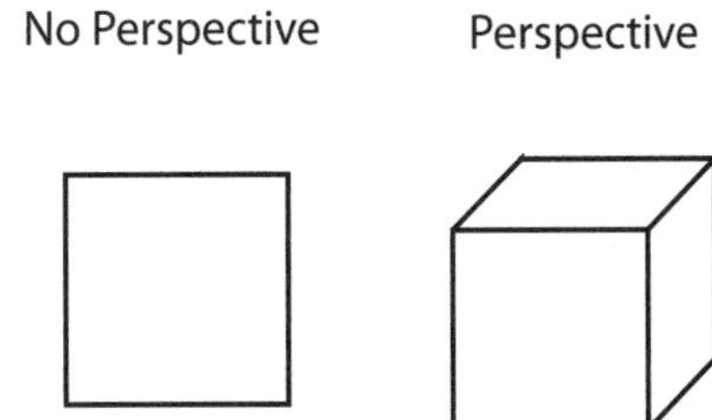

The TOP VIEW, FRONT VIEW, and END VIEW are always presented in the same positions relative to a cross on the left of the page.

The END VIEW is a lateral view of the object from the right.

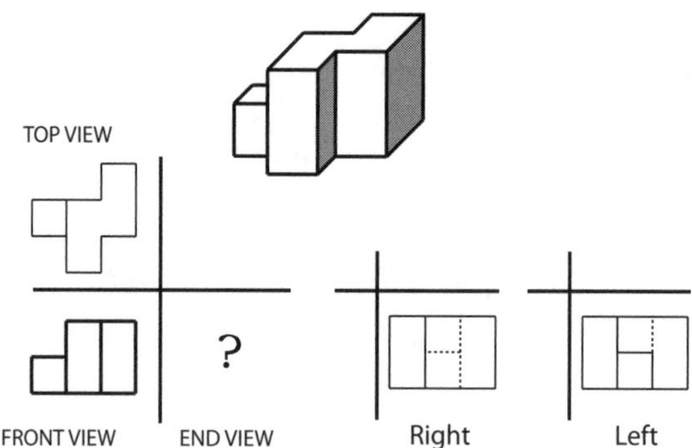

Edges of the object that cannot be seen are represented by DOTTED lines.

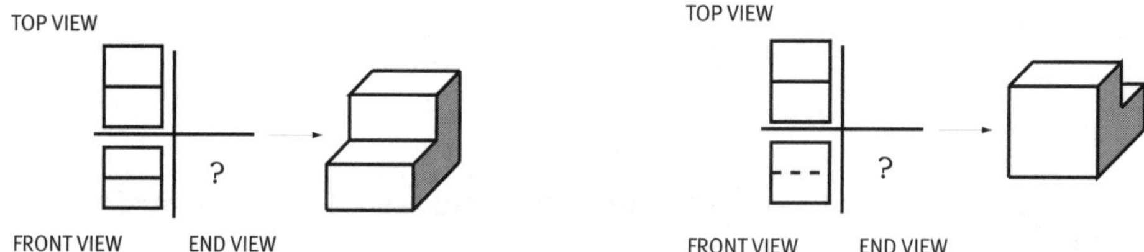

Strategies

Event Theory

- Angles
- Edges
- Lines

Fold the Quadrants

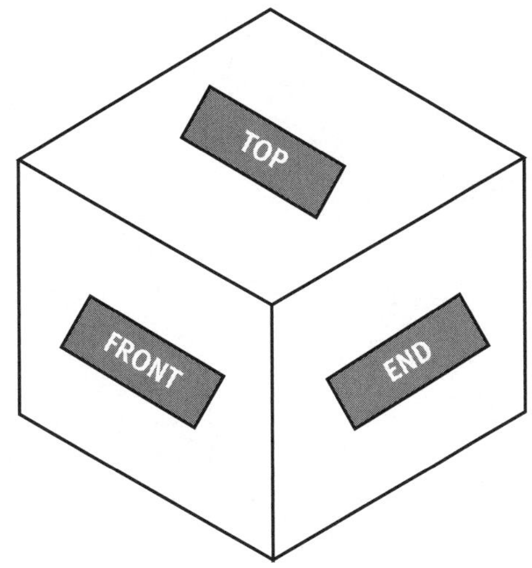

Hidden vs. Visible Events

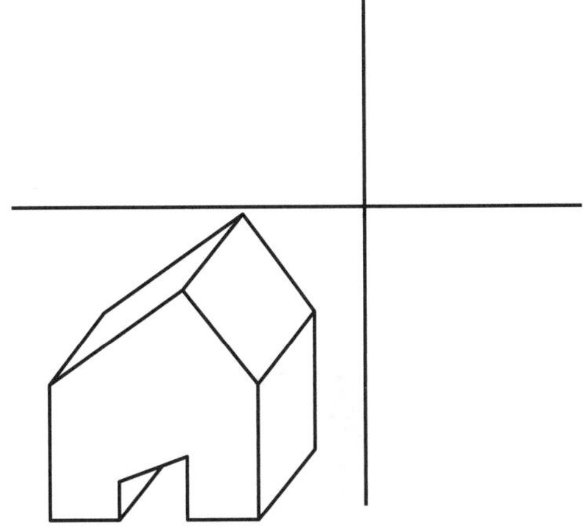

Practice Questions

9. Choose the correct **END VIEW.**

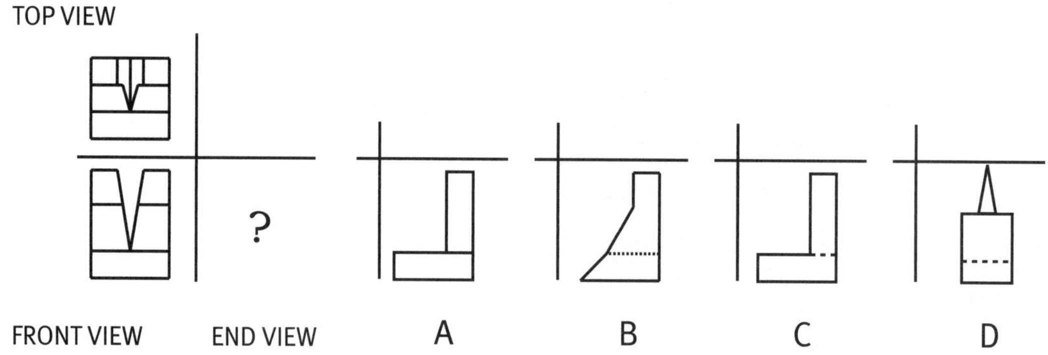

10. Choose the correct **TOP VIEW.**

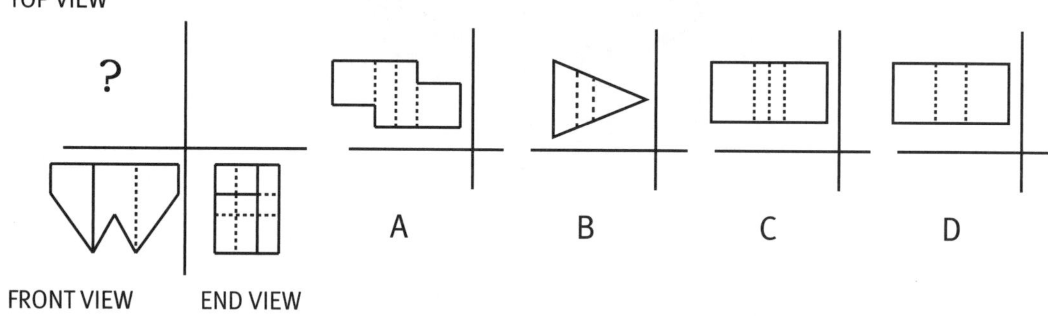

Practice Questions

11. Choose the correct **END VIEW**.

TOP VIEW

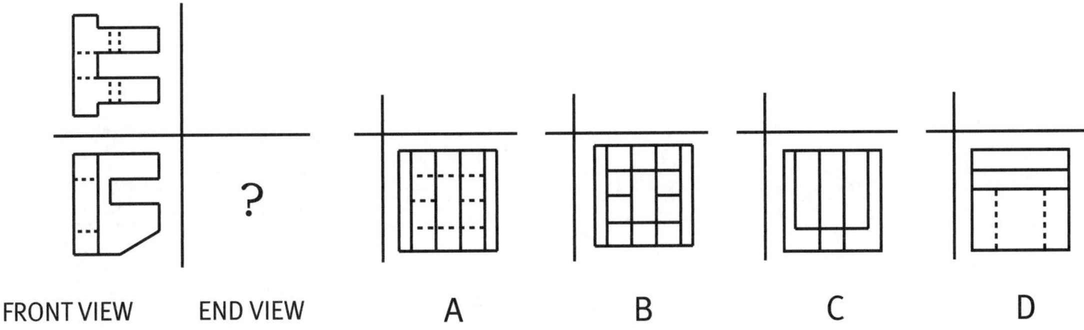

12. Choose the correct **FRONT VIEW**.

TOP VIEW

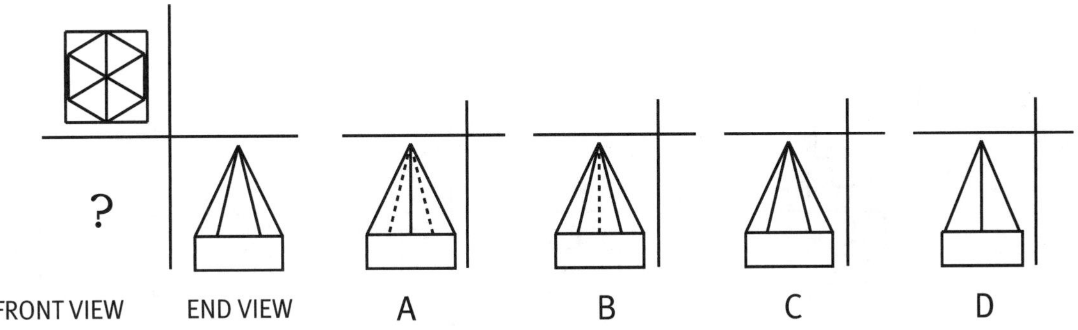

Practice Questions

13. Choose the correct **FRONT VIEW.**

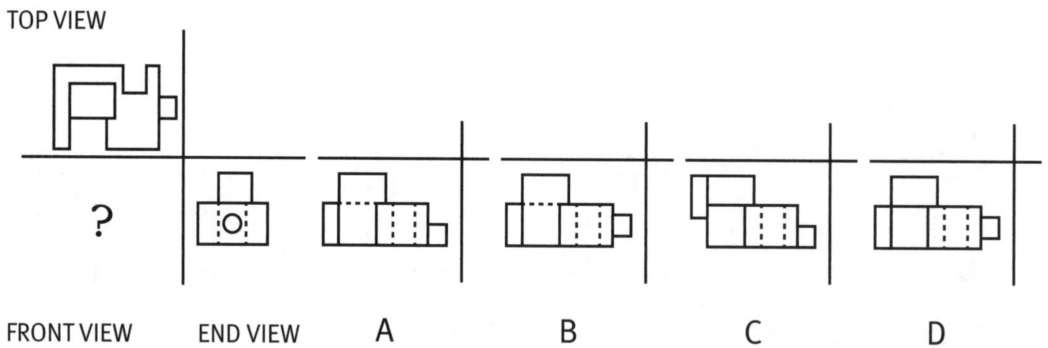

14. Choose the correct **END VIEW.**

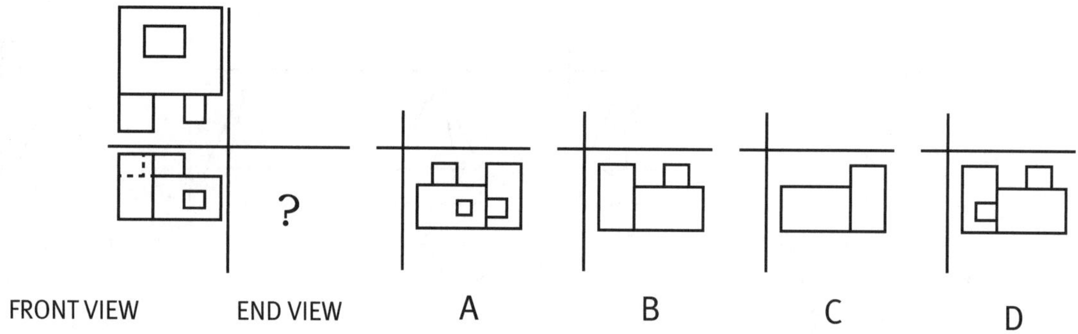

Practice Questions

15. Choose the correct **FRONT VIEW**.

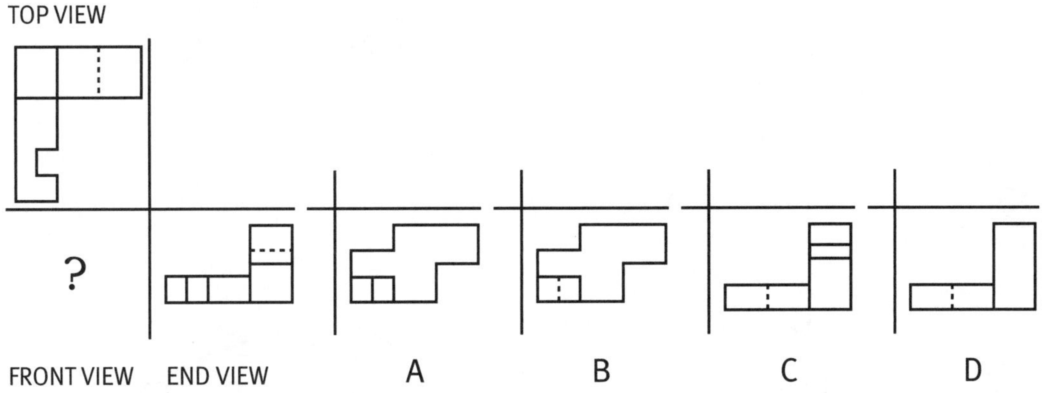

16. Choose the correct **END VIEW**.

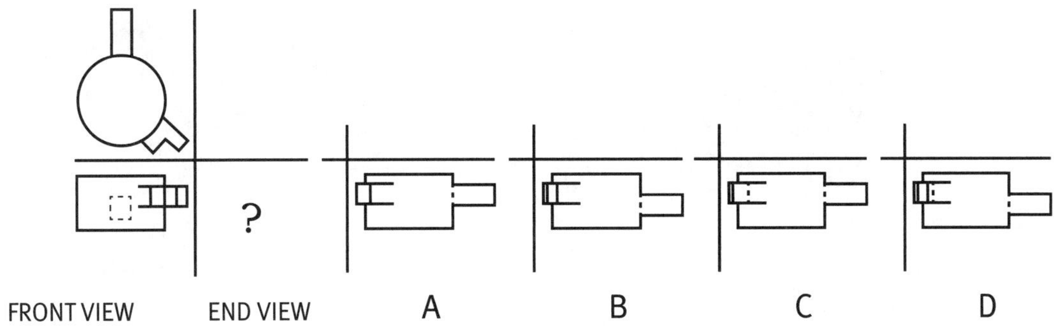

Top-Front-End 3D Images

9.

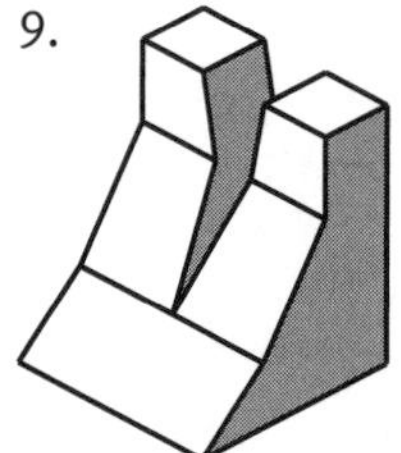

13.

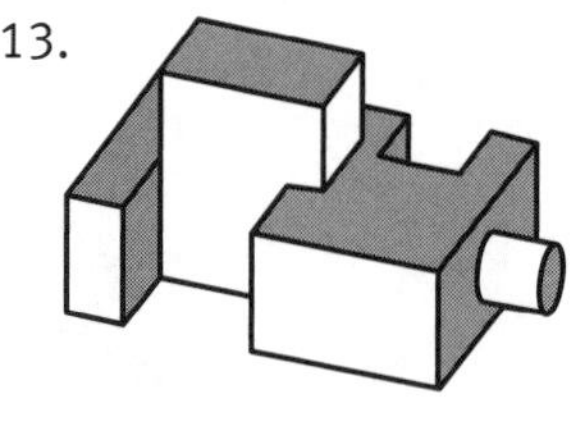

10.

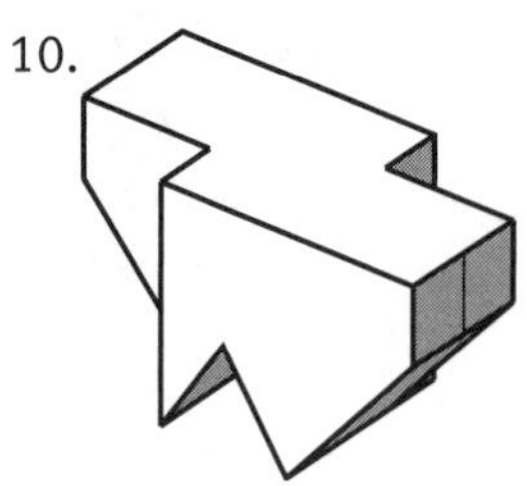

14.

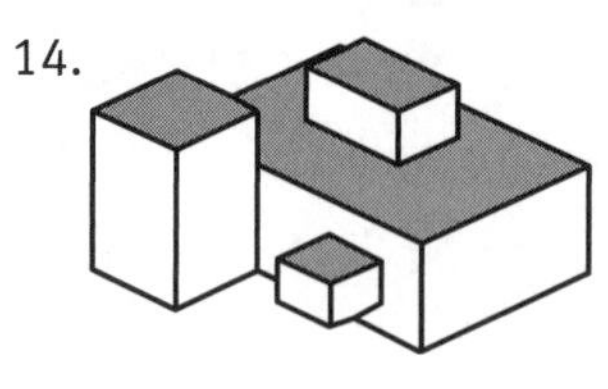

11.

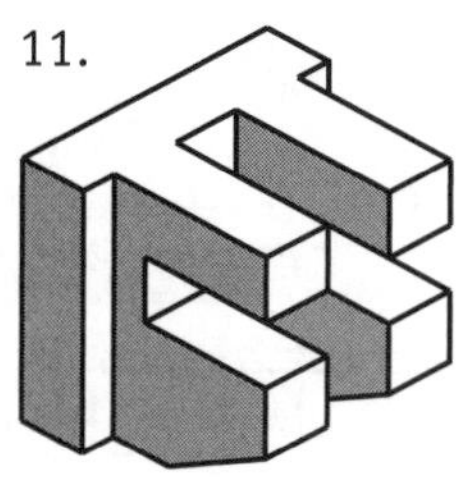

15.

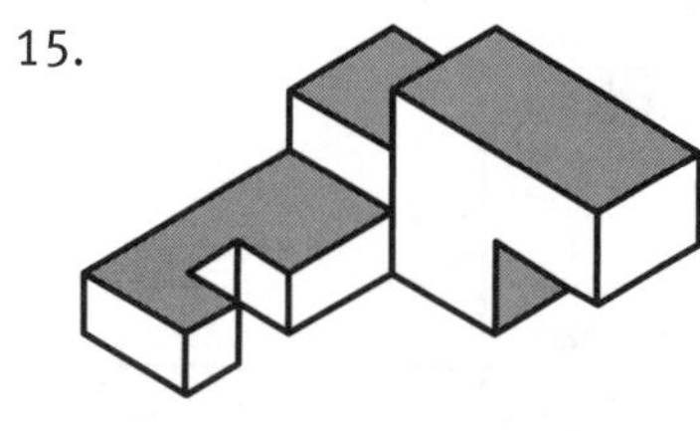

12.

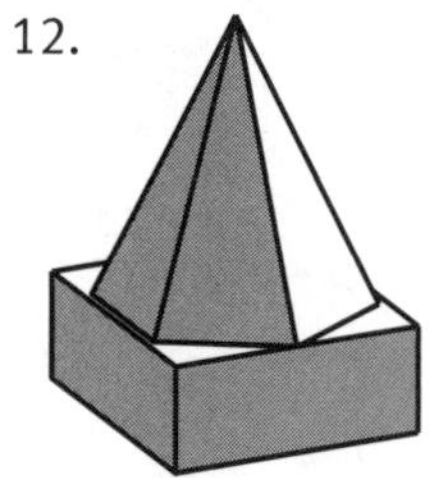

16.

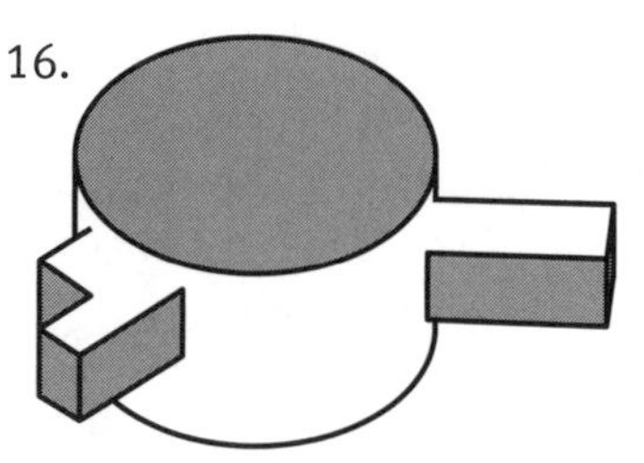

Angle Ranking

PART 3

Each question in this section presents four INTERIOR angles, labeled 1 through 4. Examine the four interior angles presented in each question.

Rank each question's angles in order from smallest to largest. Select the answer choice that represents the correct ranking. Try the following example:

Example

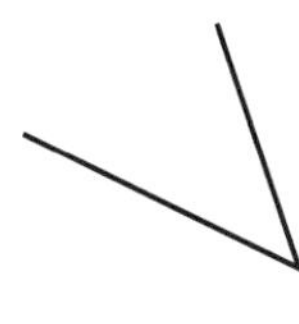

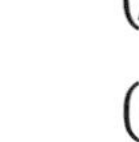

1 2 3 4

(A) 4-1-2-3
(B) 2-1-4-3
(C) 1-4-2-3
(D) 3-2-1-4

The correct ranking of the angles from small to large is 4-1-2-3. Therefore, the correct answer is choice (A).

Proceed to Questions

Overview

Four angles are given and must be ranked in order of increasing angle.

The Rules

Each question in this section presents four INTERIOR angles, labeled 1 through 4.

Strategies

Smallest and Largest Angles

Blocking

Stacking

Practice Questions

17.

1 2 3 4

(A) 2-1-4-3

(B) 2-3-4-1

(C) 2-4-1-3

(D) 1-2-3-4

18.

1 2 3 4

(A) 1-3-4-2

(B) 1-2-4-3

(C) 2-1-3-4

(D) 1-2-3-4

19.

1 2 3 4

(A) 1-2-3-4

(B) 2-1-3-4

(C) 2-1-4-3

(D) 1-4-2-3

20.

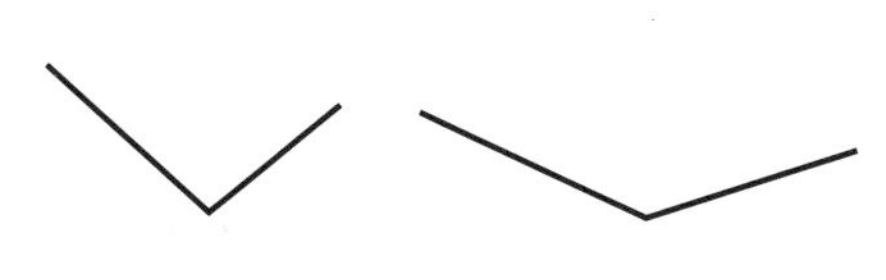
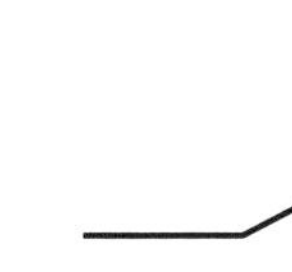

1 2 3 4

(A) 4-1-3-2

(B) 2-3-4-1

(C) 1-4-2-3

(D) 1-4-3-2

Practice Questions

21.

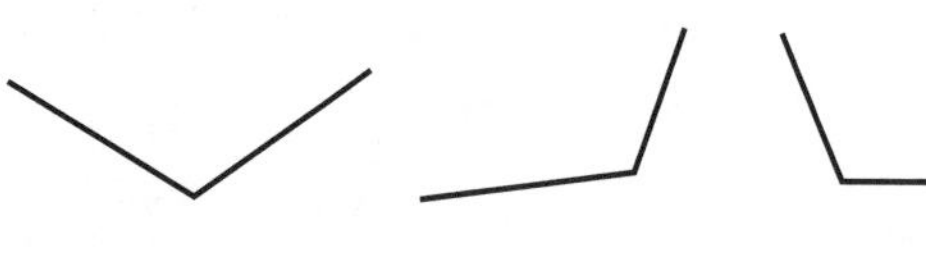

1 2 3 4

(A) 1-3-2-4
(B) 3-1-2-4
(C) 3-1-4-2
(D) 1-3-4-2

22.

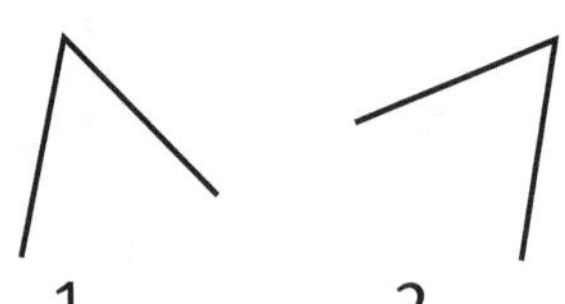

1 2 3 4

(A) 1-3-2-4
(B) 1-2-3-4
(C) 3-1-2-4
(D) 3-2-1-4

23.

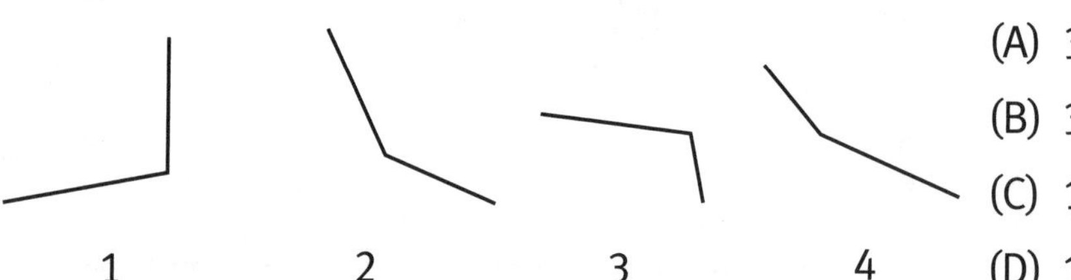

1 2 3 4

(A) 3-1-2-4
(B) 3-1-4-2
(C) 1-3-2-4
(D) 1-3-4-2

24.

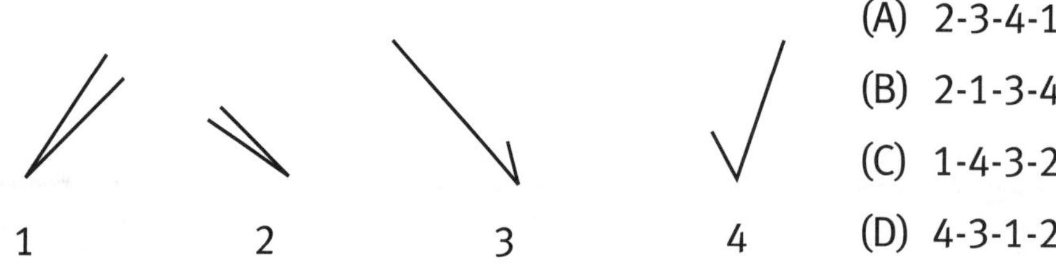

1 2 3 4

(A) 2-3-4-1
(B) 2-1-3-4
(C) 1-4-3-2
(D) 4-3-1-2

Hole Punching

PART 4

In these questions, a flat, square piece of paper is folded one or more times. Broken lines indicate the original position of the paper, and solid lines indicate the position of the folded paper. The folded paper remains within the boundaries of the original, flat sheet. The paper is not turned or twisted. There are one, two, or three folds per question.

After the final fold is performed, a hole is punched in the paper. Once the hole is punched, mentally unfold the paper and determine the position(s) of the hole(s) on the original flat sheet.

Select the answer choice that represents the same pattern of dark circles that would reflect the position of holes on the unfolded sheet. There is only one correct pattern for each question. Try the following example:

Example

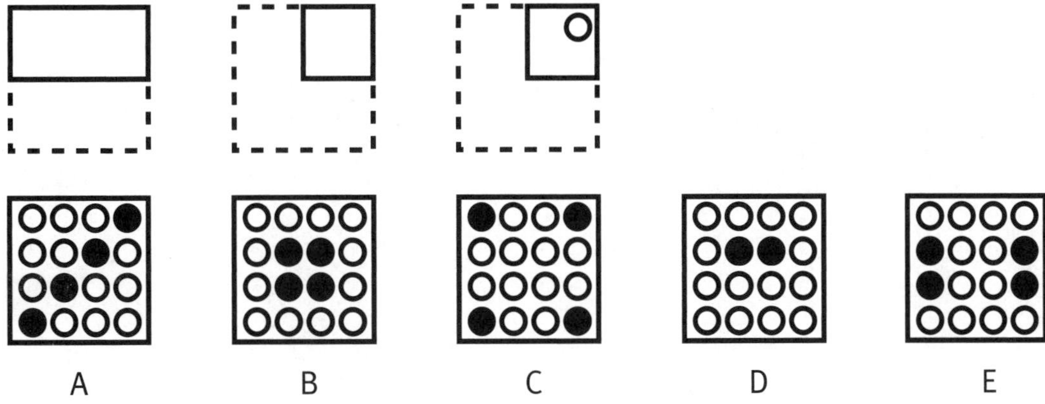

The correct answer is choice (C).

Proceed to Questions

Overview

You must identify where the holes punched in a folded piece of paper will be when the piece of paper is unfolded.

The Rules

A flat, square piece of paper is folded one or more times.

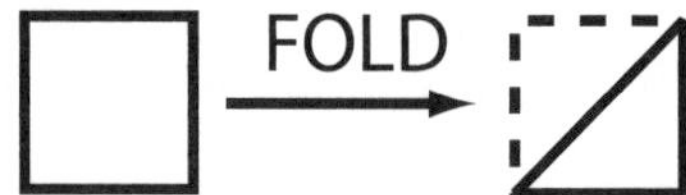

Broken lines indicate the original position of the paper, and solid lines indicate the position of the folded paper. The folded paper remains within the boundaries of the original, flat sheet. The paper is not turned or twisted.

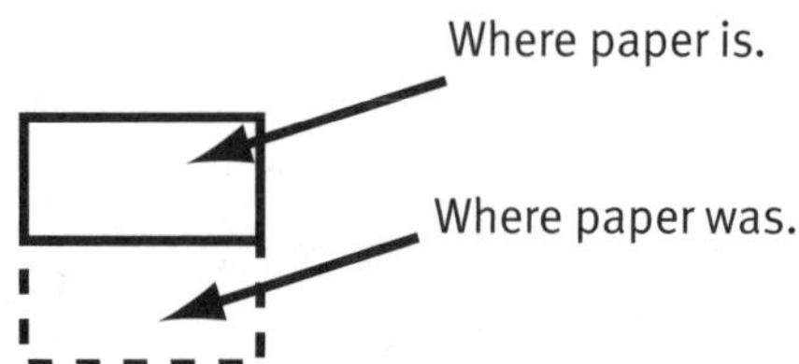

Determine how the paper was folded by looking at its position before and after the fold.

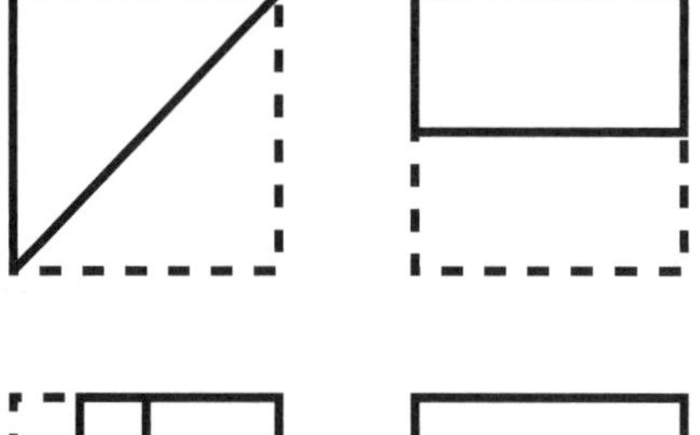

These are the possible first folds.

There are one, two, or three folds per question.

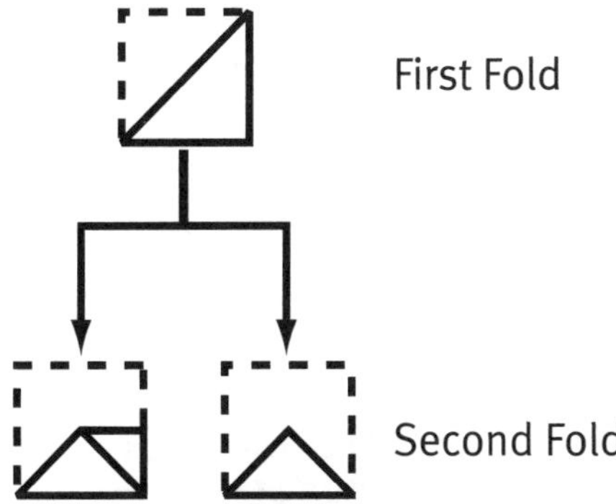

Here are two of the many possible second folds following the given first fold.

After the final fold is performed, one or more holes are punched in the paper. Once the holes are punched, mentally unfold the paper and ascertain the positions of the holes on the original flat sheet.

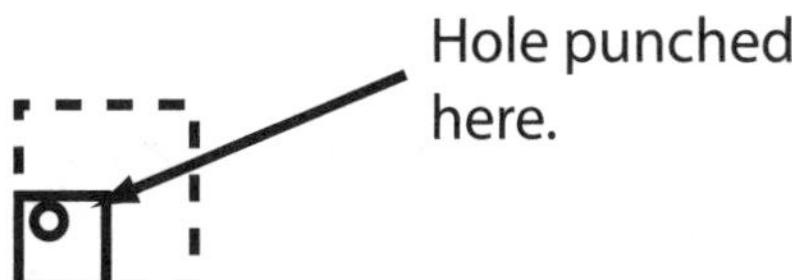

Notice that the location of the hole being punched is indicated by the outline of a circle.

The location of the hole punched is constrained by the fact that no "half " holes are generated. However, a hole may be punched along a fold so that when the paper is unfolded, a single "whole" hole results from the "half" punch.

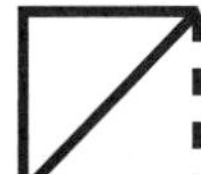  

Strategies

First Fold Line of Symmetry

The first fold is particularly important for determining the symmetry of the final solution.

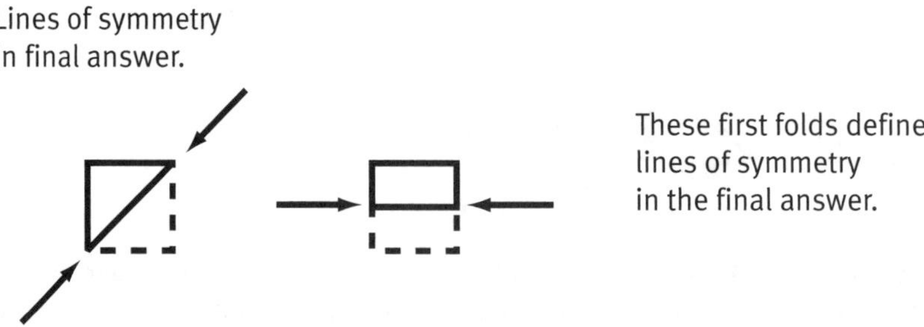

Practice with Lines of Symmetry

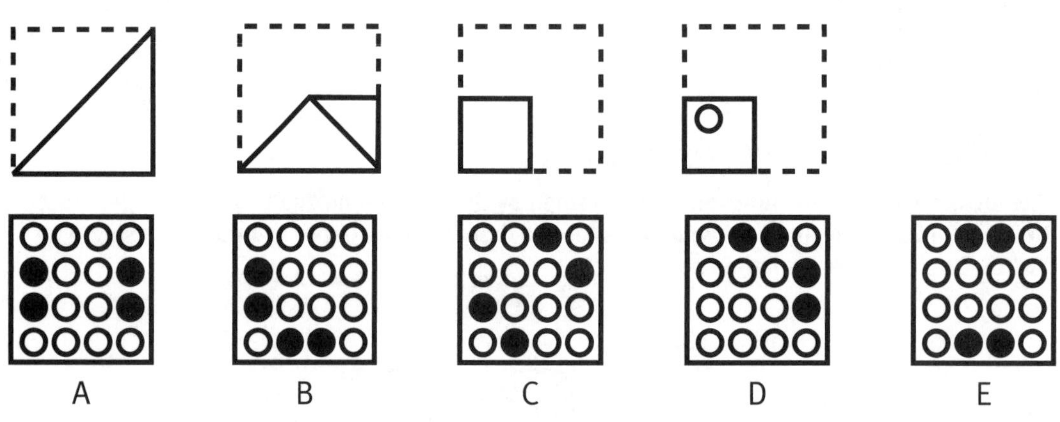

Number of Folds

Layers of Paper

Practice with Number of Folds and Layers of Paper

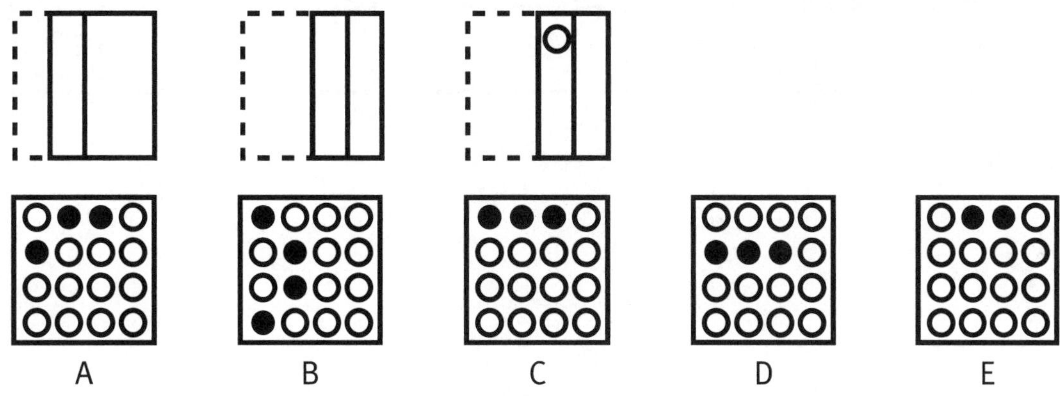

Number of Punches

Practice with Number of Punches

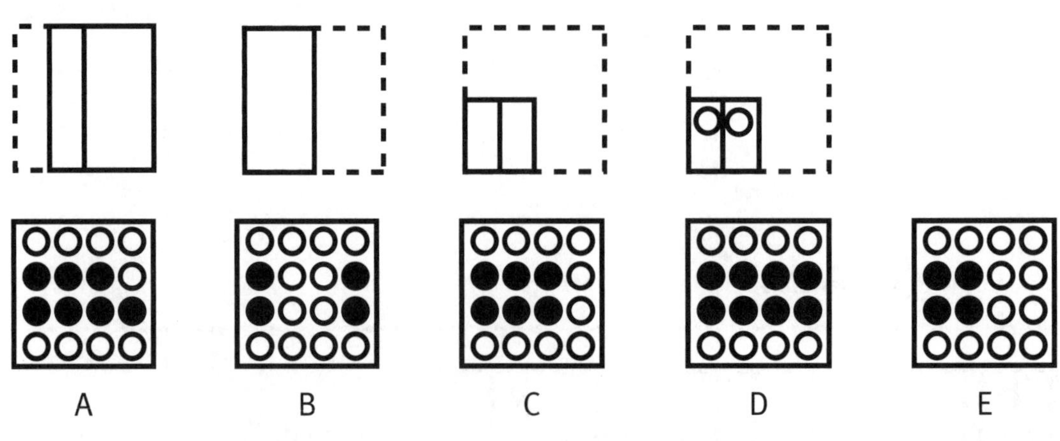

Practice Questions

25.

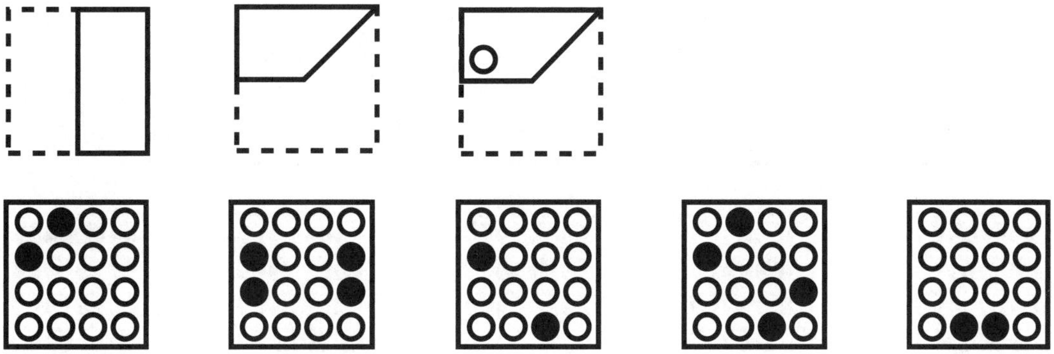

A B C D E

26.

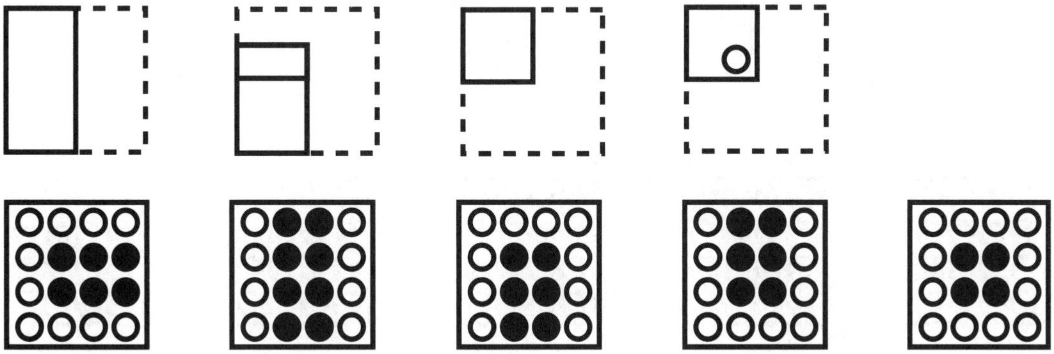

A B C D E

Practice Questions

27.

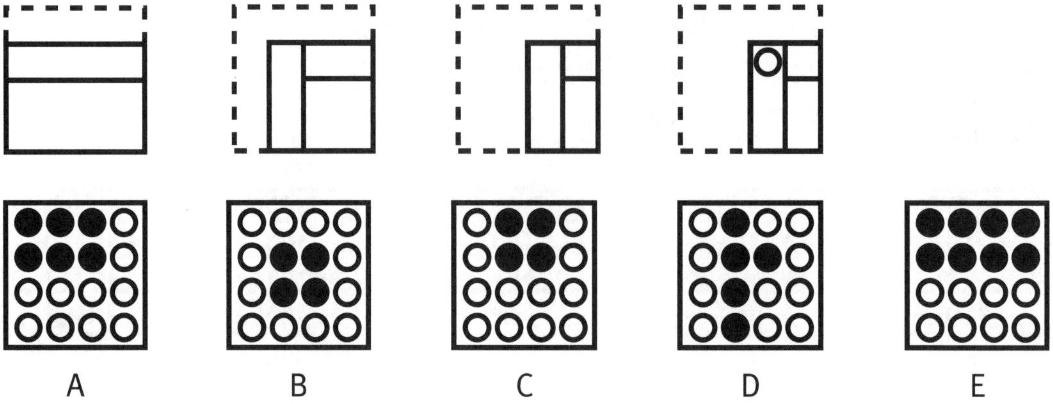

A B C D E

28.

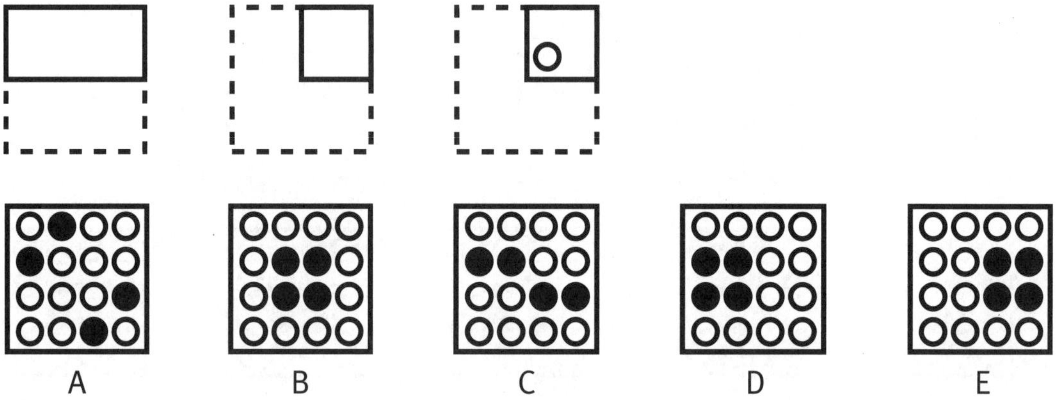

A B C D E

Practice Questions

29.

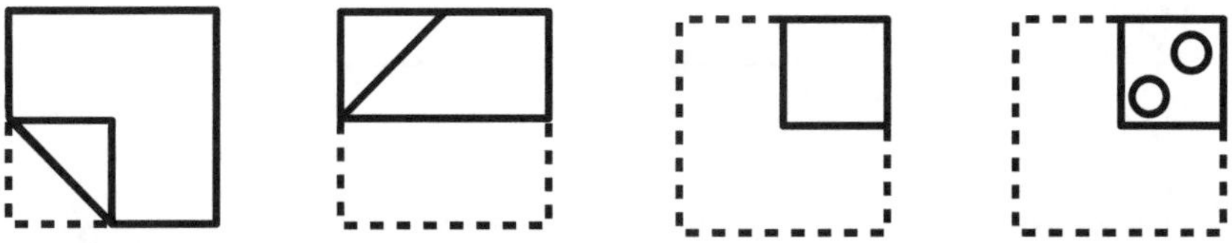

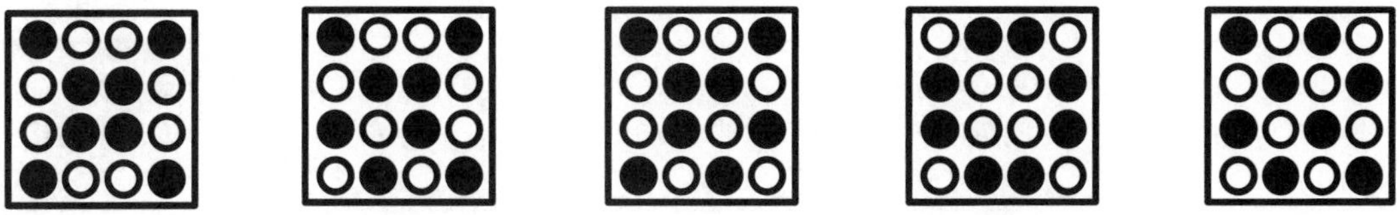

A B C D E

30.

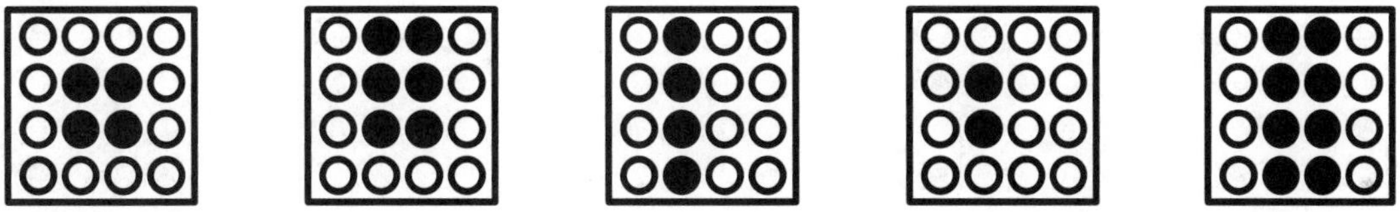

A B C D E

Practice Questions

31.

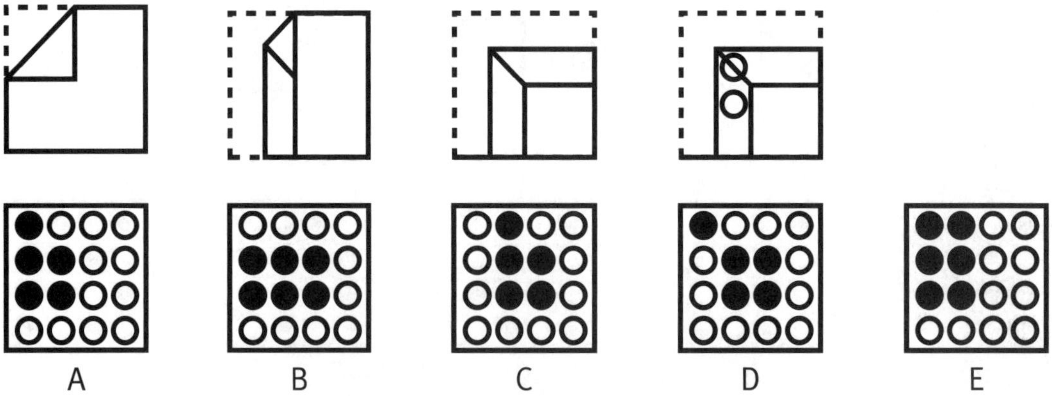

A B C D E

32.

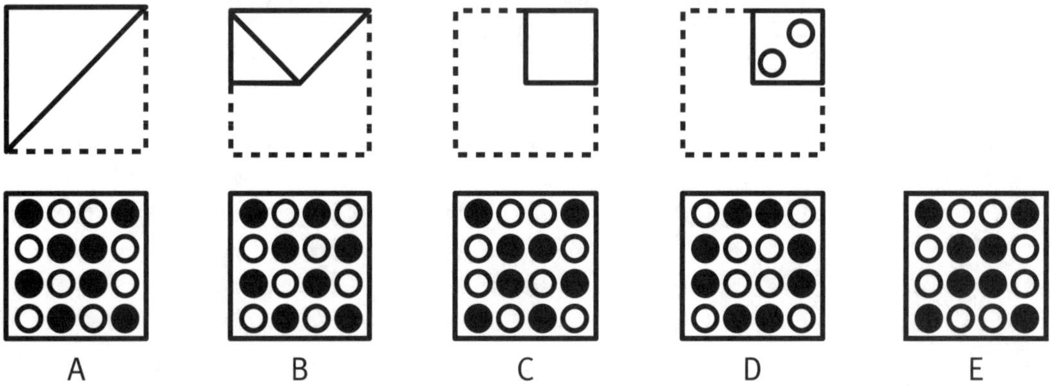

A B C D E

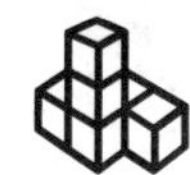

Cube Counting

PART 5

Each figure presented in this section has been constructed by cementing together identical cubes. After being cemented, each figure was varnished on all sides EXCEPT for the bottom (the side on which the figure rests). The only hidden cubes are the ones necessary to support other cubes in the figure.

Examine each figure carefully regarding the number of sides on each cube that have been varnished. The following questions ask for this information. Select the correct answer choice from the ones provided. Try the following example:

Example

In the Example Figure, how many cubes have two of their exposed sides painted?

A. 1 cube
B. 2 cubes
C. 3 cubes
D. 4 cubes
E. 5 cubes

Example Figure

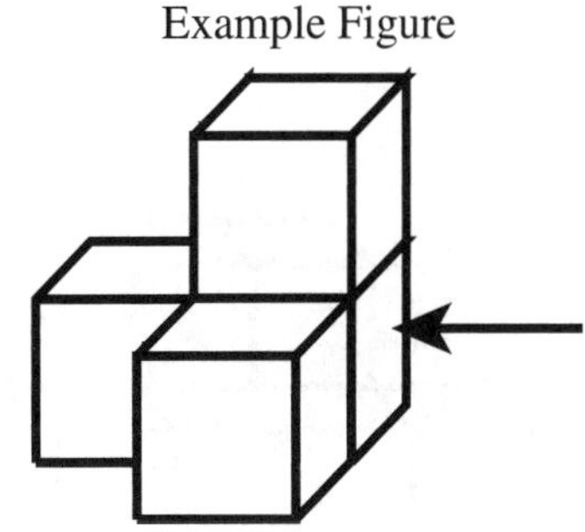

The correct answer is choice A. The cube is indicated with an arrow above.

Proceed to Questions

Overview

A stack of cubes is given. You must determine how many cubes have a particular number of exposed sides.

The Rules

Each figure has been constructed by cementing together identical cubes.

After being cemented, each figure was painted on all sides EXCEPT for the bottom (the side on which the figure rests).

The only hidden cubes are the ones necessary to support other cubes in the figure.

How many cubes are in this stack?

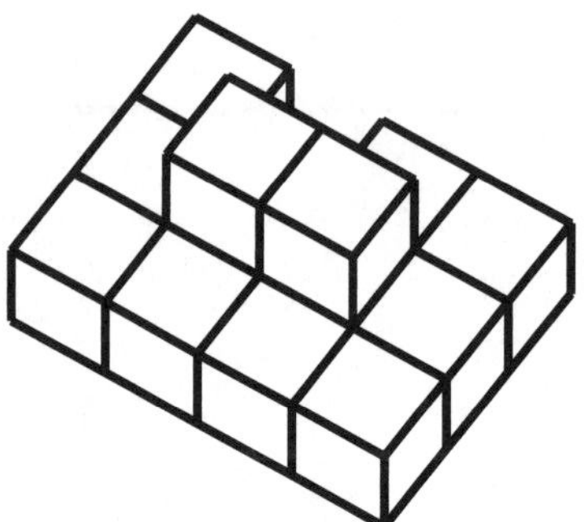

This is how you should interpret the stack of cubes shown above.

The Six Cubes of the PAT

One-Sider

In the diagram below, shade the cubes that have one side exposed.

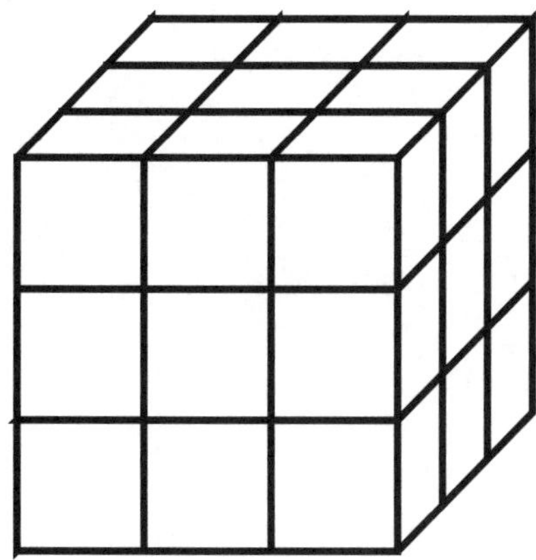

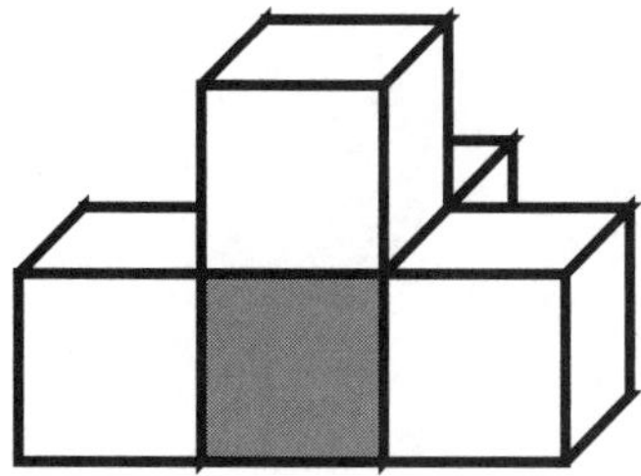

The One-Sider appears on the faces of complex figures.

Two-Sider

In the diagram below, shade the cubes that have two sides exposed.

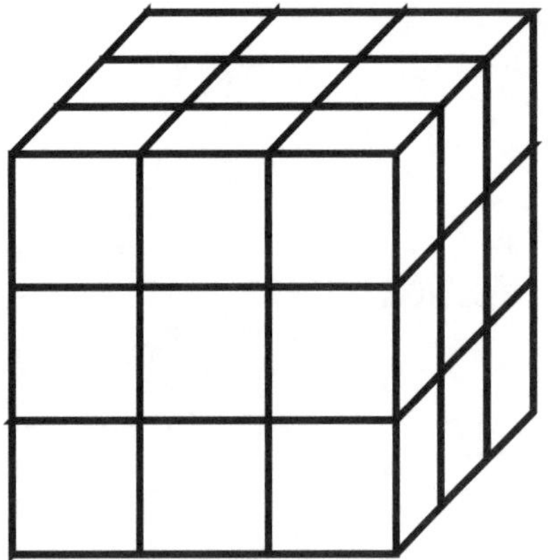

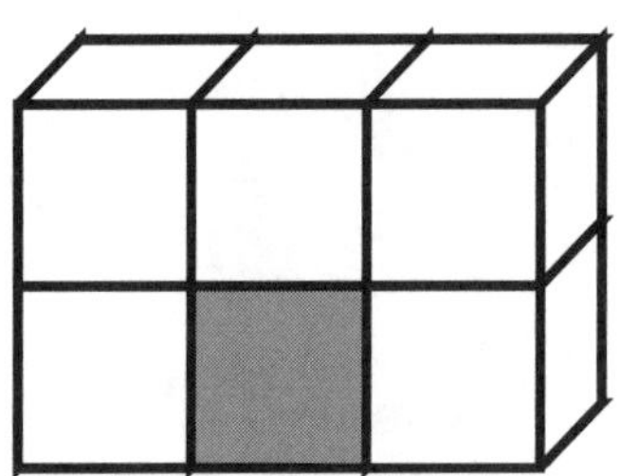

The Two-Sider appears on the bottoms of walls.

Three-Sider

In the diagram below, shade the cubes that have three sides exposed.

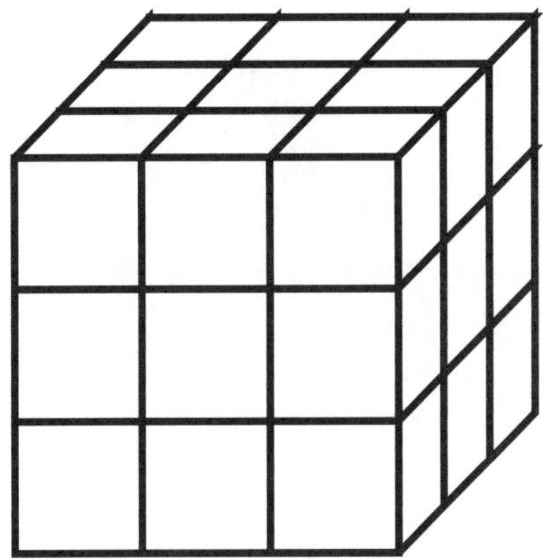

The Three-Sider appears on the edges of a wall of cubes.

Four-Sider

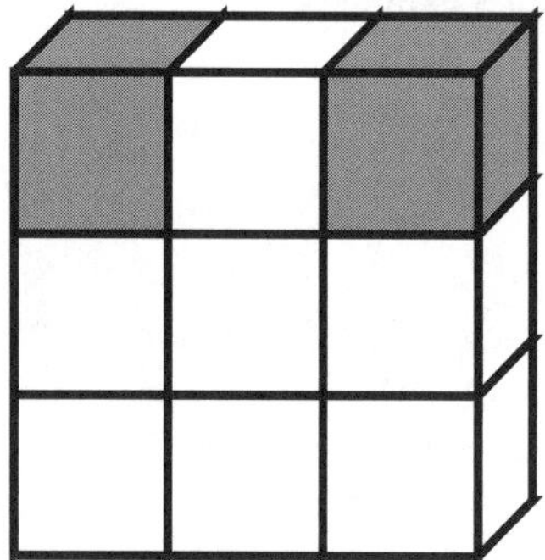

The Four-Sider appears on the corners of a wall of cubes.

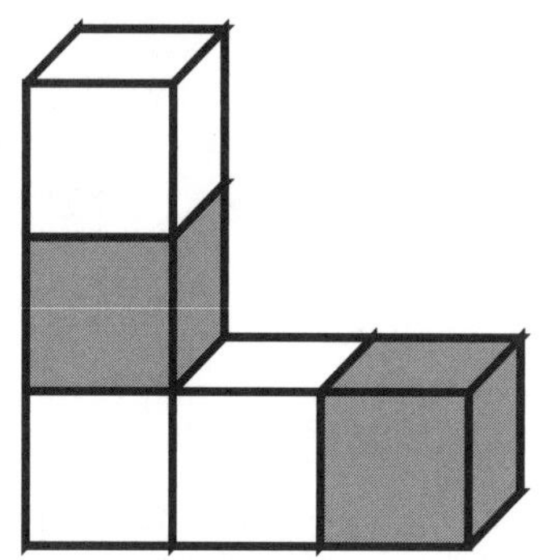

The Four-Sider can also appear within a column of cubes.

Five-Sider

The cube with five sides exposed can only appear in the following way:

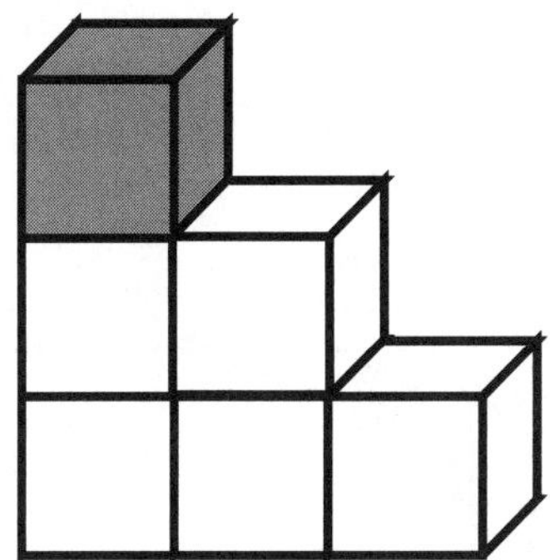

The Five-Sider sits up on a column of cubes.

No-Sider

The cube with no exposed side can appear in the following way:

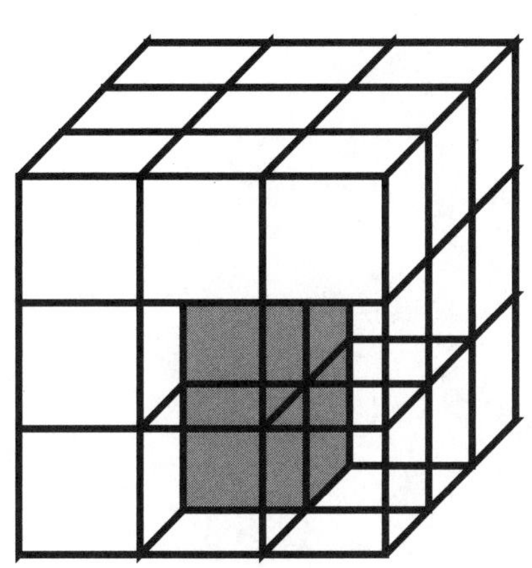

The No-Sider exists in the core of a complex figure.

Tallying the Cubes

Figure A

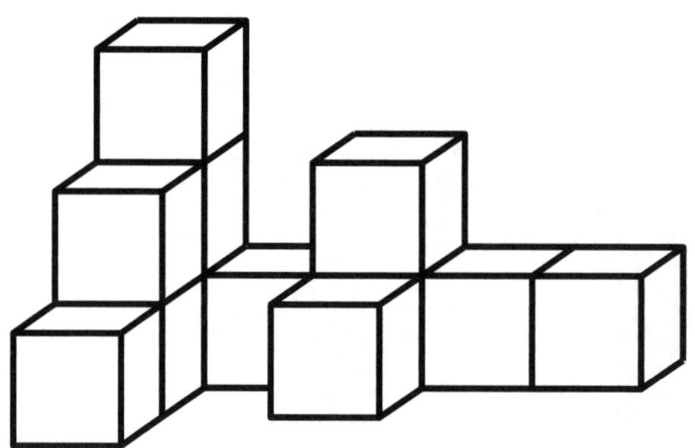

Sides	#
0	
1	
2	
3	
4	
5	
Total	

Practice Questions

33. In Figure A, how many cubes have two of their exposed sides painted?

    A. 1 cube
    B. 2 cubes
    C. 3 cubes
    D. 4 cubes
    E. 5 cubes

34. In Figure A, how many cubes have four of their exposed sides painted?

    A. 1 cube
    B. 2 cubes
    C. 3 cubes
    D. 4 cubes
    E. 5 cubes

35. In Figure A, how many cubes have five of their exposed sides painted?

    A. 1 cube
    B. 2 cubes
    C. 3 cubes
    D. 4 cubes
    E. 5 cubes

Tallying the Cubes

Figure B

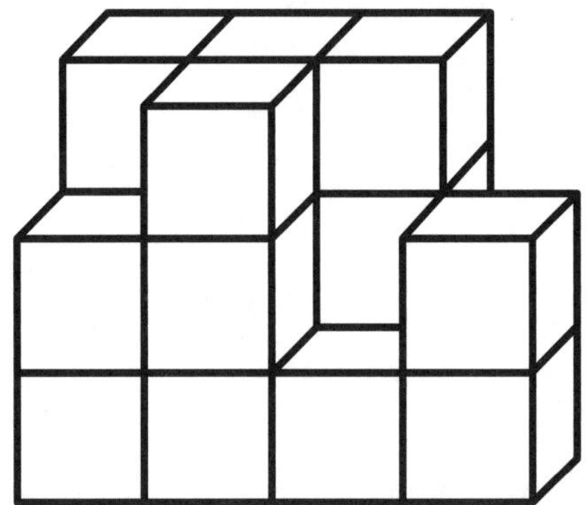

Sides	#
0	
1	
2	
3	
4	
5	
Total	

Practice Questions

36. In Figure B, how many cubes have one of their exposed sides painted?

 A. 1 cube
 B. 2 cubes
 C. 3 cubes
 D. 4 cubes
 E. 5 cubes

37. In Figure B, how many cubes have three of their exposed sides painted?

 A. 1 cube
 B. 2 cubes
 C. 3 cubes
 D. 4 cubes
 E. 5 cubes

38. In Figure B, how many cubes have five of their exposed sides painted?

 A. 1 cube
 B. 2 cubes
 C. 3 cubes
 D. 4 cubes
 E. 5 cubes

Pattern Folding

PART 6

In the following questions, a flat pattern is presented. This pattern will be folded into a three-dimensional figure, and the correct three-dimensional figure is one of the four answer choices illustrated at the right of the pattern. There is only one correct three-dimensional figure for each question. The pattern at left represents the outside of the figure.

Select the three-dimensional figure that directly corresponds to the pattern at left. Choose the appropriate answer choice. Try the following example:

Example

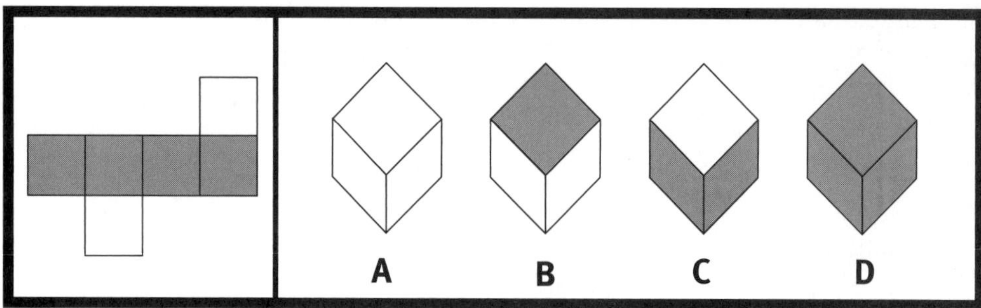

The correct answer is choice (C).

Proceed to Questions

Overview

Determine which three-dimensional shape is produced by folding a two-dimensional pattern.

The Rules

A flat pattern is presented at left.

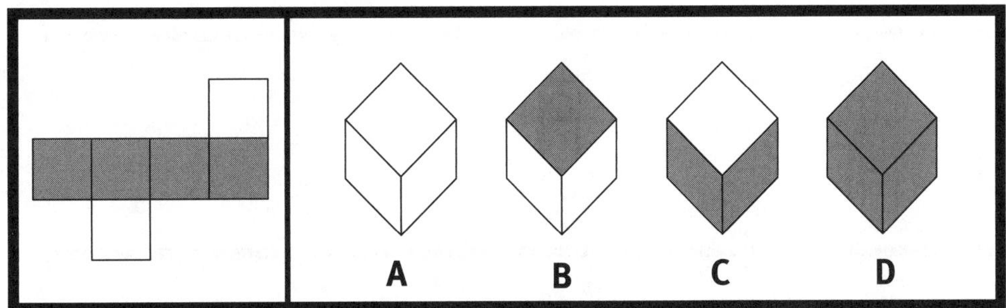

There is only one correct three-dimensional figure for each question.

This means if two choices are different views of the same object, then neither is correct.

The flat pattern represents the *outside* of the figure.

This means fold the flat pattern *into the page* in order to produce a three-dimensional object with the pattern facing out.

Strategies

Unique Shape

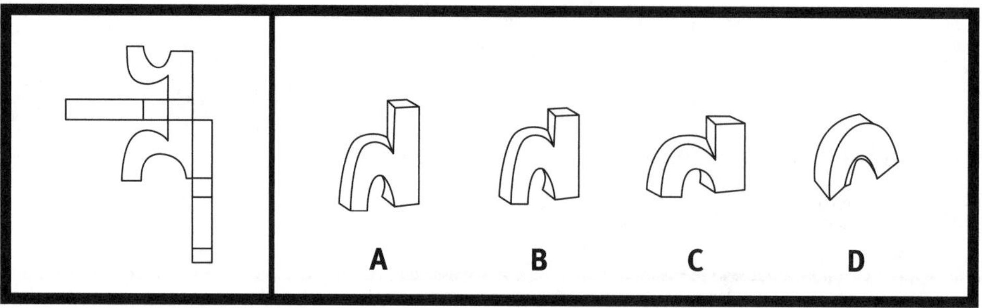

Unique Shading

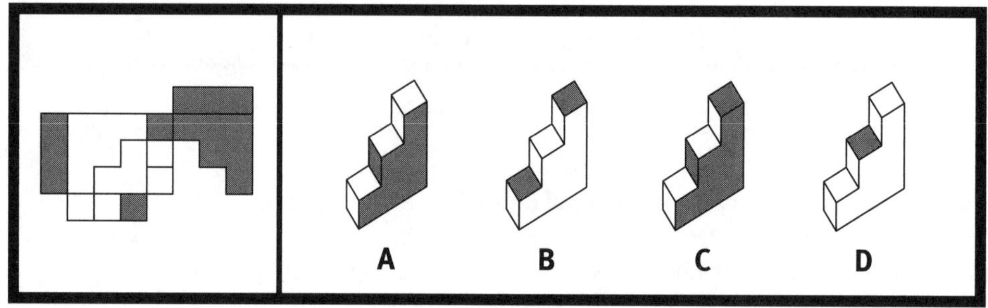

Key Landmark

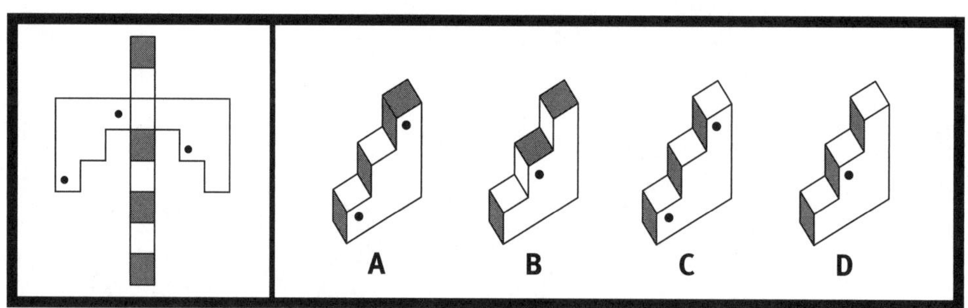

Practice Questions

39.

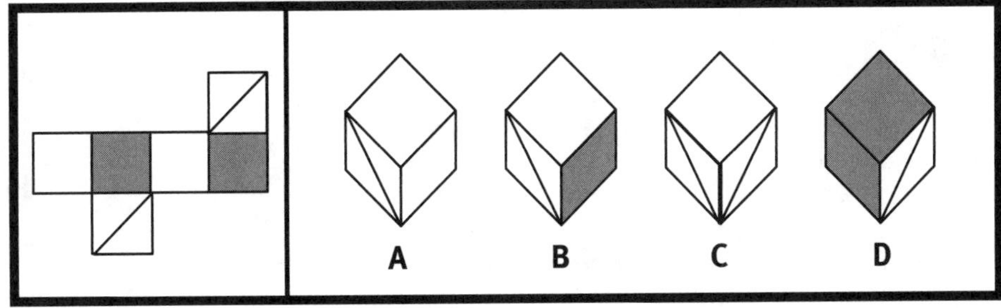

40.

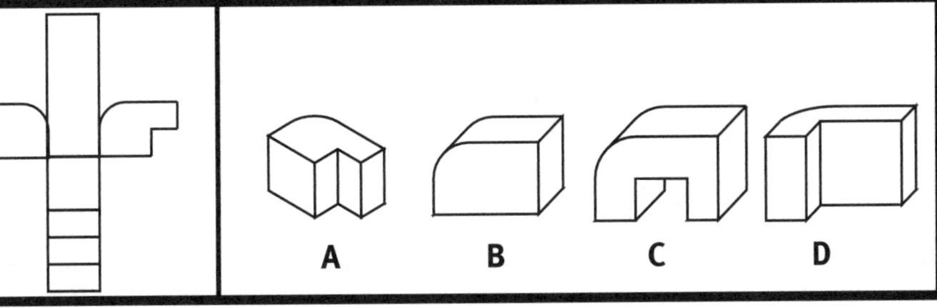

41.

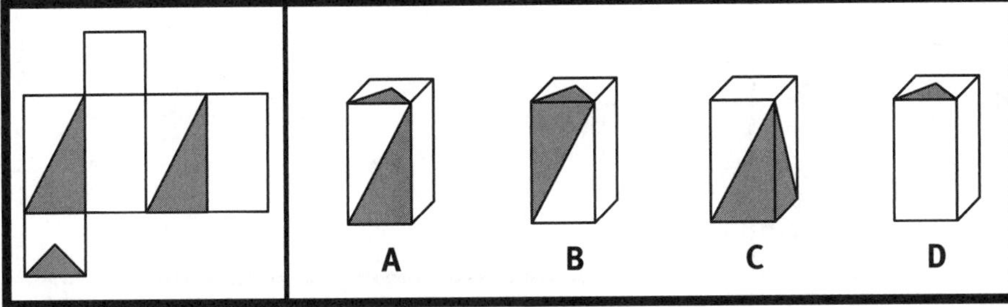

42.

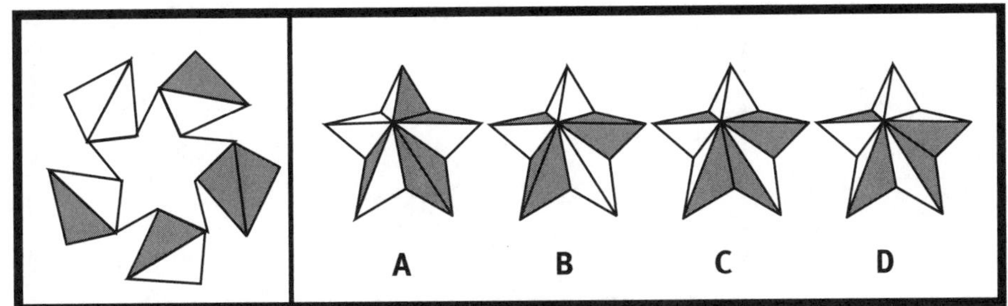

Practice Questions

43.

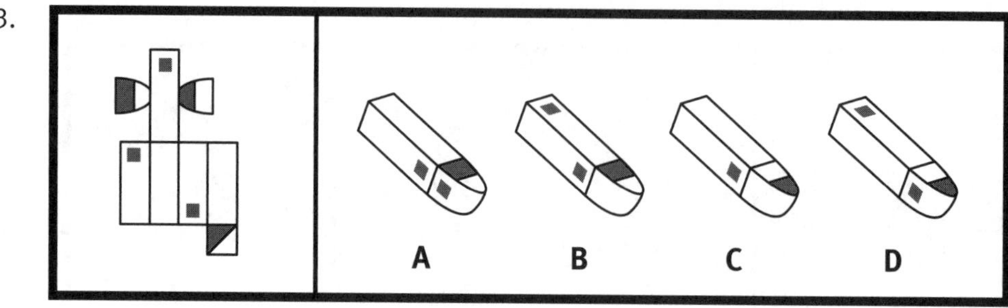

44.

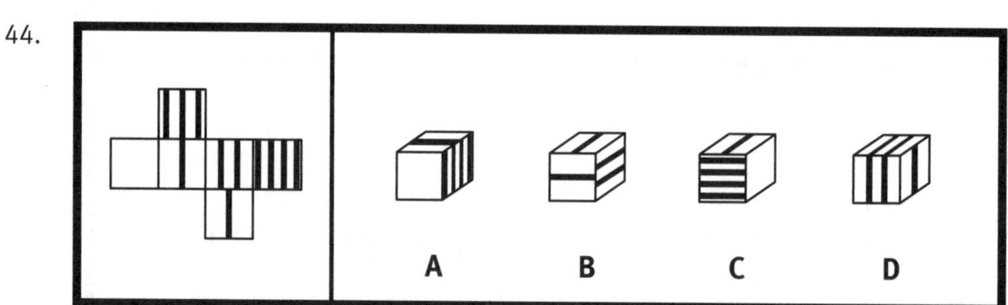

45.

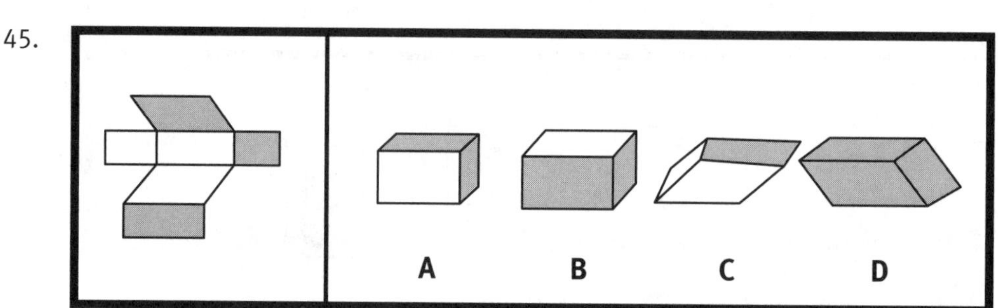

46.

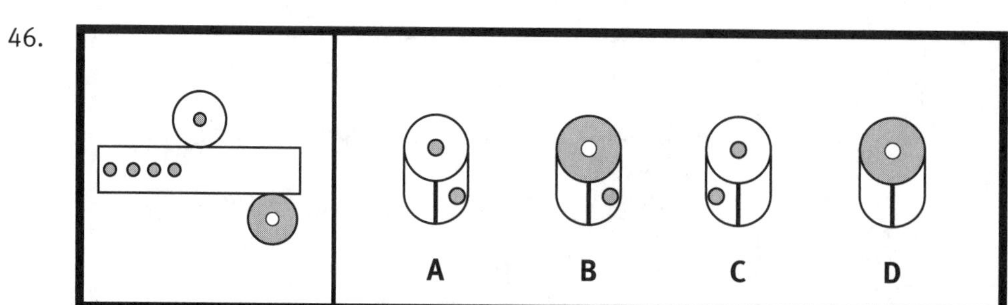

Study Plan

After Class: Perceptual Ability 1		
Complete Remaining *Lesson Book* Practice Questions	30m	
Practice with Tests and Quizzes		
Before Class: Quantitative Reasoning 1		
Read *Review Notes* Chapters 55–57	1h 30m	
Problem Solving Basics Workshop	45m	
Arithmetic Fundamentals Workshop	45m	

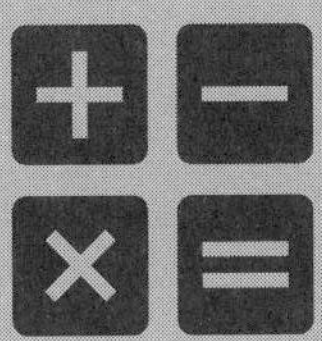

QUANTITATIVE REASONING 1

TOPICS COVERED

- The Quantitative Reasoning Section
- Quantitative Reasoning Strategic Overview
- Numerical Calculations
- Algebra

After this session you will be able to:

- Identify opportunities to apply Traditional Math, Picking Numbers, Backsolving, Educated Guessing, and Estimation to math problems
- Calculate numerical problems involving fractions, decimals, exponents, and absolute values
- Calculate algebra problems using equations and inequalities
- Analyze the properties of graphs and figures

The Quantitative Reasoning Section

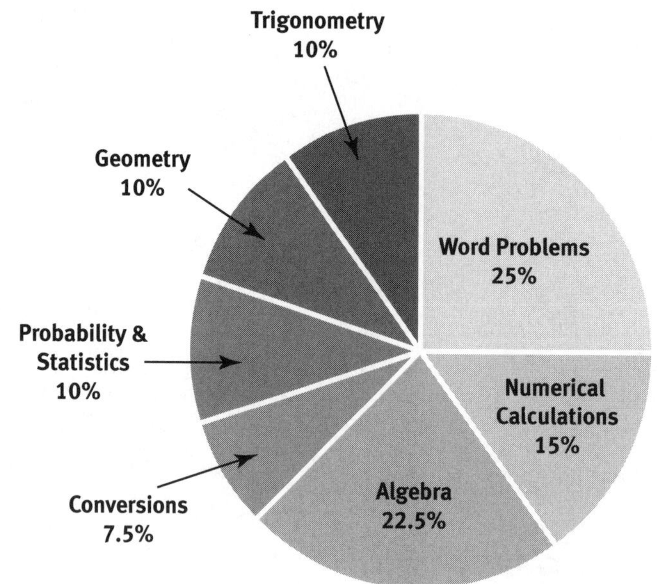

The distribution of Quantitative Reasoning questions

Overview

- 40 questions in 45 minutes

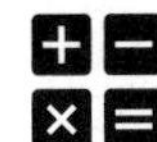

Topics

Numerical Calculations (6)

- Fractions and Decimals
- Percentages
- Approximation
- Scientific Notation

Algebra (9)

- Equations and Expressions
- Inequalities
- Exponential Notation
- Absolute Value
- Ratios and Proportions
- Graphical Analysis

Applied Mathematics (Word) Problems (10)

Conversions (3)

- Equations and Expressions
- Inequalities
- Exponential Notation
- Absolute Value
- Ratios and Proportions
- Graphical Analysis

Probability and Statistics (4)

Geometry (4)

Trigonometry (4)

The Kaplan Method for Quantitative Reasoning

STOP

➜ Read the question and characterize the answer choices.

THINK

➜ What is the question really asking?

➜ Pick the strategy to quickly and accurately solve the problem.

- **Picking Numbers:** Use manageable numbers in place of variables.
- **Backsolving:** Plug answers into question stem.
- **Educated Guessing:** Avoid trap answers.
- **Estimating:** Find a solution close to the correct answer.
- **Traditional Math:** Apply classic math formulas.

PREDICT

➜ Use the chosen strategy to formulate a framework or prediction for your answer.

MATCH

➜ Select the answer that truly meets the requirements of the prediction.

Quantitative Reasoning Strategic Overview

Picking Numbers

Why to Pick Numbers

- Many people find it easier to perform calculations with numbers than with variables.

When to Pick Numbers

- Variables are in the answer choices.
- Percents are in the answer choices.
- Number property questions.

How to Pick Numbers

- Pick numbers that are permissible by the rules of the question.
- Pick easy, manageable numbers.
- Avoid numbers with unusual properties, such as one and zero.
- When needed, try sets of numbers that have different properties, such as positives and negatives or odds and evens.

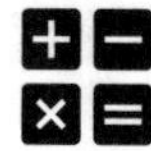

Variables in the Answer Choices

When the answer choices contain variables, consider using Picking Numbers to solve the problem. After choosing numbers, reread the question stem, substituting your numbers for the variables. Finally, plug your numbers into every answer choice.

Example:

1. C individuals pledged to pay equal contributions so that a charity's goal of $\$x$ could be reached. If d of the contributors failed to pay their share, which of the following represents the additional number of dollars that each of the remaining individuals had to pay in order for the charity to reach its goal?

A. $\frac{dx}{c}$

B. $\frac{x}{c-d}$

C. $\frac{d}{c-dx}$

D. $\frac{x}{c(c-d)}$

E. $\frac{dx}{c(c-d)}$

Number Properties

Picking numbers is especially useful for questions that are abstract or that would be difficult to solve using traditional math, such as those involving number properties (e.g., positive vs. negative, odd vs. even, factors vs. multiples). As with other questions with variables in the answer choices, test your numbers with every answer choice.

Example:

2. If x and y are integers such that $x > y$, which of the following CANNOT be a positive integer?

   I. $y(y - x)$

   II. $y(x - y)$

   III. $\frac{(x - y)}{(y - x)}$

   A. I

   B. II

   C. III

   D. I and II

   E. II and III

Percentages

Picking numbers also works well on percentage questions when the actual values aren't given in the question stem. When picking numbers on a percentage problem, always pick the number 100; this will get you the correct answer more directly.

Example:

3. Over the course of a year, a certain factory increased its output by 90%. At the same time, it decreased its total working hours by 20%. By what percentage did the factory increase its output per hour?

   A. 70%
   B. 110%
   C. 112.5%
   D. 137.5%
   E. 237.5%

Backsolving

Backsolving is a quick method to use when the answer choices are numbers. To backsolve, use the answer choices to plug back into the question stem and identify which one works.

Examples:

4. In a class of 7 students, the average score on a test is 80. If 6 of the 7 students scored a 78 on the test, what did the seventh student score?

   A. 85
   B. 88
   C. 90
   D. 92
   E. 95

5. Jacob is now 12 years younger than Michael. If in 9 years Michael will be twice as old as Jacob, how old will Jacob be in 4 years?

   A. 3
   B. 7
   C. 9
   D. 12
   E. 15

Estimation

Estimation is useful on problems for which a math formula could solve for the right answer but would take a long time. Estimation saves time and still allows you to get an answer that is close to the correct choice.

Example:

6. A county contains two voting districts. District A has 5,492 registered voters, and district B has 8,445 registered voters. Assuming a 25% turnout for voting on a ballot that contains separate votes for 8 different candidates, how many total votes will need to be counted for the entire county?

A. 13,937
B. 20,984
C. 27,874
D. 30,827
E. 73,052

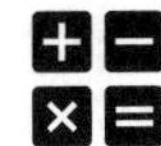

Educated Guessing

Educated Guessing is helpful when a problem is difficult to solve but some of the answer choices can easily be eliminated as incorrect. Educated Guessing can be used to select an answer more accurately before marking and skipping a question and as a safeguard for catching arithmetic mistakes that result in a calculated answer that isn't logically correct.

Example:

7. A vat can be filled by a certain faucet in 20 minutes. Another faucet can fill the same vat in 12 minutes. If both faucets are used to fill up the vat simultaneously, how long will it take the vat to fill?

   A. 3 minutes
   B. 7.5 minutes
   C. 15 minutes
   D. 20 minutes
   E. 32 minutes

Quantitative Reasoning Strategies Summary

Test Day Strategy	When to Use
Traditional Math	
Picking Numbers	
Backsolving	
Estimation	
Educated Guessing	

TAKEAWAY
Sometimes the best approach for tackling a question is to combine two methods. Determine your approach, then let the methods do the work.

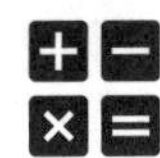

Numerical Calculations

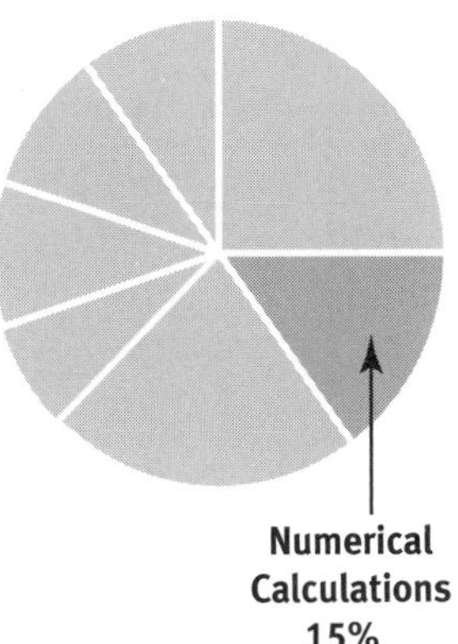

Fractions

Adding and subtracting fractions: Utilize a common denominator to add or subtract numerators.

Example:

$$\frac{3}{4}+\frac{5}{7}=\frac{21}{28}+\frac{20}{28}=\frac{41}{28}$$

Multiplying fractions: Multiply numerators together and multiply denominators together.

Example:

$$\frac{3}{4}\times\frac{5}{7}=\frac{15}{28}$$

Dividing fractions: Multiply fraction in numerator by inverse of fraction in denominator.

Example:

$$\frac{\frac{3}{4}}{\frac{5}{7}}=\frac{3}{4}\div\frac{5}{7}=\frac{3}{4}\times\frac{7}{5}=\frac{21}{20}$$

Example:

8. $\dfrac{2}{3-\frac{1}{\frac{2}{3}}}+2=?$

   A. $\frac{3}{10}$

   B. $\frac{8}{3}$

   C. 3

   D. $\frac{10}{3}$

   E. $\frac{9}{2}$

Practice Questions

9. Which of the following is a possible value for n if $\frac{3}{4} - \frac{1}{2} + \frac{n}{12}$ is an integer?

   A. $\frac{3}{4}$

   B. $\frac{12}{7}$

   C. 6

   D. 21

   E. 24

10. $\frac{2a}{2a+3b} - \left(\frac{3b}{2a+3b} - 1\right) =$

   A. 0

   B. 2

   C. $\frac{6b}{2a+3b}$

   D. $\frac{2a}{2a+3b}$

   E. $\frac{4a}{2a+3b}$

11. Which of the following must be true if $\frac{12c}{7c-d} = 2$?

   A. $c = 2$

   B. $d = 0$

   C. $d = 7$

   D. $c = d$

   E. $c = 2d$

Ratios

Ratios represent the proportion of one quantity to another and can be written as fractions or in the form *c*:*d*.

A ratio does not, by itself, represent the number of each item present.

Two types of ratios:

- Part-to-whole: numerator or first number is the part; denominator or second number is the whole.
- Part-to-part: both numerator and denominator represent different parts; parts add up to the whole.

Examples:

12. What is the ratio of men's to women's average scores on a test if the scores are as follows?

Students	Scores
Student 1 (male)	76
Student 2 (male)	90
Student 3 (male)	85
Student 4 (female)	66
Student 5 (female)	95
Student 6 (female)	87

A. $\frac{25}{26}$

B. $\frac{251}{248}$

C. $\frac{85}{80}$

D. $\frac{250}{227}$

E. $\frac{91}{81}$

13. If there are 14 sofa beds and the ratio of sofa beds to futons is 7:6, what is the combined number of sofa beds and futons?

A. 26

B. 28

C. 30

D. 32

E. 34

Practice Questions

14. At a floral shop, the rules require that all flower arrangements have 6 daisies for every 3 roses and 2 lilies for every 4 daisies. If a floral arrangement has one dozen roses, how many daises and lilies must also be present?

A. 4 lilies and 8 daisies
B. 6 lilies and 12 daisies
C. 12 lilies and 24 daisies
D. 9 lilies and 18 daisies
E. 6 lilies and 24 daisies

15. If $x = \frac{1}{y} = 2$, what is the ratio of x^4 to y^4?

A. $\frac{1}{16}$

B. $\frac{1}{2}$

C. $\frac{1}{1}$

D. $\frac{32}{1}$

E. $\frac{256}{1}$

16. If a solution of iodine and alcohol contains 4 ounces of iodine and 16 ounces of alcohol, how many ounces of alcohol need to evaporate to make the ratio of ounces of iodine to ounces of solution 2 to 3?

A. 6
B. 7
C. 8
D. 10
E. 14

Percentages

Percentage Formula:

$$\text{Percent} = \frac{\text{Part}}{\text{Total}} \times 100\%$$

To increase a number by a percentage, add the percentage to 100%, convert to a decimal, and multiply by the original value.

Example:

A child blows into a balloon originally containing 2 L of gas, causing the volume of the balloon to expand by 30%. What is the new volume of gas in the balloon?

To decrease a number by a percentage, subtract the percentage from 100%, convert to a decimal, and multiply by the original value.

Example:

While shopping for bargains, a customer chooses to buy a shirt that originally cost $35 but is on sale for 20% off the original price. How much must the customer now pay for the shirt?

Example:

17. A broker buys $2,500 worth of a certain stock. If the stock price rises by 40% and then falls by 15%, how much would the stock be worth in the end?

    A. $1,375
    B. $2,125
    C. $2,975
    D. $3,125
    E. $3,500

Practice Questions

18. In 1980, the population of a certain district was 9,000 people. The district was divided into two counties: p people lived in County A, and the rest lived in County B. Over the next ten years, the population of County A increased by 9% and the population of County B increased by 5%. By how many people did the population of the entire district increase, in terms of p?

A. $4p + 45{,}000$
B. $450 - 0.14p$
C. $450 + 0.04p$
D. $-4p + 810$
E. $810 + 0.04p$

19. From June to September, the volume of water held in a certain reservoir fell by 40%. From September to November, the volume of water held by the reservoir increased by 40%. What was the percentage change in volume from June to November?

A. A decrease of 80%
B. A decrease of 16%
C. No change
D. An increase of 36%
E. An increase of 84%

20. In a recent survey, 80% of the people polled were registered voters, and 75% of registered voters voted in the last election. What fraction of all those surveyed were registered voters who did not vote in the last election?

A. $\frac{1}{10}$
B. $\frac{1}{5}$
C. $\frac{1}{4}$
D. $\frac{3}{10}$
E. $\frac{1}{3}$

Scientific Notation

Scientific notation is used to simplify calculations with very large or very small numbers.

The general format is $a \times 10^b$, where b is an integer exponent of 10.

To convert a regular number into scientific notation:

- Insert a decimal point after the leftmost non-zero digit; this gives you a.
- Count the number of digits the original decimal point needed to be moved to reach its new position; this is the numerical value of b.
- If the original number was less than one, make b negative.

Example:

21. Which of the following represents the number 25,630,000 correctly written in scientific notation?

A. 2.563×10^{-7}
B. 0.2563×10^{-7}
C. 2.563×10^{7}
D. 2.563×10^{8}
E. 25.63×10^{6}

TEST DAY TIP

Even though you'll have a calculator on Test Day, sometimes it's faster to answer questions without it. Using the calculator can be time-consuming and tedious.

Practice Questions

22. Which of the following is equivalent to 3.7×10^3?

    A. 0.370
    B. 0.0037
    C. 370
    D. 3700
    E. 37000

23. What is the approximate sum of 10,485,456 and 650,987,498?

    A. 6.6×10^7
    B. 7.5×10^7
    C. 6.6×10^8
    D. 7.5×10^8
    E. 6.5×10^9

24. Which of the following is equivalent to 2.21×10^{-5}?

    A. 0.0000221
    B. 0.000221
    C. 0.00221
    D. 0.02210
    E. 0.22100

Algebra

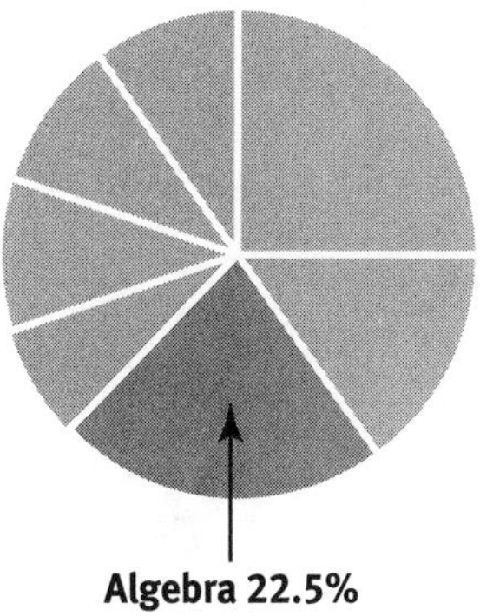

Exponential Notation

A power is a base raised to an exponent.

An example of a power is $3x^2$. In the example, x is the base and 2 is the exponent.

The exponent refers to the number of times the base is a factor in the product.

Exponent Rules

$x^0 = 1$

$x^{-n} = \frac{1}{x^n}$

$x^a \cdot x^b = x^{a+b}$

$(x^a)^b = x^{ab}$

$\frac{x^a}{x^b} = x^{a-b}$

$(xy)^a = x^a y^a$

Example:

25. Which of the following is equal to the ratio of $\left(\frac{3}{8}\right)^5$ to $\left(\frac{3}{8}\right)^6$?

A. $\frac{9}{64}$

B. $\frac{1}{3}$

C. $\frac{3}{8}$

D. $\frac{8}{3}$

E. 3

Practice Questions

26. If $4^{2x+2} = 16^{3x-1}$, what is the value of x?

   A. 0
   B. 1
   C. 2
   D. 3
   E. 4

27. $\dfrac{2^{21}}{4^4\left(4^4 + 4^5\right)} =$

   A. $\frac{1}{4^4}$
   B. $\frac{1}{2^7}$
   C. $\frac{2^1}{2^5}$
   D. $\frac{2^5}{5}$
   E. $\frac{2^9}{17}$

28. What is the value of x if $(4^{2x})(4^x)(2^3) = 128$?

   A. $\frac{2}{3}$
   B. $\frac{3}{4}$
   C. $\frac{4}{3}$
   D. $\frac{3}{2}$
   E. 3

Roots

A square root of a non-negative number *x* is a number that when multiplied by itself results in *x*. The square root is indicated by the radical sign ($\sqrt{}$).

Important Rules

$$\sqrt{a} \times \sqrt{b} = \sqrt{a \times b}$$

$$a\sqrt{c} + b\sqrt{c} = (a + b)\sqrt{c}$$

$$\frac{\sqrt{a}}{\sqrt{b}} = \sqrt{\frac{a}{b}}$$

But:

$$\sqrt{a} + \sqrt{b} \neq \sqrt{a + b}$$

Example:

29. $\sqrt{75} + 3\sqrt{12} =$

A. $11\sqrt{3}$
B. $11\sqrt{6}$
C. $17\sqrt{3}$
D. $4\sqrt{87}$
E. $30\sqrt{3}$

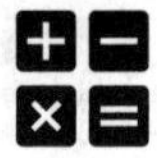

Practice Questions

30. $\sqrt{0.0064} =$

    A. 0.0008
    B. 0.0032
    C. 0.008
    D. 0.032
    E. 0.08

31. $\dfrac{x^3yz^2}{\sqrt[3]{x^6y^4z^6}} =$

    A. $\dfrac{x}{y^{\frac{1}{2}}}$
    B. $\dfrac{x}{y^{\frac{1}{3}}}$
    C. $\dfrac{xz}{y^3}$
    D. $\dfrac{z}{y^{\frac{1}{3}}}$
    E. $\dfrac{x}{y^3}$

32. The positive fourth root of x^3 times the positive square root of x equals 32. What is the value of x?

    A. 2
    B. 8
    C. 10
    D. 16
    E. 32

Equations

An equation is composed of two expressions on opposite sides of an equal sign where at least one of those expressions contains a variable representing an unknown value.

Setting up an equation or expression often involves translating a written scenario into mathematical terms.

Addition: *add, sum, total, net, together, gain*

Subtraction: *minus, difference, fewer, left, less, remaining, take away, remove*

Multiplication: *multiple, product, at this rate, times*

Division: *divide, factor, per, each, quotient, ratio*

Example:

33. Which of the following expressions represents the difference of two times the sum of x and y and three less than x?

    A. $(x + y) - (3 - x)$
    B. $2(x - y) + (3 - x)$
    C. $2x + 3y - 3$
    D. $(x - 3) - 2(x + y)$
    E. $2(x + y) - (x - 3)$

To solve an equation involving one variable, isolate the variable. Be sure to perform the same operation on both sides of the equation.

Example:

34. What is the value of s if 68% of $\frac{7}{s} = 5$?

    A. 0.485
    B. 0.867
    C. 0.952
    D. 1.05
    E. 2.05

Practice Questions

35. What is the value of d if $\sqrt{(50 + 2d)} = 1 + d$?

    A. 6
    B. 7
    C. 8
    D. 9
    E. 10

36. Which of the following equations can be used to find the value of y if 5 times the sum of y and 4 is 2 less than y?

    A. $y - 2 = 5(y + 4)$
    B. $y = 5(y + 4) - 2$
    C. $y - 2 = 5y + 4$
    D. $5(y + 2) = y + 4$
    E. $y = 5(y + 4 + 2)$

37. If $0.1m = 1$, what is the value of $1.1m$?

    A. 1.1
    B. 2
    C. 9.9
    D. 10.1
    E. 11

Practice Questions

38. If Larry's weight were to decrease by 20 pounds, his new weight would be 7/8 of his current weight. What is his current weight?

A. 17.5 lb
B. 22.9 lb
C. 160 lb
D. 180 lb
E. 200 lb

39. A certain phone company charges $4.50 for the first 5 minutes of an international phone call. Additional time is charged at $0.50 per minute. How much would a customer be charged for an international phone call that started at 9:35 p.m. and ended at 11:15 p.m. the same day?

A. $45.00
B. $47.50
C. $50.00
D. $52.00
E. $52.50

40. The daily cost of running a certain air conditioner is 12 cents per hour for the first 8 hours and 10 cents per hour for each additional hour over 8 hours. Which of the following expressions represents the cost in dollars of running this air conditioner for h hours each day for 90 days if $8 < h < 24$?

A. $90(0.12) + 9(h - 8)$
B. $90(0.12)h + h - 8$
C. $90(0.12)h + 9(h - 8)$
D. $90(0.12)(8) + 9(h - 8)$
E. $90(0.12)(8) + (h - 8)$

Polynomials

Polynomials are algebraic expressions with more than one term (e.g., $x^2 + 2x$). The answers to polynomial equations often contain two possible values.

To multiply polynomials, use FOIL (multiply the First, then the Outer, then the Inner, then the Last terms).

Example:

$(x + 3)(x + 4)$

First terms:

Outer terms:

Inner terms:

Last terms:

Solution:

The most frequently tested polynomial problem solutions are below:

$a^2 + 2ab + b^2 = (a + b)^2$

$a^2 - 2ab + b^2 = (a - b)^2$

$a^2 - b^2 = (a - b)\,(a + b)$

Practice Questions

41. If $n > 2$, which of the following expressions is equivalent to $\frac{3(n-2)+1}{(n+5)(n-2)}$?

    A. $\frac{3n-5}{n^2+3n-10}$

    B. $\frac{4}{n+5}$

    C. $3n - \frac{1}{n^2+3n-10}$

    D. $-\frac{5}{n^2-10}$

    E. $\frac{3n-3}{n^2+3n-3}$

42. What are the possible values of n in $n^2 + 7n - 5 = 3$?

    A. $\{-8, 1\}$
    B. $\{8, -1\}$
    C. $\{-3, 5\}$
    D. $\{2, -5\}$
    E. $\{-2, 5\}$

43. What is the value of the expression $3(x - 5)^2$?

    A. $x^2 - 10x + 25$
    B. $3x^2 - 30x + 75$
    C. $3x^2 - 9x + 25$
    D. $(3x - 15)^2$
    E. $x^2 - 30x + 75$

Practice Questions

44. Factor $x^6 - 9y^4$ into the product of two binomial pairs.

  A. $(x^3 + 3y^2)(x^3 - 3y^2)$
  B. $(3x^3 + 3y^2)(3x^3 - 3y^2)$
  C. $(3x^3 + y^2)(3x^3 - y^2)$
  D. $(x^3 + 9y^2)(x^3 - 9y^2)$
  E. $(x^3 - 3y^2)(x^3 - 3y^2)$

45. If x does not equal zero, and $x - \frac{2 - x^2}{x} = \frac{y}{x}$, then $y =$

  A. -2
  B. $-2 - 3x^2$
  C. $2x^2 - 2$
  D. $x^2 - 2$
  E. $x - 2 - x^2$

46. If $x > y > 0$ and a fraction with a numerator equal to the sum of x and 3 and a denominator equal to the positive difference of x and y is equal to 56, then y is equal to

  A. $\frac{53x - 3}{56}$
  B. $\frac{53x}{56}$
  C. $\frac{53x - 3}{53}$
  D. $\frac{55x}{56}$
  E. $\frac{55x - 3}{56}$

Simultaneous Equations

Simultaneous equations include more than one variable.

There are two techniques for solving simultaneous equations.

Substitution

In this method, one equation is solved by isolating one variable. The resulting expression is substituted into the other equation to solve for the other variable.

Example:

Solve for x and y if:

$4x + 3y = 8$ and $x + y = 3$

$y = 3 - x$	Solve one equation for one variable.
$4x + (3)(3 - x) = 8$	Substitute $(3 - x)$ for y into the other equation.
$4x + 9 - 3x = 8$	
$x = -1$	Solve for the variable.

From here you can solve for y by plugging $x = -1$ into $x + y = 3$.

Combination

In this method, the equations are aligned such that a variable can be eliminated by subtraction.

Example:

Solve for x and y if:

$4x + 3y = 8$ and $x + y = 3$

$$\begin{array}{r} 4x + 3y = 8 \\ -(x + y = 3) \\ \hline \end{array}$$

Align the equations like a subtraction problem.

$$\begin{array}{r} 4x + 3y = 8 \\ -(3x + 3y = 9) \\ \hline x + 0 = -1 \\ x = -1 \end{array}$$

Multiply the bottom equation by 3 so the y terms will cancel out. Subtract the bottom equation from the top equation. Solve for x.

From here you can solve for y by plugging $x = -1$ into either of the original equations.

Example:

47. If $3a + 7b = 12$ and $a - b + 1 = 0$, what are the values of a and b?

A. $a = \frac{1}{2}, b = \frac{3}{2}$

B. $a = \frac{3}{2}, b = \frac{1}{2}$

C. $a = -\frac{1}{11}, b = \frac{10}{11}$

D. $a = \frac{10}{11}, b = -\frac{1}{11}$

E. $a = 2, b = 3$

Substitution

Combination

Practice Questions

48. If $a = 3 + 3w$, $b = 5w - 7$, and $4a = 3b$, what does w equal?

A. 10
B. 11
C. 12
D. 13
E. 15

49. A theater charges $12 for seats in the orchestra and $8 for seats in the balcony. On a certain night, a total of 350 tickets were sold, resulting in a total revenue of $3,320. How many more tickets were sold that night for seats in the balcony than for seats in the orchestra?

A. 90
B. 110
C. 120
D. 130
E. 220

50. If $p + 2q = 8$ and $2p - q = 11$, then $p = ?$

A. 1
B. 6
C. 7
D. 8
E. 9

Absolute Value

The absolute value sign indicates the distance a number is from zero on a number line.

When solving for a variable within the absolute value sign, separate the term within the absolute value sign into a positive and negative version and solve for both.

Example:

51. If $|x - 2| = 6$, which of the following sets represents all possible values of x?

   A. $\{8\}$
   B. $\{-4, 4\}$
   C. $\{-8, 8\}$
   D. $\{4, -8\}$
   E. $\{-4, 8\}$

Practice Questions

52. $\dfrac{|14 \times -6|}{|19 - 5|} =$

    A. -6

    B. $\dfrac{-7}{2}$

    C. $\dfrac{8}{14}$

    D. $\dfrac{7}{2}$

    E. 6

53. If $|18 - 6|x = 48$, then $x =$

    A. $\{4\}$

    B. $\{-4, 4\}$

    C. $\{4, 12\}$

    D. $\{12\}$

    E. $\{-12, 12\}$

54. If $-6|4x + 2| = 96$, then x must

    A. be greater than 2.

    B. be an odd number.

    C. be an even number.

    D. not be a positive number.

    E. not be a real number.

Inequalities

To solve an inequality, do what is necessary to both sides to isolate the variable.

If solving the inequality requires multiplying or dividing by a negative number, you must reverse the inequality sign.

When solving an inequality with an absolute value sign, solve both a positive and a negative version of the equation within the absolute value sign.

Example:

55. If $|x + 4| > 1$, what are all possible values of x?

A. $x > 3$ and $x < 5$

B. $x > 3$ or $x < -5$

C. $x > -3$ or $x < -5$

D. $x > -3$ and $x < 5$

E. $x > 3$

Practice Questions

56. If $8(z + 3) < 5z + 12$, which of the following is always true?

A. $z > 12$
B. $z > 8$
C. $z < -6$
D. $z < -4$
E. $z < -12$

57. What are all the values of x for which $(x - 2)(x + 5) < 0$?

A. $2 < x < 5$
B. $-2 < x < 5$
C. $-5 < x < 2$
D. $x < -5$
E. $x > 2$

58. How many integer values exist for x such that $1 < 3x + 5 < 17$?

A. 1
B. 3
C. 5
D. 6
E. 8

Graphical Analysis

A function is a mapping of inputs to outputs.

The inputs are usually *x* values on the horizontal axis; the outputs are usually *y* values on the vertical axis.

A function can have only one output for each input. Many inputs can share the same output.

The inputs to a function are called the domain, and the outputs of the function are called the range.

Example:

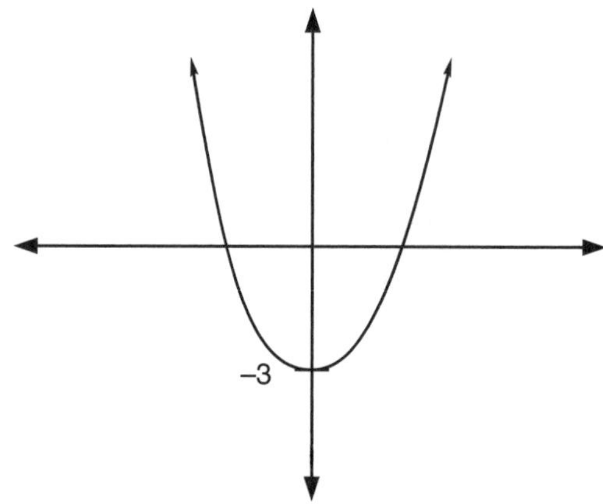

59. What are the domain and range of the above function?

A. Domain: all values of x; range: $y \geq -3$
B. Domain: $y \geq -3$; range: all values of x
C. Domain: $y \geq -3$; range: $x \geq 0$
D. Domain: $x \geq -3$; range: $y \geq -3$
E. Domain: $x \geq -3$; range: $y \geq 0$

TAKEAWAY

Algebra is tested not only on its own but also in the context of word problems. Brush up on any unfamiliar topics to ensure you're ready to handle all of the Quantitative Reasoning questions efficiently and effectively.

Practice Questions

60. Which function has a range containing only negative numbers?

A. $y = -x^2$
B. $y = -|x|$
C. $y = -x^2 - 1$
D. $y = -x^3$
E. $y = x^3$

61. The graph below is best represented by the function

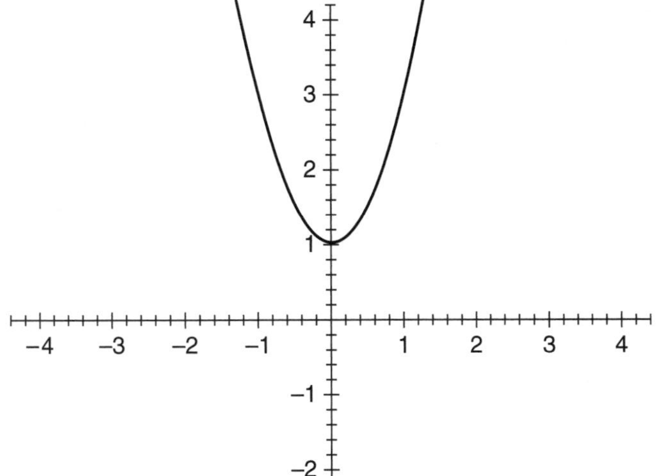

A. $y = ax + b$
B. $y = ax^2 + b$
C. $y = ax^3 + b$
D. $x = ay + b$
E. $x = ay^2 + b$

62. What is the domain of the function $y = \frac{27}{x^3}$?

A. $x < 0 \cup x > 0$
B. $x < 3 \cup x > 3$
C. All positive numbers
D. All negative numbers
E. All real numbers

Study Plan

After Class: Quantitative Reasoning 1		
Complete Remaining *Lesson Book* Practice Questions	30m	
Practice with Tests and Quizzes		

Before Class: General Chemistry 1		
Read *Review Notes* Chapters 22–27, 31–33	4h 30m	
Quantum Number and Electron Configuration Workshop	45m	
Chemical Kinetics Workshop	45m	
Thermodynamics Workshop	45m	

GENERAL CHEMISTRY 1

TOPICS COVERED

- The General Chemistry Subsection
- Atomic and Molecular Structure
- Periodic Properties
- Stoichiometry
- Thermochemistry
- Equilibria
- Kinetics

After this session you will be able to:

- Differentiate between the different types of intramolecular and intermolecular bonds
- Predict properties based on those bonds and the periodic table
- Calculate stoichiometric values and balanced chemical equations
- Calculate energies based on thermodynamics
- Calculate properties of systems at equilibrium
- Determine chemical rate laws

The General Chemistry Subsection

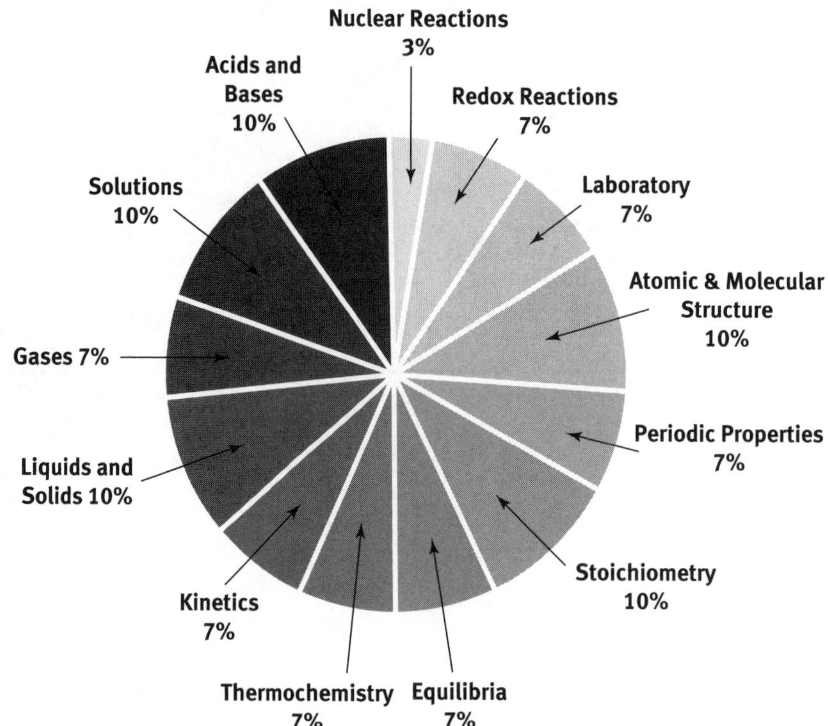

The distribution of General Chemistry questions

Overview

- 30 questions (30% of the Survey of Natural Sciences section)

Topics

Atomic and Molecular Structure (3)

- Electron Configuration
- Orbital Types
- Lewis-Dot Diagrams
- Atomic Theory
- Quantum Theory
- Molecular Geometry
- Bond Types
- Subatomic Particles

Periodic Properties (2)

- Representative Elements
- Transition Elements
- Periodic Trends
- Descriptive Chemistry

Stoichiometry (3)

- Percent Composition
- Empirical Formulas
- Balancing Equations
- Molecular Formulas
- Molar Mass
- Density
- Calculations from Equations

Chemical Equilibria (2)

- Molecular
- Acids/Bases
- Precipitation
- Calculations
- Le Châtelier's Principle

Thermochemistry (2)

- Laws of Thermodynamics
- Hess's Law
- Spontaneity
- Enthalpies and Entropies
- Heat Transfer

Chemical Kinetics (2)

- Rate Laws
- Activation Energy
- Half-Life

Liquids and Solids (3)

- Intermolecular Forces
- Phase Changes
- Vapor Pressure
- Structures
- Polarity
- Properties

Gases (2)

- Kinetic Theory of Gases
- Dalton's Gas Law
- Boyle's Gas Law
- Charles's Gas Law
- Ideal Gas Law

Solutions (3)

- Polarity
- Colligative Properties
- Forces
- Concentration Calculations

Acids and Bases (3)

- pH
- Strength
- Brønsted-Lowry Reactions
- Calculations

Nuclear Reactions (1)

- Balancing Equations
- Binding Energy
- Decay Processes
- Particles
- Terminology

Oxidation-Reduction Reactions (2)

- Balancing Equations
- Oxidation Numbers
- Electrochemistry Calculations
- Electrochemistry Concepts

Laboratory (2)

- Basic Techniques
- Equipment
- Error Analysis
- Safety
- Data Analysis

The Kaplan Question Strategy

STOP

→ Characterize the answer choices.

THINK

→ What is the question really asking?

→ What relevant information do you need?

PREDICT

→ Formulate a framework or prediction for your answer.

MATCH

→ Select the answer that truly meets the requirements of the prediction.

Atomic and Molecular Structure

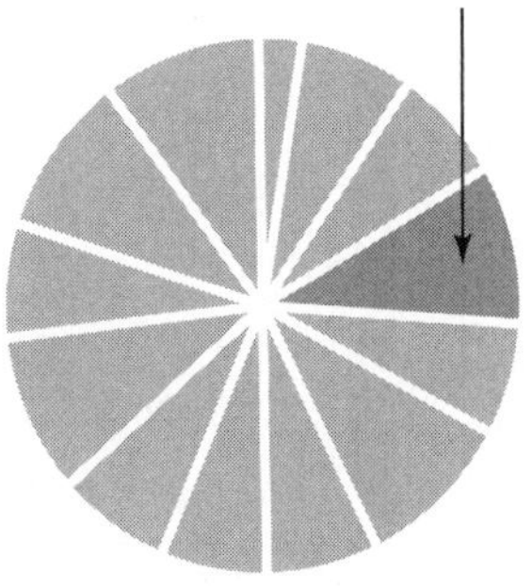

Intramolecular Bonds

Ionic

Covalent

Metallic

Lewis-Dot Diagrams

Octet Rule

Formal Charge

Formal charge = valence e^- − number of π and σ bonds attached − nonbonding e^-

Resonance Structures

Practice Questions

1. Which of the following Lewis structures represents a compound free of formal charge that consists of one carbon atom, one hydrogen atom, one nitrogen atom, and one oxygen atom?

   I. $\ddot{\underset{..}{O}}$=C=$\ddot{N}$–H

   II. :N≡C–$\ddot{\underset{..}{O}}$–H

   III. H–$\underset{..}{O}$=C=$\underset{..}{\ddot{N}}$

   A. I

   B. II

   C. I and II

   D. II and III

   E. I, II, and III

2. Possible structures of perchloric acid are shown below. Which is most stable?

   A. H—Ö—Cl≡O: (with —:Ö: above Cl and —:Ö: below Cl, single bonds)

   B. H—Ö—Cl—Ö: (with —:Ö: above Cl and —:Ö: below Cl, single bonds)

   C. H—Ö—Cl=Ö (with =:O: above Cl and =:O: below Cl, double bonds)

   D. H—Ö—Cl—Ö: (with =:O: above Cl and =:O: below Cl, double bonds)

   E. H—Ö=Cl=Ö (with —:Ö: above Cl and —:Ö: below Cl, single bonds)

3. The correct order of decreasing individual bond strength between the nitrogen and oxygen atoms in the nitrate ion (NO_3^-), hydroxylamine (NH_2OH), the nitrosyl ion (NO^+), and the nitryl ion (NO_2^+) is

   A. $NO_3^- > NH_2OH > NO^+ > NO_2^+$

   B. $NO^+ > NO_2^+ > NO_3^- > NH_2OH$

   C. $NO^+ > NO_3^- > NO_2^+ > NH_2OH$

   D. $NH_2OH > NO_3^- > NO_2^+ > NO^+$

   E. $NO_3^- > NO^+ > NH_2OH > NO_2^+$

Molecular Geometry

Valence Shell Electron-Pair Repulsion Theory (VSEPR)

Bonding Pairs vs. Nonbonding Pairs

Electronic Geometry vs. Molecular Geometry

Electron Pairs	Nonbonding Pairs	Example	Geometric Arrangement	Shape	Angles
2	0	$BeCl_2$	X — A — X	Linear	
3	0	BH_3	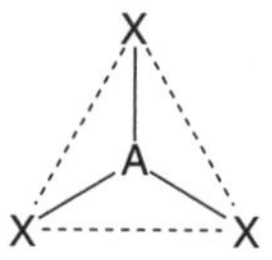	Trigonal Planar	
4	0	CH_4	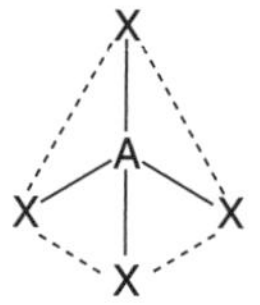	Tetrahedral	
4	1	NH_3	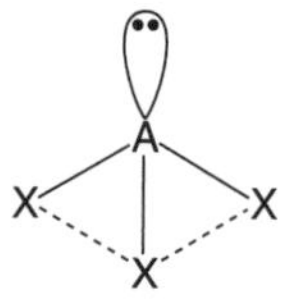	Trigonal Pyramidal	
4	2	H_2O	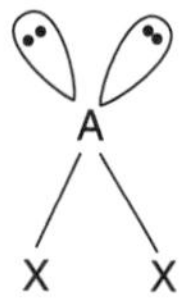	Bent	
5	0	PCl_5	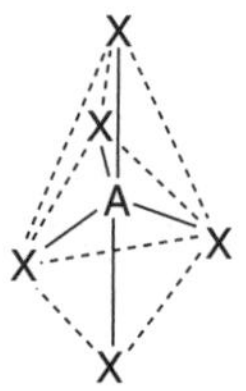	Trigonal Bipyramidal	
6	0	SF_6	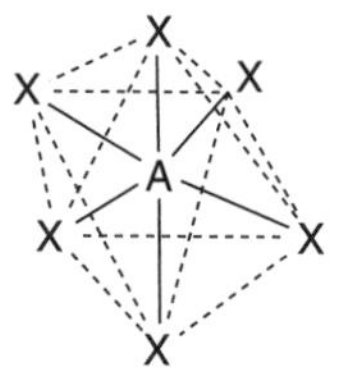	Octahedral	

Practice Questions

4. Which of the following molecules has the smallest bond angle?

   A. CH_4
   B. NH_3
   C. H_2O
   D. BH_3
   E. CO_2

5. Which of the following has a tetrahedral molecular geometry?

   A. ClO_3^-
   B. C_2H_4
   C. SO_4^{2-}
   D. H_2S
   E. NH_3

6. Which of the following does NOT have a tetrahedral electronic geometry?

   A. ClO_3^-
   B. C_2H_4
   C. SO_4^{2-}
   D. H_2S
   E. NH_3

Molecular Dipoles

Molecular dipoles depend on both individual bond dipoles and molecular geometry.

Intermolecular Forces

Intermolecular forces are a result of electrostatic interactions between charges or partial charges on different molecules.

Decreasing Strength ↓

1. ______________________________
2. ______________________________
3. ______________________________
4. ______________________________
5. ______________________________

Practice Questions

7. Which of the following participate(s) in hydrogen bonding?

   A. Methanol
   B. Methane
   C. Methanal
   D. Bromomethane
   E. All of the above

8. Which substance boils at the highest temperature?

   A. Dimethyl ether (CH_3OCH_3)
   B. Ethanol (CH_3CH_2OH)
   C. Ethane (CH_3CH_3)
   D. Chloroethane (CH_3CH_2Cl)
   E. Ethanal (CH_3CHO)

9. Which represents the correct order of increasing boiling point?

   A. Water < acetone < methane < acetic acid
   B. Acetone < methane < acetic acid < water
   C. Methane < acetone < acetic acid < water
   D. Methane < acetone < water < acetic acid
   E. Acetone < water < methane < acetic acid

Quantum Numbers

Principal (n)

Angular (l)

Magnetic (m_l)

Spin (m_s)

Electron Configuration

Spectroscopic Notation

Hund's Rules

Aufbau Principle

STUDY TIP

Master the basics of General Chemistry first, starting with the level of the atom and building up to how different elements interact with one another. Progressing from small- to large-scale will help keep everything in perspective.

Practice Questions

10. What is the maximum number of electrons that can occupy a shell with a principal quantum number $n = 4$?

A. 4
B. 8
C. 16
D. 18
E. 32

11. All of the following are possible principal and magnetic quantum numbers for an electron of a carbon atom in its ground state EXCEPT one. Which one is the EXCEPTION?

A. $n = 1, \quad m_1 = 0$
B. $n = 2, \quad m_1 = 0$
C. $n = 2, \quad m_1 = -1$
D. $n = 2, \quad m_1 = 1$
E. $n = 3, \quad m_1 = -1$

12. Which of the following subshells will fill first?

A. 5d
B. 5f
C. 6s
D. 6p
E. 4f

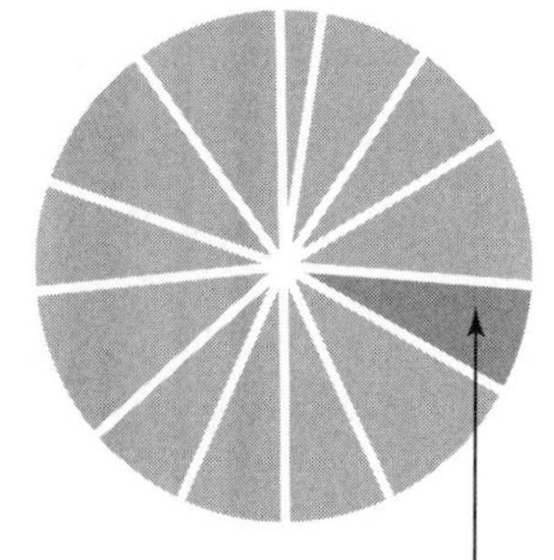

Periodic Properties

Isotope Notation

The Periodic Table

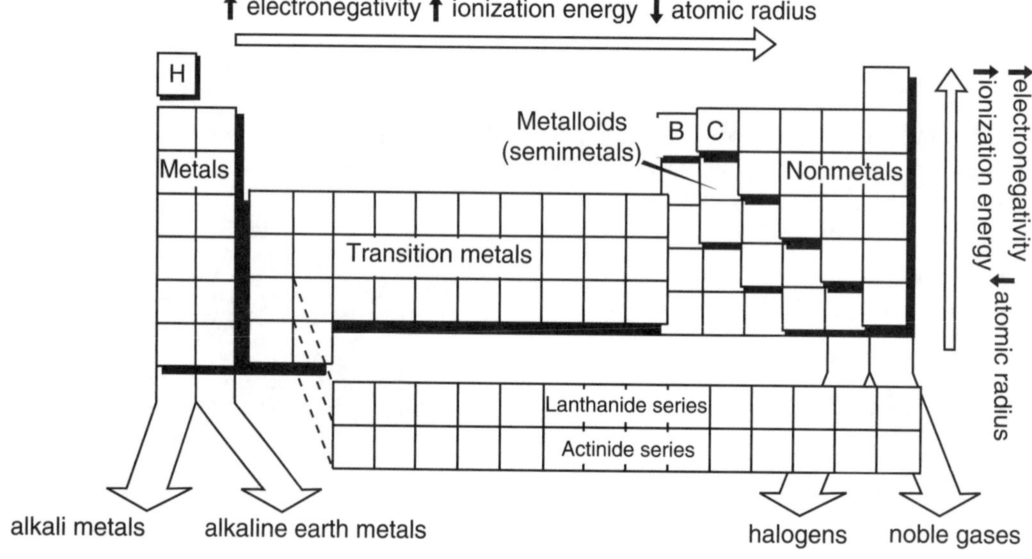

Representative Elements

Alkali Metals

Alkaline Earth Metals

Carbon Family

Nitrogen Family

Oxygen Family

Halogens

Noble Gases

Types of Elements

Metals

Nonmetals

Transition Metals

Metalloids

Periodic Trends

Effective Nuclear Charge (Z_{eff})

Atomic Radius

Electronegativity

Ionization Energy

Electron Affinity

TAKEAWAY

Knowing how the subatomic particles within an atom interact, especially in terms of Z_{eff}, makes understanding and memorizing all the periodic trends much easier.

Practice Questions

13. Isotopes always have the same

    A. atomic mass.
    B. mass number.
    C. atomic number.
    D. quantum number.
    E. molecular mass.

14. Among the transition metals essential to life one finds V, Cr, Mn, Fe, Co, Ni, Cu, and Zn but not Sc or Ti. Which one of the following elements is also likely to be biologically important?

    A. Zr
    B. La
    C. Hf
    D. Mo
    E. Y

15. What is the electronic configuration of a free Fe^{3+} ion?

    A. $[Ar]3d^5$
    B. $[Ar]3d^6$
    C. $[Ar]3d^6 4s^2$
    D. $[Ar]4s^2 4p^3$
    E. $[Ar]4s^1 4d^4$

Practice Questions

16. Which of the following has the greatest atomic radius?

    A. Ca^{2+}
    B. F^{-}
    C. Ar
    D. O^{2-}
    E. He

17. Which of the following would require the greatest energy to remove an electron?

    A. K
    B. K^{+}
    C. K^{-}
    D. Na
    E. Na^{+}

18. The ionization energies below most likely correspond to which of the following elements?

First Ionization Energy	590 kJ/mol
Second Ionization Energy	1145 kJ/mol
Third Ionization Energy	4912 kJ/mol

    A. Na
    B. Ca
    C. N
    D. Ne
    E. P

Stoichiometry

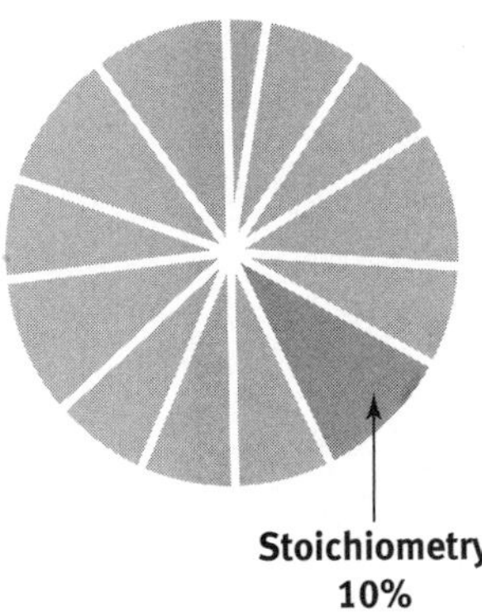

Compound vs. Molecule

Molecular Mass vs. Molar Mass

Empirical vs. Molecular Formula

Percent Composition: percentage of mass contributed by each element in a compound

$$\%\ \text{composition} = \frac{\text{Mass of X in formula}}{\text{Formula weight of compound}}$$

Practice Questions

19. What is the percent composition of chromium in $K_2Cr_2O_7$ (294.2 g•mol^{-1})?

    A. 18.2%
    B. 35.4%
    C. 44.4%
    D. 48.6%
    E. 52.0%

20. A compound with the empirical formula CH_2O has a weight of 180 g/mol. What is the molecular formula?

    A. CH_2O
    B. $C_2H_4O_2$
    C. $C_2H_6O_2$
    D. $C_6H_{12}O_6$
    E. $C_8H_{20}O_4$

21. What is the molecular formula of a compound composed of 40.9% carbon, 4.58% hydrogen, and 54.52% oxygen with a molecular weight of 264 g/mol?

    A. $C_9H_{12}O_9$
    B. CHO
    C. CH_2O
    D. $C_3H_4O_3$
    E. $C_{10}H_{10}O$

Balancing Equations

$$\_\_\_\_ NaHCO_3 \rightarrow \_\_\_\_ Na_2CO_3 + \_\_\_\_ CO_2 + \_\_\_\_ H_2O$$

1. Write the unbalanced equation without coefficients.
2. Balance molecules containing the least represented element, found in the fewest number of reactants and products, first.
3. Balance remaining molecules, saving highly represented elements (often H and O) and elements by themselves (e.g., C (*s*)) for last.
4. If fractions are present, multiply every coefficient by the least common denominator so that all coefficients become whole numbers.
5. Check that the sums of elements and charges are equal on both sides of the equation.

Limiting Reactant

Stoichiometric Ratios

Theoretical Yield

Actual Yield

$$\text{Percent Yield} = \frac{\text{Actual Yield}}{\text{Theoretical Yield}} \times 100\%$$

TAKEAWAY

A calculator will not be available during the Survey of Natural Sciences section, so practice performing arithmetic mentally and by hand to quickly move through these types of calculations.

Practice Questions

22. When the following chemical reaction is balanced, what is the coefficient for O_2?

$$C_4H_{10}\,(l) + O_2\,(g) \rightarrow CO_2\,(g) + H_2O\,(l)$$

A. 1
B. 3
C. 8
D. 10
E. 13

23. According to the following equation, if there is 1 mol of A and 1 mol of B, which is the limiting reagent?

$$2\,A + B \rightarrow 2\,C + D$$

A. A
B. B
C. C
D. D
E. Both A and B

24. How many moles of B are needed to completely react with 1 mol of A given the following equation?

$$2\,A + 3\,B \rightarrow C$$

A. 1
B. 1.5
C. 2
D. 2.5
E. 3

25. How many grams of calcium chloride are needed to prepare 72.0 g of silver chloride according to the following equation?

$$CaCl_2\,(aq) + 2\,AgNO_3\,(aq) \rightarrow Ca(NO_3)_2\,(aq) + 2\,AgCl\,(s)$$

A. 14.0 g
B. 27.9 g
C. 36.0 g
D. 55.8 g
E. 72.0 g

Thermochemistry

Thermochemistry
7%

Enthalpy (ΔH)

Exothermic Reaction

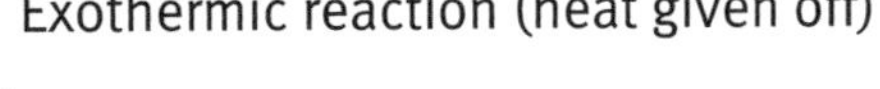

Exothermic reaction (heat given off)

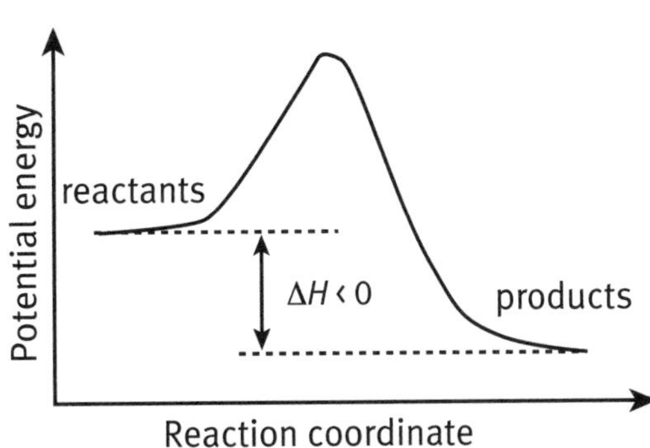

Endothermic Reaction

Endothermic reaction (heat taken in)

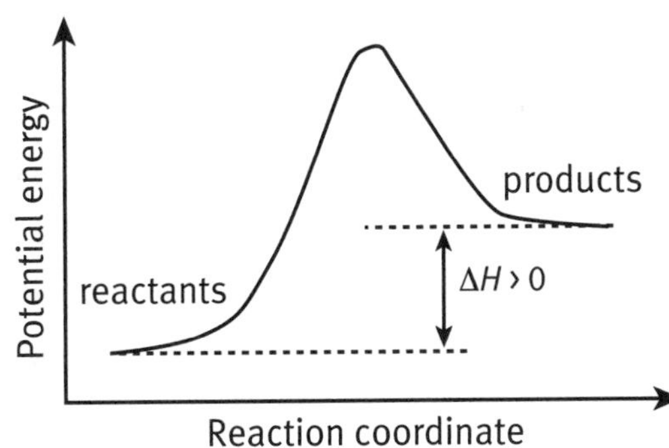

Transfer of Heat

$\Delta U = Q - W_{by\ system}$

Radiation

Conduction

Convection

Bond Energy

Standard Heat of Formation (ΔH_f°)

$\Delta H_{rxn}^\circ = (\text{sum of } \Delta H_{products}^\circ) - (\text{sum of } \Delta H_{reactants}^\circ)$

Hess's Law

If a reaction can be broken down into a series of steps, the enthalpy change for the overall net reaction is the sum of the enthalpies of each step.

Practice Questions

26. Given the thermochemical equations below, calculate ΔH_{rxn}° for the reaction.

$$3\,C\,(s) + 4\,H_2\,(g) \rightarrow C_3H_8\,(g)$$

a) $C_3H_8\,(g) + 5\,O_2\,(g) \rightarrow 3\,CO_2\,(g) + 4\,H_2O\,(l)$ $\Delta H_a^{\circ} = -2220.1$ kJ

b) $C\,(s) + O_2\,(g) \rightarrow CO_2\,(g)$ $\Delta H_b^{\circ} = -393.5$ kJ

c) $H_2\,(g) + \frac{1}{2}\,O_2\,(g) \rightarrow H_2O\,(l)$ $\Delta H_c^{\circ} = -285.8$ kJ

A. −4544 kJ/mol
B. −2872 kJ/mol
C. −103.6 kJ/mol
D. 467.9 kJ/mol
E. 1541 kJ/mol

27. The bond energy of the N–H bond is 389 kJ/mol, the bond energy of the O=O bond is 498, and the bond enthalpy of the N≡N bond is 941 kJ/mol. Given the following chemical reaction, what is the bond energy of the O–H bond?

$4\,NH_3 + 3\,O_2 \rightarrow 2\,N_2 + 6\,H_2O$ $\Delta H_{rxn}^{\circ} = -1266$ kJ

A. 71 kJ/mol
B. 251 kJ/mol
C. 324 kJ/mol
D. 462 kJ/mol
E. 1033 kJ/mol

28. Consider the following reaction:

$C_2H_2 + \frac{5}{2}\,O_2 \rightarrow 2\,CO_2 + H_2O$ $\Delta H_{rxn}^{\circ} = -1255.5$ kJ/mol

If the ΔH_f° of CO_2 is −393.5 kJ/mol and the ΔH_f° of H_2O is −241.8 kJ/mol, what is the ΔH_f° of acetylene, C_2H_2?

A. −620.1 kJ/mol
B. −226.6 kJ/mol
C. 0 kJ/mol
D. 226.6 kJ/mol
E. 620.1 kJ/mol

Entropy (ΔS)

Gibbs Free Energy (ΔG)

$\Delta G = \Delta H - T\Delta S$

$\Delta G < 0$: ____________________

$\Delta G = 0$: ____________________

$\Delta G > 0$: ____________________

STUDY TIP

Be careful with the minus signs! Focus on whether energy is leaving or being added rather than attempting to follow the thermochemistry equations strictly.

Practice Questions

29. Which of the following occurs when frozen ice melts into liquid water?

    A. The enthalpy increases, and the entropy increases.
    B. The enthalpy decreases, and the entropy increases.
    C. The enthalpy increases, and the entropy decreases.
    D. The enthalpy decreases, and the entropy decreases.
    E. The enthalpy increases, and the entropy remains the same.

30. Which of the following defines a reaction that is temperature-dependent?

    I. Positive ΔH, positive ΔS
    II. Positive ΔH, negative ΔS
    III. Negative ΔH, positive ΔS
    IV. Negative ΔH, negative ΔS

    A. I and II
    B. I and III
    C. I and IV
    D. II and III
    E. III and IV

31. While standing in the ocean, you begin to feel cold. This is because heat is transferring from you to the water, which mainly occurs through the process of

    A. radiation.
    B. conduction.
    C. convection.
    D. advection.
    E. changing phase.

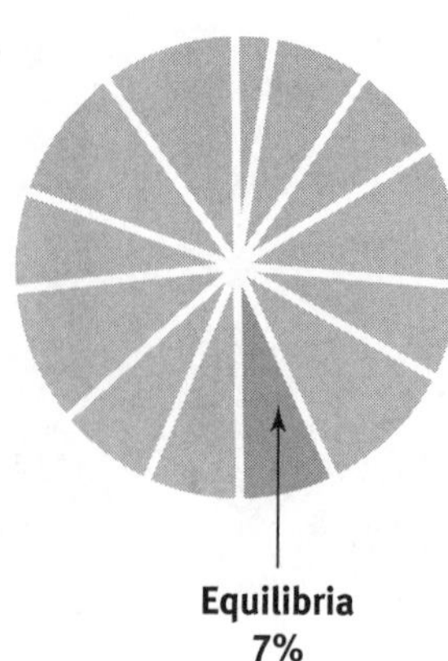

Equilibria

Molecular Equilibrium

Reaction Quotient (Q)

For a reaction aA + bB $\leftrightharpoons$ cC + dD,

$$Q = \frac{[\text{products}]}{[\text{reactants}]} = \frac{[C]^c[D]^d}{[A]^a[B]^b}$$

Equilibrium Constant (K_{eq})

$K_{eq} > Q$: ______________________

$K_{eq} = Q$: ______________________

$K_{eq} < Q$: ______________________

Le Châtelier's Principle

If a stress (a change in concentration, pressure, or temperature) is applied to a system at equilibrium, the system will shift in such a way as to relieve the applied stress.

Solution Equilibrium

Ion Product (Q_{sp})

Solubility Product Constant (K_{sp})

$K_{sp} > Q_{sp}$: ______________________________

$K_{sp} = Q_{sp}$: ______________________________

$K_{sp} < Q_{sp}$: ______________________________

Molar Solubility

Common Ion Effect

Kaplan Method for Equilibrium Questions

1. Write down a balanced reaction for the dissociation reaction (if not given).
2. Find the expression for the K_{eq}.
3. Plug into the K_{eq} expression.

TEST DAY TIP

Questions regarding Stoichiometry, Balancing Equations, and Equilibrium can be very time-consuming on Test Day, so triage them for later if they will involve heavy calculations.

Practice Questions

System 1

$$2\ PbSO_4\ (s) + 2\ H_2O\ (l) \rightleftharpoons Pb\ (s) + PbO_2\ (s) + 2\ HSO_4^-\ (aq) + 2\ H^+\ (aq)$$

32. What effect would increasing the amount of Pb(*s*) have on system 1?

    A. The reaction would proceed in reverse to form more of both reactants.
    B. The reaction would proceed in reverse to produce more $PbSO_4$ only.
    C. The reaction would proceed forward to form more of all the products.
    D. The reaction would proceed forward to produce more H^+ only.
    E. There would be no net effect.

33. What would happen if the pH of system 1 were increased?

    A. The reaction would proceed in reverse to form more of both reactants.
    B. The reaction would proceed in reverse to produce more $PbSO_4$ only.
    C. The reaction would proceed forward to form more of all the products.
    D. The reaction would proceed forward to produce more H^+ only.
    E. There would be no net effect.

34. What would happen to system 1 if the pressure were increased?

    A. The reaction would proceed in reverse to form more of both reactants.
    B. The reaction would proceed in reverse to produce more $PbSO_4$ only.
    C. The reaction would proceed forward to form more of all the products.
    D. The reaction would proceed forward to produce more H^+ only.
    E. There would be no net effect.

Practice Questions

35. The solubility of FeF_2 in an aqueous solution was determined to be 1.9×10^{-2} mol/L. What is the value of the K_{sp} for FeF_2?

   A. 3.3×10^{-10}
   B. 6.8×10^{-6}
   C. 2.7×10^{-5}
   D. 1.4×10^{-3}
   E. 1.4×10^{-1}

36. What is the molar solubility of silver chloride solution in a 0.1 M solution of table salt ($K_{sp} = 1.6 \times 10^{-10}$)?

   A. 2.6×10^{-20}
   B. 1.6×10^{-9}
   C. 4.0×10^{-5}
   D. 1.6×10^{-5}
   E. 4.0×10^{-4}

37. If 1.0 mL of a 1.0×10^{-5} M NaSCN solution is added to 3.0 mL of a 1.0×10^{-5} M $AgNO_3$ solution, will there be any precipitate? (K_{sp} of AgSCN = 1.0×10^{-12})

   A. No, both NaSCN and $AgNO_3$ are completely soluble.
   B. No, all ion concentrations are at or below saturation levels.
   C. No, NaSCN is hygroscopic so will undergo a side reaction with water.
   D. Yes, both AgSN and $NaNO_3$ are completely insoluble.
   E. Yes, Ag^+ and SCN^- concentrations are above saturation levels.

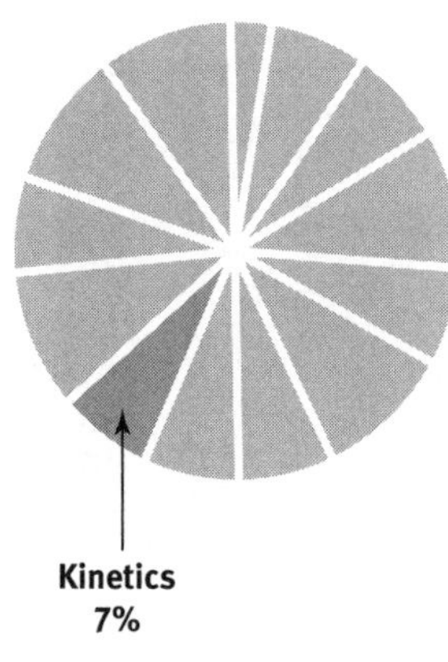

Kinetics

Rate Laws

For a reaction $aA + bB \rightleftharpoons cC + dD$,

Rate $= k\,[A]^X\,[B]^Y$

$k =$ rate constant

$X + Y =$ order of reaction

Reaction Orders

Zero order

First order

Second order

Determining Orders

Trial	$[A]_{initial}$ (M)	$[B]_{initial}$ (M)	$r_{initial}$ (M/sec)
1	1.0	1.0	2.0
2	1.0	2.0	8.1
3	2.0	2.0	15.9

Factors Affecting Rate

Reaction Concentration

Temperature

Medium

Catalyst

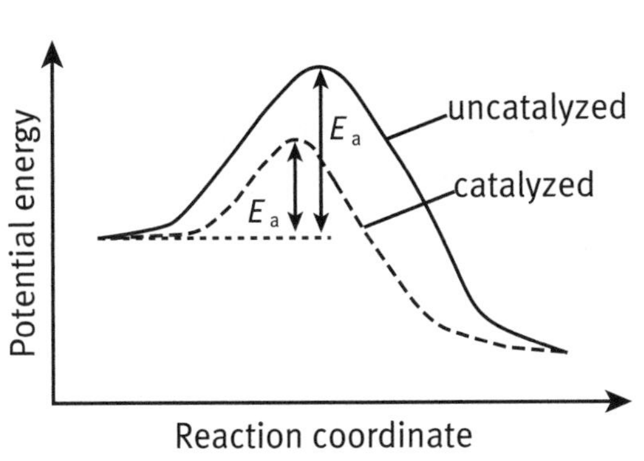

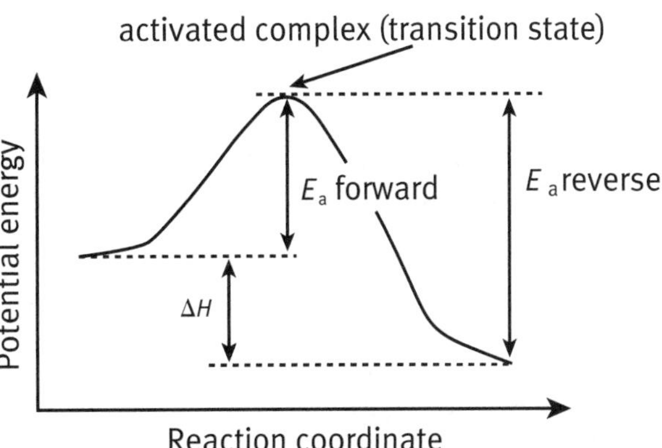

TAKEAWAY

Although their equations may look similar, Equilibria and Kinetics are completely different topics, especially because a rate law cannot be determined from a balanced equation alone. Be careful not to confuse the two topics on Test Day.

Practice Questions

38. Given the experimental data below, determine the rate law for the following reaction.

$$2\,H_2O_2\,(aq) + I^-\,(aq) \rightarrow O_2\,(g) + 2\,H_2O\,(l) + I^-\,(aq)$$

Trial	$[KI]_{initial}$ (M)	$[H_2O_2]_{initial}$ (M)	Rate of O_2 Formation (mol • L^{-1} • s^{-1})
1	0.060	0.040	3.61×10^{-8}
2	0.060	0.080	7.25×10^{-8}
3	0.090	0.040	5.39×10^{-8}

A. Rate = $k[H_2O_2]$
B. Rate = $k[I^-][H_2O_2]$
C. Rate = $k[I^-][H_2O_2]^2$
D. Rate = $k[I^-]^2[H_2O_2]$
E. Rate = $k[I^-]^2[H_2O_2]^2$

39. If the rate law of the reaction that follows the mechanism below is determined to be $k[H^+][I^-][H_2O_2]$, then what is the rate-limiting step?

$H_2O_2 + H^+ \rightleftharpoons H_3O_2^+$	Step 1
$I^- + H_3O_2^+ \rightarrow HOI + H_2O$	Step 2
$I^- + HOI \rightarrow I_2 + OH^-$	Step 3
$H^+ + OH^- \rightarrow H_2O$	Step 4

A. Step 1
B. Step 2
C. Step 3
D. Step 4
E. Cannot be determined

40. Which of the following is least likely to increase the rate of a reaction not at equilibrium?

A. Increasing the temperature
B. Adding more reactant
C. Removing product
D. Adding a catalyst
E. Adding an enzyme

Study Plan

After Class: General Chemistry 1		
Complete Remaining *Lesson Book* Practice Questions	30m	
Practice with Tests and Quizzes		

Before Class: Organic Chemistry 1		
Read *Review Notes* Chapters 38–43	3h 0m	
Nomenclature and Functional Groups Workshop	45m	

ORGANIC CHEMISTRY 1

TOPICS COVERED

- The Organic Chemistry Subsection
- Nomenclature
- Stereochemistry
- Mechanisms

After this session you will be able to:

- Assign names to molecules
- Differentiate among different types of isomers
- Identify types of substitution, elimination, and addition reactions
- Describe the properties of those reactions

The Organic Chemistry Subsection

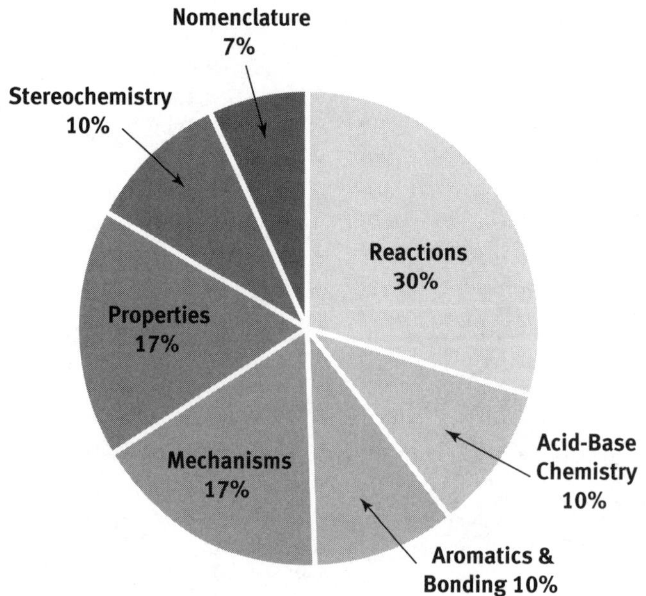

The distribution of Organic Chemistry questions

Overview

- 30 questions (30% of the Survey of the Natural Sciences section)

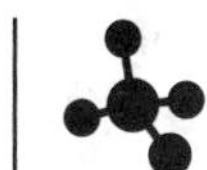

Topics

Mechanisms: Energetics, Structure, and Stability of Intermediates (5)

- Elimination
- Addition
- Free Radical
- Substitution

Chemical and Physical Properties of Molecules and Organic Analysis (5)

- Intermolecular Forces
  1. Solubility
  2. Melting/Boiling Points
- Laboratory Theory and Techniques
  1. TLC
  2. Separation
- Spectroscopy
  1. ^{1}H NMR
  2. ^{13}C NMR
  3. Infrared
  4. Multi-spectra
- Polarity

Stereochemistry (3)

- Chirality
- Isomer Relationships
- Conformations

Nomenclature (2)

- IUPAC Rules
- Functional Groups in Molecules

Reactions of the Major Functional Groups (9)

- Alkene/Alkyne
- Aromatic
- Substitution/Elimination
- Aldehyde/Ketone
- Carboxylic Acids and Derivatives

Acid-Base Chemistry (3)

- Ranking Acidity/Basicity
  1. Structure Analysis
  2. pH/pK_a Data Analysis
- Prediction of Products and Equilibria

Aromatics and Bonding (3)

- Aromaticity
- Resonance
- Atomic/Molecular Orbitals
- Hybridization
- Bond Angles/Lengths

The Kaplan Question Strategy

STOP

➜ Characterize the answer choices.

THINK

➜ What is the question really asking?

➜ What relevant information do you need?

PREDICT

➜ Formulate a framework or prediction for your answer.

MATCH

➜ Select the answer that truly meets the requirements of the prediction.

Nomenclature

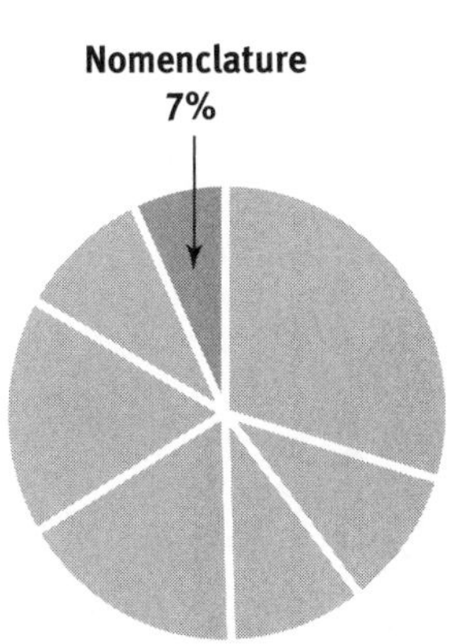

IUPAC Rules

1. Identify the longest carbon chain containing the highest-priority functional group.
2. Number the carbon chain so the highest-priority functional group receives the lowest number and becomes the suffix.
3. Number the remaining substituents accordingly, including them as prefixes in alphabetical order.

Carbon Chains

Carbons	Prefix
1	Meth-
2	Eth-
3	Prop-
4	But-
5	Pent-
6	Hex-
7	Hept-
8	Oct-
9	Non-
10	Dec-

Functional Groups

Functional Group	Structure	IUPAC
Alkane	H H | | —C—C— | | H H	-ane
Alkene	H H | | —C=C—	-ene
Alkyne	—C≡C—	-yne
Phenyl	H H \ / C=C / \ H—C C— \\ // C—C / \ H H	phenyl-
Alkyl Halide	X | —C— | (X = F, Cl, Br, I)	halo- and -halide
Acyl Halide	O || — C —X	halocarbonyl- and -oyl halide
Alcohol	OH | —C— |	hydroxy- and -ol
Aldehyde	O || —C—H	oxo- and -al
Ketone	O || —C—	oxo- and -one
Carboxylic Acid	O || —C—OH	carboxy- and -oic acid
Ether	| | —C—O—C— | |	alkoxy- and -ether
Ester	O | || | —C—O—C— |	alkoxycarbonyl- and -oate

Functional Group	Structure	IUPAC
Amine	$-\overset{\overset{\large NH_2}{\vert}}{\underset{\vert}{C}}-$	amino- and -amine
Amide	$-\overset{\overset{\large O}{\Vert}}{C}-NH_2$	amido- and -amide
Imine	$-\overset{\vert}{C}=N-$	imino- and -imine
Nitrile	$-C\equiv N$	cyano- and -nitrile
Thiol	$-\overset{\overset{\large SH}{\vert}}{\underset{\vert}{C}}-$	sulfhydryl- and -thiol

TAKEAWAY

Even though Nomenclature by itself is only worth three points on Test Day, you will need to rely on your knowledge of IUPAC rules and functional groups to be able to answer many of the other questions in the Organic Chemistry section.

Practice Questions

1. Compound E reacts with semicarbazide to form the semicarbazone F according to the following equation:

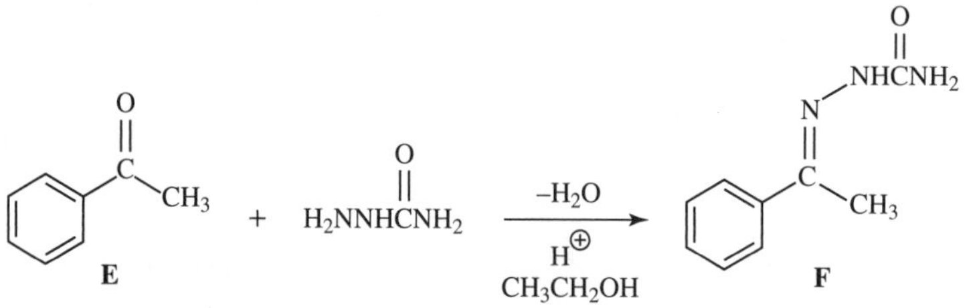

$$\underset{\textbf{E}}{C_6H_5C(=O)CH_3} + H_2NNHC(=O)NH_2 \xrightarrow[\substack{H^{\oplus} \\ CH_3CH_2OH}]{-H_2O} \underset{\textbf{F}}{C_6H_5C(=N{-}NHC(=O)NH_2)CH_3}$$

Compound F contains what functional groups?

A. Imine, amine, amide
B. Imine, amine, carbonyl
C. Amine, amide, hydroxyl
D. Phenyl, amide, imine
E. Ethyl, amide, ketone

2. What is the correct IUPAC name for the compound below?

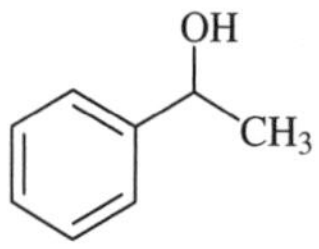

$$C_6H_5CH(OH)CH_3$$

A. 1-phenylethanol
B. 2-ethylphenol
C. 2-phenylethanol
D. Methyl phenyl ketone
E. 1-hydroxymethylphenyl

3. Name the organic reactant and product of the following reaction.

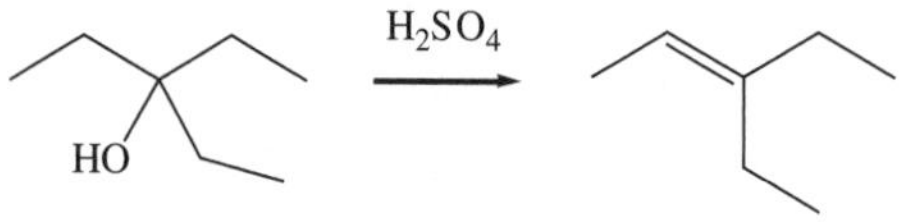

$$(CH_3CH_2)_3COH \xrightarrow{H_2SO_4} CH_3CH{=}C(CH_2CH_3)_2$$

A. 3-propylpentanol, 3-ethyl-2-pentene
B. 2-ethylbutanol, 3-ethyl-3-pentene
C. t-butylpentanol, isoheptene
D. 3-ethyl-3-pentanol, 3-ethyl-2-pentene
E. 3-ethyl-3-pentanol, isopentene

Stereochemistry

Stereochemistry
10%

Conformational Isomers

Newman Projections

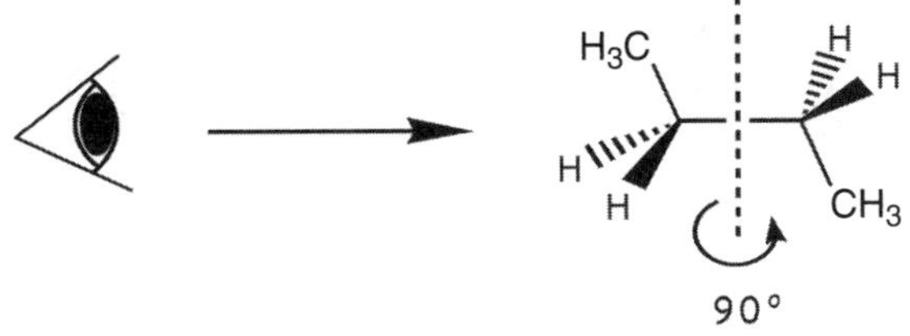

Torsional Strain

CH_3 H H H H CH_3

staggered (*anti*)

CH_3 H CH_3 H H H

staggered (*gauche*)

CH_3 CH_3 H H H H

totally eclipsed

H CH_3 H H CH_3 H

eclipsed

Cycloalkanes

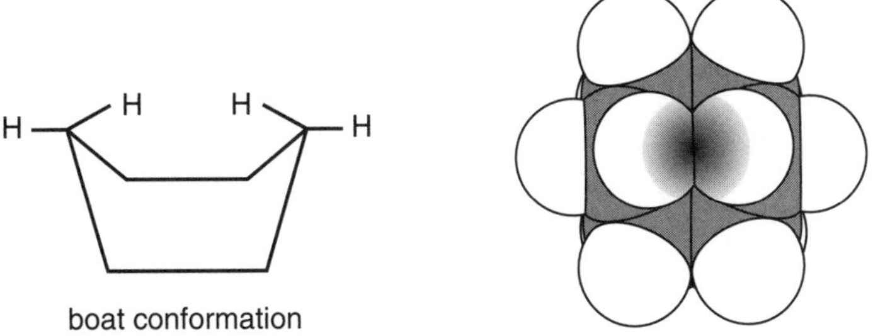

boat conformation

Substituted Cycloalkanes

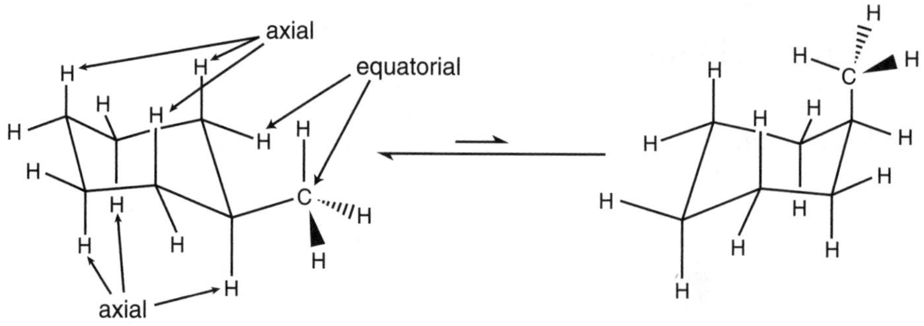

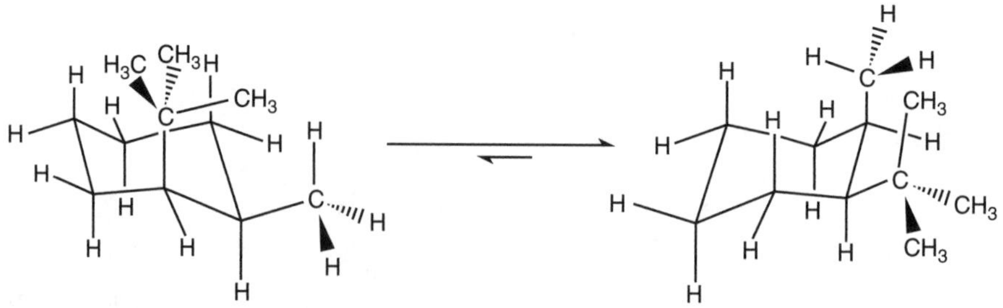

Ring Strain

Practice Questions

4. Which of the following conformations of 1-*t*-butyl-2,4-dichlorocyclohexane is the least stable?

A. 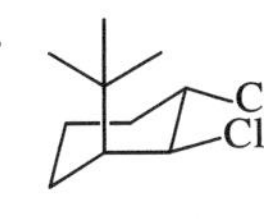

B. 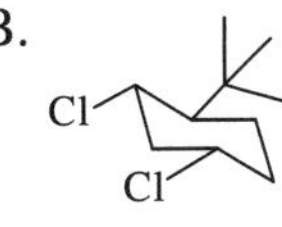

C. 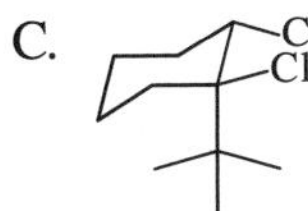

D. 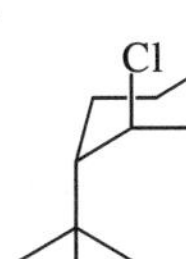

E. Cl Cl

5. Which of the following conformations is the most stable?

A. CH_3 CH_3

B. 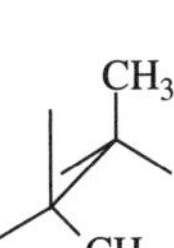

C. H_3C CH_3

D. CH_3 CH_3

E. CH_3 CH_3

6. Which of the following correctly ranks the cycloalkanes in decreasing order of ring strain?

A. Cyclobutane > cyclopentane > cyclohexane > cyclopropane
B. Cyclohexane > cyclobutane > cyclopentane > cyclopropane
C. Cyclopentane > cyclopropane > cyclobutane > cyclohexane
D. Cyclohexane > cyclopropane > cyclobutane > cyclopentane
E. Cyclopropane > cyclobutane > cyclopentane > cyclohexane

Enantiomers

Fischer Projections

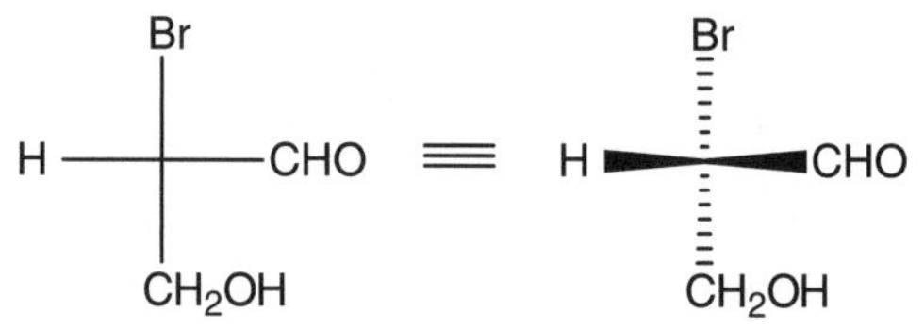

Br Br

H —CHO ≡ H CHO

CH_2OH CH_2OH

Chirality

Designating the Molecule as *R* or *S*

1. Put the atoms attached directly to the chiral center in descending order by molecular weight of the attached atom.

2. Ignore priority 4 and draw an arrow connecting $1 \rightarrow 2 \rightarrow 3$.

3. Note the direction of the arrow as clockwise (*R*) or counterclockwise (*S*).

4. If priority 4 is going into the page (going away), keep the designation as it is.
   If priority 4 is coming out of the page (coming forward), switch the designation (e.g., *R* to *S*).

Optical Activity

Racemic Mixture

Diastereomers

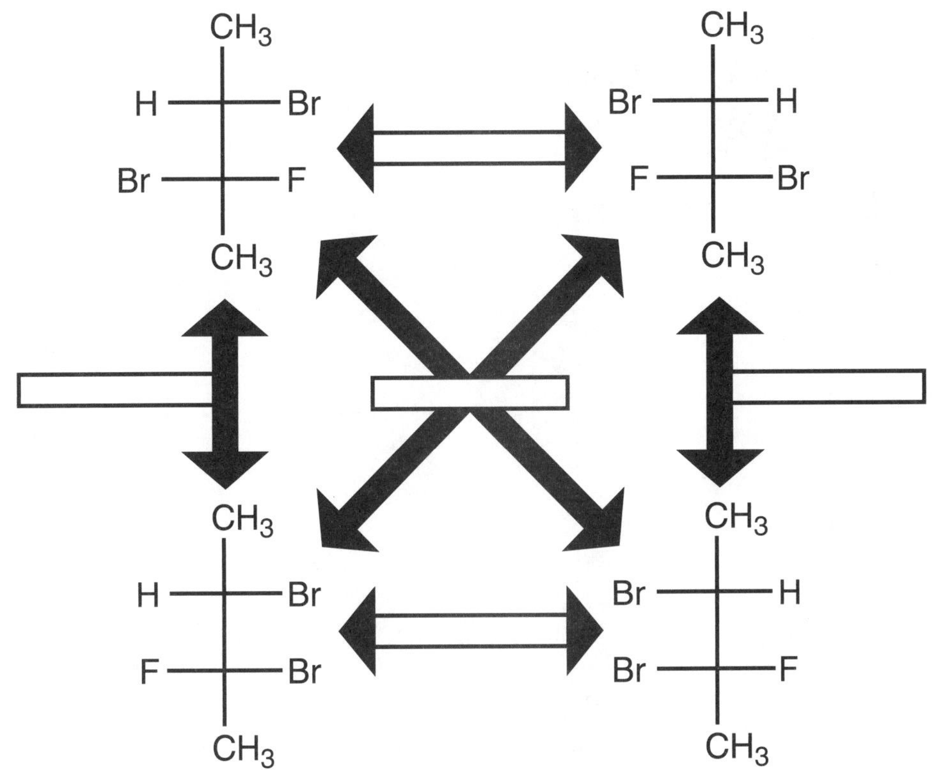

Meso Compounds

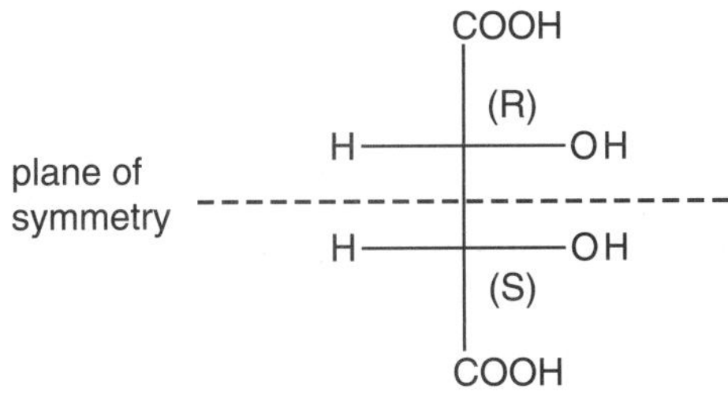

Practice Questions

7. Cholesterol, shown below, contains how many chiral centers?

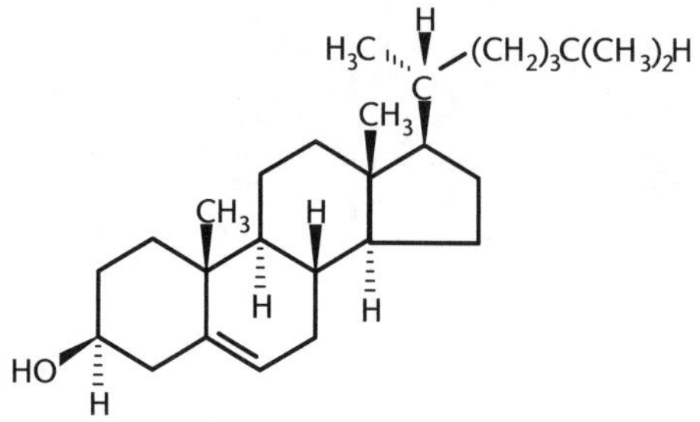

A. 5
B. 7
C. 8
D. 9
E. 11

8. Which of the following compounds is optically inactive?

A. CH_3 / H—C—Cl / Cl—C—H / CH_3

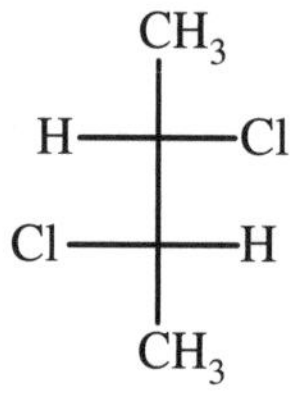

B. CH_3 / Cl—C—H / H—C—Cl / CH_3

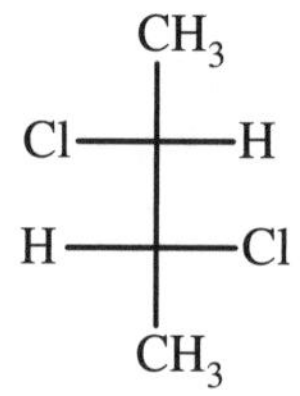

C. CH_3 / H—C—Cl / H—C—Cl / CH_3

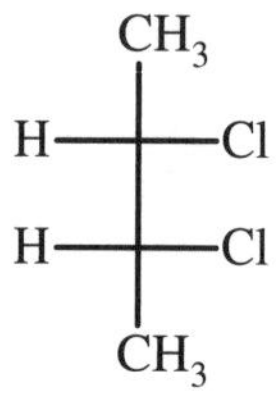

D. CH_2Cl / H—C—Cl / H—C—H / CH_3

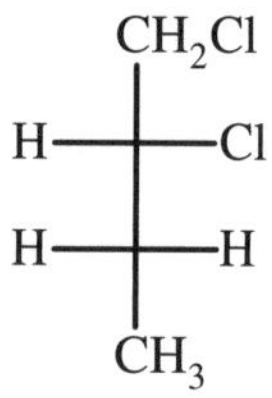

E. CH_2Cl / H—C—Cl / H—C—Cl / CH_3

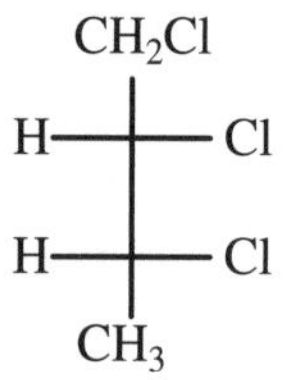

9. How many chiral centers does thyroid hormone (shown below) have, and how should the chiral center(s) be designated?

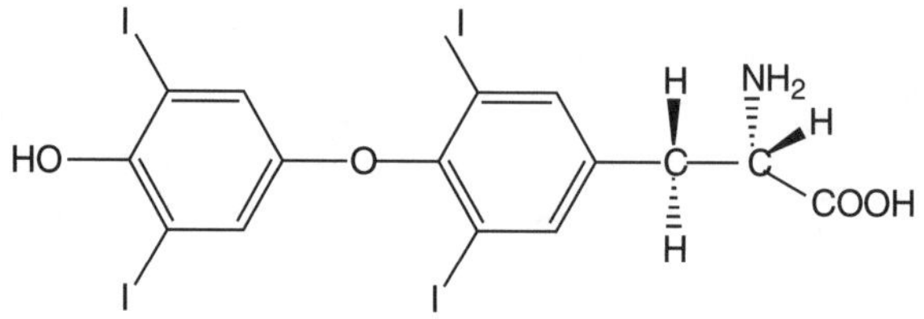

A. 1 chiral center; *R* configuration
B. 1 chiral center; *S* configuration
C. 2 chiral centers; both *R* configuration
D. 2 chiral centers; both *S* configuration
E. 2 chiral centers; one *R* configuration, one *S* configuration

Cis-Trans Isomers

$H_3CH_2C(H)C{=}C(CH_3)(H)$ ________

$H_3CH_2C(H)C{=}C(H)(CH_3)$ ________

E-Z Isomers

$H_3C(Cl)C{=}C(H)(CH_2CH_3)$ ________

$H_3C(Cl)C{=}C(CH_2CH_3)(H)$ ________

STUDY TIP

Make sure you know the definitions of each type of isomer. The test can ask you about any number of molecules, but if you know the definitions of the isomers, you'll be ready for anything thrown your way on Test Day.

Practice Questions

10. Which molecule has the lowest boiling point?

   A. *cis*-2-Butene
   B. *trans*-2-Butene
   C. *cis*-3-Hexene
   D. *trans*-3-Hexene
   E. *cis*-4-Octene

11. Which term best describes the following molecules?

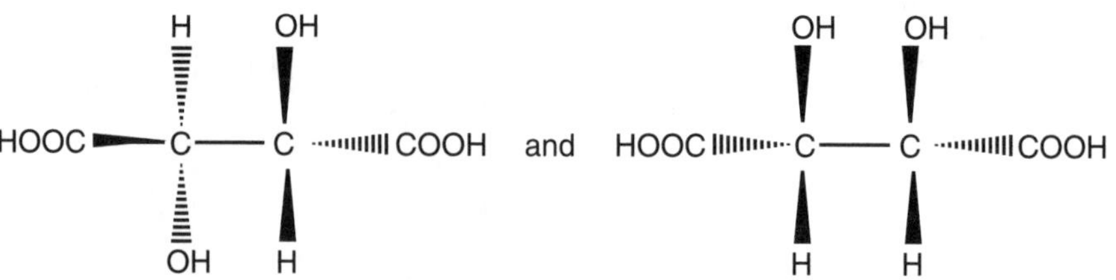

   A. Conformational isomers
   B. Identical compounds
   C. Enantiomers
   D. Geometric isomers
   E. Meso compounds

12. Which term best describes the following molecules?

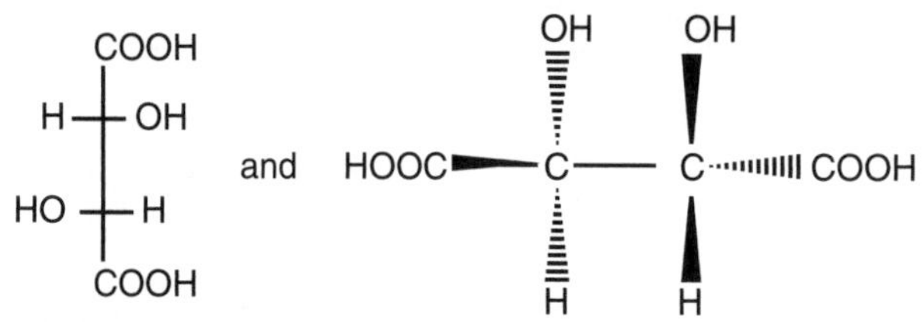

   A. Conformational isomers
   B. Identical compounds
   C. Enantiomers
   D. Geometric isomers
   E. Meso compounds

Mechanisms

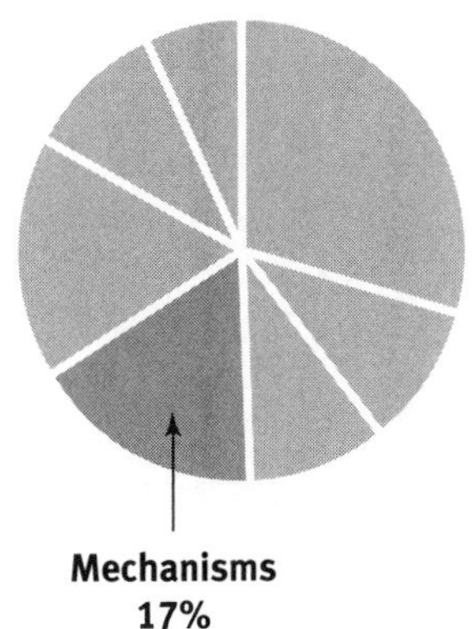

Nucleophiles

Electrophiles

Leaving Groups

Substitution: S_N1

$R_1R_2R_3C{-}X \xrightarrow{\text{slow}} R_2{-}C^{+}(R_1){-}R_3 + X^{-} \longrightarrow R_2{-}C(R_1)(Nu){-}R_3$

Alkyl halide

Carbocation intermediate

$:Nu^{-}$

Substituted product

Mechanism

Kinetics

Substrate

Nucleophiles

Leaving Groups

Solvents

Stereochemistry

$$CH_3CH_2-C(CH_3)(CH(CH_3)_2)Br \longrightarrow CH_3CH_2-\overset{+}{C}(CH_3)-CH(CH_3)_2$$

$$\xrightarrow{^-OH} CH_3CH_2-C(CH_3)(OH)-CH(CH_3)_2$$

$$\xrightarrow{^-OH} CH_3CH_3-C(CH3)(CH(CH_3)_2)-OH$$

Example

$$CH_3-\underset{CH_3}{\overset{CH_3}{C}}-Cl \xrightarrow[(-Cl^-)]{\text{slow step}} CH_3-\underset{CH_3}{\overset{CH_3}{C^+}} \xrightarrow{OH^-} CH_3-\underset{CH_3}{\overset{CH_3}{C}}-OH$$

Practice Questions

13. Which of the following is the best leaving group?

    A. F^-
    B. Cl^-
    C. Br^-
    D. I^-
    E. H^-

14. Each of the following statements correctly describes an S_N1 reaction EXCEPT one. Which one is the EXCEPTION?

    A. The reaction follows first-order kinetics.
    B. The intermediate is a carbocation.
    C. The carbocation stability follows the trend $3° > 2° > 1°$.
    D. Polar aprotic solvents stabilize the carbocation by hydrogen bonding.
    E. If the substrate is optically active, a racemic mixture results.

15. A chemist wants to increase the rate of an S_N1 reaction. Which of the following strategies would be most effective?

    A. Reacting the substrate with a stronger nucleophile.
    B. Performing the reaction in an aprotic solvent.
    C. Selecting a substrate that will form a primary carbocation.
    D. Using a substrate with a better leaving group.
    E. Replacing the weak nucleophile with an equal concentration of strong base.

Substitution: S_N2

$$:Nu^{\ominus} + R_1R_2R_3C{-}X \xrightarrow{\text{slow}} \left[\overset{\delta\ominus}{Nu}\cdots C(R_1)(R_2)(R_3) \cdots \overset{\delta\ominus}{X} \right] \longrightarrow Nu{-}C(R1)(R2)(R3) + X^{\ominus}$$

Alkyl halide — Transition state — Substituted product

(R = alkyl group or —H)

Mechanism

Kinetics

Substrates

Nucleophiles

Leaving Groups

Solvents

Stereochemistry

$CH_3CO_2^- +$ (R'')(R')(H)C—I ⟶ CH_3CO_2—C(H)(R')(R'') + I^-

Example

H—Ö: + CH_3—Cl ⇌ [H—O---C(H)(H)(H)---Cl] ⇌ HO—CH_3 + :Cl:

Transition state

Practice Questions

16. How would the reaction profile for an S_N2 reaction be different if using a secondary substrate instead of a primary substrate?

    A. The reaction with a secondary substrate would have a significantly higher activation energy.

    B. The reaction with a secondary substrate would have a significantly lower activation energy.

    C. The reaction with a secondary substrate would have a significantly higher energy of products.

    D. The reaction with a secondary substrate would have a significantly lower energy of reactants.

    E. The reaction with a secondary substrate would follow second order kinetics, while the reaction with the primary substrate would follow first order kinetics.

17. The rate law for an S_N2 reaction is best described as

    A. rate = k[nucleophile].

    B. rate = k[alkyl halide].

    C. rate = k[alkyl halide]^2.

    D. rate = k[alkyl halide][nucleophile].

    E. rate = k[alkyl halide][nucleophile]^2.

18. Which of the following alkyl halides will be the most suitable for an S_N2 reaction?

    A. CH_3Cl

    B. Cl

    C. Cl

    D. Cl

    E. Cl

Elimination: E1

Base:

slow

$X^{\ominus}$

+ HX

Alkyl halide

Carbocation intermediate

Elimination product

Mechanism

Kinetics

Substrates

Bases

Leaving Groups

Solvents

Stereochemistry

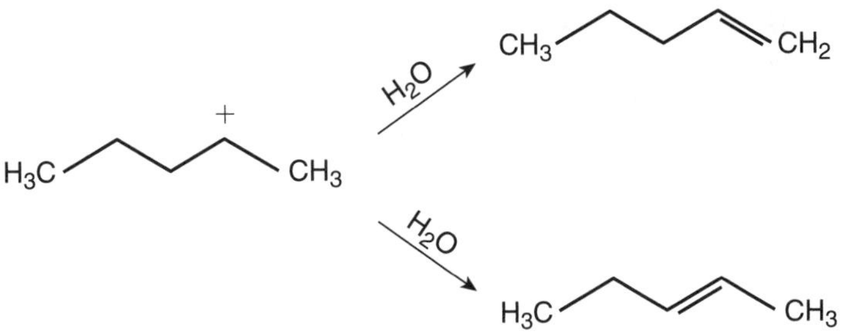

Competition

Example

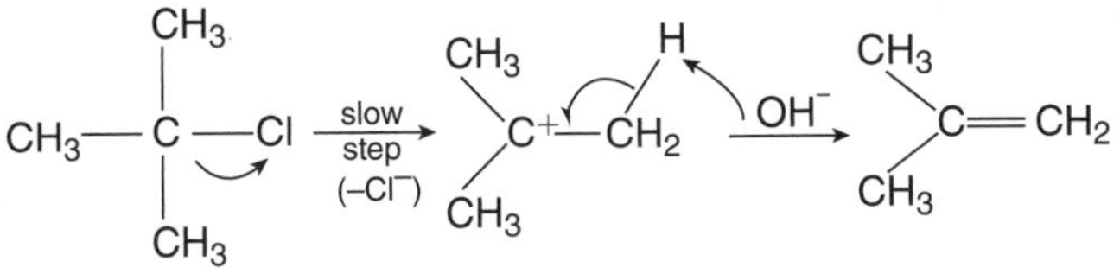

Elimination: E2

Alkyl halide

Elimination product

Mechanism

Kinetics

Substrates

Bases

Leaving Groups

Solvents

Stereochemistry

anti-periplanar
(staggered)

Competition

Example

$C_2H_5O^-$ → + C_2H_5OH + Cl^-

Practice Questions

19. Which of the following is the best solvent for an E2 reaction?

   A. Water
   B. Alcohol
   C. Acetone
   D. Hexane
   E. Ammonia

20. The rate-determining (slow) step in an E1 reaction is the

   A. nucleophilic attack on the substrate.
   B. formation of the carbocation intermediate.
   C. formation of the chiral transition state.
   D. inversion of configuration of the alkyl halide.
   E. formation of the double bond.

21. The dehydration of 2-methylcyclohexanol is an illustration of Zaitsev's rule, which states: In a β-elimination reaction, the most highly substituted alkene will be the major product. Assuming the following reaction follows an E2 mechanism, predict the product distribution.

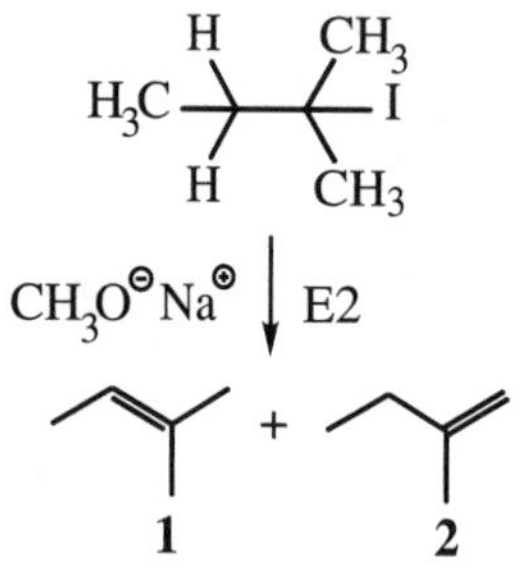

H CH$_3$
H_3C — I
H CH$_3$

$CH_3O^{\ominus}Na^{\oplus}$ ↓ E2

1 + 2

   A. Only product 1 will be formed.
   B. Only product 2 will be formed.
   C. Product 1 will be the major product, and product 2 will be the minor product.
   D. Product 2 will be the major product, and product 1 will be the minor product.
   E. Both Products 1 and 2 will be formed in equal amounts.

Substitution and Elimination Reactions Overview

When predicting the reactivity of a substrate with respect to S_N2, S_N1, E2, and E1 reactions, ask the following questions:

1. Would the carbocation be stable if the leaving group dissociated?

   If no, rule out S_N1 and E1.

2. Is there a good nucleophile?

   If no, rule out S_N2 .

3. Is there a strong base available to attack the substrate?

   If no, rule out E2 .

4. Does the nucleophile have easy access to the side of the substrate opposite the leaving group?

   If no, rule out S_N2 .

Reactivity in Aprotic Solvent

Substrate	**Good Nu:, Weak Base (e.g., Cl^-)**	**Good Nu:, Strong Base (e.g., OH^-)**	**Bulky Nu:, Strong Base (e.g., *t*-butoxide)**
Methyl			
1°			
2°			
3°			

Practice Questions

22. What is the major product of the following reaction?

$$(CH_3)_2CHCHOHCH_2CH_3 \xrightarrow[\text{Heat}]{H_2SO_4}$$

A. 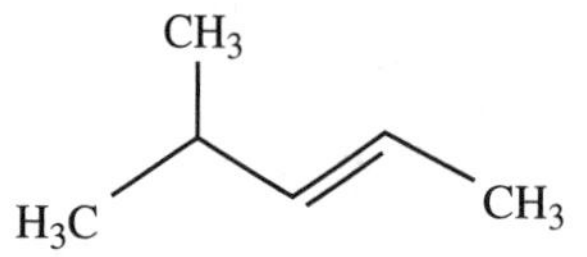 CH_3 / H_3C / CH_3

B. 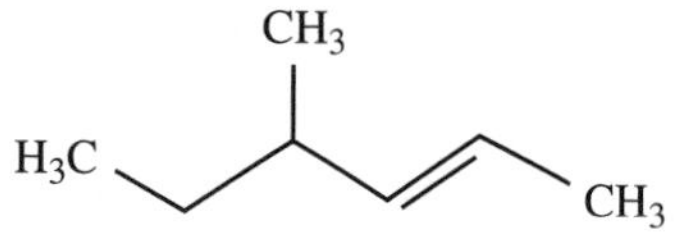 CH_3 / H_3C / CH_3

C. 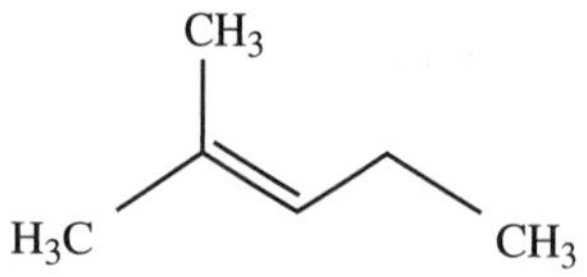 CH_3 / H_3C / CH_3

D. 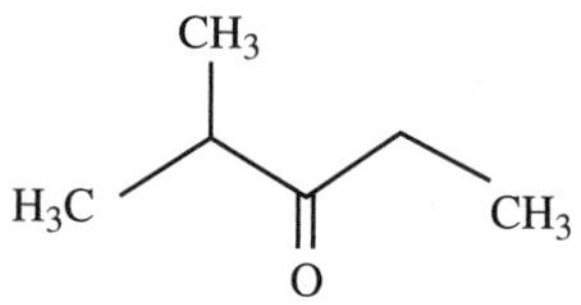 CH_3 / H_3C / CH_3 / O

E. 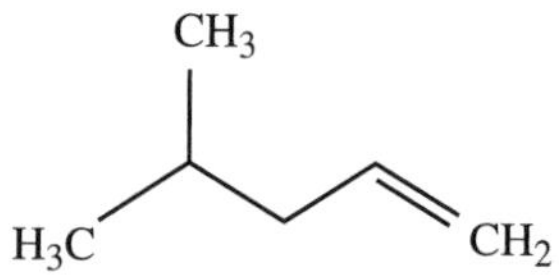 CH_3 / H_3C / CH_2

23. A chemist wants to ensure that the chemical reaction he is about to perform will follow the S_N2 mechanism. How can he promote S_N2 over E2?

A. He can use a substrate with a bulkier base.
B. He can add heat to the reaction.
C. He can use a good leaving group.
D. He can use a substrate with tertiary substitution.
E. He can use a good nucleophile that is not a strong base.

24. (*R*)-1-Fluoro-1-iodopropane is reacted with NaN_3 in HMPA. Which of the following is the major product of this reaction?

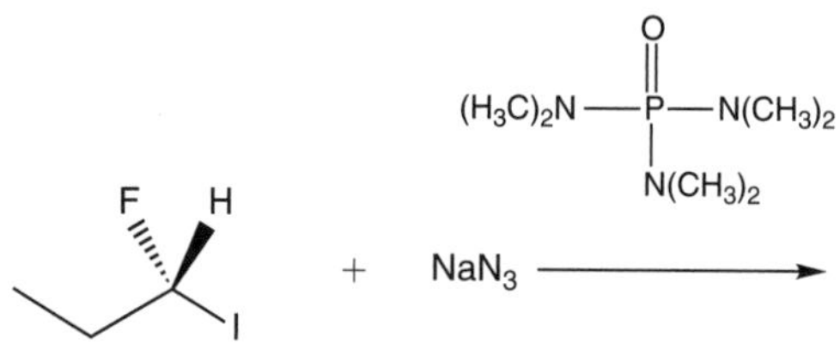

F H I + NaN_3 $\xrightarrow{(H_3C)_2N-P(=O)(N(CH_3)_2)-N(CH_3)_2}$

A. (*R*)-1-Azido-1-fluoropropane
B. (*R*)-1-Azido-1-iodopropane
C. (*S*)-1-Azido-fluoropropane
D. (*S*)-1-Azido-fluoropropene
E. A racemic mixture of (*R*)-1-azido-1-fluoropropane and (*S*)-1-azido-1-fluoropropane

Substitution: Radical

General Reactions

Initiation: $X_2 \xrightarrow[\text{or } \Delta]{h\nu} 2\,X\bullet$

Propagation: $X\bullet + RH \rightarrow HX + R\bullet$

$R\bullet + X_2 \rightarrow RX + X\bullet$

Termination: $2\,X\bullet \rightarrow X_2$

$X\bullet + R\bullet \rightarrow RX$

$2\,R\bullet \rightarrow R_2$

Practice Questions

25. Which of the following is the most likely intermediate for the following reaction?

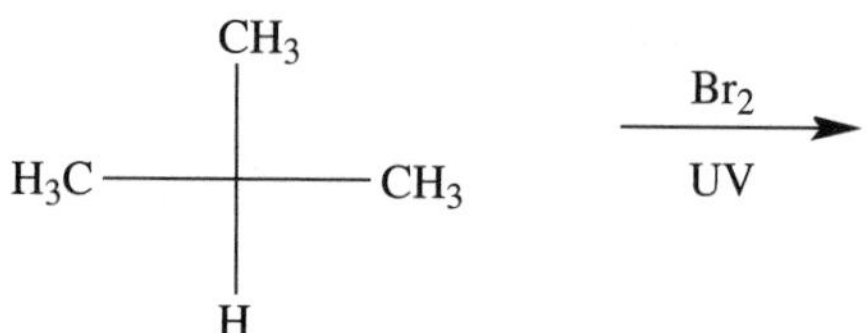

A. $H_3C—\dot{C}—CH_3$, with H_3C on the central C

B. $H_3C—C(H)(CH_3)—\dot{C}H_2$

C. $H_3C—\overset{+}{C}(CH_3)—CH_3$

D. $H_3C—\bar{C}—CH_3$, with CH_3 on the central C

E. $\dot{H_2C}—C(H)(CH_3)—\dot{C}H_2$

26. Which of the following is a chain-termination step?

A. $Cl\bullet + Cl\bullet \rightarrow Cl_2$
B. $Cl\bullet + CH_4 \rightarrow CH_3CH_3HCl$
C. $CH_3\bullet + Cl_2 \rightarrow CH_3Cl + Cl\bullet$
D. $CH_3\bullet + Cl\bullet \rightarrow CH_3Cl_2Cl + Cl\bullet$
E. $Cl_2 \rightarrow 2\,Cl\bullet$

27. What alkyl halide will be the major product from the reaction of excess butane with I_2 in the presence of light?

A. 1-Iodobutane
B. 2-Iodobutane
C. 1,2-Diiodobutane
D. Iodoethane
E. No reaction will occur.

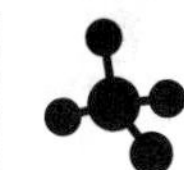

Addition

Markovnikov Addition

Alkene + Hydrogen Halide → Halogen on more-substituted carbon of alkane

Anti-Markovnikov Addition

Alkene + Halogen Radical → Halogen on less-substituted carbon of alkane

Anti Addition of Halogens

Alkene + X_2 → Halogenated Alkane

$Br^{\ominus}$

Br—Br

Br $\oplus$

Br

Br

Dibromination to Synthesize Alkynes from Alkenes

$$RHC{=}CHR + Br_2 \xrightarrow{\text{(addition rxn.)}} R{-}CH(Br){-}CH(Br){-}R$$

vic-dibromide

$$R{-}CH(Br){-}CH(Br){-}R + NH_2^- \longrightarrow R{-}CH{=}C(Br){-}R + NH_3 + Br^-$$

$$R{-}CH{=}C(Br){-}R + NH_2^- \longrightarrow R{-}C{\equiv}C{-}R + NH_3 + Br^-$$

> **STUDY TIP**
>
> Rather than trying to memorize each individual mechanism, learn the similarities and differences between substitution, elimination, and addition reactions. This will allow you to more easily understand the material and help you answer a variety of questions on Test Day.

Practice Questions

28. What is the product of the following reaction?

$$CH_3CH_2CH{=}CH_2 + HBr \longrightarrow$$

A. 1-Bromobutane
B. 2-Bromobutane
C. 1,2-Dibromobutane
D. 1-Bromopropane
E. No reaction will occur.

29. What is the product of the following reaction?

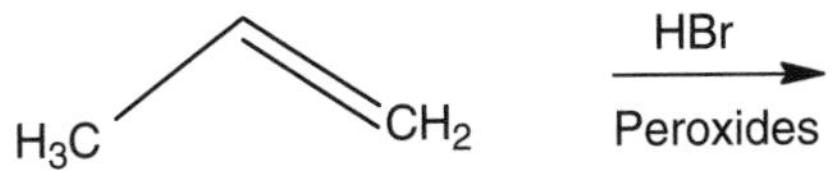

A. 1-Bromopropane
B. 2-Bromopropane
C. 1,2-Dibromopropane
D. 1-Bromopropene
E. No reaction will occur.

30. 2-Methyl-2-butene was reacted to form a tertiary alkyl halide. Which reagent is most likely to have caused this reaction?

A. HF with light
B. CH_3OOCH_3 alone
C. HI with heat
D. HCl with light
E. HBr alone

Study Plan

After Class: Organic Chemistry 1		
Complete Remaining *Lesson Book* Practice Questions	30m	
Practice with Tests and Quizzes		
Practice Tests		
Full-Length Test 1	4h 30m	
Before Class: Biology 2		
Read *Review Notes* Chapters 10–18	4h 30m	

BIOLOGY 2

TOPICS COVERED

- Anatomy and Physiology
- Cell and Molecular Biology
- Developmental Biology

After this session you will be able to:

- Recall the structures and functions of the digestive, circulatory, respiratory, musculoskeletal, nervous, endocrine, urinary, integumentary, immunological, and reproductive systems
- Describe the steps of mitosis and meiosis
- Describe the stages of embryonic development

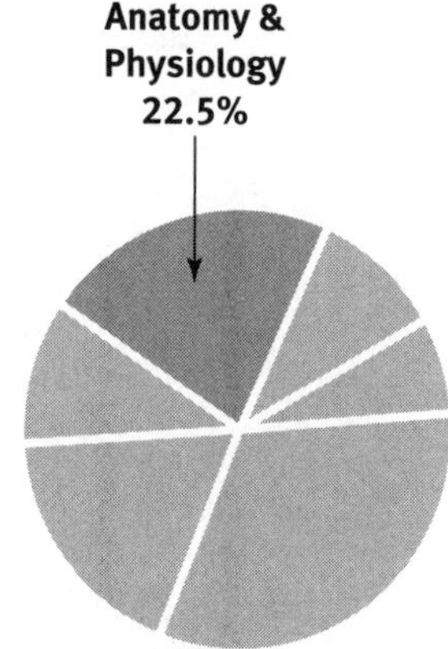

Anatomy and Physiology

Digestive System

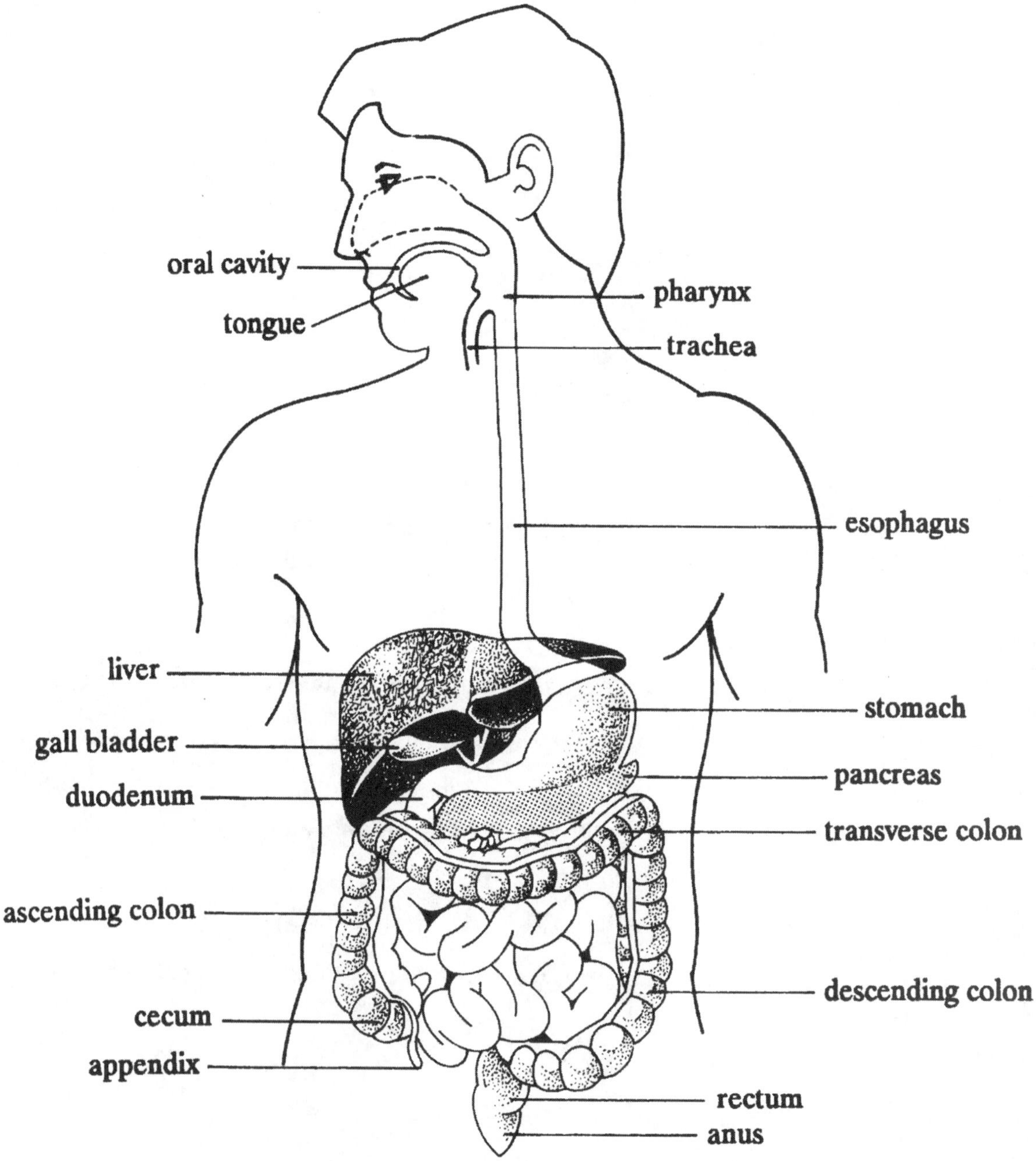

oral cavity
tongue
pharynx
trachea
esophagus
liver
gall bladder
duodenum
stomach
pancreas
transverse colon
ascending colon
descending colon
cecum
appendix
rectum
anus

Components of the Digestive Tract

Mouth

Esophagus

Stomach

Small Intestine

Large Intestine

Liver

Gall Bladder

Pancreas

Practice Questions

1. A certain individual lacks the enzyme maltase, which breaks down the disaccharide maltose into glucose monosaccharides. Which of the following is most likely to occur?

   A. Maltose will be digested by the lactase enzymes in the small intestine.
   B. Maltose will not be absorbed by active transport but will passively diffuse into the cells of the intestinal epithelium.
   C. Maltose will be anaerobically digested by the bacteria in the gut.
   D. Maltose will be flagged as a foreign body and attacked by the immune system.
   E. The individual will be susceptible to malnutrition due to an inability to absorb glucose.

2. Which biological molecules does salivary amylase break down?

   A. Proteins
   B. Lipids
   C. Monosaccharides
   D. Nucleic acids
   E. Starches

3. Which of the following best describes the role of bacteria in the human large intestine?

   A. Prevent invasion of opportunistic species
   B. Ferment undigested carbohydrates
   C. Produce vitamin K
   D. Create methane gas as a byproduct of metabolism
   E. All of the above

Circulatory System

Blood Components

Erythrocytes

Leukocytes

Thrombocytes

Plasma

Blood Types

Blood Type	Antigens	Antibodies	Receives From	Donates To
AB^+				
O^-				

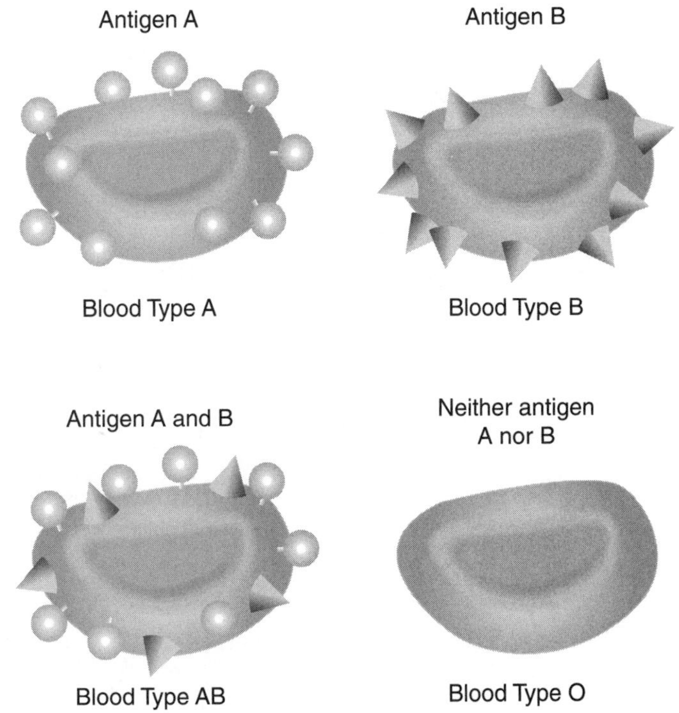

Blood Vessels

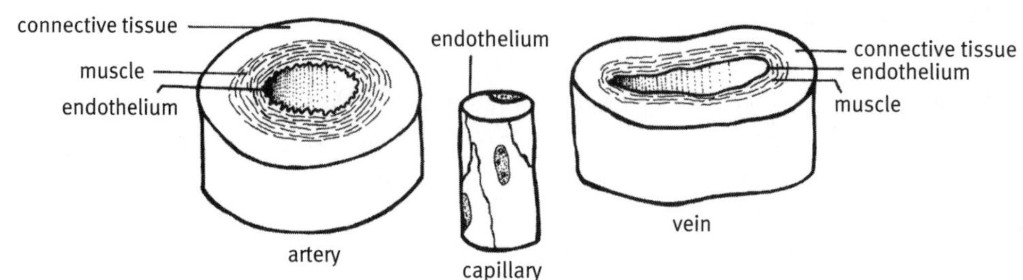

Blood Vessels	Direction	Description	Type of Blood	Valves
Arteries				
Veins				
Capillaries				

Heart

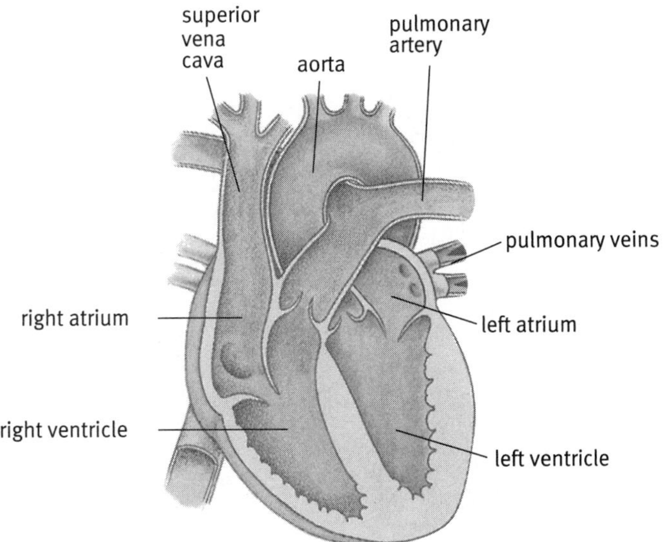

Electrical Conduction

Respiratory System

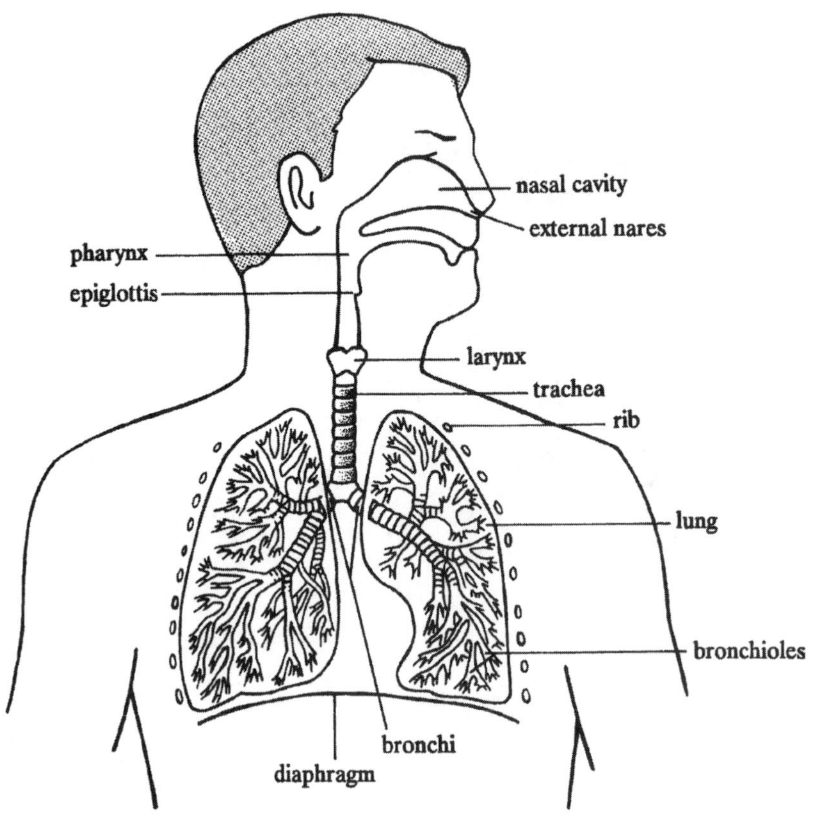

Ventilation

Practice Questions

4. After a person with B^- blood type is given a blood transfusion, hemolysis occurs. Which answer choice includes only blood types that will cause this reaction?

    A. AB^+, B^-, A^+
    B. AB^+, A^-, O^+
    C. AB^-, B^+, B^-
    D. B^+, O^-, A^+
    E. O^+, B^-, AB^-

5. A researcher wanting to study aerobic respiration in mammalian cells should not choose RBCs for her protocols because

    A. RBCs have a life span of only 120 days.
    B. aerobic respiration occurs only in the cells of alveoli.
    C. RBCs lack mitochondria and therefore attain their ATP anaerobically.
    D. RBCs consume O_2 at a faster rate than other cells.
    E. RBCs are much larger than other cells.

6. Which of the following is the correct sequence of the passages through which air travels during inhalation?

    A. Pharynx → trachea → lungs → bronchi → alveoli
    B. Larynx → pharynx → bronchi → lungs → alveoli
    C. Larynx → pharynx → trachea → bronchi → alveoli
    D. Pharynx → larynx → trachea → bronchi → alveoli
    E. Larynx → pharynx → bronchi → trachea → alveoli

Musculoskeletal System

Skeleton

Bone

Cartilage

Tendon

Ligament

Muscles

Muscle Types

Type	Striated	Nuclei	Voluntary
Skeletal			
Smooth			
Cardiac			

Sarcomere

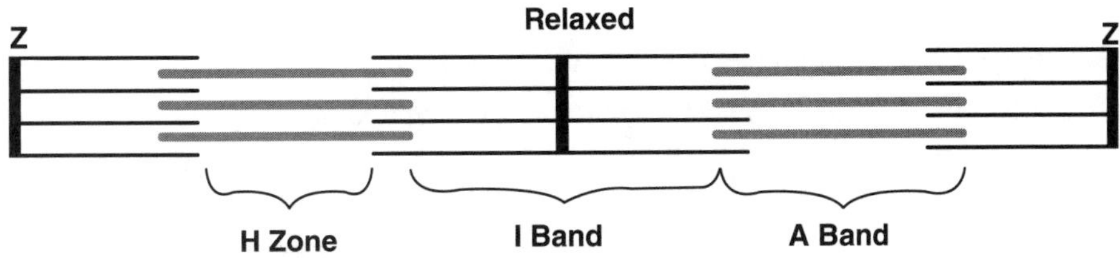

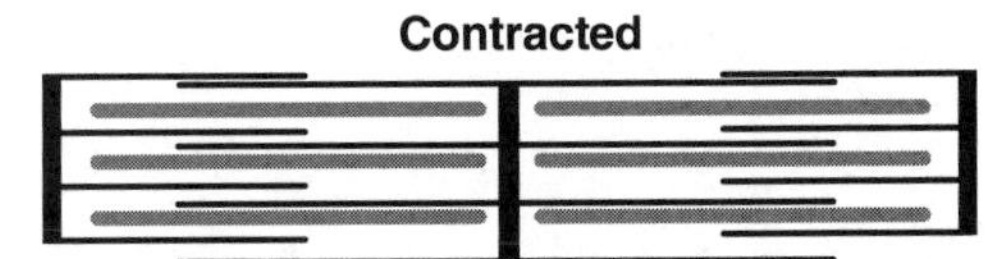

Practice Questions

7. Which of the following statements about the musculoskeletal system is FALSE?

A. Tendons join muscle to muscle; ligaments join muscle to bone.
B. Contraction is initiated in muscle tissue by a cascade of Ca^{2+} ions.
C. Specialized cells react to changing body conditions to maintain serum Ca^{2+} levels.
D. The distance between Z lines always decreases during a contraction.
E. The length of the H zone always decreases during a contraction.

8. For most muscle groups, all of the following are required for a muscle to elongate EXCEPT one. Which of the following is the EXCEPTION?

A. Influx of Ca^{2+} into that muscle's sarcoplasmic reticulum
B. Consumption of ATP by that muscle
C. Contraction of an antagonist muscle
D. Elongation of actin filaments within that muscle
E. Reduction in action potentials to that muscle's ryanodine receptors

9. If the calcium gradients of the sarcoplasmic reticulum were forced to dissipate, which immediate effect would be most likely?

A. Emesis
B. Hyperventilation
C. Paralysis
D. Relaxation
E. Drowsiness

Nervous System

Neuron

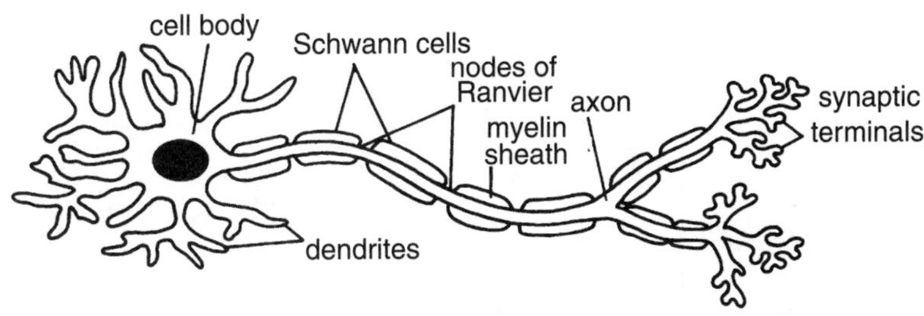

Dendrites

Cell Body

Axon

Synaptic Terminals

Myelin

Synapse

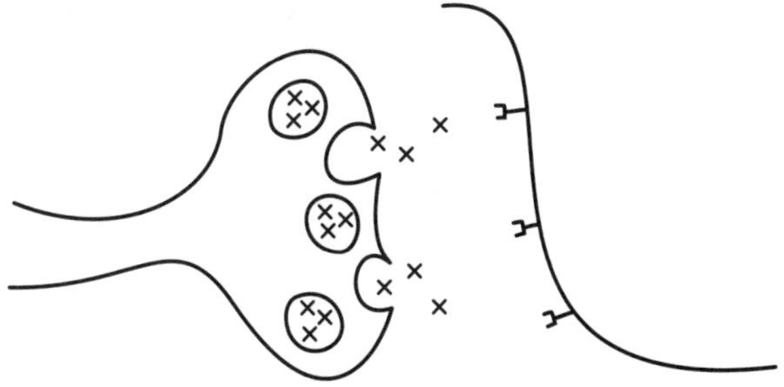

Action Potential

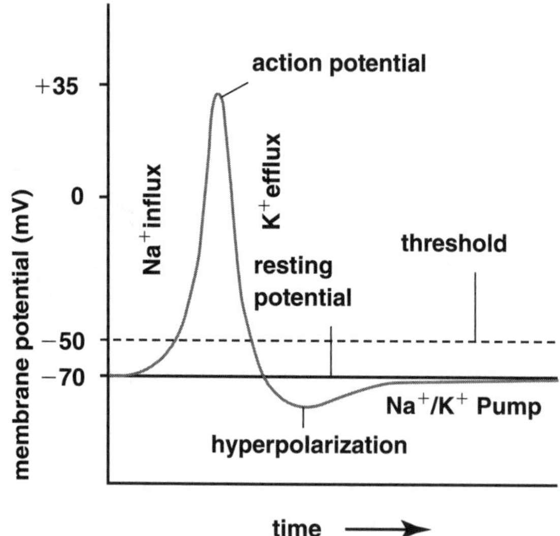

Nervous System Divisions

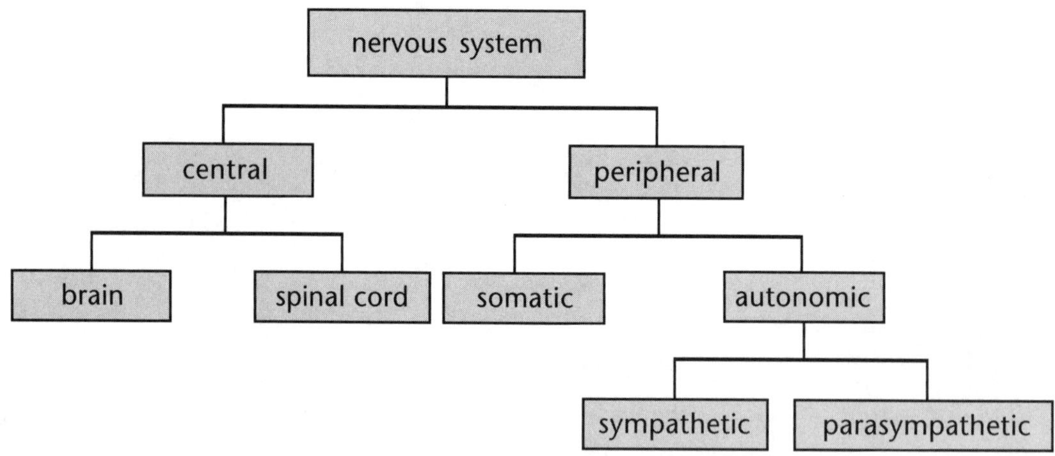

Practice Questions

10. Which of the following responses takes place upon activation of the parasympathetic nervous system?

    A. Increased dilation of pupils
    B. Increased heart rate
    C. Increased respiratory rate
    D. Decreased rate of digestion
    E. Decreased blood flow to skeletal muscles

11. Below is a model of the simple nervous system of the sea snail, *Aplysia*.

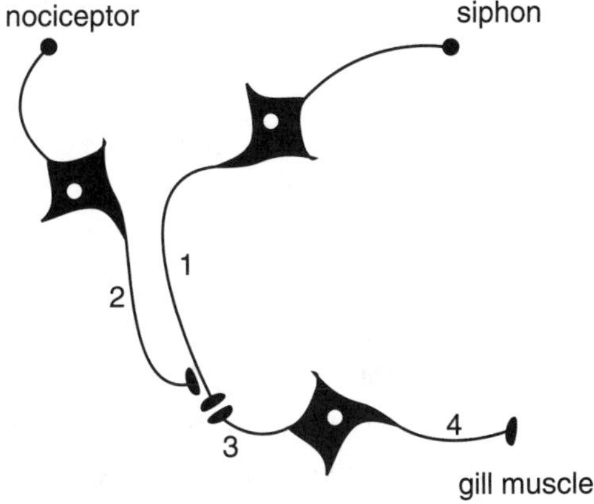

    Which of the above point(s) indicates neural axons?

    A. 2 only
    B. 1 and 2 only
    C. 1 and 3 only
    D. 2, 3, and 4 only
    E. 1, 2, and 4 only

12. The absence of myelin on neurons would be most likely to result in

    A. total paralysis.
    B. uncoordinated movement of the limbs.
    C. seizures.
    D. increased risk of myocardial infarction.
    E. frequent hyperventilation.

Practice Questions

13. After the learning process of habituation, neurons receiving a stimulus respond with less response than they would have prior to habituation. Which of the following effects of repeated stimulation is a possible explanation for habituation?

    A. Permanent closure of calcium channels in the terminal membrane
    B. Increase in the number of neurotransmitter receptors in the postsynaptic membrane
    C. Decrease in the concentrations of neurotransmitter-degrading enzymes in the synapse
    D. Neurotransmitter vesicles fusing with the terminal membrane in response to lower excitatory potentials
    E. Increase in the amount of neurotransmitter released per action potential

14. Individual neurons in the skin containing mechanoreceptors can register the difference between a slight touch and a forceful push by

    A. propagating a larger action potential due to a forceful push.
    B. decreasing the voltage of the resting potential before a light touch.
    C. releasing more frequent action potentials due to a forceful push.
    D. releasing a higher concentration of neurotransmitters for a light touch.
    E. increasing the time between action potentials due to a forceful push.

15. Sensitization allows neurons to respond more frequently to a stimulus than they would have prior to sensitization for a short period of time. What change in the axon terminal could explain this phenomenon?

    A. The axon terminal is permanently hyperpolarized.
    B. The axon terminal is permanently depolarized.
    C. The axon terminal remains polarized longer following an action potential.
    D. The axon terminal remains depolarized longer following an action potential.
    E. The axon terminal releases less neurotransmitter following an action potential.

Endocrine System

Hypothalamus

Posterior Pituitary

Anterior Pituitary

Follicle-Stimulating Hormone (FSH)

Luteinizing Hormone (LH)

Adrenocorticotropic Hormone (ACTH)

Thyroid-Stimulating Hormone (TSH)

Prolactin

Endorphins

Growth Hormone

Thyroid

Triiodothyronine

Thyroxine

Calcitonin

Parathyroid

Parathyroid Hormone

Adrenal Cortex

Glucocorticoids

Mineralocorticoids

Adrenal Medulla

Epinephrine

Pancreas

Insulin

Glucagon

Testes

Androgens

Ovaries

Estrogen

Progesterone

Practice Questions

16. Which of the following accurately describes what happens after a meal high in sugar is eaten by a healthy human?

    A. Blood glucose concentration increases, insulin levels increase, cells take up glucose.
    B. Blood glucose concentration increases, glucagon levels increase, cells break down glycogen.
    C. Blood glucose levels normalize, insulin and glucagon levels both increase.
    D. Blood glucose concentration drops, glucagon levels increase, cells take up glucose.
    E. Blood glucose concentration drops, insulin levels increase, cells break down glycogen.

17. The function of parathyroid hormone is to

    A. stimulate osteoblasts to create new bone when serum calcium is low.
    B. stimulate osteoclasts to create new bone when serum calcium is high.
    C. stimulate osteoblasts to break down bone when serum calcium is low.
    D. stimulate osteoclasts to break down bone when serum calcium is low.
    E. stimulate osteoclasts to break down bone when serum calcium is high.

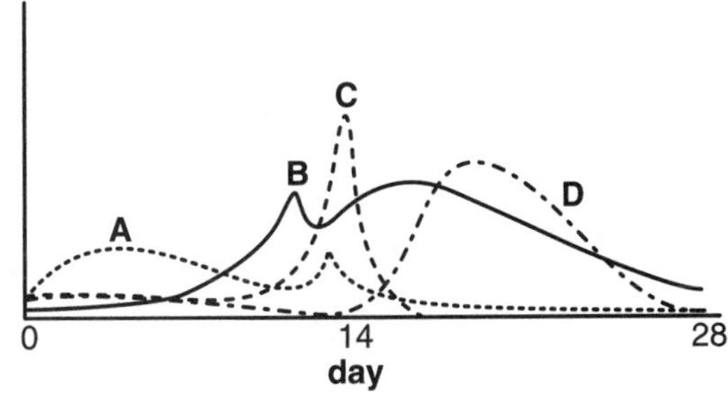

18. Which of the following lines in the chart above represents the levels of luteinizing hormone during the menstrual cycle?

    A. A
    B. B
    C. C
    D. D
    E. Both A and D

Urinary System

Kidney

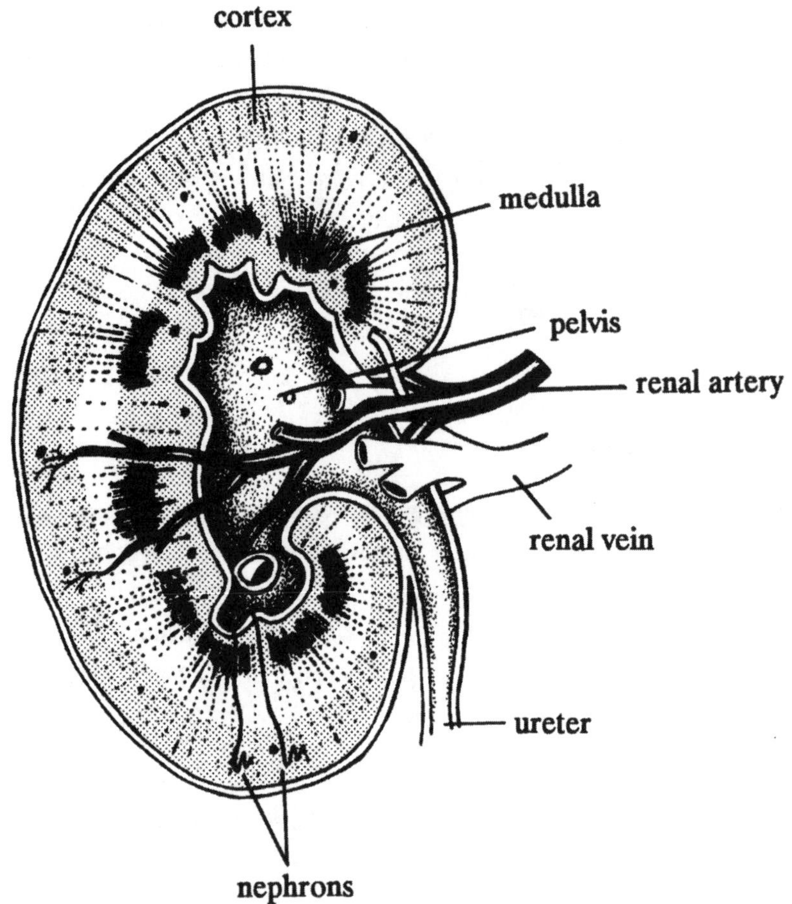

Nephron

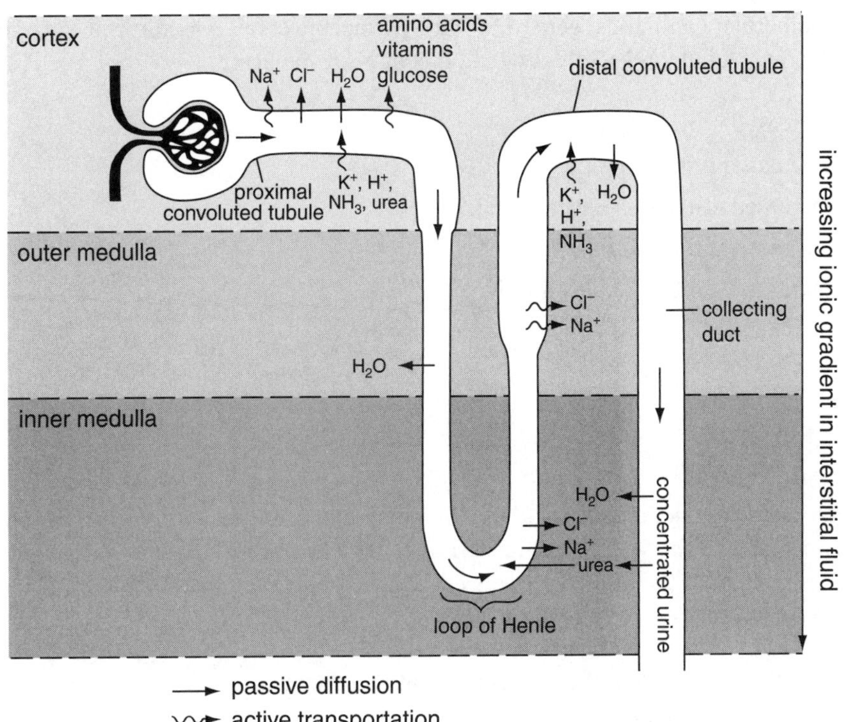

Filtration

Secretion

Reabsorption

Vasopressin (ADH)

Renin-Angiotensin-Aldosterone System

Practice Questions

19. If the glomerular capillaries were to become permeable enough to allow plasma proteins to enter the renal tubule, what effect would this have on the urine?

    A. Increased urine output
    B. Decreased urine output
    C. Increased urine urea concentration
    D. Decreased urine osmolarity
    E. Increased urine salt concentration

20. Caffeine, as a diuretic, increases urine volume by inhibiting the action of ADH. Experimental data shows that administering an injection of ADH at the same time as caffeine counteracts the diuretic effects of caffeine, indicating that caffeine's mechanism of action is to

    A. stimulate conversion of angiotensin-I into angiotensin-II.
    B. block ADH receptors.
    C. promote aldosterone secretion.
    D. inhibit ADH secretion.
    E. inhibit aldosterone secretion.

21. Which of the following is characteristic of the hormone vasopressin?

    A. It increases water reabsorption in the kidneys.
    B. It increases sodium reabsorption in the kidneys.
    C. It increases waste reabsorption in the kidneys.
    D. Its secretion is regulated by the hormone ACTH.
    E. Its secretion is regulated by the enzyme renin.

Integumentary System

Skin

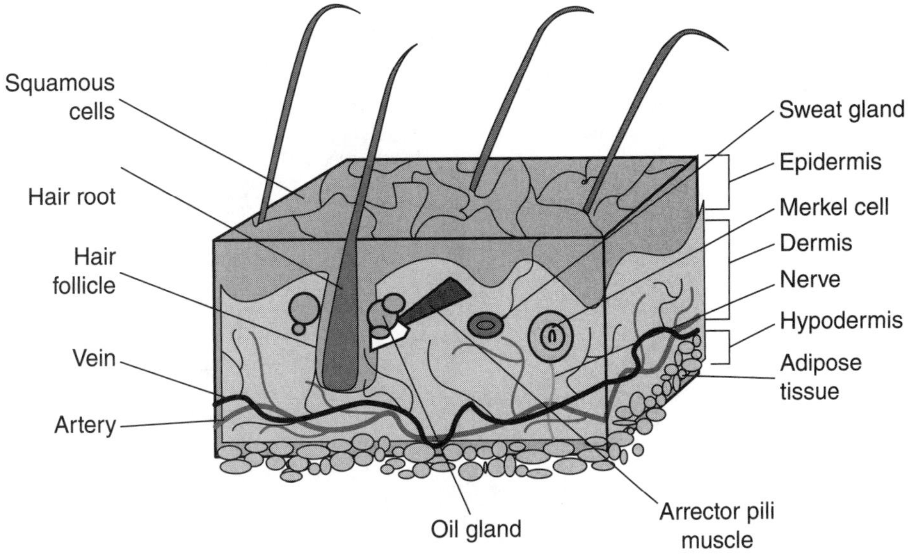

Acidity

Human Microbiome

Mucus

Mechanical Action

Blood Clotting

Immunological System

Immune Cells

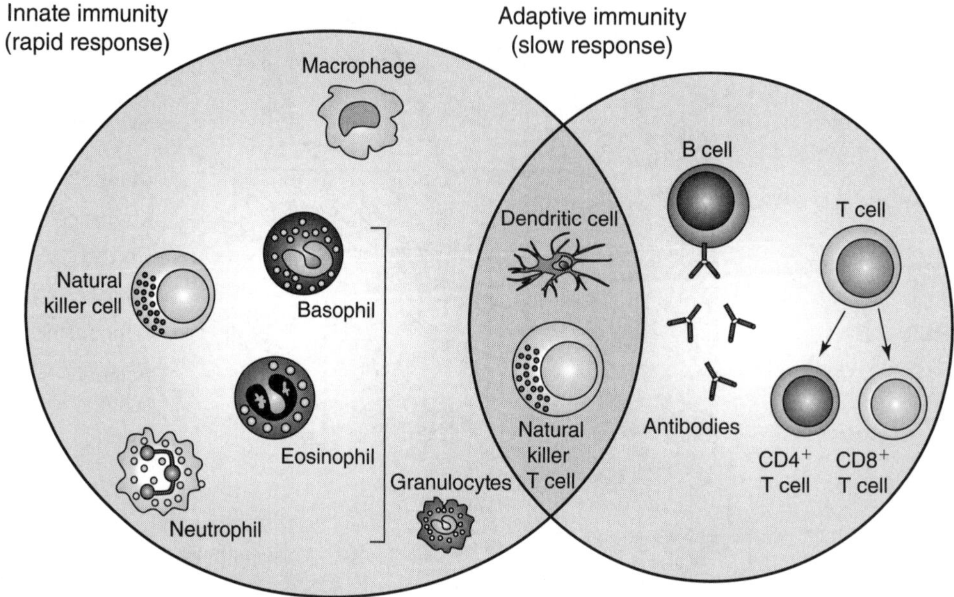

Granulocytes

Basophils/Mast Cells

Eosinophils

Neutrophils

Monocytes

Macrophages

Dendritic Cells

Lymphocytes

B Cells

T Cells

Natural Killer Cells

Practice Questions

22. An increase in serum eosinophil concentration would most likely indicate the presence of what type of agent?

    A. Bacteria
    B. Fungus
    C. Parasite
    D. Venom
    E. Virus

23. Which of the following is NOT involved in nonspecific immune defense?

    A. Skin
    B. Lysozymes
    C. Interferons
    D. Macrophages
    E. B cells

24. The main function of $CD8^+$ T cells is to

    A. promote an allergic response.
    B. stimulate other immune cells.
    C. release antibodies.
    D. destroy damaged cells.
    E. present antigens.

Reproductive System

Male Reproductive Anatomy

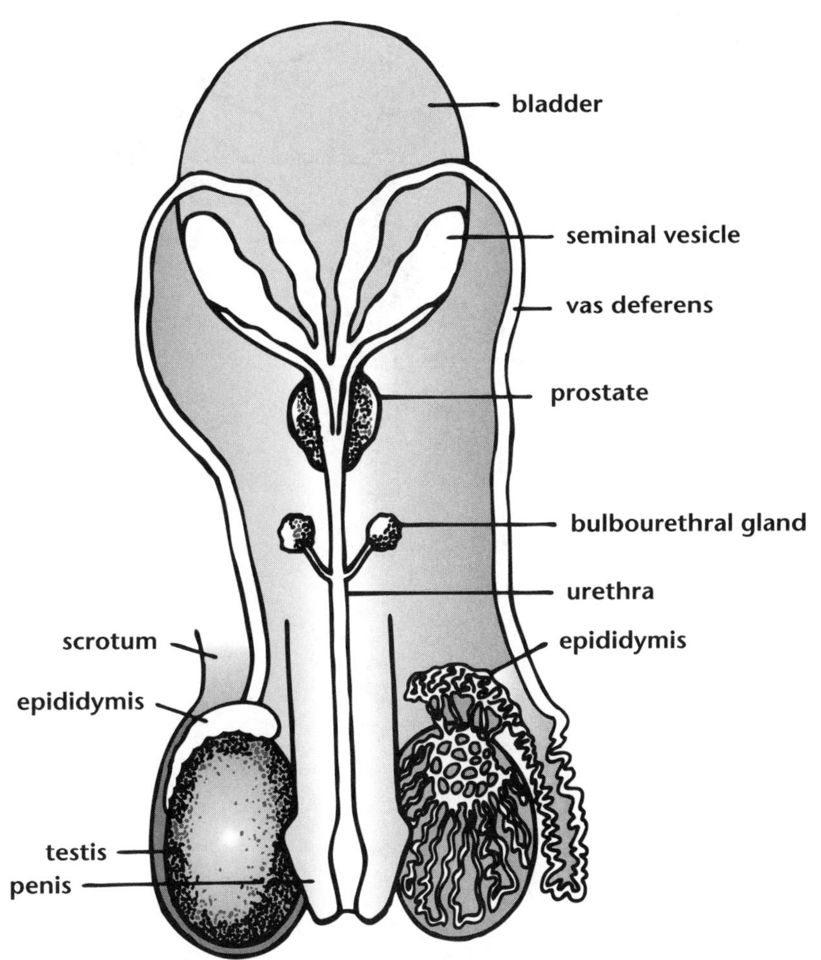

Female Reproductive Anatomy

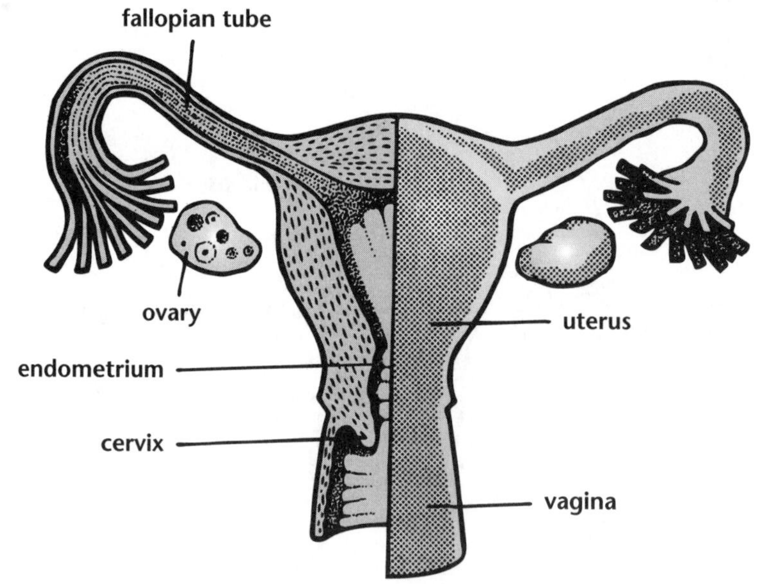

STUDY TIP

Anatomy and physiology cover a wide range of content, but don't neglect the other three-fourths of the Biology subsection. Studying this other material may earn you more points per hour of studying.

Practice Questions

25. Which of the following is FALSE with regard to the reproductive system?

    A. Fertilization of the egg takes places in the oviduct.
    B. The function of the ductus deferens is to store sperm.
    C. The function of the epididymis is to store sperm.
    D. The bulbourethral gland is present in the male reproductive system.
    E. Eggs are released by the ovarian follicle during ovulation.

26. Which of the following structures is found in both male and female systems?

    A. Epididymis
    B. Fallopian tubes
    C. Testes
    D. Urethra
    E. Uterus

27. Which of the following hormones does NOT promote production and development of sperm?

    A. Follicle-stimulating hormone
    B. Testosterone
    C. Luteinizing hormone
    D. Gonadotropin-releasing hormone
    E. Somatostatin

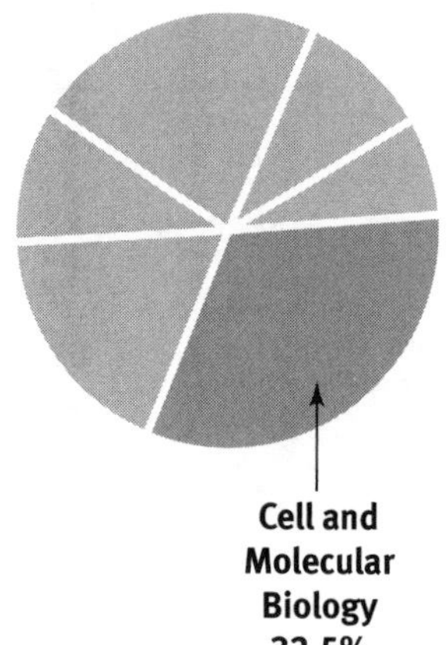

Cell and Molecular Biology

Mitosis and Meiosis

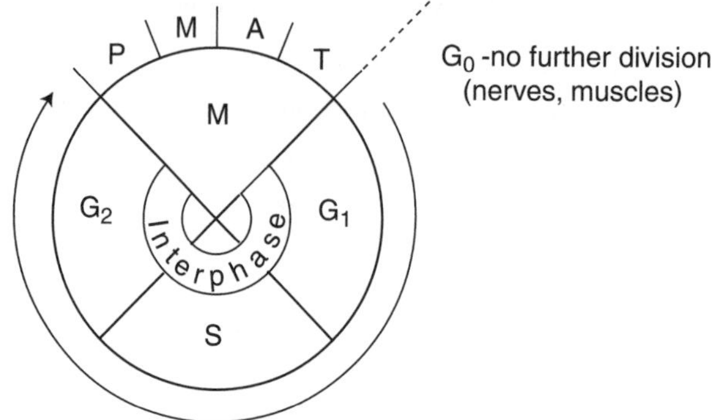

Cell Cycle

Gap

Synthesis

Mitosis

Meiosis

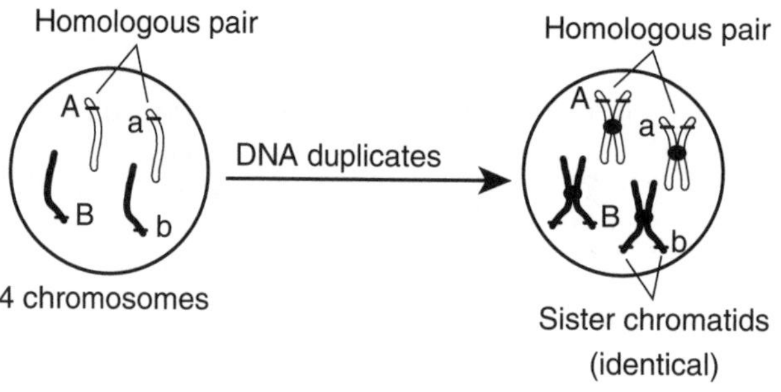

Cellular Machinery

Chromatid

Centromere

Centriole

Centrosome

Stages of Mitosis and Meiosis

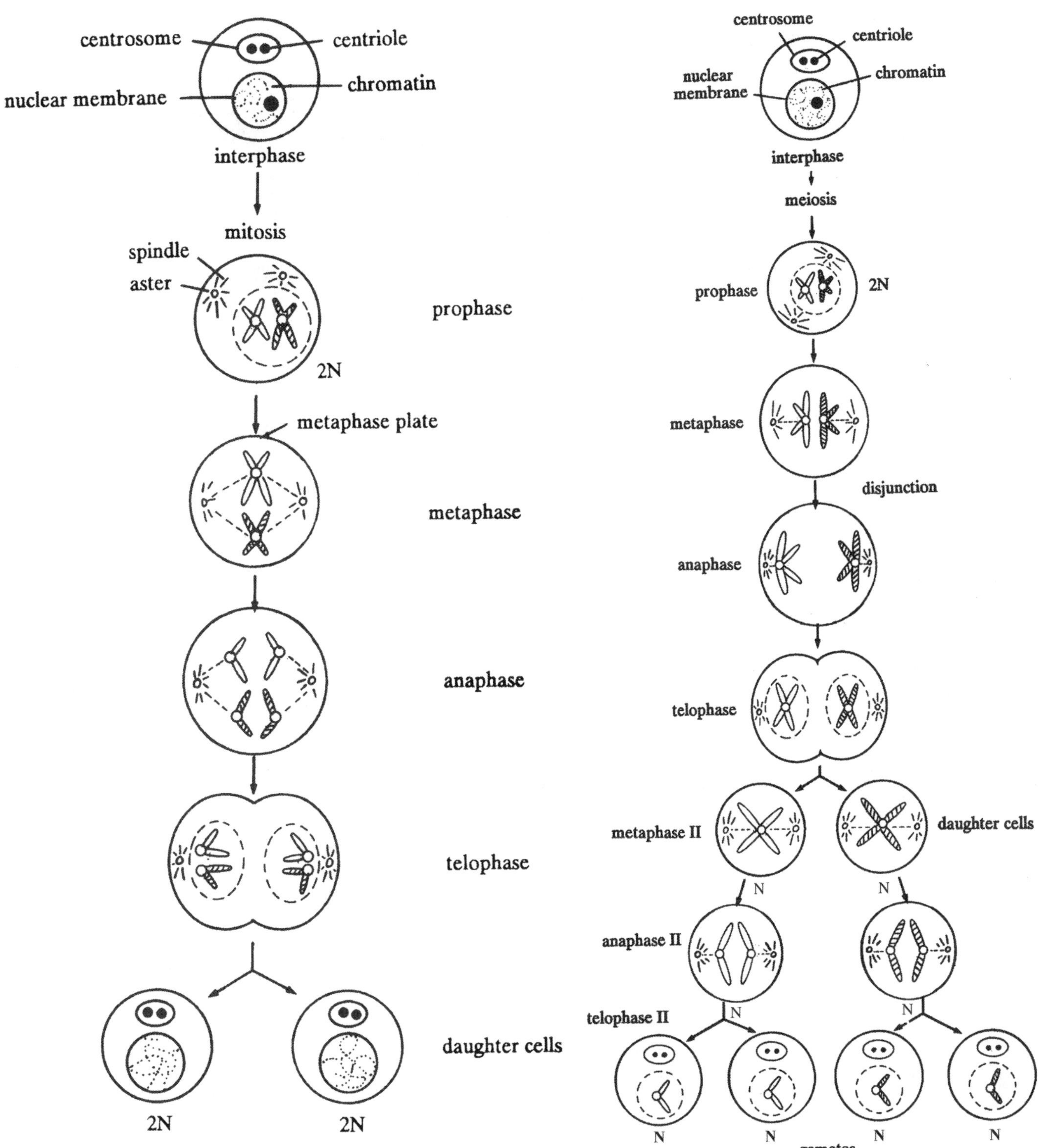

Fertilization

Spermatogenesis

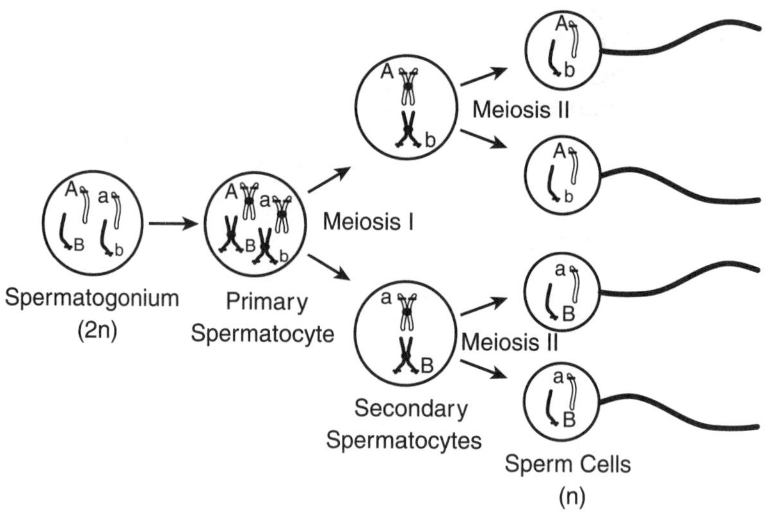

Oogenesis

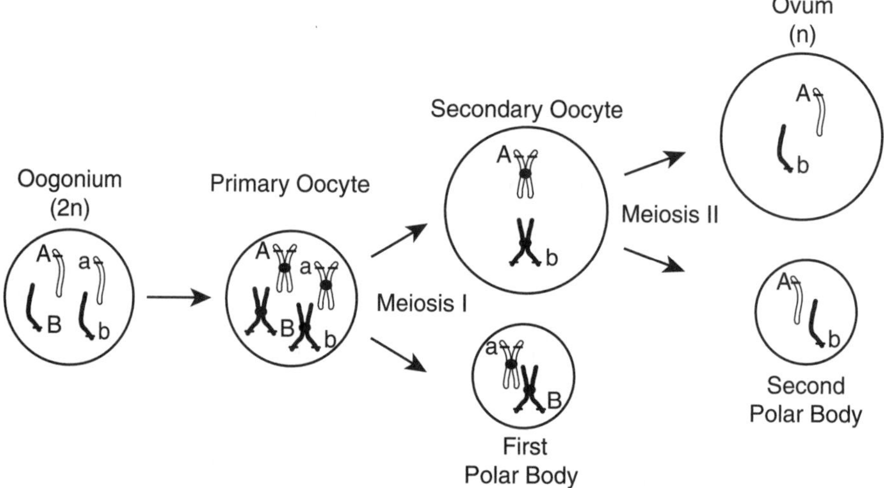

> **STUDY TIP**
>
> Cell and molecular biology is related to many other topics within biology, which is why the DAT tests it so heavily. Study this content as it relates to other topics to help you make connections on Test Day.

Practice Questions

28. After the age of 35, women experience a dramatic increase in the rate of nondisjunction, centromeres not separating correctly during meiosis. This results in

    A. total infertility.
    B. an increased likelihood of birthing identical twins.
    C. a decreased ability to have male children.
    D. a decreased chance of fertilization.
    E. an increased probability of forming zygotes with an incorrect number of chromosomes.

29. A mutation has occurred in one chromosome of a spermatogonium. This mutation will show up in how many of the gametes produced from this cell?

    A. None
    B. One
    C. Two
    D. Four
    E. Cannot be determined

30. Each stage of the cell cycle is regulated by proteins coded for by suppressor genes that control the rate of cell division. Mutations to these genes are direct risk factors for

    A. insomnia.
    B. myocardial infarction.
    C. diabetes mellitus.
    D. cancer.
    E. osteoporosis.

Developmental Biology 10%

Developmental Biology

Descriptive Embryology

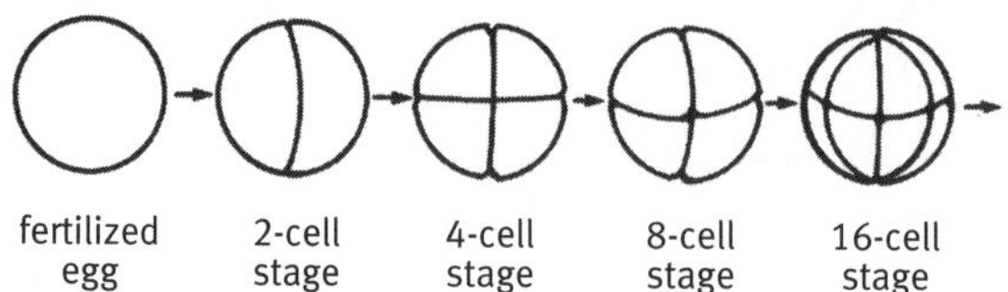

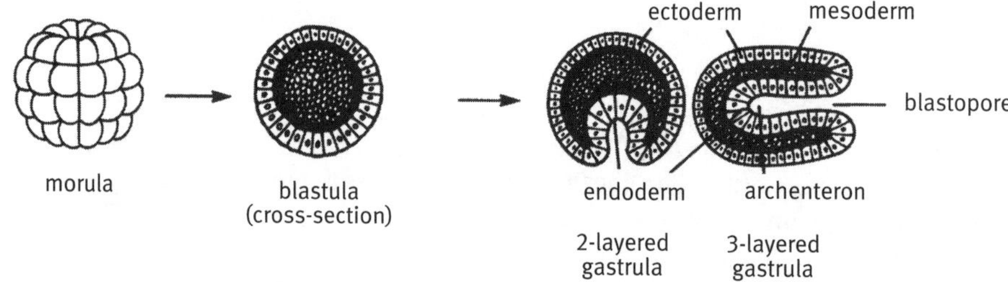

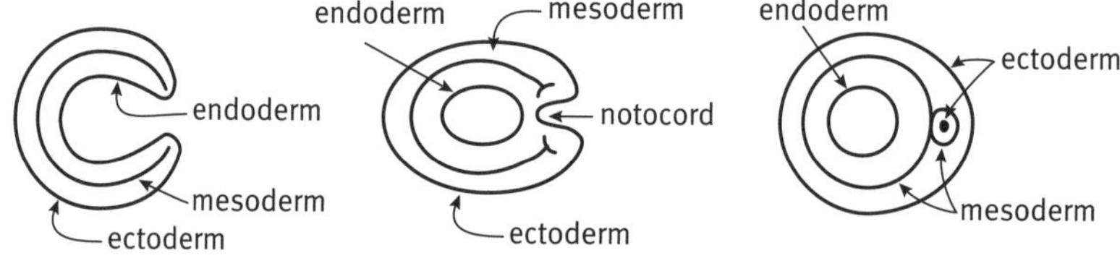

Developmental Mechanisms

Totipotent Cells

Germ Layers

Ectoderm

Mesoderm

Endoderm

Induction

STUDY TIP

Developmental biology has less content to learn than some other subject areas but is still worth four points on Test Day. Learn this material well to maximize your studying efficiency!

Practice Questions

31. Which of the following is the most likely mechanism for the formation of fraternal twins?

    A. Splitting of a 2-cell or 4-cell embryo into two organisms
    B. Collapse of a blastula into two organisms
    C. Two sperm fertilizing one ovum
    D. Two sperm fertilizing two ova
    E. One sperm fertilizing two ova

32. Individuals with a certain disorder are known to have a reduced ability to sweat, sparse body and scalp hair, and vision defects due to an abnormality arising in the

    A. ectoderm.
    B. endoderm.
    C. mesoderm.
    D. morula.
    E. blastocyst.

33. Spina bifida (myelomeningocele) is a birth defect involving the back and spinal cord caused by a problem first arising in the

    A. zygote.
    B. morula.
    C. blastocyst.
    D. neurula.
    E. fetus.

Study Plan

After Class: Biology 2		
Complete Remaining *Lesson Book* Practice Questions	30m	
Biology Test A	25m	
Practice with Tests and Quizzes		

Before Class: Perceptual Ability 2		
Read *Review Notes* Chapter 64	30m	

PERCEPTUAL ABILITY 2

TOPICS COVERED

- Kaplan Pacing Strategy
- Reviewing Your Practice Tests
- Goal Setting
- Keyholes
- Top-Front-End
- Angle Ranking
- Hole Punching
- Cube Counting
- Pattern Folding

After this session you will be able to:

- Finish the PAT subsections within the appropriate amounts of time and while using the Kaplan strategies for each subsection

Kaplan Pacing Strategy

Kaplan Triaging Strategy

Kaplan Marking Strategy

Pacing Strategies Section by Section

Reviewing Your Practice Tests

Review Every Answer

Track Answer Changes

Check Your Pacing

Complete Why I Missed It Charts

Section	Q #	Topic or Type	Why Missed
Biology	*4*	*Embryology*	*Didn't know content*
Quant	*17*	*Algebra*	*Solved for x instead of $x + 2$*
RC	*29*	*Detail Question*	*Did not go back to passage*

Goal Setting

Calendar Revision

Complete any remaining Unit 1 assignments

Recalculate time remaining until Test Day

Build in time to take additional Full-Length tests

Achieving Your Test Day Goals

Practice

Goals by Section

Overall Goals

Keyholes

Rules

1.

2.

3.

4.

5.

Strategies

Practice Questions

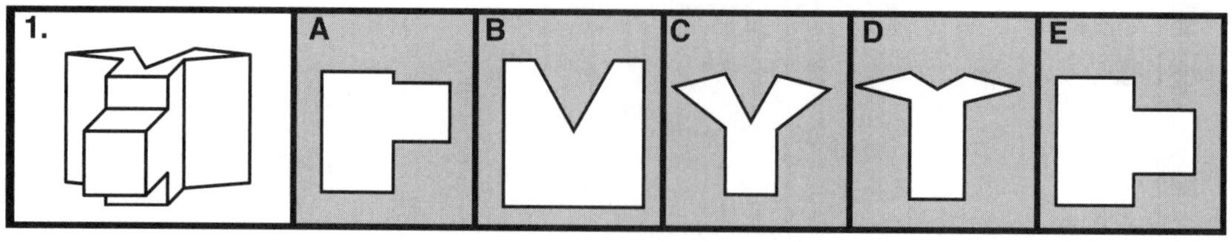

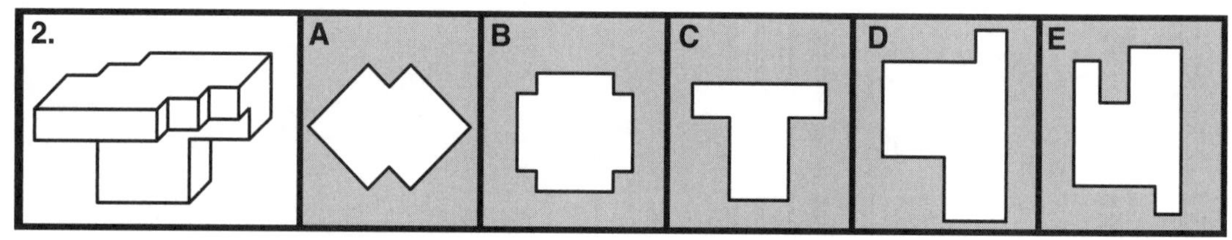

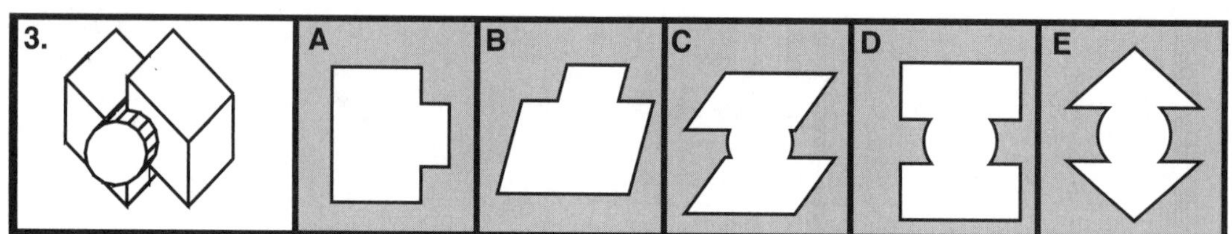

Practice Questions

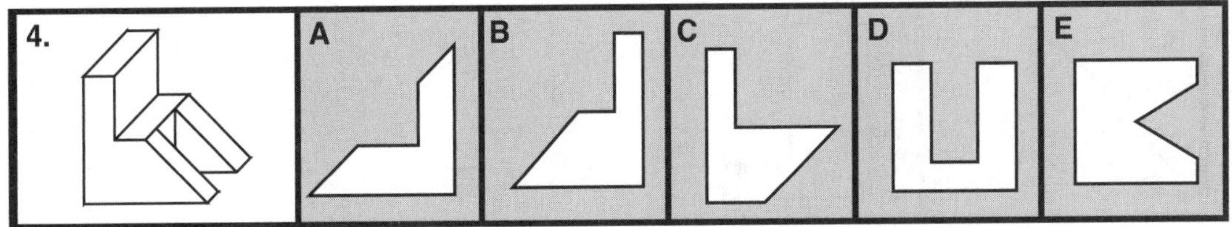

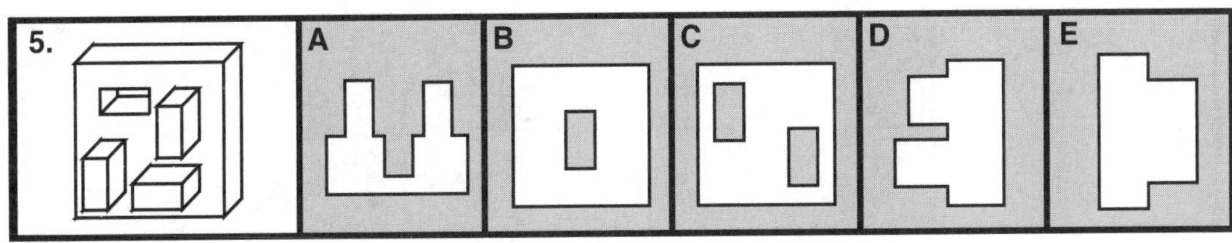

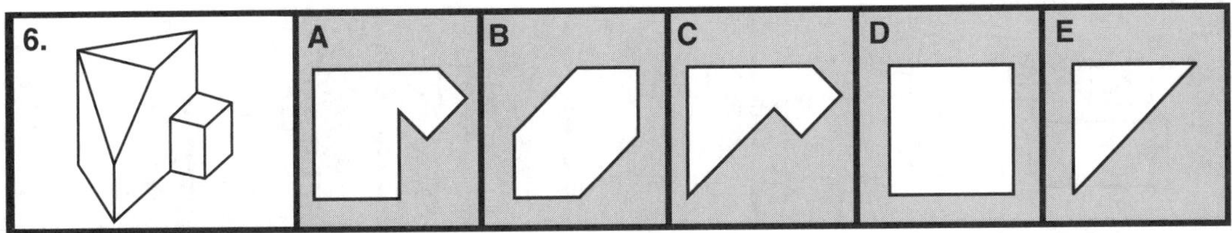

Practice Questions

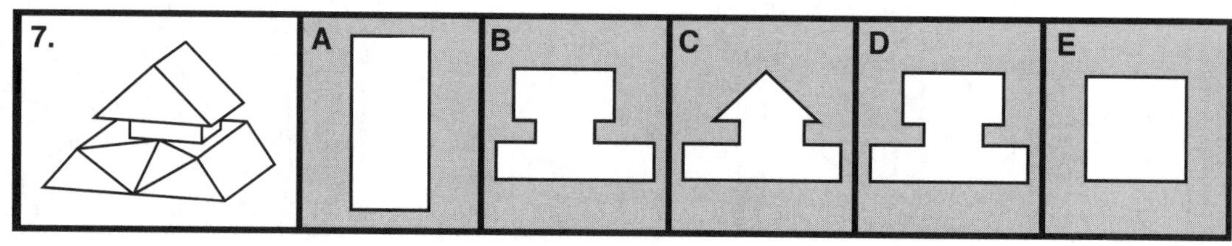

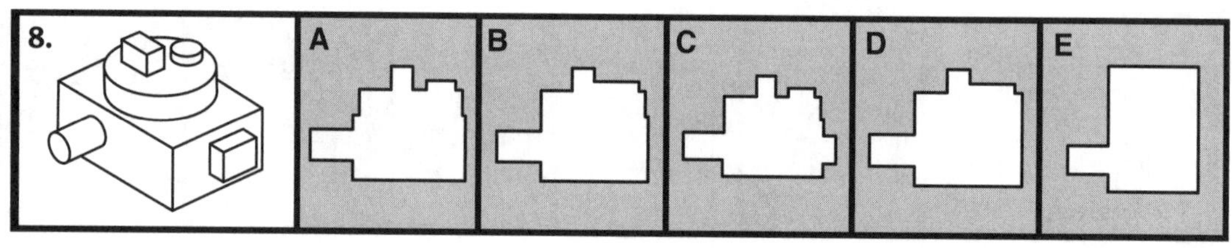

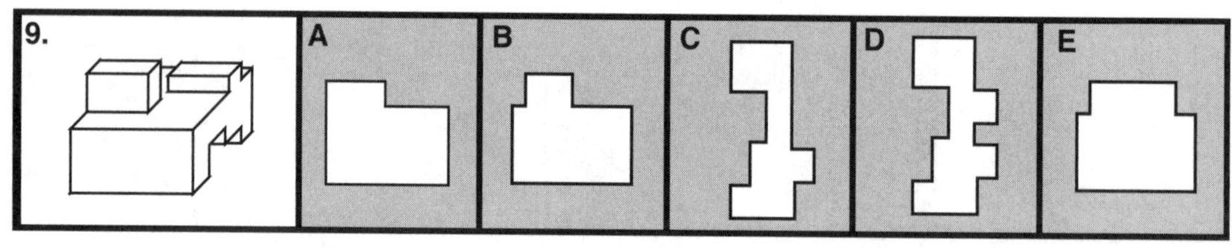

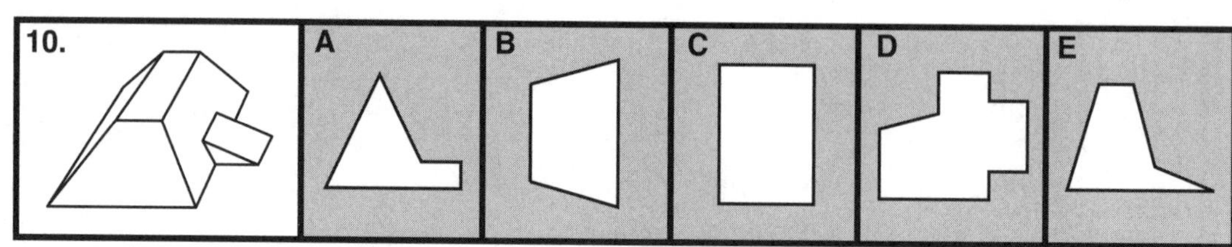

Top-Front-End

Rules

1.

2.

3.

4.

5.

Strategies

Practice Questions

11. Choose the correct **FRONT VIEW**.

TOP VIEW

?

FRONT VIEW END VIEW A B C D

12. Choose the correct **END VIEW**.

TOP VIEW

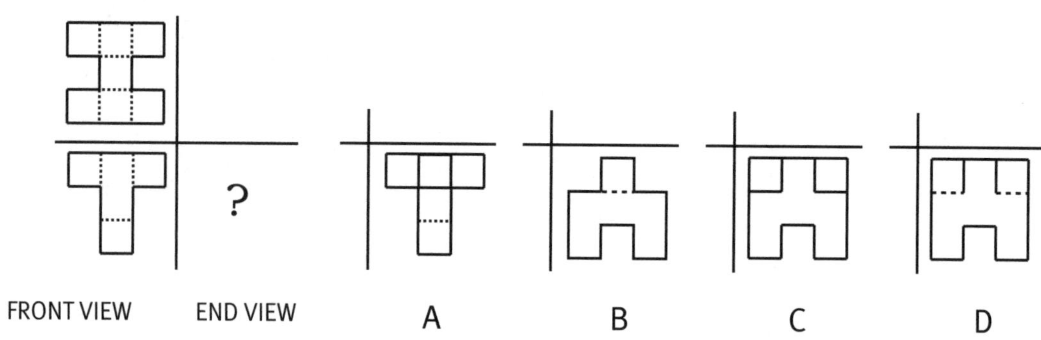

Practice Questions

13. Choose the correct **TOP VIEW**.

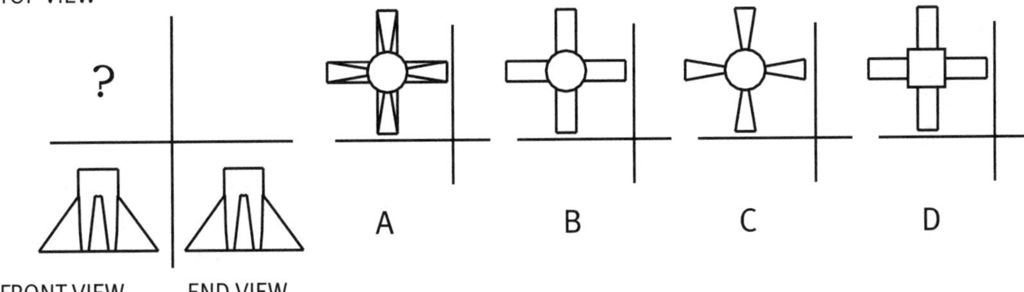

14. Choose the correct **END VIEW**.

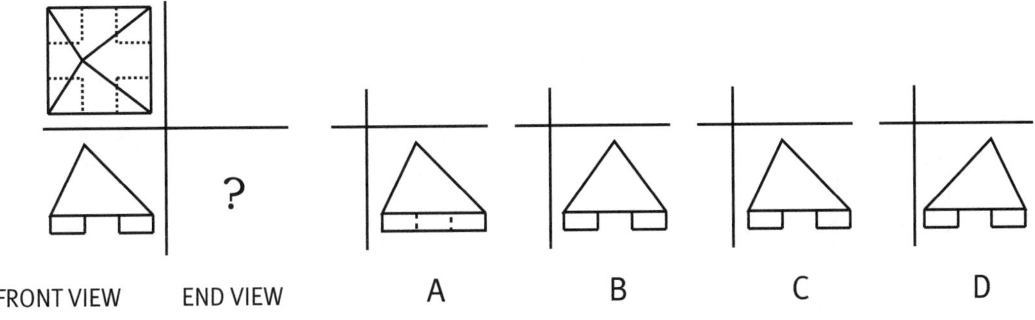

Practice Questions

15. Choose the correct **END VIEW**.

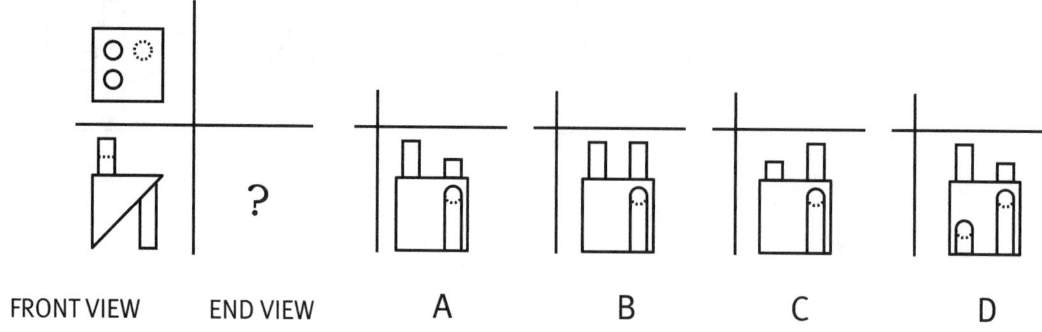

16. Choose the correct **TOP VIEW**.

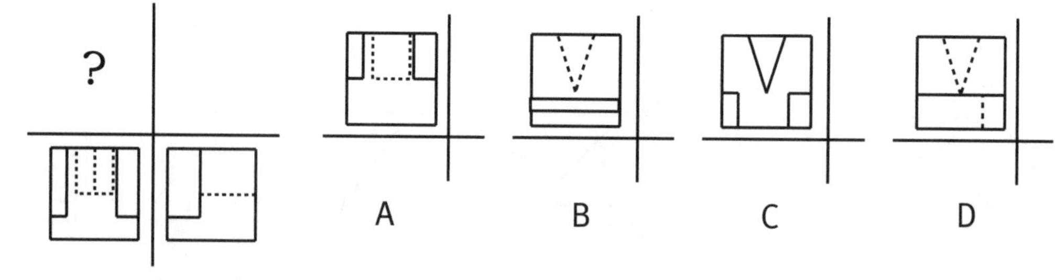

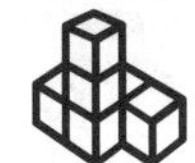

Practice Questions

17. Choose the correct **END VIEW**.

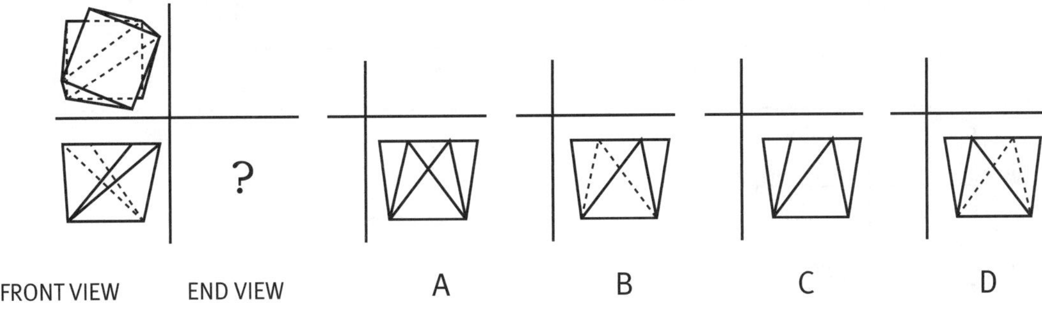

18. Choose the correct **TOP VIEW**.

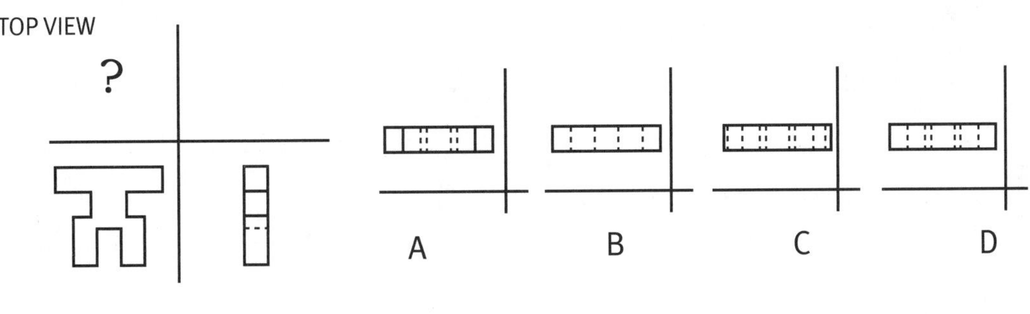

Practice Questions

19. Choose the correct **TOP VIEW**.

TOP VIEW

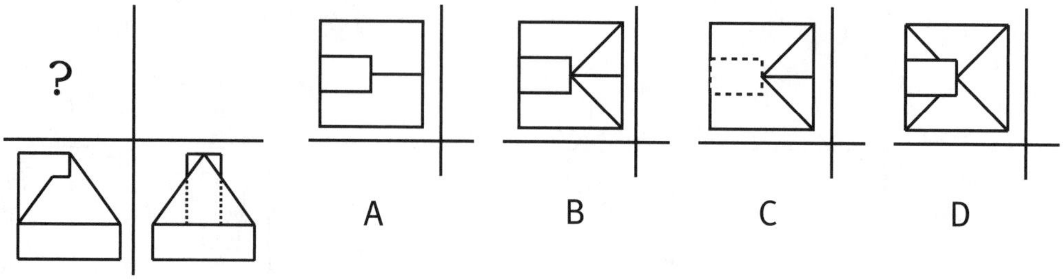

?

A B C D

FRONT VIEW END VIEW

20. Choose the correct **FRONT VIEW**.

TOP VIEW

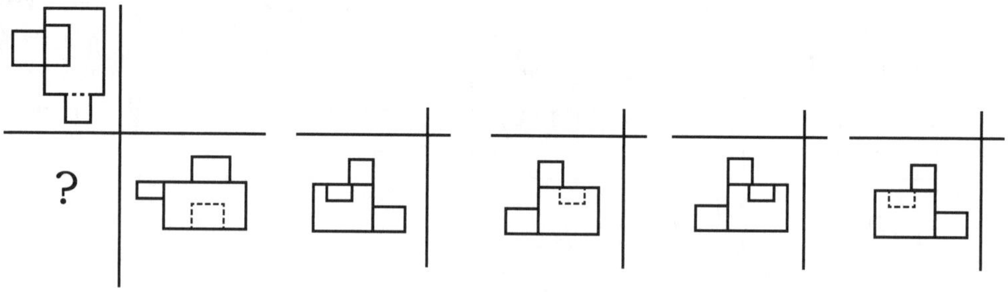

?

FRONT VIEW END VIEW A B C D

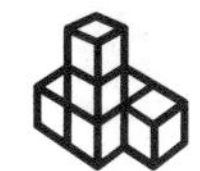

Top-Front-End 3D Images

11.

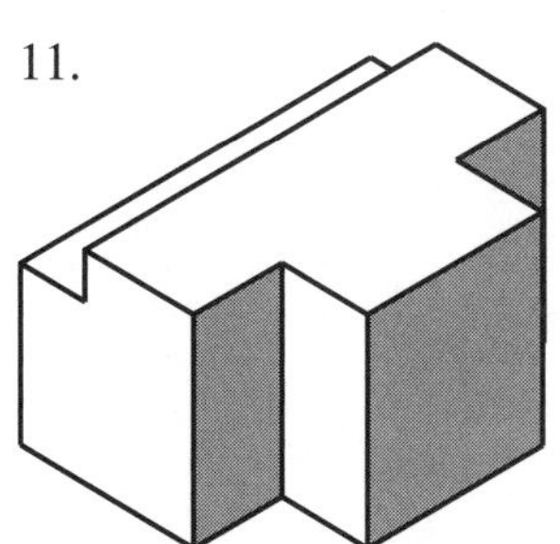

15.

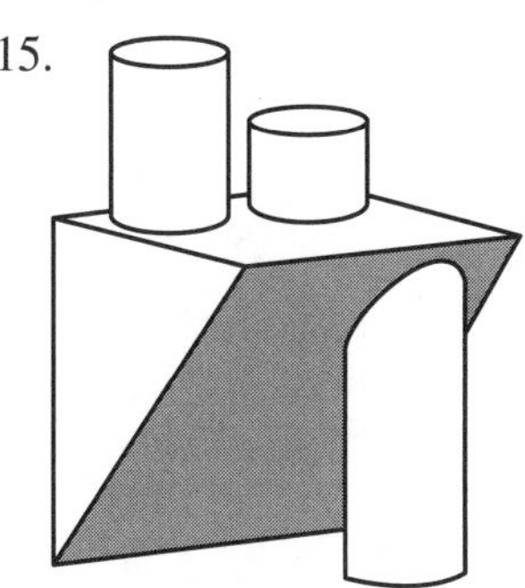

19.

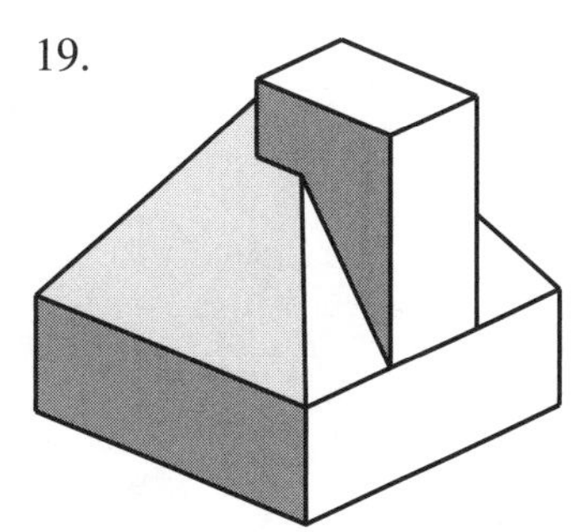

12.

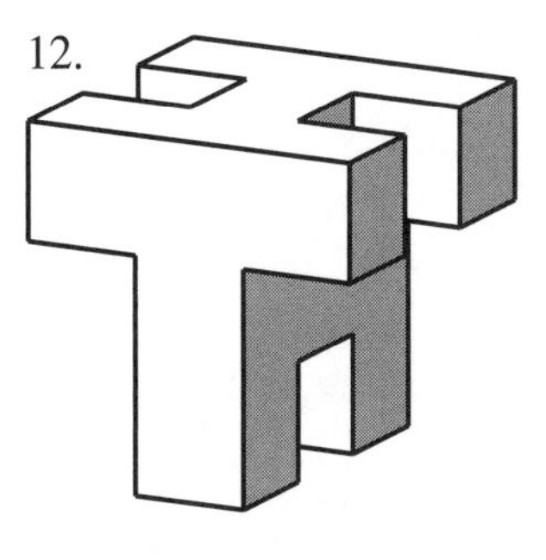

16.

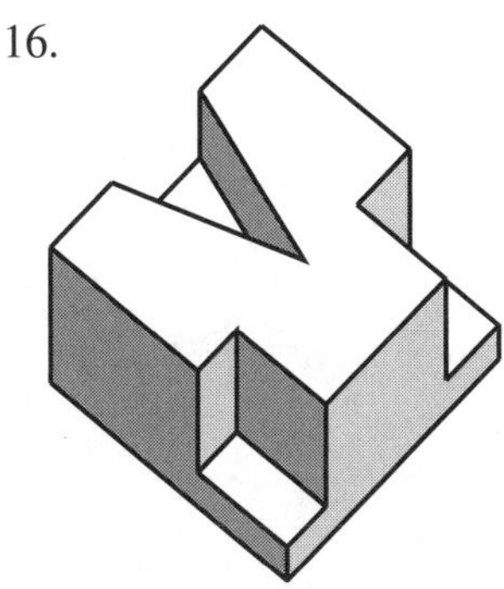

20.

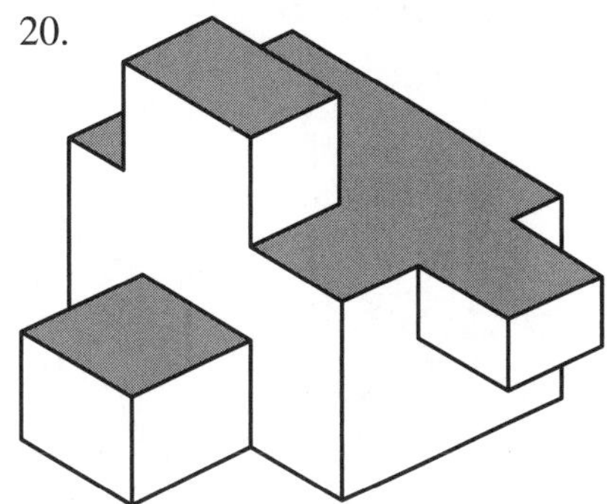

13.

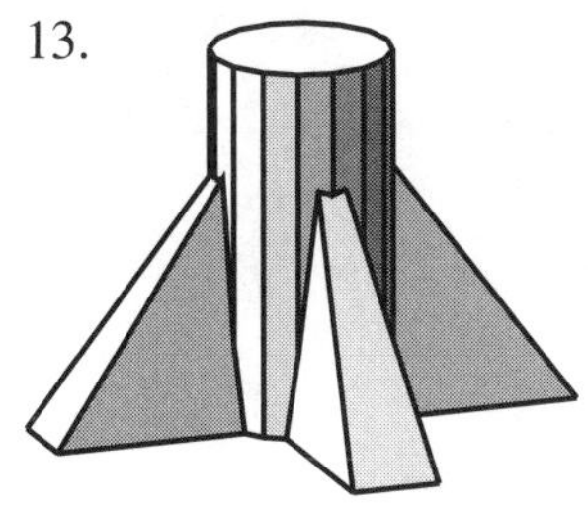

17.

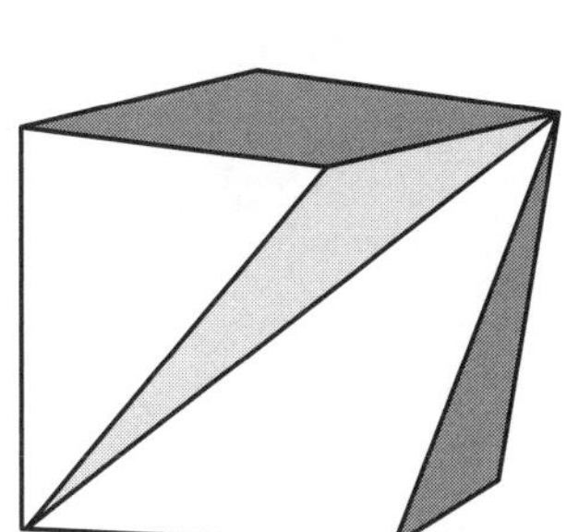

14.

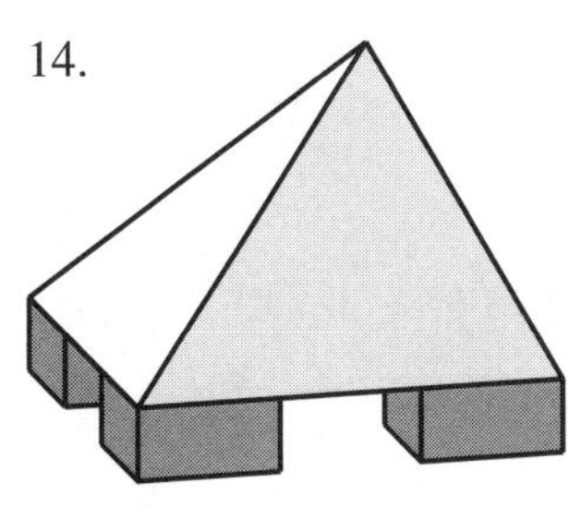

18.

Angle Ranking

Rules

1.

2.

Strategies

Practice Questions

21.

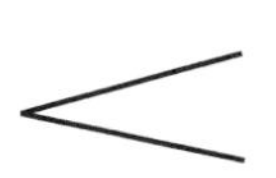   

1 2 3 4

(A) 3-2-1-4
(B) 3-1-2-4
(C) 1-3-2-4
(D) 1-3-4-2

22.

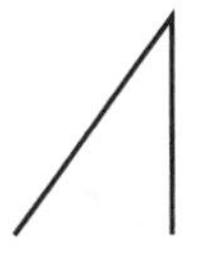   

1 2 3 4

(A) 4-3-2-1
(B) 1-4-2-3
(C) 4-2-1-3
(D) 2-4-3-1

23.

1 2 3 4

(A) 1-2-4-3
(B) 1-2-3-4
(C) 2-1-4-3
(D) 2-1-3-4

24.

1 2 3 4

(A) 1-2-3-4
(B) 4-1-2-3
(C) 2-4-1-3
(D) 1-4-2-3

Practice Questions

25.

  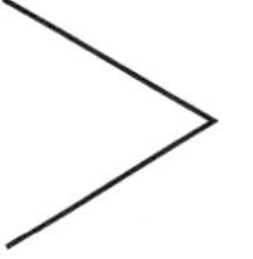 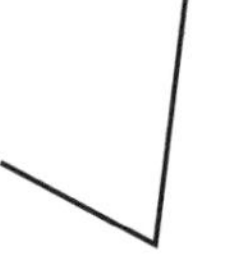

1 2 3 4

(A) 3-1-4-2
(B) 3-2-4-1
(C) 3-2-1-4
(D) 3-1-2-4

26.

1 2 3 4

(A) 1-4-3-2
(B) 4-3-1-2
(C) 2-4-3-1
(D) 4-3-2-1

27.

1 2 3 4

(A) 2-1-3-4
(B) 2-3-1-4
(C) 1-2-3-4
(D) 1-2-4-3

28.

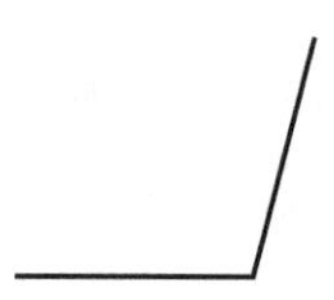 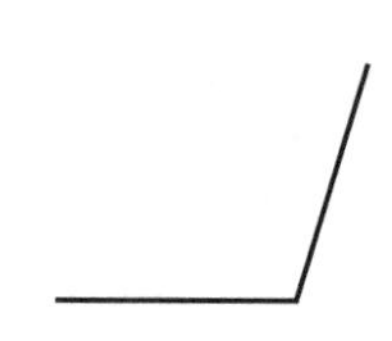 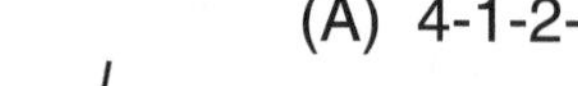

1 2 3 4

(A) 4-1-2-3
(B) 4-2-1-3
(C) 4-2-3-1
(D) 2-4-1-3

Practice Questions

29.

1 2 3 4

(A) 2-4-3-1

(B) 4-2-1-3

(C) 4-2-3-1

(D) 4-3-2-1

30.

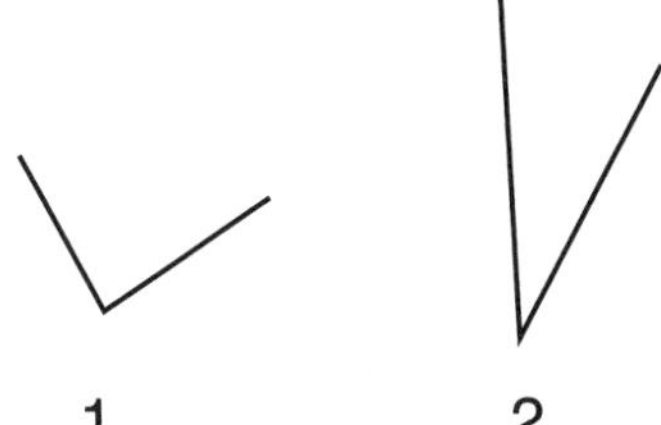

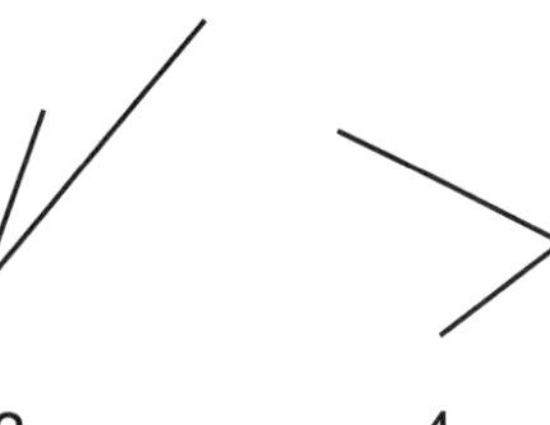

1 2 3 4

(A) 3-4-2-1

(B) 2-4-3-1

(C) 3-2-4-1

(D) 3-2-1-4

Hole Punching

Rules

1.

2.

3.

4.

5.

Strategies

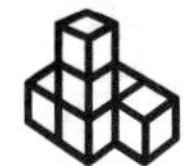

Practice Questions

31.

A B C D E

32.

A B C D E

33.

A B C D E

Practice Questions

34.

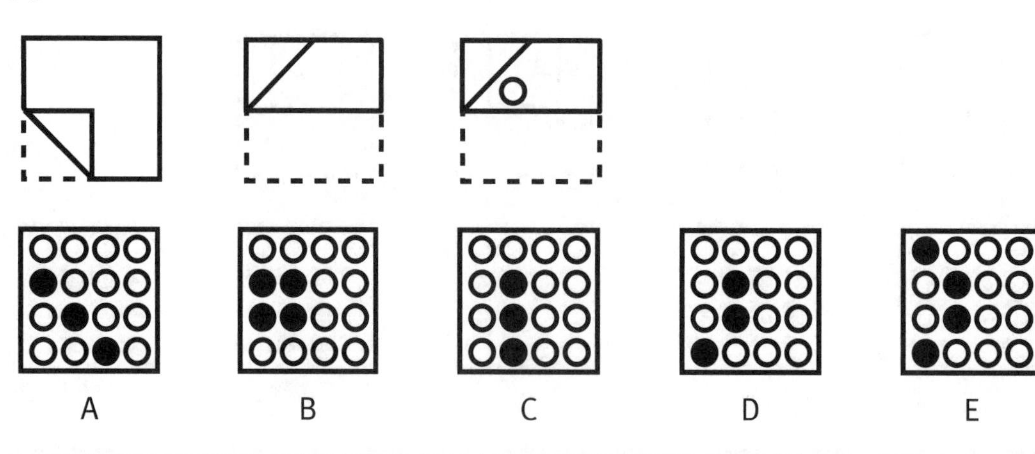

35.

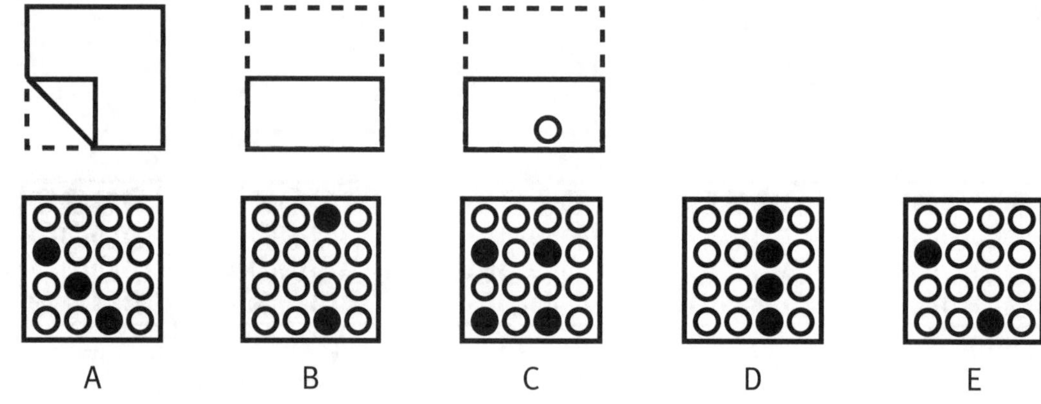

36.

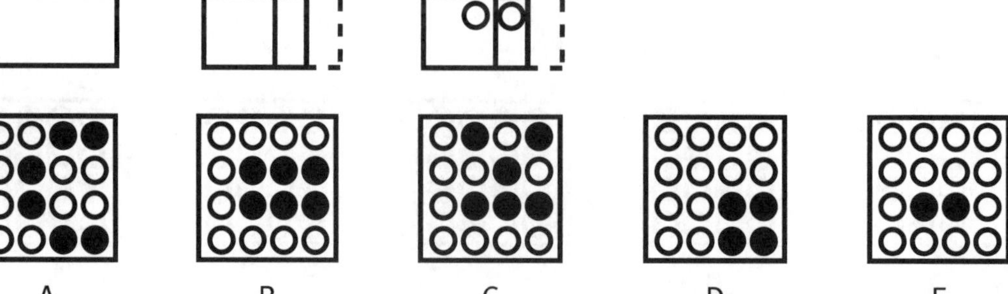

Practice Questions

37.

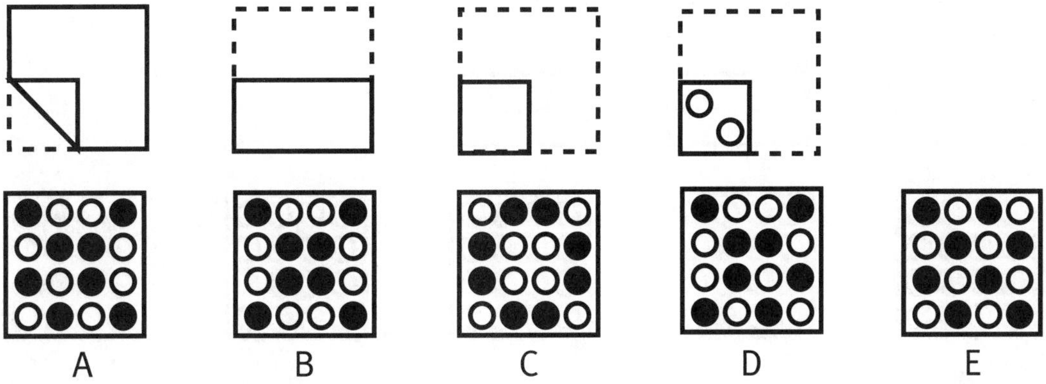

A B C D E

38.

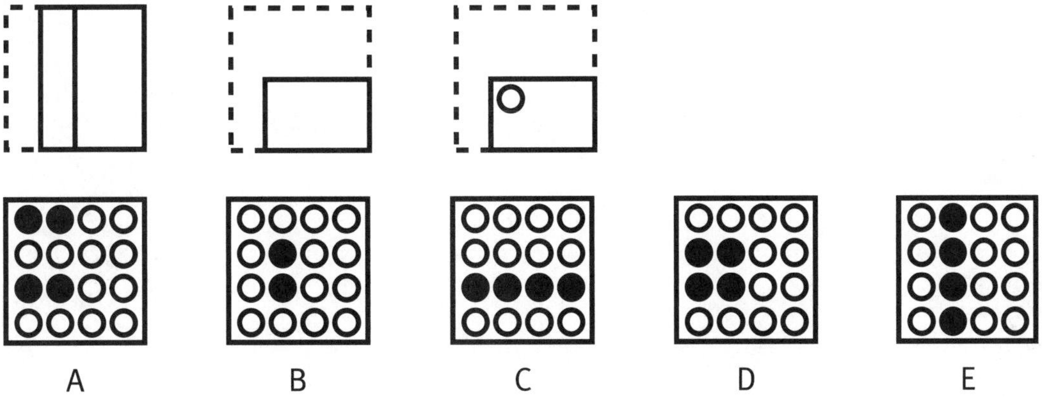

A B C D E

39.

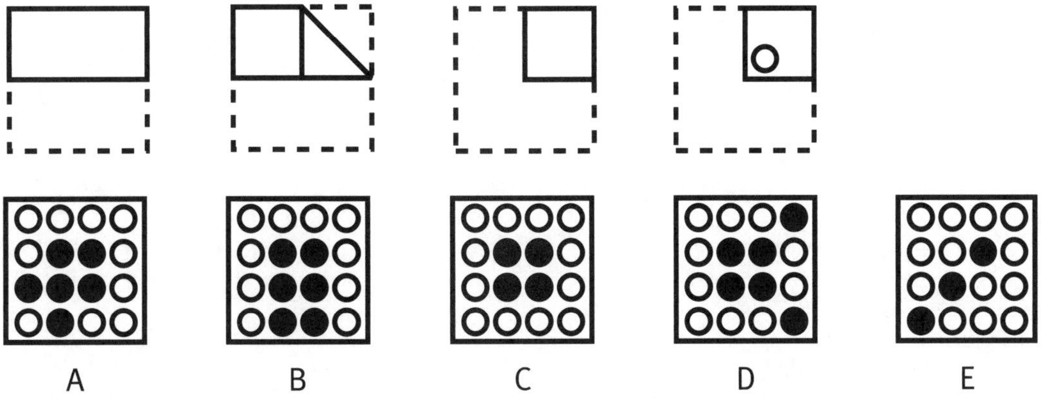

A B C D E

Practice Questions

40.

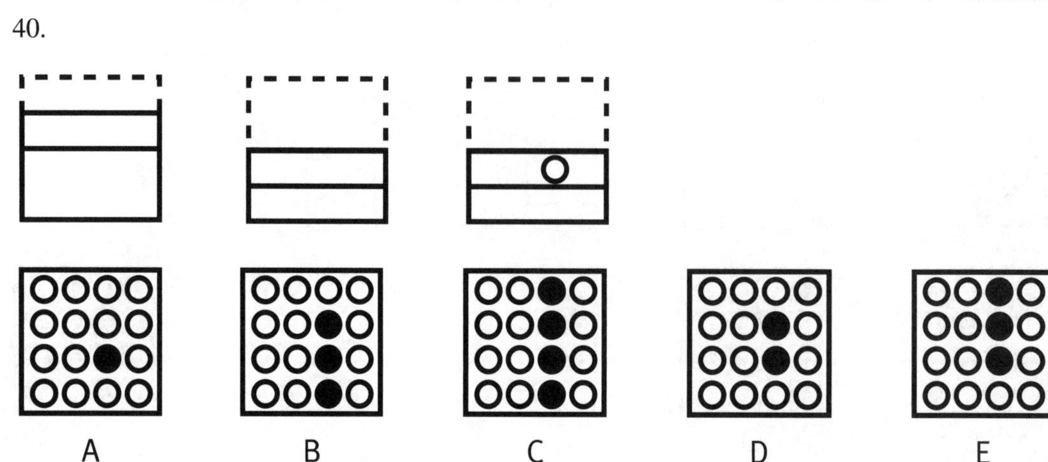

Cube Counting

Rules

1.

2.

3.

Strategies

Practice Questions

Figure A

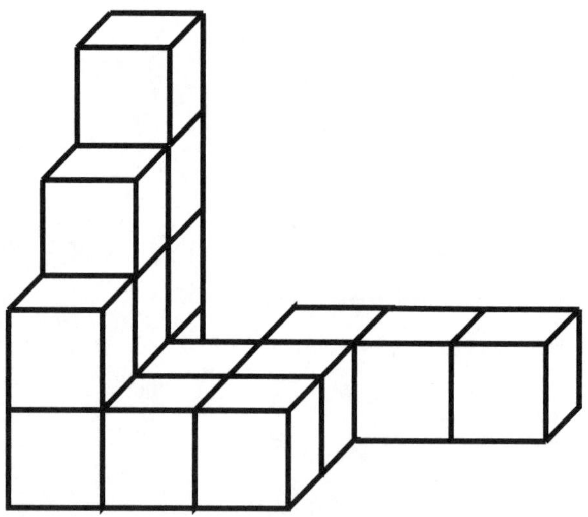

41. In Figure A, how many cubes have four of their exposed sides painted?

    A. 1 cube
    B. 2 cubes
    C. 3 cubes
    D. 4 cubes
    E. 5 cubes

42. In Figure A, how many cubes have five of their exposed sides painted?

    A. 1 cube
    B. 2 cubes
    C. 3 cubes
    D. 4 cubes
    E. 5 cubes

Practice Questions

Figure B

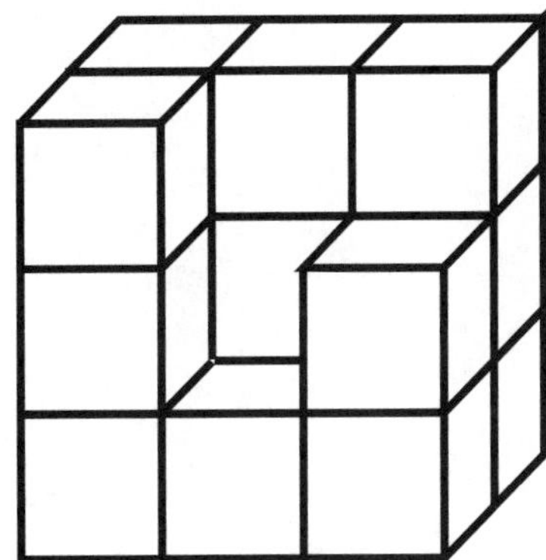

43. In Figure B, how many cubes have one of their exposed sides painted?

    A. 1 cube
    B. 2 cubes
    C. 3 cubes
    D. 4 cubes
    E. 5 cubes

44. In Figure B, how many cubes have three of their exposed sides painted?

    A. 1 cube
    B. 2 cubes
    C. 3 cubes
    D. 4 cubes
    E. 5 cubes

45. In Figure B, how many cubes have four of their exposed sides painted?

    A. 1 cube
    B. 2 cubes
    C. 3 cubes
    D. 4 cubes
    E. 5 cubes

Practice Questions

Figure C

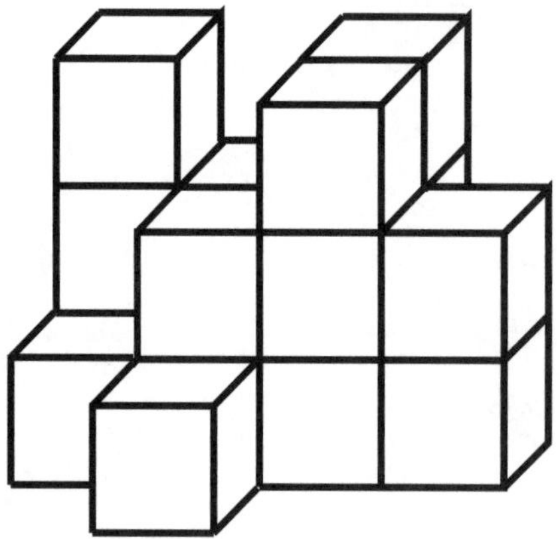

46. In Figure C, how many cubes have one of their exposed sides painted?

    A. 1 cube
    B. 2 cubes
    C. 3 cubes
    D. 4 cubes
    E. 5 cubes

47. In Figure C, how many cubes have three of their exposed sides painted?

    A. 1 cube
    B. 2 cubes
    C. 3 cubes
    D. 4 cubes
    E. 5 cubes

48. In Figure C, how many cubes have four of their exposed sides painted?

    A. 1 cube
    B. 2 cubes
    C. 3 cubes
    D. 4 cubes
    E. 5 cubes

Practice Questions

Figure D

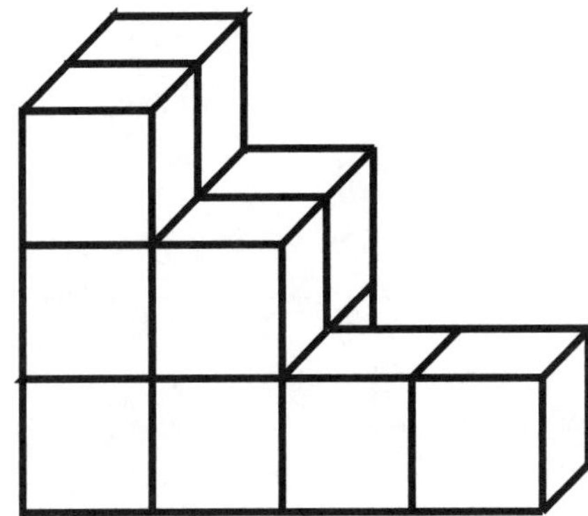

49. In Figure D, how many cubes have one of their exposed sides painted?

  A. 1 cube
  B. 2 cubes
  C. 3 cubes
  D. 4 cubes
  E. 5 cubes

50. In Figure D, how many cubes have two of their exposed sides painted?

  A. 1 cube
  B. 2 cubes
  C. 3 cubes
  D. 4 cubes
  E. 5 cubes

Pattern Folding

Rules

1.

2.

3.

Strategies

Practice Questions

51.

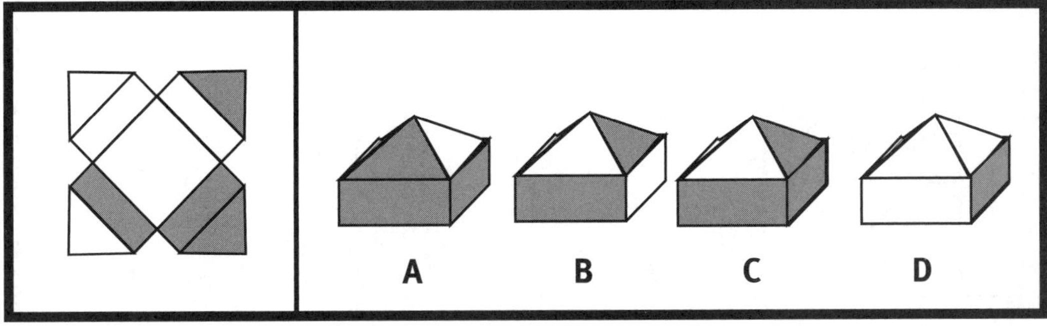

52.

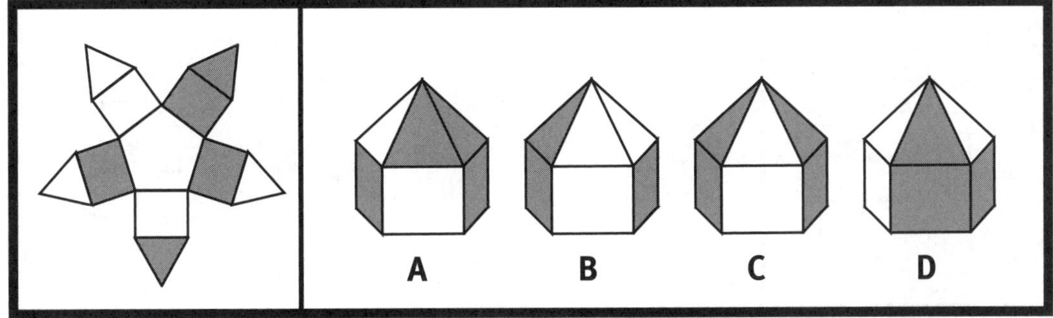

53.

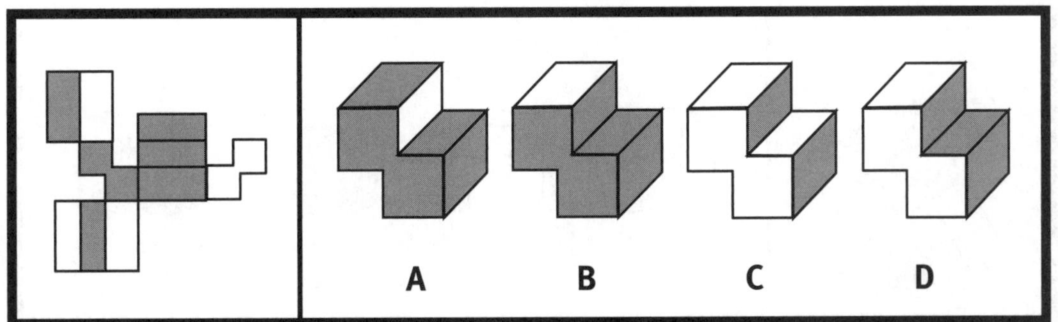

Practice Questions

54.

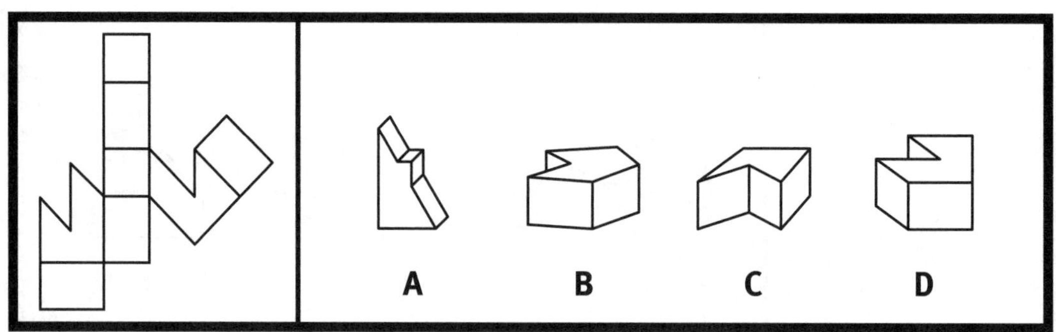

55.

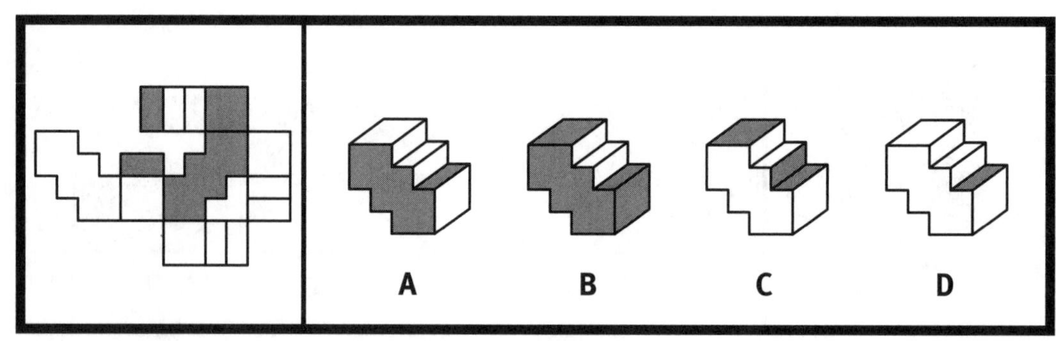

56.

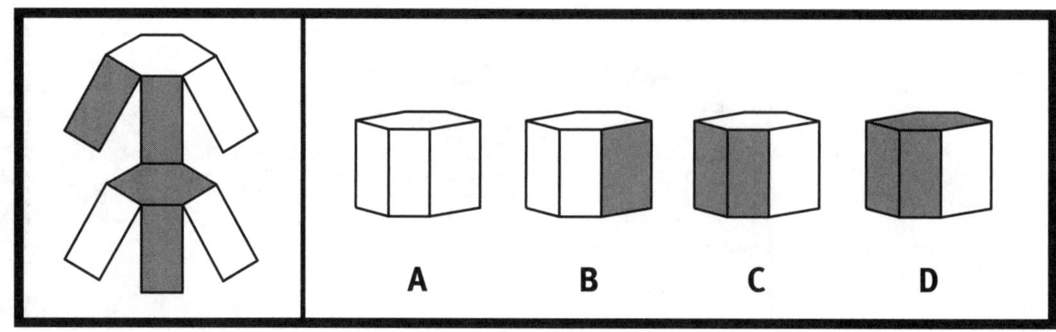

Practice Questions

57.

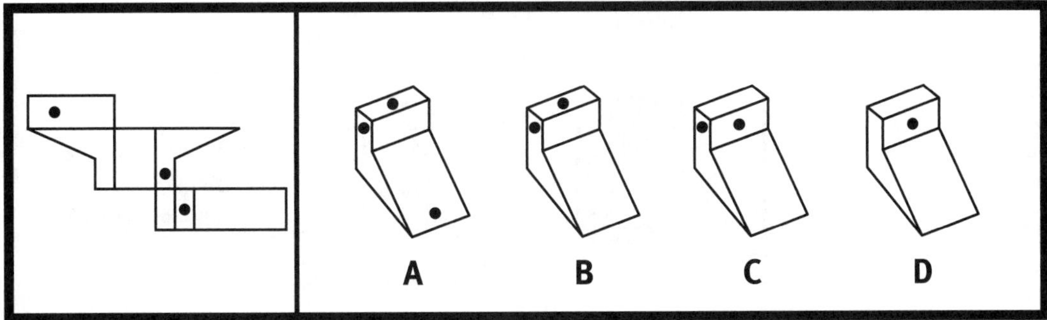

58.

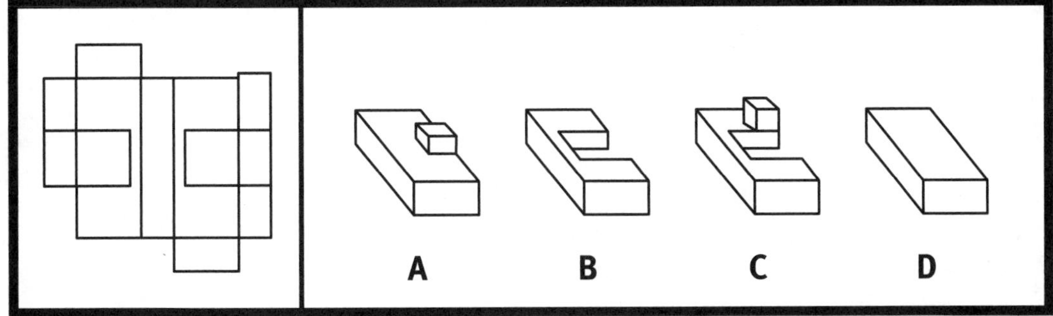

59.

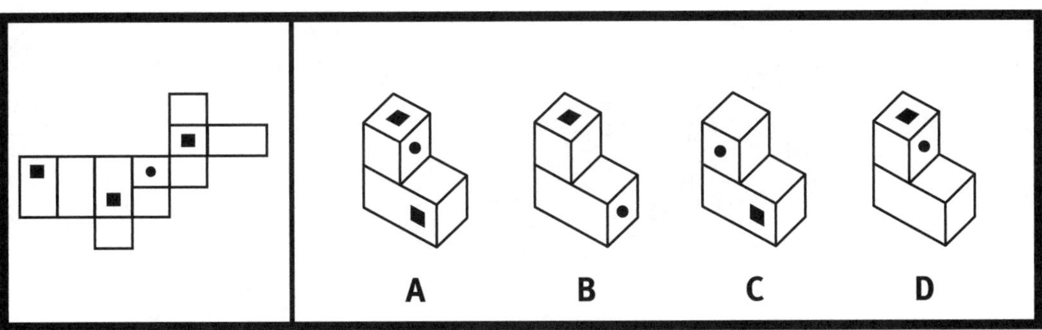

Practice Questions

60.

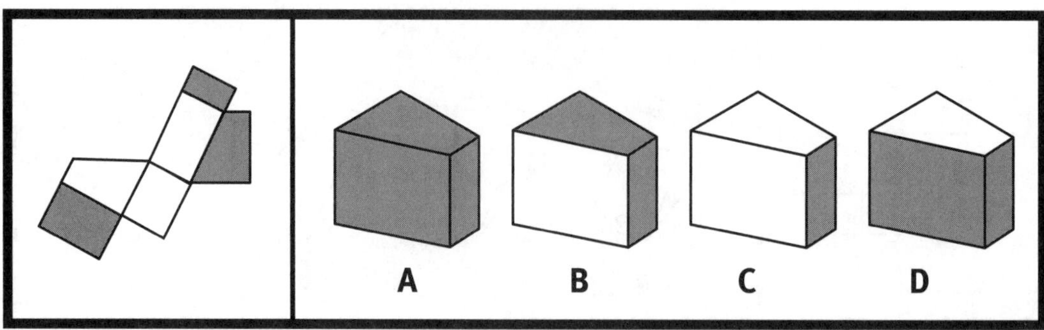

Study Plan

After Class: Perceptual Ability 2	
Complete Remaining *Lesson Book* Practice Questions	30m
Perceptual Ability Test A	1h 0m
Perceptual Ability Test B	1h 0m
Practice with Tests and Quizzes	

Before Class: Quantitative Reasoning 2	
Read *Review Notes* Chapters 58–62	1h 30m
Word Problems Workshop	45m

QUANTITATIVE REASONING 2

TOPICS COVERED

- Kaplan Strategic Math Review
- Conversions
- Probability and Statistics
- Geometry
- Trigonometry

After this session you will be able to:

- Calculate conversions
- Calculate averages, variance, and standard deviation
- Calculate probabilities
- Analyze geometric shapes
- Calculate trigonometric relationships

Kaplan Strategic Math Review

Traditional Math

Picking Numbers

Backsolving

Estimation

Educated Guessing

Strategic Math Exercise

Match each of the following question stems to the letter of the most effective strategy for solving it.

Question Stem	Strategy
$(\sqrt{3}+\sqrt{7})(\sqrt{3}-\sqrt{7})=$	
Three students are competing to collect the most stamps. They collect 103, 198, and 295 stamps, respectively. What is the average number of stamps collected per student?	
During a sale, a store sells 20% of its remaining stock each day, without replenishment. After 4 days, what fraction of its original stock has it sold?	
A truck driver drove for 2 days. On the second day he drove 3 hours longer and at an average speed of 15 miles per hour faster than he drove on the first day. If he drove a total of 1,020 miles and spent 21 hours driving during the 2 days, what was his average speed on the first day?	
Of the 150 employees at a company, 80 are full-time and 100 have worked at the company for at least a year. There are 20 employees who aren't full-time and haven't worked at the company for at least a year. How many full-time employees of this company have worked at the company for at least a year?	

Kaplan DAT Quantitative Reasoning Strategies

A. Traditional Math

B. Picking Numbers

C. Backsolving

D. Estimation

E. Educated Guessing

TEST DAY TIP

If you start using one strategy and get stuck, consider if there is another strategy you can use instead. Most questions can be solved in multiple ways.

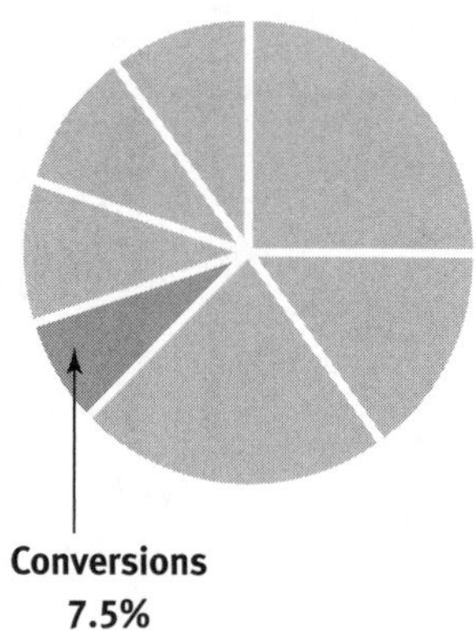

Conversions

Conversion questions ask you to switch between units of temperature, time, weight, or distance.

Common Conversions

Temperature

$K = °C + 273$

$°C = \frac{5}{9}(°F - 32)$

Time

60 seconds = 1 minute

60 minutes = 1 hour

24 hours = 1 day

365 days = 1 year

Weight

16 ounces = 1 pound

2.2 pounds = 1 kilogram

Distance

12 inches = 1 foot

3 feet = 1 yard

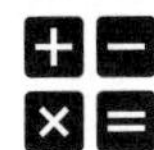

Example:

How many feet are in 65 meters? (There are 5,280 feet in one mile and 0.62 miles in one kilometer.)

$$65\text{ m}\times\left(\frac{1\text{ km}}{1000\text{ m}}\right)\times\left(\frac{0.62\text{ miles}}{1\text{ km}}\right)\times\left(\frac{5{,}280\text{ feet}}{1\text{ mile}}\right)\approx 213\text{ feet}$$

Example:

1. Two quarts equal 1.89 liters, and 1 liter equals 1 cubic decimeter. Therefore, how many cubic centimeters are in 1 gallon?

   A. 3.78 cm^3
   B. 378 cm^3
   C. 3,780 cm^3
   D. 4,780 cm^3
   E. 7,560 cm^3

TEST DAY TIP

Conversion questions are a great way to get points quickly on Test Day, but make sure to take the time to set up your scratch work so you don't make careless mistakes.

Practice Questions

2. Greg drove 400 miles at a rate of 25 miles per hour. During the same time, Andrew was driving at 30 miles per hour. How many miles farther than Greg did Andrew drive?

   A. 16
   B. 80
   C. 330
   D. 400
   E. 480

3. How many minutes does it take Alex to drive r miles if she drives at the constant rate of s miles per hour?

   A. $\frac{r}{60s}$
   B. $\frac{s}{60r}$
   C. $\frac{60s}{r}$
   D. $\frac{60r}{s}$
   E. $\frac{60}{rs}$

4. If the conversion between degrees Celsius (C) to degrees Fahrenheit (F) can be represented by the equation $C = \frac{5}{9}(F - 32)$, what temperature in degrees Fahrenheit is equivalent to 24°C?

   A. −4.40
   B. 13.3
   C. 43.2
   D. 45.3
   E. 75.2

Practice Questions

5. A company manufactures 450 widgets a day. The company sells these widgets in boxes of 200. How many days will it take the company to manufacture the number of widgets in 180 boxes of widgets?

   A. 50
   B. 80
   C. 160
   D. 415
   E. 500

6. A 120 gallon tub has a drain that, when open, drains water at a rate of 6 gallons per minute. If the tub is empty and the drain is open, at what rate must water be added to the tub so that it fills in exactly 1 hour?

   A. 6 gallons per minute
   B. 8 gallons per minute
   C. 12 gallons per minute
   D. 16 gallons per minute
   E. 18 gallons per minute

7. Magnabulk Corp sells boxes holding d magnets each. The boxes are shipped in crates, each holding b boxes. What is the price charged per magnet (in cents) if Magnabulk charges m dollars for each crate?

   A. $\frac{100bd}{m}$
   B. $\frac{100m}{bd}$
   C. $\frac{bd}{100m}$
   D. $\frac{m}{bd}$
   E. $\frac{100b}{m}$

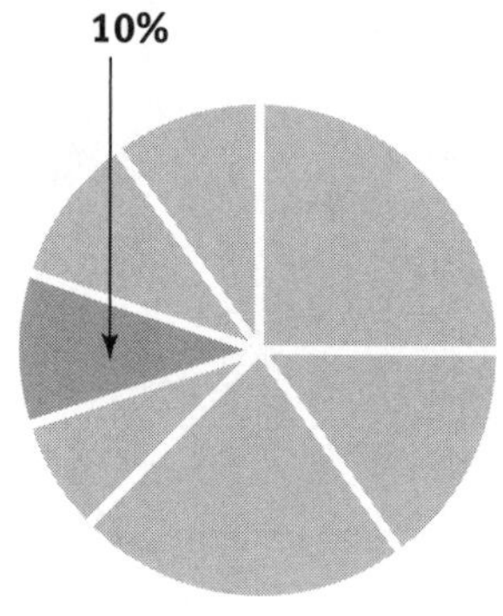

Probability and Statistics

Statistics

Mean

The mean, or average, is the sum of all the members of a list divided by the number of items in that list.

$$\text{Mean} = \frac{\text{sum of terms}}{\text{number of terms}}$$

Example:

8. Four students take a test, scoring 60, 70, 80, and 90 points out of 100, respectively. If the teacher wants to adjust the average on this quiz to be 90 by adding the same number of points to each student's score, how many additional points will each student receive?

 A. 2
 B. 5
 C. 10
 D. 15
 E. 19

Median

The median is the center number in a list arranged in numerical order.

Example:

9. What is the median for the data set below?

   4, 7, 25, 9, 16, 10, 13, 19, 22

   A. 9
   B. 10
   C. 13
   D. 14
   E. 16

Mode

The mode is the most common number in a set.

Example:

10. What is the mode of the data set below?

    7, 11, 13, 6, 7, 9, 11, 8, 11, 19, 21

    A. 7
    B. 9
    C. 11
    D. Both 7 and 9
    E. Both 7 and 11

Practice Questions

11. The ages of 4 members of a club are 6, 8, 10, and x years. If the mean age of the 4 members is 9 years, then what is the value of x?

    A. 7
    B. 8
    C. 9
    D. 10
    E. 12

12. The mean of all the scores on a certain algebra test was 90. If the average score of the 8 male students was 87 and the average grade of all the female students was 92, then how many females took the test?

    A. 5
    B. 8
    C. 10
    D. 12
    E. 15

13. Which of the following is the mean of n, $n + 2$, and $n + 7$?

    A. n
    B. $n + 3$
    C. $n + 9$
    D. $3n + 9$
    E. $\frac{(3n + 9)}{5}$

14. Esther drove at an average rate of 40 miles per hour for 2 hours and then increased her average rate by 25 percent for the next 3 hours. What was her average rate, in miles per hour, for the total 5 hours?

    A. 44
    B. 45
    C. 46
    D. 47
    E. 50

Variance

Variance, σ^2, is one way to measure the dispersion of data.

$$\sigma^2 = \frac{1}{n}\sum_{i=1}^{n}\left(x_i - \bar{x}\right)^2$$

Use the following steps to calculate variance:

1. Find the mean of the data.
2. Subtract the mean from each of the numbers in the data set.
3. Square each of the results from step 2.
4. Take the average of the numbers from step 3.

Standard Deviation

Standard deviation, σ, is the square root of variance. To calculate standard deviation, complete the steps above for variance and then perform a final step of taking the square root of the result.

$$\sigma = \sqrt{\frac{1}{n}\sum_{i=1}^{n}\left(x_i - \bar{x}\right)^2}$$

Example:

15. What are the variance and standard deviation of the data set shown below?

    4, 5, 8, 10, 13

    A. $8, \sqrt{8}$

    B. 9, 3

    C. $\frac{54}{5}, \sqrt{\frac{54}{5}}$

    D. $11, \sqrt{11}$

    E. 16, 4

Practice Questions

16. The mean weight of men aged 70–79 in North America is approximately 75 kg, with a standard deviation of 12 kg. Which best represents the minimum weight of a male in the top 5% by weight of men in their 70s?

    A. 87 kg
    B. 96 kg
    C. 99 kg
    D. 105 kg
    E. 111 kg

17. What is x if the variance of the data (1, 2, 3, 4, 5, 6, 7, x) is $\frac{21}{2}$?

    A. 8
    B. 9
    C. 10
    D. 11
    E. 12

18. What is the standard deviation of the sample: 1, 2, 2, 4, 6?

    A. $\sqrt{\frac{8}{5}}$
    B. $\sqrt{3}$
    C. $\sqrt{\frac{16}{5}}$
    D. $\sqrt{\frac{17}{5}}$
    E. $\sqrt{\frac{19}{5}}$

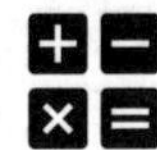

Graphical Representations of Data

Data on the DAT may be given in a list, table, or graph. If in a table or chart, data should be treated the same way as if in a list.

Example:

Trial	Outcome
1	1
2	3
3	4
4	1
5	1
6	2
7	5
8	4
9	5
10	4

19. Given the data in the table above, what are the mean and median of that data?

    A. 3, 3.5
    B. 3.5, 3
    C. 3, 4
    D. 3.5, 4.5
    E. 5.5, 5

Practice Questions

Use the chart below to answer the following questions.

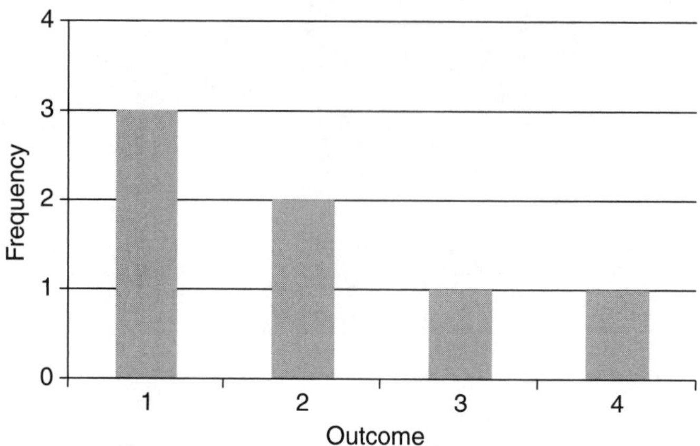

20. What is the mean of the data?

    A. 1
    B. 2
    C. 3
    D. 4
    E. 5

21. What is the median of the data?

    A. 1
    B. 2
    C. 3
    D. 4
    E. 5

22. What is the standard deviation of the data?

    A. $\sqrt{\frac{3}{5}}$
    B. $\sqrt{\frac{11}{16}}$
    C. $\sqrt{\frac{4}{5}}$
    D. 1
    E. $\sqrt{\frac{8}{7}}$

Probability

$$\text{Probability} = \frac{\text{number of desired outcomes}}{\text{total number of outcomes}}$$

The sum of the probabilities of a complete set of mutually exclusive possible outcomes is 1.

To find the probability that one *OR* another of two mutually exclusive events occurs, *ADD* the probabilities of the two events.

To find the probability that one *AND* another of two independent events occurs, *MULTIPLY* the probabilities of the two events.

Example:

23. A bowl contains only 5 bananas and 5 apples. If one piece of fruit is selected from the bowl at random and a second piece is selected from the bowl without replacing the first, what is the probability that both pieces of fruit chosen are apples?

A. $\frac{1}{10}$

B. $\frac{1}{5}$

C. $\frac{2}{9}$

D. $\frac{1}{4}$

E. $\frac{2}{5}$

Practice Questions

24. Robert tossed a fair coin 3 times. What is the probability that the coin landed heads up exactly twice?

    A. 0.125
    B. 0.250
    C. 0.375
    D. 0.500
    E. 0.750

25. All of the marbles in a bag are blue, red, or green. If a marble is withdrawn from the bag at random, the probability that it is blue is $\frac{3}{5}$ and the probability that it is red is $\frac{1}{10}$. What is the probability that a marble withdrawn from the bag is green?

    A. $\frac{3}{50}$
    B. $\frac{3}{10}$
    C. $\frac{5}{8}$
    D. $\frac{7}{10}$
    E. $\frac{5}{7}$

26. A student is entered in a college housing lottery for 2 consecutive years. Each year, 1 out of 5 students receives housing through the lottery. What is the probability that the student will receive housing through the lottery for at least 1 of these years?

    A. $\frac{1}{125}$
    B. $\frac{1}{5}$
    C. $\frac{9}{25}$
    D. $\frac{16}{25}$
    E. $\frac{4}{5}$

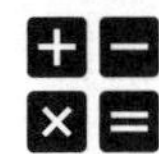

Volume

Cube, Prism, or Cylinder

$V = A \times h$

Pyramid or Cone

$V = \frac{1}{3} A \times h$

Sphere

$V = \frac{4}{3} \pi r^3$

Surface Area

Complex Shapes

Practice Questions

43. In the figure below, the base of the triangular prism is a right triangle with legs of lengths 3 and 4. If the height of this uniform solid is 6, what is the total volume?

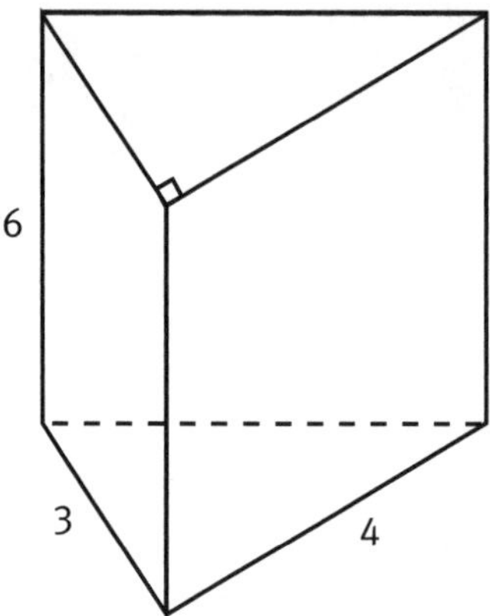

A. 12
B. 30
C. 36
D. 60
E. 72

44. An empty basin, 18" long, 10" wide, and 5" deep, was put under a leak in a pipe. After 5 hours, the water in the basin was 3" deep. What was the average rate of water loss from the leak during this time?

A. 108 in^3/hr
B. 324 in^3/hr
C. 460 in^3/hr
D. 540 in^3/hr
E. 900 in^3/hr

Practice Questions

45. What is the area of the trapezoid below?

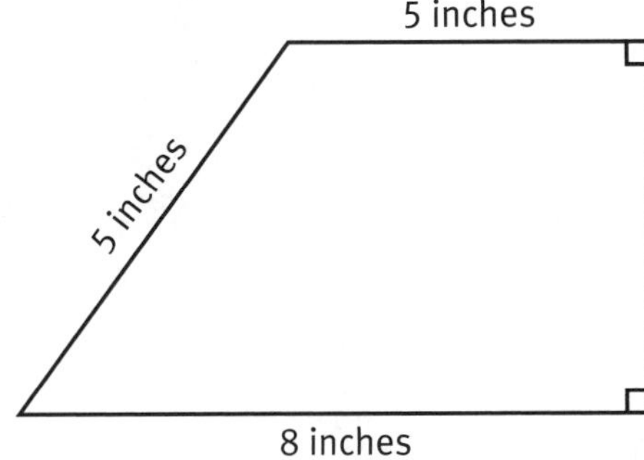

A. 22 in^2
B. 24 in^2
C. 26 in^2
D. 28 in^2
E. 32.5 in^2

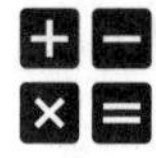

Coordinate Geometry

Slope

$m = \frac{\Delta y}{\Delta x}$

Parallel Lines

Perpendicular Lines

Slope-Intercept Equation

$y = mx + b$

Distance Formula

$d = \sqrt{(x_2 - x_1)^2 + (y_2 - y_1)^2}$

Example:

46. What is the slope of the line that passes through the points (1, 3) and (5, 11)?

A. $-\frac{1}{2}$

B. $\frac{1}{5}$

C. $\frac{1}{2}$

D. 2

E. 5

TAKEAWAY

Questions can ask you to find the area or perimeter of a figure given its coordinates, so be prepared to utilize multiple areas of your geometry expertise to solve for the correct answers on Test Day.

Practice Questions

47. What is the distance between (4, 8) and (−7, 11)?

    A. 5
    B. $4\sqrt{2}$
    C. $5\sqrt{2}$
    D. $\sqrt{130}$
    E. 14

48. Which of the following lines is perpendicular to $y = -2x + 3$ and has the same y-intercept as $y = 2x - 3$?

    A. $y = -\frac{1}{2}x + 3$
    B. $y = \frac{1}{2}x - 3$
    C. $y = \frac{1}{2}x + 3$
    D. $y = 2x + 3$
    E. $y = 2x - 3$

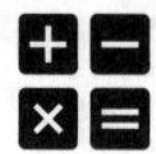

Practice Questions

49. What is the area of the figure below?

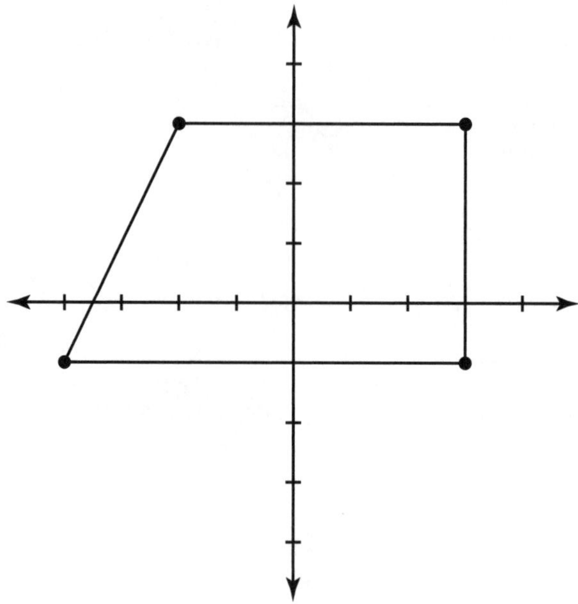

A. 13.5
B. 24.0
C. 28.0
D. 37.5
E. 45.0

Trigonometry

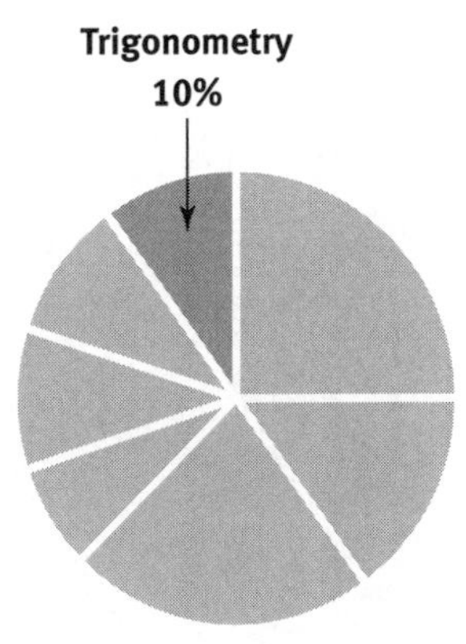

Mnemonic: SOH-CAH-TOA

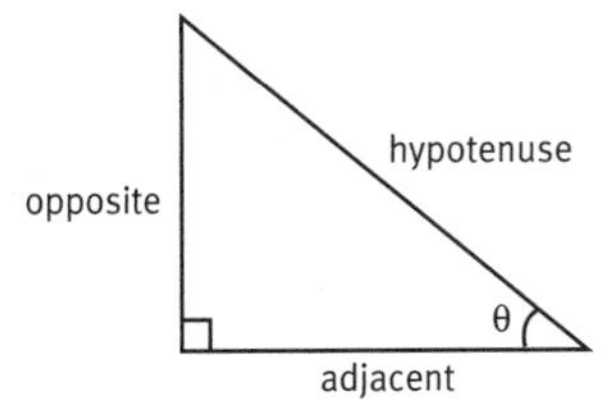

Sine

$\sin\theta = \dfrac{\text{opposite}}{\text{hypotenuse}}$

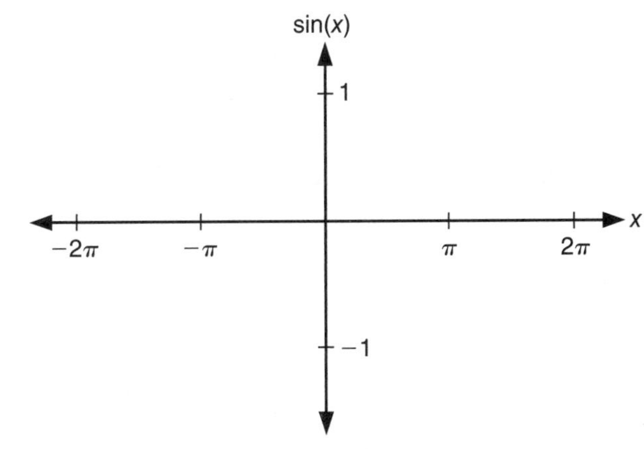

Domain: ____________ Range: ____________

x-intercepts: ____________

Example:

50. Which of the following is equal to $2 \sin\left(\frac{\pi}{2}\right)$?

A. 0
B. $\sqrt{2}$
C. 2
D. π
E. 2π

Cosine

$\cos\theta = \frac{\text{adjacent}}{\text{hypotenuse}}$

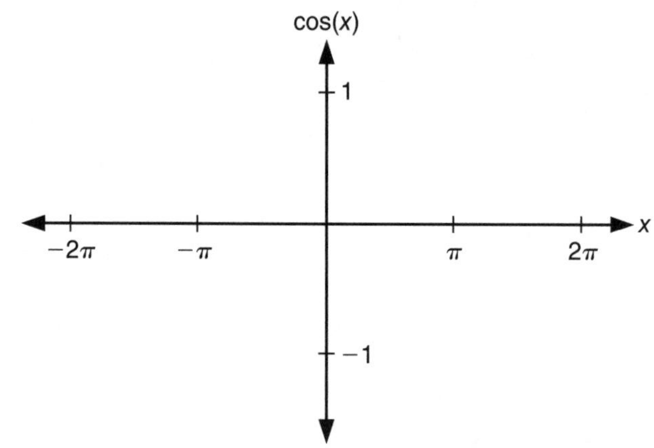

Domain: ____________ Range: ____________

x-intercepts: ____________

Example:

51. Which of the following is equal to $11\cos\left(\frac{3\pi}{2}\right)$?

A. 0

B. $\frac{3}{2}$

C. $\frac{3\pi}{2}$

D. 11

E. $\frac{33\pi}{2}$

Tangent

$\tan\theta = \frac{\text{opposite}}{\text{adjacent}} = \frac{\sin\theta}{\cos\theta}$

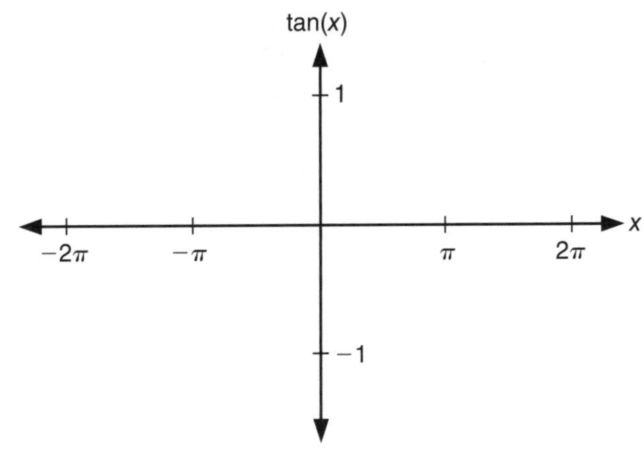

Domain: ____________________ Range: ____________________

x-intercepts: ____________________

Example

52. Which of the following is equal to 5 tan(0)?

A. 0
B. 1
C. π
D. 5
E. 5π

Practice Questions

53. In the figure below, what is the tangent of angle *ACB*?

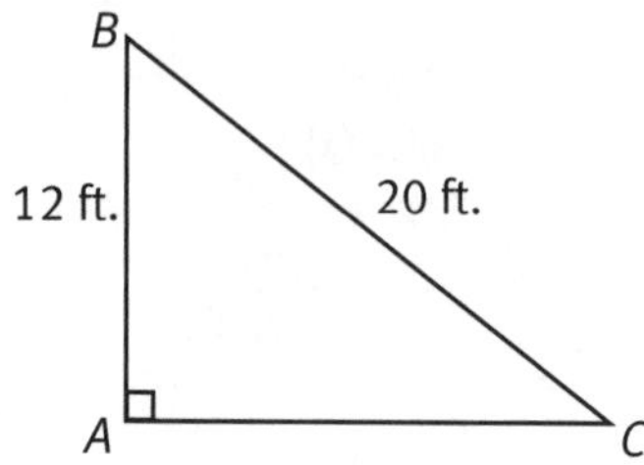

A. $\frac{3}{5}$

B. $\frac{3}{4}$

C. $\frac{12}{13}$

D. $\frac{13}{12}$

E. $\frac{4}{3}$

Practice Questions

54. To determine the height h of a tree, Roger stands b feet from the base of the tree, as shown in the figure below, and measures the angle of elevation to be θ. Which of the following illustrate the relationship between h and b?

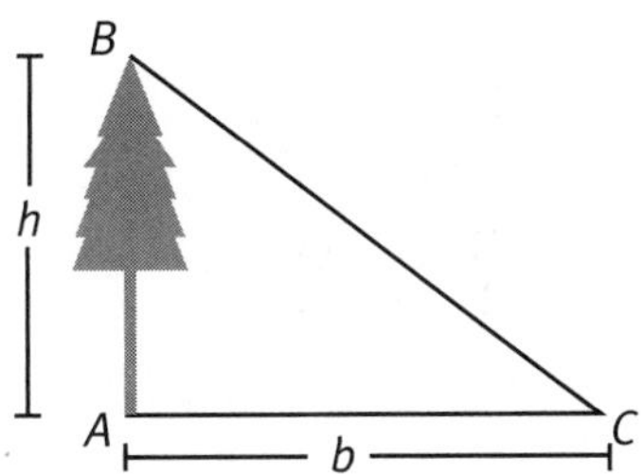

A. $\sin\theta = \frac{h}{b}$

B. $\sin\theta = \frac{b}{h}$

C. $\sin\theta = \frac{b}{\sqrt{b^2 + h^2}}$

D. $\sin\theta = \frac{h}{\sqrt{b^2 + h^2}}$

E. $\sin\theta = \frac{\sqrt{b^2 + h^2}}{b}$

55. In the figure below, if the length of line segment CB is x, what is the area of triangle ABC in terms of x and angle θ?

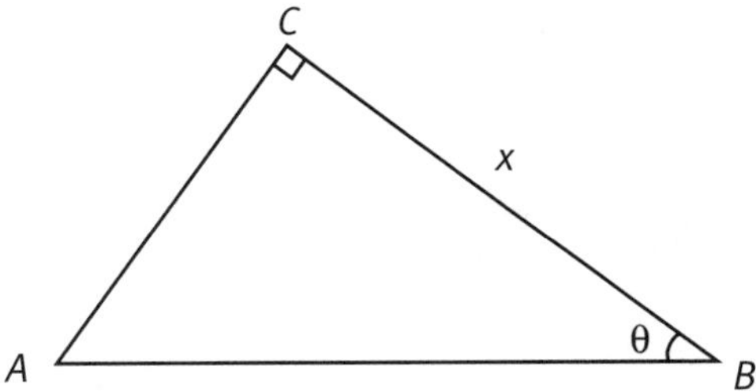

A. $\sin^2\theta + \cos^2\theta$

B. $\frac{1}{2}x^2 \tan\theta$

C. $\frac{1}{2}x^2 \sin\theta$

D. $\frac{1}{2}x^2 \cos\theta$

E. $x^2 \tan\theta$

Numerical Values for Trigonometric Functions

θ	0°	30°	45°	60°	90°
$\sin\theta$	$\frac{\sqrt{0}}{2}$	$\frac{\sqrt{1}}{2}$	$\frac{\sqrt{2}}{2}$	$\frac{\sqrt{3}}{2}$	$\frac{\sqrt{4}}{2}$
$\cos\theta$	$\frac{\sqrt{4}}{2}$	$\frac{\sqrt{3}}{2}$	$\frac{\sqrt{2}}{2}$	$\frac{\sqrt{1}}{2}$	$\frac{\sqrt{0}}{2}$

Inverse Trigonometric Functions

$\arcsin(x) = \sin^{-1}(x)$

$\arccos(x) = \cos^{-1}(x)$

$\arctan(x) = \tan^{-1}(x)$

Reciprocal Trigonometric Functions

$\csc(x) = \frac{1}{\sin(x)}$

$\sec(x) = \frac{1}{\cos(x)}$

$\cot(x) = \frac{1}{\tan(x)}$

Pythagorean Identities

$\cos^2\theta + \sin^2\theta = 1$

$1 + \tan^2\theta = \sec^2\theta$

Example:

56. Which of the following is equal to $\cos^{-1}(1)$?

A. 0

B. $\frac{\sqrt{2}}{2}$

C. 1

D. π

E. Both A and C

STUDY TIP
Use your flashcards to memorize the important trigonometry relationships.

Practice Questions

57. Which of the following is equal to $-3\cos(\pi)$?

    A. -3
    B. -1
    C. 0
    D. 1
    E. 3

58. Which of the following is equal to $\sec(-\pi)$?

    A. $-\pi$
    B. -1
    C. 0
    D. 1
    E. π

59. A 6 foot ladder is propped against a wall so that the bottom of the ladder is 30 inches from the wall. What angle does the top of the ladder make with the wall?

    A. $\arccos\left(\frac{1}{5}\right)$
    B. $\arctan\left(\frac{12}{5}\right)$
    C. $\arcsin\left(\frac{5}{12}\right)$
    D. $\arccos\left(\frac{5}{12}\right)$
    E. $\arcsin\left(\frac{12}{5}\right)$

Study Plan

After Class: Quantitative Reasoning 2		
Complete Remaining *Lesson Book* Practice Questions	30m	
Quantitative Reasoning Test A	45m	
Practice with Tests and Quizzes		

Before Class: General Chemistry 2		
Read *Review Notes* Chapters 28–30, 34–37	4h 30m	

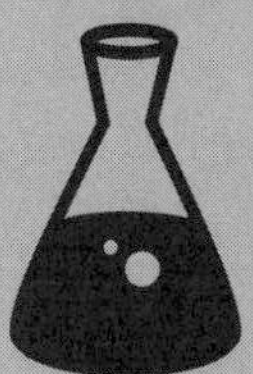

GENERAL CHEMISTRY 2

TOPICS COVERED

- Liquids and Solids
- Gases
- Solutions
- Acids and Bases
- Oxidation-Reduction Reactions
- Nuclear Reactions

After this session you will be able to:

- Calculate the energy involved in changing temperature and phase of matter
- Calculate the properties of gases using the ideal gas law
- Calculate the general and colligative properties of solutions
- Calculate pH and dissociation constant values for acids and bases
- Determine oxidizing and reducing numbers
- Calculate the energies associated with electrochemical cells
- Determine the products of radioactive decay

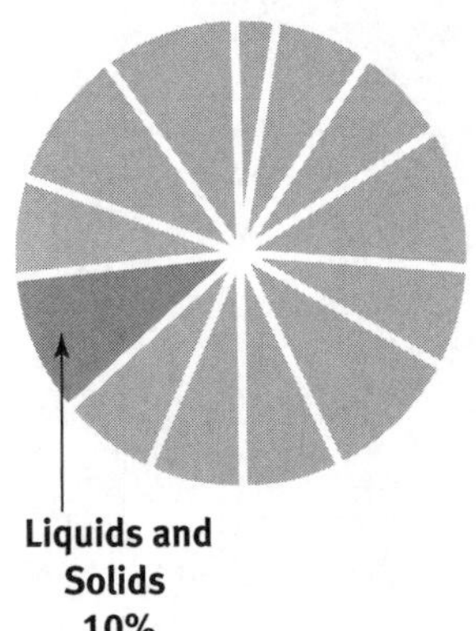

Liquids and Solids

Phases of Matter

Solid

Liquid

Gas

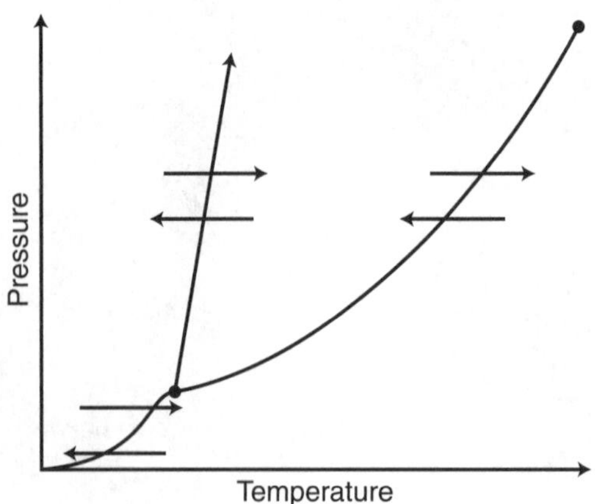

Critical Point

Triple Point

Practice Questions

1. The phase diagram for water looks different from most other phase diagrams in that its

   A. critical point does not exist.
   B. triple point is at 0 Pa.
   C. phase is not dependent on pressure.
   D. boundary line between solid and liquid phases has a negative slope.
   E. boundary line between solid and liquid phases has a positive slope.

2. Which of the following processes is endothermic?

   A. Condensation
   B. Crystallization
   C. Deposition
   D. Freezing
   E. Sublimation

3. When released in space, liquid water will first undergo vaporization but then quickly undergo deposition. What is the reason for this?

   A. Solid ice has higher entropy than liquid water or gaseous water vapor, which is opposite of the enthalpy trend.
   B. The low pressure in space allows the liquid to expand, but the low temperature leads to crystallization, which is the slower process.
   C. The water vapor interacts with dark matter particles to form a new compound with a higher boiling point.
   D. The energy within the water is converted into matter, which in turn releases energy.
   E. Gases cannot exist long-term in space, which means the majority of material must be solid or liquid.

Phase Changes

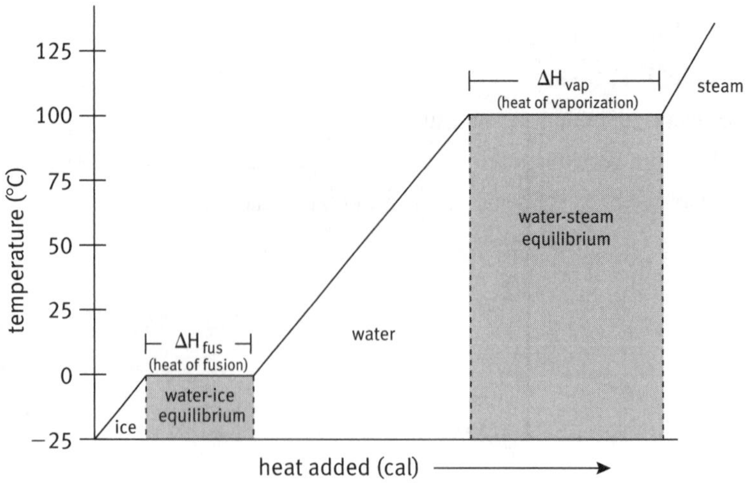

Specific Heat

Heat Capacity

$q = mc\Delta T$

Heat of Fusion

Heat of Vaporization

Vapor Pressure

TAKEAWAY

Be methodical with phase change calculations and make sure you don't miss any important pieces, whether heat capacity, heat of fusion, or heat of vaporization.

Practice Questions

4. Ice has a specific heat of 0.50 cal/g°C and a heat of fusion of 79.8 cal/g. How many calories are required to heat 12.0 g of water from –5°C to 25°C?

   A. 94.8 cal
   B. 107 cal
   C. 479 cal
   D. 1140 cal
   E. 1290 cal

5. What happens to the properties of a liquid when moved from sea level to higher altitudes?

   A. Boiling point increases.
   B. Boiling point decreases.
   C. Vapor pressure increases.
   D. Vapor pressure decreases.
   E. Heat of vaporization increases.

6. A certain 10.0 g sample of paraffin wax has a heat capacity of 25 J/K. If the sample releases 575 J as it cools to 12.0°C, what was the original temperature?

   A. 2.30°C
   B. 9.70°C
   C. 14.3°C
   D. 23.0°C
   E. 35.0°C

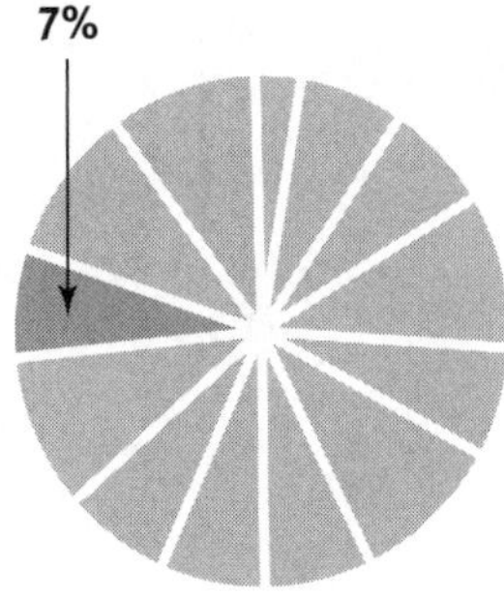

Gases

Ideal Gases

Kinetic Molecular Theory of Gases

Temperature

Pressure

Mole Fraction (*X*)

$$X_A = \frac{\text{Moles of A}}{\text{Total moles of all components}}$$

Dalton's Law of Partial Pressures

$P_{total} = P_A + P_B + P_C + ...$

$P_A = X_A P_{total}$

Boyle's Law

$P_1V_1 = P_2V_2$

Charles's Law

$\frac{V_1}{T_1} = \frac{V_2}{T_2}$

Avogadro's Law

$\frac{V_1}{n_1} = \frac{V_2}{n_2}$

Ideal Gas Law

$PV = nRT$

STUDY TIP

Many of the gas laws are just restatements of the Ideal Gas Law. If you understand the key relationships, you can answer any related questions on Test Day.

Practice Questions

7. What is the volume occupied by 3.2 g of oxygen at standard temperature and pressure?

   A. 2.24 L
   B. 4.48 L
   C. 22.4 L
   D. 32.0 L
   E. 44.8 L

8. A vessel contains 0.75 mol of nitrogen, 0.20 mol of hydrogen, and 0.05 mol of fluorine at a total pressure of 2.50 atm. What is the partial pressure of F_2?

   A. 0.050 atm
   B. 0.125 atm
   C. 0.50 atm
   D. 1.25 atm
   E. 2.50 atm

9. One mole of gas had its temperature changed to 546 K and its pressure increased to 3 atm. What is its new volume?

   A. 3.70 L
   B. 14.9 L
   C. 33.6 L
   D. 134 L
   E. 1,510 L

Solutions

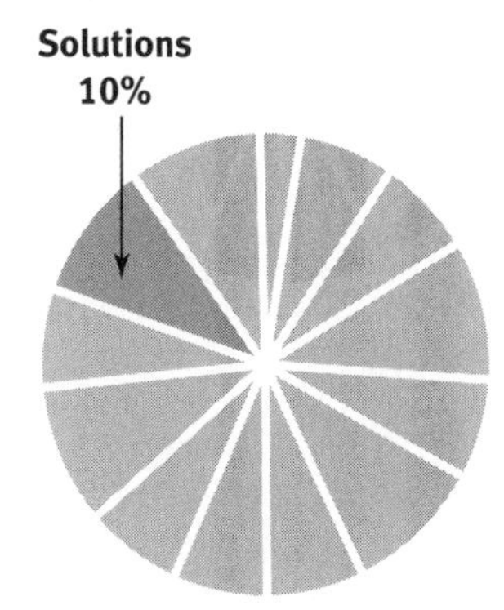

Concentration Calculations

Solute

Solvent

Molarity (M)

$$M = \frac{\text{Moles of solute}}{\text{Liters of solutions}}$$

Molality (m)

$$m = \frac{\text{Moles of solute}}{\text{Kilograms of solvents}}$$

Dilution

$$M_1V_1 = M_2V_2$$

Practice Questions

10. Two hundred milliliters of water are added to 55 mL of a 7.5 M solution of KOH (56.1 g•mol^{-1}). What is the final concentration of the solution?

    A. 0.08 M
    B. 1.6 M
    C. 6.5 M
    D. 13 M
    E. 27 M

11. If 10 g of NaOH (40.0 g•mol^{-1}) are dissolved in 500 mL of water, what is the molality of the solution if the density of water is 1 g/mL?

    A. 0.005 m
    B. 0.5 m
    C. 0.6 m
    D. 0.8 m
    E. 20 m

12. Eighty grams of NaOH (40.0 g•mol^{-1}) are added to 195 mL of water. How much additional water is needed to make a final concentration of 5 M NaOH?

    A. 160 mL
    B. 205 mL
    C. 400 mL
    D. 410 mL
    E. 3810 mL

Colligative Properties

Vapor-Pressure Depression

$\Delta P_{\text{soln}} = X_{\text{solute}} P_{\text{solvent}}^{\circ}$

Boiling-Point Elevation

$\Delta T_{\text{b}} = iK_{\text{b}}m$

Freezing-Point Depression

$\Delta T_{\text{f}} = iK_{\text{f}}m$

Osmotic Pressure

$\Pi = iM\text{R}T$

Solubility

Factors Affecting Solubility

TAKEAWAY

Many solubility calculations rely on how many total moles of solute can be dissolved, so don't forget the van't Hoff factor for molecules that dissociate in solution.

Practice Questions

13. Which solute would lower the freezing point of 1 L of water the most if 2 moles of that solute were added?

    A. NaCl
    B. KCl
    C. HCl
    D. H_2SO_4
    E. $C_6H_{12}O_6$

14. The K_b for water is 0.512°C•kg/mol. How much NaCl would need to be added to cause the boiling point of 4.0 L of water in a pot to rise by 1°C?

    A. 0.78 mol
    B. 2.0 mol
    C. 3.9 mol
    D. 7.8 mol
    E. 39 mol

15. A truck sprays a 20% by weight NaCl (58.5 $g\bullet mol^{-1}$) solution on ice covering a road, causing the ice to melt. If water was used as the solvent when creating the solution, what is the freezing point of the solution given that the K_f of water is 1.9 $K\bullet kg\bullet mol^{-1}$?

    A. −16°C
    B. −13°C
    C. −8.0°C
    D. −4.3°C
    E. −0.75°C

16. Maintaining the correct concentration of dissolved oxygen is important for aquatic life. Which change could cause an unsafe dip in oxygen levels within a fish tank?

    A. Increasing water temperature
    B. Decreasing water temperature
    C. Dissolving less salt into the water
    D. Increasing ambient pressure
    E. Decreasing the number of fish present

Acids and Bases

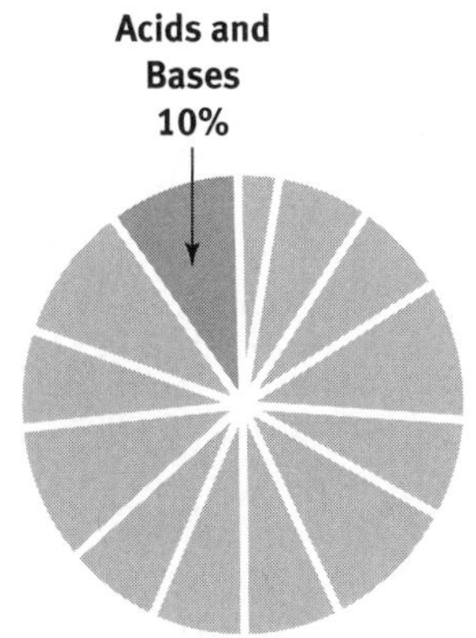

Arrhenius

Acid

Base

Brønsted-Lowry

Acid

Base

Lewis

Acid

Base

Conjugate Acids and Bases

$$CH_3COOH + H_2O \rightleftharpoons CH_3COO^- + H_3O^+$$

$$CH_3COO^- + H_2O \rightleftharpoons CH_3COOH + OH^-$$

Amphoteric Species

Autoionization of Water

$H_2O\ (l) \rightleftharpoons H^+\ (aq) + OH^-\ (aq)$

$K_w = [H^+][OH^-] = 1 \times 10^{-14}$

Acid Dissociation Constant (K_a)

$HA\ (aq) + H_2O\ (l) \rightleftharpoons A^-\ (aq) + H_3O^+\ (aq)$

$$K_a = \frac{[A^-][H_3O^+]}{[HA]}$$

Base Dissociation Constant (K_b)

$B\ (aq) + H_2O\ (l) \rightleftharpoons HB^+\ (aq) + OH^-\ (aq)$

$$K_b = \frac{[HB^+][OH^-]}{[B]}$$

p Function

p(anything) = −log[anything]

Examples:

$pK_a = -\log(K_a)$

$pK_b = -\log(K_b)$

$pH = -\log[H^+]$

Strengths of Acids and Bases

Practice Questions

17. What is the pH of a solution at 25°C with a hydronium ion concentration of 6.4×10^{-3}?

    A. 1.7
    B. 2.2
    C. 3.6
    D. 4.0
    E. 6.4

18. The K_a of acetic acid (CH_3COOH) is 1.8×10^{-5} at 25°C. What is the K_b of acetate (CH_3COO^-) at 25°C?

    A. 3.6×10^{-19}
    B. 1.8×10^{-12}
    C. 5.6×10^{-10}
    D. 1.8×10^{-5}
    E. 1.8×10^{-2}

19. The pH of a specific acetic acid solution at standard conditions is 5.5. What is the pOH of that solution?

    A. 4.5
    B. 5.5
    C. 6.5
    D. 8.5
    E. 9.5

Practice Questions

20. What is the pH of a solution when 1.0×10^{-10} mol of HCl is added to 1 L of pure water?

    A. 3.6
    B. 5.9
    C. 7.0
    D. 9.9
    E. 10.0

21. The water autoionization reaction is endothermic. If the temperature is increased, what happens to the solution?

    A. The pH of the solution increases.
    B. The pH of the solution decreases.
    C. The pH of the solution stays the same.
    D. The solution becomes more acidic.
    E. The solution becomes more basic.

22. The relative permittivity of a solvent is a measure of its polarity; the higher its value, the better the solvent is at solvating ions. Below is a list of the relative permittivity of certain solvents at 20°C.

Solvent	Relative Permittivity
Hexane	1.9
Benzene	2.3
Diethyl Ether	4.3
Methanol	30.0
Water	80.1

    If the same amount of nitric acid is added to 0.5 L of each solvent, which solvent would result in the solution with the highest pH?

    A. Hexane
    B. Benzene
    C. Diethyl Ether
    D. Methanol
    E. Water

Titration

Equivalence Point

$$V_A N_A = V_B N_B$$

Normality

$$N = M \times \frac{\text{equivalents}}{\text{mol}}$$

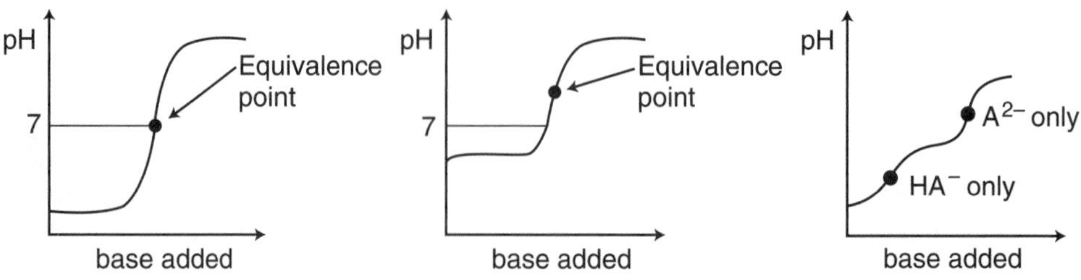

Buffers

Henderson-Hasselbalch Equation

$$pH = pK_a + \log\left[\frac{\text{conjugate base}}{\text{weak acid}}\right]$$

$$pOH = pK_b + \log\left[\frac{\text{conjugate acid}}{\text{weak base}}\right]$$

> **STUDY TIP**
> The DAT tests acids and bases using both calculation and conceptual questions. Memorizing formulas will help with calculations, but understanding relationships is essential for correctly answering conceptual questions.

Practice Questions

23. One hundred fifty milliliters of an unknown concentration of H_2SO_4 is found to reach equivalence after being titrated with 20 mL of a 2.0 M NaOH solution. What was the original H_2SO_4 concentration?

  A. 0.13 M
  B. 0.27 M
  C. 0.53 M
  D. 2.70 M
  E. 3.80 M

24. One liter of an aqueous ammonia ($K_b = 1.8 \times 10^{-5}$) solution is titrated with 1.1 N HCl *(aq)*. If 50.0 mL of the acidic solution is required to reach the equivalence point, what was the pH of the ammonia solution before the titration was begun?

  A. 3.0
  B. 5.3
  C. 6.0
  D. 7.1
  E. 11.0

25. The pK_a of methyl red is 5.2. What is the ratio of acid to conjugate base of a 1 M solution of methyl red at pH 4.2?

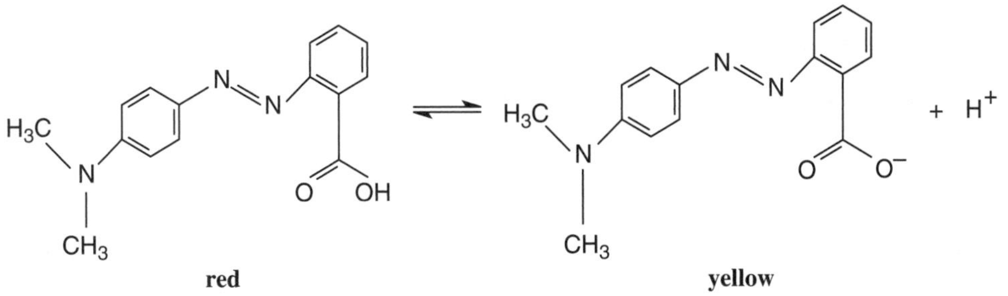

red **yellow**

  A. 10:1
  B. 7:1
  C. 1:1
  D. 1:9
  E. 1:10

Practice Questions

26. Which of the following chemicals would work best for determining the concentration of a formic acid solution via titration?

    A. Hydrochloric acid
    B. Ammonia
    C. Hydrogen sulfide
    D. Lithium hydroxide
    E. Acetone

27. To evaluate the endpoint of a titration of ammonia with a hydrobromic acid titrant, you should use the indicator

    A. methyl violet ($pK_{a2} = 1.8$).
    B. methyl orange ($pK_a = 3.7$).
    C. bromothymol blue ($pK_a = 7.0$).
    D. phenolphthalein ($pK_a = 9.3$).
    E. thymolphthalein ($pK_a = 9.9$).

28. Which of the following instruments would be most useful for measuring the amount of known base concentration added during the titration of 250 mL of an unknown acid?

    A. Pipette
    B. Burette
    C. Round-bottom flask
    D. Separatory funnel
    E. Retort

Oxidation-Reduction Reactions

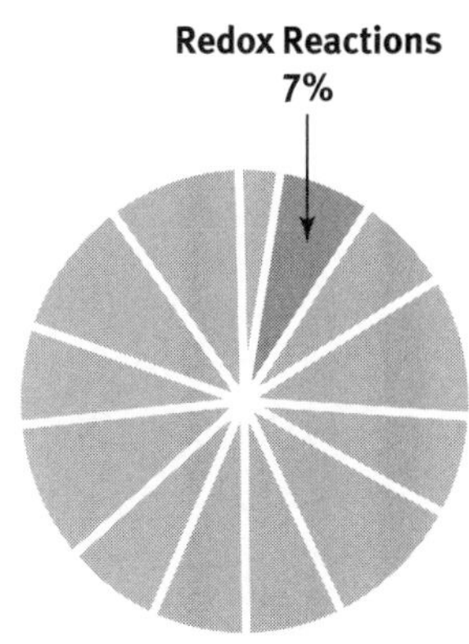

Reduction

Oxidation

Reducing Agent

Oxidizing Agent

Oxidation Numbers

Rule 1: The oxidation number of free elements equals 0.

Rule 2: The oxidation number for a monoatomic ion equals its charge.

Rule 3: In a binary compound, the oxidation number of the more electronegative element equals its usual ionic charge.

Rule 4: The sum of the oxidation numbers of the atoms in a compound equals the overall charge of the compound.

Rule 5: Some elements usually have only one oxidation number.

Balancing Redox Equations

1. Separate the two half-reactions.
2. Balance the atoms, except H and O, of each separate half-reaction.
3. Use H_2O to balance the O atoms and then H^+ to balance the H atoms.
4. Use electrons to balance the charges of each half-reaction separately and then together such that each half-reaction has the same total number of electrons.
5. Combine the half-reactions, canceling out any molecules that appear on both sides of the equation.
6. In basic solution only: Add to both sides of the equation the same number of moles of OH^- as H^+ present, combine the H^+ and OH^- to make water, and cancel out any water molecules that appear on both sides of the equation.
7. Confirm that the numbers of atoms and charges are balanced.

Example: $MnO_4^- + AsO_3^{3-} \rightarrow MnO_2 + AsO_4^{3-}$

Practice Questions

29. What are the oxidizing and reducing agents in the following reaction?

$$AgNO_3\ (aq) + CuNO_3\ (aq) \rightarrow Ag\ (s) + Cu(NO_3)_2\ (aq)$$

A. Cu is the oxidizing agent; Ag is the reducing agent.
B. Ag is the oxidizing agent; Cu is the reducing agent.
C. Ag is the oxidizing agent; NO_3 is the reducing agent.
D. NO_3 is the oxidizing agent; Cu is the reducing agent.
E. Cu is the oxidizing agent; NO_3 is the reducing agent.

30. What is the oxidation state of each nickel on the reactant side of the following reaction?

$$2\ NiO(OH) + Cd + 2\ H_2O \rightarrow 2\ Ni(OH)_2 + Cd(OH)_2$$

A. –2
B. –1
C. 0
D. +1
E. +3

31. What is the complete and balanced reaction that involves the reagents indicated below?

$$MnO_4^- + C_2O_4^{2-} \rightarrow Mn^{2+} + CO_2$$

A. $16\ H^+ + 5\ C_2O_4^{2-} + 2\ MnO_4^- \rightarrow 2\ Mn^{2+} + 10\ CO_2 + 8\ H_2O$
B. $8\ H^+ + 5\ C_2O_4^{2-} + 2\ MnO_4^- \rightarrow 2\ Mn^{2+} + 10\ CO_2 + 4\ H_2O$
C. $16\ H^+ + 5\ C_2O_4^{2-} + 2\ MnO_4^- \rightarrow 2\ Mn^{2+} + 5\ CO_2 + 8\ H_2O$
D. $8\ H^+ + 5\ C_2O_4^{2-} + 2\ MnO_4^- \rightarrow 2\ Mn^{2+} + 5\ CO_2 + 8\ H_2O$
E. $8\ H^+ + 5\ C_2O_4^{2-} + 2\ MnO_4^- \rightarrow 2\ Mn^{2+} + 10\ CO_2 + 8\ H_2O$

Electrochemistry

Galvanic/Voltaic Cells

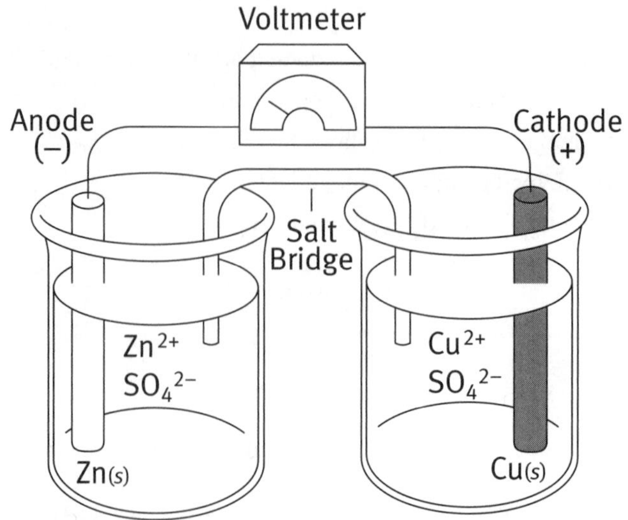

Electrolytic Cells

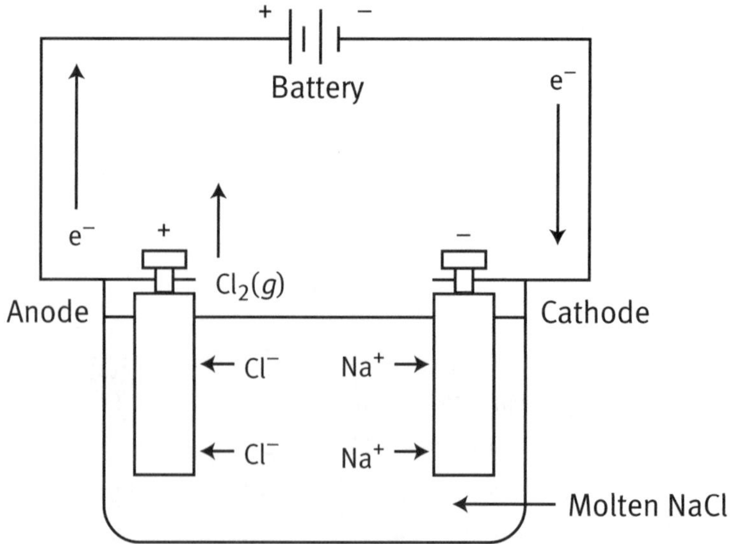

Reduction Potentials

Electromotive Force (emf)

$E_{cell}^{\circ} = E_{cathode}^{\circ} - E_{anode}^{\circ}$

Faraday's Laws of Electrolysis

$It = n\mathrm{F}$

Gibbs Free Energy

$\Delta G = -n\mathrm{F}E_{cell}^{\circ}$

$\Delta G = -\mathrm{R}T \ln K_{eq}$

$n\mathrm{F}E_{cell}^{\circ} = \mathrm{R}T \ln K_{eq}$

STUDY TIP

Use your Quick Sheets to study the important equations you need to know for Test Day.

Practice Questions

Reaction	$E_{\text{reduction}}^{\circ}$ (V)
$ZnS\ (s) + 2\ e^- \rightarrow Zn\ (s) + S^{2-}\ (aq)$	−1.440
$Zn^{2+}\ (aq) + 2\ e^- \rightarrow Zn\ (s)$	−0.763
$Cu^{2+}\ (aq) + 2\ e^- \rightarrow Cu\ (s)$	+0.337

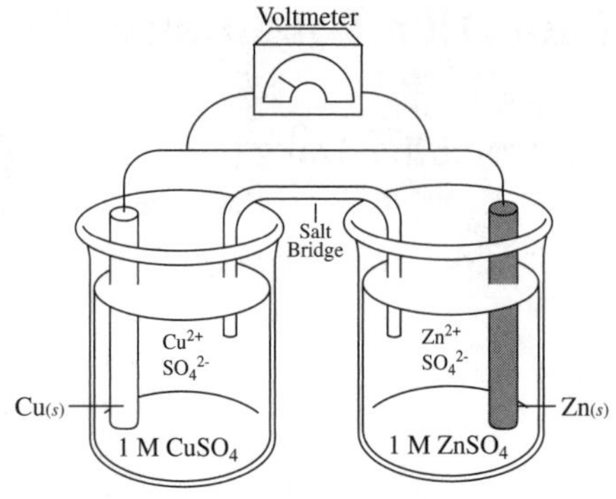

32. The cell above is an example of

    A. a galvanic cell with a zinc cathode and a copper anode.
    B. an electrolytic cell with a zinc cathode and a copper anode.
    C. a galvanic cell with a zinc anode and a copper cathode.
    D. an electrolytic cell with a zinc anode and a copper cathode.
    E. a galvanic cell with a zinc anode and a sulfur cathode.

33. What is the standard cell potential of the above cell?

    A. −1.10 V
    B. −0.430 V
    C. +0.430 V
    D. 1.10 V
    E. 1.78 V

34. If the following reaction produces a current of 3 A for 2.0 seconds, how many moles of Na (*s*) are consumed?

$$CO^{3+}\ (aq) + Na\ (s) \rightarrow CO^{2+}\ (aq) + Na^{+}\ (aq)$$

    A. 6.0×10^{-5}
    B. 6.0×10^{-4}
    C. 1.5×10^{-4}
    D. 1.5×10^{4}
    E. 6.0×10^{5}

Nuclear Reactions

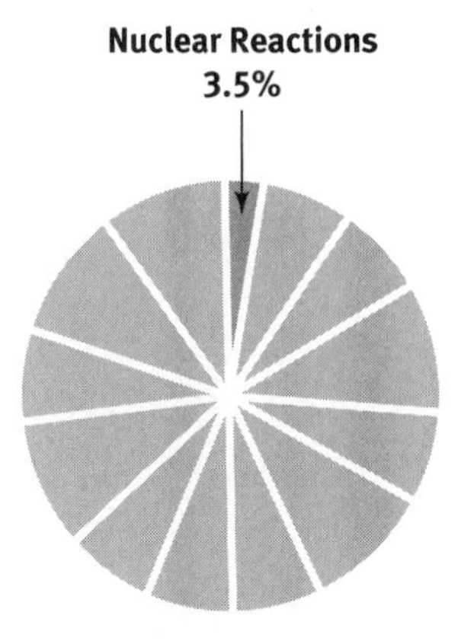

Alpha Decay (α)

$${}^{A}_{Z}X \rightarrow {}^{A-4}_{Z-2}Y + \alpha$$

Beta Minus Decay (β^-): Electron Emission

$${}^{A}_{Z}X \rightarrow {}^{A}_{Z+1}Y + e^-$$

Electron Capture

$${}^{A}_{Z}X + e^- \rightarrow {}^{A}_{Z-1}Y$$

Beta Plus Decay (β^+): Positron Emission

$${}^{A}_{Z}X \rightarrow {}^{A}_{Z-1}Y + e^+$$

Gamma Decay (γ)

$${}^{A}_{Z}X^* \rightarrow {}^{A}_{Z}X + \gamma$$

Half-Life ($t_{1/2}$)

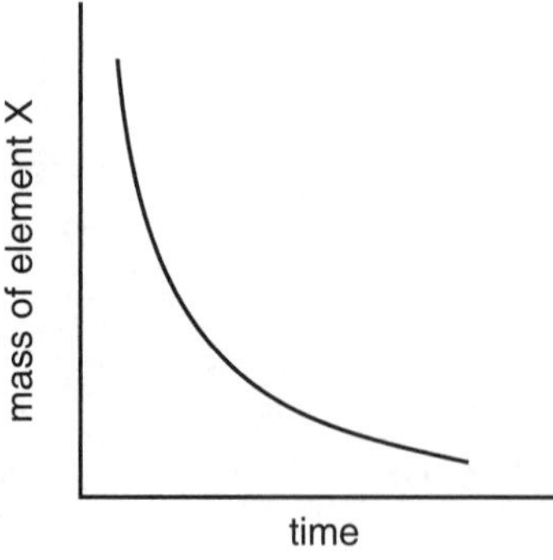

Time Elapsed	Sample Remaining
0 half-life	100%
1 half-life	50%
2 half-lives	25%
3 half-lives	12.5%

Fraction remaining after n half-lives $= \left(\frac{1}{2}\right)^n$

Fraction of nuclei decayed after n half-lives $= 1 - \left(\frac{1}{2}\right)^n$

STUDY TIP

In-depth knowledge of quantum physics isn't necessary for Test Day. Memorize the effects of each nuclear reaction so you can move on to study higher-yield topics.

Practice Questions

35. Uranium-238 ($Z = 92$) can undergo a single alpha decay to form a daughter with a mass number of

    A. 234.
    B. 236.
    C. 238.
    D. 240
    E. 242.

36. Plutonium-241 ($Z = 94$) can transform into americium-241 ($Z = 95$). This is an example of

    A. alpha decay.
    B. beta minus decay.
    C. beta plus decay.
    D. electron capture.
    E. gamma decay.

37. After 82 days, $\frac{15}{16}$ of a sample of einsteinium-253 has decayed. What is the $t_{1/2}$ of einsteinium-253?

    A. 4.0 days
    B. 5.1 days
    C. 20.5 days
    D. 27.3 days
    E. 328 days

Study Plan

After Class: General Chemistry 2		
Complete Remaining *Lesson Book* Practice Questions	30m	
General Chemistry Test A	40m	
Practice with Tests and Quizzes		
Before Class: Organic Chemistry 2		
Read *Review Notes* Chapters 44–51	3h 0m	

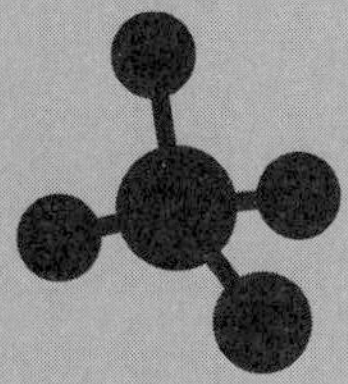

ORGANIC CHEMISTRY 2

TOPICS COVERED

- Aromatics and Bonding
- Reactions
- Acid-Base Chemistry
- Properties of Molecules and Organic Analysis

After this session you will be able to:

- Determine aromaticity
- Describe the properties of and predict the products of reactions involving aromatics, alcohols, ethers, carbonyls, and carboxylic acid derivatives
- Identify specific named chemical reactions
- Determine the relative strengths of acids and bases
- Interpret results from IR and NMR spectroscopy
- Evaluate the separation methods of extraction and distillation

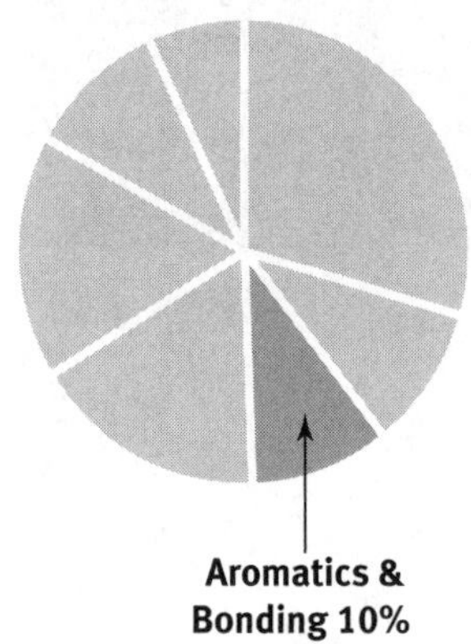

Aromatics and Bonding

Bond Types

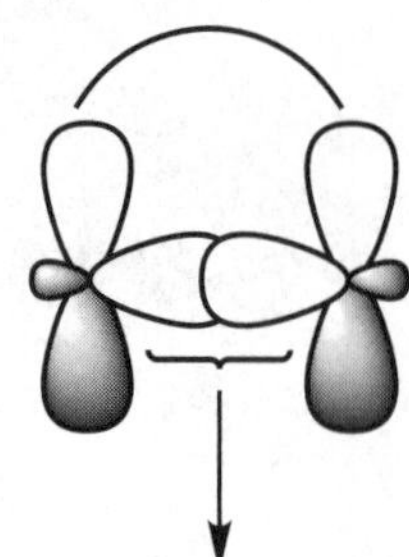

Sigma (σ)

Pi (π)

Hybridization

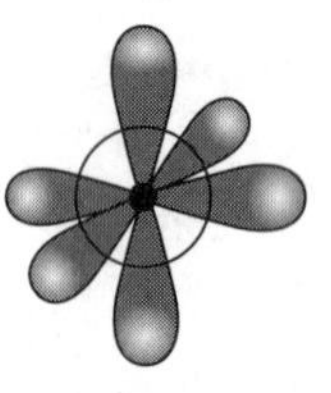 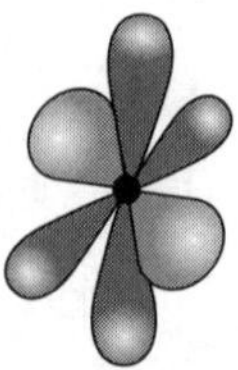 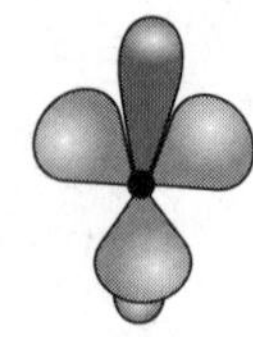 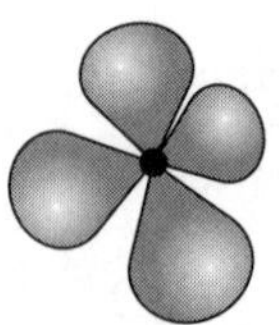

Hybridization	# of σ Bonds	Bond Angle
sp^3		
sp^2		
sp		

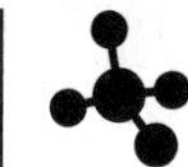

Conjugation

α, β-unsaturated carbonyl

1, 3 diene

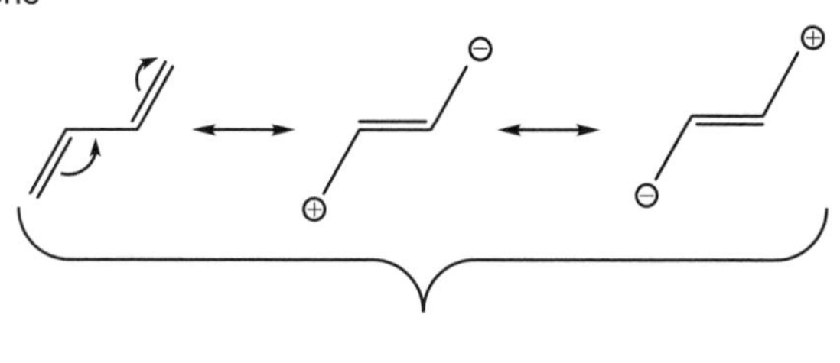

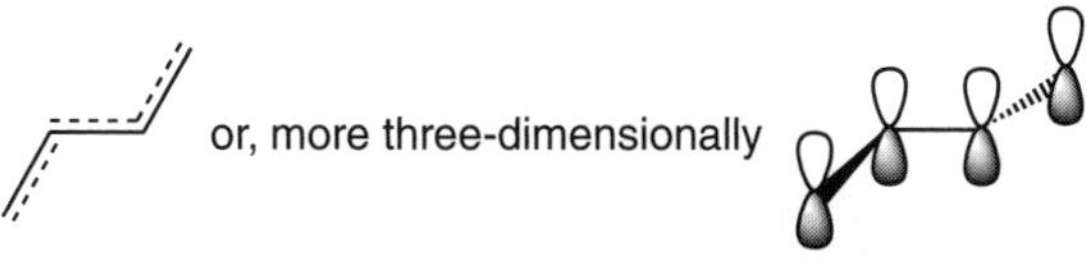

Aromaticity

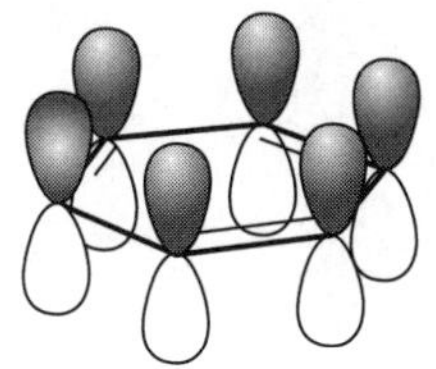

Practice Questions

```
                 H
                /
       H—C=C
         |      \
         |       H
H—C≡C—C—H
         |
         H
```

1. How many sigma bonds are in the above molecule?

   A. 4
   B. 7
   C. 8
   D. 10
   E. 13

2. How many pi bonds are in the above molecule?

   A. 1
   B. 2
   C. 3
   D. 4
   E. 5

3. What is the angle between any two of the hydrogens in ammonia, NH_3?

   A. 104.5°
   B. 107°
   C. 109.5°
   D. 120°
   E. 180°

Practice Questions

4. What is the hybridization of the two carbons in ethene, C_2H_4?

   A. sp^0 (none)
   B. sp
   C. sp^2
   D. sp^3
   E. Both sp^2 and sp^3

5. Is the following compound aromatic?

   A. Yes, because the compound is conjugated.
   B. Yes, because the compound is cyclic.
   C. Yes, because the molecule emits a pleasant odor.
   D. No, because the compound has six pi electrons.
   E. No, because the molecule violates Hückel's rule.

6. Which of the following compounds is aromatic?

   I. 

   II.

   III.

   A. II
   B. III
   C. II and III
   D. I, II, and III
   E. None of the above

Electrophilic Aromatic Substitution

General Mechanism

(addition)

(elimination)

Substituent Effects in EAS Reactions

ortho

meta

para

Activators vs. Deactivators

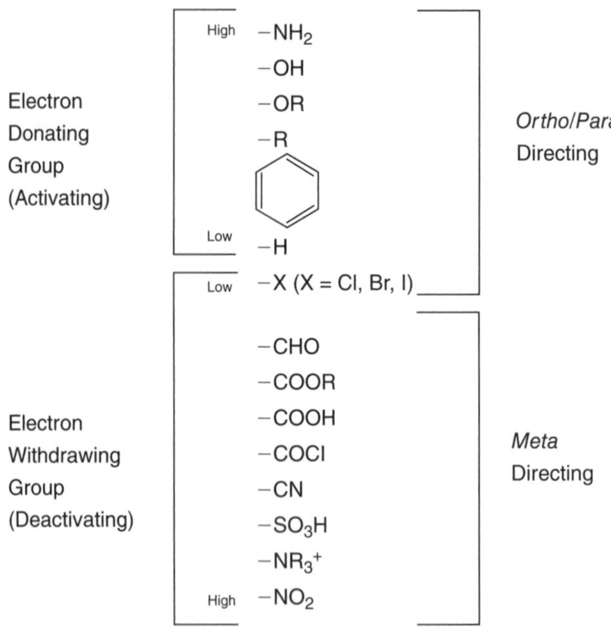

STUDY TIP

Although you won't have many questions directly related to EAS, understanding electron-withdrawing and electron-donating groups will help you earn many points on questions about various other reactions.

Practice Questions

7. A chemist used electrophilic aromatic substitution in order to complete the following reaction. In what order must the substituents have been added?

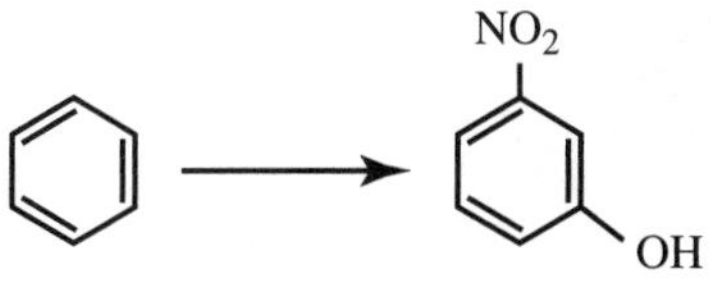

NO_2

OH

A. The nitro group was added first, then the alcohol group was added.
B. The alcohol group was added first, then the nitro group was added.
C. Both were added at the same time in the presence of heat.
D. The order in which the groups were added does not matter.
E. One group was added at a time, but the order cannot be determined.

8. What will be the product(s) of the following reaction?

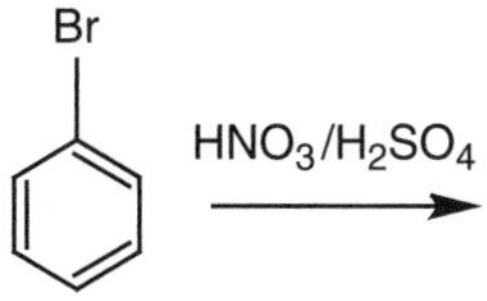

Br

HNO_3/H_2SO_4

A. 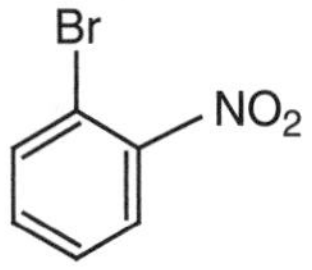 Br, NO_2

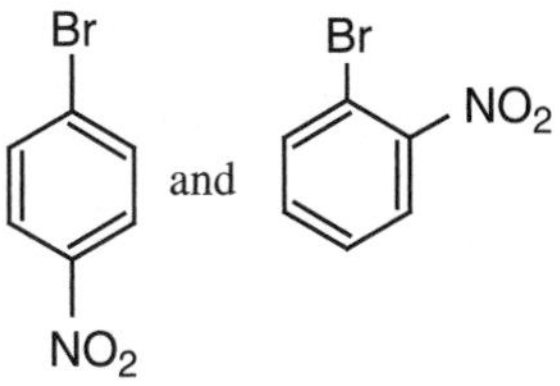

D. 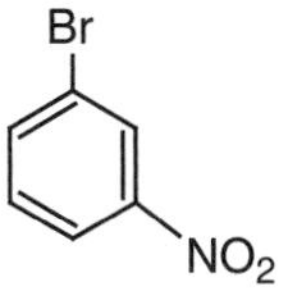 Br, NO_2

B. Br, NO_2

E. 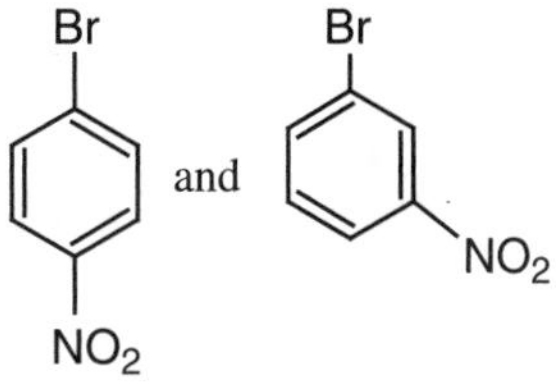 Br, NO_2 and Br, NO_2

C. Br, NO_2 and Br, NO_2

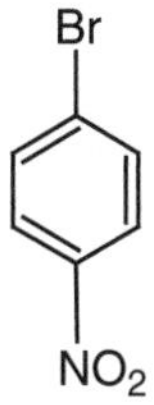

9. Each of the following is an electron-donating group EXCEPT one. Which one is the EXCEPTION?

A. OH
B. CH_3
C. NH_2
D. C_6H_6
E. Cl

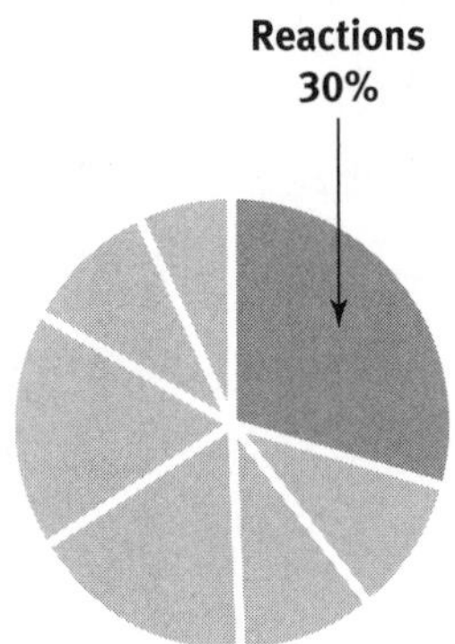

Reactions

Alcohols and Ethers

R—OH R—O—R'

Nomenclature

Electrophile

Nucleophile

Leaving Group

$$R{-}OH \xrightarrow{H^+} R{-}OH_2$$

Acidity

$$R{-}OH \longrightarrow R{-}O^- + H^+$$

Alcohol Synthesis

Alkene + H_2O → Alcohol

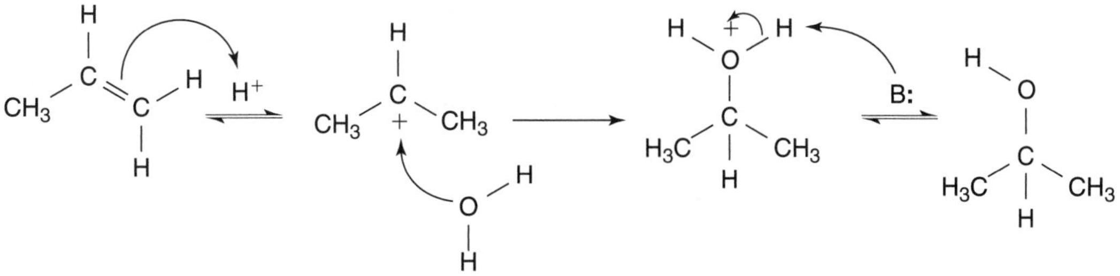

Ether Synthesis

2 Alcohol → Ether + Water

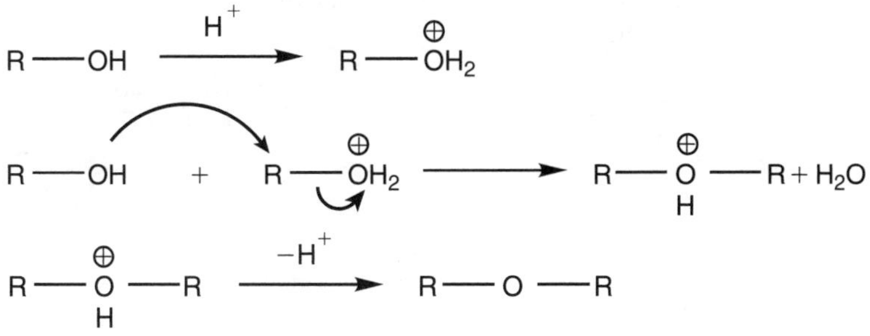

$$R{-}OH \xrightarrow{H^+} R{-}\overset{\oplus}{O}H_2$$

$$R{-}OH + R{-}\overset{\oplus}{O}H_2 \longrightarrow R{-}\underset{H}{\overset{\oplus}{O}}{-}R + H_2O$$

$$R{-}\underset{H}{\overset{\oplus}{O}}{-}R \xrightarrow{-H^+} R{-}O{-}R$$

Williamson Ether Synthesis

Alcohol + Alkyl Halide → Ether + Salt

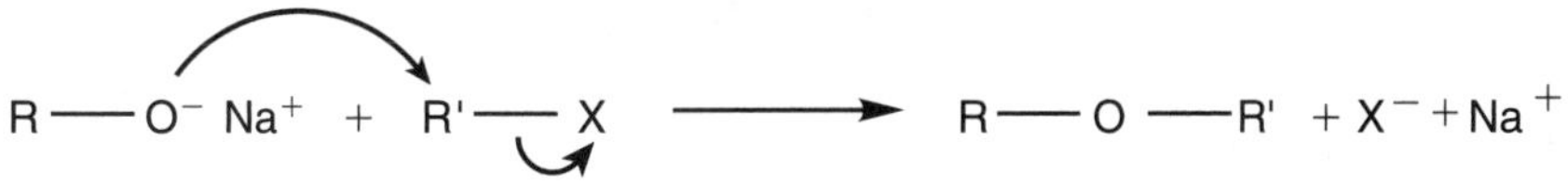

$$R{-}O^- Na^+ + R'{-}X \longrightarrow R{-}O{-}R' + X^- + Na^+$$

Practice Questions

10. Treatment of diisopropyl ether with two equivalents of hydrogen bromide (below) yields what product(s)?

$$CH_3-\overset{\overset{\displaystyle CH_3}{|}}{CH}-O-\overset{\overset{\displaystyle CH_3}{|}}{CH}-CH_3 + 2\,HBr \longrightarrow$$

A. 1-Bromopropane
B. 1-Bromopentane
C. 2-Bromopropane
D. 2-Bromopropanol
E. 1-Bromopropane and 1-propanol

11. Ethene can be reacted with steam to form ethanol via a hydration reaction; yields from this reaction are low but can be improved by

A. adding base.
B. adding H_2 and Pd.
C. removing water.
D. removing heat.
E. removing ethanol product.

12. Why do alcohols generally have higher boiling points than ethers?

A. Ethers are more polar than alcohols.
B. Alcohols have hydrogen bonding but ethers do not.
C. Ethers have lower atomic weights than alcohols.
D. Ethers cannot form ions.
E. Alcohols have more branching in their side chains.

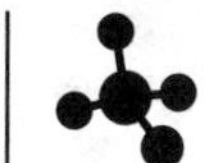

Carbonyls: Aldehydes and Ketones

$$R-\overset{\overset{\displaystyle O}{\|}}{C}-H \qquad\qquad R-\overset{\overset{\displaystyle O}{\|}}{C}-R'$$

Nomenclature

Electrophile

Nucleophile

$$RC(=O)R' \xrightarrow{H^+} RC(=\overset{\oplus}{O}H)R' \longleftrightarrow R\overset{\oplus}{C}(OH)R'$$

Carbonyl Synthesis

Alkyne + H_2O → Carbonyl

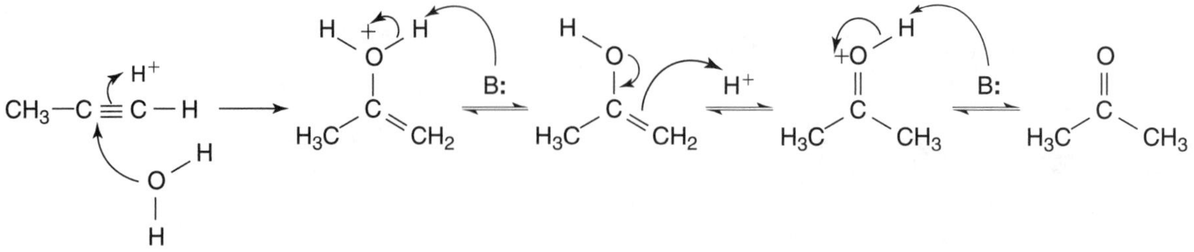

General Carbonyl Reactions

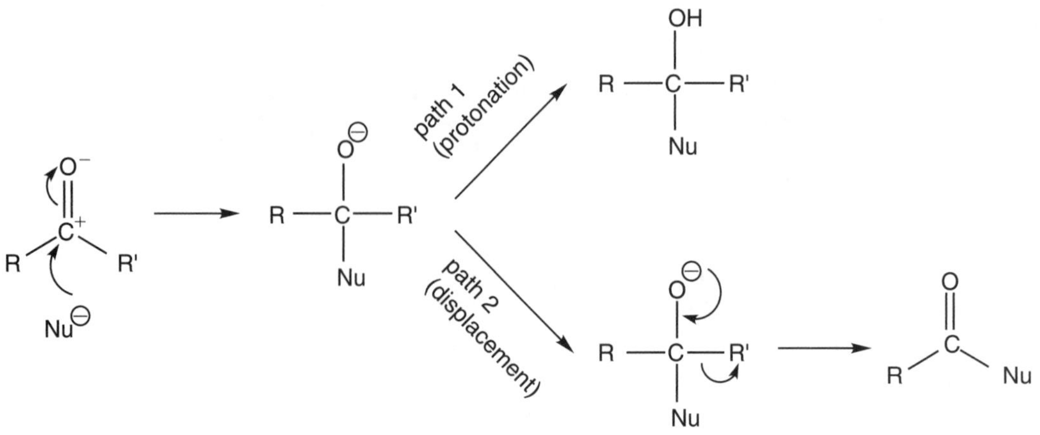

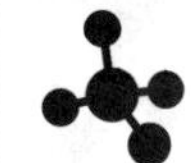

Acidity and Alpha Hydrogen

Keto-Enol Tautomerism

Aldol Reactions

Aldol Addition

Aldol Condensation

Practice Questions

13. What is the product of the following reaction?

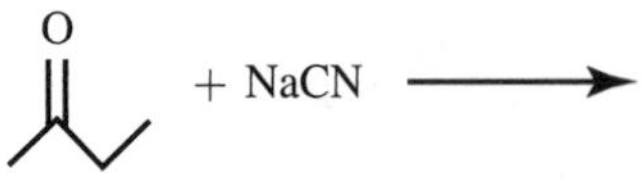

A.
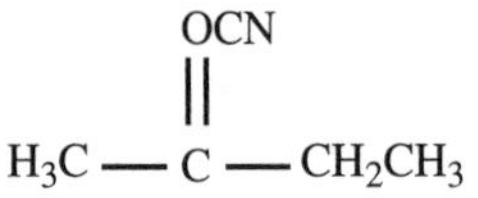

D.
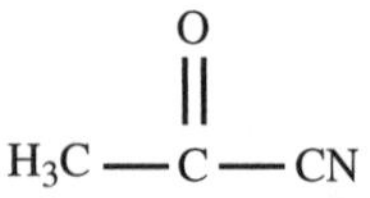

B.
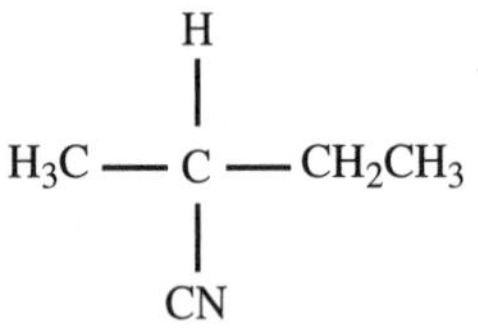

E.
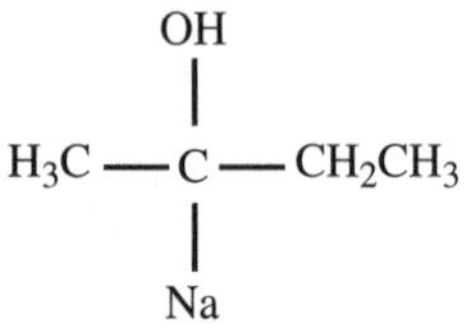

C.
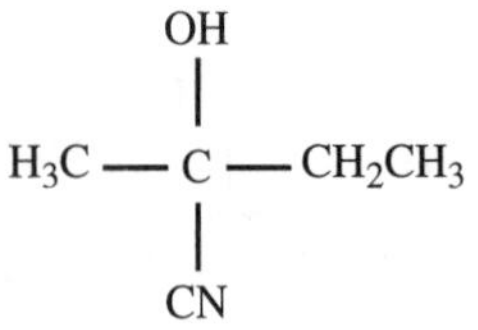

14. Which of the following reactions produces the below compound?

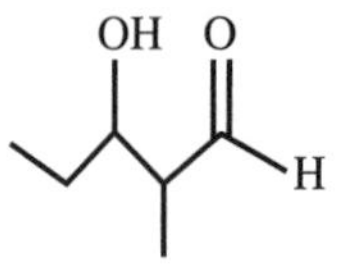

A. $CH_3CHO + CH_3CH_2CH_2CHO \rightarrow$
B. $CH_3COCH_3 + CH_3CH_2CH_2CHO \rightarrow$
C. $CH_3CH_2COCH_3 + CH_3CHO \rightarrow$
D. $CH_3CH_2CHO + CH_3CH_2CHO \rightarrow$
E. $CH_3CHO + CH_3COCH_3 \rightarrow$

15. Which hydrogen atom in the below compound is the most acidic?

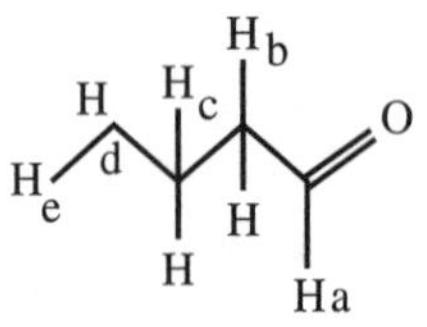

A. a
B. b
C. c
D. d
E. e

Carbonyls: Carboxylic Acids

$$RCOOH \longrightarrow [RCOO^- \longleftrightarrow RCOO^-] + H^+$$

Nomenclature

Electrophile

Nucleophile

Leaving Group

Acidity

Carboxylic Acid Synthesis

Amide/Ester + Water → Carboxylic Acid

$$R_1C(=O)NHR_2 \xrightarrow{H_2O} R_1C(=O)OH + H_2NR_2$$

$$R_1C(=O)OR_2 \xrightarrow{H_2O} R_1C(=O)O^{\ominus} + R_2OH$$

Carbonyls: Carboxylic Acid Derivatives

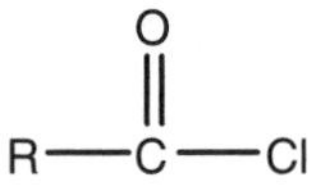

$R-C(=O)-Cl$

acyl halide

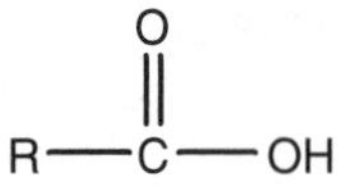

$R-C(=O)-OH$

carboxylic acid

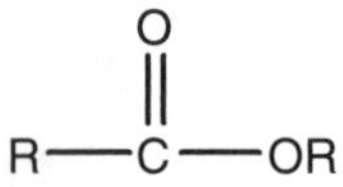

$R-C(=O)-OR$

ester

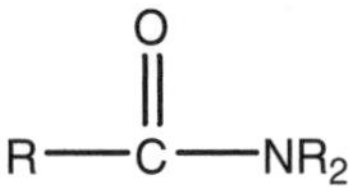

$R-C(=O)-NR_2$

amide

$R-C(=O)-O-C(=O)-R$

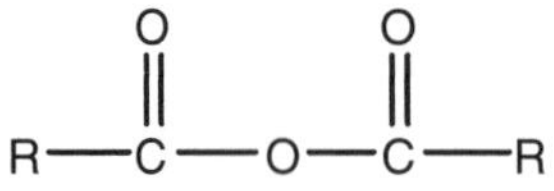

acid anhydride

Reactivity

most reactive

least reactive

General Substitution Reaction

Carboxylic Acid + Nucleophile → Carboxylic Acid Derivative

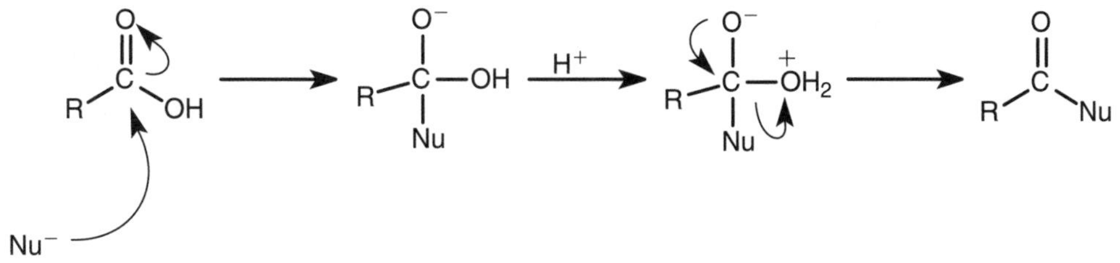

Acyl Halide Formation

Carboxylic Acid + Thionyl Chloride → Acyl Chloride

$$\text{CH}_3\text{COOH} + SOCl_2 \xrightarrow{H^+} \text{CH}_3\text{COCl}$$

Ester Formation

Carboxylic Acid + Alcohol → Ester

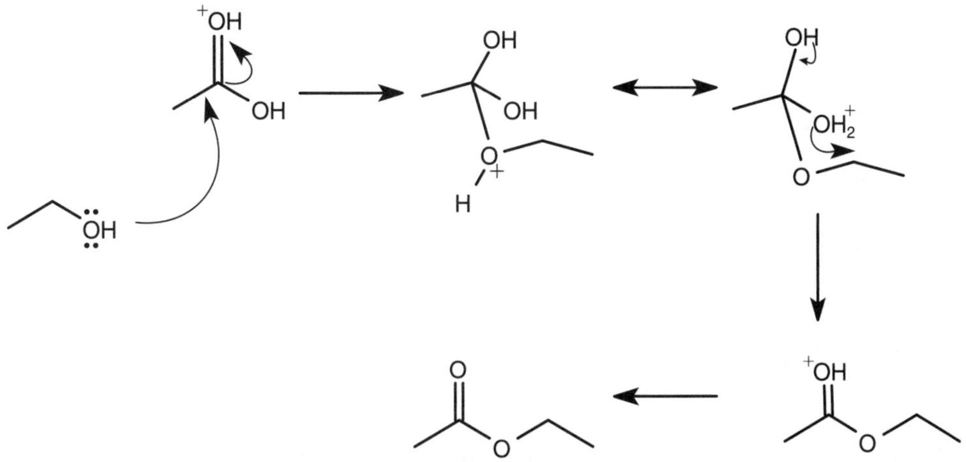

Practice Questions

16. What type of reaction is represented below?

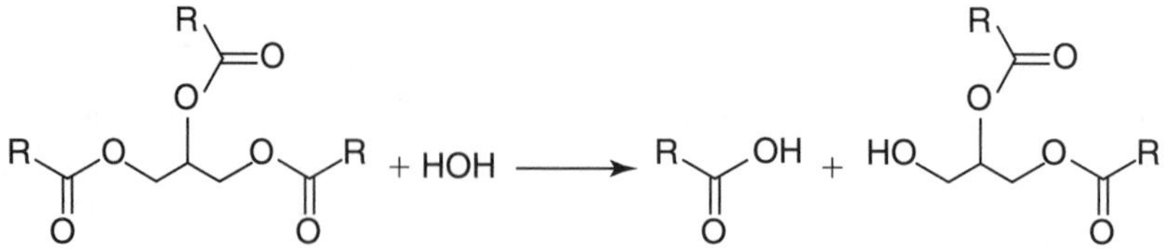

triacylglyceride + HOH → fatty acid + diacylglyceride

A. Hydration
B. Hydrolysis
C. Hydrogenation
D. Dehydration
E. Esterification

17. Which of the following will undergo ester hydrolysis most rapidly?

A. 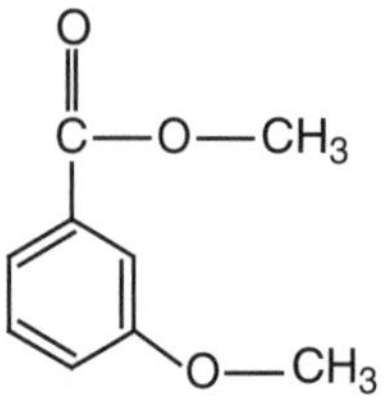 $C_6H_4(COOCH_3)(OCH_3)$ (meta: C(=O)—O—CH_3, O—CH_3)

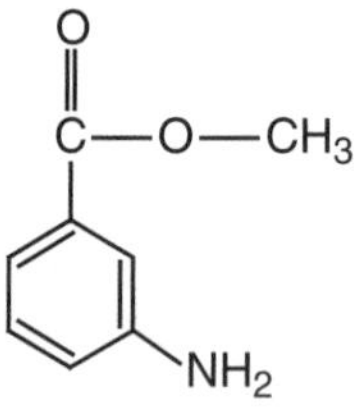

D. 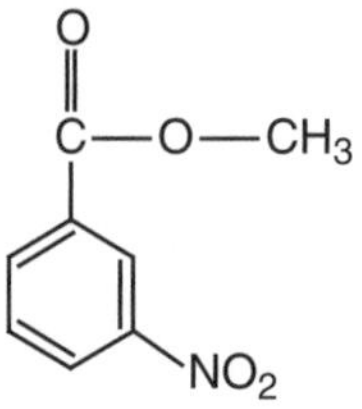 C(=O)—O—CH_3, NO_2

B. 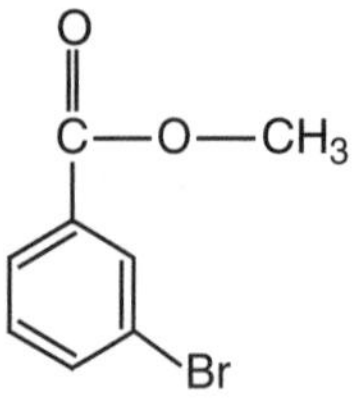 C(=O)—O—CH_3, Br

E. C(=O)—O—CH_3, NH_2

C. C(=O)—O—CH_3, CH_3

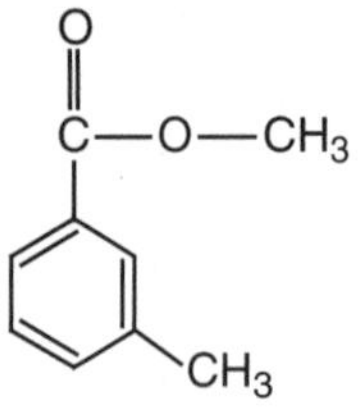

18. Why should esterification reactions not be carried out in water?

A. Acid is insoluble in water.
B. The polar nature of water overshadows the polar nature of the carboxyl group.
C. The extensive hydrogen bonding of water interferes with the S_N2 reaction mechanism.
D. Water molecules would hydrolyze useful products back to the parent carboxylic acid.
E. Water would cause the carboxylic acid to ionize, so no reaction would occur.

Named Reactions

Grignard Reaction

Carbonyl + Grignard Reagent → Alcohol

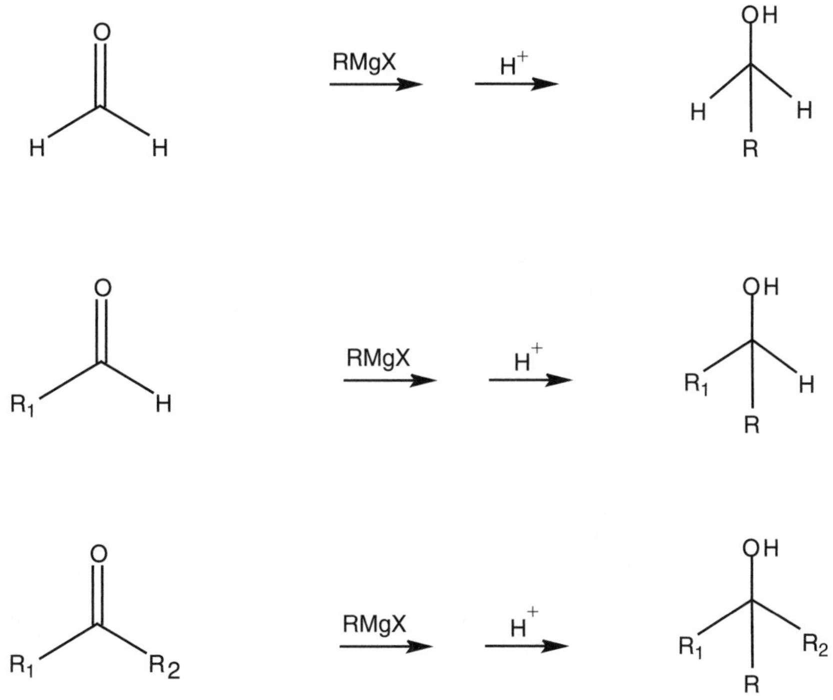

Diels-Alder Reaction

Diels-Alder Reaction

Diene + Dienophile → Ring

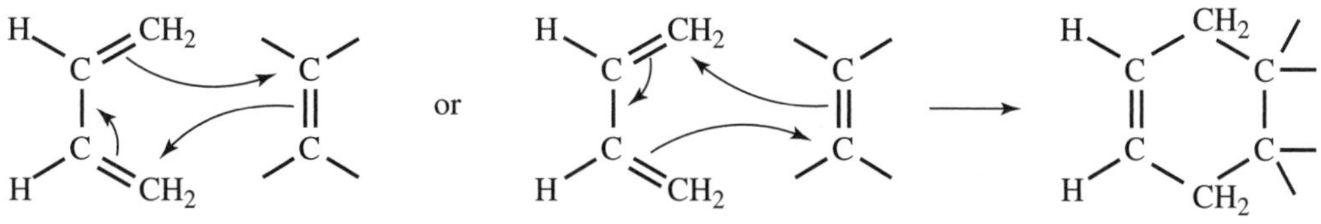

Wittig Alkene Synthesis

Aldehyde/Ketone + Triphenyl Phosphonium Ylide → Alkene

$$R_1R_2C{=}O + Ph_3P^{+}{-}C^{-}R_3R_4 \longrightarrow R_1R_2C{=}CR_3R_4 + Ph_3P{=}O$$

$$Ph_3\overset{+}{P}{-}CH^{-}R_1 + HC(O)R_2 \rightleftharpoons Ph_3\overset{+}{P}{-}CH(R_1){-}CH(R_2){-}O^{-} \rightleftharpoons \text{(rotamer)} \rightleftharpoons \text{oxaphosphetane} \longrightarrow HR_1C{=}CHR_2 + Ph_3PO$$

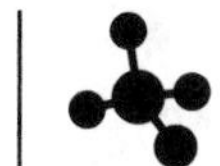

Practice Questions

19. What is the product of the following reaction?

$$C_6H_5C(=O)CH_3 + CH_3CH_2CH_2MgBr \longrightarrow \xrightarrow{H_2O}$$

A. 1-Phenyl-1-butanol
B. 1-Phenyl-2-butanol
C. 1-Methyl-1-phenyl-1-propanol
D. 2-Phenyl-2-butanol
E. 2-Phenyl-2-pentanol

20. Why must a diene be able to exist in the *cis* conformation to undergo the Diels-Alder reaction?

A. The energy of the products is lower than that of the reactants when using the *trans* conformation.
B. The *trans* conformations of dienes have too many electron-donating groups.
C. The double bonds in the *trans* conformation are too close together to allow reaction.
D. Only the *cis* conformation shows conjugation, which is required for the reaction to proceed.
E. If the *trans* conformation is too sterically hindered to rotate about the bond, a ring cannot form.

21. Which of the following most accurately describes the mechanism of the Wittig reaction?

A. The first step is nucleophilic attack on the carbonyl carbon.
B. The electrophile is the anionic carbon of the ylide.
C. Phosphorous bonds with oxygen to stabilize the alkene final product.
D. The mechanism can only proceed if the ylid reacts with a ketone.
E. The final step of the mechanism is hydrolysis of the four-membered oxaphosphetane ring.

Oxidation-Reduction Reactions

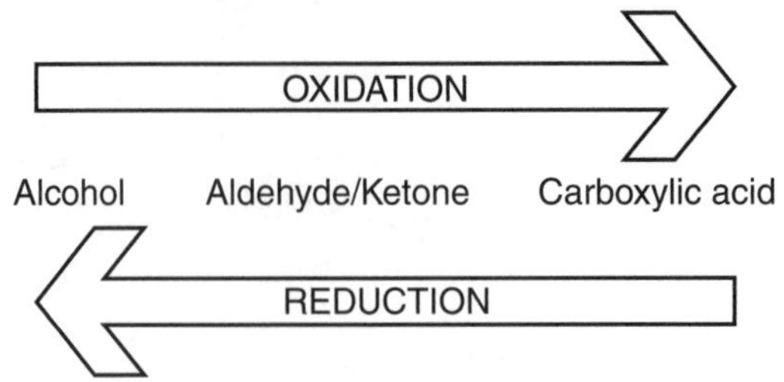

Reducing Agents

Oxidizing Agents

General Oxidation Reactions

Primary Alcohols

OH
H_3C H H
PCC $\rightarrow$
H_3C O H
Tollens' Reagent $\rightarrow$
H_3C O OH

$KMnO_4$, $K_2Cr_2O_7$, etc.

Secondary Alcohols

OH
H_3C CH_3 $\rightarrow$ H_3C O CH_3

Tertiary Alcohols

OH
H_3C CH_3 CH_3 $\not\rightarrow$ H_3C O C CH_3 CH_3

Oxidative Cleavage of Alkenes

Alkene + Oxidizing Agent → 2 Carbonyls

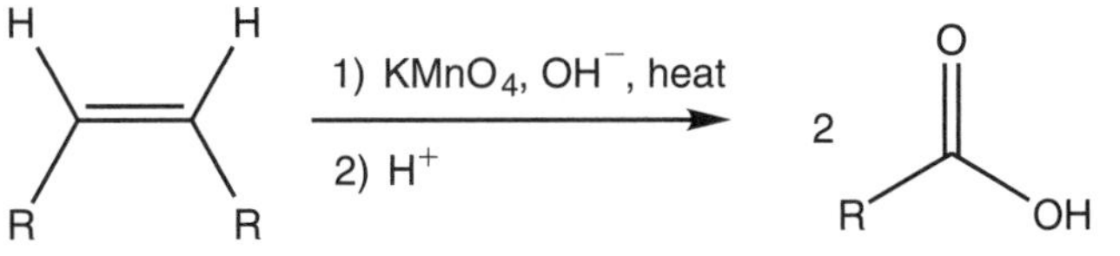

H H R R; 1) $KMnO_4$, OH^-, heat; 2) H^+ → 2 R(C=O)OH

non-terminal alkene

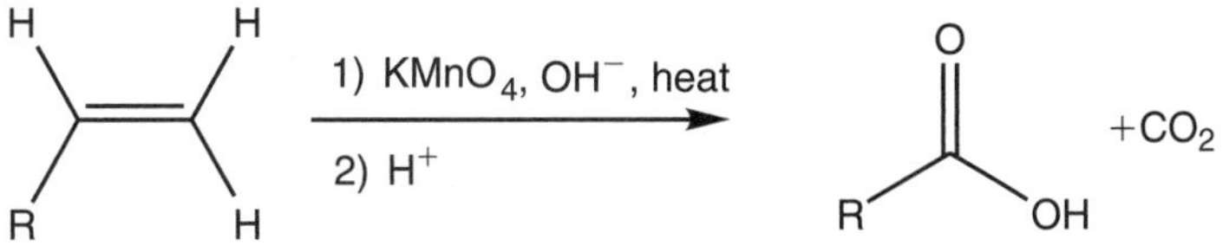

H H R H; 1) $KMnO_4$, OH^-, heat; 2) H^+ → R(C=O)OH $+CO_2$

terminal alkene

H H R R; 1) O_3, CH_2Cl_2; 2) Zn/H_2O → 2 R(C=O)H

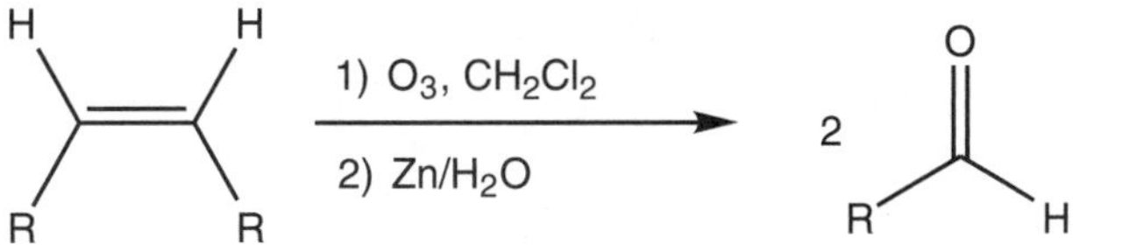

non-terminal alkene

General Reduction Reactions

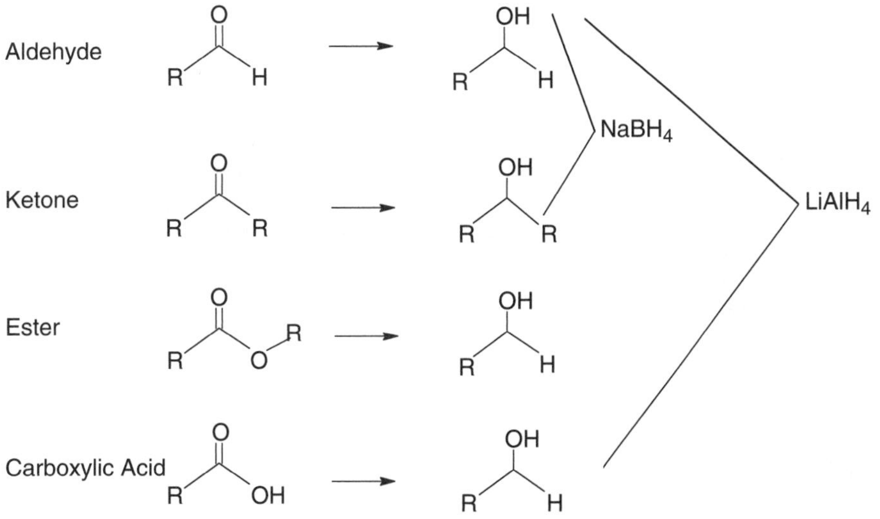

Aldehyde R(C=O)H → R–CH(OH)–H

Ketone R(C=O)R → R–CH(OH)–R

Ester R(C=O)OR → R–CH(OH)–H

Carboxylic Acid R(C=O)OH → R–CH(OH)–H

$NaBH_4$ (aldehyde, ketone)

$LiAlH_4$ (aldehyde, ketone, ester, carboxylic acid)

STUDY TIP

Take the time to understand reactivity trends throughout Organic Chemistry. If you understand the trends, you'll be able to answer conceptual questions more easily and won't waste time trying to memorize every single reaction.

Practice Questions

22. What is the product of the following reaction?

$$(CH_3)_2CHCH_2OH \xrightarrow{KMnO_4}$$

A. 2-Methylethanal
B. 2-Methylpropanal
C. 2-Methylpropanoic acid
D. Butanal
E. Butanoic acid

23. Upon ozonolysis of an unknown alkene, the following two compounds were formed.

$$\overset{O}{\overset{\|}{C}}HCH_2CH_3 \quad \text{and} \quad CH_3\overset{O}{\overset{\|}{C}}CH_3$$

What was the original alkene?

A. 2-methyl-2-butene
B. 2-methyl-2-pentene
C. 2-methyl-2-hexene
D. 3-methyl-2-pentene
E. 3-methyl-2-hexene

24. Which of the following would NOT react in the presence of $NaBH_4$?

A. Cyclohexanone
B. Ethyl ethanoate
C. Formaldehyde
D. Propanal
E. All of the above would react in the presence of $NaBH_4$.

Acid-Base Chemistry

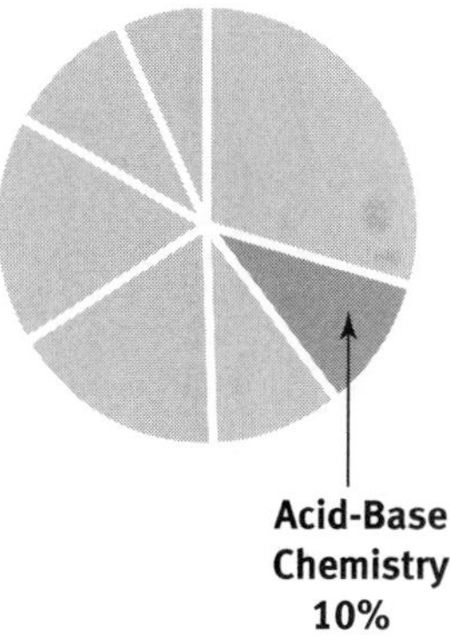

Determining Acid Strength

Resonance Effects

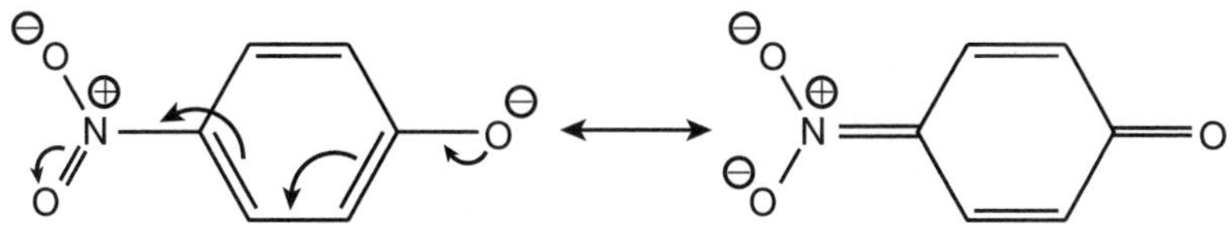

Induction: Electron-Withdrawing Groups

(1) The closer the electron-withdrawing group to the acidic hydrogen, the stronger the acid.

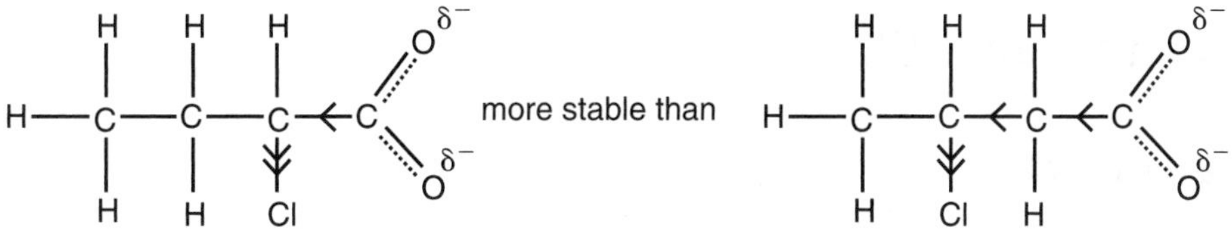

more stable than

(2) The more electronegative the electron-withdrawing group, the stronger the acid.

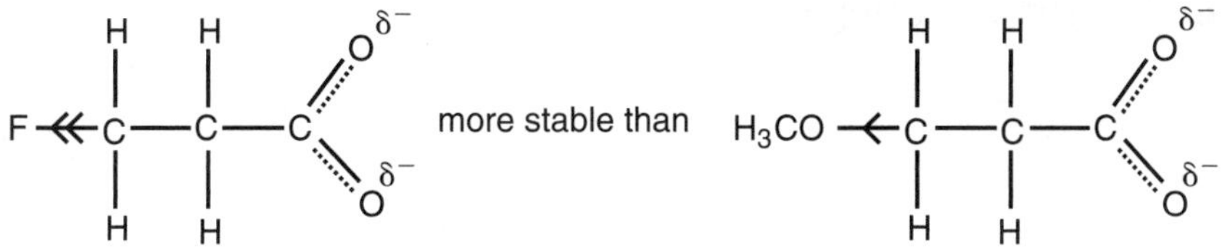

more stable than

(3) The larger the number of electron-withdrawing groups, the stronger the acid.

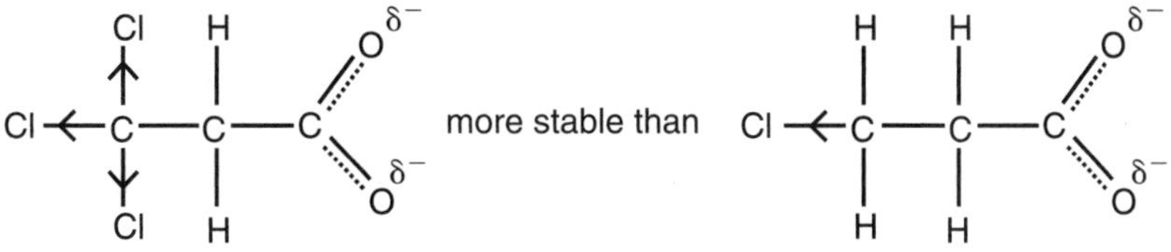

more stable than

Hybridization

$$R{-}C{\equiv}C{-}H \longrightarrow R{-}C{\equiv}C{:}^{\ominus} \qquad pK_a \approx 22$$

$$RHC{=}CH_2 \longrightarrow RHC{=}\ddot{C}H^{\ominus} \qquad pK_a \approx 40$$

$$R{-}CH_2{-}CH_2{-}H \longrightarrow R{-}CH_2{-}CH_2{:}^{\ominus} \qquad pK_a \approx 60$$

Determining Base Strength

Resonance Effects

Induction: Electron-Donating Groups

Hybridization and Non-Bonded Electron Pairs

> **STUDY TIP**
> Acids and bases are tested in both the General Chemistry and the Organic Chemistry sections of the Survey of the Natural Sciences. Study all of this content together to help you make better connections and earn more points for your effort.

Practice Questions

25. Which represents the order of increasing basicity for the following compounds?

I. (benzene ring)—NH_2

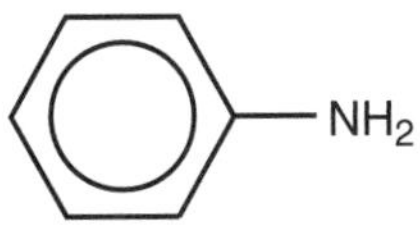

II.

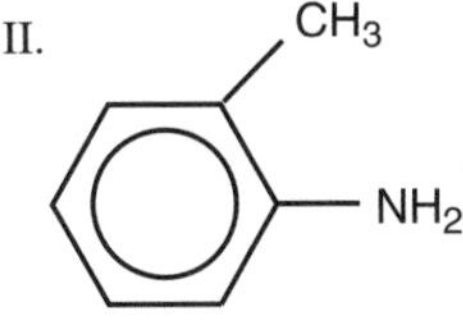

III.

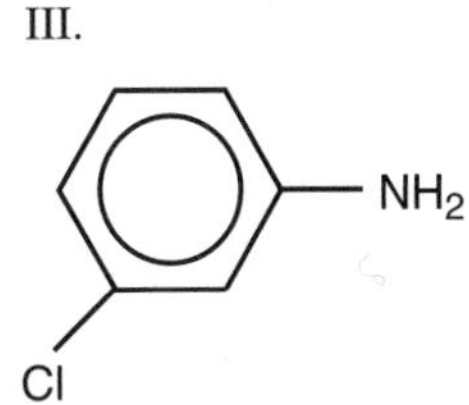

A. I < II < III
B. II < III < I
C. II < I < III
D. III < I < II
E. III < II < I

26. Which represents the order of increasing acidity for the following compounds?

I. COOH, CH_3

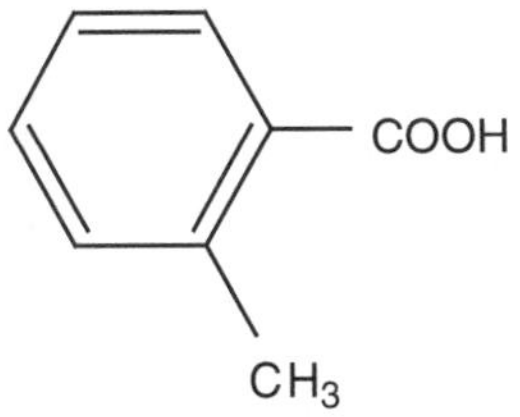

III. Br, COOH, Br

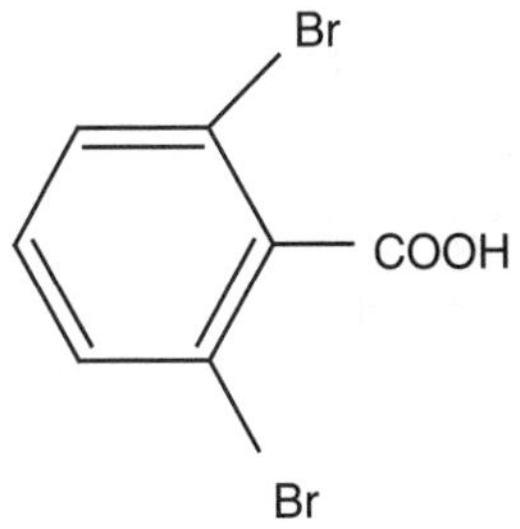

II. COOH, Br

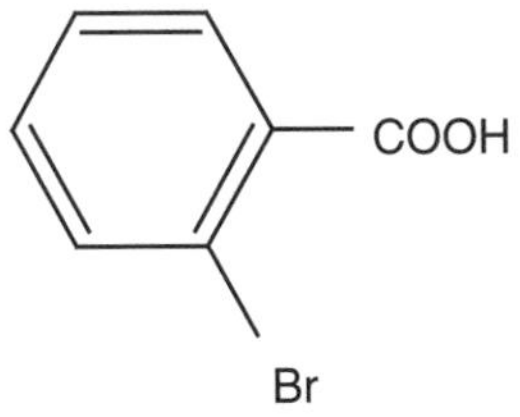

IV. Br, COOH, O, Br

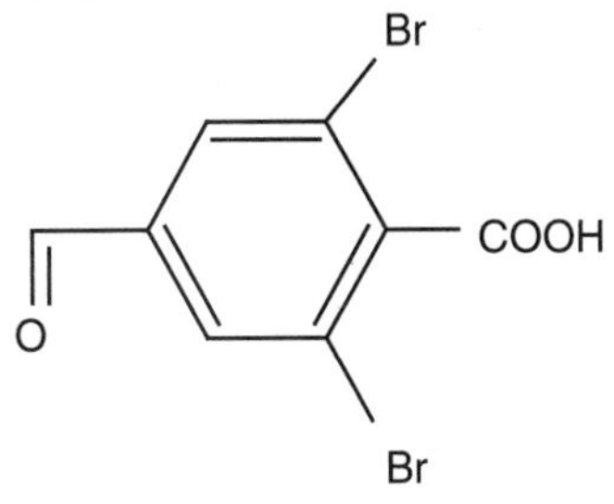

A. I < II < III < IV
B. I < II < IV < III
C. II < I < III < IV
D. II < I < IV < III
E. IV < III < II < I

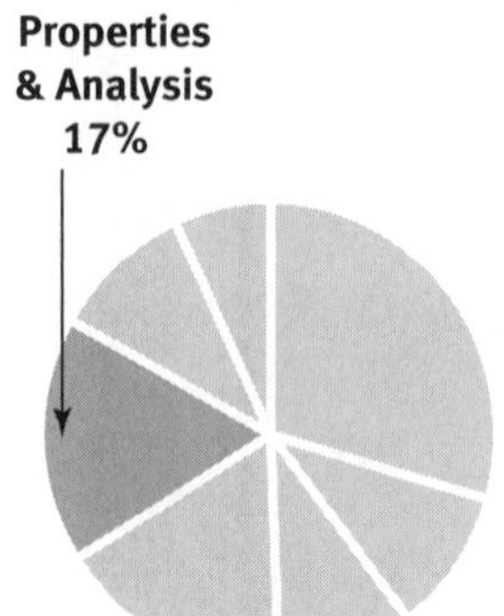

Properties of Molecules and Organic Analysis

Spectroscopy

IR

Practice Questions

27. A student attempting to determine the identity of an unknown sample employs IR spectroscopy to analyze it and obtains the following spectrum:

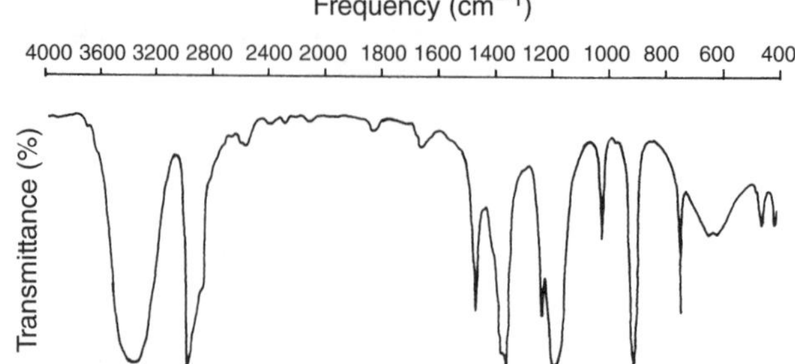

Based on the spectrum, the identity of the unknown compound is most likely to be

A. butanamine.
B. benzaldehyde.
C. hexane.
D. propanol.
E. pentanone.

28. A chemist performs an organic synthesis that requires the oxidation of *sec*-butanol to 2-butanone. Based on the following IR spectrum, which of the following would provide the best evidence that he successfully completed this conversion?

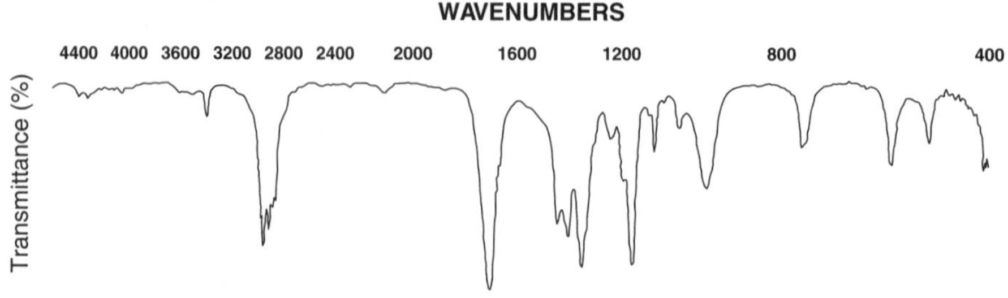

A. Noting the appearance of a broad absorption peak in the region of 1000–800 cm^{-1}
B. Noting the appearance of a strong absorption peak in the region of 1700 cm^{-1}
C. Noting the appearance of two sharp peaks at 3000 cm^{-1}
D. Noting the appearance of multiple peaks in the fingerprint region
E. Noting the appearance of a broad absorption peak in the region of 1900–2700 cm^{-1}

Nuclear Magnetic Resonance (NMR)

^{1}H NMR

Practice Questions

29. Which of the following compounds will produce the given ^{1}H NMR spectrum?

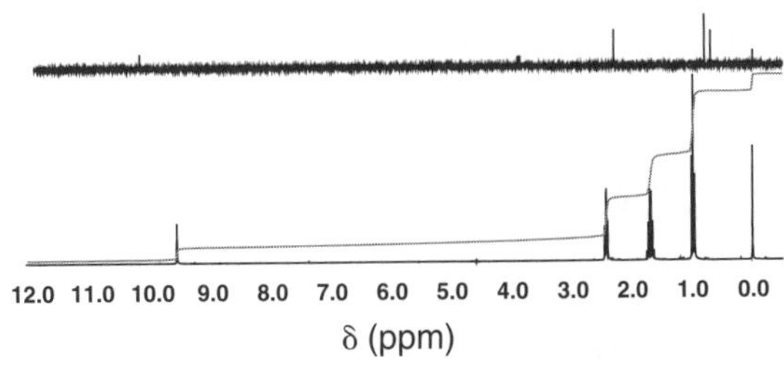

A. 2-Chloropentane
B. Butanal
C. Benzoic acid
D. Methanal
E. 2-Pentene

30. Which of the following compounds will produce the given ^{1}H NMR spectrum?

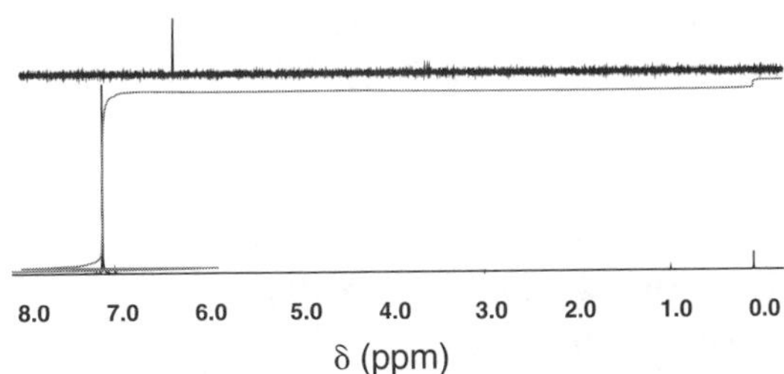

A. Benzene
B. Benzoic acid
C. Acetone
D. Methane
E. Octene

^{13}C NMR

Practice Questions

31. How many peaks would you expect to see on a ^{13}C NMR spectrum of toluene, shown below?

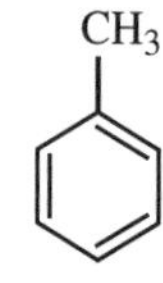

toluene

A. 1
B. 3
C. 5
D. 7
E. 9

32. Which of the following spectra most likely corresponds to alanine, shown below?

alanine

A. 168.10 ppm, 159.91 ppm, 144.05 ppm, 95.79 ppm
B. 207.85 ppm, 172.69 ppm, 29.29 ppm
C. 178.54 ppm, 53.25 ppm, 18.95 ppm
D. 183.81 ppm, 182. 63 ppm, 73.06 ppm, 45.35 ppm
E. 167.9 ppm, 136.5 ppm, 125.4 ppm, 51.8 ppm, 18.4 ppm

Practice Questions

33. A chemist observes a broad IR stretch at 3,400 cm^{-1}. Which of the following groups is being observed?

    A. C=O
    B. N–H
    C. O–H
    D. C=C
    E. C–H

34. How many peaks would you expect to see on a proton NMR spectrum of (*E*)-buten-2-ol?

    A. 0
    B. 1
    C. 2
    D. 3
    E. 4

35. A proton is one bond away from only a methyl group of which all protons are equivalent. What is the splitting pattern seen on the first proton?

    A. Singlet
    B. Doublet
    C. Triplet
    D. Quadruplet
    E. No splitting is seen.

Separation

Extraction

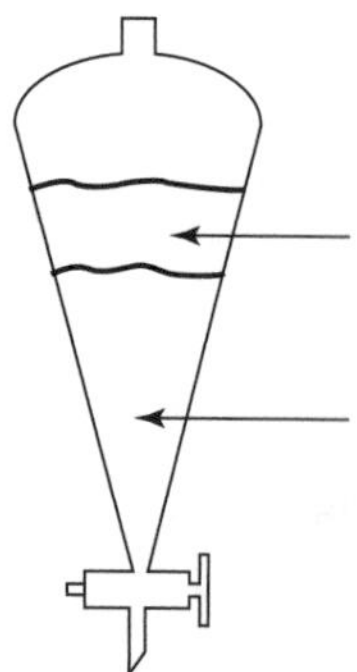

Aqueous Layer

Organic Layer

Intermolecular Forces

Using Acids and Bases

Distillation

Simple

Fractional

Vacuum

> **STUDY TIP**
> The DAT does not expect you to be an organic lab expert. Memorize the key values for spectroscopy, but otherwise focus on the concepts behind how lab techniques work rather than every specific detail.

Practice Questions

36. A chemist plans to purify a mixture of two liquids by using distillation followed by recrystallization. What must be true of the two liquids in order for this technique to be successful?

    A. The liquids must have different solubilities.
    B. The liquids must have different molecular weights.
    C. The liquids must have different densities.
    D. The liquids must have different precipitates.
    E. The liquids must have different boiling points.

37. At the end of an experiment, a solution of benzoic acid is contaminated with cresol. A student attempts to isolate benzoic acid by carrying out two extraction experiments. Part of the mixture is extracted using NaOH and the other part is extracted using $NaHCO_3$. Spectroscopic data shows that the extraction was more successful using $NaHCO_3$. Why would these results be observed?

    A. $NaHCO_3$ is a weak base and only deprotonates cresol, whereas NaOH protonates both cresol and benzoic acid.
    B. $NaHCO_3$ is a weak base and only deprotonates benzoic acid, whereas NaOH reacts with both cresol and benzoic acid.
    C. $NaHCO_3$ is a weak base and only protonates cresol, whereas NaOH protonates both cresol and benzoic acid.
    D. $NaHCO_3$ is a strong base and protonates both benzoic acid and cresol, but NaOH only reacts with benzoic acid.
    E. $NaHCO_3$ is a strong base and only protonates benzoic acid, whereas NaOH reacts with both cresol and benzoic acid.

38. An alcohol distillery wants to obtain 100% ethanol. They currently have an azeotropic mixture of 95% ethanol, which means that the ethanol and water boil at the same temperature. What technique should be used to separate this mixture?

    A. Simple distillation
    B. Fractional distillation
    C. Vacuum distillation
    D. Recrystallization
    E. It is impossible to separate an azeotropic mixture.

Study Plan

After Class: Organic Chemistry 2		
Complete Remaining *Lesson Book* Practice Questions	30m	
Organic Chemistry Test A	30m	
Practice with Tests and Quizzes		
Before Class: Reading Comprehension 2		
Read *Review Notes* Chapter 54	60m	

READING COMPREHENSION 2

TOPICS COVERED

- Kaplan Reading Comprehension Strategy Review
- Running Out of Time Strategy

After this session you will be able to:

- Apply the strategies you have already learned to any question on your exam

Kaplan Reading Comprehension Strategy Review

READ STRATEGICALLY

- ➜ Preview the passage for Topic
- ➜ Anticipate while reading using Keywords
- ➜ Map each paragraph's Scope
- ➜ Determine the author's Tone
- ➜ Identify the author's overall Purpose

The Kaplan Question Strategy

STOP

- ➜ Characterize the question type.

THINK

- ➜ What is the question really asking?
- ➜ Where is the relevant information you need?

PREDICT

- ➜ Formulate a framework or prediction for your answer.

MATCH

- ➜ Select the answer that truly meets the requirements of the prediction.

Question Types

Type	Task
Global	
Detail	
Detail EXCEPT	
Tone	
Function	
Inference	
Strengthen/Weaken	

Identify the question type for the following question stems:

1. According to the passage, the goal of Flowers's experiment was to
2. The author mentions excavations at Susa in order to
3. Which of the following most accurately describes the passage?
4. Which of the following would most weaken Janis's hypothesis?
5. Each of the following is listed as an example of a difference between the giant panda and a typical bear EXCEPT one. Which is the EXCEPTION?
6. Which of the following best describes the author's tone in the passage?
7. It can be inferred from the passage that some researchers believe that the site discovered in the Yucatan

a. Global

b. Detail

c. Detail EXCEPT

d. Tone

e. Function

f. Inference

g. Strengthen/ Weaken

Kaplan Answer Choice Strategy

Wrong Answer Choice Pathologies

Pathology	Why It's Wrong	Why It's Seductive
Faulty Use of Detail		
Opposite		
Distortion		
Out of Scope		

Passage 1

Mapping Exercise

Heart Disease

(1). Today, there is a fairly standard model of the factors leading to heart disease. Most heart disease is caused by the growth of fatty deposits, known as atherosclerotic plaques, in coronary artery walls. Plaques narrow the width of arteries and also lead to the formation of clots that can block the flow of blood, eventually causing a heart attack. Factors such as high blood pressure, smoking, and diabetes increase the risk of heart disease. High levels of cholesterol and saturated fats in the diet also increase the risk because they contribute to plaque formation.

(2). A sizable minority of coronary patients, however, experience heart attacks even though they display few or no standard risk factors. Recent research by Richard M. Lawn suggests that lipoprotein(a), a blood protein first isolated in the 1960s, may play a major role in such cases. Excessive levels of lipoprotein(a) are associated with strokes, heart attacks, and the narrowing of coronary arteries. In fact, males with high lipoprotein(a) levels account for about one quarter of male heart attack victims under the age of 60.

(3). Lipoprotein(a) is closely related to low-density lipoprotein (LDL), a major contributor to atherosclerosis. As a group, lipoproteins absorb and transport fatty substances, including cholesterol, to various sites in the body. High-density lipoproteins, or HDLs, are protective and carry cholesterol to the liver for later use in the synthesis of important hormones; LDLs, however, deposit cholesterol in the bloodstream, including in coronary arteries, where it contributes to plaque formation. Lipoprotein(a) has almost the same complex structure as LDL, with an additional surface protein called apolipoprotein(a). Apolipoprotein(a) resembles plasminogen, a protein that binds with and dissolves fibrin, a key component of blood clots. Unlike plasminogen, however, apolipoprotein(a) does not dissolve fibrin.

(4). A theory that would adequately explain how lipoprotein(a) operates has yet to be developed. But there is speculation that when too much lipoprotein(a) is present in the arteries, it may compete with plasminogen for access to fibrin in arterial blood clots. Since lipoprotein(a) cannot dissolve fibrin, the dissolution of clots is hampered, increasing the risk of arterial blockage. Another negative function has been suggested as well: Lipoprotein(a), which enters blood vessel walls inside white blood cells known as macrophages, may prompt the release of growth factors by macrophages that thicken artery walls.

Predicting Exercise

Read each question stem, then Stop – Think – Predict. Write down your prediction for each question in a few words.

8. The passage is primarily concerned with

9. Which of the following statements best describes the author's view about research on lipoprotein(a)?

10. According to the passage, which of the following is a difference between lipoprotein(a) and low-density lipoprotein?

11. The author suggests which of the following about the "standard model" (paragraph 1) of the causes of heart disease?

12. According to the passage, research has shown that lipoprotein(a)

13. The passage implies that three-fourths of heart attacks in males under age 60 must occur from

14. Which of the following, if true, would strengthen the theory that lipoprotein(a) contributes to heart disease?

15. The author refers to lipoprotein(a)'s competition with plasminogen (paragraph 4) in order to

Matching Exercise

8. The passage is primarily concerned with

   A. discussing the possible role of lipoprotein(a) in some cases of heart disease.
   B. refuting the standard model of risk factors that may lead to heart disease.
   C. examining the evidence for two opposing theories about the function of lipoprotein(a).
   D. proposing that the structure of plasminogen is similar to the structure of apolipoprotein(a).
   E. explaining the cause of heart disease seen in the majority of patients.

9. Which of the following statements best describes the author's view about research on lipoprotein(a)?

   A. Although lipoprotein(a) contributes to heart disease, research on its specific functions has not yet begun.
   B. Research has provided some insight into lipoprotein(a)'s role in heart disease.
   C. Lipoprotein(a) is believed to cause heart disease, but further study of its role has been delayed by technical problems.
   D. Recent test results have determined that lipoprotein(a) does not contribute to heart disease among males under 60.
   E. The research conducted by Richard Lawn is outdated and should not be considered valid.

10. According to the passage, which of the following is a difference between lipoprotein(a) and low-density lipoprotein?

   A. Lipoprotein(a) causes damage to the liver, while low-density lipoprotein causes damage to arteries.
   B. Lipoprotein(a) has only positive functions, while low-density lipoprotein has only negative functions.
   C. Lipoprotein(a)'s functions are taken into account by the standard model of heart disease, while the functions of low-density lipoprotein are not.
   D. Lipoprotein(a) probably contributes to plaque formation by releasing growth factors, while low-density lipoprotein contributes to plaque formation by putting cholesterol into the bloodstream.
   E. Lipoprotein(a) dissolves fibrin to aid in blood clotting, while low-density lipoprotein carries cholesterol to the liver to be used in hormone synthesis.

11. The author suggests which of the following about the "standard model" (paragraph 1) of the causes of heart disease?

    A. It misidentifies the most frequent causes of heart disease.
    B. It has been undermined by research on lipoprotein(a).
    C. It does not account for a significant number of heart disease cases.
    D. It is no longer credible to most heart disease researchers.
    E. It also explains the increased number of strokes in heart disease patients.

12. According to the passage, research has shown that lipoprotein(a)

    A. is more closely related to plasminogen than to low-density lipoprotein.
    B. functions in the same way as low-density lipoprotein.
    C. may decrease the risk of heart disease for some people.
    D. resembles low-density lipoprotein in structure.
    E. contributes to atherosclerosis by attacking the liver.

13. The passage implies that three-fourths of heart attacks in males under age 60 must occur from

    A. high lipoprotein(a) levels.
    B. high levels of low-density lipoprotein.
    C. high levels of high-density lipoproteins.
    D. the inability to dissolve fibrin.
    E. factors other than high lipoprotein(a) levels.

14. Which of the following, if true, would strengthen the theory that lipoprotein(a) contributes to heart disease?

    A. It interferes with clot formation in coronary arteries.
    B. It is more closely related to high-density lipoprotein than to low-density lipoprotein.
    C. It assists in transporting cholesterol to the liver.
    D. It is unable to absorb and transport fatty substances within the body.
    E. It causes the release of growth factors in blood vessels.

15. The author refers to lipoprotein(a)'s competition with plasminogen (paragraph 4) in order to

    A. provide evidence for the standard model of heart disease.
    B. speculate about lipoprotein(a)'s correlation to growth factor release.
    C. suggest how lipoprotein(a) may increase the risk of arterial blockage.
    D. describe the way fibrin dissolves lipoprotein(a) instead of plasminogen.
    E. explain how lipoprotein(a) can enter blood vessels through macrophages.

STUDY TIP

You can re-create this exercise on your own with any of your Reading Comprehension practice passages. Continue to practice mapping, predicting, and matching to become an expert at the Kaplan Methods.

Running Out of Time Strategy

READ LESS OF THE PASSAGE

- ➜ Read only the first and last paragraphs completely.
- ➜ Read only the first sentence of each body paragraph.
- ➜ Make a shorter map
- ➜ Skim for proper nouns when tackling questions.

TRIAGE THE QUESTIONS MORE

- ➜ Select an answer for every question.
- ➜ Complete the least time-consuming questions first.
- ➜ Avoid trap answers.

DON'T PANIC

Risk Assessment

(1). Over 40 years ago, former President Nixon signed the National Environmental Policy Act, this nation's first major federal environmental law. **Although** the nation has now witnessed several decades of continuing debate about environmental law, a relatively new element has recently entered the **controversy**: the **use of risk assessment** procedures to determine levels of acceptable risk from threats of hazardous wastes.

(2). **Before** the development of risk assessment as a decision-making tool, when a spill of a pollutant occurred, a government agency often simply told the responsible party to remove the pollutant. Blah blah blah blah. blah blah, blah blah blah. Blah blah blah blah. blah blah, blah blah blah. Blah blah blah blah. blah blah, blah blah blah. Blah blah blah blah. blah blah, blah blah blah. Blah blah blah blah. blah blah, blah blah blah. Blah blah blah blah. blah blah, blah blah blah. Blah blah blah blah. blah blah, blah blah blah. Blah blah blah blah. blah blah, blah blah blah. Blah blah blah blah. blah blah, blah blah blah. Blah blah blah blah. blah blah, blah blah blah. Blah blah blah blah. blah blah, blah blah blah. Blah blah blah blah. blah blah, blah blah blah.

(3). **But** are risk assessments really neutral scientific procedures? Blah blah blah blah. blah blah, blah blah blah.

(4). Environmental decisions based on **current risk assessment procedures** should therefore be viewed primarily as **ethical choices** rather than as technically dictated conclusions. Blah blah blah blah. blah blah, blah blah blah. Blah blah blah blah. blah blah, blah blah blah. Blah blah blah blah. blah blah, blah blah blah. Blah blah blah blah. blah blah, blah blah blah. Blah blah blah blah. blah blah, blah blah blah. Blah blah blah blah. blah blah, blah blah blah. Blah blah blah blah. blah blah, blah blah blah. Blah blah blah blah. blah blah, blah blah blah.

16. Which one of the following best expresses the main point of the passage?

    A. Risk assessment is an improvement over past cleanup methods because it is based more on factual evidence than on intuition.
    B. Former President Nixon did more than his predecessors to protect the environment from pollutants by approving the use of risk assessment.
    C. The EPA should mandate the use of thoroughly tested scientific procedures proven to be most effective in removing hazardous waste.
    D. While the concept of risk assessment is enticing from a scientific viewpoint, this method is so expensive that its use is impractical on a large scale.
    E. Though risk assessment is perhaps more scientific than previous pollution control measures, the claim that risk assessment is a value-free process is not wholly credible.

17. Each of the following is explicitly mentioned in the passage as part of the risk assessment process EXCEPT one. Which one is the EXCEPTION?

    A. Visual observation
    B. Exposure assessment
    C. Hazard identification
    D. Risk characterization
    E. Chemical neutralization

18. The author most probably mentions confidence levels (paragraph 3) in order to

    A. demonstrate that risk assessment is more scientific than past cleanup methods.
    B. question the accuracy of post-cleanup visual observations currently in use.
    C. suggest that the government should eliminate ambiguities in its environmental cleanup agenda.
    D. show that nonscientific principles can affect the results of scientific processes.
    E. defend the procedures currently in use for hazard identification and risk characterization.

19. The author suggests which one of the following about pollution cleanup methods that predated the development of risk assessment?

 A. They are considered to be completely ineffective in protecting the environment.
 B. Many environmental professionals are not satisfied with the results produced by these methods.
 C. They are often difficult to apply because they depend on precise scientific measurements.
 D. The best features of these methods should be integrated into the risk assessment process.
 E. They were more effective and less expensive because they did not involve any ethical choices.

20. The passage's reference to the factual and scientific basis of the risk assessment process in paragraph 2 serves which one of the following functions?

 A. It explains the government's unwillingness to choose between older pollution cleanup methods and risk assessment.
 B. It provides background information about how hazardous waste was handled prior to environmental law.
 C. It introduces pollution control policy choices for which there is no a priori assessment method.
 D. It highlights the attitude of environmentalists toward the National Environmental Policy Act.
 E. It underscores the belief of environmentalists that risk assessment is a useful method for controlling pollution.

21. The author of the passage is primarily concerned with

 A. explaining why government should make explicit the ethical choices involved in environmental cleanup.
 B. highlighting government's inability to deal effectively with pollution cleanup.
 C. reviewing the evolution of pollution cleanup methods over the past two decades.
 D. proposing a new method for environmental cleanup that incorporates the best features of risk assessment.
 E. suggesting that government complete additional research on hazardous waste before signing environmental laws.

TAKEAWAY

You can still get points on Test Day even if you don't have time to read every word of the passage. Always use the Kaplan Method to get your easiest points first.

Passage 2

The Corpus Callosum

(1). The evolution of the vertebrate brain occurred primarily in the cerebrum, not the brainstem. The brainstems of all vertebrates, no matter their complexity, are roughly the same size, but this is not so for their cerebrums. The mammal cerebrum has grown so large that it folds in on itself to form a right and left hemisphere, connected by a dense network of neurons called commissures. The most significant of the commissures is the corpus callosum, whose size dwarfs that of the other parts of the mammalian brain.

(2). There is a division of labor in the brain, as in all other parts of the body. There are divisions between the cerebrum and the brainstem, as well as within the various regions of each hemisphere of the cerebrum. However, more interesting for our purposes are the divisions across hemispheres and the role of the corpus callosum, especially in the human brain.

(3). It has long been known that the effects of damage to one hemisphere of the brain often differ radically from the effects of similar damage to the other hemisphere. For instance, injury to the left hemisphere of the human brain often impairs or destroys speech ability, whereas an analogous injury to the right hemisphere does not. For this reason, the left hemisphere has long been regarded as the hemisphere that controls speech and language and that therefore is dominant over its right hemisphere counterpart, which has been characterized as mute, minor, or passive.

(4). However, this reasoning can be misleading in several ways. First, a sizable minority, 10 percent of right-handed people and 35 percent of left-handed people, have their speech areas in the right hemisphere. Second, it has been documented that if the damage to one hemisphere occurs early enough in infant development, the other hemisphere may eventually adapt and take over the tasks usually carried out by its now-damaged counterpart. Indeed, in the mid-nineteenth century, A. L. Wigan, a British physician, performed autopsies on men who apparently led normal lives, yet had only half a brain.

(5). Third, and most importantly, the right hemisphere, though not usually the control center for speech, is far from passive. It controls many visual-motor tasks, so that a person whose right hemisphere is damaged may have difficulty navigating in new areas and fail to recognize familiar surroundings and people. It also seems to be the center for musical talent, so that damage to the right hemisphere may result in a loss of musical ability and yet leave speech unimpaired.

(6). Because of these and other similar facts, people who excel in analytical and verbal tasks, or who are logical and sequential in their problem-solving approaches, are often called left-brained, whereas people who excel at visual and creative tasks, or who are more holistic and novel in the problem-solving are called right-brained. Of course, such characterizations can also be quite misleading.

(7). Of much recent interest is the role played by the corpus callosum, specifically whether—and in what ways—the two hemispheres of the brain can interact when the corpus callosum is severed. In the late 1930s, neurosurgeons discovered that severing the corpus callosum significantly retarded the severity of, or even halted altogether the occurrence of, seizures in certain epileptic patients. More remarkably, these patients seemed to suffer no side effects in personality, behavior, or otherwise. All outward appearances in such patients seemed not to change after their radical treatment. One patient, his sense of humor still intact, even wryly complained of having a "splitting headache."

(8). This naturally led scientists to wonder about the function of the corpus callosum. In the early 1960s, psychobiologist Roger Sperry of the California Institute of Technology began groundbreaking research on just this question. He and his associates designed tests to investigate the behavior of the epileptics who had undergone this radical treatment. In general, the research indicated that in most situations these patients were able to function normally, but placing them under certain carefully controlled conditions led to surprising results. In brief, in certain situations these patients seemed to behave as if they had two separate brains, hence the name "split-brain patient."

(9). Brain wiring is in many cases contralateral, and this holds for the processing of visual information. Thus, information from the right visual field is processed in the left hemisphere of the brain, and likewise information from the left visual field is processed in the right hemisphere of the brain. The same holds true for hand and finger control: The right hemisphere controls the left hand, and the left hemisphere controls the right hand.

(10). Perhaps the most striking of Sperry's discoveries was that visual information could no longer move between the two sides of the brain. In these tests, the subjects were seated in front of a screen on which images could be flashed to either side of her visual field but not the other. The subject's hands were also kept from her own view. This way, the information processed in each hemisphere could be isolated and controlled.

(11). Sperry discovered that if an image was projected to the right visual field of a split-brain patient, thereby being processed in the left hemisphere, the patient could easily describe the image vocally because the left hemisphere controls speech. However, the same image projected only to the opposite, left visual field could not be likewise described; the patient would draw a blank when asked to describe what she saw. Yet in this case, if the patient were asked to point to an object similar to the image seen, she could do so with ease. For instance, in one test, the researchers flashed a dollar sign image to the right visual field of one subject and a question mark to his left visual field. When asked to draw what he saw, he drew the question mark, the image that had been processed in the right hemisphere. When asked to state what he saw, without hesitation he said "a dollar sign," corresponding to the image processed in the left hemisphere. This suggests that the right hemisphere can process the image as well as the left and can even mobilize a non-verbal response, but it cannot provide speech about what it sees in the way that the left hemisphere can.

(12). The same results applied in similar tests for touch, smell, and sound. For instance, when a spoon was placed in the right hand of a test subject, it could be easily identified orally because the left hemisphere controls the right hand; however, the same spoon placed in the subject's left hand could not likewise be identified. One subject even complained about his sinister left hand, which continually tried to undo the work of his right hand, e.g., pulling down his trousers as his right hand attempted to put them on.

(13). These findings initially created quite a stir, sparking a flurry of popular interest in the psychological consequences of these "two realms of consciousness," but most such speculations proved unwarranted by the hard data. Still, the results have had lasting scientific significance, enough to earn Sperry the Nobel Prize in medicine in 1981. They strongly suggest a very sharp and intricate division of labor between the two hemispheres of the brain and also answer, at least partially, the riddle of the corpus callosum: Its function, or at least one of its functions, is to integrate all of the different roles performed by the two hemispheres of the brain.

(14). Of course, the brain is one of the least understood organs of the body, and many questions still remain unanswered. Some researchers are currently investigating the role of the more minor commissures between the hemispheres, and whether these lesser neural pathways can serve to conduct information between the hemispheres even when the corpus callosum is severed. Some scientists also speculate as to the evolutionary reasons behind such lateralization, or specialization between hemispheres. Suffice it to say that Sperry's findings, like all groundbreaking research, both answered many significant questions and raised many new ones.

22. Each of the following kinds of division of labor is specifically mentioned in the passage EXCEPT one. Which one is the EXCEPTION?

    A. That between different types of commissures
    B. That between different areas within the same hemisphere
    C. That between different hemispheres
    D. That between the brainstem and cerebrum
    E. That between different parts of the body in general

23. According to the passage, which of the following actions might result in improvement in a person's seizures?

    A. Removing a portion of the left hemisphere
    B. Removing a portion of the right hemisphere
    C. Severing the corpus callosum
    D. Limiting the visual material presented to the left hemisphere
    E. Providing anticonvulsant drug therapy

24. Which of the following best describes the goal of the passage?

    A. To explain the research conducted by Roger Sperry
    B. To evaluate the effectiveness of split-brain studies
    C. To recommend that split-brain patients receive adequate treatment
    D. To convey details of case studies of split-brain patients
    E. To describe the role of the corpus callosum based on research

25. A brain-damaged patient who is easily disoriented and who fails to recognize family members but whose speech is unimpaired is most likely brain-damaged in which of the following areas?

    A. The right hemisphere
    B. The left hemisphere
    C. Both hemispheres
    D. The corpus callosum
    E. The evidence is inconclusive

26. A person with left hemisphere brain damage will definitely display which of the following characteristics?

    A. Slurring of speech and diminished writing ability
    B. Loss of musical and artistic ability
    C. Split-brain personality
    D. None, except under carefully controlled situations
    E. The age of the patient at the time of the damage determines what effects would be displayed.

27. Which of the following is NOT among the reasons the author cites to support the principle that most changes in the brain leading up to the vertebrate brain occurred in the cerebrum?

    A. The size of the cerebrum
    B. The complexity of the cerebrum
    C. How the cerebrum differs from other parts of the mammalian brain
    D. The lack of correlation between the size of the brainstem and the complexity of the vertebrate
    E. The large number of neuronal connections in the corpus callosum

28. Which of the following best describes the author's tone used when describing Sperry's research?

    A. Laudatory, because Sperry's research explained the evolutionary advantage for lateralization
    B. Nostalgic about the way that Sperry's findings were able confirm the results of Wigan's previous research
    C. Cynical about the ability of the results to help answer the riddle of the corpus callosum
    D. Intrigued by the possibility that Sperry's findings may help treat epileptic patients without severed corpora callosa
    E. Earnest about the significance of Sperry's research in determining the function of the corpus callosum

29. The author sometimes speaks loosely of the left and right hemispheres of the brain, but more precisely the hemispheres are of the

    A. brainstem.
    B. cerebrum.
    C. corpus callosum.
    D. commissures.
    E. cerebellum.

30. Which of the following most clearly states the riddle of the corpus callosum?

    A. Severing the corpus callosum seemed to have no ill effect on subjects.
    B. Severing the corpus callosum leads to split-brain personalities.
    C. The difference in function between the corpus callosum and the other commissures was unclear.
    D. Severing the corpus callosum can result in impairment of both right-brain and left-brain functions.
    E. The corpus callosum's function in humans differs from that in other mammals.

31. Which of the following would most weaken the conclusions of Sperry's research?

    A. A subject with a severed corpus callosum is prevented from retrieving an object because her right and left hands work against each other.
    B. A subject with a severed corpus callosum cannot orally describe an object placed in her left hand.
    C. A subject with a severed corpus callosum cannot point to an object similar to one seen in her right visual field.
    D. A subject with an intact corpus callosum cannot orally describe an object seen in her left visual field.
    E. A subject with a severed corpus callosum could draw with her left hand an object seen in her right visual field.

32. The author mentions that "brain wiring is in many cases contralateral" (paragraph 9) in order to

    A. provide another way to talk about split-brain patients.
    B. compare the anatomy of the mammalian brain to the brains of other vertebrates.
    C. describe why the methods of Sperry's research were successful.
    D. explain how the right hemisphere controls the left hand and vice versa.
    E. introduce the reader to a scientific term critical to understanding the passage.

33. The passage suggests that a more complex vertebrate has a brain with

    A. a left and right hemisphere.
    B. a larger brainstem.
    C. more commissures.
    D. a larger cerebrum.
    E. a larger corpus callosum.

34. It can be inferred from the passage that the author believes which of the following regarding the relationship between the left and right hemispheres of the brain?

A. The left hemisphere dominates the right.
B. The right hemisphere dominates the left.
C. Neither hemisphere dominates; each carries out the same functions.
D. Neither hemisphere dominates; each carries out different functions.
E. The dominating hemisphere is determined by handedness.

35. Which of the following best illustrates the concept of lateralization?

A. The right hemisphere of the brain controls the left hand; the left hemisphere controls the right hand.
B. Damage to one hemisphere of the brain in young-enough subjects can sometimes be compensated for by the other hemisphere.
C. Visual and auditory information is conveyed across the brain hemispheres by the corpus callosum.
D. The speech center for a significant number of left-handed people resides in the right hemisphere of their brains.
E. The right hemisphere of the brain controls musical ability; the left hemisphere controls speech.

36. Which of the following symptoms is likely to be experienced by a patient with a severed corpus callosum under normal conditions?

A. Loss of musical ability
B. Debilitating headaches
C. Development of a wry sense of humor
D. Impaired speech
E. Usually no symptoms are present under normal conditions.

37. What is the purpose of paragraph 4 in the context of the passage?

A. To introduce Wigan's research as the precedent for Sperry's research
B. To correct a misconception about the dominance of the left brain
C. To provide examples of anomalies in infant development
D. To show that some people might have their speech areas in the right hemisphere
E. To present evidence that humans are able to adapt after a traumatic brain injury

Passage 3

Health Benefits of Eye Exams

(1). While eye exams are commonly used to measure and correct vision, they serve an important preventative function as well. There are many different components to a routine eye exam designed to gather information far beyond a patient's visual acuity. Optometrists check each patient's cornea, retina, pupil, iris, optic nerve, ocular pressure, and veins and arteries during an exam. While many of the tests an optometrist completes are intended to provide information about eye health, exams may also reveal important information about overall health, leading to diagnoses of other diseases.

(2). One common component of an eye exam is eye tracking. The patient is asked to look at a target, and his eye movements are recorded while the target moves slightly. This test helps measure eye muscle strength and control, but recent research suggests that eye tracking tests can also serve as an early detection method for Alzheimer's disease. In two studies, the Retinal Amyloid Index and Sapphire II, participants diagnosed with Alzheimer's disease or Parkinson's disease and healthy individuals of various ages were asked to track a light and then look away. It was found that participants with Alzheimer's were up to ten times more likely to make mistakes during these experiments. Healthcare professionals are excited about the possibility that this simple test can help diagnose Alzheimer's because early diagnosis is essential to successful management of the disease.

(3). Pupil dilation is also commonly used as part of an eye exam. When the pupil is dilated, the optometrist can effectively examine the retina and other structures behind the eye. During this part of the exam, special attention is paid to the blood vessels; abnormalities with the vascular system attached to the eye can be a sign of larger cardiovascular problems or diabetes. Sometimes these abnormalities may occur even before other risk factors are apparent.

(4). More specifically, patients may have signs of retinopathy that could be caused by hypertension or diabetes. A patient with retinopathy may have bleeding or oozing, blood vessel narrowing, or damage to the macula or optic nerve. Patients with diabetes are at risk of diabetic retinopathy, which can lead to blindness. In fact, preventive eye care is an important part of the treatment plan for patients diagnosed with diabetes. These patients are at greater risk for glaucoma, cataracts, and other changes in vision.

(5). Interestingly, another disease that can be diagnosed by examining the retina is familial colorectal polyposis. Also known as Gardner syndrome, this autosomal dominant disease is characterized by polyps in the colon. There is no cure for Gardner syndrome, but treatment can help reduce the risk of colon cancer in affected patients. Optometrists may notice specific lesions on the retina that can tip them off to potential problems in the colon. When these lesions are accompanied by scarring without a known reason, such as trauma or other illness, the optometrist will likely inquire about colon health and may send the patient to a gastroenterologist for further examination.

(6). While many of the aforementioned diseases may be diagnosed despite the patient not experiencing other symptoms, sometimes patients will specifically schedule an appointment with an optometrist because they are experiencing eye-related symptoms. These eye-related symptoms may be limited to problems with the eye, oftentimes indicated by changes in vision. For example, blurred, dim, or hazy vision could indicate cataracts, which is a reversible clouding of the vision due to deposits on the lens of the eye. But several symptoms that may point to cataracts could also be indicative of alternate diagnoses.

(7). Many patients affected by cataracts have difficulty with night vision. However, decreased night vision can also be a sign of vitamin A deficiency. Vitamin A can be found in several foods including liver, leafy greens, and carrots. In the eye, vitamin A is used in the form of retinal and combines with the protein opsin to make rhodopsin. Rhodopsin is critical for night and low-light vision. If left untreated, a deficiency of vitamin A can lead to ulcers on the cornea, which can progress to irreversible blindness. Thus, when a patient complains of difficulty seeing in low light, an optometrist will investigate the root of the cause since it could potentially be very serious.

(8). Another symptom that may be concerning to a patient is yellowing of the whites of the eyes, which are known as the sclerae. Yellowing of the eyes is related to jaundice, which also causes yellowing of the skin. The eyes will sometimes yellow before the skin, so this symptom can be an early indicator of an underlying issue. Jaundice is most commonly caused by problems with the liver but can also be a symptom of gall bladder or pancreatic issues. The yellowing is a result of excess bilirubin, which is a product of broken down red blood cells. Increased levels of bilirubin can be a side effect of some medications as well as chemotherapy but can also indicate a serious underlying condition such as bile duct obstruction, liver failure, or pancreatic cancer.

(9). Many other eye-related symptoms can point to still more diseases. Bulging eyes are a symptom of Grave's disease, an autoimmune disease that leads to hyperthyroidism. Chronic drooping eyelids can be caused by the autoimmune disease myasthenia gravis, whereas an acute eyelid droop could potentially be a symptom of a brain aneurysm. The inability to close one eye may be due to Bell's palsy. Sudden changes in vision can also indicate a stroke or a risk of stroke, so medical attention should be sought immediately when these symptoms are experienced.

(10). Healthcare professionals suggest that annual eye exams are important not only for tracking changes in vision but for monitoring overall health as well. At-risk patients such as diabetics should be especially sure to visit their optometrists every year. Healthy adults with no vision problems under the age of 60 may choose to visit an optometrist biannually. Older patients should go to their eye doctors yearly because vision changes more quickly with age. Regardless of patient age, the benefits of regular eye exams are clear.

38. Why are healthcare professionals excited about the results of the Retinal Amyloid Index study?

    A. Participants with Alzheimer's disease were much more likely to make mistakes in the experiment than other participants.
    B. Measurements of eye-muscle strength and control can help prevent the development of Alzheimer's disease.
    C. Previous tests using eye tracking required a target other than light in order to produce meaningful results.
    D. The test used in the study can be used to diagnose Alzheimer's disease earlier for more effective disease management.
    E. Eye tracking is already a commonly used test in most routine eye exams performed by optometrists.

39. According to the passage, each of the following is commonly completed as part of an eye exam EXCEPT one. Which one is the EXCEPTION?

    A. Eye tracking
    B. Low-light ocular test
    C. Pupil dilation
    D. Iris examination
    E. Visual acuity measurement

40. According to the passage, which of the following is an example of an eye-related disease that patients with diabetes are at greater risk for developing?

    A. Grave's disease
    B. Bell's palsy
    C. Cataracts
    D. Hypertensive retinopathy
    E. Jaundice

41. The author discusses the eye-related symptoms of each of the following conditions EXCEPT one. Which one is the EXCEPTION?

    A. Gardner syndrome
    B. Myasthenia gravis
    C. Rhodopsin deficiency
    D. Drug intoxication
    E. Retinopathy

42. The author's tone in the passage can best be described as

    A. introspective.
    B. theoretical.
    C. patronizing.
    D. restrained.
    E. positive.

43. Which of the following most accurately depicts the Retinal Amyloid Index as described in the passage?

    A. The Retinal Amyloid Index was created based on the findings from the Sapphire II experiments.
    B. Participants who were not previously diagnosed with Alzheimer's were diagnosed with the disease during the study.
    C. The participants with Alzheimer's and the participants with Parkinson's performed similarly.
    D. Younger, healthy participants were less likely to make eye tracking mistakes than older, healthy participants.
    E. Eye tracking as used in the study may help with early detection of Alzheimer's disease in patients.

44. The passage implies that any patient who is having trouble seeing in low light is

    A. most likely to be experiencing vitamin A deficiency.
    B. unable to produce rhodopsin because of a deficiency of retinal.
    C. at greater risk of irreversible blindness if the cause is vitamin A deficiency than if the cause is cataracts.
    D. likely to develop ulcers on the cornea that will eventually lead to irreversible blindness.
    E. also likely to experience blurred, dim, or hazy vision due to problems with the lens of the eye.

45. The passage is primarily concerned with

    A. detailing the components and patient experience of a typical eye exam.
    B. outlining a recommended schedule for routine visits to an optometrist.
    C. describing the symptoms of diseases an optometrist might diagnose.
    D. comparing the diagnostic ability of optometrists and primary care physicians.
    E. providing additional reasons to visit an optometrist beyond routine visual acuity checks.

46. Which of the following is NOT provided in the passage as a sign of retinopathy?

   A. Retinal lesions
   B. Bleeding and oozing
   C. Damage to the optic nerve
   D. Blood vessel narrowing
   E. Damage to the macula

47. When a patient presents with yellowing of the sclerae, the optometrist can be confident that

   A. the patient has an obstructed bile duct.
   B. the patient is at greater risk for pancreatic cancer.
   C. the patient has excess systemic bilirubin.
   D. the patient's liver is failing.
   E. the patient is undergoing chemotherapy.

48. Which of the following best aligns with the author's recommendations regarding eye exam frequency?

   A. A healthy 52-year-old patient visits her optometrist every other year.
   B. A 33-year-old patient with diabetes visits his optometrist every other year.
   C. A 47-year-old patient with a family history of Grave's disease visits his optometrist biannually.
   D. A 67-year-old patient with no known health issues visits her optometrist biannually.
   E. A healthy 21-year-old patient visits his optometrist every three years.

49. Which of the following, if true, would most strengthen the author's argument about the health benefits of eye exams?

   A. Optometrists in some states are now legally able to provide immunizations.
   B. Many health insurance providers do not cover eye care in basic health insurance packages.
   C. Early treatment of colorectal polyposis reduces the risk of colon cancer by more than 60 percent.
   D. Vitamin A deficiency has been virtually eradicated in most industrialized nations.
   E. Periodic acute increases in serum bilirubin occur in 40 percent of people and are usually benign.

50. The sudden onset of eyelid droop may be a symptom of

A. hypothyroidism.
B. a brain aneurysm.
C. myasthenia gravis.
D. diabetes.
E. macular degeneration.

51. The author briefly discusses the symptoms associated with cataracts in paragraph 6 in order to

A. compare the symptoms associated with cataracts with the symptoms associated with vitamin A deficiency.
B. provide examples of symptoms that may prompt a patient to schedule an exam with an optometrist.
C. recommend that any patient who experiences any of the symptoms seek treatment from an optometrist.
D. explain how the optometrist's examination of the lens of the eye can support the diagnosis of cataracts.
E. express concerns that serve as a warning about the dangers of letting cataracts go undiagnosed and untreated.

52. According to the passage, how does pupil dilation help an optometrist perform an eye exam?

A. Pupil dilation helps the optometrist to measure visual acuity.
B. Pupil dilation can be used in place of the eye tracking test.
C. Pupil dilation improves the optometrist's ability to view the cornea and iris.
D. Pupil dilation allows the optometrist to examine the retina and blood vessels.
E. Pupil dilation is only utilized to rule out damage to the vascular system.

53. An optometrist is most likely to refer a patient to a gastroenterologist upon observing

A. sudden changes in vision in an otherwise healthy patient.
B. yellowing of the sclerae unaccompanied by yellowing of the skin.
C. the patient's inability to see in low light.
D. drastic changes in vision in a patient with diabetes.
E. lesions and scarring on the patient's retina.

Study Plan

After Class: Reading Comprehension 2		
Complete Remaining *Lesson Book* Practice Questions	30m	
Reading Comprehension Test B	60m	
Practice with Tests and Quizzes		

Practice Tests		
Full-Length Test 2	4h 30m	
Full-Length Test 3	4h 30m	
Full-Length Test 4	4h 30m	
Full-Length Test 5	4h 30m	

STRATEGY 2

TOPICS COVERED

- Strategy Review
- Test Day Preparation
- Test Day Countdown

After this session you will be able to:

- Plan your study calendar appropriately so you know what to do from now until Test Day

Strategy Review

The Kaplan Question Strategy

Step	Purpose	Action
Stop		
Think		
Predict		
Match		

Crisis Prevention

What if I am spending too long on a question?

What if I can't identify what the question is really asking?

What if I can't formulate a prediction?

What if I don't see my prediction in the answer choices?

Kaplan Strategy for Science

STOP

- ➜ Characterize the answer choices.

THINK

- ➜ What is the question really asking?
- ➜ What relevant information do you need?

PREDICT

- ➜ Formulate a framework or prediction for your answer.

MATCH

- ➜ Select the answer that truly meets the requirements of the prediction.

Kaplan Strategy for Reading Comprehension

READ STRATEGICALLY

- ➜ Preview the passage for Topic.
- ➜ Anticipate while reading using Keywords.
- ➜ Map each paragraph's Scope.
- ➜ Determine the author's Tone.
- ➜ Identify the author's overall Purpose.

STOP

- ➜ Characterize the question type.

THINK

- ➜ What is the question really asking?
- ➜ Where is the relevant information you need?

PREDICT

- ➜ Formulate a framework or prediction for your answer.

MATCH

- ➜ Select the answer that truly meets the requirements of the prediction.

Kaplan Strategy for Quantitative Reasoning

STOP

➜ Read the question and characterize the answer choices.

THINK

➜ What is the question really asking?

➜ Choose the best strategy to quickly and accurately solve the problem.

- **Picking Numbers:** Use manageable numbers in place of variables.
- **Backsolving:** Plug answers into question stem.
- **Educated Guessing:** Avoid trap answers.
- **Estimating:** Find an answer close to the correct answer.
- **Traditional Math:** Apply classic math formulas.

PREDICT

➜ Use the chosen strategy to formulate a framework or prediction for your answer.

MATCH

➜ Select the answer that truly meets the requirements of the prediction.

Kaplan Pacing Strategy

Kaplan Triaging Strategy

Kaplan Marking Strategy

Pacing Strategies Section by Section

Test Day Preparation

Am I Ready to Take the DAT?

✓ Have I completed all of my Kaplan assignments?

✓ Have I taken enough full-length practice tests to have a sense of my preparedness?

✓ Am I consistently scoring in my desired score range?

✓ Do I have a healthy amount of test anxiety or do I have legitimate areas of concern?

Common Testing Challenges

Symptom	Diagnosis	Prescription
Not finishing sections in time		
Needing to read the same thing over and over		
Narrowing questions down to two answers but picking the wrong choice		
Feeling burned out by Quantitative Reasoning and not performing as well in that section as possible		

Calendar Revision

- Complete any remaining course assignments.
- Recalculate time remaining until Test Day.
- Build in time to take additional full-length tests.

Higher Score Guarantee

- Attend or watch all required sessions. If you are in an instructor-led course, you can use a maximum of two Lessons On Demand as make-up sessions.
- Take all scheduled practice tests.
- Complete the required homework for your course prior to your course expiration date or exam date, whichever is earlier.

Test Day Countdown

The Day Before Test Day

- Plan your day in advance.
- Avoid studying.
- Avoid talking about the DAT.
- Relax.
- Think about your post-test activities.
- Do something you enjoy.
- Eat balanced meals.
- Gather your test materials using the Test Day Checklist.
- Get a good night's sleep.

Test Day Checklist

- ❑ Printout of your confirmation email
- ❑ Personal identification (two)
- ❑ Directions to the test center
- ❑ Kaplan Flashcards or Quick Sheets
- ❑ Extra layers of clothing
- ❑ Snacks and sports drink
- ❑ Earplugs
- ❑ Tissues
- ❑ Cough drops
- ❑ Painkillers
- ❑ Antacid

The Day of the Test

Before the Test

- Wake up on time.
- Eat your normal breakfast.
- Warm up physically and mentally.
- Wear comfortable clothing and dress in layers.
- Bring all your testing materials.
- Arrive at the test site with time to spare.

During the Test

- Do the tutorial.
- Get comfortable with the computer.
- Triage difficult questions for later.
- Answer every question.
- Reset your mind during the break.
- Focus on what is in front of you.
- Don't discuss the test during the break or after the exam.

After the Test

- Relax and celebrate!
- Tell us about your scores.
- Continue building a strong application.
- Secure letters of recommendation.
- Work on your personal statement.

Test Day Crisis Prevention

What should I do if I . . .

- start to lose confidence?

- start to lose concentration?

- take too long at the break?

- find the test environment too distracting?

What to Do Now

- Determine whether you are ready to take your test.
- Update your calendar in preparation for Test Day.
- Build your stamina and endurance.
- Contact your teachers if questions still remain.
- Remember that the entire team at Kaplan is here to help you.
- Focus on your successes!

APPENDIX

ANSWERS AND EXPLANATIONS

Reading Comprehension 1

1. C	7. E	13. C
2. A	8. A	14. A
3. D	9. C	15. A
4. B	10. D	16. C
5. D	11. C	17. D
6. D	12. D	18. D

Roadmap Sample Questions

1. C

Stop: This is a Global question because it asks about the passage as a whole.

Think: Consider the overall purpose of the passage.

Predict: The passage explains the use and advancement of refractor and reflector telescopes throughout history.

Match: The correct answer is (C). Answer choice (A) is a Faulty Use of Detail. While the different shapes of lenses is discussed in paragraph 2, that is not globally what the passage is about. Answer choice (B) is Opposite since the final paragraph states that reflectors are now preferred to refractors. Answer choice (D) is Out of Scope. The passage's scope is limited to refractor and reflector telescopes through history—not the course of science as a whole. Answer choice (E) is another Faulty Use of Detail. Dispersion is discussed in paragraphs 1 and 3, but it is not the subject of the entire passage.

2. A

Stop: The phrase "in order to" at the end of the question makes this a Function question; it asks why the author did something in the passage.

Think: Since the reference to Sir Isaac Newton is contained in paragraph 2, its purpose will be in line with paragraph 2's overall purpose. Refer to the map for paragraph 2 to determine the purpose of that paragraph. Also look for Keywords in or near the sentence referring to Sir Isaac Newton.

Predict: According to the map, paragraph 2's purpose is to outline how reflectors were tried (after problems were found with refractors in paragraph 1) and how there were also problems with the reflector telescopes. The Newton detail must support this purpose. Since the sentence referring to Newton begins with "When," it implies a causal relationship between Newton's announcement and scientists' change to reflector telescopes. In this instance "when" can be thought of as similar to "because" since Newton's announcement is the cause of the scientists' actions.

Match: The correct answer is (A). Answer choice (B) is a Faulty Use of Detail. While spherical aberrations are mentioned in paragraph 2, that is not the overall purpose of paragraph 2. Answer choice (C) is Out of Scope. The author never tries to show that early scientists frequently drew erroneous conclusions. Answer choice (D) is also Out of Scope; the author isn't concerned with analyzing Newton. Plus, if the author actually challenged Newton's brilliance, why would he mention that all it took was Newton's opinion to cause other scientists to explore reflectors? Choice (E) is another Out of Scope answer choice. As your prediction notes, paragraph 2 is about reflectors, not refractors.

3. D

Stop: This is a Detail question. "According to the passage" is the indicative language in this question stem.

Think: Locate "chromatic aberration" in your passage map. You should refer to paragraph 3. Once in paragraph 3, locate the detail that explains how chromatic aberration can be corrected. [Note that in class, this is as far as you would get in the problem since you did not actually read this passage. However, if you use the passage found at the beginning of the Reading Comprehension 1 lesson in your Lesson Book, you can continue with this problem.]

Predict: According to the passage, the problem of chromatic aberration could be corrected by using a compound lens. There are multiple ways to create a compound lens provided in the passage, so any one of those options would be correct.

Match: The correct answer is (D). This matches with Euler's approach to creating a compound lens described in paragraph 3. Answer choice (A) is a Faulty Use of Detail. A lens with a rounded surface could result in a spherical aberration, but would not correct a chromatic aberration. Answer choice (B) is also a Faulty Use of Detail. Metal alloys are related to problems found with reflectors as discussed in paragraph 2. Answer choice (C) is also a Faulty Use of Detail. This solution was given in paragraph 2 as a way to fix the light absorption problems seen in reflector telescopes. Answer choice (E) is Out of Scope, as rotating lenses aren't ever discussed.

Passage 1—The Harbor Seal

Map

Paragraph 1: harbor seal adaptations

Paragraph 2: ear

Paragraph 3: eye

Paragraph 4: echolocation

Paragraph 5: whiskers

Paragraph 6: +

Purpose: explain the harbor seal's adaptations to land and water environments

Questions

4. B

Stop: This is a Global question. The phrase "main purpose of the passage" is the clue.

Think: Refer to the overall purpose of the passage.

Predict: The purpose of the passage is to explain the harbor seal's adaptations to its two distinct habitats, land and water.

Match: Answer choice (B) matches the prediction almost exactly. Answer choices (A), (C), and (D) are all Faulty Uses of Detail. They come from paragraphs 1, 2, and 4, respectively, but none addresses the passage's main purpose. When a detail is limited to just one paragraph, it is very unlikely to be the answer to a "main purpose" question. Choice (E) is Out of Scope; while a seal's vision is discussed, the author does not compare it to the vision of any other mammal except for that of a human.

5. D

Stop: This is a Detail question. "According to the passage" is an immediate clue.

Think: Based on the map, the "sensitivity of the harbor seal's whiskers to vibrations" is discussed in paragraph 5. Refer back to that paragraph to determine why this sensitivity exists.

Predict: According to the passage, the vibrissae "may sense wave disturbances produced by nearby moving fish, allowing the seal to home in on and capture prey." This can serve as your prediction.

Match: Answer choice (D) matches this sentence in the passage. Answer choice (A) is a Distortion as the whiskers don't trigger fish to move about but instead sense when fish are already moving about. Answer choice (B) is Out of Scope as smell is not discussed in the passage. Answer choice (C) is Out of Scope as well, as balance on land is never discussed. Answer choice (E) is also Out of Scope since the passage does not relate the vibrissae to echolocation nor to sensing other seals. (E) uses the detail of "echolocation" in a faulty way, too.

6. D

Stop: This is a Detail EXCEPT question—it is looking for the detail that is not included in the passage. The word "EXCEPT" is critical to this question stem. This kind of Detail question can be more time-consuming on Test Day, as it requires you to confirm that 4 choices *are* present in the passage.

Think: The question stem refers to the "quadraphonic hearing system," which is discussed in paragraph 2. The one right answer will be an answer that is not a detail included in the passage. The four other answers will be details from the passage.

Predict: Here, the only prediction that can be made is that the four wrong answers will be details provided in paragraph 2. The one right answer will not be included in the passage, will distort a detail in the passage, or will be a detail that is not about the quadraphonic hearing system and thus will not be in paragraph 2.

Match: Each answer choice must be evaluated here to determine if the detail is included in the passage. Answer choices (A), (B), (C), and (E) are all stated in paragraph 2 of the passage and therefore can be eliminated. Answer choice (D), which says that the quadraphonic hearing system is "used most on land," contradicts the idea in paragraph 2 that quadraphonic hearing developed in response to sonic conditions in water and especially contrasts the final sentence of the paragraph. Therefore, answer choice (D) is the correct answer.

7. E

Stop: This is a Tone question.

Think: Refer to the passage map for any places where the author was positive or negative. Also check for Keywords—especially Emphasis keywords—which can indicate the author's feelings. Note "one of the most interesting animals on earth" and "matched by few other mammals" in paragraph 6.

Predict: The author had a slightly positive tone.

Match: The correct answer is (E). "Admiration" captures the slightly positive tone in the passage, and the passage's last sentence even references the harbor seal's "sensory acuity and flexibility." Answer choice (A) is a Distortion because it is too Extreme. There are no passage keywords to indicate that the author is "astonished." Also, "astonished' means that the author would not have expected these adaptations, which is not supported by the text. Answer choice (B) is Out of Scope, as "skeptics of the theory of evolution" are never discussed in the passage. Answer choice (C) is Opposite because the author is not "ambivalent" or neutral in the passage; he uses positive language to describe the seal's adaptations. Answer choice (D) is also Out of Scope, as the passage does not condemn anything.

8. A

Stop: This question stem includes the phrase "in order to," which indicates that this is a Function question.

Think: The question stem directs you to paragraph 4. According to the map, this paragraph is about echolocation. Look for the references to "bats, porpoises, and dolphins" in order to predict why the author included these, proceeding with the likely assumption that it should have something to do with echolocation.

Predict: The first sentence of paragraph 4 says that "some scientists hypothesize that harbor seals have an echolocation system akin to the sensory capabilities of bats, porpoises, and dolphins." Thus, the author is including the reference to these other mammals to show that other mammals have echolocation systems.

Match: Answer choice (A) is correct. Answer choice (B) is a Faulty Use of Detail as the stenopaic pupil is discussed in paragraph 3 and is not the reason these mammals are referenced in the passage. Answer choice (C) is a Faulty Use of Detail—the overall paragraph describes the radar and its functions, but that is not why other animals are mentioned. Answer choice (D) is Opposite because the author is trying to draw a parallel between these other mammals and the harbor seal, not make a "contrast." Answer choice (E) is Out of Scope since the passage never mentions a hypothesis that the adaptations are most important at night, even if it could be inferred that echolocation is unaffected by darkness.

9. C

Stop: Two clues in the question stem indicate that this is an Inference question: "Based on the passage" and "inferred."

Think: This question stem does not provide any clues as to where the answer the answer will be. Because this is an Inference question, the answer must be both unstated and true based on the passage.

Predict: Evaluate each answer choice individually, looking for what must be true based on the information given in passage. If an answer could be false or is definitely false, then it is not the correct answer. Find proof for the correct answer directly in the passage.

Match: Answer choice (A) is a Faulty Use of Detail. Paragraph 3 states that the human cornea "aids in the refraction and focusing of light onto the retina," not that it is astigmatic like a seal's. So, a human would not need a stenopaic pupil. Answer choice (B) is a Faulty Use of Detail from paragraph 4. While it could be true that bats, porpoises, and dolphins have an astigmatic cornea, these mammals were mentioned as examples of animals that use echolocation; nothing was ever mentioned about their eyes. Answer choice (C) refers to the seal's eye, so paragraph 3 should be examined. In the first half of paragraph 3, the seal's eye and the human eye are contrasted. Specifically, the passage explains that the human eye is equipped with a cornea that is adapted to function primarily in air, while the seal's eye has a cornea with a refractive index similar to that of water. Thus, proof for answer (C) is in the passage, so it must be true and is the correct answer. At this point on Test Day, you could move on to the next question. For reference, answer choice (D) is Opposite of paragraph 3, which states that when the seal is "in water, light rays are transmitted by the cornea without distortion." Answer choice (E) is Out of Scope because, even though the seal's cornea and the way it focuses light on the retina are compared to the human's cornea and the way it focuses light on the retina, there is never any judgment made as to which is more effective. While one might say that the seal's vision is adapted to be more effective than the human's in water, the answer choice does not mention water. It is important to not make logical leaps in an Inference question or answer choice.

10. D

Stop: The question stem starts with the word "suppose" and then provides new information that potentially affects the author's argument. This is a Strengthen/Weaken question.

Think: First, it is important to understand the new information in the question stem. A walrus, which is also a pinneped, uses its whiskers to find its prey, but it does so by detecting differences in shapes. Refer back to paragraph 5 to recall how the seal uses its whiskers. According to paragraph 5, the seal also uses its whiskers to find prey, but it does so by sensing wave disturbances rather than by detecting different shapes.

Predict: The author would see this information as another example of the way pinnepeds adapt to find prey using whiskers.

Match: Answer choice (D) is correct. Answer choice (A) is Opposite since the evidence about the walrus does not conflict with what is stated about how the seal uses its whiskers. Answer choice (B) is Out of Scope because the passage never mentions a theory that the walrus developed before the harbor seal. Answer choice (C) is Opposite but may be an especially tempting wrong answer. In the second sentence of paragraph 5, the author states "vibrissae are unusually well-developed in Pinnepedia." The author claims that the whole order, not only seals, has unusually well-developed whiskers. Thus, the new information in the question stem would support rather than conflict with his claim. Answer choice (E) is Out of Scope; the author never indicates that pinnepeds are the only animals who can use whiskers for sensory reception. The word "only" in this answer also indicates a Distortion of the author's description since it only mentions vibrissae used by pinnepeds but does not state that they are the only animals to use them.

Passage 2—Dental Caries

Map

Paragraph 1: bacteria + dental caries = destruction

Paragraph 2: studies on development

Paragraph 3: plaque + spec. bact. = caries

Paragraph 4: acidic conditions, enamel protects

Paragraph 5: bact. need carbs, saliva factor

Paragraph 6: chem. protection, ex: Fl

Paragraph 7: location of teeth = factor

P: explain factors affecting dental caries

Questions

11. C

Stop: The phrase "main point of this passage" indicates this is a Global question.

Think: Refer to the purpose in your map.

Predict: The purpose is to explain factors leading to and protecting against dental caries.

Match: Answer choice (C), while slightly more specific than the purpose you may have in your map, is correct. Bacteria, oral cavity, and teeth are all factors that are discussed throughout the passage, making answer (C) accurate in response to this Global question. If matching was challenging here, the evaluation of the other choices will show that answer (C) is the only possibility for the right answer. Answer choice (A) is a Faulty Use of Detail answer. While this sentence is true based on paragraph 5 of the passage, it is not the main point of the passage. Answer choice (B) is Out of Scope. While this could be inferred from various places in the passage, it does not even address dental caries, which absolutely needs to be mentioned in the answer to this Global question. Answer choice (D) is also Out of Scope since the point at which dental caries should be clinically recognized is not discussed in the passage. Answer choice (E) is Out of Scope—while causes of dental caries are discussed, specific prevention mechanisms are not mentioned at all in the passage.

12. D

Stop: This question stem may not be immediately identifiable as a Detail question, but on closer inspection you can see that the question stem requires you to find a specific detail in the passage. This is a Detail question rather than Inference because of the categorical language at the end of the question stem (i.e., "is").

Think: This detail is located in paragraph 3. According to the passage map, paragraph 3 is about how plaque combined with specialized bacteria lead to dental caries. This could be enough information, but looking at the specific sentence where this is mentioned will serve as a good confirmation.

Predict: According to the passage, "The preliminary event in the development of caries is deposition of plaque on the tooth's surface," so the correct answer must mention plaque.

Match: A quick scan of the answer choices reveals that only choice (D) mentions plaque. It is the correct answer. Answer choice (A) is a Distortion; the passage states that the bacteria that cause plaque are "indigenous to the human oral cavity," so "invasion" does not fit. Answer choice (B) is also a Distortion. The bacterial dextrans allow the bacteria to attach to the salivary proteins. The proteins are what are attached to the enamel, so the dextrans are not directly adhered to the enamel. Answer choice (C) is a Faulty Use of Detail as the dissolution of calcium salts is referenced in paragraph 4 and is not the initial event leading to dental caries. Answer choice (E) is a Faulty Use of Detail—the proteolytic enzymes are produced by the bacteria that are found in plaque, so plaque needs to form *before* the enzymes can be produced.

13. C

Stop: This question asks us for a specific piece of information from the passage, so it is a Detail question.

Think: The location of teeth is the scope of paragraph 7; research that paragraph to find the correct answer.

Predict: According to paragraph 7, "the teeth that are least susceptible to dental caries are the mandibular central and lateral incisors." Either of these could be the correct answer.

Match: Answer choice (C) matches. Answer choice (A) is Opposite of paragraph 7, which states that "interproximal surfaces . . . are prime sites for the initiation of caries." Answer choice (B) is also Opposite of paragraph 7, which states that the prime sites are "especially in the contact areas." Answer choice (D) actually comes from paragraph 5 but is also Opposite as the paragraph states that individuals with no salivary flow "often exhibit rampant dental caries." Answer choice (E) is Out of Scope as bicuspids are never specifically mentioned in the passage.

14. A

Stop: This is an Inference question. "Eating of ice cream" was not explicitly discussed in the passage, so this is a new scenario, and the task is to infer how the information from the passage would apply.

Think: Find an analogous scenario in the passage. Paragraph 1 discusses "pain after the consumption of sugar and a throbbing sensation association with thermal

hypersensitivity." Ice cream is full of sugar and is cold, so this fits. Read the surrounding text to find the answer to the question of what is happening to the carious lesion.

Predict: According to the passage, it is "pulpal involvement" that leads to these symptoms.

Match: Answer choice (A) matches the prediction. Answer choice (B) is a Faulty Use of Detail. Paragraph 1 indicates that the oral infection can affect systemic health if left untreated, which indicates a more progressed stage than that at which throbbing pain occurs. Answer choices (C), (D), and (E) are also Faulty Uses of Detail as these details come from other parts of the passage and are not associated with this analogous scenario found in paragraph 1.

15. A

Stop: The phrase ". . . the dentist would most likely *not* see" tells us that this is another Inference question. The first sentence provides a scenario, and the task is to determine how the passage would apply.

Think: This question asks for what the dentist would most likely *not* see, so proceed carefully. While recent immigrants from third-world countries are not explicitly mentioned in the passage, in paragraph 5 the passage talks about "the diets of many people in industrialized nations." What is true of people in industrialized nations will be unlikely to be true of people in third-world countries since the author made a deliberate distinction. Read the sentence to determine what the author says about people in industrialized nations, noting that the focus of this paragraph is on the necessity of carbohydrates for the development of dental caries.

Predict: According to the passage, people in industrialized nations have diets "high in sucrose and other sugars." The answer should reference these carbohydrates and their relationship to the development of dental caries.

Match: Answer choice (A) is the only one to mention carbohydrates, so it is likely correct, but the additional language about "damage to enamel" should be verified. Find this in the passage. This actually comes from paragraph 4, which explains that, once bacteria produce proteolytic enzymes, "calcium salts in the enamel are slowly dissolved due to the acidic conditions." Thus, choice (A) is the correct answer. Answer choice (B) is a Distortion. The passage never suggests that people who do not have diets high in sugar consumption will not have dental caries, especially because there are many other contributing factors. Answer choice (C) is a Faulty Use of Detail. Failure to form saliva is discussed in paragraph 5 but not in relation to patients living in industrialized versus third-world countries. Answer choice (D) is another Distortion. Paragraph 6 mentions application of fluoride to the teeth, not fluoride—or lack thereof—in the diet. Be wary of answers that may play on your outside knowledge, and be especially wary here since the correct answer will be something the dentist is *unlikely* to see in an immigrant from a third world country. Choice (E) is Opposite; the passage notes in paragraph 7 that mandibular central incisors are among the least susceptible teeth to dental caries.

16. C

Stop: This is a Function question, which is evident due to the phrase "primarily in order to."

Think: The question stem directs you to paragraph 2. The map for paragraph 2 serves as reminder that this paragraph is about studies on the development of dental caries. Go back to paragraph 2 to read exactly how Louis Pasteur fit in with this paragraph as a whole.

Predict: Louis Pasteur is mentioned in the context of this paragraph in order to explain the early studies on the development of dental caries that were then followed by the rat studies.

Match: Answer choice (C) matches. Answer choice (A) is a tempting Distortion. While the passage discusses studies, it mentions dental caries experiments specifically and not one scientific study in general. Answer choice (B) is Opposite. Pasteur's results were the foundation for modern knowledge and were not in opposition to it. Answer choice (D) is a Faulty Use of Detail. Several other paragraphs explain how bacteria form dental caries, but that is not relevant to this question. Answer choice (E) is Out of Scope. Paragraph 2 discusses the results of Pasteur's studies but does not question the scientific validity of the research. In fact, the author uses the studies' results to help explain how caries are formed, so he sees the research as conclusive.

17. D

Stop: This is an Inference question. Questions about the author's beliefs or attitudes fall within the Inference category.

Think: The correct answer is the one that must be true, but it could be derived from information found anywhere in the passage.

Predict: Each answer will need to be evaluated, and proof for the answer must be found.

Match: Answer choice (A) is Out of Scope. The scientific experiments that the author discusses are not deemed successful or unsuccessful. Answer choice (B) is Out of Scope and also uses Extreme language. The author does not use any language that implies that patients deserve to experience dental caries. Answer choice (C) is also Out of Scope as the success of fluoride programs is not discussed

in the passage. Answer choice (D) matches with the overall purpose of the passage and in fact matches the answer to the first question (the Global question) of this passage. It also matches the author's neutral tone, whereas the other answer choices thus far have suggested a negative or positive tone. Answer choice (E) is Out of Scope; while the author *does* talk about dental caries prevention in the passage, you do not have enough evidence to confirm this statement.

18. D

Stop: This is a Function question. Note the phrase "in order to."

Think: The stem directs you to specific quotes within paragraph 5. Read the sentences containing these quotes to understand the context.

Predict: The passage states that these diets "supply the bacterial with a preferential metabolic substrate . . . facilitating the carious process." The author mentions these diets to say that they are likely to lead to the formation of dental caries.

Match: Answer choice (D) is correct. Answer choice (A) is Out of Scope. While the author implies that people in industrialized nations eat more sugars than those in underdeveloped nations, he does not discuss caloric intake. Answer choice (B) is Out of Scope. Only the diets of people in industrialized nations are discussed, not the percentage of dental caries cases. Answer choice (C) is Out of Scope as well since diabetes is never discussed in the passage. Answer choice (E) is a Faulty Use of Detail. The author mentions salivary composition as an example of a factor other than diet that contributes to the incidence of dental caries; he does not discuss the relationship between diet and salivary composition.

Biology 1

1. E	16. D	31. C
2. C	17. D	32. E
3. D	18. A	33. A
4. C	19. B	34. C
5. D	20. A	35. D
6. D	21. E	36. A
7. A	22. C	37. B
8. A	23. C	38. A
9. A	24. E	39. C
10. E	25. B	40. D
11. D	26. D	41. E
12. A	27. C	42. C
13. C	28. E	43. B
14. D	29. E	
15. E	30. C	

1. E

Stop: Answer choices are taxonomic kingdoms.

Think: The question asks which kingdom is the best classification for a multicellular eukaryotic species with cells that have rigid walls but no cellulose.

Predict: Two eukaryotic kingdoms include multicellular organisms that have cell walls: Plantae and Fungi. But, plant cell walls contain cellulose.

Match: (E) is correct because fungi are eukaryotes whose cell walls contain chitin rather than cellulose. Not all fungi are multicellular, but many are. Monera (A) are prokaryotes. Plantae (B) have cell walls containing cellulose. Members of Animalia (C) do not have cell walls. Protista (D) usually don't have cell walls and aren't typically multicellular. Thus, Fungi (E) is the correct answer.

2. C

Stop: Answer choices are taxonomic kingdoms.

Think: The question stem asks to which kingdom Platyhelminthes belong.

Predict: Platyhelminthes are worms. Worms are animals.

Match: (C) is correct. The kingdoms Monera (A), Plantae (B), Protista (D), and Fungi (E) do not include any animals.

3. D

Stop: Answer choices are elements from the periodic table.

Think: The question asks which element would have been most important to the first living organisms on Earth.

Predict: Since elemental oxygen was not available in the early environment on Earth, organisms must have able to survive without it. All living organisms are made up of one or more cells. The first cell structure needed would have been the cell membrane. The cell membrane is made up mostly of phospholipids.

Match: (D) is correct because even the earliest, most primitive organisms needed cell membranes to separate their interiors from the environment, and cell membranes require significant amounts of phosphorus. Sulfur (A), iron (B), and calcium (E) are important for more advanced cell structures and functions that would have developed later. Oxygen (C) was not freely available, so the first organisms must have been able to survive without it.

4. C

Stop: Answer choices are organelles.

Think: The question asks which organelle is needed for autophagy. Autophagy is the breaking down of cellular components, which is also known as cellular digestion.

Predict: The lysosome is where cellular waste is lysed, or broken down.

Match: (C) is correct. The ribosome (A), Golgi apparatus (D), and rough endoplasmic reticulum (E) are involved in the synthesis, not degradation, of cellular products. Chloroplasts (B) perform photosynthesis and other synthetic functions.

5. D

Stop: Answer choices are sentences describing cellular components.

Think: The question asks which choice is false or not true about mitochondria. Predict what is true about mitochondria and then eliminate the choices that are true.

Predict: Mitochondria are the "powerhouses" of the cell. They are responsible for the production of ATP by aerobic respiration. Mitochondria have inner and outer membranes and their own DNA and ribosomes. Mitochondria exhibit similarity to bacteria; they have circular DNA and replicate by binary fission. Eliminate any of these facts.

Match: (A), (B), (C), and (E) are all true of mitochondria. This leaves (D) as the correct answer because it is false. Note that even if your prediction did not include every fact found in the wrong choices, you could still match (D) as the correct answer because mitochondria produce ATP rather than macromolecules such as carbohydrates.

6. D

Stop: Answer choices are sentences describing mechanisms of membrane traffic.

Think: The question stem asks which description is accurate, but it does not specify which mechanism, so make a general prediction about the ones mentioned in the choices.

Predict: Active transport requires ATP to move molecules against the concentration gradient (low to high). Facilitated diffusion moves molecules along the concentration gradient (high to low) with the help of a carrier protein but does not require ATP. Osmosis is the diffusion of water from low solute concentrations to high solute concentrations. Endocytosis is the active engulfing of material into vesicles within the cell. Diffusion is the passive movement of molecules along the concentration gradient (high to low).

Match: (D) is correct because it accurately describes endocytosis as an active process that is often used to move large volumes or molecules into the cell. (A) is incorrect because ATP is the source of energy in active transport. (B) is incorrect because protein, not carbohydrate, carriers are used in facilitated diffusion. (C) is incorrect because osmosis transports water, which is a polar molecule. (E) is incorrect because diffusion moves molecules from higher concentration to lower concentration, not lower to higher.

7. A

Stop: Answer choices are sentences describing the movement of water and ions into or out of a fish and the consequences.

Think: The question asks what happens to a fish when it moves from saltwater to fresh water. The fish is moving into a hypotonic environment. Draw a picture of the before and after situations if needed.

Predict: Water will move from the area of lower solute concentration to the area of higher solute concentration. The cells of the fish are permeable to water. The fish must have been isotonic with the saltwater, which makes it hypertonic to the fresh water, so water would move into the fish. If the fish cannot decrease its solute concentration, the fish's cell volume will increase dramatically.

Match: (A) is correct because it describes water moving into the fish and its cells lysing, or bursting. (B) is the opposite and would be expected if the fish moved from fresh water to saltwater. Even if the fish is permeable to ions, (C) is incorrect since solute would move toward the hypotonic environment. (D) is incorrect because ions flowing out of the fish would make it either isotonic with or hypotonic to the environment.

8. A

Stop: Answer choices are phrases describing the movement of water and ions from one compartment to another.

Think: The question asks what happens when two compartments—1.5 M NaCl on the left and 2.0 M glucose on the right—are separated by a semipermeable membrane. Draw a picture. The left compartment contains 1.5 M NaCl, which becomes 3.0 M solute after dissociating into Na^+ and Cl^-. The right side contains 2.0 M glucose, which will not dissociate.

Predict: Water will move from the area of lower solute concentration on the right to the area of higher solute concentration on the left.

Match: (A) is correct. Note that this also means the final height of the water will be higher on the left as the osmotic pressure partially counters the force of gravity. (B) is incorrect because it does not account for the dissociation of NaCl. (C), (D), and (E) can be eliminated since the membrane is not permeable to ions.

9. A

Stop: Answers choices describe how something changes but without specific numbers.

Think: The question asks what immediately happens to the rate of ATP consumption when a cell is moved to a hypotonic environment. The Na^+/K^+ pump has the net effect of pumping out one ion. The pump requires ATP, but the answer choices do not require considering specific amounts.

Predict: Moving to a hypotonic environment would cause water to rush into the cell, leading to swelling and eventual bursting. To prevent this from occurring, the cell needs to transfer solute to the environment, so the pump will need to increase its activity to increase the net movement of ions out of the cell. Increasing the activity of the pump will increase the rate of ATP consumption.

Match: (A) is correct. (C) is incorrect because the question asks what happens "immediately" after moving to a hypotonic environment, not what might happen over time. Even if true (and it might not be, depending on how leaky the cell membrane is), it does not answer the question.

10. E

Stop: Answer choices are sentences about cellular metabolism.

Think: The question stems asks which of the choices is true but does not include a specific scope or any other information, so make a general prediction.

Predict: Anaerobic respiration occurs in the cytoplasm and includes glycolysis and fermentation. Glycolysis produces a net of 2 ATP by breaking down glucose into pyruvate. Fermentation then reduces pyruvate to ethanol to regenerate the NAD^+ needed for more glycolysis. Aerobic respiration occurs in the mitochondria and includes pyruvate decarboxylation, the citric acid cycle, and oxidative phosphorylation to produce 36 net ATP.

Match: (E) is correct. Note that the question can be answered either by knowing the location of oxidative phosphorylation or by the process of elimination. Eliminate (A) because glucose, not alcohol, undergoes glycolysis. Eliminate (B) because only 2 ATP are produced from each $FADH_2$; 3 ATP can be produced from NADH. Eliminate (C) because pyruvate decarboxylation does not directly produce any ATP; instead, this process yields 2 NADH, which can be converted into 6 ATP, but no ATP is directly produced at this step. Eliminate (D) because glycolysis is an anaerobic process.

11. D

Stop: Answer choices are enzymes.

Think: The question asks for the last enzyme that is used in cellular respiration. The final process in cellular respiration is oxidative phosphorylation, which involves a series of redox reactions, at the end of which oxygen is the final electron receptor.

Predict: Since the final step in oxidative phosphorylation is the transfer of electrons to oxygen, its name should reflect that it acts on oxygen.

Match: (D) is correct. Note that the question can be answered even without recalling the role of cytochromes in the electron transport chain because (D) is the only answer that refers to oxygen—"oxi"—in the name. (A), (C), and (E) are used in anaerobic respiration. (B) is used early aerobic respiration.

12. A

Stop: Answer choices are molecules related to cellular respiration.

Think: The question asks which molecule is not necessary for oxidative phosphorylation. Predict which molecules are necessary and then eliminate them.

Predict: NADH and $FADH_2$ are electron carriers. H^+ is needed to maintain the electrochemical gradient that provides energy for phosphorylation. A phosphate must be added to ADP to create ATP. Oxygen is the final electron acceptor.

Match: (A) is correct because NAD^+ is a product of oxidative phosphorylation rather than a reagent or substrate. NAD^+ is a required reactant in glycolysis, but NADH is required for oxidative phosphorylation. (B), (C), (D), and (E) can be eliminated as predicted.

13. C

Stop: Answer choices are components of leaves and chloroplasts.

Think: The question asks where the Calvin cycle takes place. The Calvin cycle is the light–independent, or dark, reaction of photosynthesis.

Predict: Since the Calvin cycle is part of photosynthesis, it occurs in the chloroplasts. And since it is "dark", it occurs in the stroma, not the grana.

Match: (C) is correct. The cuticle (A) is a waxy coating on leaves that helps them retain water. The grana (B) are the thylakoid stacks where the light reactions of photosynthesis take place. The stomata (D) are pores in leaves that allow gas exchange. The xylem (E) are channels or vessels that allow plants to transport water and nutrients.

14. D

Stop: Answer choices are even numbers in increasing order.

Think: The question asks how many PGAL molecules must be produced for a plant to make 1 molecule of sucrose. Sucrose contains 12 carbon atoms. PGAL (also called G3P) contains 3 carbon atoms.

Predict: It would take 4 PGAL molecules to provide the 12 carbon atoms needed to produce 1 molecule of sucrose. But, the question asks how many PGAL must be produced. Only 1 out of every 6 PGAL produced is available to make sugar; the other 5 are used to maintain the photosynthetic reactions. To get 4 available PGAL, you need 6 times that many, or 24. So, 24 PGAL must be produced for the plant to make 1 molecule of sucrose.

Match: (D) is correct. (A) is the number of PGAL that would actually be used to produce the sucrose, but the question asks how many PGAL must be produced by the plant, not how many would be used. (C) is the number of carbon atoms needed for 1 molecule of sucrose. (B) and (E) are miscalculations.

15. E

Stop: Answer choices are plant adaptations.

Think: The question asks which plant adaptation would not be helpful in a drought. Predict what would be helpful and then eliminate.

Predict: During a drought, a plant must conserve water or collect it despite a limited supply. Eliminate anything that would help the plant conserve or collect additional water.

Match: (E) is correct because open stomata would allow gas exchange, which would cause the plant to lose water to the dry environment. Browning of stems and leaves (A), altering the solute concentration in its phloem (C), and slowing photosynthesis (D) would allow a plant to conserve water. Expanding its root system (B) would allow a plant to find and collect more water.

16. D

Stop: Answer choices are plots of reaction rate versus pH and temperature.

Think: The question asks which set of graphs shows the optimal pH and temperature for pepsin activity. Pepsin is a digestive enzyme in the stomach, an acidic environment.

Predict: Since pepsin acts in a highly acidic environment, the rate of reaction should be highest at low pH. And since pepsin is a biological enzyme, its optimal temperature should be around 37 °C.

Match: (D) is correct because it shows high enzyme activity when pH is low and temperature is around 37 °C. (A) shows an optimal pH near the physiological pH of 7.4, which would be ideal for many enzymes but not those in the stomach. And the temperature of 50 °C is way too high. (B) shows the correct pH but a temperature close to 100 °C, which would work only if it were measured in Fahrenheit. (C) shows a very basic pH and makes the same temperature error as (B). (E) shows the correct pH graph, but the temperature is too high, just like (A).

17. D

Stop: Answer choices are actions related to enzymes.

Think: The question asks what the role of thyroxine is in the figure. The figure shows thyroxine as a product negatively affecting an upstream reactant. Since the choices are general actions, it is not necessary to consider the specific hormones.

Predict: The curved arrow with a minus sign indicates negative feedback, which reduces the availability or activity of the upstream component acted upon, thereby decreasing downstream effects. By triggering the negative feedback, thyroxine will decrease its own production or release.

Match: (D) is correct. No information about enzyme specificity (A) or catalyst production (C) is given in the diagram. Eliminate positive feedback (B) because of the negative sign in the diagram. While thyroxine does serve as a substrate for a further reaction, the question asks about the role of thyroxine in this particular reaction, so (E) does not answer the question.

18. A

Stop: Answer choices are changes to a reaction.

Think: The question asks how an enzyme alters a reaction.

Predict: Enzymes are catalysts. They increase the rate of reaction by lowering activation energy. They have no effect on equilibrium concentrations.

Match: (A) is correct because it describes the reaction reaching equilibrium faster. Enzymes do not affect equilibrium point, which means you can eliminate (B) and (E), or the free energy absorbed or released, which means you can eliminate (D). Activation energy (C) is decreased, not increased.

19. B

Stop: Answer choices compare leading and lagging strands and the number of molecules involved in their synthesis.

Think: The question asks which daughter strand, the leading or the lagging, is more likely to have a mutation.

Predict: The lagging strand is synthesized as short Okazaki fragments that are later joined together. This process requires additional steps and machinery compared to the continuous process used to replicate the leading strand. Mutations are more likely in the more complicated, discontinuous process undergone by the lagging strand.

Match: (B) is correct. Mutations occur randomly, but the lagging strand is subjected to more steps and molecules than the leading strand, so there is a greater chance of error. (A) and (C) are incorrect because they name the wrong strand. (D) and (E) are incorrect because the lagging strand interacts with more molecules than the leading strand.

20. A

Stop: Answer choices compare the nucleotide content of two DNA fragments.

Think: The question asks how melting temperature is related to the nucleotide composition of DNA fragments. Fragment A has a significantly higher melting point than Fragment B. Adenine–thymine (A–T) pairs have two hydrogen bonds, while guanine–cytosine (G–C) pairs have three hydrogen bonds.

Predict: The presence of more hydrogen bonds results in a higher melting point, so the fragment with the higher melting temperature must have more G–C pairs. This means that fragment A must have more cytosine and guanine.

Match: (A) is correct. The extra hydrogen bond in the G–C pairs will give fragment A its higher melting point. Fragment B would not have more cytosine (B) or guanine than fragment A since it has a lower melting temperature. More thymine (C) or adenine (D) in fragment A would not result in a higher melting point. Choice (E) cannot be correct because DNA does not contain uracil.

21. E

Stop: Answer choices are components of DNA.

Think: The question asks what gives DNA its negative charge. DNA is made up of deoxyriboses, nitrogenous bases, and phosphate groups.

Predict: Of the DNA components, only phosphate is negatively charged.

Match: (E) is correct. (A), (B), and (C) are uncharged components of DNA. A hydroxyl group (D) is negatively charged when in the form of a free hydroxide ion but neutral when bonded, as in DNA.

22. C

Stop: Answer choices are DNA and RNA sequences.

Think: The question gives a sequence of DNA and asks what the sequence of mRNA transcribed from it would be. Base pairing is the same in transcription as in DNA replication except U is substituted for T and the 5′ end of the mRNA should be complementary to the 3′ strand of the DNA template.

Predict: Transcribe by matching U with A and G with C, but don't forget to reverse the sequence!

Match: (C) is correct. (A) and (B) include T, but mRNA has U in the place of T. (E) is backward because it does not align the 5′ end of the mRNA with the 3′ strand of the DNA template.

23. C

Stop: Answer choices are Roman numerals involving lactose and glucose.

Think: The question asks what happens when the promoter at the lactase gene is nonfunctional.

Predict: If the promoter region is nonfunctional, the gene will not be transcribed, so the person would be missing lactase. Lactase breaks down lactose, so without lactase, lactose cannot be digested normally.

Match: (C) is correct. Less digestion of lactose (I) matches the prediction. If someone cannot digest lactose enzymatically, intestinal bacteria must do more of the digestion, as described in (II). Eliminate (III) because glucose can be obtained from other food sources.

24. E

Stop: Answer choices describe cell responses to different signals. Two choices identify the type of cell.

Think: The question asks what would cause an increased concentration of RNA for a single gene.

Predict: Transcription is tightly regulated, but any number of signals may cause it to be upregulated. The upregulation of one gene suggests a very specific signal and response.

Match: (E) is correct. An increase in the RNA of a gene indicates that the cell is increasing transcription of the DNA for that gene in response to a particular signal. Erythrocytes (A), which are mature red blood cells, lose their nucleus, chromosomal DNA, and other organelles during their development, so they do not participate in any gene regulation or produce RNA or proteins. An infection would cause leukocytes (B) to increase the expression of multiple genes rather than a "particular" gene as described in the question stem. Translation (C) is the production of protein rather than the production of RNA itself. Downregulation (D) of a gene would decrease, not increase, the concentration of its RNA.

25. B

Stop: Answer choices are sentences about the placement of amino acids during translation.

Think: The question asks what would happen if tRNA with an anticodon for alanine carried valine instead. The tRNA anticodon pairs with the mRNA codon, and the amino acid attached to the tRNA will be added to the chain.

Predict: If the tRNA has an anticodon for alanine, it will pair with an alanine codon on the mRNA. But, since it carries valine, valine would be added to the amino acid chain where alanine should have been.

Match: (B) is correct. The tRNA is not carrying alanine, so it cannot add alanine to the peptide chain either alone (A) or with the valine (D). Since the tRNA carries valine, there is no reason to expect that it would not add an amino acid, as described in (C). (E) is incorrect because tRNA normally binds to the ribosome, so the binding would not cause translation to stop.

26. D

Stop: The answer choices are sentences describing bacteria dying when the synthesis stops.

Think: The question asks how destruction of ribosomes could kill bacteria. Ribosomes make proteins.

Predict: Destroying ribosomes would stop protein synthesis, which would cause death.

Match: (D) is correct. Plasmids (A), lipids (B), carbohydrates (C), and (E) nucleic acids are not produced by ribosomes, so destroying the ribosomes would not cause these problems.

27. C

Stop: Answer choices are processes related to translation.

Think: The question asks what process is dependent on peptidyl transferase.

Predict: Peptidyl transferase forms peptide bonds between amino acids during translation.

Match: (C) is correct. Ribosome assembly (A) occurs in the nucleolus long before the initiation of translation. (B) and (D) describe RNA interactions rather than building proteins.

28. E

Stop: Answer choices are sentences about genetic mutations.

Think: The question asks what must have happened if a mutation is noticeable.

Predict: In order for a mutation to be noticeable, it must occur in a protein coding portion of the DNA and change a protein's structure enough to change its function.

Match: (E) is correct. Note that this does not mean that the mutation will always be noticeable when a protein's function is changed, but in order for a mutation to be noticeable, protein function must be altered. Point mutations (A) may not change the amino acid sequence at all due to degeneracy in the genetic code. Substitution of a single amino acid (B) may not noticeably change the shape or function of that protein. Frequently transcribed DNA (C) is likely to be translated, but mutations may be silent. The chromosomal location (D) of the mutation does not determine its expression. So, none of (A), (B), (C), or (D) is necessary to cause a mutation to be noticeable.

29. E

Stop: Answer choices are types of mutations.

Think: The question asks which type of mutation is most likely to cause fetal death.

Predict: Chromosomal mutations usually result in embryos that are not viable because they affect hundreds or thousands of genes.

Match: (E) is correct. (A), (B), (C), and (D) would result in mutation of a single gene only.

30. C

Stop: Answer choices are Roman numerals describing codons.

Think: The question asks why some mutations are not expressed.

Predict: The genetic code has 64 codons that code for 20 amino acids. This means that some amino acids have more than one codon, which is called degeneracy. There are only 45 known tRNA anticodons, some of which pair with more than one codon by "wobble" pairing. The redundancy of both degeneracy in the amino acid codons and "wobble" pairing between codons and anticodons keep many mutations from altering the amino acid codes of proteins.

Match: (C) is correct. Although point mutations are often silent, the second position in a codon (II) is usually important in determining the corresponding amino acid. Degeneracy usually occurs in the third position of the codon.

31. C

Stop: Answer choices are percentages.

Think: The question asks what the chance is that the unaffected offspring is carrier. Carriers have the Rr genotype. The offspring cannot be rr because it does not express the gene.

Predict: If you don't have the genotype ratio of 1:2:1 memorized, make a Punnett square:

	R	r
R	RR	Rr
r	Rr	rr

Of the four options, notice that an offspring who is rr would express the recessive trait, but the generation 2 offspring is not affected (filled in), so this is not an option. Two-thirds of the remaining options are carriers.

Match: (C) is correct. (B) does not account for all of the information in the pedigree. The offspring does not express the trait, so the possibility of rr must be eliminated from consideration.

32. E

Stop: Answer choices are inheritance patterns.

Think: An equal number of males and females are affected, but no other patterns are evident.

Predict: Since males and females are equally affected, eliminate X-linked recessive. But, since no generational skipping occurs and no mating pairs share the same phenotype (see below), it is difficult to prove whether the pattern is dominant or recessive.

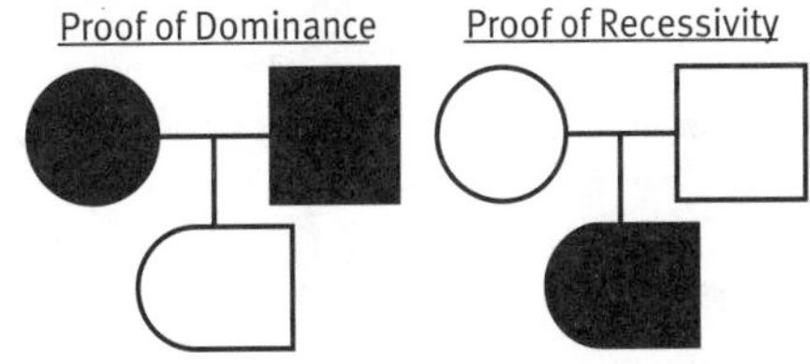

Match: (E) is correct. Although X-linked recessive (C) can be eliminated, either autosomal dominant (A) or autosomal recessive (B) could be true. Note that the absence of generational skipping does not prove that the trait is dominant. You would not want to spend the time on Test Day labeling every individual's genotype; instead, look for the patterns of generational skipping or two parents with the same phenotype giving birth to an offspring with the opposite phenotype. Nevertheless, if you did label the original pedigrees, you would find both recessive and dominant patterns work. Y-linked (D) is not a pattern of inheritance that will appear on Test Day.

33. A

Stop: Answer choices are inheritance patterns.

Think: Generational skipping occurs in the center of the pedigree when two unaffected parents produce an affected offspring. Both male and female offspring are affected in a 4:5 ratio, or almost equally.

Predict: Since generational skipping occurs, the pattern must be recessive. And since the affected ratio of men to women is nearly equal, the pattern is likely autosomal.

Match: (A) is correct. Autosomal dominant (B) and X-linked dominant (D) traits do not skip generations since it is not possible for offspring to be unaffected carriers. X-linked recessive (C) traits can only affect a woman who has an affected father, but the affected generation 2 females have an unaffected father.

34. C

Stop: Answer choices percentages.

Think: The question asks for the frequency of the recessive allele in Hardy–Weinberg equilibrium. The dominant allele is present in 84% of the population. $p^2 + 2pq + q^2 = 1$, where p represents the dominant allele and q represents the recessive allele.

Predict: 84% of the population is Rh positive, so 16% of the population is Rh negative and has the homozygous recessive genotype (q^2). $q^2 = 0.16$ and $q = 0.4$, or 40%.

Match: (C) is correct. Choice (B) is the frequency of individuals who are Rh negative or homozygous recessive, not the frequency of the recessive allele itself, which is also carried by heterozygous individuals.

35. D

Stop: Answer choices are percentages.

Think: The question asks for the frequency of the red hair allele. The allele is recessive and is only expressed by 1% of the population. $p^2 + 2pq + q^2 = 1$, where p represents the dominant allele and q represents the recessive allele.

Predict: 1% of the population is homozygous recessive, so $q^2 = 0.01$ and $q = 0.1$, or 10%.

Match: (D) is correct. Answer choice (B) is the frequency of individuals with red hair or the homozygous recessive genotype rather than the frequency of the recessive allele.

36. A

Stop: Answer choices are percentages.

Think: The question asks for the frequency of homozygous recessive individuals in a tetraploid population. The recessive allele frequency (q) is 0.20.

Predict: In a tetraploid, homozygous recessive is calculated by finding q^4 rather than q^2. If $q = 0.20$, then $q^4 = 0.0016$, or 0.16%.

Match: (A) is correct. Choice (C) results from calculating q^2 rather than q^4.

37. B

Stop: Answer choices are patterns and effects of evolution.

Think: Sharks and dolphins have different ancestors but common traits.

Predict: Separate lineages developing similar traits is called convergent evolution.

Match: (B) is correct. Divergent evolution (A) and speciation (D) occur among species with common ancestors. The founder effect (C) describes a few individuals that establish an evolutionarily isolated population. Vestigial structures (E) are either nonfunctional or lost during the life cycle of the organism.

38. A

Stop: Answer choices are patterns of evolution.

Think: The question asks what type of evolution occurs when a change in environment causes a separation of species.

Predict: Speciation occurs when one species diverges along two separate evolutionary pathways.

Match: (A) is correct. Convergent evolution (B) and coevolution (C) occur between species with no shared ancestry. Sexual selection (D) occurs when members of a species compete for mates rather than survival. Parallel evolution (E) occurs when related but distinct species independently develop a similar, rather than different, trait.

39. C

Stop: Answer choices are types of traits.

Think: The question asks how to characterize a structure that is similar in two unrelated species.

Predict: Bats and birds have no shared ancestor, but their wings have the same function, so the wings are analogous.

Match: (C) is correct. Homologous structures (B) are the opposite: structures that serve different functions but that are derived from the same ancestor.

40. D

Stop: Answer choices are types of biomes.

Think: The questions ask which biome has pines, spruces, bison, and beaver.

Predict: Boreal forest, or taiga, is characterized by these species.

Match: (D) is correct. Coniferous forest (A) contains pine trees but not spruces or large animals. Grassland (B) does not contain large trees. Rainforest (C) does not contain bison. Tundra (E) does not contain many trees.

41. E

Stop: Answer choices are animals.

Think: The question asks which animal permanently inhabits intertidal zones.

Predict: The intertidal zone is underwater at high tide but dry at low tide. Residents must be able to survive both environments.

Match: (E) is correct. Sharks (A), stingrays (B), and tuna (D) all live exclusively underwater. Seagulls (C) may spend time in the intertidal zone but are wide-ranging, so they are not permanent residents.

42. C

Stop: Answer choices are plants and animals.

Think: The question asks which species would settle on a rock after lichen.

Predict: Lichen is a symbiotic mixture of fungus and algae. An organism that settles on a rock covered with fungus and algae must not be an animal or a plant with a deep root system.

Match: (C) is correct. Moss is a plant that grows on rocks or in shallow soil. Trees (A), shrubs (B), and grass (E) require deeper soil to settle. Scrub hares (D) are animals, which would arrive much later.

43. B

Stop: Answer choices are relationships.

Think: The question asks what type of relationship exists between humans and bacteria in the gut.

Predict: Bacteria receive a stable environment. Humans receive immunity and vitamins. Both organisms benefit.

Match: (B) is correct. In commensalism (A) both organisms share nutrient sources but neither directly benefits the other. Parasitism (C) and (D) results when only one organism benefits. Predation (E) occurs when one species eats the other.

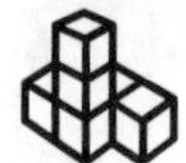

Perceptual Ability 1

1. B	17. A	33. B
2. B	18. D	34. D
3. A	19. C	35. B
4. D	20. C	36. C
5. E	21. B	37. C
6. D	22. C	38. A
7. A	23. C	39. B
8. B	24. B	40. A
9. B	25. E	41. B
10. A	26. D	42. A
11. B	27. A	43. D
12. D	28. B	44. B
13. B	29. A	45. D
14. D	30. B	46. A
15. B	31. E	
16. D	32. E	

Keyholes

1. B

The correct answer is the back projection flipped horizontally (which is also the front projection).

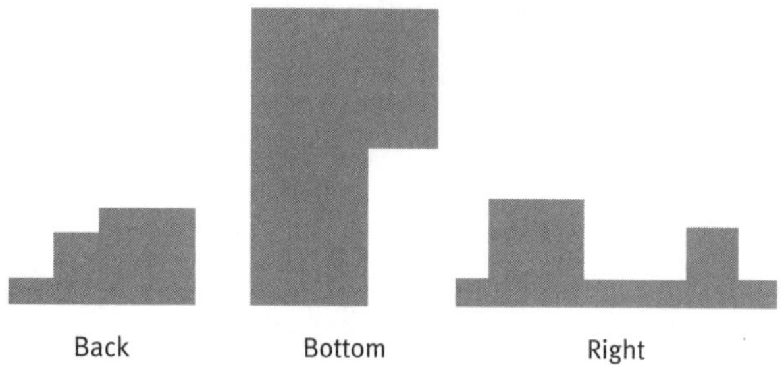

2. B

The correct answer is either the right projection flipped horizontally (which is also the left projection) or the bottom projection rotated 90° clockwise, both of which result in the same image.

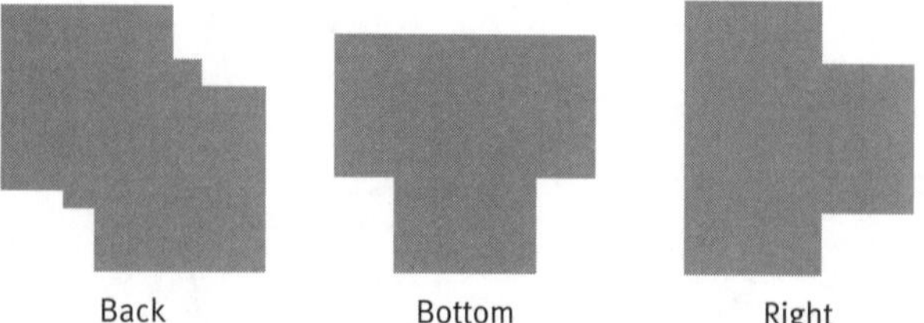

3. A

The correct answer is the right projection rotated clockwise 90°.

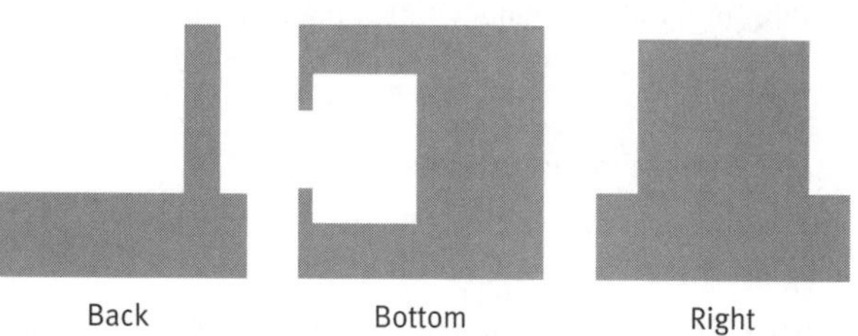

4. D

The correct answer is the bottom projection rotated counterclockwise 90°.

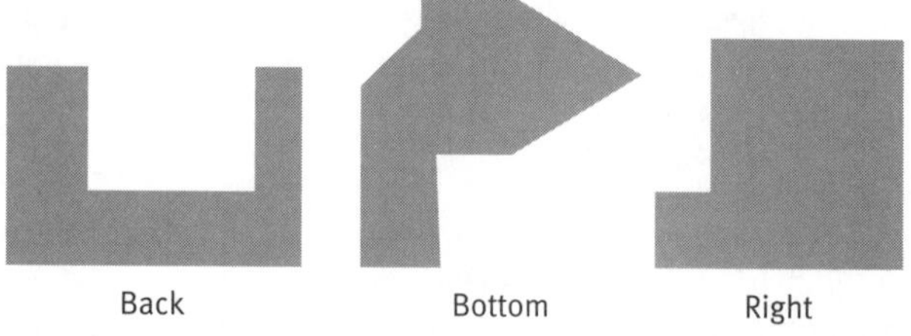

5. E

The correct answer is the back projection.

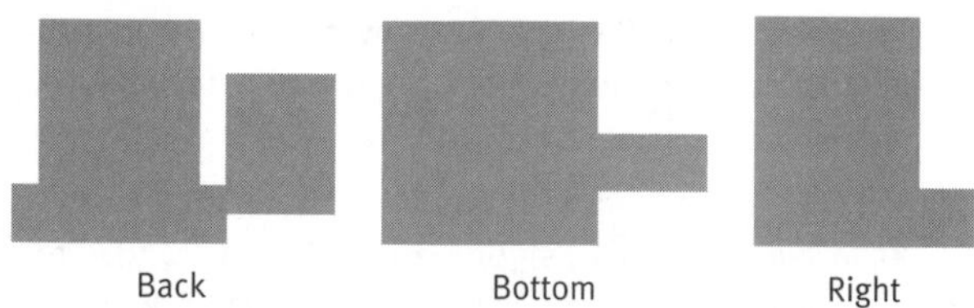

6. D

The correct answer is the back projection flipped horizontally (which is also the front projection).

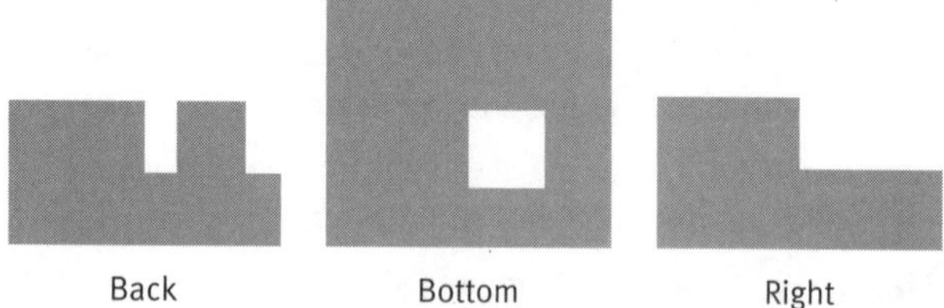

7. A

The correct answer is the bottom projection rotated clockwise 180°.

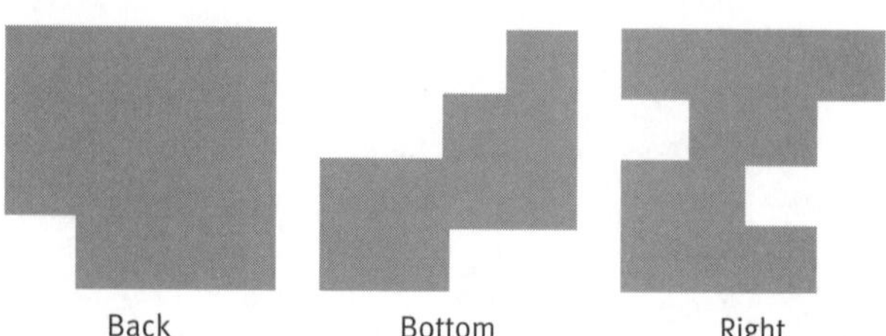

8. B

The correct answer is the right projection rotated counterclockwise 180°.

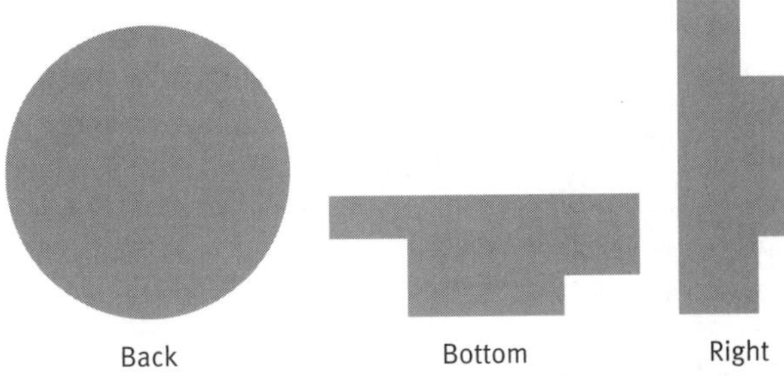

Top-Front-End

9. B

Evaluate the shared edge between the front and end views first. The front view has 5 total horizontal events, so the end must also have 5 horizontal events. Note that the third event down is really 2 events; there is a visible event that is the line on the front and is solid, and there is also the bottom of the V, which is hidden. Eliminate (A), (C), and (D), which have 3, 3, and 4 events, respectively. This leaves (B) as the correct answer.

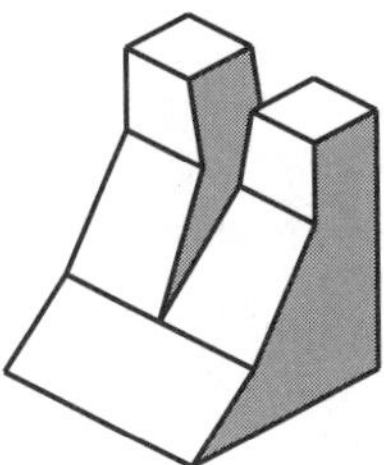

10. A

Evaluate the shared edge between the front and top views first. The front view has 5 total vertical events, so the top must also have 5 vertical events. Eliminate (B) and (D), which have 4 and 4 events, respectively. This leaves (A) and (C).

Next, evaluate the shared edge between the end and top views. The end view has 4 total vertical events, which means that the top must have 4 total horizontal events. You can eliminate (C), which only has 2 events, leaving (A) as the correct answer.

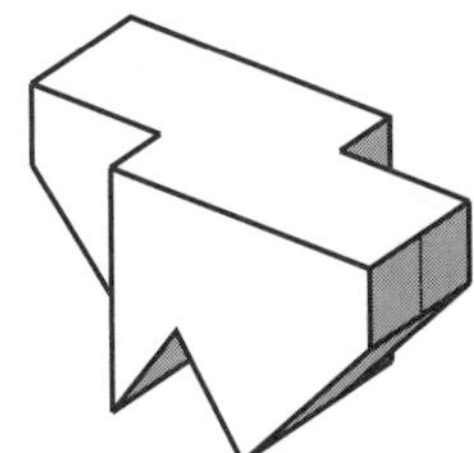

11. B

Evaluate the shared edge between the front and end views first. The front view has 5 total horizontal events, so the end must also have 5 horizontal events. Eliminate (C) and (D), which have 3 and 4 events, respectively. This leaves (A) and (B).

Next, evaluate the shared edge between the top and end views. The top view has 6 horizontal events, which means the end must have 6 total vertical events. Both (A) and (B) have 6 vertical events.

Finally, determine the number of visible and hidden events. Evaluate the shared edge between the front and end views since this is where the difference in visible and hidden is located in answers (A) and (B). The front view has 5 visible and no hidden events. Eliminate (A), which has 2 visible and 3 hidden events. This leave (B) as the correct answer.

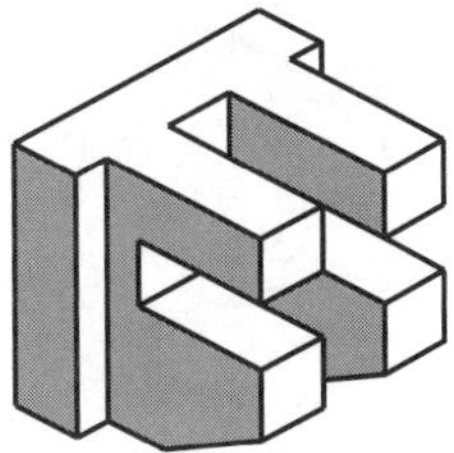

12. D

Evaluate the shared edge between the top and front view first. The top view has 3 total vertical events, so the front view must also have 3 vertical events. Eliminate (A), (B), and (C), which each have 5 vertical events, leaving (D) as the correct answer.

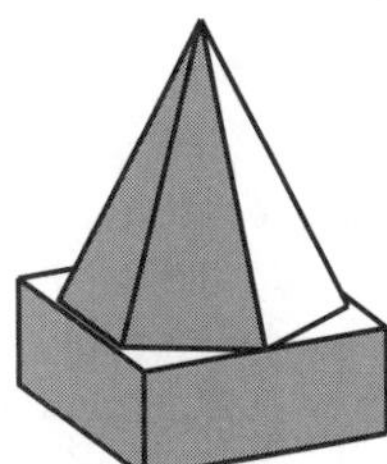

13. B

Evaluate the shared edge between the top and front view first. The top view has 8 total vertical events, so the front view must also have 8 vertical events. All of the choices have 8 vertical events.

Next, evaluate the shared edge between the end and front view. The end view has 5 horizontal events, so the front view must also have 5 horizontal events. Eliminate (A), which has 4 horizontal events. This leaves (B), (C), and (D).

Finally, determine the number of visible and hidden events using the shared edge between the end and front views. The end view has 4 visible and 1 hidden event (note that the second line from the top has a piece behind it). Eliminate (C) and (D), which both have 5 visible and no hidden events. This leaves (B) as the correct answer.

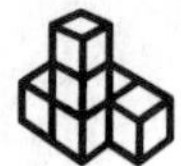

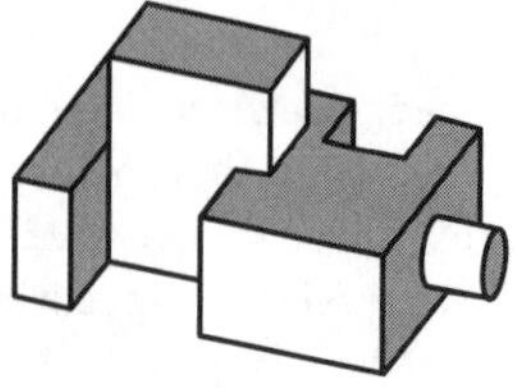

14. D

Evaluate the shared edge between the front and end view first. The front view has 5 horizontal events, so the end view must also have 5 horizontal events. Eliminate (B) and (C), which both have 3 horizontal events. This leaves (A) and (D).

Next, evaluate the shared edge between the top and end views. The top view has 6 horizontal events, so the end view must have 6 vertical events. Eliminate (A), which has 7 vertical events. The correct answer is (D).

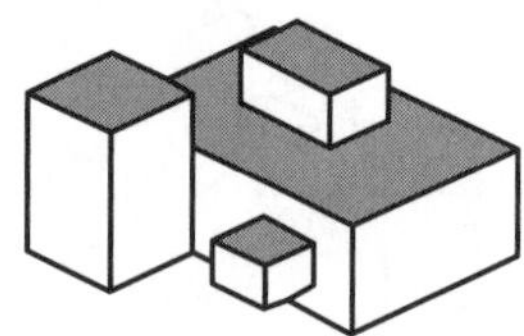

15. B

Evaluate the shared edge between the top and front view first. The top view has 5 total vertical events, so the front view must also have 5 vertical events. Eliminate (C) and (D), which both have 4 vertical events. This leaves (A) and (B).

Next, evaluate the shared edge between the end and front views. The end view has 5 total horizontal events, so the front view must have 5 horizontal events. Both (A) and (B) have 5 horizontal events.

Finally, determine the number of visible and hidden events on the shared edge between the top and front views. The top view has 4 visible and 1 hidden vertical event, so the front view must have 4 visible and 1 hidden event. Eliminate (A), which has 5 visible vertical events. This correct answer is (B).

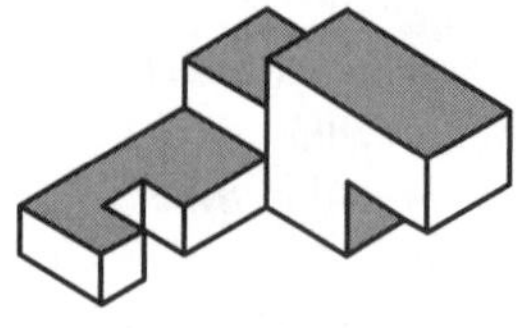

16. D

Evaluate the shared edge between the front and end views first. The front view has a total of 6 horizontal events, so the end view must also have a total of 6 horizontal events. Eliminate (A) and (C), which both have 4 horizontal events. This leaves (B) and (D).

Next, evaluate the shares edge between the top and end views. The top view has 8 horizontal events, so the end view must have 8 vertical events. Eliminate (B), which has 7 vertical events. The correct answer is (D).

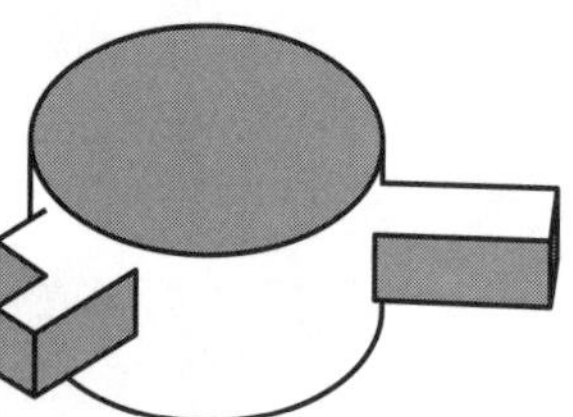

Angle Ranking

17. A

Smallest: The answer choices indicate that either angle 1 or 2 is the smallest. 2 is the smallest, so eliminate (D).

Largest: The remaining answer choices indicate that 1 or 3 is the largest. 3 is the largest, so eliminate (B).

Blocking: The vertices of 1 and 2 are aligned, so blocking shows that 2 is smaller than 1. This verifies that (D) is not correct.

Stacking: Stacking shows that 1 fits inside 4, which eliminates (C), leaving (A) as the correct answer.

18. D

Smallest: The answer choices indicate that either angle 1 or 2 is the smallest. 1 is the smallest, so eliminate (C).

Largest: The remaining answer choices indicate that 2, 3, or 4 is the largest. 4 is the largest, which eliminates (A) and (B). The correct answer is (D).

Blocking: This is a great example of when to use blocking to only look at the angles and not be distracted by the length of the lines. This directly shows you that the correct order of 1<2<3<4.

Stacking: Similarly, stacking could show the entire sequence: 1 fits inside 2, and 3 fits inside 4.

19. C

Smallest: The answer choices indicate that either angle 1 or 2 is the smallest. 2 is the smallest, so eliminate (A) and (D).

Largest: The remaining answer choices indicate that either 3 or 4 is the largest. 3 is the largest, so eliminate (B). The correct answer is (C).

Blocking: Blocking is a difficult strategy to use on this particular problem as all of the vertices are not facing the same direction.

Stacking: Stacking could show the entire sequence: 2 fits inside 1, and 4 fits inside 3.

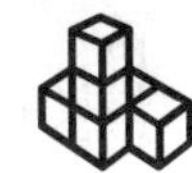

20. C

Smallest: The answer choices indicate that either 1, 2, or 4 is the smallest. 1 is very close to a 90° angle and is the smallest, so eliminate (A) and (B).

Largest: The remaining answer choices indicate that either 3 or 2 is the largest. 3 is the largest, so eliminate (D). The correct answer is (C).

Blocking: The vertices of all of the angles are aligned, so blocking shows you the correct order of $1<4<2<3$.

Stacking: Similarly, stacking could show the entire sequence: 1 fits inside 4, and 2 fits inside 3.

21. B

Smallest: The answer choices indicate that either 1 or 3 is the smallest. 3 is the smallest, so eliminate (A) and (D).

Largest: The remaining answer choices indicate that either 2 or 4 is the largest. 4 is the largest, so eliminate (C). The correct answer is (B).

Blocking: Blocking is a difficult strategy to use on this particular problem as all of the vertices are not facing the same direction.

Stacking: Stacking could show the entire sequence: 1 fits inside 3, and 2 fits inside 4.

22. C

Smallest: The answer choices indicate that either 1 or 3 is the smallest. 3 is the smallest, so eliminate (A) and (B).

Largest: The remaining answer choices both show that the largest angle is 4; use stacking to determine the middle 2 angles.

Blocking: Blocking is a difficult strategy to use on this particular problem as all of the vertices are not facing the same direction.

Stacking: Stacking shows that 1 fits inside 2, so eliminate (D). The correct answer is (C).

23. C

Smallest: The answer choices indicate that either 1 or 3 is the smallest. 1 is the smallest, so eliminate (A) and (B).

Largest: The remaining answer choices indicate that either 2 or 4 is the largest. 4 is the largest, so eliminate (D). The correct answer is (C).

Blocking: Blocking is a difficult strategy to use on this particular problem as all of the vertices are not facing the same direction.

Stacking: Stacking could show the entire sequence: 1 fits inside 3, and 2 fits inside 4. The correct answer is (C).

24. B

Smallest: The answer choices indicate that 1, 2, or 4 is the smallest. 2 is the smallest, so eliminate (C) and (D).

Largest: The remaining answer choices indicate that either 1 or 4 is the largest. 4 is the largest, so eliminate (A). The correct answer is (B).

Blocking: Blocking is a difficult strategy to use on this particular problem as all of the vertices are not facing the same direction.

Stacking: Stacking could show the entire sequence: 2 fits inside 1, and 3 fits inside 4.

Hole Punching

25. E

Symmetry: (A), (C), and (D) can be eliminated because they do not have a vertical line of symmetry.

Number of Holes: The answer choices are a mixture of 2 and 4 total holes. There are 2 layers of paper where the hole is punched, and therefore only 2 holes will result. This can eliminate (B) and verify that (D) is incorrect. The correct answer is (E).

Position: Mentally unfolding the paper from the second fold back to the first fold shows that the left-hand segment with the hole punch swings down to the bottom. This also eliminates (A) and (B) because they do not have holes in the bottom row.

26. D

Symmetry: Eliminate (A) because it does not have a vertical line of symmetry.

Number of Holes: There are 6 layers of paper where the hole is punched, creating 6 holes. This can be used to eliminate (B) and (E).

Position: Mentally unfolding the pattern from the third fold to the second fold shows that there is one hole in the second row and one in the third row, but this does not eliminate any choices. There is a hole in the top row when the second fold is reversed, which can eliminate (C) and again (E). There is not a hole in the bottom row, so you can verify that (B) is incorrect. The correct answer is (D).

27. A

Symmetry: Eliminate (B) and (D) because they do not have a horizontal line of symmetry.

Number of Holes: The answer choices are a mixture of 4, 5, 6, and 8 total holes. There are 6 layers of paper where the hole is punched creating 6 holes. This can be used to eliminate all of (B), (C), (D), and (E). The correct answer is (A).

Position: Mentally unfolding the pattern isn't necessary here. Unfolding the third fold to the second fold shows that there are holes in the second row of the second and third columns, but this does not eliminate any choices. When the second fold is reversed, there are holes in the second row of the first, second, and third columns; this eliminates (B), (C), and (D). There are no holes in the fourth column, which eliminates (E). The correct answer is still (A).

28. B

Symmetry: You can eliminate (A) and (C) because they do not have a horizontal line of symmetry.

Number of Holes: All of the answer choices have 4 holes, so none of them can be eliminated based on number of holes.

Position: Mentally unfolding the second fold indicates that there are holes in the second row of columns 2 and 3. This can be used to eliminate (D) and (E). The correct answer is (B).

29. A

Symmetry: This does not eliminate any answer choices as none violate the line of symmetry.

Number of Holes: All answer choices have 8 holes, so none of them can be eliminated based on number of holes.

Position: Looking at the third fold indicates that there are holes in the top right corner and diagonally below it, so eliminate (D) and (E). Mentally unfolding the third fold indicates that there are holes in the upper-left corner and diagonally below it; this can be used to further prove that (D) is not correct. Unfolding the second fold indicates that there are holes in the bottom right and diagonally above it, so eliminate (C). Unfolding the final fold shows that there is a hole in the bottom left and diagonally above it, so eliminate (B). The correct answer is (A).

30. B

Symmetry: (C) and (D) can be eliminated since they do not have a vertical line of symmetry.

Number of Holes: The answer choices are a mixture of 4, 6, and 8 holes. There are 6 layers of paper where the hole is punched; therefore, there are 6 holes, and you can eliminate (A) and (E). The correct answer is (B).

Position: Mentally unfolding isn't necessary here. Nevertheless, the third fold indicates that there are holes in the second and third row of the second column, so you can eliminate (C) and (D). Unfolding the second fold indicates that there are holes in the first, second, and third rows of the second and third columns, so you can eliminate (A), (C), and (D). There are no holes in the bottom row, so you can eliminate (E).

31. E

Symmetry: (B) and (C) can be eliminated since they violate the line of symmetry of the first fold.

Number of Holes: The answers are a mixture of 5 and 6 holes. There are 4 layers of paper where the top hole is punched and 2 layers of paper where the bottom hole is punched for a total of 6 holes. This eliminates (A), (C), and (D). The correct answer is (E).

Position: Mentally unfolding the third fold indicates there are holes in the top 3 rows of column 2, so eliminate (A) and (D). Unfolding the second fold indicates there are holes in the top 3 rows of columns 1 and 2, so eliminate (B) and (C). This results in the correct answer of (E).

32. E

Symmetry: Eliminate (C) because it violates the diagonal line of symmetry.

Number of Holes: All answer choices have 8 holes, so none can be eliminated based on number of holes.

Position: The position of the holes on the final fold indicates holes in the upper-right corner and diagonally below it, so eliminate (B) and (D). Mentally unfolding the third fold indicates additional holes in the upper left and diagonally below it; this confirms that (D) is not correct. Unfolding the second fold indicates additional holes in the bottom left and diagonally above it, so eliminate (A), (B), and (D). The correct answer is (E).

Cube Counting

Figure A Tally

0 siders: 0

1 siders: 1

2 siders: 2

3 siders: 3

4 siders: 4

5 siders: 2

Total: 12

33. B

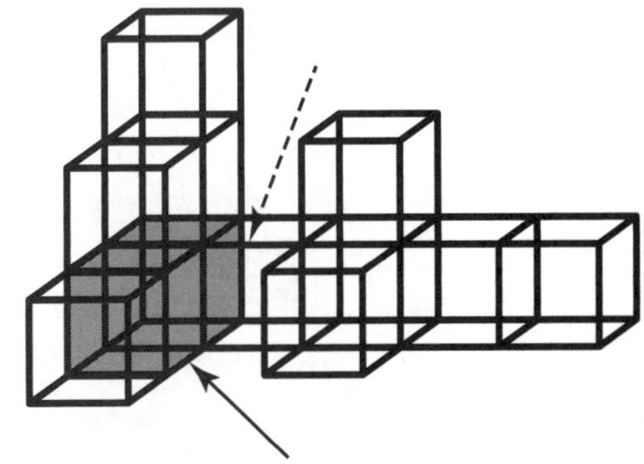

34. D

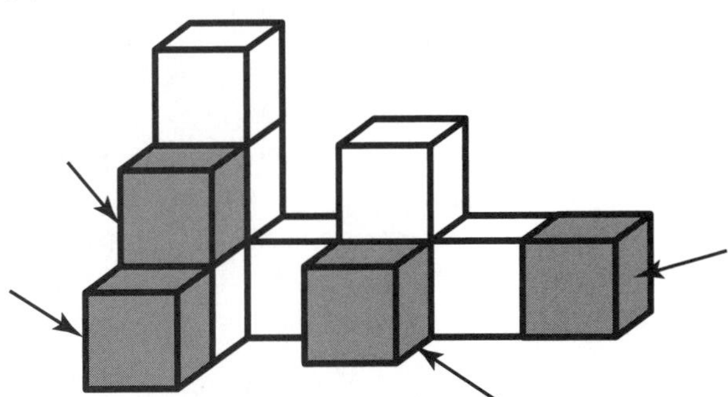

35. B

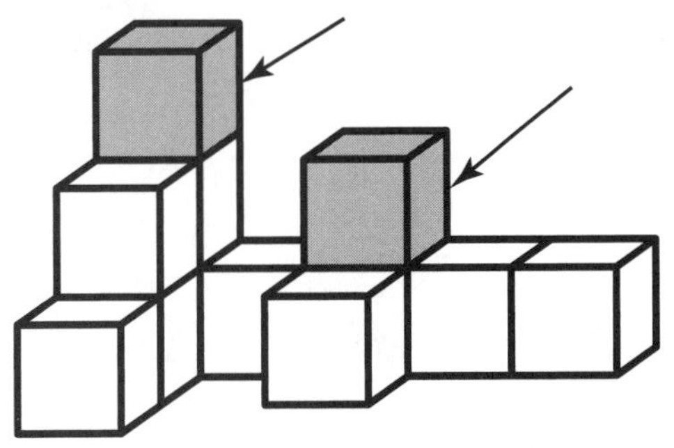

Figure B Tally

0 siders: 0

1 siders: 3

2 siders: 7

3 siders: 3

4 siders: 3

5 siders: 1

Total: 17

36. C

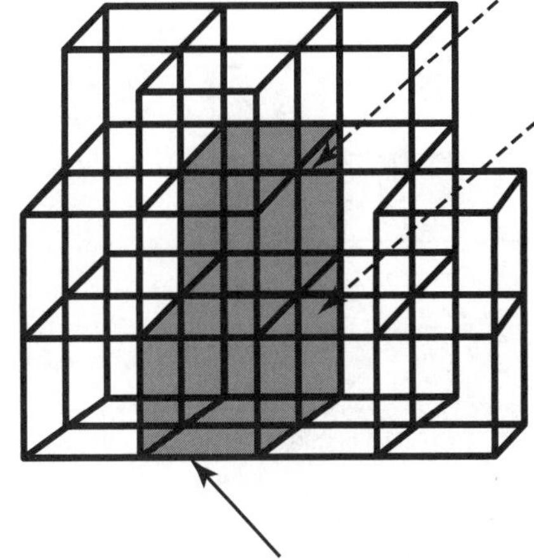

37. C

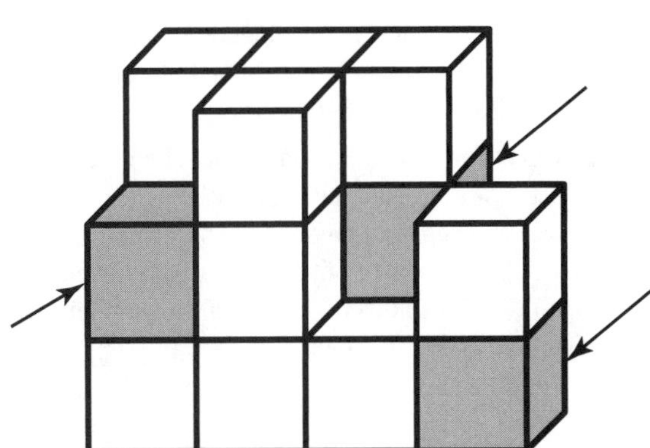

38. A

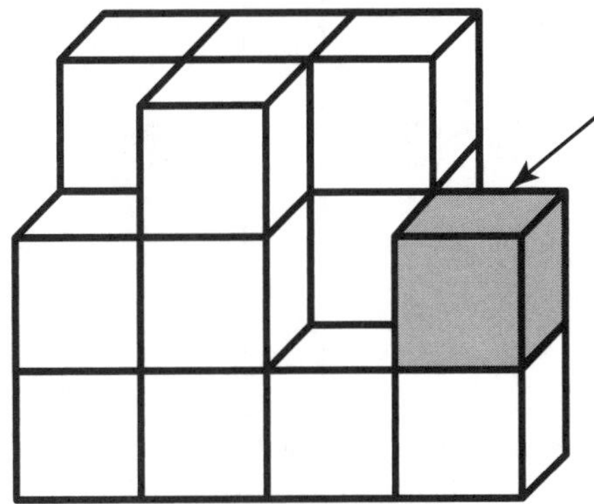

Pattern Folding

39. B

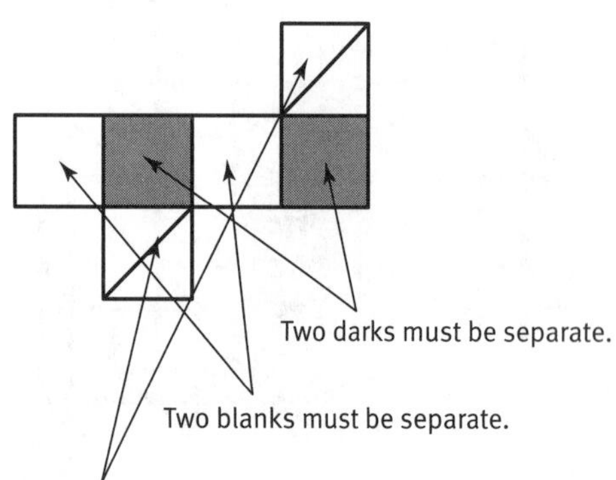

Unique shape: All sides are squares, so there isn't a unique shape.

Unique shading: The overall shading alternated between shaded and blank squares, which is best represented by choice (B). This can be verified by using key landmarks.

Key landmark: The two dark squares must be on opposite sides of the figure, so eliminate (D). Likewise, the two blank squares must be separate on opposite sides of the figure, so eliminate (A). Finally, the two squares with hashmarks must be on opposite sides of the figure, so eliminate (C). This leave (B) as the correct answer.

40. A

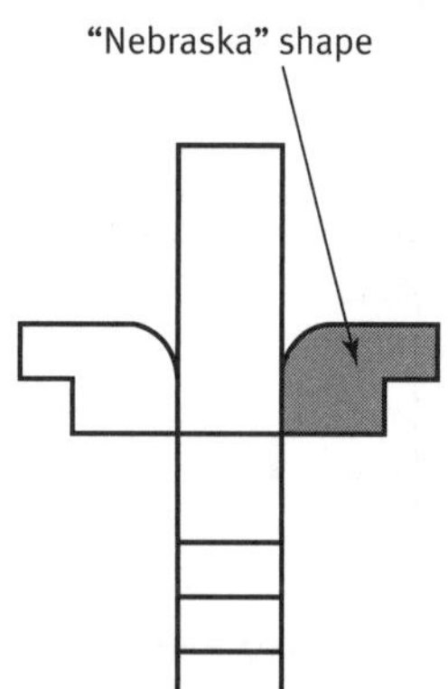

Unique shape: The left and right wing-like segments resemble the state of Nebraska and its mirror image, so the correct answer must have the same shape. (A) is the only shape that matches. If you do not see that, you can eliminate (B), which does not have the correct notch; (C), which has the notch in the middle rather than on the end; and (D), which has a notch that is too large. Eliminating all three verifies that the correct answer is (A).

Unique shading: The figure has no shading.

Key landmark: There is no need to use a key landmark since unique shape is sufficient.

41. B

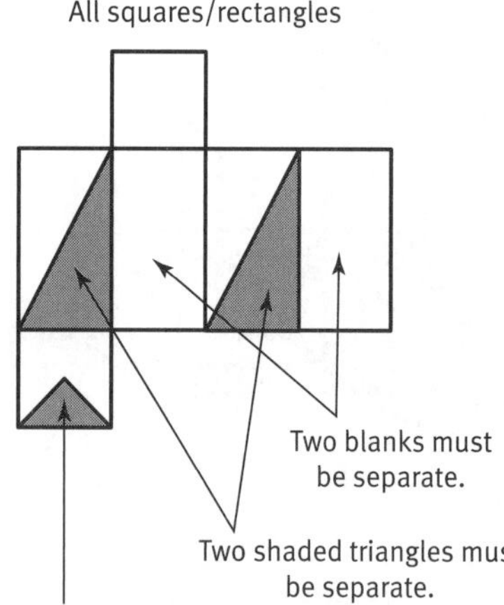

Unique shape: All sides are squares or rectangles, so there is no unique shape.

Unique shading: The overall shading alternates between half-shaded and blank rectangles, which is represented by (A) and (B) and eliminates (C) and (D).

Key landmark: The key triangle on the square on the bottom can be used to determine if the answer is (A) or (B). When the pattern is folded away from you, the bottom of the first white rectangle will be on the side, and the bottom of the half shaded rectangle with the shade will touch the triangle, so you can eliminate (A). The correct answer is (B).

42. A

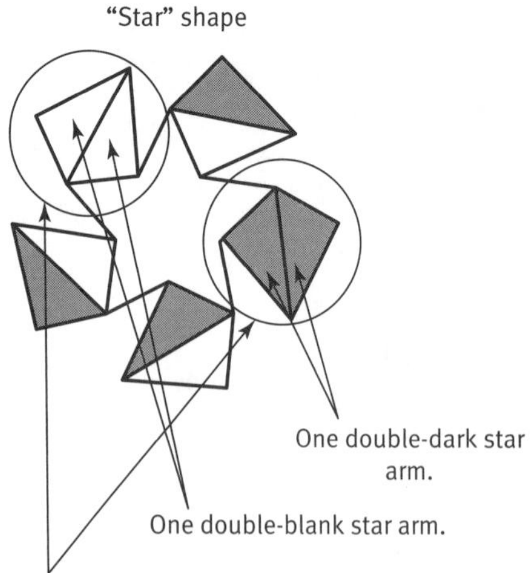

Unique shape: All the sides are arms of the star; there is no unique shape.

Unique shading: There is only one double-dark star arm, so eliminate (B), which has 2 double-dark arms, and (D), which has no double-dark arms. There is also only one

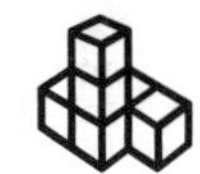

double-blank star arm, so eliminate (B), which has 2 double-blank arms.

Key landmark: The double-dark star arm and the double-blank star arm must be separated by at least 1 star arm, so eliminate (C), which has those arms next to each other. The correct answer is (A).

43. D

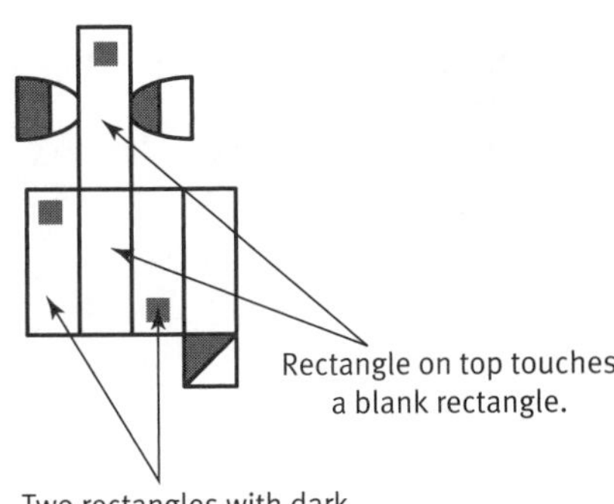

Unique shape: There is a curve on the front. All answer choices have this curve, so none can be eliminated.

Unique shading: The overall shading alternates between blank rectangles and rectangles that contain a small dark square. You can eliminate (B), which has the rectangles with the 2 small dark squares next to each other.

Key landmark: The key landmark is the piece that curves. Both ends of this piece must touch one of the blank rectangles. You can eliminate (A), (B), and (C), which all have the curved piece touching a rectangle with a dark square. The correct answer is (D).

44. B

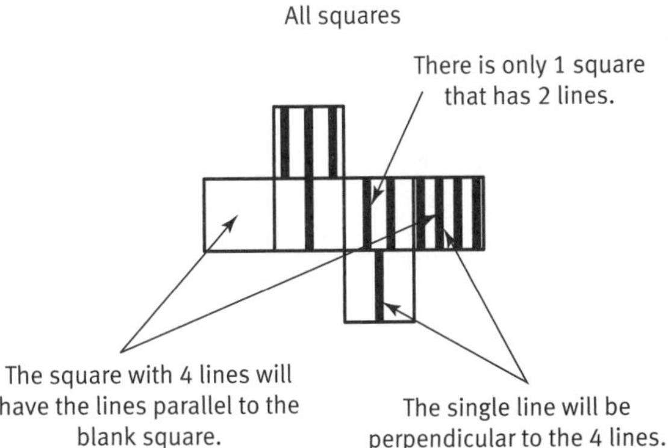

Unique shape: All sides are squares, so there is no unique face.

Unique shading: Here you want to look at the number of lines on each of the squares for unique shading. There is only one square that contains 2 lines, so you can eliminate (D), which has 2 sides with 2 lines.

Key landmark: The piece on the bottom with one line will line up perpendicular to the side on the far right with 4 lines. Therefore, you can eliminate (A), which has the lines oriented in the same direction. The square with the 4 lines on the right side will line up so that the lines are parallel to the blank square. This allows you to eliminate (C), which has the 4 lines going into the blank square. The correct answer is (B).

45. D

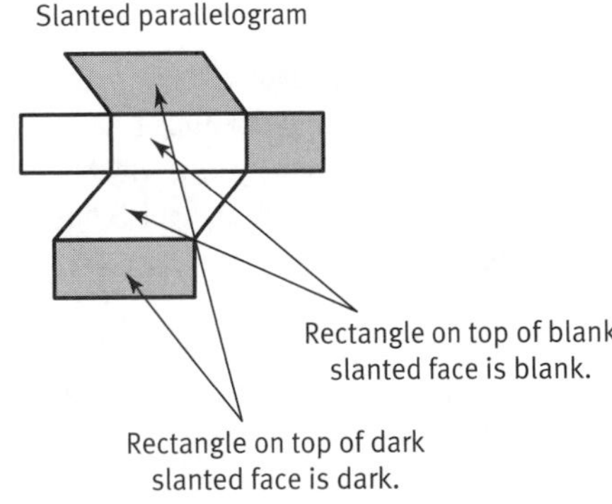

Unique shape: The main large pieces are slanted parallelograms, so eliminate (A) and (B), which are both parallelograms with 90° angles.

Unique shading: The overall shading has one shaded slanted parallelogram and one blank slanted parallelogram. The rectangles on the top and bottom of the slanted parallelogram will either be blank or shaded. Look at these as key landmarks.

Key landmark: Use the slanted faces as key landmarks, starting with the blank slanted face. The blank end will be on the left, and the rectangle on top will be blank, so eliminate (C), which has the dark rectangle on top. The correct answer is (D). Confirm answer (D) by using the dark slanted parallelogram; when the dark parallelogram is in the front, the dark end will be on the right, and the top will be dark, which matches (D).

46. A

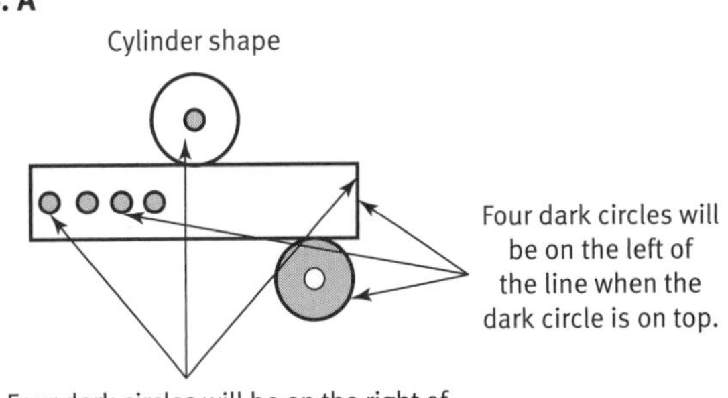

Unique shape: The circles on the top and bottom show that the rectangle will curve around them to become a cylinder. All the answers are cylinders, so none can be eliminated.

Unique shading: The circle on top will either be blank with a dark dot or dark with a blank dot. You can use the four dark circles on the rectangle as key landmarks to eliminate answer choices.

Key landmark: Start by keeping the blank circle on the top, as in the pattern. When the rectangle curls around, the 4 dark circles will be on the right of the line, so you can eliminate (C), which has the dark circles on the left of the line.

Next, put the dark circle with blank dot on top. Then, the rectangle curls around such that the circles will be to the left of the line, so you can eliminate (B), which has the dark circles to the right of the line, and (D), which has no dark circles. The correct answer is (A).

Answers and explanations continue on the next page ▶ ▶ ▶

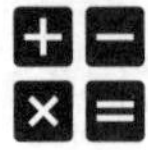

Quantitative Reasoning 1

1. E	22. D	43. B
2. C	23. C	44. A
3. D	24. A	45. C
4. D	25. D	46. E
5. B	26. B	47. A
6. C	27. D	48. B
7. B	28. A	49. A
8. D	29. A	50. B
9. D	30. E	51. E
10. E	31. B	52. E
11. D	32. D	53. A
12. B	33. E	54. E
13. A	34. C	55. C
14. C	35. B	56. D
15. E	36. A	57. C
16. E	37. E	58. C
17. C	38. C	59. A
18. C	39. D	60. C
19. B	40. D	61. B
20. B	41. A	62. A
21. C	42. A	

1. E

Stop: This is a word problem, and the choices are variable expressions with fractions.

Think: Variables in the answer choices means that Picking Numbers will work, but take care to Pick Numbers that divide easily into each other. There are three distinct variables: c, x, and d. Originally, there were c people who would contribute equal amounts to raise a total of x dollars. But, d people dropped out. The question asks how many extra dollars must be raised by each remaining person in order to meet the dollar goal.

Predict: Most of the choices have x on top of the fraction and c and/or $(c - d)$ on the bottom. To keep the arithmetic simple, Pick Numbers such that x divides nicely by both c and $(c - d)$. And, while the problem doesn't explicitly say so, c must be greater than d because there can't be more people dropping out than were contributing in the first place.

Here's one set of numbers:

$x = 12$

$c = 6$

$d = 4$

Replacing variables with numbers makes it much easier to solve the problem. Originally, 6 people had to come up with a total of \$12, so each person would have had to pay $\frac{\$12}{6} = \$2$. After 4 people drop out, there are $6 - 4 = 2$ people left, but the amount to be raised is still \$12. With only 2 people sticking around, they need to pay $\frac{\$12}{2} = \$6$ each. Remember that the question asked how much extra each person would need to pay. The original contribution per person was \$2. Now, it's \$6. So, the additional number of dollars each contributor must pay is \$4.

Match: Since the choices are variable expressions, plug the numbers into each choice to make sure that only one choice produces the correct answer of \$4.

(A) $\frac{4(12)}{6} = \frac{48}{6} = 8$ Eliminate.

(B) $\frac{12}{6-4} = \frac{12}{2} = 6$ Eliminate.

(C) $\frac{4}{6-4(12)} = \frac{4}{6-48}$ Eliminate. Don't waste time with this arithmetic on Test Day! The fraction is not going to equal 4.

(D) $\frac{12}{6(6-4)} = \frac{12}{6(2)} = \frac{12}{12} = 1$ Eliminate. Either select (E), the only remaining choice, or plug in the numbers to confirm.

(E) $\frac{4(12)}{6(6-4)} = \frac{48}{6(2)} = \frac{48}{12} = 4$ Matches the prediction.

2. C

Stop: This is a number properties question with Roman numeral answer choices. The Roman numeral statements are variable expressions.

Think: The question asks which of the expressions *cannot* be a positive integer. This means that you can eliminate a statement as soon as you determine that it *can* be a positive integer. It doesn't have to *always* be a positive integer; you need to find only one scenario in which the expression can be a positive integer in order to eliminate it. Both x and y are integers and x is greater than y. Use Kaplan's Roman Numeral Strategy and consider Picking Numbers. Start with the statement that appears most often in the answer choices. If plugging in the numbers results in a positive integer, eliminate the choices that include that statement. If it results in a negative integer, pick another set of numbers that might change the sign of the outcome.

Predict: Start with Roman numeral II since it appears in three of the answer choices. Pick Numbers. One manageable set is $x = 3$ and $y = 2$. Plugging those numbers into Roman numeral II gives you:

II. $y(x - y) = 2(3 - 2) = 2(1) = 2$

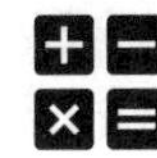

The expression in statement II can be a positive integer, so eliminate choices (B), (D), and (E). The remaining options are (A) and (C). Statement I (A) is easier to evaluate than statement III (C), so start with statement I. Notice that the structure of the expression is the same as in statement II and that the sign of the result depends upon the signs of the numbers being multiplied. Looking at the terms strategically, you can see that $(y - x)$ will be negative if both variables are positive because y is less than x. Multiplying that negative term by a positive y will yield a negative result. But, what if the numbers are negative? Try $x = -3$ and $y = -4$:

I. $y(y - x) = -4(-4 - (-3)) = -4(-1) = 4$

So, statement I can be positive. Eliminate choice (A).

Match: (C) is correct because statements I and II can result in positive integers. Without even testing statement III, you know that it cannot be a positive integer because the others can be. You may note, though, that the numerator and denominator of the fraction are each the difference between x and y, just in the opposite directions. This answer would therefore yield −1.

3. D

Stop: This is a word problem with unknown values. The choices are percentages, and two of them have decimals. Careful arithmetic work will be needed in this problem.

Think: Output increased by 90% while working hours decreased by 20%. The question asks for the percent increase in output per hour. Since both the original output and the original hours are unknowns, Picking Numbers is a solid approach. For percentage problems like this one, 100 is the best number to pick because the value and the percent will be the same.

Predict: Let the original output and hours both equal 100. Also, compute the original output per hour since that's what the question asks about:

Original output $= 100$

Original hours $= 100$

Original output per hour $= \frac{100}{100} = 1$

Output increases by 90 percent, which is 90, since any number as a percent out of 100 is just itself. Similarly, hours decrease by 20. Write down the new values and compute the new output per hour:

New output $= 100 + 90 = 190$

New hours $= 100 - 20 = 80$

New output per hour $= \frac{190}{80} = \frac{19}{8} = 2\frac{3}{8} = 2.375$

Note that the decimal equivalents of eighths $\left(\frac{1}{8} = 0.125\right)$ are very handy to know on Test Day. Now, be sure to answer the question: the *increase* in the output per hour:

New – Original $= 2.375 - 1 = 1.375 = \frac{137.5}{100} = 137.5\%$

Match: (D) is correct. (E) is the new output per hour as a percent of the original.

4. D

Stop: This is an averages problem, and the answers are numbers, so calculations must be made.

Think: The average test score in a class of 7 is 80. The average score of 6 of the 7 students is 78. The question asks what the seventh score is. Backsolving would work here since the choices contain easy numbers to plug in.

Predict: Use the formula for averages and Backsolve starting with (B) and (D) looking for the final average to be 80. (B) (88) and try the averages formula.

(B) $\frac{6(78)+88}{7} = 79.4$ This is too low, so you need a higher number.

(D) $\frac{6(78)+92}{7} = 80$ This matches the information in the question stem.

Match: (D) is correct. Backsolving worked very well, but you can also use critical thinking to balance the average. Six of the seven students average a 78, so each of them is an average of 2 points shy of the overall class average. So, as a group, they bring down the average by $(2)(6) = 12$ points. To balance the average, the seventh student needs to make up that 12 point shortfall: $80 + 12 = 92$. Finally, you could set up the average formula and solve for x instead of Backsolving:

$$\text{sum} = (\text{average})(\text{number})$$

$$(6)(78) + x = (80)(7)$$

$$468 + x = 560$$

$$x = 560 - 468 = 92$$

5. B

Stop: The question relates two people's ages, and the choices are small, manageable integers.

Think: Michael is 12 years older than Jake and will be twice as old as Jacob in 9 years. The question asks for Jacob's age in 4 years. Since the choices are numbers and the only unknown value is the one the question asks for, Backsolving will work here.

Predict: Start Backsolving with (B) since Jacob is the younger boy. If Jacob will be 7 in 4 years, then he's 3 years old right now. Michael is 12 years older, making him $3 + 12 = 15$ years old. Now, look nine years ahead. Michael will be $15 + 9 = 24$, and Jacob will be $3 + 9 = 12$. Check whether this fits the problem. It does! Nine years from now, Mike is twice as old (24 years) as Jake (12 years).

Match: (B) is correct.

6. C

Stop: The question includes percentages and actual values. The answer choices are large values and are very far apart. This means that you can round the numbers in the problem and not worry that you'll accidentally reach an incorrect answer.

Think: The question asks for the total number of votes that must be counted. First, find the number of registered voters. Then, calculate 25% of the total number of registered voters in the county. Finally, multiply the number of ballots cast by 8 since each ballot contains 8 votes. Use estimation to find the answer more quickly.

Predict: The total number of voters is 5,492 + 8,445, which is slightly lower than 14,000. Take 25% of this estimate: 25% of 14,000 = $\frac{14{,}000}{4}$ = 3,500. Each voter would vote 8 times. 3,500 × 8 = 28,000. The number that is closest (yet still lower) is 27,874 or answer choice (C).

Match: The number that is closest yet still lower is 27,874. Choice (C) is correct.

7. B

Stop: This is a combined work problem, and the answer choices are times. The choices are spread pretty far apart, so estimation will be an effective approach.

Think: One faucet takes 20 minutes to fill a vat, while another takes 12 minutes. The question asks how long the faucets will take to fill the vat when working together. Educated Guessing and Traditional Math are both effective approaches on this question.

Predict: Before doing any math, think intuitively about the problem. One of the faucets can fill the vat in 12 minutes by itself, so the two faucets working together would not take longer than 12 minutes. Eliminate all choices greater than 12: (C), (D), and (E). Continue to think critically. If either faucet could get the job done in 12 minutes, then working together, they'd be twice as fast, and the vat would be full after 6 minutes. But one of the faucets is slower than that, so the answer must be longer than 6 minutes. Eliminate any choice that is 6 minutes or less: (A).

Match: Only one choice is greater than 6 minutes but less than 12 minutes. (B) is correct. If the choices were closer together, the combined work formula would make short work of this problem too:

$$\text{Total time} = \frac{(\text{Rate A})(\text{Rate B})}{(\text{Rate A} + \text{Rate B})} = \frac{(12)(20)}{(12+20)} = 7.5$$

8. D

Stop: The question is an expression with a complex fraction and numerals. No variables are included. Most of the choices are fractions.

Think: Use Traditional Math. Note that since most of the choices are fractions, you'll want to keep your work in fraction form rather than simplifying to decimals.

Predict: Start with the most nested fraction: $\frac{1}{\frac{2}{3}} = \frac{3}{2}$. Now, calculate:

$$\frac{2}{3-\frac{3}{2}}+2=$$

$$\frac{2}{\frac{6}{2}-\frac{3}{2}}+2=$$

$$\frac{2}{\frac{3}{2}}+2=$$

$$\frac{2}{1}\times\frac{2}{3}+2=$$

$$\frac{4}{3}+2=$$

$$\frac{4}{3}+\frac{4}{2}=$$

$$\frac{8}{6}+\frac{12}{6}=\frac{20}{6}=\frac{10}{3}$$

Match: (D) is correct.

9. D

Stop: The question tests fractions and arithmetic. The choices are numbers; some are fractions and some are integers.

Think: The question asks for a permissible value of n, given that $\frac{3}{4}-\frac{1}{2}+\frac{n}{12}$ is an integer. The question looks tricky, so simplifying the given expression by using Traditional Math will be helpful.

Predict: The common denominator of $\frac{3}{4}$, $\frac{1}{2}$, and $\frac{n}{12}$ is 12. Use this to simplify the expression:

$$\frac{9}{12}-\frac{6}{12}+\frac{n}{12}=\frac{9-6+n}{12}=\frac{3+n}{12}$$

Now, think critically. If $\frac{3+n}{12}$ is an integer, then $3+n$ must be a multiple of 12.

Match: (D) is correct because 3 + 21 = 24, which is a multiple of 12. Choice (E) is a multiple of 12, but $3+n$ should be a multiple of 12, not n.

10. E

Stop: The question stem includes complex fractions with two variables. The choices are a mix of simple whole numbers and complicated fractions with variables. You're likely to be tested on your ability to cancel accurately. Either the variables will cancel out, or they won't.

Think: Fraction algebra will work on this problem, but it looks pretty complicated. Consider Picking Numbers here since there are variables.

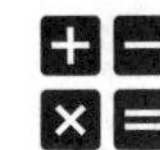

Predict: There aren't any restrictions for a and b, so pick small numbers that are easy to work with:

$$a = 2$$
$$b = 3$$

$$\frac{2\times 2}{(2\times 2)+(3\times 3)} - \left(\frac{3\times 3}{(2\times 2)+(3\times 3)} - 1\right) = \frac{4}{13} - \left(\frac{9}{13} - 1\right)$$
$$= \frac{4}{13} - \frac{9}{13} + \frac{13}{13} = \frac{8}{13}$$

Match: Since the answer will be a fraction, eliminate (A) and (B). Plug $a = 2$ and $b = 3$ into the remaining choices to find the one that matches.

(C) $\frac{6\times 3}{(2\times 2)+(3\times 3)} = \frac{18}{13}$ Eliminate.

(D) $\frac{2\times 2}{(2\times 2)+(3\times 3)} = \frac{4}{13}$ Eliminate.

(E) $\frac{4\times 2}{(2\times 2)+(3\times 3)} = \frac{8}{13}$ Match.

(E) is correct.

To solve with algebra, you would replace 1 with $\frac{2a+3b}{2a+3b}$ and then add the terms in the numerator and set the sum over the common denominator.

11. D

Stop: This is a "must be true" question with an equation. The choices are variables set equal to either numbers or other variables.

Think: What must be true isn't immediately evident from the equation given, so simplify the equation by using Traditional Math.

Predict: The first step to simplifying any equation is to get rid of the fractions. Multiply both sides by $(7c - d)$:

$12c = 2(7c - d)$

$12c = 14c - 2d$

Now, subtract $14c$ from both sides to get all of the like terms together:

$12c - 14c = -2d$

$-2c = -2d$

Finally, divide both sides by -2:

$c = d$

This means that any values for c and d would work as long as they're equal to each other.

Match: (D) is correct. Neither c nor d has to have any particular value.

12. B

Stop: This is a ratio question. The answer choices are written as fractions.

Think: You're looking for the ratio of men's to women's average scores. Traditional math will work best here.

Predict: Use the average formula to find the men's and women's average scores:

Men's average $= \frac{76+90+85}{3} = \frac{251}{3}$

Women's average $= \frac{66+95+87}{3} = \frac{248}{3}$

Men's average:Women's average

$= \frac{251}{3} \div \frac{248}{3} = \frac{251}{3} \times \frac{3}{248} = \frac{251}{248}$

Match: (B) is correct.

13. A

Stop: This is a ratio question, and the choices are whole numbers closely packed together, so estimation probably won't work.

Think: There are 7 sofas for every 6 futons, and 14 total sofas. The question asks for the combined number of sofas and futons, which can be found using Traditional Math.

Predict: You can solve ratios by setting up an equation, but here the answer can be found quickly by thinking critically. Since there are 14 sofas and 14 equals 7×2, the number of futons must be 6×2, or 12. The combined number of sofas and futons is therefore $14 + 12 = 26$.

Match: (A) is correct. On Test Day, the number of futons (12) could have been a trap choice.

14. C

Stop: This question includes multiple ratios. The choices provide numbers of lilies and daisies.

Think: The question provides three concrete facts: there are 12 roses, 6 daisies for every 3 roses, and 4 daisies for every 2 lilies. Your task is to compute the number of daisies and lilies using Traditional Math.

Predict: To make working with ratios simpler, translate them into equations:

daisies:roses = 6:3

daisies:lilies = 4:2

You have the number of roses and a ratio of roses to daisies, so you can figure out the number of daisies right away. The number of roses, 12, is 3×4, so the number of daisies must be 6×4, or 24. Eliminate any choice in which the number of daisies isn't 24: (A), (B), and (D). Since there are 2 daisies for every lily, the number of lilies must be 12.

Match: (C) is correct.

15. E

Stop: This question involves fractions, ratios, and exponents. The choices are fractions, but three of them have a 1 in the denominator, so they could just as easily be whole numbers. The correct answer may or may not be an integer.

Think: You know that $x = 2$ and that $\frac{1}{y} = 2$. The question asks for the ratio of x^4 to y^4, or the value of $\frac{x^4}{y^4}$ Traditional math should be used here.

Predict: Approach this question methodically. You already know that $x = 2$, so find the value of y. Given that $\frac{1}{y} = 2$, $y = \frac{1}{2}$. Plug in the values of x and y into the expression:

$$\frac{2^4}{\left(\frac{1}{2}\right)^4} = 16 \times 16 = 256$$

Match: (E) is correct.

16. E

Stop: The choices are whole numbers, and the question contains a chemical solution and a ratio. This is a mixture problem.

Think: Right now there are 4 ounces of iodine and 16 ounces of alcohol. Some alcohol will evaporate, and the final ratio of iodine to solution must be 2:3. Since the numbers are manageable integers, Backsolving is a nice way to avoid some messy equations here.

Predict: Starting with either (B) or (D) will work. For choice (B), 16 ounces of alcohol – 7 ounces evaporated = 9 ounces left. The amount of iodine stays steady at 4 ounces, so there are 4 + 9 = 13 total ounces of solution. The ratio of iodine to solution is therefore 4:13. Is this right? No. The problem says that the ratio of iodine to solution should be 2:3. At this point, a bit of critical thinking goes a long way. In order for the ratio of iodine to solution to increase, more alcohol needs to evaporate. If more alcohol evaporates, there'll be less total solution, which means a higher proportion of it will be iodine. Since you need a bigger answer, eliminate both (A) and (B). Try choice (D). 16 ounces of alcohol – 10 ounces evaporate = 6 ounces left. The amount of iodine is still 4 ounces, so there are 4 + 6 = 10 total ounces of solution. The ratio of iodine to solution is now 4:10, or 2:5. This still isn't enough, so eliminate (D) and (C).

Match: (E) is correct because it is the only choice that evaporates more alcohol than (D), which was too small. Beware of the wrong–ratio trap seen in (D): if 10 ounces of alcohol evaporate, the ratio of iodine to alcohol would be 2:3, not the ratio of iodine to solution.

17. C

Stop: This is a percent question. The answer choices are whole numbers, but they're fairly close together. Precise calculation will be required.

Think: The original stock price is \$2,500. The price increases by 40% then decreases by 15%. You're tasked with finding the final value. Use Traditional Math.

Predict: A common trap answer will combine the two percentages. Don't do this! Instead, compute the percent change one change at a time. First, the stock rises by 40%. Since $40\% = \frac{2}{5}$, you can find 40% of 2,500 quickly: one–fifth of 2500 is 500, so two–fifths is $500 \times 2 = 1000$. The new price is \$2,500 + \$1,000 = \$3,500. Next, the stock falls by 15%. Again, clever arithmetic is the way to go. Ten percent of 3500 is 350, and 15 is one and a half times as much as 10. So, 15% of 3,500 is $350 \times 1.5 = 350 + 175 = 525$. The final price is \$3,500 – \$525 = \$2,975.

Match: (C) is correct. Don't fall for choice (D), which is what you'd get if you tried to combine the percent changes. Note that you also could have used the on-screen calculator here instead of mental math.

18. C

Stop: This is a long word problem with variables in the answer choices. It looks difficult, but Picking Numbers might work. On Test Day, this may be one to skip and return to later.

Think: This problem is complex, but there's just one variable, p, and it looks like you can Pick Numbers for it just fine. The question asks how many people were added to the district.

Predict: To keep things simple, let $p = 9{,}000$. This way, everybody lives in County A, while County B's population is zero. Sure, it's a bit strange, but there's nothing against it in the problem, and it simplifies your work. Now, solve the problem. In 1980, there were 9,000 people in County A and 0 people in County B. Over the next ten years, the population of County A increased by 9%. Since the question asks for the increase, not the total, find just the increase:

$$9\% \text{ of } 9{,}000 = \frac{9}{100} \times 9{,}000 = \frac{81000}{100} = 810$$

The population of County B increased by 5%, but 5% of 0 is 0. Since County B remained empty, the total population increase was just 810 people.

Match: At first glance, it may look difficult to plug $p = 9{,}000$ into the choices. When the arithmetic looks difficult on Test Day, use critical thinking to shortcut your work.

(A) is huge. It's 45,000 plus something, so it's way bigger than 810.

(B) is 450 minus a positive number. This will be much less than 810.

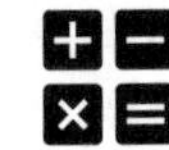

(C) might be right at first glance.

(D) includes 810—the number you're looking for—but minus some number, so it won't be 810 exactly.

(E) includes 810—again, the number you're looking for—but plus some number, so it will be too large.

(C) is correct. It's not necessary to do the arithmetic since you've eliminated all of the other choices.

19. B

Stop: This is a percent problem. The choices indicate percent change. They cover a wide spread, so Estimation will work on this problem.

Think: The volume of water fell by 40% and then rose by 40%. Your goal is to find the total percent change. Picking Numbers would work here, but Estimation is even faster.

Predict: Since the volume of water rose after falling by 40%, there's no way the total decrease is greater than 40%, so eliminate (A). At the same time, there had to have been some overall decrease, since 40% of the original, larger value would have been greater than 40% of the new, smaller value, so eliminate (D) and (E). Remember that you cannot combine percent changes, so eliminate (C), which assumes that the 40% decrease is cancelled out by the 40% increase. The correct value should be somewhere between 0 and 40.

Match: (B) is correct because it is the only choice with a decrease between 0 and 40.

20. B

Stop: The choices are fractions, while the question contains percentages. Conversion between fractions and percentages will be required.

Think: Eighty percent of the poll's respondents are registered voters, and 75% of those people voted. The question asks for the percentage of survey respondents who were registered voters and did *not* vote. Since there are percentages and one unknown value, Pick Numbers.

Predict: Let the number of respondents be 100 since 100 is the best number to use with percentages. If 100 people responded to the poll, then 80 people are registered voters. Seventy-five percent of the registered voters voted in the last election, so compute 75% of 80. The quickest way to do this is to note that 75% is $\frac{3}{4}$, and $\frac{3}{4}$ of 80 is 60. But, the question asks for the percent of people who were registered voters but *didn't* vote. Since 60 registered voters voted, $80 - 60 = 20$ did not. Thus, 20 out of 100, or 1 in 5, of the poll's respondents are registered voters who didn't vote.

Match: (B) is correct. Watch out for choice (C), which is the fraction of *registered voters* who didn't vote, not the fraction of *survey respondents* who were registered but didn't vote.

21. C

Stop: This is a scientific notation question.

Think: You need to rewrite this number in scientific notation. Remember the definition of how to express numbers in scientific notation: $a \times 10^b$.

Predict: The first non-zero number is 2, so the decimal point goes just to the right of this value: 2.563×10^b. Next, count up the number of places that you needed to move the decimal point in order for it to be in between the 2 and the 5: 7.

Substituting in the values for a and b makes your expression 2.563×10^7.

Match: (C) is correct. On Test Day, it is useful to remember that 10^0 is 1, 10^3 is a thousand, 10^6 is a million, and 10^9 is a billion. This will help you narrow the possibilities for b.

22. D

Stop: This is a scientific notation question. The number in the question is in scientific notation but the answer choices are not.

Think: You're given a number written in scientific notation, and you need to convert it to simple decimal form. Determine how many digits you'll need to move the decimal point.

Predict: The 10 has an exponent of positive 3, so you'll move the decimal point 3 places to the right. Moving the decimal point on 3.7 by 3 digits gives you 3,700.

Match: (D) is correct. Notice that because the exponent is positive, the value of the expression is greater than 1. Answer choices (A) and (B) can thus be eliminated right away, leaving you with only three choices.

23. C

Stop: The question uses very large numbers in the stem and scientific notation in the choices. While the numbers in this question look daunting, you can use critical thinking to determine which answer choice is correct without doing extensive addition of large terms.

Think: The question asks for the approximate sum, so you can round the numbers in the question stem, find a, and then count the number of places that you must move the decimal point to find the b exponent.

Predict: Round 10,485,456 to 10,500,000 and 650,987,498, to 651,000,000. Adding these numbers gives you a sum of 661,500,000. You'll need to move the decimal point 8 places to the left in order to put it in

between the first two digits. So, the correct answer will begin with approximately 6.6, and the 10 will have an exponent of 8.

Match: (C) is correct. Notice that if you needed to save time, you could recognize that the correct answer needed an exponent of 8 on the 10, which eliminates every choice except for (C) and (D). Alternatively, as soon as you realized that the correct answer needed to begin with 6.6, you could narrow things down to choices (A) and (C).

24. A

Stop: The question contains scientific notation with answer choices in decimal form.

Think: You need to rewrite the expression in decimal form. Recognizing how many digits you'll need to move the decimal point will allow you to calculate the correct answer.

Predict: The *b* value, or the exponent on the 10, is –5; you'll need to move the decimal point 5 places to the left. Moving the decimal point one digit to the left creates the number 0.21. In order to move it another four digits to the left, you'll need to add four 0s between 2 and the decimal point.

Match: (A) is correct.

25. D

Stop: The choices are fractions, while the question contains fractions, exponents, and a ratio. Get ready for lots of careful arithmetic.

Think: You need to find the ratio of $\left(\frac{3}{8}\right)^5$ to $\left(\frac{3}{8}\right)^6$. There aren't any variables or unknowns, and the fractional answer choices make estimation difficult. It's time to do arithmetic using Traditional Math.

Predict: Use the exponent properties to simplify the numbers. Powers can be distributed across multiplication and division:

$\left(\frac{3}{8}\right)^5 = \frac{3^5}{8^5}$ and $\left(\frac{3}{8}\right)^6 = \frac{3^6}{8^6}$

Since the choices are fractions, write the ratio as division:

$\frac{3^5}{8^5} \div \frac{3^6}{8^6}$

Recall that dividing by a fraction is the same as multiplying by its reciprocal:

$\frac{3^5}{8^5} \times \frac{8^6}{3^6}$

Now use the exponent properties to simplify the 3 and 8 terms individually:

$\frac{3^5}{3^6} = 3^{5-6} = 3^{-1} = \frac{1}{3}$

$\frac{8^6}{8^5} = 8^{6-5} = 8^1 = 8$

The answer:

$\frac{1}{3} \times 8 = \frac{8}{3}$

Match: (D) is correct.

26. B

Stop: The choices are small integers, while the question contains an equation with a variable in the exponents.

Think: You need to solve for *x*. Since the choices are numbers, Backsolving is an option. In this case, however, the exponent rules lead to simple arithmetic, so use Traditional Math.

Predict: Whenever you have variables in exponents, try to convert all of the bases to be the same. In this problem, $16 = 4^2$, so plug 4^2 in place of the 16 on the right side of the equation:

$4^{2x+2} = (4^2)^{3x-1}$

Now use exponent properties to simplify the right side:

$4^{2x+2} = 4^{(2)(3x-1)} = 4^{6x-2}$

This is why you want the bases to be the same. If 4 to one power equals 4 raised to another power, then the powers have to be the same. There's no way you can take the same number to two different powers and get the same result. Thus, the 4 drop out, leaving you a straightforward equation to solve.

$2x + 2 = 6x - 2$

$-4x = -4$

$x = 1$

Match: (B) is correct. You can Backsolve to confirm: $4^{2+2} = 16^{3-1}$ and $4^4 = 16^2 = 256$.

27. D

Stop: The choices are fractions with exponents, while the question is a complex fraction with even more unsimplified exponents. Looks like you'll have to use the exponent properties here but not find an exact value.

Think: The question asks for the simplified expression. With no variables and fractions in the choices, you'll have to use Traditional Math.

Predict: Addition and subtraction don't work well with exponents; the exponent properties only work across division and multiplication. Thus, in exponent problems, always factor to eliminate as many addition and subtraction signs between bases as possible. The most that you can factor out of $4^4 + 4^5$ is 4^4:

$$\frac{2^{21}}{4^4(4^4+4^5)} = \frac{2^{21}}{(4^4)(4^4)(1+4)} = \frac{2^{21}}{(4^4)(4^4)(5)}$$

Next, use exponent properties to combine $4^4 \times 4^4$:

$$\frac{2^{21}}{(4^4)(4^4)(5)} = \frac{2^{21}}{(4^8)(5)}$$

When working with exponents, try to make all the bases the same so that you can use the exponent properties. Here, $4 = 2^2$, so insert 2^2 in place of the 4:

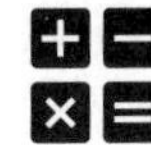

$$\frac{2^{21}}{(4^8)(5)} = \frac{2^{21}}{(2^2)^8(5)} = \frac{2^{21}}{(2^{16})(5)}$$

Finally, apply the exponent property of division to simplify:

$$\frac{2^{21}}{(2^{16})(5)} = \frac{2^5}{5}$$

Match: (D) is correct.

28. A

Stop: The choices are numbers, and most of them are fractions. The question includes an equation with variable exponents.

Think: The question asks for the value of *x*. You could Backsolve since this is the only unknown. However, fractions would make it complicated. Using exponent properties and algebra will be best.

Predict: When you work with exponents, try to make all the bases the same. Here, $4 = 2^2$ so you can replace each 4 with 2^2. Notice also that 128 is a power of 2: 2^7.

$$(4^{2x})(4^x)(2^3) = 128$$

$$(2^2)^{2x} \times (2^2)^x \times 2^3 = 2^7$$

You can now use the exponent properties to simplify the left side:

$$2^{4x} \times 2^{2x} \times 2^3 = 2^7$$

$$2^{4x + 2x + 3} = 2^7$$

$$2^{6x + 3} = 2^7$$

At this point, the bases drop out, leaving you with an equation to solve for *x*:

$$6x + 3 = 7$$

$$6x = 4$$

$$x = \frac{4}{6} = \frac{2}{3}$$

Match: (A) is correct.

29. A

Stop: The question and answer choices are numbers with radicals. The properties of roots being tested.

Think: The question is an expression with radicals, which you need to simplify. You'll have to use Traditional Math, since there aren't any variables or unknowns.

Predict: Factor each radical to pull out the perfect squares. 75 is 25×3, and 12 is 4×3. So:

$$\sqrt{25 \times 3} + (3)\left(\sqrt{4 \times 3}\right) = 5\sqrt{3} + 6\sqrt{3} = 11\sqrt{3}$$

Match: (A) is correct.

30. E

Stop: The choices are small decimals, while the question is a radical of a decimal.

Think: There are no unknowns, so use radical arithmetic to calculate the value.

Predict: Taking square roots of decimals can be tricky. If you're not sure of the answer, convert the decimal to a fraction and apply the radical properties instead. The number 0.0064 is the same as 64/10,000.

$$\sqrt{\frac{64}{10000}} = \frac{\sqrt{64}}{\sqrt{10000}} = \frac{8}{100} = 0.08$$

The square root of 64 is 8, and the square root of 10,000 is 100. So the answer is 8/100, or 0.08.

Match: (E) is correct. Don't be trapped by choice (B); it's half of 0.0064, not the square root of 0.0064.

31. B

Stop: The choices are expressions with variables and fractional powers, while the question is a variable expression with exponents and a radical.

Think: The question asks you to simplify the expression. With all these variables, Picking Numbers is an option. However, the large powers and the fractional powers will make it hard to compute a value. On this problem, straightforward algebra is best.

Predict: Taking the *n*th root of something is the same as raising it to the 1/*n*th power. So, rewrite the denominator as a power of $\frac{1}{3}$ and use the exponent property of multiplication to simplify:

$$\frac{x^3y^1z^2}{(x^6y^4z^6)^{\frac{1}{3}}} = \frac{x^3y^1z^2}{(x^6)^{\frac{1}{3}}(y^4)^{\frac{1}{3}}(z^6)^{\frac{1}{3}}} = \frac{x^3y^1z^2}{x^2y^{\frac{4}{3}}z^2}$$

To simplify the fraction further, use the exponent property of division:

$$\frac{x^3y^1z^2}{x^2y^{\frac{4}{3}}z^2} = (x^{3-2})\,y^{1-\frac{4}{3}}\,(z^{2-2}) = xy^{-\frac{1}{3}}z^0 = \frac{x}{y^{\frac{1}{3}}}$$

Match: (B) is correct.

32. D

Stop: The choices are simple integers, while the question describes exponents and roots. Accurate translation will be important.

Think: Solve for *x*. Backsolving is a possibility, but the powers and roots will make calculation difficult. This is another case when Traditional Math is best.

Predict: Translate the first sentence, one piece at a time. The positive fourth root of x^3 is $x^{\frac{3}{4}}$. The positive square root of *x* is $x^{\frac{1}{2}}$. Note that if you write the roots as fractional exponents, you can combine them:

$(x^{\frac{3}{4}})(x^{\frac{1}{2}}) = 32$

$x^{\frac{3}{4}+\frac{1}{2}} = 32$

$x^{\frac{5}{4}} = 32$

To clear the exponent from the x, you need to raise both sides of the equation to $\frac{4}{5}$, since $\frac{5}{4} \times \frac{4}{5} = 1$.

$x = 32^{\frac{4}{5}}$

$32^{\frac{4}{5}}$ is prohibitively difficult to compute. When this happens on Test Day, look for simpler bases to substitute into the problem. For instance, 32 is 2^5. Powers of 2 are very handy to know on Test Day.

$x = (2^5)^{\frac{4}{5}} = 2^4 = 16$

Match: (D) is correct. If you were stumped by $32^{\frac{4}{5}}$, you could use estimation to make an Educated Guess. Since the exponent is just a bit less than 1, the answer must be less than 32. This would eliminate (E), and (D) is the next closest choice to the estimated value.

33. E

Stop: The question asks you to translate the given information into an algebraic expression. The choices are expressions.

Think: Translate one piece of information at a time.

Predict: You're taking the difference of two terms: "two times the sum of x and y" and "three less than x." The first can be written as $2(x + y)$. The second is equal to $x - 3$. (If you thought about translating this as $3 - x$, you can pick a number to help you see the distinction. If you said "3 less than 7", for example, then you would calculate that as $7 - 3$.) The correct answer is the difference between these two terms: $2(x + y) - (x - 3)$.

Match: (E) is correct.

34. C

Stop: The choices are small decimals, and the question includes a percentage and a fraction. Be prepared to do conversions.

Think: The question asks for the value of s. Since there is a variable in the equation and there are numbers in the choices, so you could Backsolve, but the decimals would make it more difficult than traditional algebra.

Predict: Recall that percentages are out of 100. So 68% of $\frac{7}{s}$ is the same as $\frac{68}{100} \times \frac{7}{s}$.

$\frac{68}{100} \times \frac{7}{s} = 5$

First, eliminate the fraction by multiplying both sides by 100s:

$68 \times 7 = 500s$

Then divide by 500 to get s alone:

$\frac{68 \times 7}{500} = s$

$\frac{476}{500} = s$

This is hard arithmetic. When you run up against prohibitively long division on Test Day, see if estimation can carry you the final steps across the finish line. The fraction is a little less than 1.

Match: Eliminate (A), (D), and (E) since the number must be just slightly less than 1. (B) is just below 0.9, while (C) is just above 0.9. The equivalent fraction for 0.9 is $\frac{450}{500}$. Since 476 is greater than 450, the answer must be larger than 0.9. (C) is correct.

35. B

Stop: The choices are manageable integers, while the problem has an equation with a radical and a single variable.

Think: You can Backsolve for d, or you can solve for d with traditional algebra. Since the answer choices are integers, what's under the radical must be a perfect square. As a result, Backsolving beats the algebra.

Predict: You know that $50 + 2d$ must be a perfect square. This makes it straightforward to test the choices. Start with (B).

Choice (B), $d = 7$, yields $50 + 2(7) = 50 + 14 = 64$, which is a perfect square. Check the full equation:

$\sqrt{50 + 2(d)} = 1 + d$

$\sqrt{50 + 2(7)} = 1 + 7$

$\sqrt{64} = 8$

Match: (B) is correct. Be careful not to select (C). Each side of the equation is equal to 8, but the question asks for the value of d rather than the value of the expression on either side.

36. A

Stop: The choices are equations while the question describes an equation in a sentence. This suggests that this problem is about setting something up rather than solving it. Note that the equations in the choices aren't fully simplified.

Think: The question asks for the correct equation. You'll need to translate the question stem in order to deduce which equation fits it.

Predict: The sentence you need to translate is "5 times the sum of y and 4 is 2 less than y." Don't try to do it all at once. Instead, translate piece by piece, from left to right. "5 times" means $5 \times$. Next, "the sum of y and 4" is $y + 4$.

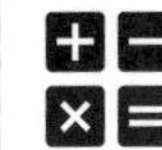

The word "is" means "equals." Thus, so far you have $5(y + 4) =$. The last piece is "2 less than y." Be careful with the order here; this is $y - 2$. Altogether, then, $5(y + 4) = y - 2$.

Match: (A) is correct. Don't do any extra work. Use the Stop step to determine how much work needs to be done.

37. E

Stop: Choices are numbers, mostly in decimal form, and some of the choices are very close together. In the question stem, there's an equation with only one variable.

Think: The question asks for the value of $1.1m$ rather than m itself. The best way to solve this problem is to do the algebra. Picking Numbers is often impractical with equations, and Backsolving is difficult here since you'd be Backsolving for $1.1m$ rather than m.

Predict: To solve $0.1m = 1$ for m, divide both sides by 0.1:

$$m = \frac{1}{0.1} = 10$$

Since $m = 10$, $1.1m$ must equal 1.1×10, which is 11.

Match: (E) is correct. (D) is a trap choice. Be sure to multiply correctly.

38. C

Stop: Choices are weights. Some are integer values, and some have decimals. The question describes an algebraic relationship.

Think: You're asked to calculate Larry's current weight; call this L. You're given enough information to write an equation involving L. Translate one piece at a time.

Predict: The first clause says "If Larry's weight [his current weight, or L] decreased by 20 pounds." This translates to $L - 20$. The sentence continues and tells you that this value would be equal to "$\frac{7}{8}$ of his current weight". This translates to $\frac{7}{8}L$. Set these two terms equal to each other and solve for L:

$$L - 20 = \frac{7}{8}L$$

$$8(L - 20) = 7L$$

$$8L - 160 = 7L$$

$$L = 160$$

Match: (C) is correct.

39. D

Stop: This is a word problem with answer choices representing costs. The answer choices are very close together, so careful calculation is needed.

Think: You need to calculate the cost of a phone call. In order to find the cost, you can set up an equation with the information given.

Predict: The company charges \$4.50—a fixed cost—for the first 5 minutes of a call. The remaining minutes cost \$.50/minute. So if c is the total cost and m is the number of minutes that the call lasts, you can say that $c = 4.5 + 0.5(m - 5)$. This accounts for both the fixed cost, and the fact that the \$0.50/minute charge begins only after the first 5 minutes of the call. The call in question lasts from 9:35–11:15 pm. So, the call lasts for a total of 1 hour and 40 minutes total, which is $60 + 40 = 100$ minutes. This is the value that you'll plug in for m.

$$c = 4.5 + 0.5(100 - 5)$$

$$c = 4.5 + 0.5(95)$$

$$c = 4.5 + 47.5$$

$$c = 52$$

Match: (D) is correct.

40. D

Stop: This is another word problem about costs, but the answer choices are unsolved expressions with the variable h. You don't need to calculate any specific values in this question, but you will need to translate the given information into an equation.

Think: Translate to find an expression for the cost of running an AC unit for h hours/day for 90 days. Start with any fixed costs, and then add the variable costs.

Predict: The air conditioner costs \$0.12/hour for the first 8 hours. This is a fixed cost. Since this air conditioner is being run for 90 days, this fixed cost will be calculated as (90 days)(\$0.12/hour)(8 hours). For any hours over 8, the cost is (90 days)(\$0.10/hour)(h – 8 hours). Put together, the final expression should be $(90)(0.12)(8) + (90)(0.10)(h - 8)$. Simplify this to $(90)(0.12)(8) + (9)(h - 8)$.

Match: (D) is correct. Notice that only answer choices (D) and (E) have the correct terms for fixed cost multiplied together, so you could eliminate choices (A), (B), and (C) before calculating the variable cost.

41. A

Stop: The question gives you a polynomial fraction, and the answer choices are in the same format.

Think: The question asks for an equivalent expression. Picking a number for n is an option. However, algebra is faster.

Predict: This problem is as much a test of what you *can't* do as it is of what you *can* do. Much as you'd like to cancel out that $(n - 2)$ from both sides of the fraction, the "+1" in the numerator prevents any such canceling. All you can do is expand the polynomials and see which answer matches. On top of the fraction you get:

$$3(n - 2) + 1 = 3n - 6 + 1 = 3n - 5$$

Foiling the denominator yields:

$(n + 5)(n - 2) =$
$n^2 - 2n + 5n - 10 = n^2 + 3n - 10$

Altogether, then, the simplified fraction equals $\frac{3n-5}{n^2+3n-10}$.

Match: (A) is correct.

42. A

Stop: The choices are number pairs, while the question contains a quadratic equation.

Think: Solve for n by either Backsolving or using algebra. Algebra is likely to be faster, though, since the equation is relatively simple.

Predict: First, set the equation equal to 0 by subtracting 3 from both sides:

$n^2 + 7n - 8 = 0$

You now need to reverse–FOIL. To do this, look for two numbers that multiply to equal –8 and add to equal 7. Look to the choices for a hint, if needed. 8 and –1 work.

$(n + 8)(n - 1) = 0$

$n = -8$ or 1

Match: (A) is correct. Watch out for choice (B), in which the signs are flipped. This choice is easily selected when you're in a hurry. When choices have the same numbers but different signs, confirm that your signs are right.

43. B

Stop: The choices are quadratic polynomials, and the question asks you to expand a binomial.

Think: As with many polynomial problems, picking a number for x will get the job done, but doing the algebra is faster.

Predict: To simplify $3(x - 5)^2$, begin by squaring the binomial $(x - 5)$. You should know the following property on Test Day: $(a - b)^2 = a^2 - 2ab + b^2$. Use the property as follows:

$3(x - 5)^2 = 3(x^2 - 2(5x) + 5^2) = 3(x^2 - 10x + 25) =$
$3x^2 - 30x + 75$

Match: (B) is correct.

44. A

Stop: Polynomials are in the question stem and the choices.

Think: The question asks you to factor. You could Pick Numbers for x and y, but that would be tedious with all of the exponents and multiplication. Algebra is easier.

Predict: On Test Day, you must know how to recognize the difference of squares: $a^2 - b^2 = (a + b)(a - b)$. Here, x^6 and $9y^4$ are both perfect squares; the square root of x^6 is x^3, and the square root of $9y^4$ is $3y^2$. So:

$x^6 - 9y^4 = (x^3 + 3y^2)(x^3 - 3y^2)$

Match: (A) is correct. Beware of choice (D), which is what you'd get if you forgot to take the square root of the 9 in $9y^4$. You have to take the square root of the whole term, not just the variable component.

45. C

Stop: The choices are polynomial expressions, and the question gives a quadratic equation.

Think: Solve for y. You could pick a number for x or use algebra to solve the equation. Given the relative simplicity of the expression, either approach would work. Careful algebra to eliminate the fractions is probably easiest.

Predict: First, distribute the negative sign on the left:

$$x - \frac{2 - x^2}{x} = \frac{y}{x}$$
$$x - \frac{2}{x} + \frac{x^2}{x} = \frac{y}{x}$$
$$x - \frac{2}{x} + x = \frac{y}{x}$$

Next, multiply both sides of the equation by x to get y by itself:

$$2x - \frac{2}{x} = \frac{y}{x}$$
$$2x^2 - 2 = y$$

Match: (C) is correct.

46. E

Stop: The question describes an equation with a complex fraction, and the answer choices are complex fractions. You need to find an expression for the value of y. In order to do so, you can translate the given information into an equation and isolate it for y.

Think: You need to find an expression for the value of y. In order to do so, you can translate the given information into an equation and then isolate y.

Predict: The stem tells you that the numerator of a fraction equals "the sum of x and 3." This is translated as $x + 3$. The denominator is "equal to the difference of x and y", which is translated as $x - y$. The stem then states that this fraction is equal to 56. So, the equation looks like this:

$$\frac{x+3}{x-y} = 56$$

Isolate y as follows:

$$(x + 3) = (56)(x - y)$$
$$(x + 3) = 56x - 56y$$
$$(x + 3) - 56x = -56y$$
$$-55x + 3 = -56y$$

$$\frac{-55x+3}{-56} = y$$

$$\frac{55x-3}{56} = y$$

Match: (E) is correct.

47. A

Stop: The answers are what values for a and b, and the question stem provides two equations. This question is testing simultaneous equations.

Think: Traditional algebra will work here. The substitution and combination methods will both work, so use the more comfortable method.

Predict: To use substitution, first rearrange the simpler equation:

$a - b + 1 = 0$ to $b = a + 1$

Then, plug this expression for b into the first equation:

$$3a + 7(a + 1) = 12$$
$$10a + 7 = 12$$
$$10a = 5$$
$$a = 0.5$$

To use combination, multiply the simpler equation by 7 and then add the equations to cancel the b terms:

$$3a + 7b = 12$$
$$\underline{+\ 7(a - b = -1)}$$
$$10a = 5$$
$$a = 0.5$$

For either method, once you have the a value, plug it into the simpler equation to find b:

$$b = a + 1$$
$$b = 0.5 + 1 = 1.5$$

Match: (A) is correct.

48. B

Stop: The choices are manageable integers. The question has several variables and equations, so this is a simultaneous equations problem.

Think: The question asks for the value of w. Picking Numbers and Backsolving are often difficult in simultaneous equations problems. Algebra is the way to go.

Predict: With three variables and three equations, it pays to take a moment to plot out the fastest course through the problem. Since you're solving for w, you want to get rid of a and b. And since the first two equations give you a and b in terms of w, you can plug those values into the third equation:

$a = 3 + 3w$ and $b = 5w - 7$

$$4a = 3b$$
$$4(3 + 3w) = 3(5w - 7)$$
$$12 + 12w = 15w - 21$$
$$33 = 3w$$
$$11 = w$$

Match: (B) is correct.

49. A

Stop: The choices are multiples of 10, while the question is a long word problem. Translation will be essential.

Think: The question asks for the difference between the number of balcony seats and the number or orchestra seats. Both of these are unknowns. Since there's only one permissible value for each variable, Picking Numbers won't work. And, since the question asks for the difference between the variables rather than for one of the variables directly, Backsolving won't be effective either. You need to translate and use algebra.

Predict: Let b be the number of balcony tickets and r be the number of orchestra tickets. (Avoid using o as a variable since it's too easy to confuse with the number 0.) A total of 350 tickets were sold, which gives you one equation:

$$b + r = 350$$

Orchestra tickets are \$12, while balcony tickets are \$8. The total income was \$3,320, so that's another equation:

$$8b + 12r = 3{,}320$$

Note that every term in the second equation is a multiple of 4, so you can simplify the equation considerably:

$$2b + 3r = 830$$

You now have two variables and two equations, so either combination or substitution will work. Let's try combination. Multiply the first equation by −2 and add the equations:

$$-2b - 2r = -700$$
$$\underline{+\ 2b + 3r = 830}$$
$$r = 130$$

Plug this value back into the first equation to solve for b:

$$b + 130 = 350$$
$$b = 220$$

Finally, make sure that you answer the question. There were $220 - 130 = 90$ more tickets sold for the balcony than for the orchestra.

Match: (A) is correct. Notice that (D) is the number of orchestra tickets and (E) is the number of balcony tickets. Be sure to always answer the question asked instead of just selecting the first number that you calculate.

50. B

Stop: The choices are simple numbers, while the question gives two equations with two unknowns. This is a classic simultaneous equations problem.

Think: Solve for p using Traditional Math.

Predict: Since the problem asks for only p, use combination to get rid of q:

$p + 2q = 8$

$2p - q = 11$

The easiest way to get rid of q is to multiply the second equation by 2, then add:

$$\begin{array}{r} p + 2q = 8 \\ + \; 4p - 2q = 22 \\ \hline 5p = 30 \\ p = 6 \end{array}$$

Match: (B) is correct. Don't waste time calculating q.

51. E

Stop: The choices are values, and the question stem contains an equation with absolute value. You need to find the possible value(s) of x.

Think: You need to find the possible values of x. Since this is an absolute value equation, you know that x has two possible values. This question can be answered with Backsolving, but the algebra is simple and probably faster.

Predict: To calculate the values of x, set the terms in the absolute value sign equal to both 6 and −6, and isolate x. Start by setting the terms equal to 6:

$x - 2 = 6$

$x = 8$

Now, calculate the value of x when the terms in between the absolute value signs equal −6:

$x - 2 = -6$

$x = -4$

Match: (E) is correct. (A) could be eliminated immediately because it has only one value, but variables inside absolute value signs always have two values. (B) and (D) can be eliminated once you have the first value.

52. E

Stop: This problem has numbers in both the question stem and the answer choices. The question stem includes absolute values symbols.

Think: To solve, you'll need to apply the order of operations to these absolute value expressions in order to determine the correct answer. Traditional math is usually required when there are no variables.

Predict: Start with the numerator:

$|14 \times -6| = |-84| = 84$

The denominator equals $|19 - 5| = 14$.

The final result will be $\frac{84}{14} = \frac{42}{7} = 6$.

Match: (E) is correct.

53. A

Stop: The choices are values, and the question stem gives an equation with absolute value.

Think: The question asks you to solve for x. Backsolving is possible, but the traditional algebra is simpler and, therefore, likely faster.

Predict: Start with the absolute value signs, and then isolate x:

$|18 - 6|x = 48$

$12x = 48$

$x = 4$

Match: (A) is correct.

54. E

Stop: This is a must be true question with absolute value in an equation.

Think: Isolate x to determine what must be true about it.

Predict: Begin by simplifying the equation given. Divide both sides by −6 to isolate the terms in the absolute value signs. As soon as you perform this step, you should see a problem. $\frac{96}{-6}$ will yield a negative result, but taking the absolute value of $(4x + 2)$ can only give a result that is either positive or 0. This equation is mathematically impossible, so x cannot be a real number.

Match: (E) is correct.

55. C

Stop: The choices give ranges for x, while the question has an inequality with absolute value.

Think: Special steps must be taken when solving inequalities with absolute value, so Traditional Math should be used carefully.

Predict: Set up the algebra with both a positive and negative version of the absolute value part. The positive expression:

$(x + 4) > 1$

$x > -3$

The negative expression:

$-(x + 4) > 1$

$-x - 4 < 1$

$-x > 5$

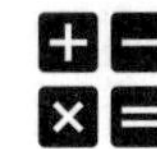

$x < -5$ (Remember to flip the inequality sign whenever you multiply or divide by a negative.)

So, $x > -3$ or $x < -5$. If you find this difficult to visualize, consider the solution on a number line:

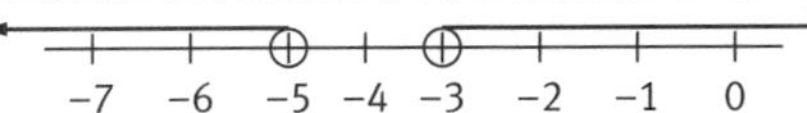

Match: (C) is correct.

56. D

Stop: The choices and question stem are inequalities. Algebra will likely be required.

Think: Since the inequality uses simple numbers, algebra is indeed the quickest way to go.

Predict: Treat the inequality as an equation, and then solve:

$8(z + 3) < 5z + 12$

$8z + 24 < 5z + 12$

$3z < -12$

$z < -4$

Match: (D) is correct. (C) and (E) are trap choices. While *z* could be less than −6 or −12, it isn't always that way. *Z* could be −5 or −4.5 or lots of other numbers in between.

57. C

Stop: The choices are ranges for the variable *x*, while the question gives a quadratic inequality.

Think: You're given the inequality $(x - 2)(x + 5) < 0$ and asked what must be true. When inequalities are nonlinear, consider Picking Numbers or Backsolving. Here, you can use both.

Predict: To solve the problem using Picking Numbers, pick values for *x* that are allowed by some choices but not others. For instance, when $x = 4$, you get $2(9) = 18$, which is not less than 0. Since $x = 4$ is an illegal value, eliminate choices (A), (B), and (E), which include it. Next, try $x = 0$, which is allowed by choice (C) but not choice (D). $(-2)(5) = -10 < 0$, so $x = 0$ is valid. Eliminate choice (D).

Match: (C) is correct. Critical thinking also works on this problem. In order for $(x - 2)(x + 5)$ to be less than 0, one of $(x - 2)$ or $(x + 5)$ must be positive and other negative. But, whenever $(x + 5)$ is negative, $(x - 2)$ is negative as well. Thus, $x + 5$ must be positive, while $x - 2$ is negative.

58. C

Stop: The choices are integers. The question gives you two inequalities.

Think: The question asks how many integer values there are for *x* rather than for the values themselves. This makes Backsolving inefficient, so do the Traditional Math. Don't be trapped by a chain of inequalities. They're no harder to solve than regular ones.

Predict: First, isolate *x*:

$1 < 3x + 5 < 17$

$-4 < 3x < 12$

$-\frac{4}{3} < x < 4$

Then, count the integer values for *x* that fit within the inequality:

−1, 0, 1, 2, and 3 = 5 integer values

Match: (C) is correct.

59. A

Stop: The answer choices of this coordinate geometry problem indicate that your task is to specify the domain and range of a function.

Think: Your task is to accurately define the domain and range of the function in the diagram. Use Traditional Math.

Predict: The domain of a function is the set of all the possible values of *x*, while the range is the set of all the possible values of *y*. Here, *x* could be anything, while *y* can be anything from −3 on up.

Match: (A) is correct. Choice (B) reverses the domain and the range.

60. C

Stop: The choices are equations for *y*. The question stem reveals that this is a range problem.

Think: Your task is to select the function that yields only negative *y* values. Pick Numbers to narrow the choices.

Predict: Critical thinking and a little bit of knowledge go a long way. Recall that 0 is neither positive nor negative. Thus, in a function with an all–negative range, *y* cannot equal 0. Since $y = 0$ when $x = 0$ for choices (A), (B), (D), and (E), none of them is right.

Match: (C) is correct. The maximum value of $-x^2$ is 0, and subtracting 1 ensures that *y* is always negative.

61. B

Stop: The choices are functions. The graph shows a parabola.

Think: Notice that the answer choices do not have any real values; you're just looking for the approximate equation. Use the graph's shape and position to predict its function.

Predict: The figure a parabola, which is created by a quadratic function. Along the parabola, *x* can have both positive and negative values, but *y* values are only positive.

Match: Eliminate choices (A), (C), and (D) because they are not quadratic functions. (B) is correct. Notice that all of the terms are positive. Squaring *x* will always yield a positive result; parabolas facing upward have positive *a* values; the *y*–intercept that is added is positive, as seen on the graph.

62. A

Stop: Choices are ranges of values. The question mentions a domain and includes an equation.

Think: You're asked to find the domain of the function. Recall that a function's domain is the set of all possible input, or *x*, values. The function in this case is a fraction: $y=\frac{27}{x^3}$. Consider what values must be excluded from the domain.

Predict: The only value of *x* that cannot be included is 0 because it would make the fraction's denominator equal 0. All other values are permissible and therefore included in the domain.

Match: The union of all positive and all negative numbers (A) is correct.

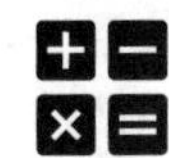

Answers and explanations continue on the next page ▶ ▶ ▶

General Chemistry 1

1. C	15. A	29. A
2. C	16. C	30. C
3. B	17. E	31. B
4. C	18. B	32. E
5. C	19. B	33. C
6. B	20. D	34. E
7. A	21. A	35. C
8. B	22. E	36. B
9. D	23. A	37. E
10. E	24. B	38. B
11. E	25. B	39. B
12. C	26. C	40. C
13. C	27. D	
14. D	28. D	

1. C

Stop: This is a Roman numeral question. Predict if possible or use Kaplan's Elimination strategy.

Think: The question asks which compounds have no formal charges. An atom's formal charge is given by the equation formal charge = (# of valence electrons) – (# of π and σ bonds attached) – (# of nonbonding electrons) or, more simply, formal charge = (# of valence electrons) – (sticks plus dots). Calculate this for each atom in the molecule, and eliminate any compound that has any nonzero values.

Predict: Since the answer cannot be Predicted based on the question stem, use Kaplan's elimination strategy. (I) and (II) appear with equal frequency. Remember to eliminate anything with a formal charge. Calculate formal charges for compound (I) as follows:

O: 6 valence electrons – (2 sticks + 4 dots) = 0

C: 4 valence electrons – (4 sticks + 0 dots) = 0

N: 5 valence electrons – (3 sticks + 2 dots) = 0

H: 1 valence electron – (1 stick + 0 dots) = 0

Compound (I) has no formal charges, so eliminate all choices that do not include it. (B) and (D) are out.

In the remaining answer choices, (II) shows up most frequently, so calculate its formal charges as follows:

N: 5 valence electrons – (3 sticks + 2 dots) = 0

C: 4 valence electrons – (4 sticks + 0 dots) = 0

O: 6 valence electrons – (2 sticks + 4 dots) = 0

H: 1 valence electron – (1 stick + 0 dots) = 0

Compound (II) has no formal charges, so eliminate all choices that do not include it. (A) is eliminated.

Since two choices remain, calculate formal charges for compound (III) as follows:

H: 1 valence electron – (1 stick + 0 dots) = 0

O: 6 valence electrons – (3 sticks + 2 dots) = +1

Stop here! Since oxygen has a formal charge, (III) cannot be included in the answer.

Match: Eliminate (E). (C) is correct.

2. C

Stop: Answer choices are resonance structures of perchloric acid.

Think: The question asks which is most stable. Where resonance structures exist, formal charges are often present. The most stable form of a molecule is the one that has the fewest formal charges. So, one way to solve this problem is to calculate the formal charges on every atom in each molecule. However, a much simpler way is to recognize that, because it has six valence electrons, oxygen forms two covalent bonds to reach an octet. Otherwise, it has a formal charge and is less stable.

Predict: The structure in which the greatest number of oxygen atoms form two covalent bonds is the most stable.

Match: (C) is correct. To confirm, calculate the formal charge on each atom: zero. Notice that chlorine forms seven total bonds in this structure, and is thus in violation of the octet rule. However, because chlorine is in the third row of the periodic table, it has access to the 3d subshell, which can accept additional electrons. Because this structure gives chlorine a formal charge of zero, chlorine is stable with more than the normal octet.

3. B

Stop: Answer choices are rankings of the same molecules. Strategic elimination may be possible.

Think: The question asks you to rank N–O bond strength from strongest to weakest. Bond strength is a function of the number of bonds: double bonds are stronger than single bonds, and triple bonds are stronger than double bonds. Convert the molecular formulas to structures. Nitrogen has five valence electrons, so it will form three bonds—unless it is charged. In hydroxylamine (NH_2OH), there is no charge, so nitrogen will make three single bonds. In the nitrosyl ion (NO^+), nitrogen again makes three bonds but all of them with the one oxygen, creating a triple bond and leaving a positive charge on the oxygen. In the nitryl ion (NO_2^+), nitrogen forms double bonds to each of the oxygen atoms. The oxygen atoms are uncharged, but nitrogen has a positive charge because it is making four bonds rather than three.

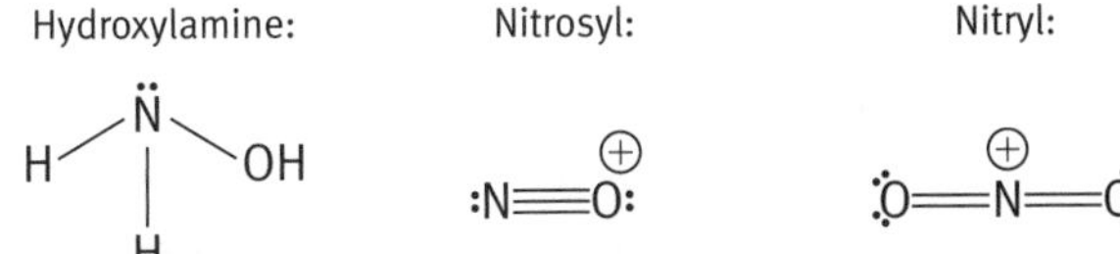

Finally, the nitrate ion (NO_3^-) consists of a central nitrogen atom bound to the three oxygen atoms. If each of these bonds is a single bond, then the three oxygen atoms would each have a negative formal charge, but the ion has a net charge of −1, so that cannot be the case. If, instead, one of the nitrogen-oxygen bonds is a double bond, then the double-bound oxygen will have no formal charge, and the nitrogen, making four bonds instead of three, will have a positive formal charge, so the net charge is −1. But, which oxygen will get the double bond? They all do. The double bond is distributed in three equivalent resonance structures. This means that each nitrogen-oxygen bond is neither a true single bond nor a true double bond but rather a partial double bond.

Nitrate:

Predict: NH_2OH with all single N–O bonds will rank weakest. NO^+ with the triple bond will rank strongest. True double bonds are stronger than partial double bonds, so NO_2^+ will rank stronger than NO_3^-. The ranking will be:

NO^+ (triple bond) > NO_2^+ (double bonds) > NO_3^- (partial double bond) > NH_2OH (all single bonds)

Match: (B) is correct. Notice that (A), (D), and (E) can be eliminated after determining the strongest and weakest bonds.

4. C

Stop: Answer choices are commonly encountered molecules with traditional geometries and no more than four bonds.

Think: The question asks which has the smallest bond angle. When considering bond angles, use VSEPR to determine the molecular geometries. Linear molecules have the greatest bond angle at 180 degrees. Tetrahedral molecules, which have no lone pairs, have smaller ideal bond angles at 109.5 degrees. Replacing atoms with lone pairs further decreases the bond angles, so trigonal pyramidal (one lone pair) has a smaller angle, followed by bent (two lone pairs) which has the smallest.

Predict: Look for a bent molecule. If none appears, then look for a molecule with trigonal planar geometry.

Match: Water is bent, so (C) is correct. For the record, though, methane (A) has a tetrahedral geometry; ammonia (B) a trigonal pyramidal shape because of the single lone pair of electrons on the nitrogen; borane (D) has a trigonal planar geometry; and carbon dioxide (E) is linear with two double bonds and no lone pairs on the carbon.

5. C

Stop: Answer choices are molecules—some charged and some neutral.

Think: The question asks for the one with tetrahedral molecular geometry. One central atom must be bound to four other atoms.

Predict: Look for the molecule with one single atom bound to four others.

Match: (C) is correct. (A), (D), and (E) have central atoms bound to too few other atoms. Ethene (B) has no central atom because of the double bond between the carbon atoms.

6. B

Stop: Answer choices are again molecules—some charged and some neutral.

Think: The question asks for the one that does not have tetrahedral electronic geometry. Be careful! Unlike molecular geometry, electronic geometry considers both bonding electron pairs and lone, or nonbonding, pairs. But, one trick is to recognize that if a molecule has a tetrahedral molecular geometry, its electronic geometry will also be tetrahedral. In general, atoms that are sp^3 hybridized will have a tetrahedral electronic geometry.

Predict: Look for a molecule that is unable to form a tetrahedron when both lone pairs and bonded electrons are taken into account.

Match: Ethene (B) has a carbon-carbon double bond, so both carbons have sp^2 hybridization. This molecule is planar. Drawing the structures for the incorrect choices will reveal tetrahedral electronic geometry.

7. A

Stop: Answer choices are molecules or functional groups, each containing one carbon.

Think: The question asks which will participate in hydrogen bonding. Molecules capable of hydrogen bonding feature a highly electronegative element (F, O, or N) bound directly to a hydrogen atom. Note that it is not enough for a molecule to simply have hydrogen atoms and mixed with electronegative atoms; the hydrogen and electronegative atoms must be bound to one another.

Predict: Look for hydrogens bound to oxygens. The molecule with the –OH bond will be capable of hydrogen bonding.

Match: Methanol with its –OH group (A) is correct. Methane (B) and bromomethane (D) have no bonds between hydrogen and oxygen, so they cannot form hydrogen bonds. Methanal (C) is an aldehyde (CH_3CHO). But, although it has an oxygen, there is no hydrogen attached directly to the oxygen, so it cannot form hydrogen bonds.

8. B

Stop: Answer choices are two-carbon molecules or functional groups.

Think: The question asks which has the highest boiling point. Since boiling point is a function of the strength of intermolecular forces, the question can be rephrased as follows: "Which molecule has the strongest intermolecular forces?"

Predict: The molecule with the strongest intermolecular forces will have the highest boiling point. The strongest intermolecular forces are hydrogen bonds, so look for a molecule that participates in hydrogen bonding.

Match: (B) is correct since ethanol can hydrogen bond. (A), (D), and (E) have dipole-dipole interactions, and ethane (C) experiences London dispersion forces, but hydrogen bonding is a stronger force than either. Remember that the oxygen in ethanal (E) is not bound to any hydrogens, so it does not participate in hydrogen bonding.

9. D

Stop: Answer choices are rankings of common molecules. Strategic elimination may be possible.

Think: The question asks you to rank boiling point from lowest to highest. This is the same as ranking the intermolecular forces from weakest to strongest. If two molecules experience equivalent intermolecular forces, the one with the higher molecular weight usually will have the higher boiling point.

Predict: Molecules with hydrogen bonds should be ranked higher, and among them the ones with molecular weight should be highest. Both water and acetic acid can hydrogen bond, but acetic acid is significantly larger than water, so acetic acid ranks higher. Methane, which only has London dispersion forces, has the lowest boiling point. Acetone, which has dipole-dipole interactions, has the third-highest boiling point, after water and acetic acid.

Match: (D) is correct. Notice that (D) is the only choice that ranks methane lowest and acetic acid highest. Strategic elimination on Test Day will help narrow down lengthy choices and increase efficiency during the Match step.

10. E

Stop: Answers are whole numbers.

Think: The question asks for the maximum number of electrons when $n = 4$. The maximum number of electrons in a given energy shell is equal to $2n^2$.

Predict: Maximum # of electrons $= 2 \times 4^2 = 2 \times 16 = 32$

Match: (E) is correct.

11. E

Stop: Answer choices are combinations of principle quantum number, n, and magnetic quantum number, m_l. Strategic elimination may be possible once you find one of the numbers.

Think: Be careful with questions containing the word EXCEPT in the stem. The question asks which set of quantum numbers is impossible when carbon is in its ground state. Although the answer choices include the magnetic quantum number, m_l, this information is not necessary to find the correct answer. Since carbon is in its ground state, all of its electrons are in the lowest energy states possible. Because carbon is found in the second row of the periodic table, its electrons will have $n = 1$ or 2.

Predict: The question asks for what is impossible. Any answer that includes a principle quantum number with value higher than $n = 2$ is impossible when carbon is in its ground state.

Match: (E) is correct.

12. C

Stop: Answer choices are high-energy subshells.

Think: The question asks which fills first. According to the Aufbau principle, this will be the subshell with the lowest overall energy. The energy of a subshell is a function of both its principle quantum number (n) and azimuthal quantum number (l), so assign each subshell its value for n and l and then use the $n + l$ rule to find the lowest energy.

Predict: The subshell with the lowest $n + l$ will be the answer.

Match: Calculate the $n + l$ for each choice as follows:

(A) 5d: $n = 5, l = 2, n + l = 7$

(B) 5f: $n = 5, l = 3, n + l = 8$ Eliminate (B).

(C) 6s: $n = 6, l = 0, n + l = 6$ Eliminate (A) since this is lower.

(D) 6p: $n = 6, l = 1, n + l = 7$ Eliminate (D).

(E) 4f; $n = 4, l = 3, n + l = 7$ Eliminate (E).

(C) is correct.

13. C

Stop: Answer choices are numbers related to atoms.

Think: The question asks for what remains constant among isotopes.

Predict: Atomic number, or the number of protons, is the same because this is what identifies an atom.

Match: (C) is correct.

14. D

Stop: Answer choices are elements, none of which are commonly used, so you'll need the periodic table.

Think: The question asks which element is important to life and gives lists of transition metals that are and are not. Elements that are found in the same group of the periodic table share the same valence electron configuration and, therefore, similar chemical properties. Find the "essential to life" list in the stem (V–Zn) and look for an element in one of the same groups. Also, find the two elements not essential—Sc and Ti—and eliminate anything in their groups.

Predict: The "essential to life" list in the stem is in row four of the periodic table in the d block. The right answer will be underneath one of these and not underneath Sc or Ti to their left.

Match: Mo (D), directly beneath Cr, is correct. The other choices are found in the same group as either Sc (Y and La) or Ti (Zr and Hf).

15. A

Stop: Answer choices are electronic configurations in spectroscopic notation.

Think: The question asks for the configuration of Fe^{3+}. Start with the electron configuration of a neutral Fe atom, and then remove three electrons. When removing electrons, simply take electrons first from the subshell with the highest principle quantum number.

Predict: Start with neutral Fe, which is $[Ar]4s^23d^6$. Remove electrons one at a time starting from the highest numbered subshell, which in this case is 4s. Removing the two 4s electrons and then one 3d electron leaves you with $Fe^{3+} = [Ar]3d^5$.

Match: (A) is correct. Note that answer choices (B) and (C) can be eliminated because they contain the wrong total number of electrons. Answer choice (D) and (E) are incorrect because they show electrons in the 4p and 4d orbitals.

16. C

Stop: Answer choices are common ions or neutral elements.

Think: The question asks for the greatest atomic radius. The combined effects of effective nuclear charge and total number of electrons must be used to determine the net effect on radius. High nuclear charge tends to decrease the radius, while a high number of total electrons tends to increase the radius. Look first for the total number of electrons since increasing the maximum *n* will significantly increase the radius.

Predict: The atom with the largest radius will have the largest number of electrons. If the number of electrons is equal, the one with fewer protons will be larger.

Match: (C) is correct. Both Ca^{2+} (A) and argon (C) have electrons in the 3s and 3p subshells. This significantly increases their size relative to the period 2 ions (B) and (D) and helium (E) in period 1. (Be careful not to assume that anions are larger when comparing them to other elements or ions; the extra electrons here are added to fill the $n = 2$ subshells.) The Ca^{2+} cation (A) has lost its 4s electrons and is now isoelectronic with argon. But, Ca^{2+} has 20 protons, whereas argon has 19 protons. So, the electrons of Ca^{2+} will be pulled in tighter than the electrons of argon, leaving argon with a slightly greater atomic radius.

17. E

Stop: Answer choices are neutral or ionized sodium and potassium.

Think: The question asks for the species that requires the most energy to remove a valence electron. In other words, which has the highest ionization energy? Ionization energy is directly correlated with effective nuclear charge, Z_{eff}; the higher the effective nuclear charge, the tighter the valence electrons are held, requiring more energy to pull one off. In this question, only sodium and potassium are considered, and sodium is just above potassium in group 1. Z_{eff} decreases down a group.

Predict: It is relatively easy to remove an electron from a group 1 element, since it has only one valence electron, so neutral sodium and potassium would have low ionization energies. But, it would be much more difficult to remove a second electron, since the $+1$ cations have completely full shells. The answer is either sodium cation or potassium cation. Effective nuclear charge decreases down a group, and potassium is below sodium, so the Z_{eff} for sodium is higher.

Match: (E) is correct.

18. B

Stop: Answers choices are commonly encountered elements.

Think: The question asks which matches the ionization energies in the table. The ionization energies increase, but the first and second ionization energies are much lower than the third. Approximately twice the amount of energy is required to remove the second electron, but there is a huge leap in energy (more than 400%) between the second and third ionization energies. So, the first two electrons come off relatively easily, and then the third electron is extremely hard to remove. These data describe an atom described that has two valence electrons. The third ionization energy is so high because the third electron being removed requires destroying the noble gas configuration of the next innermost shell.

Predict: The third ionization energy is so high because the third electron being removed requires destroying the noble gas configuration of the next innermost shell, so the atom has two valence electrons.

Match: (B) is correct because calcium is in group 2.

19. B

Stop: Answers are percentages with decimals, some of which are very close together. Calculation will probably be required.

Think: The question asks for percent composition of chromium and gives the molecular formula and the molecular weight of the molecule. Percent composition is the mass of an individual element in a molecule divided by the mass of the whole molecule. To find the molecular weight of chromium, refer to the periodic table; it's about 52 g/mol.

Predict: Molecular weight of chromium = 2 × 52 = 104 g/mol

Total molecular weight of $K_2Cr_2O_7$ = 294 g/mol

$$\% \text{ Composition Cr} = \frac{\text{mass}_{\text{chromium}}}{\text{mass}_{\text{total}}} = \frac{104\text{ g}}{294\text{ g}} \cong \frac{100}{300} \cong \frac{1}{3}$$

Match: (B) is correct.

20. D

Stop: Answers are formulas for molecules containing only carbon, hydrogen, and oxygen.

Think: The question asks for the molecular formula and gives the empirical formula (CH_2O) and the molecular weight (180 g/mol). The empirical formula is the smallest whole number ratio of the different atoms in a molecule. The molecular weight can be found by summing the weight of the individual atoms that make up a molecule.

Predict: The answer must have exactly twice as many hydrogens as it does carbons and oxygens. And the mass of all of the atoms must sum to 180. The empirical formula's mass = C + 2H + O = 12 g/mol + (2 × 1 g/mol) + 16 g/mol = 30 g/mol. So, the molecular formula is multiplied by six: $C_6H_{12}O_6$.

Match: (D) is correct.

21. A

Stop: Answer choices are again formulas for molecules made up of carbon, oxygen, and hydrogen.

Think: The question asks for the molecular formula given the percent composition of each element and the total molecular weight. There are two approaches to solving this problem: calculate using percent composition and molecular weight or Backsolve by finding the molecular weight of answer choices. Backsolving proves to be much simpler.

Predict: To Backsolve start with the simplest answer choice, CHO (B). The molecular weight of CH_2O is equal to (1 × 12) + (2 × 1) + (1 × 16), or 30 g/mol. However, the molecular weight of the molecule in the question stem is 264, which is almost nine times as large. The correct answer should have about nine times as many carbon and oxygen atoms. This will require nine times as many carbons and oxygens as CH_2O, and only answer choice (A) matches this with $C_9H_{12}O_9$.

Match: Choice (A) with $C_9H_{12}O_9$ is the only answer anywhere close to the prediction, and it is correct. (E) appears similar at first glance, but there are far too few oxygens to reach 264 g/mol since the hydrogens will add very little weight. To find the answer with Traditional Math, choose the simplest element to work with in the formula. In this case, hydrogen is easiest because its molecular weight is 1 g/mol, and its percent composition is easy to round up to 5%. Take 10% and divide by one-half to make the calculation easier.

$$\text{mass of Hydrogen per molecule (g)} = \left(264\frac{\text{g}}{\text{mol}}\right) \times (4.58\%)$$

$$\cong 264 \times 0.05 \cong \frac{(264 \times 0.10)}{2}$$

$$\cong \frac{26.4}{2} \cong 13.2\text{ g}$$

In each mole of the molecule, about 13 grams will be hydrogen, and since 13 grams of hydrogen is 13 moles of hydrogen, hydrogen needs to have a subscript of approximately 13 in the molecular formula. Choice (A) is closest with 12.

22. E

Stop: Answer choices are small whole numbers.

Think: The question asks for the coefficient of oxygen when the equation is balanced. Just balance the equation.

Predict: Balancing reactions is most easily accomplished by balancing any molecules consisting of only one element last, so balance O_2 last.

$\_C_4H_{10} + \_O_2 \rightarrow \_CO_2 + \_H_2O$

Four carbon atoms in C_4H_{10} on the left results in four CO_2 molecules on the right:

$1\ C_4H_{10} + \_\_O_2 \rightarrow 4\ CO_2 + \_\_H_2O$

Ten hydrogen atoms in C_4H_{10} on the left results in five H_2O molecules on the right:

$1\ C_4H_{10} + \_\_O_2 \rightarrow 4\ CO_2 + 5\ H_2O$

There are already 13 oxygen atoms on the right, so balance the left by adding the appropriate coefficient to O_2:

$1\ C_4H_{10} + \left(\frac{13}{2}\right) O_2 \rightarrow 4\ CO_2 + 5\ H_2O$

To remove the fractional coefficient, multiply the entire equation by 2, leaving O_2 with 13.

Match: (E) is correct.

23. A

Stop: Answer choices are generalized molecules from the equation, so this is a conceptual question.

Think: The question asks what the limiting reagent is. The limiting reagent is the reactant that is used up first.

Predict: There is 1 mol each of reactants A and B, but it takes twice as many moles of A as moles of B to produce the products. So, A is used up twice as quickly.

Match: (A) is correct. Note that (C) and (D) can be eliminated quickly because they are products.

24. B

Stop: Answer choices are small numbers that are 0.5 apart.

Think: The question asks how many moles of B are needed to completely react with 1 mole of A. Three moles of B are required to react with moles of A. Set up a simple ratio.

Predict: $\frac{2A}{3B} = \frac{1A}{x\,B}$

$x = \frac{3 \times 1}{2} = 1.5 \text{ moles B}$

Match: (B) is correct.

25. B

Stop: Answer choices are masses with decimals, but the values are reasonably far apart, so rounding and estimating should be possible.

Think: The question asks you to solve for the amount of $CaCl_2$ needed to yield 72.0 g of AgCl. Use dimensional analysis, but estimate whenever possible to make the division easier.

Predict: Mass AgCl produced $= 72\text{ g} \cong 75\text{ g}$

Molar mass AgCl $= 143.4\text{ g/mol} \cong 150\text{ g/mol}$

Molar mass $CaCl_2 = 111.1\text{ g/mol} \cong 100\text{ g/mol}$

Ratio of $CaCl_2/AgCl = \frac{1}{2}$

$$\text{g } CaCl_2 \cong \frac{100\text{ g } CaCl_2}{1\text{ mol } CaCl_2} \times \frac{1\text{ mol } CaCl_2}{2\text{ mol AgCl}} \times \frac{1\text{ mol AgCl}}{150\text{ g AgCl}} \times 75\text{ g AgCl}$$

Simplifying, this gives:

$$\text{g } CaCl_2 \cong \frac{100}{2} \times \frac{75}{150} \cong 50 \times \frac{1}{2} \cong 25\ \text{g } CaCl_2$$

Match: (B) is correct.

26. C

Stop: Answer choices are enthalpies and are widely separated. Rounding and estimating can be used to simplify any math, but there is undoubtedly a lot of math to be done, so this probably should be triaged on Test Day.

Think: The question asks for the enthalpy change for a reaction that is the sum of three other reaction. Use Hess's Law: the enthalpy of a reaction can be calculated by summing the enthalpies for each step in the reaction mechanism.

Predict: Overall reaction: $3\ C\ (s) + 4\ H_2\ (g) \rightarrow C_3H_8\ (g)$

Step (a) has a reaction mechanism that shows C_3H_8 as a reactant and must be reversed to align C_3H_8 as a product. Once reversed, the change in enthalpy is now positive, making ΔH_a positive:

$3\ CO_2\ (g) + 4\ H_2O\ (l) \rightarrow C_3H_8\ (g) + 5\ O_2\ (g)$
$\Delta H_a = +2220.1\text{ kJ} \cong +2200\text{ kJ}$

Step (b) is in the correct direction but has only 1 mole of carbon. Multiply by 3 to match the overall reaction:

$3\ C\ (s) + 3\ O_2\ (g) \rightarrow 3\ CO_2\ (g)$
$\Delta H_b = 3 \times (-393.5\text{ kJ}) \cong 3 \times (-400) \cong -1200\text{ kJ}$

Step (c) is in the correct direction but has only 1 mole of H_2. Multiply by 4 to match the overall reaction:

$4\ H_2\ (g) + 2\ O_2\ (g) \rightarrow 4\ H_2O\ (l)$
$\Delta H_c = 4 \times (-285.8\text{ kJ}) \cong 4 \times (-275) \cong -1100$

Now, sum the estimated change in enthalpy of each of the three steps:

$2200 + (-1200) + (-1100) = 2200 + (-2300) = -100\text{ kJ}$

Match: (C) is correct.

27. D

Stop: Answer choices are enthalpies and are widely separated. Rounding and estimating can be used here.

Think: The question asks for the energy in an O–H bond. You are given the change in enthalpy for the reaction and the bond enthalpies for the other bonds in the reaction: the nitrogen-nitrogen triple bond, the oxygen-oxygen double bond, and the nitrogen-hydrogen single bonds. Setting up an equation with the bond enthalpies and overall change in enthalpy and then solving for the O–H bond will work, but that will take awhile. Before triaging, think critically. So much information is given in the stem, and the bond energies are easy to compare.

Predict: The O–H bond has a lower energy than the double and triple bonds and is most similar to the N–H bond.

Match: (C) and (D) are both less than the double bond energy of 498 kJ/mol. (C) is less than the energy for N–H, while (D) is greater. Oxygen is more electronegative than nitrogen, making the O–H bond stronger and therefore more energetic. So, (D) is correct. Wow! A little critical thinking eliminated a ton of time-consuming work. However, the calculations are as follows:

$\Delta H_{rxn} = [\Delta H \text{ of bonds broken}] + [\Delta H \text{ of bonds formed}] =$ total energy input – total energy released

For this reaction, ΔH_{rxn} is given, along with bond enthalpies for all but the required O–H bond. The bond enthalphies given are also known as bond dissociation energies. Thus, they are the correct values for bonds broken. However, for bonds formed, the sign must be reversed, so instead of adding the enthalpies of the bonds formed, subtract them. And remember to multiple the bond enthalpies by their coefficients.

$\Delta H_{rxn} = -1{,}266 \text{ kJ} = [(12 \times \Delta H_{N\text{–}H}) + (3 \times \Delta H_{O=O})] - [(2 \times \Delta H_{N\equiv N}) + (12 \times \Delta H_{O\text{–}H})]$

$-1{,}266 = [(12 \times 389) + (3 \times 498)] - [(2 \times 941) + (12 \times \Delta H_{O\text{–}H})]$

$-1{,}300 \cong [(12 \times 400) + (3 \times 500)] - [2(1{,}000) + (12 \times \Delta H_{O\text{–}H})]$

$-1{,}300 \cong 6{,}300 - 2{,}000 - (12 \times \Delta H_{O\text{–}H})$

$-5{,}600 \cong (-12 \times \Delta H_{O\text{–}H})$

$450 \text{ kJ} \cong \Delta H_{O\text{–}H}$

28. D

Stop: Answer choices are enthalpies and are widely separated. Rounding and estimating can be used to simplify any math. Be sure to get the sign correct since this likely will be necessary to determine the right answer.

Think: The question asks for the enthalpy of formation for one reagent in a chemical reaction given the ΔH_f for other compounds and the overall enthalpy of reaction. This problem will involve significant calculations and should be considered for triage until the end of the section.

Predict: $\Delta H_{rxn} = [\Delta H_f \text{ of products}] - [\Delta H \text{ of reactants}]$.

$-1256 = [(2 \times -393) + (-242)] - [0 + \Delta H_f \text{ for acetylene}]$

Note that ΔH_f for CO_2 must be doubled because it has a coefficient of 2 in the balanced reaction, and ΔH_f for O_2 is zero because oxygen is in its standard state.

ΔH_f for acetylene $= 1256 - (2 \times 393) - 242 \cong 1250 - 800 - 250 \cong 200$ kJ/mol

Match: (D) is correct. Keep the signs straight to avoid the trap answer (B).

29. A

Stop: Answer choices are about changes to both enthalpy and entropy.

Think: The question asks what happens when water undergoes a phase change from solid to liquid.

Predict: Liquids also have higher entropy than and enthalpy than solids, so both increase.

Match: (A) is correct.

30. C

Stop: This is a Roman numeral question. The statements require you to decide the sign of the changes in enthalpy and entropy. Either Predict or use Kaplan's Elimination strategy.

Think: The question asks what proves that a reaction is temperature-dependent. Temperature, ΔH, and ΔS are related through the Gibbs free energy equation: $\Delta G = \Delta H - T\Delta S$. Find where the temperature can determine the sign of ΔG.

Predict: If ΔH and ΔS have different signs, ΔG will either always be negative (when $-\Delta H$ and $+\Delta S$) or always be positive (when $+\Delta H$ and $-\Delta S$) regardless of the temperature. If ΔH and ΔS have the same sign, then the value of ΔG will depend on the relative size of ΔH and ΔS and the value for temperature. So, the signs are the same when a reaction is temperature-dependent. (If you have difficulty determining this, try Picking Numbers with simple positive and negative numbers and evaluate the results.) Roman numerals (I) and (IV) have same signs for ΔH and ΔS, so they are included in the right answer, while (II) and (III) are not.

Match: (C) is correct.

31. B

Stop: Answer choices are mechanisms of heat transfer.

Think: The question stem asks about transfer of heat from your body to the water when you're in the ocean.

Predict: Your body is in direct contact with the ocean, so the transfer of heat is by direct contact, or conduction. Note that although there is moving water in the ocean, the heat transfer is not by convection; the heat is carried away by convection of the ocean water, but there is no bulk transfer of fluid from your body to the ocean water.

Match: (B) is correct. (C) is a trap. The heat transfer from your body is not by convection. Rather, once the heat has

been conducted from your body to the water, the heat is carried away, or moved through the water, by convection. The Think step will keep you from answering the wrong question.

32. E

Stop: Answer choices represent some kind of shift in equilibrium.

Think: The question asks about the effect of changing the amount of a product. However, the product is a solid, which is not part of the equilibrium constant.

Predict: There will be no shift because solids do not affect the equilibrium.

Match: (E) is correct. (A) and (B) are traps, but remembering the rule about solids will help you avoid this trap on Test Day.

33. C

Stop: Answer choices represent shifts in equilibrium.

Think: The question asks what would happen if you increased the pH. An increase in pH means a decrease in $[H^+]$, which is a product in the reaction.

Predict: Decreasing the concentration of a nonsolid on the product side of equilibrium will shift the reaction forward to form more products.

Match: (C) is correct. (A) is Opposite and the result of forgetting that increasing pH means decreasing hydrogen ions.

34. E

Stop: Answer choices again represent shifts in equilibrium.

Think: The question asks what will happen if the pressure is increased. Changing pressure can influence equilibrium but only when gases are present.

Predict: There are no gaseous species in this reaction, thus pressure changes will not have an effect.

Match: (E) is correct.

35. C

Stop: Answer choices are in scientific notation and differ by at least one factor of ten. Either the leading value or the decimal place could eliminate all but one choice. Be careful with the decimal place if the number is some multiple of 1.4 because of answers (D) and (E).

Think: This question gives molar solubility, and asks for the K_{sp}. Molar solubility is the amount of solid FeF_2 that dissolves in solution to reach an equilibrium state and is represented as x in solubility calculations. Use the Kaplan Method for Equilibrium Questions.

Predict: 1. Find a balanced chemical reaction:

$$FeF_2\ (s) \rightleftharpoons Fe^{2+}\ (aq) + 2\ F^-\ (aq)$$

2. Find the expression for the K_{sp}:

$$K_{sp} = [Fe^{2+}][F^-]^2$$

3. Plug molar solubility, x, into the K_{sp} expression:

$$K_{sp} = [x][2x]^2$$

Remember to use the coefficients from step 1 twice: once as the exponents in the expression in step 2 and again as coefficients for x in step 3. Now solve as follows:

$$\begin{aligned} K_{sp} &= 4x^3 \\ &= 4 \times (1.9 \times 10^{-2})^3 \cong 4 \times (8 \times 10^{-6}) \cong 32 \times 10^{-6} \\ &\cong 3.2 \times 10^{-5} \end{aligned}$$

Match: The Match is a bit tricky here. The 3.2 appears to Match (A), but the exponent is way off. A quick review of the math shows that the exponent is correct. Recall that 1.9^3 was rounded up, so the estimated value is higher than the actual value, and (C) is correct.

36. B

Stop: Answer choices are in scientific notation, and some of the values and exponents are very similar, so careful calculation will be needed.

Think: This question provides K_{sp} and asks for molar solubility. This question also tests your knowledge of the common ion effect because the chloride ion donated to solution by table salt (NaCl) will influence the molar solubility of AgCl. In other words, chloride is the ion that is common to both AgCl and NaCl. Use Kaplan's three-step method for solubility questions.

Predict: 1. Find a balanced chemical equation:

$$AgCl\ (s) \rightleftharpoons Ag^+\ (aq) + Cl^-\ (aq)$$

2. Find the expression for the K_{sp}:

$$K_{sp} = [Ag^+][Cl^-]$$

3. Plug molar solubility, x, into the K_{sp} expression:

$$K_{sp} = [x][0.1 + x]$$

There are two sources of chloride ion in this solution. NaCl donates 0.1 M Cl^-, and AgCl itself donates x amount of Cl^- ion. So, the total $[Cl^-] = [0.1 + x]$. However, the K_{sp} value of AgCl is extremely small, which indicates that very little of the AgCl actually dissociates. So, approximate the Cl^- comes entirely from the NaCl:

$$K_{sp} = 1.6 \times 10^{-10} = [Ag^+][Cl^-] = [x][0.1] = 0.1x$$

$$1.6 \times 10^{-10} = 0.1x$$

$$x = 1.6 \times 10^{-9}$$

Match: (B) is correct.

37. E

Stop: Answer choices display a "yes/no and why" pattern.

Think: The question asks if there will be any AgSCN precipitate, but you know from the Stop step that you must also determine why or why not. NaSCN and $AgNO_3$ are in solution, so they will dissociate into their constituent ions. The question gives the K_{sp}. A precipitate will form if the $[Ag^+]$ and $[SCN^-]$ are above the saturation concentrations described by the K_{sp} value of 1×10^{-12}.

Predict: $AgSCN \rightarrow Ag^+ + SCN^-$

$$K_{sp} = [Ag^+][SCN^-]$$

To solve the problem, you must calculate the concentrations of the ions, multiply their concentrations together, and compare the result with the K_{sp} value. Note that in this question 1 mL of one solution is added to 3 mL of another solution. This detail is important because the new solution will have a total volume of 4 mL. Increasing the volume dilutes each ion's concentration. It is therefore necessary to recalculate the concentrations using the formula $M_1V_1{=}M_2V_2$.

For SCN^-:

$$M_2 = \frac{M_2 \times V_2}{V_2} = \frac{(1 \times 10^{-5}) \times 1}{4} = 0.25 \times 10^{-5} = 2.5 \times 10^{-6}$$

For Ag^+:

$$M_2 = \frac{M_2 \times V_2}{V_2} = \frac{(1 \times 10^{-5}) \times 3}{4} = 0.75 \times 10^{-5} = 7.5 \times 10^{-6}$$

Finally, multiply these two concentrations together and compare to the K_{sp} value:

$[Ag^+][SCN^-] = [7.5 \times 10^{-6}][2.5 \times 10^{-6}] \cong (8 \times 10^{-6}) \times (2 \times 10^{-6}) \cong 16 \times 10^{-12} \cong 1.6 \times 10^{-11} > K_{sp} = 1 \times 10^{-12}$

Because the concentrations of Ag^+ and SCN^- in the mixture are above saturation levels, a solid precipitate will form.

Match: (E) is correct.

38. B

Stop: Answer choices are rate laws.

Think: A table of concentration versus rate is given. Use the data and the general form of the law (rate $= k[I^-]^x[H_2O_2]^y$) to determine the values of x and y.

Predict: The first two rows keep the concentration of I^- constant while changing the concentration of H_2O_2. The concentration of H_2O_2 doubles from row 1 to 2, and so does the rate. Doubling the concentration of $[H_2O_2]$ doubles the rate. This is a linear change, so the y exponent on $[H_2O_2]$ must be 1. Next, check the answer choices and eliminate any that do not have 1 as the exponent for $[H_2O_2]$. Check the choices to see if this is enough. It isn't, but you can eliminate (C) and (E). Now repeat the process, with rows 1 and 3 where the concentration of H_2O_2 is constant and only the concentration of I^- changes. When the concentration of I^- is increased by 1.5, the rate is increased by approximately 1.5. Following the same logic as before, the x exponent on $[I^-]$ must be 1.

Rate $= k[I^-][H_2O_2]$

Match: (B) is correct.

39. B

Stop: Answer choices are steps in the reaction.

Think: The question is asking which step is rate-limiting given that rate $= k[H^+][I^-][H_2O_2]$. The rate-limiting step, by definition, determines the rate law. The rate-limiting step will be the one that is influenced by all three concentrations.

Predict: The rate-limiting step must have all three of the reactants shown in the rate law, because the concentration of each has an impact on the rate of reaction. However, no single step of the reaction shows all three of these reactants. Inspection of the reaction shows that step 1 has reactants H^+ or H_2O_2, while step 2 has I^-. However, the $H_3O_2^+$ in step 2 is produced from H^+ or H_2O_2 in step 1. Thus, the rate of step 2 is determined by the concentrations of H^+, I^-, and H_2O_2, making step 2 the rate-limiting step.

Match: (B) is correct.

40. C

Stop: Answer choices describe changes that can affect the rate of a reaction.

Think: The question asks for the one factor that will NOT increase the rate of the forward reaction. Predict what will, and then eliminate.

Predict: Increased temperature increases the rate of reaction because raising temperature provides energy. The rate law is given by rate $= k[\text{reactants}]^x$. Therefore, increasing reactant concentration will increase the rate of reaction. Catalysts, by definition, increase the reaction rate. Eliminate all choices containing these factors.

Match: (C) is correct. Although changing the amount of product will shift a reaction that is at equilibrium, products are not included in the forward rate law, so removing them will not affect the rate.

Answers and explanations continue on the next page ▶ ▶ ▶

Organic Chemistry 1

1. D	11. A	21. C
2. A	12. C	22. C
3. D	13. D	23. E
4. D	14. D	24. A
5. E	15. D	25. A
6. E	16. A	26. A
7. C	17. D	27. E
8. C	18. A	28. B
9. B	19. C	29. A
10. B	20. B	30. E

1. D

Stop: Answer choices are lists of functional groups.

Think: The question asks for the functional groups in compound F. Ignore the reaction and focus instead on the functional groups in compound F.

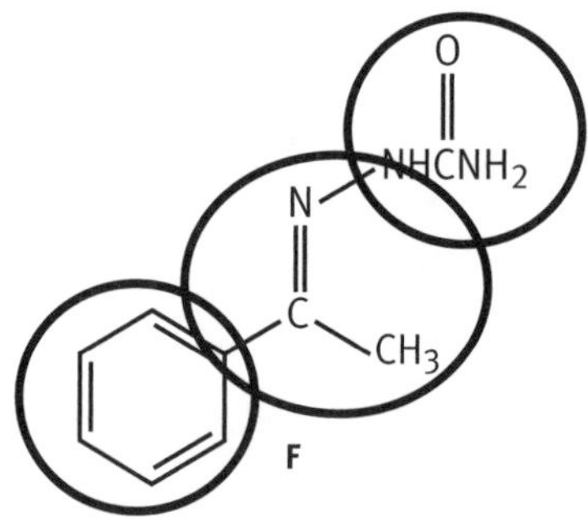

Predict: phenyl, imine, amide

Match: (D) is correct. Note that the question does not require the groups to be listed in any particular order.

2. A

Stop: Answer choices are IUPAC names.

Think: Name the compound. Identify the principal functional group: hydroxyl. Identify the longest chain containing the functional group: two carbons. Identify the substituents: a phenyl group. Finally, number the chain so that the principal functional group has the lowest possible number. Both the hydroxyl and phenyl groups are on carbon 1.

Predict: The two carbon chain is translated "eth." The principal functional group, the hydroxyl, provides the suffix "–ol" and receives a 1. The phenyl group is a prefix and is also attached to carbon 1. So, the compound is 1–phenylethanol.

Match: (A) is correct.

3. D

Stop: Answer choices are pairs of IUPAC names. Strategic elimination may be possible.

Think: The question asks for the names of the reactant and product. Name the reactant and then check the choices to see if that has answered the question. If not, name the product as well. Name the reactant as follows:

Identify the principal functional group: hydroxyl (–ol).

Identify the longest chain containing the functional group: 5 carbons (pent–).

Identify the substituents: an ethyl group (ethyl–).

Number the chain: The hydroxyl and ethyl groups are on carbon 3.

Predict and check the choices to see if this eliminates all but one choice. It doesn't, so name the product as follows:

Identify the principal functional group: the alkene (–ene).

Identify the longest chain containing the functional group: 5 carbons (pent–).

Identify the substituents: an ethyl group (ethyl–).

Number the chain: The double bond is on carbon 2 and the ethyl group is on carbon 3.

Predict: The reactant is 3–ethyl–3–pentanol. The product is 3–ethyl–2–pentene.

Match: (D) is correct. Notice that correctly naming the reactant eliminates (A), (B), and (C) and that correctly naming the product eliminates (B), (C), and (E). Use strategic elimination when needed on Test Day.

4. D

Stop: Answer choices are structures.

Think: The question asks which conformation is the least stable for a cyclohexane. Putting the largest substituents in the equatorial positions will confer the most stability. The opposite is also true: Having the largest substituents in axial positions will confer the least stability.

Predict: The conformation that puts the largest groups in the axial positions will be the least stable.

Match: (D) is correct. All of the chlorines and *t*–butyl groups are in axial positions. (A) and (C) show not only the wrong conformation but also the wrong molecule; the functional groups are attached to the wrong carbons. This is an easy way to eliminate choices on Test Day. (B) is Opposite; this configuration is the most stable because all groups are in equatorial positions. Be careful on Test Day not to automatically look for stability. Similarly, (E) has one of the chlorines in an equatorial position, making it less stable than (B) but too stable to be the answer.

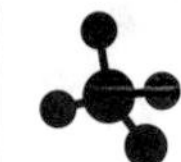

5. E

Stop: Answer choices are Newman projections.

Think: The question asks which conformation is the most stable. The methyl groups are the largest functional groups.

Predict: The methyl groups should be separated as much as possible to avoid steric hindrance. An *anti* staggered conformation in which the two methyl groups are separated by a 180 degree angle would be the most stable.

Match: (E) is correct.

6. E

Stop: Answer choices are cycloalkanes arranged from greatest to least. Strategic elimination may be possible.

Think: The question asks you to rank the ring strain of the molecules from most strain to least strain. Angle strain occurs when the bond angle deviates from the angle predicted by VSEPR. Alkanes should have a 109.5 degree angle. Cyclopropane. cyclobutane, cyclopentane, and cyclohexane have approximate angles of 60, 90, 108, and 109.5 degrees, respectively.

Predict: Cyclopropane deviates the most from 109.5, so it has the most strain. Cyclohexane has the least strain because its angles deviate the least.

Match: (E) is correct. Notice that only this choice ranks cyclopropane the highest. And, this is the only choice that puts the molecules in order of their number of carbons. Use strategic thinking like this on Test Day to save time and to help when you are not sure of the answer.

7. C

Stop: Answer choices are small integers.

Think: The question asks how many chiral carbons are in cholesterol. Use the figure to locate and count the chiral carbons. To be chiral the carbon needs to be asymmetrical and attached to four different atoms or groups.

Predict: There are eight carbons attached to four different groups, as shown in the figure below. Each black dot represents a chiral carbon.

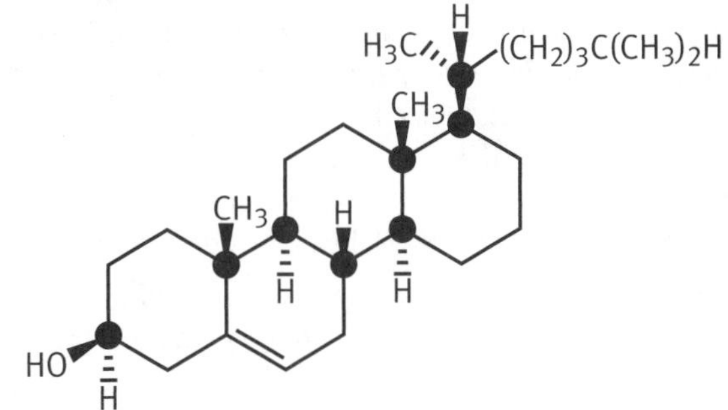

Match: (C) is correct.

8. C

Stop: Answer choices are Fischer projections.

Think: The question asks which compound is optically inactive. All of the answer choices have two chiral centers, so the optically inactive compound will be a *meso* compound.

Predict: The correct answer will have an internal plane of symmetry.

Match: (C) is correct.

9. B

Stop: Answer choices show that this a configuration problem. The question will require counting chiral centers and determining the designation of each.

Think: To be chiral, a carbon needs to be attached to be asymmetrical and attached to four different atoms or groups. To determine whether it is *R* or *S* configuration, look at the substituents and determine their priorities. Clockwise is *R*; counterclockwise is *S*. But, remember to invert the answer if the lowest priority group is coming out of the page.

Predict: The carbon on the far right is attached to an amino group, a carboxylic acid, a methylene group, and a hydrogen. This carbon is the only chiral center in the molecule. Assigning priority to the substituents: first is the amino group; second is the carboxylic acid; third is the methylene; fourth is the hydrogen. Going in order (one, two, three) results in a clockwise rotation, which would be an *R* configuration. However, the hydrogen is the lowest priority group, and it is coming out of the page instead of going in, so it is an *S* configuration.

Match: (B) matches the prediction. There are a couple of traps to avoid on this question. First, not every carbon that is drawn with wedges and dashes is a chiral carbon. Check for chirality rather than just visually assessing the size or complexity of the molecule. Second, don't forget to invert the configuration as choice (A) does.

10. B

Stop: Answer choices are *cis–trans* isomers.

Think: The question asks which molecule has the lowest boiling point. Boiling point is determined mostly by the strength of intermolecular forces. The lower the strength, the lower the boiling point. *Trans* isomers generally have lower boiling points than their corresponding *cis* isomers because *trans* isomers have some symmetry and therefore weaker net molecular dipoles due to individual bond dipole vectors canceling out when added together. Also, smaller molecules will have lesser London dispersion forces and therefore lower boiling points.

Predict: Smaller molecules will have lower boiling points, and the *trans* isomer will have a lower boiling point than the *cis* isomer.

Match: (B) is correct. Notice that (C), (D), and (E) can be eliminated quickly because hexane and octane are larger than butane.

11. A

Stop: Answer choices are types of isomers.

Think: The question is straightforward: what type of isomers are these molecules? Determine the absolute configuration of the two molecules to determine their relationship.

Predict: The molecule on the left has a configuration of *R,S*. The molecule on the right also has a configuration of *R,S*. Since the molecules have the same absolute configurations, they are conformational isomers of one another. (The left half of the molecule on the left is rotated by 180 degrees in the right molecule.).

Match: (A) is correct. Conformational isomers are stereoisomers that have the same connectivity but different rotation about a single bond.

12. C

Stop: Answer choices are types of isomers.

Think: The question is straightforward: what is the relationship between the molecules. Determine the absolute configuration of each to determine their relationship.

Predict: The molecule on the left has a configuration of *R,R*. The molecule on the right has a configuration of *S,S*. These two molecules are opposite at every chiral center, so they are enantiomers.

Match: (C) is correct.

13. D

Stop: Answer choices are halide ions.

Think: The question asks for the best leaving group. Weak bases, or the conjugate bases of strong acids, make excellent leaving groups. And, the larger the halide conjugate base, the less the electron affinity, making its acid more readily ionized and thus a stronger acid.

Predict: The ion that forms the strongest acid will make the best leaving group. The largest halide ion will likely make the strongest acid.

Match: (D) is correct. Rank the choices as acids from most to least acidic: $HI > HBr > HCl > HF > H_2$. Also, I is the largest halide ion listed.

14. D

STOP: Answer choices are statements about S_N1 reactions.

THINK: The question asks for what is not true about S_N1 reactions. Predict what is true, and then eliminate.

PREDICT: The S_N1 reaction occurs in two steps and follows first-order kinetics. The first step is the rate limiting step, results in the formation of the carbocation. Substitution stabilizes the carbocation, and a protic solvent will stabilize the leaving group; both of these make the mechanism more favorable. The second step is the nucleophilic attack on the carbocation, which forms a new bond.

MATCH: (D) is correct because it is not true. Polar protic, not aprotic, solvents stabilize leaving groups, not carbocations, by hydrogen bonding.

15. D

Stop: Answer choices describe changes made to a reaction. Reaction mechanisms are being tested.

Think: The question asks how to increase the rate of an S_N1 reaction. The rate of an S_N1 reaction depends on the first step, which is the loss of the leaving group and formation of the carbocation.

Predict: Anything that makes the loss of the leaving group more favorable will increase the rate of reaction.

Match: (D) is correct. A more electronegative leaving group will make the loss of the leaving group more favorable. (A) and (E) can be eliminated quickly because they involve the nucleophile, which is part of the fast second step and therefore has no bearing on the rate of the reaction. (B) would make the leaving group less stable, and (C) describes an extremely unstable carbocation; both of these conditions are unfavorable for S_N1.

16. A

Stop: Answer choices are long but parallel sentences describing energy states and kinetics in a reaction.

Think: The question asks how using a secondary substrate rather than a primary substrate would change an S_N2 reaction profile. S_N2 reactions occur via a concerted, or one-step, mechanism; the addition of the nucleophile to the electrophile and the departure of the leaving group occur simultaneously. Since the nucleophile must have room to attack from the back of the substrate, minimizing steric hindrance is important. A secondary substrate is more substituted, so there will be more steric hindrance.

Predict: Since steric hindrance will be increased with the secondary substrate, the reaction will have a higher activation energy.

Match: (A) is correct. (B) is Opposite.

17. D

Stop: Answer choices are rate laws.

Think: The question asks for the rate law for S_N2. S_N2 stands for bimolecular nucleophilic substitution. Since it is bimolecular, the rate depends on both the nucleophile and the electrophile.

Predict: The rate law should include both the nucleophile and the alkyl halide.

Match: (D) is correct. The nucleophile concentration does not affect the rate more than the concentration of the leaving group, as is depicted in (E).

18. A

Stop: Answer choices are structures.

Think: The question asks which substrate would be best for an S_N2 reaction. The nucleophile must attack an electrophilic carbon. Steric hindrance should be avoided.

Predict: The least substituted alkyl halide will provide the least hindrance and be the best substrate.

Match: (A) is correct. Remember that S_N2 reactions prefer methyl and primary alkyl halides.

19. C

Stop: Answer choices are solvents.

Think: The question asks for the best solvent for E2 reactions. E2 reactions are similar to S_N2 reactions; they require a good base and a good leaving group. The best solvent will react with the base and stabilize the leaving group.

Predict: Protic solvents increase H^+ in solution, which will react with the base instead of allowing it to perform E2. Polar aprotic solvents don't weaken the base as much but do increase the stability of the leaving group. Nonpolar solvents would not stabilize the leaving group sufficiently. Look for a polar aprotic solvent.

Match: (C) is correct because acetone is a polar aprotic solvent. Water (A), alcohol (B), and ammonia (E) are polar protic solvents. Hexanes (D) are nonpolar. Note that E2 reactions are commonly performed in the conjugate acid of the base, which will form as one of the products naturally anyway, but this is not required.

20. B

Stop: Answer choices describe steps in a reaction.

Think: The question asks for the rate–determining step in an E1 reaction. E1 reactions occur in two steps. The first and rate–limiting step is the formation of the carbocation—just like in S_N1. The carbocation is a positively charged carbon. Spontaneously breaking apart the original molecule to create this charge requires energy input and is much slower than the reaction of carbocation and nucleophile, which is fast since it is energetically favorable.

Predict: The formation of the carbocation, which requires energy, is the rate–limiting step.

Match: (B) is correct. Note that (C) and (D) are not describing E1 but S_N2.

21. C

Stop: Answer choices describe the number and distribution of products.

Think: The question asks for the distribution of products resulting from an E2 reaction. The reaction follows Zaitsev's rule: The most highly substituted product will be the major product. Product 1 has the double bond between the secondary and tertiary carbons, whereas product 2 has the double bond between the primary and tertiary carbons.

Predict: Product 1 is the most substituted, so it will be favored and the major product.

Match: (C) is correct. (A) is Extreme: Product 1 is favored, but it is not the only product since product 2 is possible. (D) is Opposite.

22. C

STOP: Answer choices are structures.

THINK: The question asks for the product. Heat and strong acid are added to an alkyl halide—classic E1 reaction conditions.

PREDICT: The OH group will be protonated by the acid to form water. Since water is a good leaving group, it will leave, forming the most substituted carbocation. Next, the proton on the adjacent carbon that forms the most substituted alkene will be abstracted either by H_2O or SO_4^{2-} in solution.

MATCH: (C) is correct. (A) and (E) have less substituted double bonds. (B) has too many carbons—seven instead of the six available. (D) has a ketone, which would not form.

23. E

Stop: Answer choices describe manipulating variables in substitution and elimination reactions.

Think: The question asks how to promote S_N2 over E2. These are competitive reactions. Without a strong base E2 reactions cannot occur.

Predict: Using a weak base that is a strong nucleophile will favor substitution over elimination.

Match: (E) is correct. Using a bulkier base (A), adding heat (B), or using a tertiary halide (D) will make E2 more favorable. Using a good leaving group (C) will make both reactions more favorable.

24. A

STOP: Answer choices are IUPAC names with *R*/*S* configuration. The question will test both nomenclature and stereochemistry.

THINK: The question asks for the major product. HMPA, the solvent, is polar aprotic, which will make an S_N2 reaction favorable. The electrophile contains iodine and fluorine. Iodine is a much better leaving group than fluorine, so when the nucleophile, N_3^-, completes the backside attack, iodine will leave and be replaced by the azido group. Although the product will be inverted, the nucleophile being added, N, has a lower priority than the leaving group, I, so reversal of *R* to *S* cannot be assumed. The absolute configuration must be determined again using the new product.

Predict: The product will be 1–azido–1–fluoropropane. Determining the absolute configuration of the new product shows that it remains *R*.

MATCH: (A) is correct. (B) indicates that fluorine leaves, but it is a bad leaving group due to its small size. (C) incorrectly assumes that inversion will lead to a reversal of *R* to *S*. An alkene (D) indicates an elimination rather than substitution. A racemic mixture (E) would result from an S_N1 reaction.

25. A

Stop: Answer choices are structures, and some are radicals.

Think: The question asks for the intermediate when reacting $CH(CH_3)_3$ with bromine in the presence of ultraviolet light—a classic radical reaction.

Predict: The intermediates for a radical reaction will be in the propagation step. Therefore, expect X• or R•. None of the answer choices includes the bromine, (X), so look for a stable radical of $CH(CH_3)_3$. The most stable radical will have the unpaired electron on the most substituted carbon.

Match: (A) is correct because it shows the unpaired electron on the most substituted carbon. (B) and (E) have unpaired electrons on the wrong carbon(s). The central carbon will not have a formal charge, so (C) and (D) cannot be correct.

26. A

Stop: Answer choices are reactions that involve radicals.

Think: The question asks for the termination step. The termination step is the last part of a radical reaction, during which the radicals formed during initiation and propagation steps come together to form a non–radical.

Predict: The reaction must combine two radicals to form a non–radical.

Match: (A) is correct. (E) is Opposite.

27. E

Stop: Answer choices are molecules. A closer look reveals that they are all alkyl halides containing iodine.

Think: The question describes the reaction of butane and iodine in the presence of light—a classic radical reaction—and asks for the major product.

Predict: Although iodine will form radicals, these radicals are not very reactive. The initial product that would normally be formed with radical halogenation, HI, is an extremely strong acid. It takes more energy to form HI than for the iodine to remain a radical. Because of this, radical reactions with iodine generally do not occur.

Match: (E) is correct.

28. B

Stop: Answer choices are molecules.

Think: The question asks for the product when HBr is added to an alkene. No radicals are involved. When an alkene and a hydrogen halide react, the hydrogen and the halogen will be added via Markovnikov addition.

Predict: The bromine will be added onto the more substituted carbon from the double bond, and the hydrogen will be added onto the less substituted carbon from the double bond.

Match: (B) is correct. Note that (D) can be eliminated easily since propane has the wrong number of carbons.

29. A

Stop: Answer choices are molecules, and all include bromine and three carbons.

Think: The question asks for the product when hydrogen bromine is added to an alkene in the presence of peroxides, which form radicals. The peroxides will generate bromine radicals. When an alkene and a halogen radical react, there will be an anti–Markovnikov addition.

Predict: The bromine will be added onto the less substituted carbon, and the hydrogen will add to the more substituted carbon.

Match: (A) is correct. The alkene in (D) can be eliminated quickly since the double bond is broken.

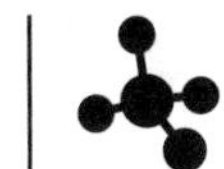

30. E

Stop: Answer choices are reactants.

Think: The question stem wants to turn $(CH_3)_2CCHCH_3$ into a tertiary alkyl halide, presumably $(CH_3)_2CXCH_2CH_3$.

Predict: The halide needs to add to the more substituted carbon. It will be added to the less substituted carbon if any radicals are generated, so exclude light, peroxides, or other radical–generating reactants.

Match: (E) is correct because it is the only answer that will add the hydrogen halide in a Markovnikov addition. (A), (C), and (D) are Opposite. (B) will not provide the halide.

Biology 2

1. C	13. A	25. B
2. E	14. C	26. D
3. E	15. D	27. E
4. B	16. A	28. E
5. C	17. D	29. C
6. D	18. C	30. D
7. A	19. A	31. D
8. D	20. D	32. A
9. C	21. A	33. D
10. E	22. C	
11. E	23. E	
12. B	24. D	

1. C

Stop: Answer choices are all sentences describing sugars, mostly maltose.

Think: The question asks what would happen in an individual who lacks the enzyme maltase. Maltase breaks maltose, a disaccharide, down into glucose monosaccharides. Think about what enzyme deficiency is similar. Lactose intolerance is the inability to break lactose down into glucose molecules due to lactase deficiency. Just as individuals who lack lactase cannot enzymatically digest lactose, individuals who lack maltase will not be able to enzymatically digest maltose.

Predict: Without maltase, maltose will not be digested in the small intestine. The small intestine is able to absorb only monosaccharides, so maltose will pass through to the large intestine. The bacteria in the large intestine will digest the maltose. When the same process occurs with lactose, the result is flatulence and diarrhea.

Match: (C) is correct. Lactase (A) is specific to lactose, so it will not digest maltose. Maltose (B) cannot passively diffuse into the cells because the interstitial epithelium is not permeable to complex sugars. Maltose is a normal product of starch digestion, so the immune system (D) would not attack it. A maltase deficiency does not affect absorption of glucose (E) but rather the ability to get glucose from maltose, and there are many other dietary sources of glucose.

2. E

Stop: Answer choices are types of biological molecules.

Think: The question stem asks what type of molecule is broken down by salivary amylase. Most digestive enzymes are named for their substrates.

Predict: Starch is made of amylose and amylopectin.

Match: (E) is correct. Proteins (A) are broken down by proteases. Lipids (B) are broken down by lipases. Nucleic acids (D) are broken down by nucleases. Monosaccharides (C) do not require enzymatic digestion; they are absorbed in the small intestine.

3. E

Stop: Answer choices are biologic functions.

Think: The question stem asks what bacteria do in the large intestine.

Predict: Bacteria in the gut have several functions. They perform some digestion, prevent infection, and produce some nutrients.

Match: (E) is correct. Notice that you do not need to evaluate all of the choices. Once you find two choices that describe functions of intestinal bacteria, select (E).

4. B

Stop: Answer choices are lists of blood types.

Think: The question asks which list contains only blood types that would cause hemolysis in a person with B^- blood. When a donor's blood contains an antigen that the recipient does not have, the recipient forms antibodies against the foreign antigen, resulting in hemolysis.

Predict: B^- blood contains the B antigen but not the A or Rh antigens. Any blood type that includes the A antigen or is Rh^+ will cause hemolysis. The list cannot contain blood types that will not cause hemolysis, so B^- (the same blood type as the recipient) and O^- (the universal donor) cannot be included.

Match: (B) is correct because all three blood types contain either the A antigen, Rh antigens, or both. Note that this choice can be matched directly or by eliminating (A), (C), and (E) because they contain B^- and (D) because it contains O^-.

5. C

Stop: Answer choices are phrases about red blood cells (RBCs) and cellular respiration.

Think: The question asks why NOT to use mammalian RBCs to study aerobic respiration. The primary function of RBCs is to transport oxygen. Mature mammalian RBCs do not have organelles.

Predict: Since mammalian RBCs do not have mitochondria, aerobic respiration cannot occur in RBCs.

Match: (C) is correct. Since RBCs lack mitochondria, they must attain their ATP anaerobically via glycolysis rather than through aerobic respiration. (A) is a faulty use of detail; it is true that RBCs live only about 120 days, but that does not answer the question. (B), (D), and (E) are false statements. Aerobic respiration occurs in many cells, not just those in the alveoli, as described in (B). RBCs do not consume oxygen (D) and are smaller, not larger (E), than many other cells.

6. D

Stop: Answer choices are pathways through anatomical structures of the human respiratory system.

Think: The question asks for the correct order of structures through which air travels during inhalation.

Predict: Air flows into the mouth and nose, through the pharynx, and down to the larynx, which sits atop the trachea. The trachea then branches into the left and right bronchi, which further branch into bronchioles that terminate in the alveoli.

Match: (D) is correct. If you can't recall the correct order, eliminate choices piece-by-piece, starting with the first and last elements. Alveoli appear at the end of every list, so disregard. Eliminate (B), (C), and (E) because each starts with the larynx. Eliminate (A) because it puts the lungs before the bronchi.

7. A

Stop: Answer choices are sentences; most are about muscle contraction.

Think: This question asks which statement is false, or not true, but does not include any additional clues. Predict what is true, and then eliminate.

Predict: Neuronal stimulus triggers an action potential that ultimately causes Ca^{2+} to flow out the sarcoplasmic reticulum. The rush of Ca^{2+} initiates the binding of actin and myosin filaments, which contract the sarcomere. During contraction, the Z lines are pulled closer together, the entire sarcomere and H and I bands shorten, and the A band lengthens. Eliminate any true statements.

Match: (A) is correct because it is not true. Tendons connect muscle to bone; ligaments connect bone to bone. (B), (D), and (E) are true as predicted. Specialized cells (C) work to maintain serum Ca^{2+} levels. Osteoclasts increase or decrease their activity to maintain serum Ca^{2+} levels in response to parathyroid hormone, which is regulated by serum Ca^{2+}.

8. D

Stop: Answer choices are statements about muscle contraction.

Think: This question asks for what is NOT required for a muscle to elongate, or relax. Predict what is required, and then eliminate. Remember that elongation is the opposite of contraction, so whatever occurs during contraction is generally reversed in elongation.

Predict: Action potentials stimulate Ca^{2+} release from the sarcoplasmic reticulum to initiate contraction. Ca^{2+} causes a conformational change along the actin filament that allows myosin to bind. ATP is hydrolyzed as myosin prepares to bind to actin, leaving ADP and inorganic phosphate bound to the myosin filament until they are released during contraction. For relaxation to occur, this must all be reversed. ATP must bind again to myosin, and Ca^{2+} must detach from the actin filament complex and be re-sequestered by the sarcoplasmic reticulum via its Ca^{2+} ATPase (SERCA) pumps. Once contraction has stopped, the action of an antagonist group pulls the muscle to elongate it, e.g., the opposing actions of biceps and triceps.

Match: (D) is correct because it is not required for elongation. The statement is also inaccurate. The actin filaments themselves do change length during contraction and elongation but instead move closer and farther apart from one another. (A), (B), and (C) are all required as predicted. Ryanodine receptors (E) are what allow the Ca^{2+} release from the sarcoplasmic reticulum in response to an action potential, so reducing the action potential signal is required for relaxation, or elongation.

9. C

Stop: Answer choices are clinical signs or conditions.

Think: The question asks what would happen if the Ca^{2+} gradient across the sarcoplasmic reticulum (SR) were lost. Ca^{2+} concentration is much higher in the SR than in the cytosol. The movement of Ca^{2+} into the cytosol initiates contraction, and the active transport of Ca^{2+} back into the SR maintains the gradient and allows relaxation.

Predict: If the gradient were not maintained, the cytosol would be overwhelmed with Ca^{2+}, and the muscles would become rigid and unable to relax.

Match: (C) is correct. Emesis, or vomiting, (A) and hyperventilation (B) require muscle contraction. Relaxation (D) is the opposite of what would happen because muscle cells cannot relax in the presence of high levels of Ca^{2+}. Drowsiness (E) is a neurological effect.

10. E

Stop: Answer choices are actions of the autonomic nervous system.

Think: The question asks what happens if the parasympathetic nervous system is activated.

Predict: The parasympathetic nervous system stimulates "rest and digest."

Match: (E) is correct because blood is directed away from skeletal muscles by the parasympathetic nervous system.

(A), (B), (C), and (D) all occur in response to sympathetic, not parasympathetic, activation.

11. E

Stop: Answers are points on the figure.

Think: The question asks which point identifies an axon. The axon is the cell projection that transmits signals away from the cell body.

Predict: 1, 2, and 4 are axons since they transfer a signal to another neuron or to the gill muscle.

Match: (E) is correct. Although 3 does not appear different from an axon in this image, it is receiving info, so it must be a dendrite.

12. B

Stop: Answer choices are disorders.

Think: The question asks what would happen without myelin. Myelin insulates neurons to speed up propagation of neuronal action potentials.

Predict: When myelin is damaged, relays between neurons become slow or disrupted. This is especially evident in neurons with long axons, such as those originating in the spinal cord and traveling through the limbs. Slowed or disrupted action potentials in the limbs cause problems with motor control and uncoordinated movement.

Match: (B) is correct. Total paralysis (A) would not occur since many neurons function without myelin. Seizures (C) result from excessive neuronal stimulation not usually associated with loss of myelin.

13. A

Stop: The question stem and answer choices are long, so you may want to triage this one. The choices are sentences about neurotransmitters.

Think: The question asks how repeated stimulation could cause habituation. Once habituated, neurons do not respond to stimuli as strongly as they would have before habituation. A weaker response indicates that either action potentials are less frequent or less neurotransmitter is released per action potential.

Predict: Fewer action potentials could result if the neuron has fewer dendrites or a lower resting potential. Or, the neuron could produce or release less neurotransmitter if there is less influx of calcium, which stimulates binding and release of the synaptic vesicles.

Match: (A) is correct. If calcium channels in the terminal membrane are closed, neurotransmitter will not be released in response to an action potential. Choices (B), (C), (D), and (E) are Opposite because they describe mechanisms for increasing neuronal response rather than decreasing it. Increasing number of receptors (B) makes it easier for neurotransmitters to bind and cause action potentials. Decreasing the concentration of neurotransmitter-degrading enzymes (C) or increasing the amount of neurotransmitter released per action potential (E) would increase the availability of neurotransmitters. If anything happens at a lower (more negative) excitatory potential (D), action potentials will happen more readily, so less, not more, stimulation is required.

14. C

Stop: Answer choices complete a long sentence about resting, action potentials, and neurotransmission.

Think: The question asks how neurons distinguish between weaker and stronger stimuli. A stimulus that is more intense or longer in duration will produce more frequent action potentials.

Predict: When the stimulus is stronger, neurons will produce more frequent action potentials and release more neurotransmitters. When the stimulus is weaker, neurons will produce action potentials less frequently and release less neurotransmitter.

Match: (C) is correct. Larger action potentials (A) are not possible; action potentials are "all or nothing." Decreasing the voltage of the resting potential (B) also would not occur since resting potential is roughly constant. The voltage does drop below the normal resting potential, but this occurs after any action potential. Decreasing the voltage of the threshold potential (D) and (E) are Opposite. Releasing a higher concentration of neurotransmitters (D) would happen in response to the forceful push rather than the light touch. Conversely, increasing the time between action potentials (E) would be a response to the light touch rather than the forceful push.

15. D

Stop: Answer choices are statements about the polarization of the axon terminal.

Think: The question asks what happens to the axon terminal to allow sensitization. Sensitized neurons respond more frequently to a stimulus than unsensitized neurons do.

Predict: During an action potential, K^+ functions to repolarize the cell membrane after the Na^+ influx depolarizes it. Without this repolarization, the axon terminal will remain depolarized for a longer period of time.

Match: (D) is correct. If the axon terminal remains depolarized for a longer period of time following action potential, the sensitized neuron will continue releasing neurotransmitter, causing more activation of the postsynaptic neuron. (A) and (B) are Extreme since these effects are described as *permanent* rather than of short duration, and they would entirely disable the neuron. Longer polarization (C) is Opposite since this would delay the next action potential. Decreased neurotransmitter release (E) is also Opposite; this describes habituation rather than sensitization.

16. A

Stop: Answer choices are patterns of blood sugar and hormone levels.

Think: The question asks how the body responds to sugar intake.

Predict: Sugar is digested and absorbed, causing blood glucose concentration to increase. The pancreas releases insulin to cause cellular uptake of glucose and thereby reduce the blood glucose concentration.

Match: (A) is correct. Glucagon (B) is released in response to low, rather than high, blood sugar. (C) is incorrect because insulin follows blood glucose; it would not increase when blood glucose normalizes. Blood glucose would not drop after eating sugar as in (D) and (E).

17. D

Stop: Answer choices are sentences about the activity of osteoblasts and osteoclasts in response to calcium levels.

Think: The question stem asks how parathyroid hormone (PTH) affects serum calcium.

Predict: PTH is released when blood calcium is low. It causes osteoclasts to break down bone, releasing free calcium and increasing calcium levels in the blood.

Match: (D) is correct. Osteoblasts (A) and (C) build new bone, reduce blood calcium, and are stimulated by calcitonin. Osteoclasts break down, not create (B), bone and are released when blood calcium is low, not high (E).

18. C

Stop: Answer choices are points or labels on a chart.

Think: The question asks which line on the chart corresponds to luteinizing hormone (LH).

Predict: LH is named for the corpus luteum, which forms upon ovulation. The LH surge is the only time during the cycle in which LH is present at high levels.

Match: (C) is correct. FSH (A) maintains the follicular phase of the cycle and then falls in the luteal phase. Estrogen (B) rises before the LH surge and is elevated during the luteal phase. Progesterone (D) rises only during the luteal phase to prepare for implantation of the egg.

19. A

Stop: Answer choices are related to a change in urine volume and composition.

Think: The question asks what would happen to urine if the glomerulus filtered plasma proteins so that they passed into the renal tubule. The glomerulus normally filters small molecules and water into the tubule while keeping almost all proteins and cells in the blood.

Predict: If proteins freely pass into the renal tubule, most of them will not be reabsorbed, or taken back out, because the proximal tubule can only reabsorb a very small amount of protein. The proteins will increase the concentration of the filtrate, which will raise the osmotic pressure and cause water to move into the tubule. The increase in water will cause an increase in urine output.

Match: (A) is correct. (B) is the opposite. Increased urea concentration (C), increased sodium concentration (E), or decreased osmolarity (D) would not be expected since the additional solute has been added in the form of protein. If anything, the opposite would be expected to in response to the presence of large amounts of protein in the filtrate.

20. D

Stop: Answer choices are related to the renin–angiotensin–aldosterone system and antidiuretic hormone (ADH).

Think: The question asks how caffeine inhibits ADH. Administering ADH with caffeine counteracts the inhibition.

Predict: If an injection of ADH counteracts the effect of caffeine, then caffeine must have been preventing the availability of ADH.

Match: (D) is correct. (A), (C), and (E) are irrelevant since the renin–angiotensin–aldosterone system is independent of ADH. If caffeine blocked ADH receptors (B), then administration of ADH could not counteract the effects of caffeine.

21. A

Stop: Answer choices are statements describing regulation related to the renal system.

Think: The question asks what is true of vasopressin, which is also called antidiuretic hormone (ADH).

Predict: Vasopressin promotes water reabsorption by increasing the permeability of the distal convoluted tubule and collecting duct to water. Vasopressin is synthesized in the hypothalamus and stored in the posterior pituitary.

Match: Answer (A) is correct. Choices (B), (D), and (E) relate to the renin–angiotensin–aldosterone system, which is independent of ADH. Wastes are secreted in the kidneys, not reabsorbed (C).

22. C

Stop: Answer choices are infectious agents

Think: The questions ask what stimulates an increase in eosinophils.

Predict: Eosinophils fight large multicellular parasites, such as worms.

Match: (C) is correct. Bacteria (A), fungi (B), and viruses (E) are fought by other immune cells. Venoms (D) are antigens that can be neutralized by antibodies.

23. E

Stop: Answer choices are components of the immune system.

Think: The question asks which component is not involved in nonspecific immune response. This is the same as asking which component provides only specific, or adaptive, immunity.

Predict: B cells produce specific antibodies. T lymphocytes, except the natural killer T cells, also provide only specific response.

Match: (E) is correct because B cells produce specific antibodies to specific antigens. Skin (A) and lysozymes (B) prevent a wide variety of infectious agents from entering the body. Interferons (C) are released in response to a wide variety of pathogens and coordinate the immune response among both nonspecific and specific immune cells. Macrophages (D) indiscriminately engulf and destroy foreign particles.

24. D

Stop: Answer choices are functions related to the immune system.

Think: The question asks what function CD8+ cells serve.

Predict: CD8+ cells are also known as cytotoxic or "killer" T cells.

Match: (D) is correct because cytotoxic T cells directly destroy cells that are cancerous, virally infected, or otherwise damaged. Allergies (A) are mediated by mast cells. Helper T cells (CD4+) stimulate other immune cells (B). Antibodies (C) are produced by B cells. Antigen-presenting cells (E) include dendritic cells, macrophages, and B cells.

25. B

Stop: Answer choices are reproductive functions.

Think: The question asks which choice is false, or not true, of the reproductive system but does not provide any additional scope or clues. Predict what is true, and then eliminate.

Predict: Sperm is made in the testes, stored in the epididymis, and then travels through the vas deferens and urethra during ejaculation. Glands including the prostate and bulbourethral gland contribute to the seminal fluid. Ova mature in follicles, are released during ovulation, and then travel down the fallopian tubes, where fertilization occurs. Remember to eliminate what is true.

Match: (B) is correct because the ductus deferens, a.k.a. the vas deferens, is what carries the sperm from the testes to the urethra rather than storing them. (A) is true; the fallopian tubes are also known as oviducts. (C), (D), and (E) are true, as predicted.

26. D

Stop: Answer choices are anatomical structures in the reproductive system.

Think: The question asks which structure is found in both males and females. Consider what specific function the reproductive system carries out in both males and females.

Predict: Male and female reproductive systems are very different, but urination is very similar.

Match: (D) is correct; both males and females have a urethra that carries urine to exit the body. (A) and (C) are found only in males. (B) and (E) are found only in females.

27. E

Stop: Answer choices are hormones. Most are related to the reproductive system.

Think: The question asks which hormone is not involved in sperm production and development. Predict which hormones are, and then eliminate.

Predict: Gonadotropin-releasing hormone (GnRH) stimulates release of LH and FSH. LH stimulates Leydig cells to produce testosterone. FSH and testosterone act on Sertoli cells to stimulate production of sperm.

Match: (E) is correct. Somatostatin is unrelated to the reproductive system. It moderates many hormones of the anterior pituitary and digestive system.

28. E

Stop: Answer choices describe reproduction outcomes.

Think: The question asks what happens when nondisjunction, or the failure of the centromeres to separate, occurs in meiosis. A nondisjunction event during meiosis results in some gametes with two copies of a chromosome and some gametes with zero copies of that chromosome.

Predict: Fertilization of such ova (two copies or zero copies) with healthy sperm (one copy) would result in zygotes with either three copies (trisomy) or one copy (monosomy).

Match: (E) is correct. (A) is incorrect because some trisomy zygotes are viable and because if nondisjunction occurs in the second meiosis division, not every gamete would have a chromosomal mutation. Identical twins (B) are formed when one zygote or blastula divides, which occurs after fertilization rather than during meiosis. (C) is incorrect because the gender of human offspring is determined by the presence or absence of the Y chromosome, which is carried by the male's sperm, not the woman's ovum, so the ovum's chromosomes are irrelevant. (D) is incorrect because chromosomal mutations are not known to affect fertilization, although the resulting embryo may not survive.

29. C

Stop: Answer choices are numbers but small ones.

Think: The question asks how many gametes will be affected if there is a mutation in one chromosome of a spermatogonium. One spermatogonium forms four sperm by replicating its DNA during the S phase and then dividing twice, once during meiosis I and again during meiosis II.

Predict: The original mutation will be replicated in S phase, resulting in a diploid primary spermatocyte with two copies of the mutation. When the primary spermatocyte divides in meiosis I, it will pass on both copies of the mutation to one of the two secondary spermatocytes, leaving the other secondary spermatocyte unaffected. Each secondary spermatocyte will divide into two sperm cells. The two sperm cells from the affected spermatocyte will have the mutation. The two from the unaffected spermatocyte will not. So, two of four gametes will be affected.

Match: (C) is correct. (A) is incorrect because the mutation cannot be eliminated from this line of spermatogenesis. (B) is incorrect because the genetic material duplicates, resulting in two copies. (D) is incorrect because both copies go to the same secondary spermatocyte, leaving one unaffected spermatocyte that will produce two unaffected sperm. (E) is incorrect. Note that chromosomal crossing over during meiosis would not affect the total number of mutated copies but instead merely change which chromatids have the mutations.

30. D

Stop: Answer choices are disorders, diseases, and maladies.

Think: The question asks which disease people are at risk for if they have mutations in genes that suppress cell division. Mutations will make suppressor genes inactive, removing suppression and thereby increasing the rate of cell division. Paraphrasing question stems is especially helpful when dealing with double negatives; inactivating suppression means activating!

Predict: Cancer involves unregulated cell division.

Match: (D) is correct. Insomnia (A) is a sleep disorder. Myocardial infarction (B) is also known as a heart attack, which is caused by disruption of blood supply to the heart. Diabetes mellitus (C) is a hormonal disease. Osteoporosis (E) is a gradual weakening of bone structure. None of these is caused by uncontrolled cell division.

31. D

Stop: Answer choices are statements about fertilization and embryogenesis.

Think: The question asks how fraternal twins develop.

Predict: Fraternal twins are dizygotic: They result when two completely separate zygotes implant in the uterine wall.

Match: (D) is correct; each zygote is made from one sperm and one egg. (A) or (B) would result in monozygotic twins. Multiple sperm fertilizing an egg (C) and a single sperm fertilizing more than one egg (E) are not possible.

32. A

Stop: Answer choices are germ layers and embryo stages.

Think: The question asks which germ layer the skin and eye arise from.

Predict: The skin and the lens of the eye arise from the ectoderm.

Match: (A) is correct. The endoderm (B) forms the lining of the gut and other organs. The mesoderm (C) forms muscle, kidneys, and gonads. (D) and (E) are embryonic stages that have not yet developed germ layers.

33. D

Stop: Answer choices are stages of embryonic development.

Think: The question asks when spina bifida develops. Spina bifida affects the formation of the spine.

Predict: Neurulation, the process by which the neural plate closes to become the neural tube that later develops into the spinal cord, occurs in the neurula.

Match: (D) is correct. Spina bifida is specific to the spine, which does not start forming until neurulation, so the zygote (A), morula (B), and blastocyst (C) are not developed enough to manifest this disorder. The fetus (E) would exhibit spina bifida but would have developed it as a neurula.

Perceptual Ability 2

1. E	21. B	41. C
2. D	22. C	42. A
3. A	23. A	43. A
4. B	24. B	44. C
5. E	25. D	45. C
6. C	26. D	46. C
7. B	27. A	47. D
8. A	28. B	48. D
9. A	29. C	49. A
10. B	30. C	50. E
11. C	31. C	51. A
12. C	32. E	52. D
13. A	33. A	53. B
14. B	34. D	54. D
15. A	35. B	55. C
16. C	36. B	56. C
17. B	37. C	57. D
18. D	38. D	58. B
19. D	39. D	59. A
20. C	40. E	60. A

Keyholes

1. E

The correct answer is the right projection.

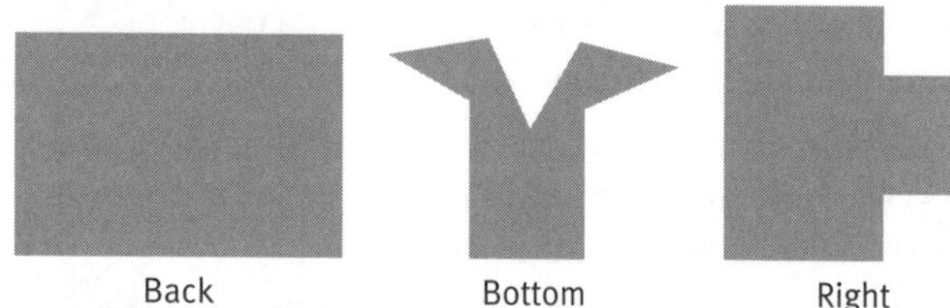

2. D

The correct answer is the back projection rotated clockwise 90°.

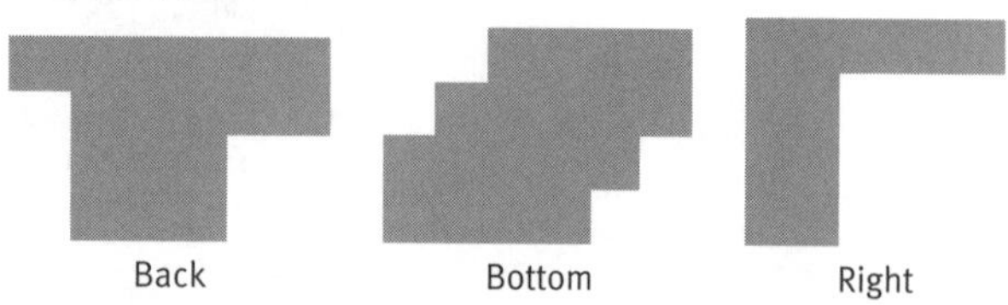

3. A

The correct answer is the bottom projection rotated counterclockwise 90°.

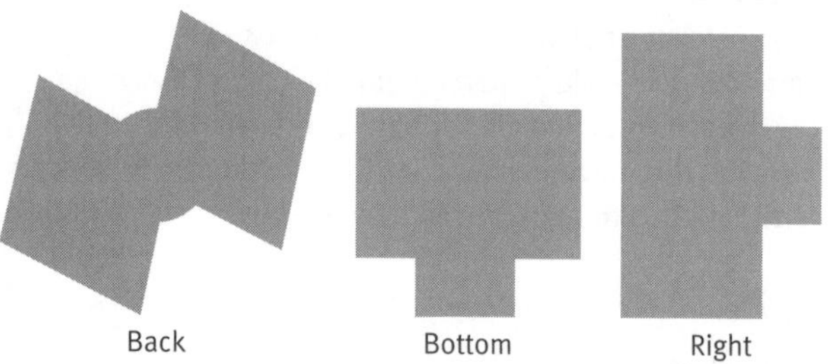

4. B

The correct answer is the back projection flipped horizontally (which is the front projection).

5. E

The correct answer is the right projection.

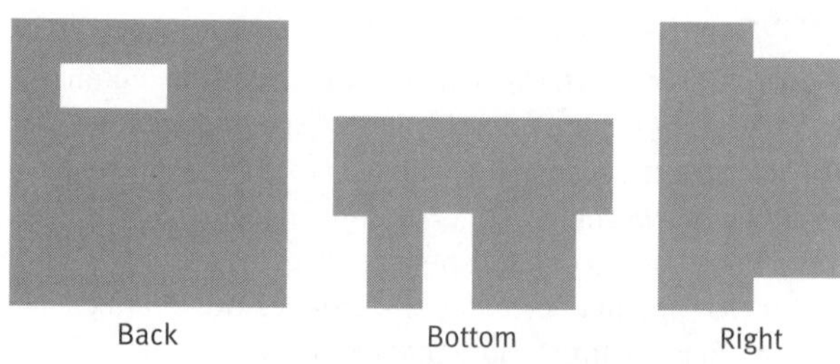

6. C

The correct answer is the bottom projection.

7. B

The correct answer is the right projection.

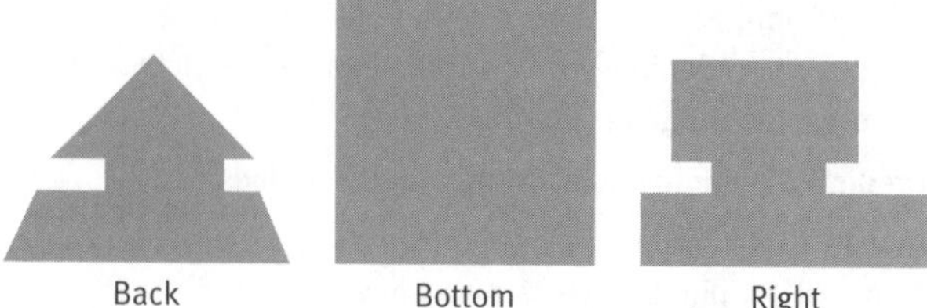

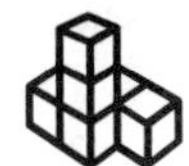

8. A

The correct answer is the right projection flipped horizontally (which is the left projection).

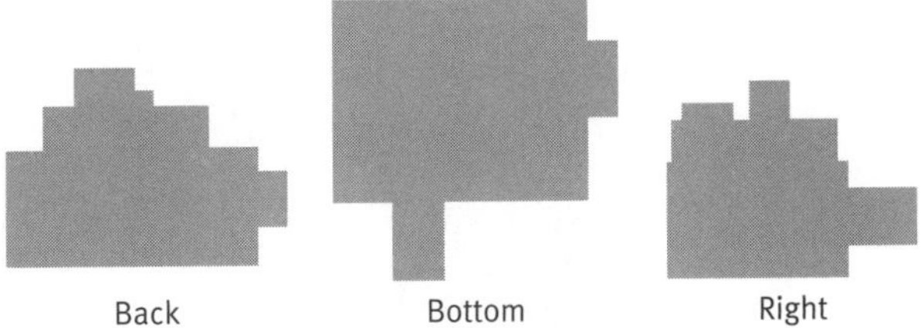

9. A

The correct answer is the back projection.

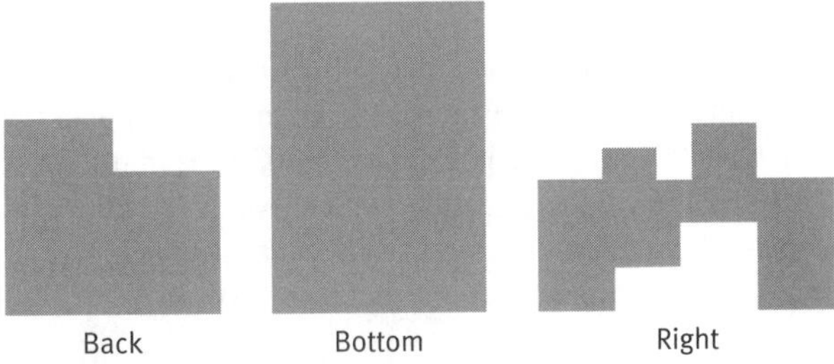

10. B

The correct answer is the right projection rotated counterclockwise 90°.

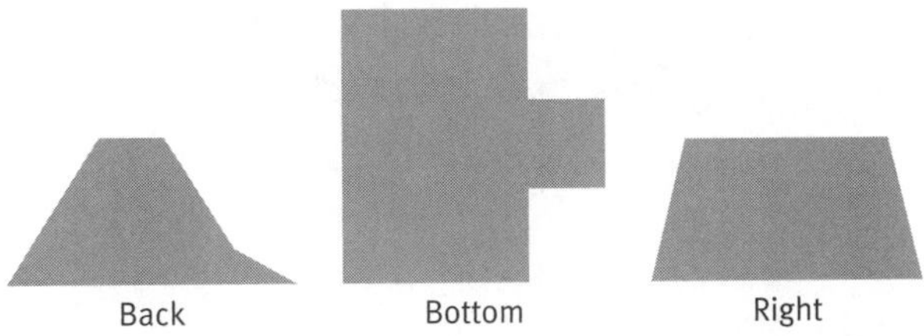

Top-Front-End

11. C

Evaluate the shared edge between the top and front views first. The top view has 4 vertical events, so the end must also have 4 vertical events. Eliminate (A), which has 3 events. This leaves (B), (C), and (D).

Next, evaluate the shared edge between the end and front views. The end view has 3 horizontal events, so the front view must also have 3 horizontal events. This confirms that (A) is not the correct answer but still leaves (B), (C), and (D).

Finally, determine the number of visible and hidden events. Start by evaluating the shared edge between the top and front views. The top view has 4 visible and no hidden events. Eliminate (D), which has 3 visible and 1 hidden event. This leaves (B) and (C). Now, evaluate the shared edge between the end and front views. The end view has 2 visible and 1 hidden event. You can eliminate (B), which has 3 visible and no hidden events. The correct answer is (C).

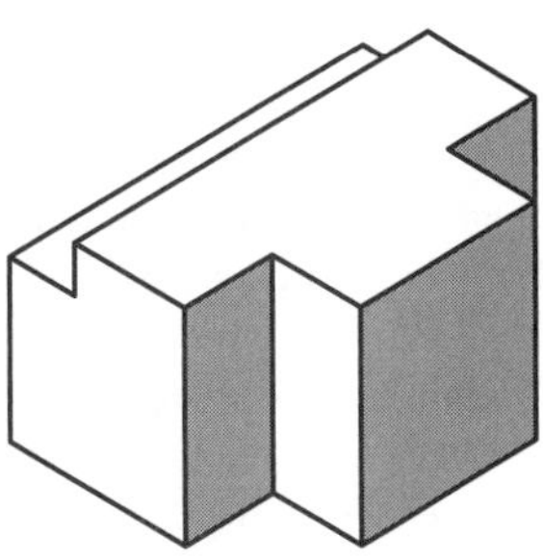

12. C

Evaluate the shared edge between the front and end views. The front view has 4 horizontal events, so the end view must have 4 horizontal events. All answers have 4 horizontal events.

Next, evaluate the shared edge between the top and end views. The top view has 4 horizontal events, so the end view must have 4 vertical events. All answers also have 4 vertical events.

Finally, determine the number of events that are visible and hidden using the shared edge between the front and end views. The front view has 3 visible and 1 hidden events. Eliminate (D), which has 2 visible and 2 hidden events. This leaves (A), (B) and (C). Now, evaluate the visible and hidden events using the shared edge between the top and end views. The top view has 4 visible and no hidden events.

You need to look at the figure as a whole to eliminate. The hidden event on the front view cannot be hidden on the end view as the lines go all of the way to the edge. This tells you that it must be seen from the end view. Eliminate (A), which also has a hidden edge. This leaves (B) and (C). The boxes on the top view must be seen from the end view. Eliminate (B), which does not have boxes on the top edge of the figure. The correct answer is therefore (C).

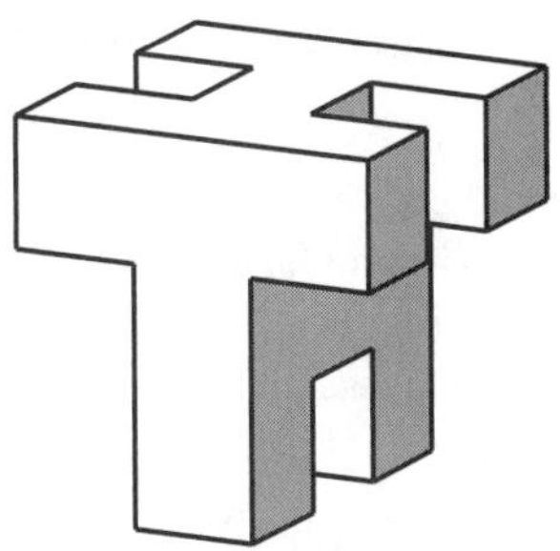

13. A

Evaluate the shared edge between the front and top views first. The front view has 8 vertical events, so the top view must also have 8 vertical events. Eliminate (B) and (D), which both have 6 visible and no hidden events. This leaves (A) and (C).

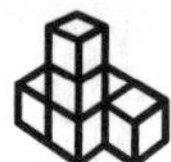

Next, evaluate the shared edge between the end and top views. The end view has 8 vertical events, so the top view must have 8 horizontal events. Both (A) and (C) have 8 horizontal events.

Finally, determine the number of visible and hidden events using the shared edge between the front and top views. The front view has 8 visible and no hidden events, so the top view must have 8 visible and no hidden events. This eliminate (B), (C), and (D) which have 6 visible and no hidden events, 6 visible and 2 hidden events, and 6 visible and no hidden events, respectively. The correct answer must be (A).

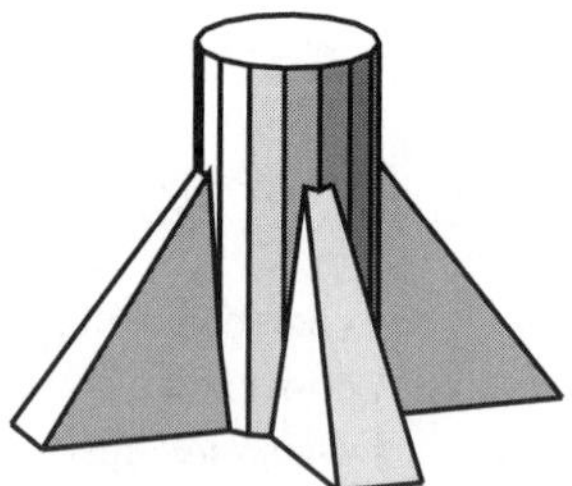

14. B

A quick glance at the answer choices shows that this is a question where you should focus on a key landmark rather than counting events because all of the choices have the same number of total, hidden, and visible events. Instead, focus on the differences among the choices: where the peak is. In the top view, the peak is in the center vertically. This means that the peak should be in the center of the end view, and only answer choice (B) reflects that.

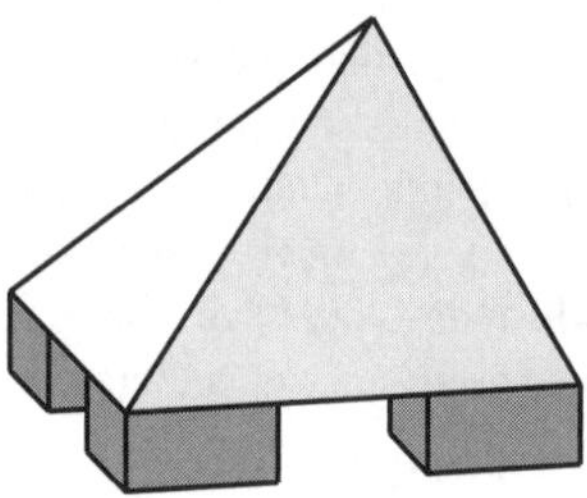

15. A

Evaluate the shared edge between the front and end views. The front view has 6 horizontal events, so the end view must also have 6 horizontal events. Eliminate (B) and (D), which have 5 horizontal events and 8 horizontal events, respectively. This leaves (A) and (C).

Next, evaluate the shared edge between the top and end views. The top view has 6 horizontal events, so the end view must have 6 visible and no hidden vertical events. But all of the remaining answers have 6 vertical events.

Finally, determine the number of visible and hidden events using the shared edge between the front and end views. The front view has 4 visible and 2 hidden horizontal events, so the end view must have 4 visible and 2 hidden horizontal events. Eliminate (C), which has 5 visible and 1 hidden horizontal event. The correct answer is (A).

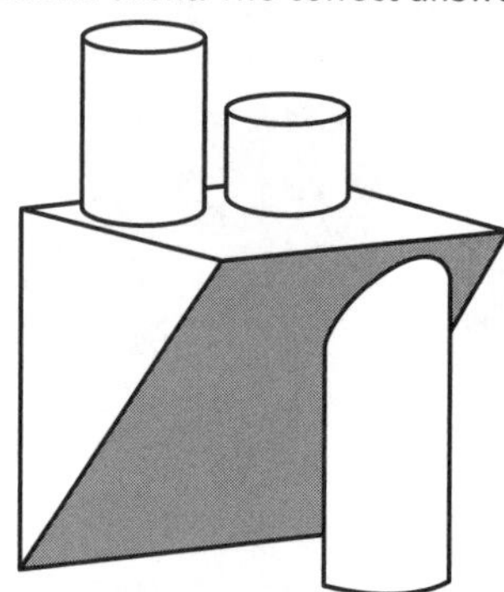

16. C

Evaluate the shared edge between the front and top views. The front view has 7 vertical events, so the top view must also have 7 vertical events. Eliminate (A), (B), and (D), which have 6 vertical events, 5 vertical events, and 6 vertical events, respectively. The correct answer is (C), and there's no need to evaluate further

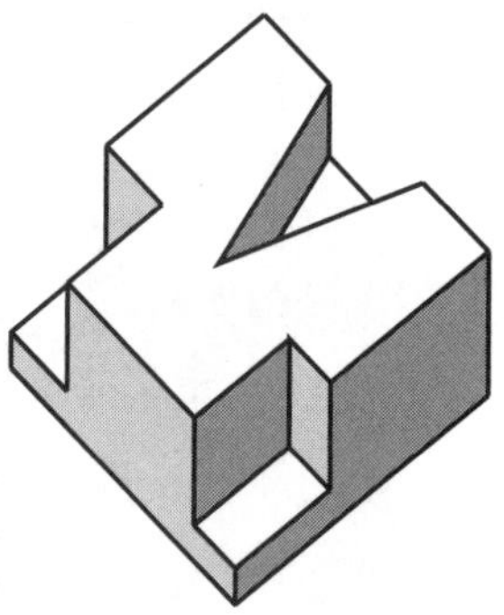

17. B

A quick glance at the answer choices shows that (A), (B), and (D) have the same number of total, visible, and hidden events but vary only in their placement. By evaluating the shared edge between the front and end views, you can see the front view has 3 horizontal events, so the end view must also have 3 horizontal events. This eliminates (C), which has 2 horizontal events, and verifies that one of (A), (B), or (D) will be correct.

From here, look at the shape as a whole to determine the answer. Note that there is a triangle in back that is hidden. Eliminate (A), which has both angles on the front. From the top view, notice that the angle on the end view will lean toward the right (it is on the top of the top view). Eliminate (D), which has the angle leaning to the left. This leaves only the correct answer of (B).

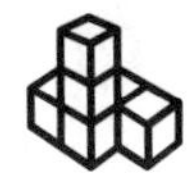

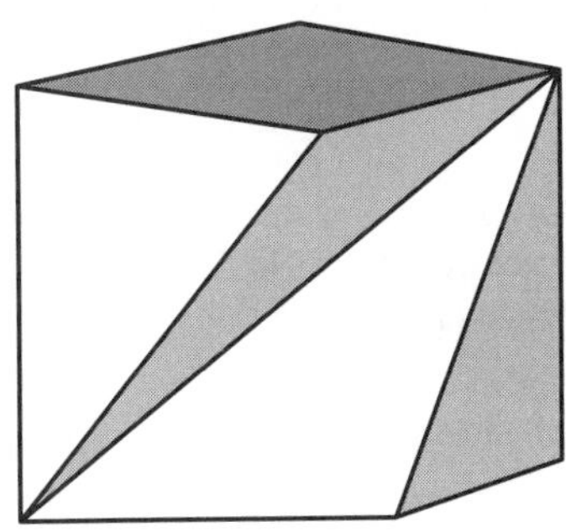

18. D

Evaluate the shared edge between the front and top views. The front view has 8 vertical events, so the top view must also have 8 vertical events. Eliminate (B) and (C), which have 6 and 10 vertical events, respectively. This leave (A) and (D).

Next, evaluate the shared edge between the end and top views. The end view has 2 vertical events, so the top view must have 2 horizontal events. But both of the remaining answers have 2 horizontal events.

Finally, determine the number of visible and hidden events using the shared edge between the front and top views. The front view has 2 visible and 6 hidden vertical events, so the end view must have 2 visible and 6 hidden vertical events. Eliminate (A), which has 4 visible and 4 hidden vertical events, leaving the correct answer to be (D).

19. D

Evaluate the shared edge between the front and top views. The front view has 4 vertical events, so the top view must also have 4 vertical events. Eliminate (A), (B), and (C), which have 3, 3, and 5 vertical events, respectively. The correct answer is (D), and you can stop evaluating here.

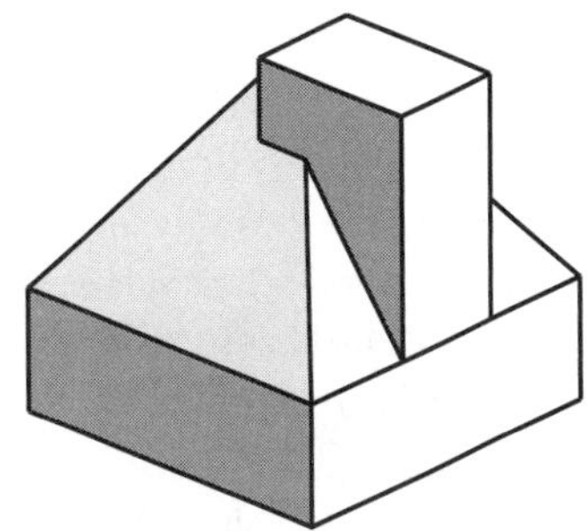

20. C

First, notice that the correct answers are mirror images of one another with differences in which edges are visible versus hidden. This means evaluating total number of events alone won't eliminate any choices, so start examining hidden versus visible right away.

The top view has 6 visible and no hidden vertical events, so the front view must also have 6 visible and no hidden vertical events. Eliminate (B) and (D), which both have 5 visible and 1 hidden vertical event. This leaves (A) and (C).

Next, identify that that the end view has 5 visible and no hidden horizontal events. Both (A) And (C) have 5 visible and no hidden events, leaving both as possibilities.

Finally, look at the shape as a whole to determine the answer. Note that on the top view, there is a rectangle that is sticking out on the left side. Eliminate (A), which has the rectangle on the right. The correct answer is (C).

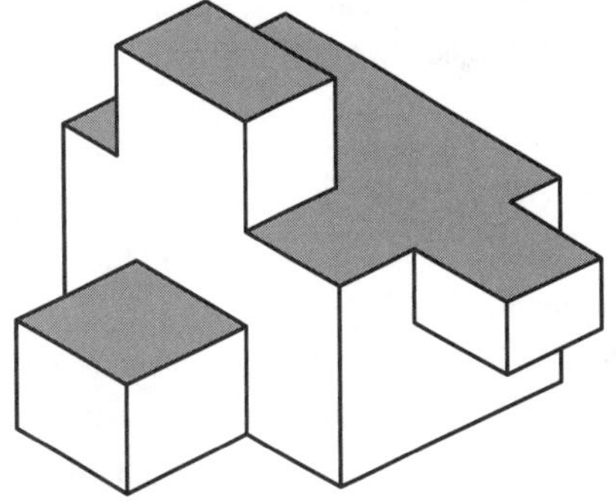

Angle Ranking

21. B

Smallest: The answer choices indicate that either angle 1 or 3 is the smallest. Angle 3 is the smallest, so eliminate (C) and (D), leaving (A) and (B).

Largest: The remaining answers choices both state that 4 is the largest.

Blocking: Blocking is a difficult strategy to use on this particular problem as all of the vertices are not facing the same direction.

Stacking: Stacking shows that 1 fits inside 2, which eliminates (A). The correct answer is (B).

22. C

Smallest: The answer choices indicate that either angle 1, 2, or 4 is the smallest. Angle 4 is the smallest, so eliminate (B) and (D), leaving (A) and (C).

Largest: The remaining answer choices indicate that either 1 or 3 is the largest. 3 is the largest, so eliminate (A), leaving (C) as the correct answer.

Blocking: Blocking could be used here to determine the exact order of angles 1, 2, and 3 since all of the vertices are facing the same direction. This directly shows the correct order of $2<1<3$. (C) is the only answer choice that has the angles in that order and has 4 as the smallest angle.

Stacking: Similarly, stacking could show the entire sequence: 4 fits inside 2, and 1 fits inside 3.

23. A

Smallest: The answer choices indicate that either 1 or 2 is the smallest. Angle 1 is the smallest, so eliminate (C) and (D). This leaves (A) and (B).

Largest: The remaining answer choices indicate that either 3 or 4 is the largest. 3 is the largest, so eliminate (B). The correct answer is (A).

Blocking: Blocking could be used here to determine the exact order of the angles since all of the vertices are facing the same direction. This directly shows the correct order of $1<2<4<3$.

Stacking: Similarly, stacking could show the entire sequence: 1 fits inside 2, and 4 fits inside 3.

24. B

Smallest: The answer choices indicate that 1, 2, or 4 is the smallest. 4 is the smallest, so eliminate (A), (C) and (D). The correct answer is (B).

Largest: You do not need to look at the largest angle since identifying the smallest angle already narrowed down to (B).

Blocking: Blocking could be used here to determine the exact order of the angles since all of the vertices are facing the same direction. This directly shows the correct order of $4<1<2<3$.

Stacking: Similarly, stacking could show the entire sequence: 4 fits inside 1, and 2 fits inside 3.

25. D

Smallest: The answer choices all indicate that 3 is the smallest.

Largest: The answer choices indicate that either 1, 2, or 4 is the largest. 4 is the largest, so eliminate (A) and (B), leaving (C) and (D).

Blocking: Blocking is a difficult strategy to use on this particular problem as all of the vertices are not facing the same direction.

Stacking: Stacking could show the entire sequence: 3 fits inside 1, and 2 fits inside 4. The correct answer is (D).

26. D

Smallest: The answer choices indicate that 1, 2, or 4 is the smallest. 4 is the smallest, so eliminate (A) and (C), leaving (B) and (D).

Largest: The remaining answer choices indicate that either 1 or 2 is the largest. 1 is the largest, so eliminate (B). The correct answer is (D).

Blocking: Blocking is a difficult strategy to use on this particular problem as all of the vertices are not facing the same direction.

Stacking: Stacking could show you the entire sequence: 4 fits inside 3, and 2 fits inside 1.

27. A

Smallest: The answer choices indicate that either 1 or 2 is the smallest. 2 is the smallest, so eliminate (C) and (D), leaving (A) and (B).

Largest: The remaining answer choices indicate that 4 is the largest.

Blocking: Blocking is a difficult strategy to use on this particular problem as all of the vertices are not facing the same direction.

Stacking: Stacking could show the entire sequence: 2 fits inside 1, and 3 fits inside 4. The correct answer is (A).

28. B

Smallest: The answer choices indicate that either 2 or 4 is the smallest. 4 is the smallest, so eliminate (D), leaving (A), (B), and (C).

Largest: The remaining answer choices indicate that either 1 or 3 is the largest. 3 is the largest, so eliminate (C), leaving (A) and (B).

Blocking: Blocking could be used here to determine the entire sequence since the vertices are facing the same direction. The sequence is $4<2<1<3$. The correct answer is (B).

Stacking: Similarly, stacking could show the entire sequence: 4 fits inside 2, and 1 fits inside 3.

29. C

Smallest: The answer choices indicate that either 2 or 4 is the smallest. 4 is the smallest, so eliminate (A), leaving (B), (C), and (D).

Largest: The remaining answer choices indicate that either 1 or 3 is the largest. 1 is the largest, so eliminate (B), leaving (C) and (D).

Blocking: Blocking is a difficult strategy to use on this particular problem as all of the vertices are not facing the same direction.

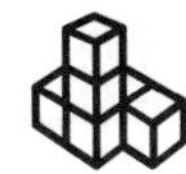

Stacking: Stacking could show the entire sequence: 4 fits inside 2, and 3 fits inside 1. The correct answer is (C).

30. C

Smallest: The answer choices indicate that either 2 or 3 is the smallest. 3 is the smallest, so eliminate (B), leaving (A), (C), and (D).

Largest: The remaining answer choices indicate that either 1 or 4 is the largest. 1 is the largest, so eliminate (D), leaving (A) and (C).

Blocking: Blocking is a difficult strategy to use on this particular problem as all of the vertices are not facing the same direction.

Stacking: Stacking could show the entire sequence: 3 fits inside 2, and 4 fits inside 1. The correct answer is (C).

Hole Punching

31. C

Symmetry: (A), (D), and (E) can be eliminated because they do not have a vertical line of symmetry. This leaves (B) and (C).

Number of holes: The remaining answers have 4 or 8 holes. There are 4 layers of paper where the hole is punched; therefore, 4 holes will result. Eliminate (B), leaving (C) as the correct answer.

Position: Mentally unfolding is not necessary for this question.

32. E

Symmetry: (A) and (C) can be eliminated because they do not have a horizontal line of symmetry. This leaves (B), (D), and (E).

Number of holes: The remaining answers are a mixture of 4 and 8 holes. There are 8 layers of paper where the hole is punched; therefore, 8 holes will result. Eliminate (B) and (D), leaving (E) as the correct answer.

Position: Although not necessary, mentally unfolding the third fold back to the second fold shows that there are holes in the top row in the first and second column. This eliminates both (B) and (D).

33. A

Symmetry: All answer choices have a diagonal line of symmetry.

Number of holes: The remaining answers are a mixture of 4 and 6 holes. There are 4 layers of paper where the hole is punched; therefore, 4 holes will result. Eliminate (C), leaving (A), (B), (D), and (E) as potential answers.

Position: Mentally unfolding the second fold back to the first fold shows that there are holes in the second row, first column and in the fourth row, third column. This eliminates both (B), (D), and (E). The correct answer is (A).

34. D

Symmetry: (A), (B), and (C) can be eliminated because they do not have a diagonal line of symmetry. This leaves (D) and (E).

Number of holes: The remaining answers are a mixture of 3 and 4 holes. There are 3 layers of paper where the hole is punched, so 3 holes will result. Eliminate (E), leaving (D) as the correct answer.

Position: Although not necessary, mentally unfolding the second fold back to the first fold shows that there are holes in the second and third row, second column. This leaves (D) and (E).

35. B

Symmetry: (A) and (C) can be eliminated because they do not have a diagonal line of symmetry. This leaves (B), (D), and (E).

Number of holes: The remaining answers are a mixture of 2 and 4 holes. There are 2 layers of paper where the hole is punched, and 2 holes will result. Eliminate (D), leaving (B) and (E).

Position: Mentally unfolding the second fold back to the first fold shows that there are holes in the first and fourth row, third column. Eliminate (E), leaving (B) as the correct answer.

36. B

Symmetry: (C), (D), and (E) can be eliminated because they do not have a horizontal line of symmetry. This leaves (A) and (B).

Number of holes: The remaining answers both have 6 holes, so counting the number of folds will not allow you to eliminate.

Position: Mentally unfolding the second fold back to the first fold shows that there are holes in the third row, second, third, and fourth column. Eliminate (A), leaving (B) as the correct answer.

37. C

Symmetry: All answer choices have a diagonal line of symmetry.

Number of holes: All answer choices have 8 holes, so the number of holes will not allow you to eliminate.

Position: Mentally unfolding the third fold back to the second fold shows that there are holes in the third row of the first and fourth column and the fourth row of the second and third columns. Eliminate (A), (B), (D), and (E), leaving (C) as the correct answer.

38. D

Symmetry: (B) and (E) can be eliminated because they do not have vertical lines of symmetry. This leaves (A), (C), and (D).

Number of holes: All of the remaining answer choices have 4 holes, so the number of holes will not allow you to eliminate.

Position: Mentally unfolding the second fold back to the first fold shows that there are holes in the second and third row in the second column. Eliminate (A) and (C), leaving (D) as the correct answer.

39. D

Symmetry: (A), (B), and (E) can be eliminated because they do not have a horizontal line of symmetry. This leaves (C) and (D).

Number of holes: The remaining answers are a mixture of 4 and 6 holes. There are 6 layers of paper where the hole is punched, so 6 holes will result. Eliminate (C), leaving (D) as the correct answer.

Position: Mentally unfolding is unnecessary and could be difficult here.

40. E

Symmetry: (B) and (D) can be eliminated because they do not have a horizontal line of symmetry. This leaves (A), (C), and (E).

Number of holes: The remaining answers are a mixture of 1, 3, and 4 holes. There are 3 layers of paper where the hole is punched; therefore, 3 holes will result. Eliminate (A) and (C), leaving (E) as the correct answer.

Position: Mentally unfolding the second fold back to the first fold shows that there are holes in the second and third rows of the third column, so eliminate (A). Mentally unfolding the first fold back to the original paper shows that there are holes in the first, second, and third rows of the third column, so eliminate (C), leaving (E) as the correct answer.

Cube counting

Figure A Tally

0 siders: 0

1 siders: 1

2 siders: 5

3 siders: 6

4 siders: 3

5 siders: 1

Total: 16

41. C

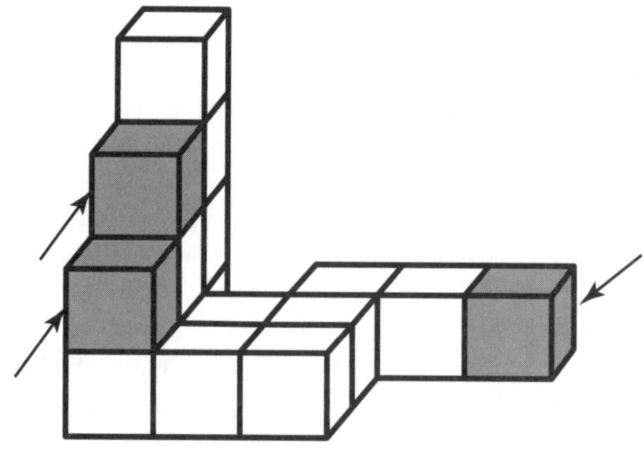

42. A

Figure B Tally

0 siders: 0

1 siders: 1

2 siders: 8

3 siders: 3

4 siders: 3

5 siders: 0

Total: 15

43. A

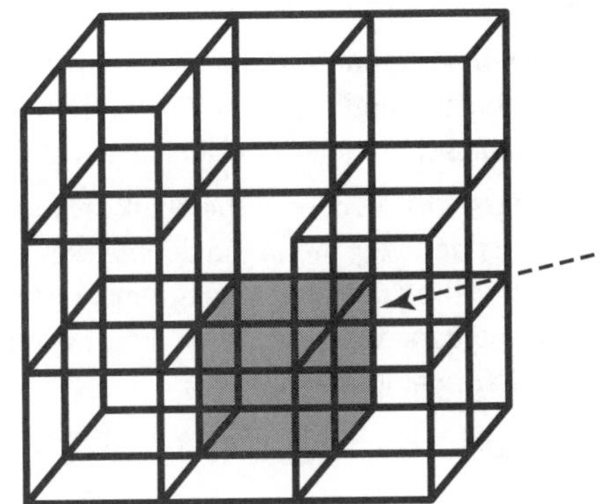

44. C

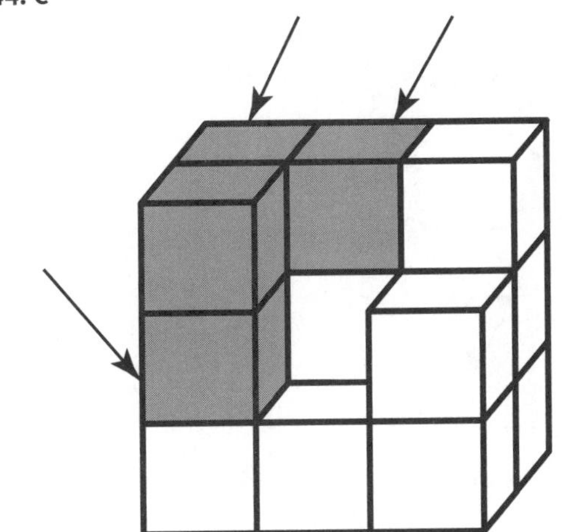

45. C

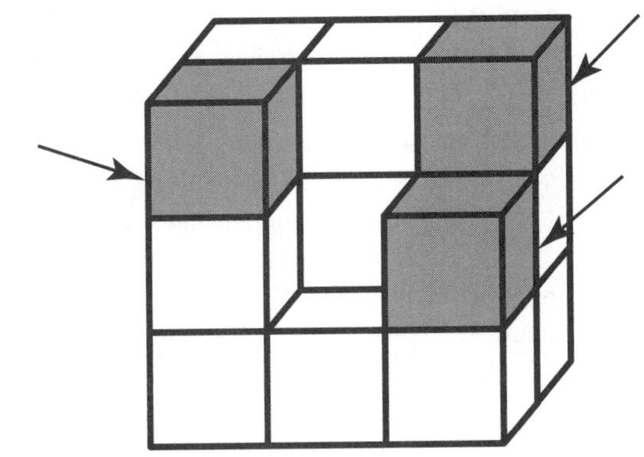

Figure C Tally

0 siders: 1

1 siders: 3

2 siders: 4

3 siders: 4

4 siders: 4

5 siders: 1

Total: 17

46. C

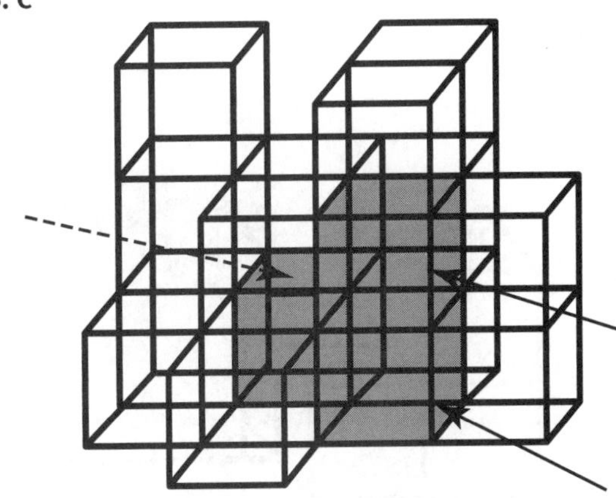

47. D

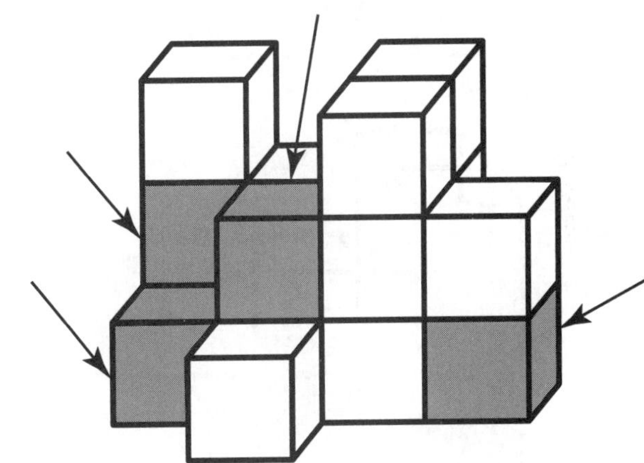

48. D

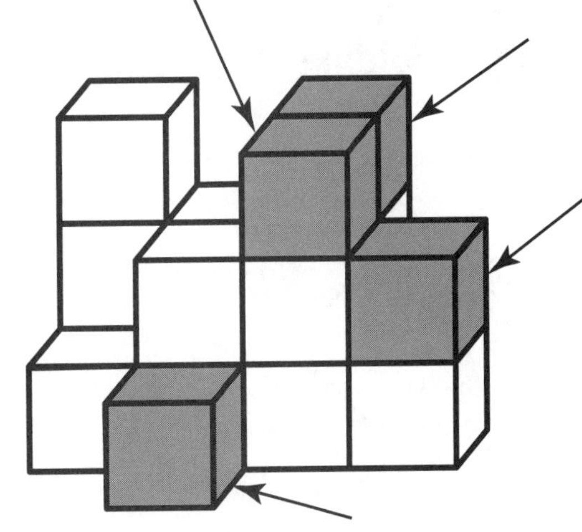

Figure D Tally

0 siders: 0

1 siders: 1

2 siders: 5

3 siders: 3

4 siders: 3

5 siders: 0

Total: 12

49. A

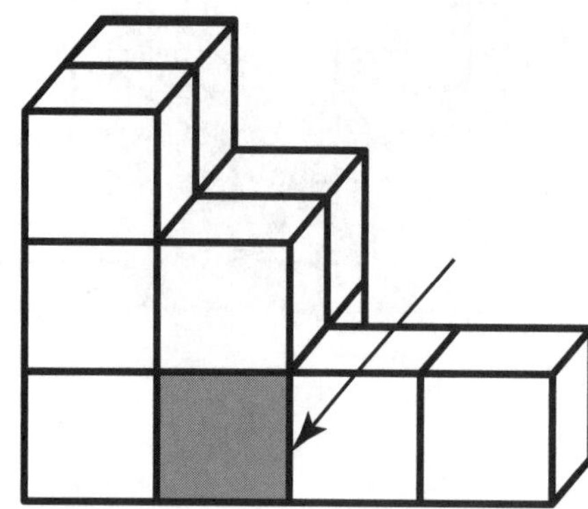

50. E

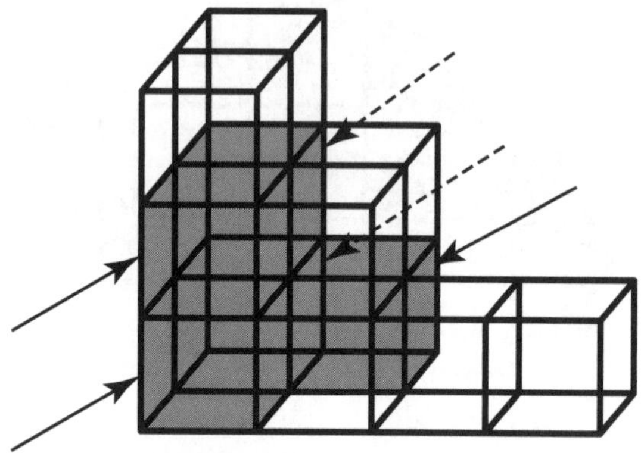

Pattern Folding

51. A

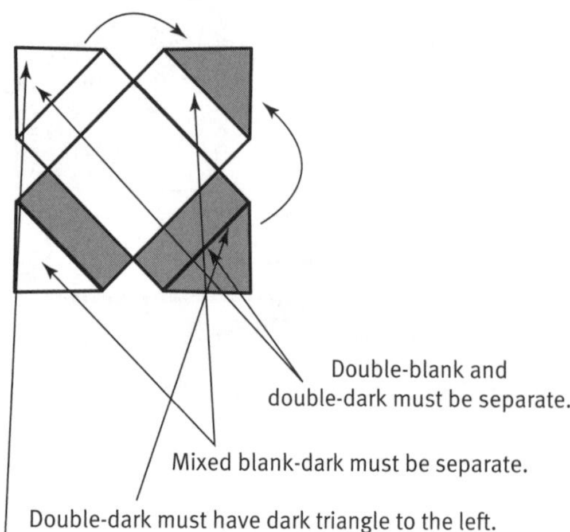

Unique shape: All the faces are standard shapes, so no answer choices can be eliminated.

Unique shading: The overall shading alternates between shaded rectangles and triangles. The mixed blank and dark sides must be separate, which eliminates (B).

Key landmark: The piece with the blank rectangle and dark triangle must be to the left of the double dark piece, so eliminate (C). The double blank piece must have the blank rectangle and dark triangle to the right, so eliminate (D). The correct answer is (A).

52. D

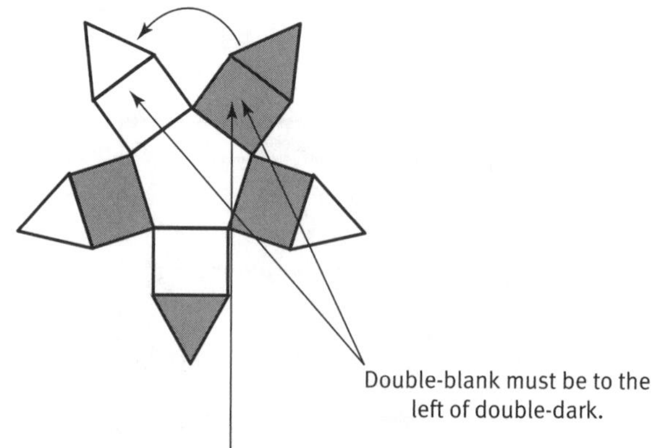

Unique shape: All standard shapes means there is no unique shape.

Unique shading: The overall shading alternates between shaded squares and triangles. There is only 1 double-dark side; eliminate (C), which has 2 double-dark sides.

Key landmark: Determine the placement of the double-blank and double-dark sides. The double-blank side must be to the left of the double-dark side, so eliminate (A) and (B), which have the mixed side to the left of the double dark and the double blank to the right of the double-dark side, respectively. The correct answer is therefore (D).

53. B

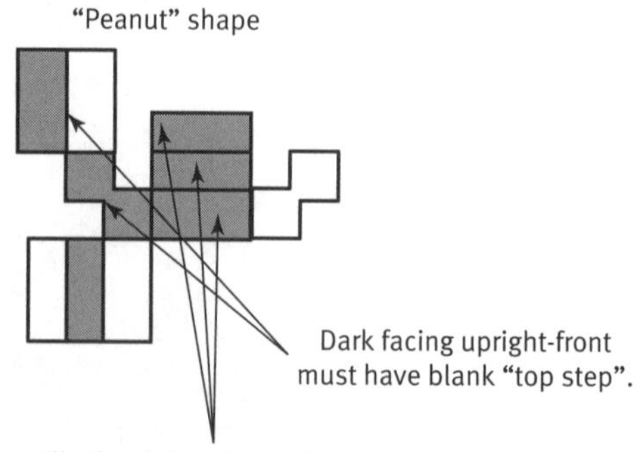

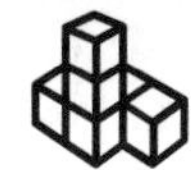

Unique shape: The main face is in the shape of a peanut; this is the piece that will be the front of the figure.

Unique shading: Begin by noticing that the dark peanut shape is facing the same direction as the answer choices; this peanut must be keep in front, so eliminate (C) and (D).

Key landmark: When the dark peanut is facing the front, the top step must be blank. Eliminate (A), which has a dark top step. Next, look at the remaining steps that make up the peanut, which are all dark; this shows that (B) is the correct answer.

54. D

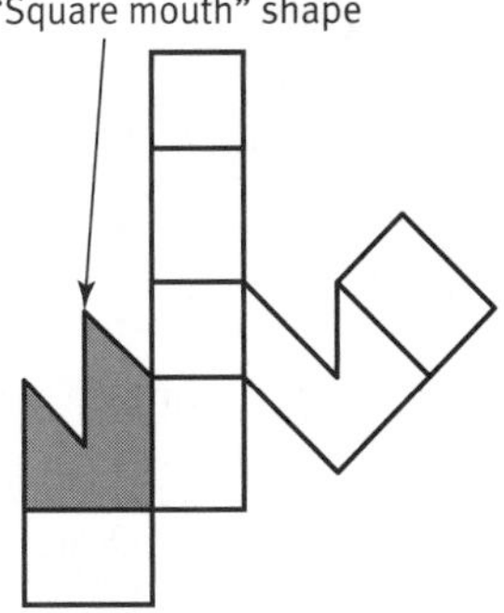

Unique shape: The unique shape is a "square mouth" shape, so the correct answer must have the same shape. (D) is the only shape that matches. Eliminate (A), which has a piece sticking out, (B), which is a chevron shape, and (C), which is too rectangular. The correct answer is (D).

Unique shading: The figure has minimal shading.

Key landmark: There is no need to use key landmark since unique shape is sufficient.

55. C

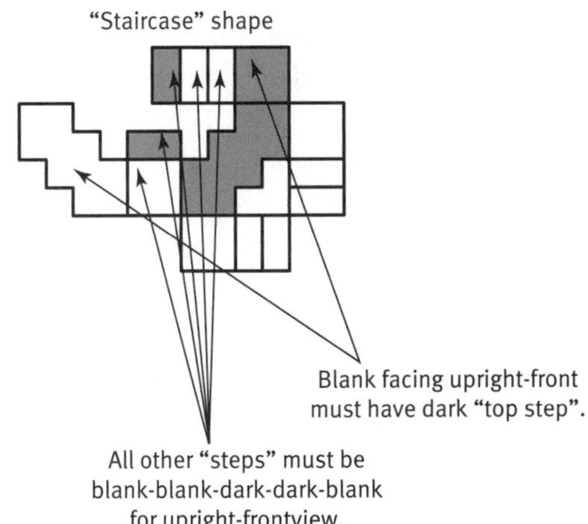

Unique shape: The main face is in the shape of a staircase; this is the piece that will be the front of the figure.

Unique shading: The blank staircase shape is facing the same direction as the answer choices; this is the staircase to keep in front. Eliminate (A) and (B), which do not do so.

Key landmark: When the blank staircase is facing the front, the top step must be dark, so eliminate (D), which has a blank top step. Next, look at the remaining steps, which are blank-blank-dark-dark-blank. This shows that (C) is the correct answer.

56. C

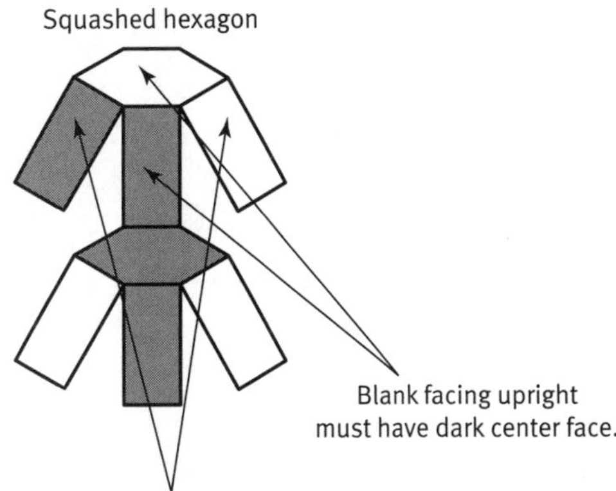

Unique shape: The shape is a squashed hexagon, which can be seen on the top of the pattern.

Unique shading: The shading alternates between dark and blank rectangles on the front and is dependent upon the dark or blank squashed hexagon being on the top of the figure.

Key landmark: If the blank squashed hexagon is on the top of the figure, the center faces on the front and the back will both be dark, eliminating (A) and (B). The two side faces must be one dark and one blank, so (C) is the correct answer. Note that (D) is incorrect because the dark and blank sides should be reversed.

57. D

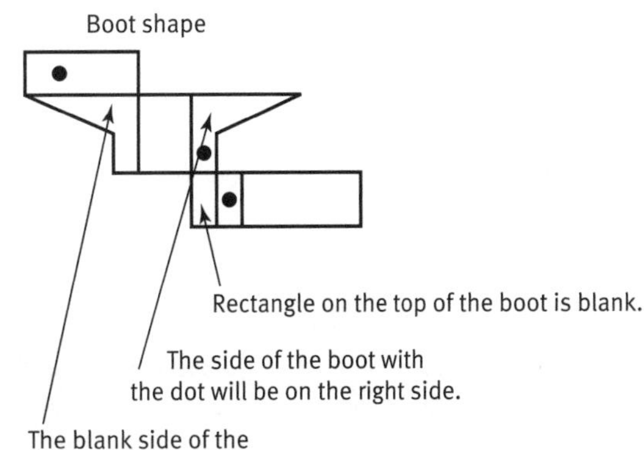

Unique shape: This shape is a pointed boot.

Unique shading: The unique shading is the dark circles. The side of the boot visible in the answer choices has no shading, and only choice (D) matches that prediction.

Key landmark: Although identifying key landmarks is not necessary, noticing that the rectangle on the top of the boot is blank quickly eliminates (A) and (B), which each have a dot on the top.

58. B

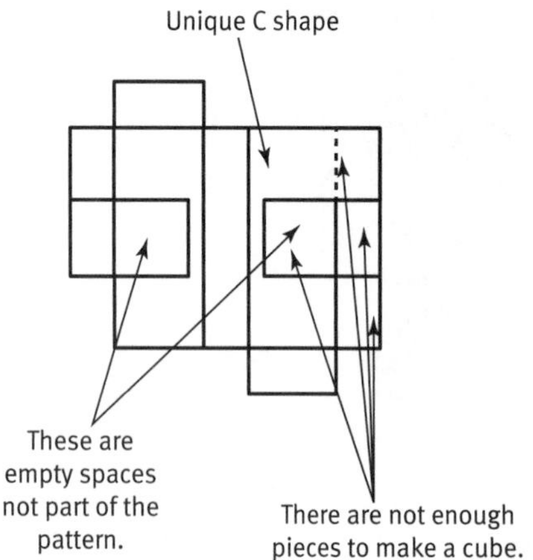

Unique shape: The C is a unique shape. (A) has a C that is too thick in the center, and (D) does not have a C shape at all, so eliminate both.

Unique shading: There is no shading on this figure.

Key landmark: Looking at the answer choices, note that (C) has a cube on top of the figure and therefore can be eliminated because there are not enough pieces to make that cube. This leaves (B) as the correct answer.

59. A

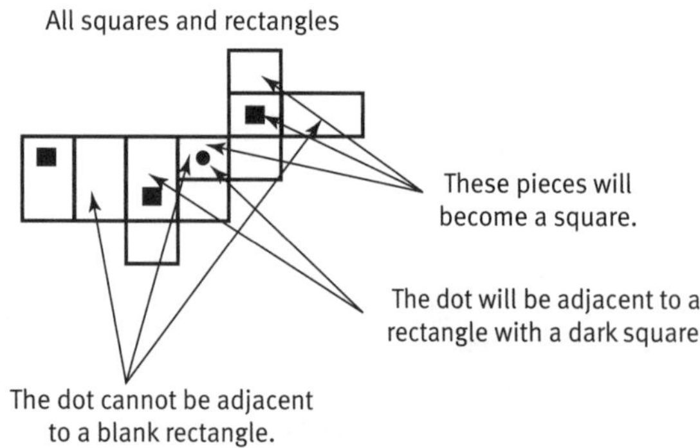

Unique shape: All the shapes are squares and rectangles. You can use the answer choices to see that this makes a stair step.

Unique shading: The unique shading is dark squares and a circle. There is no way that the dark circle can be adjacent to a long blank rectangle, so eliminate (B).

Key landmark: When the pieces on the upper right fold to become a square, the dark dot will be adjacent to the small piece with the dark square, so eliminate (C). The square on top will be next to a rectangle containing a dark square, so eliminate (D). The correct answer is (A). Note that the dashed line will be cut to make the top square.

60. A

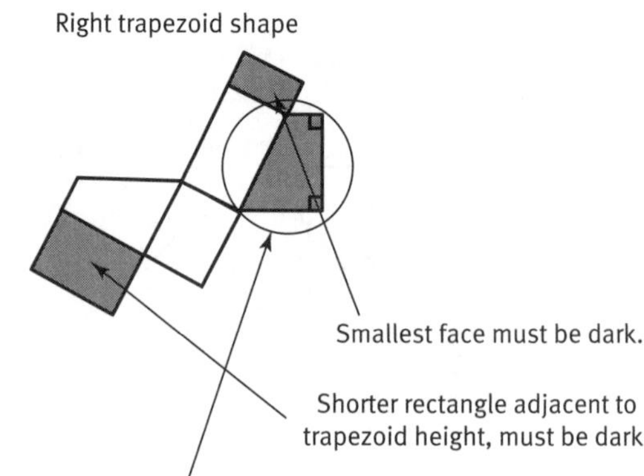

Unique shape: The shape is a right trapezoid.

Unique shading: The smallest face must be dark. The right trapezoids are blank and dark.

Key landmark: The dark right trapezoid must be on top since the 3D image shows the small dark piece facing out to the right; this eliminates (C) and (D), since they both have the blank right trapezoid on top, which would cause the smallest dark piece to be facing to the back left. Next, look at the right angles on the dark right trapezoid shape, which must be adjacent to the dark rectangle. Eliminate (B), which has the right angles adjacent to the blank rectangle. The correct answer is (A).

Answers and explanations continue on the next page ▶ ▶ ▶

Quantitative Reasoning 2

1. C	21. B	41. A
2. B	22. E	42. C
3. D	23. C	43. C
4. E	24. C	44. A
5. B	25. B	45. C
6. B	26. C	46. D
7. B	27. D	47. D
8. D	28. D	48. B
9. C	29. C	49. B
10. C	30. E	50. C
11. E	31. B	51. A
12. D	32. D	52. A
13. B	33. C	53. B
14. C	34. B	54. D
15. C	35. D	55. B
16. B	36. E	56. A
17. E	37. B	57. E
18. C	38. B	58. B
19. A	39. D	59. C
20. B	40. D	

1. C

Stop: The question contains measurements with different units. The choices are measurements in cubic centimeters, and three of them are 378 multiplied by a power of ten. Unit conversion and keeping track of the decimal point will be essential.

Think: The question asks for the conversion of 1 gallon to cubic centimeters, so conversion arithmetic (Traditional Math) is the only option. Two quarts equal 1.89 liters, and 1 liter equals 1 cubic decimeter. Recall that there are 4 quarts in a gallon.

Predict: Set up the conversion so that the units cancel until you're left with liters:

$$1 \text{ gallon}\left(\frac{4 \text{ quarts}}{1 \text{ gallon}}\right)\left(\frac{1.89 \text{ liters}}{2 \text{ quarts}}\right) = \left(\frac{4}{2}\right)(1.89 \text{ liters})$$
$$= (2)(1.89 \text{ liters}) = 3.78 \text{ liters}$$

This is where the variations on 378 in the choices come from. The question says that 1 liter equals a cubic decimeter, so 3.78 liters = 3.78 cubic decimeters. However, the question asks for the number of cubic centimeters, not decimeters. Take care when doing cubic unit conversions. Since the units are cubed, the conversion factor must be cubed as well. For example, just as there are 3 feet in a yard, there are $3^3 = 27$ cubic feet in a cubic yard. Similarly, since there are 10 centimeters in a decimeter, there are $10^3 = 1{,}000$ cubic centimeters in 1 cubic decimeter. Do the final conversion:

$$(3.78 \text{ cubic decimeters})\left(\frac{1{,}000 \text{ cubic centimeters}}{1 \text{ cubic decimeter}}\right) =$$
$$(3.78)(1{,}000) = 3{,}780 \text{ cubic centimeters}$$

Match: (C) is correct. Note that (A) is the number of cubic decimeters, not cubic centimeters.

2. B

Stop: The question indicates a rate problem. The choices are whole numbers with a wide range.

Think: The question asks for the difference between the number of miles that Greg drove and the number of miles that Andrew drove. Greg drove 400 miles at 25 miles/hour while Andrew drove for the same amount of time at 30 miles/hour. Use the distance formula ($d = rt$).

Predict:

First, calculate the driving time for both men:

$$d = rt$$
$$400 \text{ mi} = 25\frac{\text{mi}}{\text{hr}}\ (t)$$
$$16 \text{ hr} = t$$

Then, use the calculated time to find the distance Andrew drives in that time:

$$d = rt$$
$$d = 30\frac{\text{mi}}{\text{hr}} \times 16 \text{ hr}$$
$$d = 480 \text{ miles}$$

Finally, solve for the difference between the distances traveled:

480 miles – 400 miles = 80 miles

Match: (B) is correct. Be careful not to choose (E), which is the distance driven by Andrew.

3. D

Stop: This is a rate problem with multiple variables in the question and variable expressions in the choices. This looks like a great time to Pick Numbers.

Think: The question asks for the time—in minutes rather than hours—to drive r miles at s miles/hour. Pick Numbers for r and s, and use the distance formula to calculate a value for time. Then, plug the numbers into each choice, looking for the one that matches the calculated value.

Predict: The distance formula is distance = (rate)(time). In this case, r is the distance and s is the rate, so you can say that $r = s$ (time) and $t = \frac{r}{s}$. You'll want to choose numbers that make the math easy. Since you'll be dividing r by s to solve for the time, make the value you pick for r divisible by the value you pick for s. Let $r = 60$ miles, and $s = 10$ miles per hour.

Plug the numbers you chose into the formula:

$$t = \frac{r}{s}$$

$$t = \frac{60}{10} = 6\text{ hr}$$

Don't forget to check the units. The question asks for the answer to be expressed in minutes. So, convert:

$$(6\text{ hr})\left(\frac{60\text{ min}}{1\text{ hr}}\right) = 360\text{ min}$$

Match: Plug the values for r and s into each choice to determine whether it matches your target value of 360 minutes:

(A) $\frac{60}{(60)(10)} = \frac{60}{600}$, which will be a value less than 1. Eliminate.

(B) $\frac{10}{(60)(60)} = \frac{10}{3{,}600}$; this will also be less than 1. Eliminate.

(C) $\frac{(60)(10)}{60} = \frac{600}{60} = 10$. Eliminate.

(D) $\frac{(60)(60)}{10} = \frac{3{,}600}{10} = 360$. This matches; check choice (E) to confirm that (D) is the only choice that matches.

(E) $\frac{60}{(60)(10)} = \frac{60}{600}$, which will be a value less than 1. Eliminate.

(D) is correct.

4. E

Stop: The question includes the formula to convert between Fahrenheit and Celsius, so this is likely a straightforward conversion problem.

Think: The question asks for the Fahrenheit equivalent of 24°C. The question provides the equation that allows you to convert between Fahrenheit and Celsius, so you can plug in 24°C and solve for Fahrenheit.

Predict:

$$C = \frac{5}{9}(F - 32)$$

$$24 = \frac{5}{9}(F - 32)$$

$$24\left(\frac{9}{5}\right) = (F - 32)$$

$$\frac{216}{5} = (F - 32)$$

$$75.2 = F$$

Match: (E) is correct.

5. B

Stop: This is a word problem, and the choices are numbers spread pretty far apart, so Backsolving or Estimation might work.

Think: The question asks how many days it takes to make 180 boxes of widgets. The company makes 450 widgets/day and sells 200 widgets/box. The combination of different rates would make Estimation difficult, and the large answer choices would make Backsolving difficult. Traditional Math with rate conversion and arithmetic is the way to go.

Predict: The question asks for the number of days, so cancel out the units until only days are left:

$$\frac{(180\text{ boxes})(200\text{ widgets})}{(1\text{ box})} = 36{,}000\text{ widgets}$$

$$\frac{(36{,}000\text{ widgets})(1\text{ day})}{(450\text{ widgets})} = \frac{36{,}000}{450\text{ days}}$$

Simplify the fraction:

$$\frac{36{,}000}{450} = \frac{3{,}600}{45} = \frac{720}{9} = 80\text{ days}$$

Match: (B) is correct.

6. B

Stop: This is a rate problem with answer choices in gallons per minute. The numbers in the choices are easy to work with.

Think: The question asks you to determine how quickly water must be poured into a 120 gallon tub so that it fills in 1 hour. But, the tub is draining water at a rate of 6 gallons/minute. The simple numbers in the answer choices make this a prime Backsolving question.

Predict: You would ordinarily want to start with answer choice (B) when Backsolving, but think strategically: (A) cannot be correct because if water were both poured into and drained out of the tub at 6 gallons/minute, then it would never fill. So, eliminate choice (A) and start Backsolving with choice (C), one of the two middle choices of the four remaining answers.

(C) says that water is poured in at a rate of 12 gallons/minute. Let's see how much water is in the tub after one hour at this rate:

$$\left(12\frac{\text{gal}}{\text{min}}\right)(60\text{ min}) - \left(6\frac{\text{gal}}{\text{min}}\right)(60\text{ min}) =$$

$$\left(12 - 6\frac{\text{gal}}{\text{min}}\right)(60\text{ min}) =$$

$$\left(6\frac{\text{gal}}{\text{min}}\right)(60\text{ min}) = 360\text{ gal}$$

The tub only holds 120 gallons, so 360 gallons is far too much water, and water must be poured in at a slower rate than 12 gallons/minute.

Match: Of the remaining choices, only (B) is smaller than 12. (B) is correct.

7. B

Stop: The choices are variable expressions, while the question is a word problem with several rates. The arrangement of units in the conversion or combination will be important.

Think: The question asks for the price per magnet as cents/magnet. Each box holds d magnets, and each crate holds b boxes. The price is m dollars/crate. Picking

Numbers is an attractive option given the variables and the expressions in the choices, but algebraic unit conversion will also work. To practice unit conversion, do the latter.

Predict: Begin by noting all of the concrete information:
d magnets/box

b boxes/crate

m dollars/crate

100 cents/dollar

Line up all of these conversions so that all units will cancel except for cents and magnets. A good way to do this is to start with cents on top so that magnets will end up on the bottom.

$$\left(100\frac{\text{cents}}{\text{dollar}}\right)\times\left(m\frac{\text{dollars}}{\text{crate}}\right)\times\left(\frac{1\text{ crate}}{b\text{ boxes}}\right)\times\left(\frac{1\text{ box}}{d\text{ magnets}}\right)$$

$$\frac{(100m\text{ cents})}{(bd\text{ magnets})}$$

Match: (B) is correct. Choice (C) is the number of magnets per cent instead of the number of cents per magnet.

8. D

Stop: This is an averages problem, and the choices are integers. The average formula might come in handy here.

Think: The question asks how many points need to be added to each of four scores to bring the average up to 90. The four test scores are 60, 70, 80, and 90. Doing algebra with the average formula would solve the problem, but, since the problem is full of numbers and the only unknown is the one represented by the choices, Backsolving is even faster.

Predict: When you Backsolve, try to make an educated guess as to whether (B) or (D) is more likely. The professor wants to make the average 90. Right now, 90 is the high score. This suggests that the students will need a hefty helping of the professor's generosity, so start with (D) because it is larger.

(D) If 15 points are added to each student's score, the new scores will be 75, 85, 95, 105. In a list of evenly spaced numbers, the mean is the median. The median of this list is halfway between 85 and 95, or 90. Thus, the average is 90.

Match: (D) is correct. You could also solve this problem with the average formula: $\frac{\text{sum}}{\text{number}}$ = average, or sum = average × number. Originally, the sum of the students' scores is $60 + 70 + 80 + 90 = 300$. If the average were 90, the sum of scores would be $90 \times 4 = 360$. Thus, the average needs to be $360 - 300 = 60$ points higher. Since you need 60 more points, each of the four students would need to pick up $\frac{60}{4} = 15$ points of the slack. Yet another way to solve this problem is to use the sum of the differences between each score and the desired average. 60 is 30 less, 70 is 20 less, and 80 is 10 less, so 60 points $(30 + 20 + 10)$ total need to be added, 15 per test.

9. C

Stop: The choices are small integers. The question gives a list of integers and asks about median. This is definitely a stats problem.

Think: You need to find the median of this list of the list. Use Traditional Math for this straightforward problem.

Predict: The median of a list is the number in the middle. The easiest way to find the middle number is to rewrite the list in ascending order: 4, 7, 9, 10, 13, 16, 19, 22, 25. With nine numbers in the list, the middle number is the fifth one: 13.

Match: (C) is correct.

10. C

Stop: The choices are small integers, and the question gives a list of integers and asks about mode. This is a stats problem. You need to find the mode, or most frequently occurring number or numbers in this set.

Think: Use the definition of mode and examine the list to find the answer.

Predict: First, put the terms in ascending order: 6, 7, 7, 8, 9, 11, 11, 11, 13, 19, 21. The term that appears the most often in this set is 11; it appears 3 times.

Match: (C) is correct.

11. E

Stop: The choices are small integers, and the question mentions an average, several values, and an unknown. Either the average formula or Backsolving could work.

Think: The question asks for the value of x. The average age of four people aged 6, 8, 10, and x is 9. Backsolving, Traditional Math using the average formula, and critical thinking to make an Educated Guess will work. Since the numbers are so simple, try to use critical thinking.

Predict: The numbers in a list must balance on either side of the average. Notice that the numbers 8 and 10 are already balanced around the average; 8 and 10 are one down and one up from 9. The other two numbers in the list are 6 and x. Since 6 is 3 less than 9, x must be 3 greater than 9, or 12.

Match: (E) is correct. Traditional Math yields the same result:

$$\begin{aligned} \text{sum} &= (\text{average})(\text{number}) \\ 6 + 8 + 10 + x &= 9 \times 4 \\ 24 + x &= 36 \\ x &= 12 \end{aligned}$$

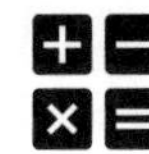

12. D

Stop: The choices are small integers, and the lengthy word problem mentions averages. This is a familiar type of problem, which is often susceptible to Educated Guessing, Backsolving, or the traditional average formula.

Think: The question asks how many females took the test. Eight men took the test and averaged 87 points. The women averaged 92, and the overall average was 90. Before Backsolving or using the average formula, try to get to the answer by using critical thinking.

Predict: Each of the men scored 3 points less than the average ($87 - 90 = -3$), and there were 8 men. This means that the men, as a group, dragged things down by $8 \times (-3) = -24$ points. Each woman scored 2 points higher than the average ($92 - 90 = 2$). Thus, to make up the -24 point deficit from the men, there would need to be $\frac{24}{2} = 12$ of them.

Match: (D) is correct. The average formula yields the same results when you solve for f, the number of females:

$$\text{average} = \frac{\text{sum}}{\text{number}}$$

$$90 = \frac{[(87 \times 8) + (f \times 92)]}{(8 + f)}$$

$$720 + 90f = 696 + 92f$$

$$24 = 2f$$

$$12 = f$$

Notice that the math is much more tedious than the critical thinking approach. Finally, note that estimation can help you eliminate: If the men were on average 3 points short and the women were on average only 2 points up, then there would need to be more women than men in order to make things balance out, so you can quickly eliminate choices (A) and (B).

13. B

Stop: The choices of this average problem are variable expressions, so either Picking Numbers or the average formula will be used.

Think: You need to find the average of n, $n + 2$, and $n + 7$. Picking a Number for n would work, but the expressions are so straightforward here that algebra is even faster.

Predict:

$$\frac{\text{sum}}{\text{number}} = \text{average}$$

$$\frac{[n + (n + 2) + (n + 7)]}{3} = \text{average}$$

$$\frac{(3n + 9)}{3} = \text{average}$$

$$n + 3 = \text{average}$$

Match: (B) is correct.

14. C

Stop: The choices are relatively large integers packed very closely together, so be careful if trying Estimation. The problem mentions several averages and speeds.

Think: The question asks for average speed over 5 hours. The journey is in two stages. First, Esther drove 40 miles/hour for 2 hours. Then, she increased her speed by 25% and drove another 3 hours. There's a formula for this, so Traditional Math is best. Use the average speed formula.

Predict: Start by doing a bit of translation. Twenty-five percent of 40 is a one-fourth of 40, or 10. So, Esther's second speed was $40 + 10$, or 50 miles/hour. The classic trap in this problem is to average the two speeds: $\frac{(40 + 50)}{2} = 45$. However, this can't be Esther's average speed for the whole journey since she spent more time traveling at the faster speed of 50 miles/hour. Thus, her average speed must be higher than the midpoint between the speeds. This eliminates (A) and (B).

Use the average speed formula:

$$\text{average speed} = \frac{(\text{total distance})}{(\text{total time})}$$

Find the components of the formula individually:

$$\text{total time} = 2 \text{ hr} + 3 \text{ hr} = 5 \text{ hr}$$

$$\text{total distance} = (2 \text{ hr})\left(40\frac{\text{mi}}{\text{hr}}\right) + (3 \text{ hr})\left(50\frac{\text{mi}}{\text{hr}}\right) = 80 \text{ mi} + 150 \text{ mi} = 230 \text{ mi}$$

Then, calculate average speed:

$$\text{average speed} = \frac{230 \text{ mi}}{5 \text{ hr}} = 46\frac{\text{mi}}{\text{hr}}$$

Match: (C) is correct. Remember to never average the given speeds on an average speed problem. Instead, use that trap to eliminate incorrect choices.

15. C

Stop: This problem is very straightforward. The answer choices each have two values, one for variance and one for standard deviation. In each choice, the second number is simply the square root of the first number, just as standard deviation is the square root of variance.

Think: Use the formula to find the variance of the list: 4, 5, 8, 10, 13. Note that you don't need to calculate the standard deviation since the choices do that for you!

Predict: Follow the steps for computing variance:

1. Find the mean of the data:
$\frac{(4 + 5 + 8 + 10 + 13)}{5} = \frac{40}{5} = 8.$

2. Subtract the mean (8) from each of the numbers in the data set:

$-4, -3, 0, 2, 5$

3. Square each of the results from step 2:

16, 9, 0, 4, 25

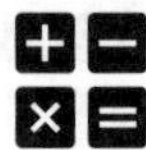

4. Take the average of the numbers from step 3.

$\frac{(0+4+9+16+25)}{5} = \frac{54}{5}$

Match: (C) is correct.

16. B

Stop: The question gives a mean and standard deviation. The answer choices are weights in kilograms. You're already given the mean and standard deviation of the set, so there won't be a lot of complicated math to do.

Think: This question asks for the minimum weight of someone in the top 5% by weight in the group. The mean is 75, and the standard deviation is 12. Recall that approximately 95% of a data set falls within 2 standard deviations of the mean. Use Estimation.

Predict: Two standard deviations is 24 kilograms, so 95% of the men will be within 24 of the mean. Two standard deviations below the mean is $75 - 24 = 51$, and two standard deviations above the mean is $75 + 24 = 99$. Half of the remaining 5% of men will have weights that are either less than 51 kilograms or greater than 99 kilograms. So, only 2.5% of men will be above 99 kilograms. You thus need a value that's just a bit smaller than 99 kg.

Match: (B) is correct. (C) is a trap because only half of that outlying 5% will be greater than 99 kilograms. This value represents the minimum weight of the top 2.5% rather than the minimum weight of the top 5%. And, since (C) is too large, so are (D) and (E).

17. E

Stop: This variance problem has small integers that are close together in the choices. This time-consuming question should be marked and skipped. If you do have time to complete it at the end of the section, Backsolving will be helpful since one of the numbers is a variable.

Think: The question asks for the value of x given that the variance of $\{1, 2, 3, 4, 5, 6, 7, x\}$ is $\frac{21}{2}$, or 10.5. To calculate variance, find the mean of the your set of numbers, subtract each number from that mean, square each difference, and then find the mean of the new set.

Predict: Since the variance provided is large despite the known numbers in the set being relatively close together, start Backsolving with D. If $x = 11$, the mean is $\frac{39}{8} = 4.875$. Although it's possible the variance could work out as evenly as $\frac{21}{2}$ with this value, it's unlikely, so move on and try the next larger answer, E.

If $x = 12$, then the mean is 5, which is much easier to work with. The differences are −4, −3, −2, −1, 0, 1, 2, 7; squared, they are 16, 9, 4, 1, 0, 1, 4, 49. The mean of these differences is $\frac{84}{8} = \frac{21}{2}$, which matches the variance provided.

Match: (E) is correct.

18. C

Stop: This straightforward problem gives you a list and asks you to find the standard deviation. The choices are all square roots.

Think: The list is 1, 2, 2, 4, 6. There's nothing to do but to use the variance formula. The right answer will be the square root of whatever you get for variance since standard deviation is the square root of variance.

Predict: Here's the procedure to find variance:

1. Find the mean of the data:

$\frac{(1+2+2+4+6)}{5} = \frac{15}{5} = 3$

2. Subtract the mean from each of the numbers in the data set:

−2, −1, −1, 1, 3

3. Square each of the results from step 2:

4, 1, 1, 1, 9

4. Take the mean of the numbers from step 3:

$\frac{(4+1+1+1+9)}{5} = \frac{16}{5}$

Match: The answer is the square root of the calculated variance. (C) is correct.

19. A

Stop: The problem provides a table of data. The choices are pairs of numbers representing mean and median. Some of the choices have the same first number, but the second number is different for each choices.

Think: The question asks for the mean and median, but since the median given for each choice is different, you don't actually need to calculate the mean; just find the median and you get the mean for free! The easiest way to find the median of a list is to write the numbers in order.

Predict: The list of numbers in order is: 1, 1, 1, 2, 3, 4, 4, 4, 5, 5 (Ignore the left column of numbers. Those are just the trial numbers, not the actual data points.) In a list with an even number of terms, the median is halfway between the middle two. The middle two numbers of this list are 3 and 4, so the median is 3.5.

Match: (A) is correct. Be careful not to confuse the mean and median, as is done in choice (B).

20. B

Stop: The choices are consecutive small integers, and the problem gives you a graph.

Think: The question asks for the mean. The numbers are small, so use straightforward arithmetic, but be sure to interpret the graph correctly.

Predict: The *y*-axis measures frequency, or how many times something appears. The *x*-axis labels the outcome, or the actual value. So, the graph shows that there were three 1s, two 2s, one 3, and one 4. In list form, this would be: 1, 1, 1, 2, 2, 3, 4.

Now, calculate the mean:

$\frac{(1+1+1+2+2+3+4)}{7} = \frac{14}{7} = 2.$

Match: (B) is correct.

21. B

Stop: This question uses the same graph and answer choices as #20 does but asks for the median.

Think: The data haven't changed, so recycle the work from #20.

Predict: The list of numbers is 1, 1, 1, 2, 2, 3, 4. Because the median of a list is the middle number, the median of this list is the fourth number out of seven, which is 2.

Match: (B) is correct.

22. E

Stop: This question again uses the graph from #20 for a stats problem, but the choices and question are different.

Think: This time you have to find the standard deviation. Mercifully, the numbers are small and easy to work with, so using the variance formula to calculate the answer will be manageable.

Predict: Use the variance formula to find the variance of the list, which you already know is 1, 1, 1, 2, 2, 3, 4. Then, take the square root of your answer to find the standard deviation. Recall the variance procedure:

1. Find the mean of the data:

You already found the mean on problem #20: it's 2.

2. Subtract the mean from each of the numbers in the data set:

−1, −1, −1, 0, 0, 1, 2

3. Square each of the results from step 2:

1, 1, 1, 0, 0, 1, 4

4. Take the average of the numbers from step 3:

$\frac{8}{7}$

The standard deviation is the square root of the variance, or $\sqrt{\frac{8}{7}}$.

Match: (E) is correct.

23. C

Stop: The choices are fractions, and the question asks about probability.

Think: There are 5 apples and 5 bananas, and you draw two pieces of fruit without replacement. The question asks the probability of picking 2 apples. This is straightforward enough that Traditional Math is the best approach.

Predict: There are 10 total pieces of fruit in the bowl (5 apples + 5 bananas). Thus, the probability that your first pick is an apple is $\frac{5}{10}$, or $\frac{1}{2}$. After that, 4 apples remain in the bowl, and there are 9 total pieces of fruit (4 apples + 5 bananas). The probability of drawing a second apple is then $\frac{4}{9}$. To find the probability that one event and another independent event both happen, multiply the two independent probabilities:

$\frac{1}{2} \times \frac{4}{9} = \frac{2}{9}$

Match: (C) is correct.

24. C

Stop: The choices are fairly precise decimals. Closer inspection indicates that they are each multiples of $\frac{1}{8}$, or 0.125.

Think: The question asks the probability of flipping exactly 2 heads in 3 flips of a coin. Because they usually lack variables and unknowns, probability problems rarely lend themselves Backsolving or Picking Numbers. Careful set-up and calculation are required.

Predict: Recall that

$\text{probability} = \frac{\text{(number of desired outcomes)}}{\text{(number of possible outcomes)}}$. Find each component of the formula carefully.

First, determine the number of desired outcomes. There are three ways that Robert can flip a coin and get exactly two heads:

H H T

H T H

T H H

Next, determine the number of possible outcomes. A common error at this point is to do $2 \times 3 = 6$ because there are 3 flips and 2 possible outcomes per flip. But, if there are 2 possible outcomes on the first flip, 2 on the second, and 2 on the third, then the actual number of possible outcomes is $2 \times 2 \times 2$, or 2^3, which equals 8.

Altogether, then, the probability is $\frac{3}{8}$, or 0.375. (Remember that eighths are useful to know on Test Day.)

Match: (C) is correct.

25. B

Stop: This is a probability problem, and the choices are fractions.

Think: The question asks the probability of drawing a green marble from a bag of blue, red, and green marbles. The probability of drawing blue is $\frac{3}{5}$, and the probability of drawing red is $\frac{1}{10}$. This straightforward problem calls for Traditional Math.

Predict: For a given event, the probabilities of all the different outcomes must add up to 1. If you reach into the bag and pull out a marble, you have to get one of the three colors. This means that $P_{\text{blue}} + P_{\text{red}} + P_{\text{green}} = 1$. Solve for P_{green}:

$$P_{\text{green}} = 1 - P_{\text{blue}} - P_{\text{red}}$$
$$P_{\text{green}} = 1 - \frac{3}{5} - \frac{1}{10}$$
$$P_{\text{green}} = \frac{10}{10} - \frac{6}{10} - \frac{1}{10}$$
$$P_{\text{green}} = \frac{3}{10}$$

Match: (B) is correct.

26. C

Stop: Once again, this is a probability problem that has fractions for answer choices.

Think: The question asks the probability of a student receiving housing in at least 1 of 2 years. Each year, the student has a 1 in 5 chance of emerging victorious from the housing lottery. Use Traditional Math.

Predict: The odds that something happens plus the odds that it doesn't must equal 1. This makes sense: something either happens or it doesn't. This idea is important in probability problems because it's sometimes easier to compute the opposite of what you are asked for and then subtract that from 1 to get the answer. Here, the probability that the student receives housing is $\frac{1}{5}$, so the probability that she *doesn't* win housing in a given year is $\frac{4}{5}$. Thus, the probability that the student *won't* get housing both years is $\frac{4}{5} \times \frac{4}{5}$, or $\frac{16}{25}$. It follows, therefore, that the probability that the student *will* get housing at least once is $1 - \frac{16}{25}$, or $\frac{25}{25} - \frac{16}{25} = \frac{9}{25}$.

Match: (C) is correct. (D) is the opposite or the result of forgetting the last step; this is the probability that the student will not get housing at all.

27. D

Stop: The choices to this problem are whole numbers spread far apart. The phrase "how many" in the question indicates that this is a counting problem.

Think: Amanda must pick 1 ball out of 3 and 3 board games out of 6. Your task is to count Amanda's total number of possible selections. You'll need the combinations formula for this one.

Predict: Compute the selections for balls and board games individually. Start with balls since that's easier: there are 3 balls, and Amanda grabs only 1. That's 3 possibilities. Next, consider the board games. Amanda picks 3 out of 6, and since order doesn't matter, that's a combination. Use the combination formula:

$$\begin{aligned} {}_6C_3 &= \frac{6!}{(3!(6-3)!)} \\ &= \frac{6 \times 5 \times 4 \times 3 \times 2}{(3 \times 2)(3 \times 2)} \\ &= \frac{6 \times 5 \times 4}{(3 \times 2)} \\ &= 5 \times 4 \\ &= 20 \end{aligned}$$

For each of the 20 possible board game selections, there are 3 balls Amanda could pair it with. Thus, there are $20 \times 3 = 60$ total selections.

Match: (D) is correct. Choice (A) is just 3×6. Avoid choices that simply combine the numbers from the problem, as this one does.

28. D

Stop: The choices are integers, and "how many" in the question indicates a counting problem.

Think: Four people stand in a line. Your task is to count the number of possible arrangements. Note that order does matter here because you are using all four people, and it's a question of the total number of ways they can be lined up.

Predict: There are 4 candidates for the first spot in the line. Once someone's been chosen to lead the line, 3 candidates remain for the second spot. That leaves 2 candidates for the third spot, and the last person goes fourth. Thus, the total number of arrangements is $4 \times 3 \times 2 \times 1$, or $4! = 24$.

Match: (D) is correct.

29. C

Stop: The choices are mostly large numbers, and "how many" in the question indicates a counting problem.

Think: A code consists of 3 As, 2 Bs, and a C and a D. Your task is to count how many possible codes there are. Counting problems, like probability problems, often require Traditional Math.

Predict: On problems like this, begin by imagining that all the letters are different. If you had 7 different letters, the number of possible codes would be 7!. This isn't the final answer, though, since there are duplicates: 3! ways that the three As can be arranged without changing the code, and

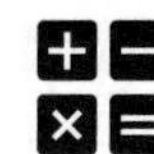

2! ways that the Bs can be arranged without changing the code. So, divide these duplicate scenarios out:

$$\frac{7!}{(2!\times3!)}=\frac{7\times6\times5\times4\times3\times2}{(2\times3\times2)}$$

$= 7 \times 6 \times 5 \times 2 = 7 \times 30 \times 2 = 7 \times 60 = 420$

Match: (C) is correct. If you need to make an Educated Guess, eliminate (E) since it is 7! and ignores the duplicate scenarios, as well as (A) since seems much too small and is the product of the total number of letters in the code multiplied by the number of different letters to be used.

30. E

Stop: The choices are small whole numbers, and the question asks you to count the number of possible combinations.

Think: There are 2 TV and 3 phone wires. Your task is to count the number of ways to pick 3 wires such that at least one of the wires is for TV. The stop step helps here! Since the choices are small, you know that it must be possible to just count the scenarios by hand and avoid any complicated combination math.

Predict: Call the TV wires T1 and T2 and the phone wires P1, P2, and P3. Then, list out all of the combinations that have at least one TV wire:

T1 T2 P1

T1 T2 P2

T1 T2 P3

T1 P1 P2

T1 P1 P3

T1 P2 P3

T2 P1 P2

T2 P1 P3

T2 P2 P3

Count up the possibilities; there are 9.

Match: (E) is correct. If you'd rather do the math: the condition "at least one TV wire" means that there are either two TV wires or just one. If there are two TV wires, then there's one phone wire. That's ${}_2C_2 \times {}_3C_1 = 1 \times 3 = 3$ possibilities. If there's just one TV wire, then two of the wires have to be phone wires. That's another ${}_2C_1 \times {}_3C_2 = 2 \times 3 = 6$ possibilities. $6 + 3 = 9$ total possibilities.

31. B

Stop: This is a geometry problem with several quadrilaterals, and the choices are integers with a wide range.

Think: You need to find the area of rectangle *STUZ* and the area of rectangle *YZWX* in order to find their sum. Since you know the perimeter of each of the two squares, you can determine the side length of each. This will allow you to find the side lengths of the rectangles, and thus their areas.

Predict: Square *RSZY* has a perimeter of 28, so it has a side length of 7. Square *ZUVW* has a perimeter of 16, so its side length is 4. Now, label the dimensions of rectangles *STUZ* and *YZWX*. *STUZ* has a vertical height of 7 and a horizontal width of 4, and *YZWX* has a vertical height of 4 and a horizontal width of 7. Since each rectangle has dimensions of 4 by 7, each one has an area of $(4)(7) = 28$. Doubling this yields 56.

Match: (B) is correct.

32. D

Stop: The choices are ratios, and the question includes several rectangles nested within each other with side lengths expressed with variables. Values for the variables are given, though, so this may not be as difficult as the figure makes it appear.

Think: You need to find the ratio of the smaller shaded area to the larger shaded area. Since you have values for *x* and *y*, you can plug them in to calculate the area of each rectangle and then find the ratio of the areas.

Predict: Start with the larger shaded area. You can calculate it by finding the area of the largest rectangle in the figure, and then subtracting the area of the next-largest rectangle.

The largest rectangle has dimensions of $x + 3$ and $y + 3$. Since $x = 2$ and $y = 1$, these side lengths are actually $(2 + 3)$ and $(1 + 3)$, or 5 and 4. So this rectangle's area is $(5)(4)$, which equals 20. The next-largest rectangle has dimensions of $x + 2$ and $y + 2$, so its side lengths are 4 and 3. So, its area is $(4)(3)$, which equals 12. The larger shaded area is thus equal to $20 - 12$, which is 8.

Now calculate the smaller shaded area. You can calculate this by subtracting the area of the smallest white rectangle from the area of the next-largest rectangle. The smallest rectangle's area is just *xy*, which is $(2)(1) = 2$. The rectangle that encloses the smallest rectangle has dimensions of $x + 1$ and $y + 1$, so it measures 3 by 2 and its area is $(3)(2) = 6$. So, the smaller shaded area is $6 - 2 = 4$.

Finally, the ratio of the smaller shaded area is 4:8, which reduces to 1:2.

Match: (D) is correct.

33. C

Stop: Choices are small, mostly whole, numbers, and the question describes a rectangle.

Think: The question asks how many times one side of the rectangle is than the other. The rectangle's perimeter is 12 times its width. Since there are multiple unknown values (the length, width, and perimeter of the rectangle), Picking Numbers is a great approach.

Predict: Start by picking a value for the width: $w = 3$. The rectangle's perimeter is $12w$, so the perimeter is $(12)(3) = 36$.

Use this value to calculate the rectangle's length. The perimeter is the sum of the four sides, so:

$$\begin{aligned} \text{perimeter} = 36 &= 3 + 3 + \text{length} + \text{length} \\ 36 &= 6 + 2(\text{length}) \\ 30 &= 2(\text{length}) \\ 15 &= \text{length} \end{aligned}$$

Now, determine how many times greater the length is than the width: $\frac{15}{3} = 5$.

Match: (C) is correct. This can be calculated using straightforward math. Since the perimeter is $2w + 2l$ and equal to $12w$, solve for l in terms of w:

$$\begin{aligned} 2w + 2l &= 12w \\ 2l &= 10w \\ l &= 5w \end{aligned}$$

34. B

Stop: This is a triangle problem with answer choices in degrees.

Think: The question asks for an interior angle of a triangle. Remember that a triangle's interior angles add up to 180 degrees. So, if you know the values of the other two angles in this triangle, you can subtract them from 180° to find the value of the missing angle.

Predict: Angle *SRQ* measures 90 degrees. And, since angles that add up to a straight line have a sum of 180° degrees, angle *QSR* is 40 degrees. Angle *RQS* = 180 – 90 – 40 = 50°.

Match: (B) is correct.

35. D

Stop: The figure shows three triangles, and the choices are small numbers that are very close together.

Think: The question asks for the length of *DE*. Notice that since lines *DE* and *BC* are both perpendicular to line *AC*, triangles *ABC* and *ADE* are similar. You can use the fact that these are similar triangles to establish the ratio between side lengths. The ratio of length *BC* to length *DE* is the same as the ratio of length *AC* to length *AE*. Find the length of *AC* in order to determine the ratio.

Predict: Triangle *ABC* has an area of 24, and its height is 6. Use these numbers to calculate the base, which is line *AC*:

$$A = \tfrac{1}{2}bh$$

$$24 = \tfrac{1}{2}(b)(6)$$

$$24 = 3b$$

$$8 = b$$

Line $AC = 8$, so the ratio of *AC* to *AE* is 8:6, or 4:3. Lines *BC* and *DE* must have the same ratio: $6{:}DE = 4{:}3$. Rewrite this in fraction form and isolate the value of *DE*:

$$\frac{6}{DE} = \frac{4}{3}$$

$$\frac{18}{DE} = 4$$

$$18 = 4(DE)$$

$$\frac{18}{4} = DE$$

$$4.5 = DE$$

Match: (D) is correct.

36. E

Stop: This is a triangle problem with two figures. The choices are lengths, some of which include radicals.

Think: You need to find the length of side *XZ* in triangle *XYZ*. The larger triangle *QRS* has an area of 100 square feet. This is 4 times the smaller triangle's area, which is 25 square feet. The two triangles are similar, and the base of the larger triangle is 16 feet long. Calling triangle *QRS* triangle 1 and triangle *XYZ* triangle 2, their areas are related as follows:

$$\begin{aligned} A_1 &= (4)(A_2) \\ (\tfrac{1}{2})(b_1)(h_1) &= (4)(\tfrac{1}{2})(b_2)(h_2) \\ (b_1)(h_1) &= 4(b_2)(h_2) \end{aligned}$$

Now, it would be very easy to assume that b_1, *QS*, is 4 times b_2, *XZ*, based on this equation. But if the base of the smaller triangle were multiplied by 4 to get the base of the larger triangle, then the triangles would need to have the same heights in order to have areas of 100 and 25. In order for the triangles to be similar, the base and height of the smaller triangle need to be multiplied by a common term in order to find the values of the larger triangle.

So rewrite $(b_1)(h_1) = 4(b_2)(h_2)$ as follows:

$$(b_1)(h_1) = (2)(b_2)(2)(h_2)$$

Now, instead of calculating the values of the larger triangle by multiplying one side of the smaller triangle by 4 (and leaving the other one untouched), you are multiplying each piece of the smaller triangle by 2, thus creating similar triangles. In other words, the ratio of each similar side (base and height) must be the same between the two similar triangles.

Predict: Now that you've established that the base and height of the larger triangle are each twice as long as the corresponding lengths of the smaller triangle, you can answer the question. If side *QS* of triangle *QRS* is 16 and the corresponding side on triangle *XYZ* is half of that length, then side *XZ* must be $\frac{16}{2} = 8$ feet long.

Match: (E) is correct. Answer choice (A) is a trap answer for anyone who assumed that the ratio of the sides would be the same as the ratio of the areas. Remember that the area is in square feet, while the sides are in feet, so the relationship between the areas and the relationship between the sides will not be the same.

37. B

Stop: This is a triangle problem with radicals in the choices.

Think: The question asks for the length of *BD*, which is the height of an equilateral triangle. Notice that two right triangles are formed by *BD*: *ABD* and *BCD*. Each of these right triangles has angle measures of 30, 60, and 90 degrees. Use the special side ratios of the 30:60:90 right triangle to find the length of *BD*.

Predict: A 30:60:90 right triangle's side lengths are in the ratio of $x : x\sqrt{3} : 2x$. *BD* will equal $x\sqrt{3}$ because it is opposite the 60 degree angle. The length $4\sqrt{2}$ is opposite the right angle, so it is equal to 2*x*. Therefore, *x* is equal to half of this, or $2\sqrt{2}$.

$BD = (2\sqrt{2})(\sqrt{3}) = 2\sqrt{6}$

Match: (B) is correct.

38. B

Stop: This is another triangle problem with choices that appear to be lengths.

Think: The question asks you to find the hypotenuse of a 45:45:90 right triangle. The ratio of the sides is $x:x:x\sqrt{2}$, and the triangle's area is 50. Use the area to find the length of the triangle's two equal legs (x) and then multiply by $\sqrt{2}$.

Predict:

$A = 50 = (1/2)bh$

$50 = (1/2)(x^2)$

$100 = x^2$

$10 = x$

Now that you know the value for *x*, find $x\sqrt{2} : (10)(\sqrt{2}) = 10\sqrt{2}$.

Match: (B) is correct.

39. D

Stop: The choices are distances. The question describes a figure. Draw the set-up.

Think: The question asks how far Joe walks. Joe and Conrad start at the same place. Conrad walks 5 miles in a straight line to Bel Air, while Joe walks 4 miles east and then an unknown number of miles north to arrive at the same destination. The three lines (one line for Conrad's straight path northeast and two lines for the two legs of Joe's journey) form a right triangle with sides of 4 and 5 miles. Use the 3:4:5 right triangle ratios.

Predict: Conrad's path is the hypotenuse of the right triangle and is 5 miles long. Joe's path east, which is one leg of the triangle, is 4 miles long. This is a 3:4:5 right triangle, so the unknown length, which is Joe's path north, is 3 miles long. Joe walks 4 miles east + 3 miles north = 7 miles.

Match: (D) is the correct answer.

40. D

Stop: This is a circle problem, and the choices are multiples of 10.

Think: The question asks for the sum of the two vertical central angles *a* and *b*. There are four central angles in the figure, and all can be related based on the measure of one of them and their relationships with each other.

Predict: Angle *a* and the 110 degree angle form a straight line, so they must sum up 180 degrees. So, $a = 70$ degrees. And angles *a* and *b* are vertical angles, so they are equal to each other. Therefore, angle *b* is also 70 degrees. Since both angle *a* and angle *b* equal 70 degrees, their sum is

$70 + 70 = 140$ degrees.

Match: (D) is correct. (B) is a trap. 70 degrees is the measure of both *a* and *b* but not their sum.

41. A

Stop: This is a circle problem, and the choices are areas given in cm^2.

Think: The question asks for the area of a sector with a central angle of 60 degrees. The diameter is 6 centimeters. Recall the ratio that relates sector and area:

$\frac{\text{(central angle)}}{\text{360 degrees}} = \frac{\text{sector}}{\text{area}}$.

Predict: First, calculate the circle's area:

Since the diameter is 6 cm, the radius is half of that, or 3 cm.

$A = \pi r^2$

$A = \pi(3^2)$

$A = 9\pi$

Now, use the ratio to calculate the area of the sector:

$$\frac{60}{360} = \frac{\text{sector}}{9\pi}$$

$$\frac{1}{6} = \frac{\text{sector}}{9\pi}$$

$$(6)(\text{sector}) = 9\pi$$

$$\text{sector} = \frac{9\pi}{6}$$

$$\text{sector} = \frac{3\pi}{2}$$

Match: (A) is correct. (C) is a trap, the result of using the diameter instead of the radius when calculating the area.

42. C

Stop: The question describes a circle inscribed in a square. You are given the square's area and need to use this information to find the area of the circle.

Think: Whenever working with combined figures, determine what lengths or angle measures they have in common. When a circle is inscribed in a square, the circle's diameter is equal to the square's side length.

Predict: Since the square's area is 144, its side length is equal to $\sqrt{144}$, or 12. This is also the circle's diameter. Since the circle's diameter is equal to 12, its radius is half of that, or 6. Substitute this value into the formula for the area of a circle:

$A = \pi r^2$
$A = \pi (6^2)$
$A = 36\pi$

Match: (C) is correct. (E) uses the diameter, instead of the radius, in the area calculation. When working with circles, always be sure to check whether you should use the radius or the diameter.

43. C

Stop: The question is about a solid triangular prism, and the choices are multiples of 6.

Think: The question asks for the volume. To find the volume of any uniform solid, multiply the area of the base by its height. The height is 6, so you just need to calculate the area of the triangular base and multiply by 6 in order to find the volume.

Predict: Since the base is a right triangle, its legs of 3 and 4 are also the base and height. Calculate the area:

$A = \frac{1}{2}bh$

$A = \frac{1}{2}(3)(4)$

$A = 6$

Now that you have the area of the base, multiply it by the height of the figure:

$V = (6)(6)$

$V = 36$

Match: (C) is correct. (E) is the result of using the area formula for quadrilaterals. The sides of the figure are quadrilaterals, but the bases are triangles.

44. A

Stop: The question is related to volume and the rate of flow. The choices are rates in volume/time.

Think: You're asked to calculate the rate at which water fills a basin. In order to determine the rate at which water leaked from the pipe into the basin, you first need to know exactly how much water was in the basin after the 5 hours and then divide the volume by the time. The basin is a rectangular prism, so volume = (length)(width)(height). The length and width are the length and width of the basin (18 and 10 inches), but the height of the water is not the height of the basin. The height is only 3 inches.

Predict: $V = (18)(10)(3) = 540 \text{ in}^3$. Divide this by the 5 hours in order to determine the hourly rate:

$\frac{540 \text{ in}^3}{5 \text{ hr}} = 108 \text{ in}^3/\text{hr}$

Match: (A) is correct. The number in (D) is the volume of water without dividing by the time to get the rate. (E) is the volume of the basin, obtained by multiplying the first three values given in the problem. Always be sure to answer the question that was asked.

45. C

Stop: This is a straightforward problem asking for the area of the trapezoid in the figure.

Think: Use the formula for a trapezoid's area: Area = $\frac{1}{2}(\text{base}_1 + \text{base}_2)(\text{height})$, where the two bases are the figure's parallel sides. The figure provides the length of the two bases but not the height. Draw the height into the figure by adding a line on the left side of the figure that is perpendicular to the base and that divides the figure up into a rectangle and a right triangle.

Predict: The triangle formed by drawing the height has a base that is equal to the difference between the two trapezoid bases: (8 inches – 5 inches) = 3 inches. This is a 3:4:5 right triangle, so the height of the triangle and the trapezoid is 4 inches. Now that you have a value for each base and for the height, you can apply the area formula:

$A = \frac{1}{2}(5 + 8)(4)$

$A = \frac{1}{2}(13)(4)$

$A = \frac{1}{2}(52)$

$A = 26$

Match: (C) is correct. (E) is the result of using the triangle's hypotenuse in the area formula instead of calculating the height. Remember that a figure's height and base are always perpendicular to each other.

46. D

Stop: This is a coordinate geometry problem. Some choices are fractions, and some are integers.

Think: The question asks for the slope. Two points are provided. To calculate a line's slope, use the slope formula: $\frac{y_2 - y_1}{x_2 - x_1}$, where (x_1, y_1) and (x_2, y_2) are two points on the line. It does not matter which of the two points given you label (x_1, y_1) and which one you label (x_2, y_2); the resulting slope will be the same either way.

Predict: Use (1,3) as (x_1, y_1) and (5,11) as (x_2, y_2). Plug these values into the slope formula:

Slope $= \frac{11 - 3}{5 - 1}$

Slope $= \frac{8}{4}$

Slope $= 2$

Match: (D) is correct.

47. D

Stop: This is a coordinate geometry problem. Some of the choices include radicals.

Think: The question asks for the distance between two points. To find the distance between two points on the coordinate plane, use the distance formula: $d = \sqrt{(x_2 - x_1)^2 + (y_2 - y_1)^2}$. It does not matter which of the two points given is substituted in for (x_1, y_1) and which one is substituted in for (x_2, y_2).

Predict: Use (4, 8) for (x_1, y_1) and (−7, 11) for (x_2, y_2). Plug these values into the distance formula:

$d = \sqrt{(-7-4)^2 + (11-8)^2}$

$d = \sqrt{(-11)^2 + (3)^2}$

$d = \sqrt{121 + 9}$

$d = \sqrt{130}$

Match: (D) is correct. While the distance formula may look intimidating, apply all of the terms that you're given in their proper place, and the terms will simplify within just a couple of steps. Note that the distance formula is really another way of using the Pythagorean Theorem since the *x* and *y* distances create a right angle and the distance between those two points is the hypotenuse.

48. B

Stop: The question includes the equations for two lines, and the choices are line equations in the same format. The relationships among the lines are being tested.

Think: The question asks for the equation of a new line based on the two in the question stem. You'll need to take specific components of the two equations given to write the new line's equation.

Predict: Start with the *y*-intercept. The question says that the new line must have the same *y*-intercept as the line $y = 2x - 3$. This line has a *y*-intercept of −3, so the correct answer must also have a −3 as its final term. Next, find the new line's slope. The question says that the new line is perpendicular to the line $y = -2x + 3$. Perpendicular lines have opposite reciprocal slopes. So, to find the slope of the new line, take the reciprocal of the slope in this line and change the sign. The reciprocal of −2 is −½, and when you change the sign, it becomes positive ½. The new line will have a slope of ½ and a *y*-intercept of −3. The equation is $y = \frac{1}{2}x - 3$.

Match: (B) is correct.

49. B

Stop: The question asks for the area of a trapezoid positioned in a coordinate plane. Some choices are whole numbers; others are decimals.

Think: Remember the formula for the area of a trapezoid: Area = ½(base_1 + base_2)(height) where the two bases are the figure's parallel sides. Find the coordinates of the corners and use them to find the lengths of the bases and the height. Then, calculate the area.

Predict: The figure's top side, or base_1, extends from −2 to 3 on the *x*-axis, so it is 3 − (−2) = 5 units long. The bottom side, or base_2, extends from −4 to 3 on the *x*-axis, so it is 3 − (−4) = 7 units long. Finally, the height extends from −1 to 3 on the *y*-axis, so this length is 3 − (−1) = 4 units. Substitute these values into the trapezoid area formula:

$A = \frac{1}{2}(5 + 7)(4)$

$A = \frac{1}{2}(12)(4)$

$A = \frac{1}{2}(48)$

$A = 24$

Match: (B) is correct.

50. C

Stop: This problem tests your knowledge of the sine function.

Think: Compute $2 \sin\left(\frac{\pi}{2}\right)$.

Predict: The sine of $\frac{\pi}{2}$ is 1. Therefore, $2 \sin\left(\frac{\pi}{2}\right) = 2(1) = 2$.

Match: (C) is correct.

51. A

Stop: The problem tests knowledge of cosine.

Think: Compute $11 \cos\left(\frac{3\pi}{2}\right)$.

Predict: The cosine of $\frac{3\pi}{2}$ is 0, so the entire expression equals 0.

Match: (A) is correct.

52. A

Stop: This problem tests your knowledge of tangents.

Think: Compute 5 tan(0). Remember that $\tan(x) = \frac{\sin(x)}{\cos(x)}$.

Predict: $\text{Tan}(0) = \frac{\sin(0)}{\cos(0)} = \frac{0}{1} = 0$. So, tan(0) is also 0.

Match: (A) is correct.

53. B

Stop: This is a triangle problem, but the question mentions the tangent, so trigonometry is being tested. The choices are fractions.

Think: In order to find the tangent of angle *ACB*, find the lengths of the opposite and adjacent sides because $\text{tangent} = \frac{\text{(opposite leg)}}{\text{(adjacent leg)}}$.

Predict: The figure shows that the opposite leg is 12 feet long. To find the value of the adjacent leg, notice that the two given side lengths, 12 and 20, are in a ratio of 3 to 5. So, this is a multiple of a 3:4:5 right triangle, and each term in the ratio is multiplied by 4. The triangle's other leg must be 16. Now, calculate the tangent:

$$\text{tangent} = \frac{\text{(opposite leg)}}{\text{(adjacent leg)}} = \frac{12}{16} = \frac{3}{4}$$

Match: (B) is correct. (A) is the angle's sine, and (E) is the cotangent. On trigonometry problems, there will always be trap answers for those who solve for the wrong function.

54. D

Stop: The figure is a triangle, and the question asks about the relationship between two sides. This is somewhat vague, but the answer choices are expressions for the sine function.

Think: To find an expression for sin θ, find terms for the leg opposite the angle, and the hypotenuse.

Predict: The opposite leg is already labeled h, but you need a term to represent the hypotenuse. Since this is a right triangle, use the Pythagorean theorem to write an expression: $h^2 + b^2 = \text{hypotenuse}^2$. The hypotenuse is thus equal to $\sqrt{h^2 + b^2}$. The expression for the sine of θ is $\frac{\text{opposite}}{\text{hypotenuse}}$, or $\frac{h}{\sqrt{h^2 + b^2}}$.

Match: (D) is correct. If you weren't sure how to tackle this problem, you still could have noticed that sin θ required having an expression for the triangle's hypotenuse. This eliminates (A) and (B), which use only the other sides.

55. B

Stop: This is a trigonometry problem with several functions appearing in the choices.

Think: Triangle *ABC* is a right triangle, and you need to calculate its area in terms of the only labeled side length, *x*, and angle θ. Side *x* is one of the right triangle's two legs, so you need an expression for the value of the triangle's other leg, *AC*, in order to write an expression for the triangle's area.

Predict: *AC* needs to be expressed in terms of *x* and angle θ, so think about the relationship between these two sides and the angle. Tan θ is equal to the opposite leg over the adjacent leg, or $\frac{AC}{x}$. Rewrite this as an expression for the value of *AC*:

$\tan \theta = \frac{AC}{x}$

$(x) \tan \theta = AC$

Now, write an expression for the triangle's area:

$A = ½(\text{base})(\text{height})$

$A = ½(x)(x) \tan \theta$

$A = ½(x^2) \tan \theta$

Match: (B) is correct. This is a difficult problem, but following the method and being comfortable looking at parts of a figure in a variety of ways will serve you well on Test Day.

56. A

Stop: This problem tests your understanding of inverse trig functions.

Think: You need to compute $\cos^{-1}(1)$. Nothing besides your knowledge of the arccos function is needed.

Predict: $\cos^{-1}(1)$ means the angle that has a cosine of 1. Only one angle gives a cosine of 1: zero degrees.

Match: (A) is correct.

57. E

Stop: This problem tests your knowledge of cosine.

Think: Compute $-3\cos(\pi)$ directly.

Predict: The cosine of π is -1. Thus, $-3\cos(\pi) = -3(-1) = 3$.

Match: (E) is correct.

58. B

Stop: This problem tests your understanding of secant.

Think: Compute $\sec(-\pi)$ directly.

Predict: Several concepts are needed to crack this one. First, $-\pi$ is the same angle as $+\pi$, so this problem is really just $\sec(\pi)$. Next, recall that secant is the reciprocal of cosine. Thus, $\sec(\pi) = \frac{1}{\cos(\pi)} = \frac{1}{-1} = -1$.

Match: (B) is correct.

59. C

Stop: The question describes a figure. The choices are different inverse trigonometric functions with different angles, although some of the angles are the same among choices.

Think: The question asks for the angle created between the top of a 6 foot ladder and the wall that it's leaning against, but the angle will be expressed as an inverse trigonometric function. While a regular trig function uses side lengths of a triangle to determine an angle's sine (or cosine, tangent, etc.), the inverse function allows you to input an angle's sine (or cosine, tangent, etc.) and determine what the angle measure is.

Predict: The ladder is the triangle's hypotenuse, and the length of the base is 30 inches, which is 2.5 feet. Draw a diagram so that you can visualize the relationship between the two sides and the angle formed by the ladder and the wall. The 6 foot ladder is the hypotenuse, and the 2.5 foot base is the opposite leg. So, the sine of the angle is $\frac{2.5}{6}$. In order to avoid having a decimal in the fraction, multiply both the numerator and denominator of the fraction by 2:

$$\frac{2.5 \times 2}{6 \times 2} = \frac{5}{12}$$

The angle can be found by taking the arcsine of this value.

Match: (C) is correct.

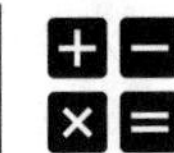

Answers and explanations continue on the next page ▶ ▶ ▶

General Chemistry 2

1. D	14. C	27. B
2. E	15. A	28. B
3. B	16. A	29. B
4. E	17. B	30. E
5. B	18. C	31. A
6. E	19. D	32. C
7. A	20. C	33. D
8. B	21. B	34. A
9. B	22. A	35. A
10. B	23. A	36. B
11. B	24. E	37. C
12. B	25. A	
13. D	26. D	

1. D

Stop: Answer choices are phrases, which suggest a critical thinking question about phase changes.

Think: The question asks what is unique about the water phase diagram. Unlike the density of most liquids, the density of water decreases as it moves from a liquid to solid state. Due to its crystal structure, water is denser as a liquid than it is as a solid.

Predict: Because water is denser as a liquid than it is as a solid, the slope for the solid–liquid boundary on water's phase diagram is negative, whereas the solid–liquid boundary for most substances has a positive slope.

Match: (D) is correct. (E) is Opposite.

2. E

Stop: Answer choices are phase changes.

Think: The question asks which phase change is an endothermic process. An endothermic process is one that has a positive ΔH, meaning that heat energy is put into the process. In general, the lowest energy phase is solid, followed by liquid, followed by gas. So, it will take energy input to move phases toward the gaseous state.

Predict: Melting—solid turning to liquid, vaporization—liquid turning to gas, and sublimation—solid changing to a gas—require energy input and are therefore endothermic.

Match: (E) is correct. Condensation (A) is gas changing to liquid. Crystallization (B) and freezing (D) are processes by which liquid changes to solid. Deposition (C) is vapor changing to solid. All of these are exothermic processes.

3. B

Stop: Answer choices are full sentences about phases of matter. This question will require critical reasoning.

Think: The question stem describes vaporization of liquid water rapidly followed by deposition and asks why this occurs in space. Space has very low pressure and very low temperature. Vaporization changes a liquid to a gas, which can happen at high temperature or at low pressure. Deposition describes a gas changing to a solid, which typically happens at low temperature.

Predict: Vaporization occurs because of the very low pressure, but then deposition occurs because of the very low temperature.

Match: (B) is correct. Prediction helps tremendously in questions like these that have long and confusing answer choices. Notice that (A) can be eliminated no matter what because solids have lower, not higher, entropy than liquids and gases.

4. E

Stop: Answer choices are in calories.

Think: The question asks for the amount of heat energy required to change the temperature and phase of water. The 12 g sample of water starts at −5 degrees Celsius, so it starts as solid ice, which has a specific heat of 0.5 cal/g·°C (given). It then increases to 25 degrees Celsius, so it becomes liquid water, which has a specific heat of 1.0 cal/g·°C (required knowledge). The heat required in the phase change must be taken into account. This calculation will require using both $q = m\Delta H_{fus}$ and $q = mc\Delta T$. The heat of fusion is 79.8 cal/g.

Predict: Treat each step of the temperature change process individually.

Heating the ice from −5°C to 0°C:

$$q = mc\Delta T$$
$$q = 12\text{ g} \times \frac{0.5\text{ cal}}{\text{g} \times {}^\circ\text{C}} \times 5^\circ\text{C} = 30\text{ cal}$$

Melting ice into water:

$$q = m\Delta H_{fus}$$
$$q = 12\text{ g} \times 79.8\text{ cal/g} \cong 960\text{ cal}$$

Heating water from 0°C to 25°C:

$$q = mc\Delta T$$
$$q = 12\text{ g} \times \frac{1\text{ cal}}{\text{g} \times {}^\circ\text{C}} \times 25^\circ\text{C} = 300\text{ cal}$$

Calculate an approximate total amount of heat energy required by summing the q values:

$q_{total} \cong 300 + 960 + 30 \cong 1{,}290$ cal

Match: (E) is correct.

5. B

Stop: Answer choices describe changes to factors related to a liquid–vapor phase change.

Think: The question asks what will happen when changing from sea level to higher altitude. Changing from sea level to higher altitude will lower the atmospheric pressure.

Predict: The vapor pressure of a liquid increases when its temperature increases, but atmospheric pressure does not change vapor pressure. Boiling, or changing from liquid to vapor, occurs at the temperature at which vapor pressure equals atmospheric pressure. At a lower atmospheric pressure, the vapor pressure necessary for boiling is lower, so boiling point is lower.

Match: (B) is correct.

6. E

Stop: Answer choices are very specific temperatures in Celsius.

Think: The question stem provides mass, heat capacity, energy released, and ending temperature and asks for the original temperature. To solve, use the relationship $q = mc\Delta T$, remembering that heat capacity is the product of mass and specific heat (mc). The change in energy will be designated as negative in the equation since the process is exothermic.

Predict: Because the question asks for temperature change rather than absolute temperature and because both the final temperature and answer are in Celsius, the temperature does not need to be converted to kelvins.

$$q = mc\Delta T$$

$$\Delta T = \frac{q}{mc}$$

$$12 - T_{\text{initial}} = \frac{-575}{25}$$

$$12 - T_{\text{initial}} = -23$$

$$-T_{\text{initial}} = -23 - 12$$

$$T_{\text{initial}} = 35°\text{C}$$

Match: (E) is correct.

7. A

Stop: Answer choices are volumes in liters.

Think: The question stem gives grams of oxygen at STP and asks for the volume. Oxygen is a diatomic gas, and this must be taken into account when calculating its molar mass. One mole of gas occupies 22.4 L at STP. Find the number of moles of diatomic oxygen and then determine the volume using the known ratio.

Predict: The molar mass of O_2 is 16 g × 2 = 32 g. Find the number of moles in 3.2 g:

$$\frac{32\text{ g } O_2}{1\text{ mol}} = \frac{3.2\text{ g } O_2}{x\text{ mol}}$$

$$x = \frac{3.2 \times 1}{32} = 0.1\text{ mol } O_2$$

Now, use 1 mole = 22.4 L to find the volume of 0.1 moles:

$$\frac{1\text{ mol } O_2}{22.4\text{ L}} = \frac{0.1\text{ mol } O_2}{x\text{ L}}$$

$$x = \frac{22.4 \times 0.1}{1} = 2.24\text{ L}$$

Match: (A) is correct.

8. B

Stop: Answer choices are pressures in atmospheres.

Think: The question asks for the partial pressure of F_2. The number of moles of each of three gases and the total pressure are given. This is a classic Dalton's Law problem. The pressure of each gas in a mixture is directly proportional to its mole fraction in the mixture: $P_A = X_A P_{\text{total}}$. First determine the mole fraction of F_2, and then use this to determine the partial pressure of F_2.

Predict: The total number of moles in the vessel is 0.75 + 0.2 + 0.05 = 1 mole. Calculate the mole fraction of F_2:

$$\text{mole fraction} = X_{F_2} = \frac{\text{mol } F_2}{\text{total mol}} = \frac{0.05}{1} = 0.05$$

Now, calculate the partial pressure of F_2:

$$P_{F_2} = X_{F_2} P_{\text{total}} = 0.05 \times 2.5\text{ atm} = 0.125\text{ atm}$$

Match: (B) is correct.

9. B

Stop: Answer choices are volumes in liters.

Think: The question stem gives moles, final temperature, and pressure change of a gas and asks for final volume. Use the ideal gas law, $PV = nRT$.

Predict: The typical approach requires remembering the value of the gas constant R and its correct units and then doing a complex calculation. However, by using the ideal gas law to set up ratios, these tedious and time-consuming steps can be avoided. Instead, compare the final conditions to the status of the gas at STP (1 atm, 273 K, 22.4 L for 1 mole of gas). First, set the ideal gas law equal to the constant R:

$$\frac{PV}{nT} = \text{R}$$

This shows that the quantity $\frac{PV}{nT}$ is a constant, meaning that a proportion can be set up.

$$\frac{P_1V_1}{n_1T_1} = \frac{P_2V_2}{n_2T_2}$$

Since the number of moles is held constant, this simplifies as follows:

$$\frac{P_1V_1}{T_1}=\frac{P_2V_2}{T_2}$$

The starting conditions are assumed to be at STP, and the final conditions are 546 K and 3 atm. The question asks for V_2, so rearrange the proportion to isolate that variable:

$$V_2=\frac{P_1V_1}{T_1}\times\frac{T_2}{P_2}$$

$$V_2=\frac{P_1}{P_2}\times\frac{T_2}{T_1}\times V_1$$

$$V_2=\frac{1}{3}\times\frac{546}{273}\times 22.4$$

$$\cong\frac{1}{3}\times\frac{2}{1}\times 22.4$$

$$\cong\frac{1}{3}\times 44.8$$

$$\cong\frac{1}{3}\times 45\cong 15\,\text{L}$$

Match: (B) is correct.

10. B

Stop: Answer choices are concentrations given in molarity.

Think: The question asks for the final concentration of a solution after dilution. The initial volume is 55 mL, and the final volume is 255 mL. (Remember that 200 mL is the volume added to the solution, not the final volume.) The initial concentration is 7.5 mol/L. This is a classic dilution problem, so use $M_1V_1 = M_2V_2$. Since the volumes and initial molarity are given, the molar mass of KOH provided is not needed.

Predict: $M_1V_1 = M_2V_2$

(7.5 moles/liter) × (55 mL) = (M_2) × (200 + 55 mL)

Milliliters do not need to be converted to liters if the same units are used on both sides of the equation.

$$M_2=\frac{7.5\times 55}{255}\cong\frac{8\times 50}{250}\cong\frac{400}{250}\cong\frac{8}{5}\cong 1.6\,\text{moles/L}$$

Match: (B) is correct.

11. B

Stop: Answer choices are concentrations given in molality.

Think: Molality is moles of solute per kilogram of solvent. The question requires you to convert the data given in the question stem to moles and kilograms.

Predict: To find molality, the moles of NaOH must be divided by the kg of solute (H_2O). The molar mass of NaOH is given as 40 g/mol, and the 500 mL of water is equal to 500 g of water.

$$\text{mol NaOH}=\frac{10\text{ g NaOH}}{40\text{ g/mol}}=0.25\text{ mol}$$

$$\text{molality}=\frac{0.25\text{ mol NaOH}}{500\text{ g } H_2O}=\frac{0.25\text{ mol}}{0.5\text{ kg}}=0.5\,\text{m}$$

Match: (B) is correct.

12. B

Stop: Answer choices are volumes in milliliters.

Think: The question asks for the additional volume of water needed to dilute to 5 M NaOH. The question stem gives the amount of NaOH and the initial volume of water. Find the initial concentration, and then use $M_1V_1 = M_2V_2$ to find the final volume. But, remember that the question asks for how much extra water is needed, so the answer will be the difference between V_2 and V_1.

Predict: First determine the number of moles of NaOH and the initial molarity of the solution.

$$\text{mol NaOH}=\frac{80\text{ g NaOH}}{40\text{ g/mol}}=2\text{ mol}$$

$$M_1=\frac{2\text{ mol}}{195\text{ mL}}=\frac{2\text{ mol}}{0.195\text{ L}}$$

Although this looks difficult to calculate, keep in mind that you will be multiplying by V_1 in the dilution equation, so 0.195 L will cancel out. Substitute the known values directly into the dilution equation:

$$M_1V_1 = M_2V_2$$

$$\frac{2\text{ mol NaOH}}{0.195\text{ L}}\times 0.195\text{ L}=5\text{ mol/L}\times V_2$$

$$V_2=\frac{2}{0.195}\times 0.195\times\frac{1}{5}=\frac{2}{5}=0.4\text{ L}=400\text{ mL}$$

However, the question does not ask for the final volume; rather, it asks how much water must be added. So, find the difference:

400mL – 195 mL = 205 mL

Match: (B) matches the prediction. The final volume (C) is a trap. The Think step help you avoid answering the wrong question on Test Day.

13. D

Stop: Answer choices are chemical compounds.

Think: The question asks which solute would lower the freezing point the most. Freezing point depression is a colligative property. The more moles of solute there are in a solution, the more the freezing point will decrease. Salts and strong acids and bases dissociate into multiple solute particles when dissolved, which increases the net concentration of particles in solution. The number of particles is given by *i*, the van 't Hoff factor.

Predict: In this case, all of the chemicals listed have the same molality, so the van 't Hoff factor alone will determine

the greatest change in freezing point. Find the highest *i* among the answer choices.

Match: (D) is correct. Although HSO_4^- is a weak acid and does not completely dissociate to 2 H^+ and SO_4^{2-}, it will still provide a van 't Hoff factor greater than 2. (A), (B), and (C) have *i* values of 2. Notice that none of these can be right since they share the same value! (E) has an *i* value of 1 since it does not dissociate.

14. C

Stop: Answer choices are in moles.

Think: The question is asks how many moles of NaCl are needed to elevate the boiling point of 4 liters of water by 1 degree Celsius. This is a colligative property, so account for the dissociation of NaCl. The K_b for water is given. Use $\Delta T_b = iK_bm$.

Predict: NaCl will dissociate into two particles in water, so $i = 2$. The density of water is 1 g/mL, or 1 kg/L, so there is 4 kg of solute.

$$\Delta T_b = iK_bm$$

$$m = \frac{\Delta T_b}{iK_b}$$

$$m = \frac{1}{2 \times 0.512}$$

Covert molality to moles:

$$\text{moles NaCl} = \frac{\text{moles}}{\text{kg solvent}} \times \text{kg solvent}$$

$$\text{moles NaCl} = \frac{1}{2 \times 0.512} \times 4 = \frac{2}{0.512} \cong \frac{2}{\left(\frac{1}{2}\right)} \cong 4 \text{ mol NaCl}$$

Match: (C) is correct.

15. A

Stop: Answer choices are temperatures in Celsius.

Think: The question asks for the new freezing point due to a freezing point depression. Be careful: this is not the same as ΔT_f. Instead, you are looking for the final temperature after ΔT_f is applied. The initial freezing point is 0°C, so use $\Delta T_f = iK_fm$ and subtract the result from 0. K_f is given, and *i* will be 2. However, the concentration of the NaCl solution is given as 20% mass, so the question requires converting from percent mass into molality.

Predict: First, find the molality of the NaCl solution. The molar mass of NaCl is 58.5 g/mol, and the molar mass of water is 18 g/mol. Twenty percent by weight NaCl means 1 part NaCl to 5 parts of solution (part:whole), which is the same as 1 part NaCl to 4 parts water (part:part). Determine how much water is necessary to make a solution containing 1 mol of NaCl:

$$\frac{1 \text{ part NaCl}}{4 \text{ parts } H_2O} = \frac{58 \text{ g NaCl}}{x \text{ g } H_2O}$$

$$x = \frac{58 \times 4}{1} \cong 60 \times 4 \cong 240 \text{ g } H_2O$$

The freezing point depression equation uses molality, which is calculated as moles of solute over kg of solvent. Set up another ration to find the molality:

$$\frac{1 \text{ mol NaCl}}{240 \text{ g } H_2O} \cong \frac{1 \text{ mol NaCl}}{250 \text{ g } H_2O} \cong \frac{x \text{ moles NaCl}}{1000 \text{ g}}$$

$$x \cong \frac{1000}{250} \cong 4 \text{ moles NaCl/kg solvent}$$

Now, use the equation:

$$\Delta T_f = iK_fm$$

$$\Delta T_f = 2 \times 1.9 \times 4 \cong 16$$

Since this is a decrease in freezing point, the new temperature will be approximately –16°C.

Match: (A) is correct.

16. A

Stop: Answer choices discuss altering conditions, such as temperature, pressure, salinity, and population density.

Think: Although the question stem involves fish, it really is asking about what will decrease the solubility of a gas (oxygen) in a liquid.

Predict: The process of dissolving a gas into liquid is exothermic under normal conditions. Le Châtelier's principle predicts that decreasing the temperature or increasing the atmospheric pressure causes the equation to shift forward (to the right), thus increasing the solubility of gas in liquid. The reverse—increasing the temperature or decreasing the pressure—makes the gas less soluble.

Match: (A) is correct. (B) and (D) are Opposite.

17. B

Stop: Answer choices are small numbers with decimals.

Think: The question asks for the pH given the hydronium ion concentration 6.4×10^{-3}. pH = $-\log[H_3O^+]$, which can be calculated using the Kaplan shortcut.

Predict: $\text{pH} = -\log(m \times 10^{-n}) \cong (n - 1).(10 - m)$

$\text{pH} = -\log(6.4 \times 10^{-3}) \cong (3 - 1).(10 - 6.4) \cong (2).(3.6) \cong 2.36$

Match: (B) is correct.

18. C

Stop: Answer choices are numbers at least an order of magnitude apart, so estimating and rounding will work well.

Think: The question asks for the value of K_b, given the K_a of an acid. Calculation of K_b from K_a can be done using $K_w = K_a \times K_b = 10^{-14}$ at 25°C.

Predict: $K_w = K_a \times K_b$

$1 \times 10^{-14} = (1.8 \times 10^{-5}) \times K_b$

$$K_b = \frac{1\times10^{-14}}{1.8\times10^{-5}} \cong \frac{1\times10^{-14}}{2\times10^{-5}} \cong 0.5\times10^{-9} \cong 5\times10^{-10}$$

Match: (C) is correct.

19. D

Stop: Answer choices are numbers.

Think: The question asks for the pOH of a solution given a pH of 5.5 at STP. At 25°C, pH + pOH = 14.

Predict: pH + pOH = 14

pOH = 14 – pH

pH = 14 – 5.5 = 8.5

Match: (D) is correct.

20. C

Stop: Answer choices are numbers.

Think: The question asks for the pH after adding 1.0×10^{-10} moles of HCl to 1 L of water. This is a very small amount of acid being added to neutral water. Check the choices before calculating to see if you can make an Educated Guess. If calculation is necessary, first determine the total amount of $[H^+]$ in solution and then calculate the $-\log[H^+]$ to find the pH. HCl is a strong acid, so it will dissociate completely in water, and water will also autoionize to contribute more H^+.

Predict: Since a tiny amount of acid is added to a liter of water, the pH change should be negligible, and the solution should have a pH of about 7.

Match: (C) is correct. Notice that (D) and (E) are basic and can be eliminated immediately. And, considering the very small amount of HCl added, (A) and (B) are much too acidic. Calculating also shows (C) to be the answer.

The 1×10^{-10} mol of HCl will yield 1×10^{-10} mol of H^+. And, at 25°C, water has a pH of 7, meaning that $[H^+] = 1 \times 10^{-7}$ moles/L. The question specifies that 1 L of pure water is present. Totaling the number of moles of H+ present gives:

$[H^+]_{autoionization} + [H^+]_{HCl} = (1 \times 10^{-7}) + (1 \times 10^{-10}) = (1 \times 10^{-7}) + (0.001 \times 10^{-7}) = 1.001 \times 10^{-7}$ mol $[H^+]$

$pH = -\log[H^+]$

$pH = -\log(1.001 \times 10^{-7}) \cong -\log(1 \times 10^{-7}) \cong 7$

21. B

Stop: Answer choices describe pH or acidity changes.

Think: The question asks what happens when you increase the temperature during an endothermic reaction. An endothermic reaction can be thought of as: reactants + heat ⇌ products, so increasing the temperature will move the reaction to the right and generate more products.

Predict: The reaction for the autoionization of water is $H_2O\ (l) \rightleftharpoons H^+\ (aq) + OH^-\ (aq)$. A shift to the product side will increase the $[H^+]$ and $[OH^-]$. An increase in $[H^+]$ concentration will, by definition, decrease pH.

Match: (B) is correct. (A) is Opposite—a trap for those who forget that pH decreases when $[H^+]$ increases. Be careful with trap choices (C) and (D). Because $[H^+]$ and $[OH^-]$ increase the same amount, the solution remains neutral, not acidic as described in (D). However, this is not the same as the pH staying the same, as described in (C). Remember that pH + pOH = 14 is only valid at 25°C. Because the temperature has been raised, K_w no longer equals 10^{-14}.

22. A

Stop: Answer choices are compounds often used as solvents.

Think: The question asks for the solvent that would result in the highest pH. The question stem provides information about relative permittivity, which is a measure of polarity. The higher a solvent's relative permittivity, the more polar the solvent is and, therefore, the better it can solvate ions. Here, an acid is solvated.

Predict: In the case of an acidic solution, the ions are H^+ and the conjugate base. This means that the greater the solvation, the greater the H^+ concentration, the lower the pH. So, to find the highest pH, determine the solvent that will solvate the fewest ions, which means the solvent with the lowest relative permittivity.

Match: (A) is correct.

23. A

Stop: Answer choices are concentrations in molarity.

Think: The question describes a titration and asks for the original concentration of H_2SO_4, a diprotic acid. The original volume of the acid is 150 mL, and it reaches equivalence after 20 mL of 2.0 M NaOH is added. The standard equation for equivalence point is $V_aN_a = V_bN_b$.

Predict: Normality is the product of molarity and equivalence per mol. For NaOH, there is 1 equivalent of OH^- per mole of base, so the normality (N_b) is equal to molarity (M_b).

$$V_aN_a = V_bN_b$$

$$N_a = \frac{V_bN_b}{V_a}$$

$$N_a = \frac{20\,\text{mL}\times2.0\,\text{N}}{150\,\text{mL}} = \frac{40}{150} = \frac{4}{15} \cong \frac{4}{16} \cong 0.25\,\text{N}$$

However, the question asks for molarity, not molality. H_2SO_4 has two equivalents of H^+ per mole of acid:

$$N_a = M_a \times \text{equivalents/mol}$$

$$0.25 = M_a \times 2$$

$$M_a = \frac{0.25}{2} = 0.125\,\text{M}$$

Match: (A) is correct. Trap choice (B) is the result of not accounting for the difference between molarity and normality for a diprotic acid.

24. E

Stop: Answer choices are numbers.

Think: The question asks for the pH of an ammonia solution before it is titrated with 1.1 N HCl. Volumes of both acid and base and the K_b of ammonia are given. This is a multi-step problem with a significant number of calculations involved. Before calculating, check the choices to see if you can make an Educated Guess.

Predict: Ammonia is a base, so a solution of ammonia will therefore have a pH that is significantly above 7.

Match: (E) is correct. This is the only significantly basic pH in the choices. Of course, you will not always be able to find the answer this way, but you will usually be able to at least eliminate a few choices. Either way, making an Educated Guess on an extremely time-consuming question is often better than taking the time to solve. For the record, though, the calculations are included below:

First, use $V_aN_a = V_bN_b$ to find the initial normality of the base.

$$V_aN_a = V_bN_b$$
$$0.050\text{ L} \times 1.1\text{ N} = 1\text{ L} + N_b$$
$$0.055\text{ N} = N_b$$

Ammonia has 1 equivalent of base per mol, so the normality is equal to the molarity, and thus $[NH_3] = 0.055$ M.

2. Using K_b, find the pH by determining the amount of ammonia that dissociates. Assume that x amount of ammonia dissociates from the initial 0.055 M present, and that that x is a negligible quantity compared to 0.055 M because K_b is a very small number.

$$NH_3\,(aq) + H_2O\,(l) \rightleftharpoons NH_4^+\,(aq) + OH^-\,(aq)$$

$$K_b = 1.8 \times 10^{-5} = \frac{[NH_4^+][OH^-]}{[NH_3]} = \frac{(x)(x)}{0.055} = \frac{x^2}{0.055}$$

$$x^2 = (1.8 \times 10^{-5}) \times (0.005) \cong (2 \times 10^{-5}) \times (0.005)$$
$$\cong 0.110 \times 10^{-5}$$
$$\cong 1.1 \times 10^{-6}$$
$$x \cong \sqrt{1.1 \times 10^{-5}} \cong 1 \times 10^{-3}$$
$$\text{pOH} = -\log[OH^-] \cong -\log(1 \times 10^{-3}) \cong 3$$
$$\text{pH} = 14 - \text{pOH}$$
$$\text{pH} \cong 11$$

25. A

Stop: Answer choices are ratios.

Think: The question asks for the ratio of acid to conjugate base in a 1 M solution with a pH of 4. The pK_a is 5.2. All of these numbers can be related using the Henderson-Hasselbach equation. Be sure to use the right order (acid:base) when setting up the final ratio.

Predict: The Henderson-Hasselbach equation is:

$$\text{pH} = \text{pK}_a + \log\frac{[\text{conjugate base}]}{[\text{acid}]}$$

$$\text{pH} = 4.2 = 5.2 + \log\frac{[\text{conjugate base}]}{[\text{acid}]}$$

$$-1 = \log\frac{[\text{conjugate base}]}{[\text{acid}]}$$

$$\log x = -1,\text{ where } x = \frac{[\text{conjugate base}]}{[\text{acid}]}$$

$$\text{If } \log x = -1,\text{ then } x = 0.1 = \frac{1}{10} = \frac{[\text{conjugate base}]}{[\text{acid}]}$$

So, the ratio of [acid]:[conjugate base] = 10:1.

Match: (A) is correct. (E) is the ratio of base:acid.

26. D

Stop: Answer choices are compounds, mostly acids and bases.

Think: The question stem asks which reagent would be best for titration of formic acid, which is a weak acid.

Predict: To most accurately titrate a weak acid, a strong base should be used.

Match: (D) is correct because LiOH is the only strong base. (A), (C), and (E) can be eliminated immediately because none of them are basic compounds. Ammonia (B) is a weak base. Titrating a weak acid with a weak base creates a titration curve with only a small pH change, which is difficult to read at the equivalence point.

27. B

Stop: Answer choices are indicators with pK_a values.

Think: The question stem asks which indicator would be best for titration of ammonia (a weak base), using HBr (a strong acid).

Predict: A weak base has a lower pH than a strong base, so the titration curve will begin and end at a lower pH than the titration curve for a strong base would. Titrating with a strong acid will result in a significant change in pH at the equivalence point, and the pH will be somewhere below 7. The role of an indicator is to change color when the equivalence point is reached, so the indicator should have a pK_a below 7.

Match: (B) is correct.

28. B

Stop: Answer choices are types of lab equipment.

Think: The question asks which instrument would be most useful in performing a titration. Titration uses an unknown volume of titrant, so it requires accurate control and measurement of the volume dispensed.

Predict: A burette is used for titrations.

Match: (B) is correct. A burette, by definition, is designed to easily dispense, measure, and control an unknown amount of liquid using the calibrated volume markings on the tube and the stopcock at the bottom. Only answer choices (A) and (B), pipette and burette, are graduated and designed to dispense. But, a pipette is better designed for transferring constant volumes by aspirating liquid into the tube and then releasing it all at once.

29. B

Stop: Answer choices identify oxidizing and reducing agents. Since both are included, strategic elimination may be possible.

Think: Oxidizing agents cause something else to be oxidized and are therefore reduced, so they gain electrons. Reducing agents cause something else to be reduced and are therefore oxidized, so they lose electrons. Calculate the oxidation states of the different components in the reaction.

Predict: To determine oxidizing and reducing agents, first calculate the oxidation states of the different components in the reaction. The NO_3^- group has a –1 charge on both the products and reactants side and does not change its oxidation state; this is a spectator ion. Check the choices. This eliminates (C) and (E). On the reactant side, the –1 charge on NO_3^- is balanced by a single silver ion, which must be Ag^+ with an oxidation number of +1. On the product side, silver is in its solid, uncharged form and must therefore have an oxidation number of 0. Because silver has gone from +1 to 0, it has gained an electron and is thus been reduced. Ag is the oxidizing agent. Check the choices again. This eliminates (A) and (D).

Match: (B) is correct. Cu goes from +1 on the reactant side to +2 on the product side, losing an electron and being oxidized. Cu is the reducing agent.

30. E

Stop: Answer choices are whole numbers ranging from –2 to +3.

Think: The question asks for the oxidation number of each Ni on the reactant side. This allows the coefficient of 2 in front of the Ni to be ignored. Since Ni is a transition metal, it can have multiple oxidation states. Determine the oxidation numbers for –O and –OH to find the right one for Ni.

Predict: Oxygen typically has an oxidation number of –2, and hydrogen typically has an oxidation number of +1. This gives the –OH group a net oxidation number of –1. The single O is also assigned –2, giving a total of –3 for everything except the Ni. Because the molecule has a net charge of 0, the Ni must balance the –3 and have an oxidation number of +3.

Match: (E) is correct.

31. A

Stop: Answer choices have the same reaction but with different coefficients. MnO_4^- indicates redox.

Think: In order to balance the redox reaction $MnO_4^- + C_2O_4^{2-} \rightarrow Mn^{2+} + CO_2$, follow the stepwise half-reaction method. However, because the balanced reactions are provided in the answer choices, it may also be possible to determine the correct answer by eliminating unbalanced reactions. If not, then this will be a time-consuming problem, so triage it.

Predict: Start by checking for unbalanced equations. Look at the carbons on both sides first. (C) and (D) have 10 carbons on the left but only 5 on the right, so they can be eliminated. Next, check the hydrogens. (E) has 8 hydrogens on the left but 16 on the right, so it can be eliminated. Finally, consider the oxygens. (B) has 28 oxygens on the left but only 24 on the right, so it, too, is eliminated.

Match: (A) is correct because the other equations are not balanced. You wouldn't on Test Day, but for practice you can confirm that this is correct as follows:

Using the half-reaction stepwise method:

1. Separate into two half reactions.

$$MnO_4^- \rightarrow Mn^{2+}$$
$$C_2O_4^{2-} \rightarrow CO_2$$

2. Balance everything except for the H and O.

$$MnO_4^- \rightarrow Mn^{2+}$$
$$C_2O_4^{2-} \rightarrow 2\,CO_2$$

3. Use H_2O and H^+ to balance out the O and H atoms.

$$8\,H^+ + MnO_4^- \rightarrow Mn^{2+} + 4\,H_2O$$
$$C_2O_4^{2-} \rightarrow 2CO_2$$

4. Use electrons to balance out the charge of each half reaction.

$$5\,e^- + 8\,H^+ + MnO_4^- \rightarrow Mn^{2+} + 4\,H_2O$$
$$C_2O_4^{2-} \rightarrow 2\,CO_2 + 2\,e^-$$

5. Combine the half reactions such that the electrons will cancel out. In this case, multiply the first half reaction by 2 and the second half reaction by 5.

$$10\,e^- + 16\,H^+ + 2\,MnO_4^- + 5\,C_2O_4^{2-} \rightarrow 2\,Mn^{2+} + 8\,H_2O + 10\,CO_2 + 10\,e^-$$

6. Cancel out any items appearing on both sides.

$16\ H^+ + 2\ MnO_4^- + 5\ C_2O_4^{2-} \rightarrow 2\ Mn^{2+} + 8\ H_2O + 10\ CO_2$

7. Verify that the atoms and charges balance.

32. C

Stop: Answer choices are descriptions of electrochemical cells. Determining the type of cell or which metal is the anode or which metal is the cathode will eliminate several choices.

Think: The question asks what type of cell is pictured. The cell shows a salt bridge and no outside power source. Cathode and anode can be determined from the table and picture.

Predict: This is a galvanic cell because electrolytic cells must have an external power supply. Eliminate (B) and (D). The zinc half-reaction is $Zn^{2+} + 2\ e^- \rightleftharpoons Zn\ (s)$ with a reduction potential of –0.763. Note that sulfate acts as a spectator ion in the reaction and is not part of the half reaction. The copper half reaction is $Cu^{2+} + 2\ e^- \rightleftharpoons Cu\ (s)$, with a reduction potential of +0.337. In any galvanic cell, the cathode is the site of reduction and therefore has the greatest reduction potential. This makes Cu the cathode. Eliminate (A) and (E).

Match: (C) is correct.

33. D

Stop: Answer choices are cell potentials in volts.

Think: The question asks for the standard cell potential, $E°$, for the cell pictured. Since there is no outside power source, the cell is galvanic, and since copper has the highest reduction potential, it is the cathode. Zinc, with the lowest reduction potential, is the anode. Plug the values from the table into the formula

$E°_{cell} = E°_{cathode} - E°_{anode}$

Predict: $E°_{cell} = E°_{cathode} - E°_{anode}$

$E°_{cell} = 0.337 - (-0.763) = 0.337 + 0.763 = +1.10V$

Match: (D) is correct.

34. A

Stop: Answer choices are numbers with varying powers of ten.

Think: The question asks for the number of moles of solid sodium consumed during a redox reaction that generates 3 A of current for 2 seconds. This can be determined using the equation $It = n\text{F}$, where I = current, t = time, n = moles of electrons, and F = the Faraday constant.

Predict: $IT = n\text{F}$

$$n = \frac{It}{\text{F}}$$

$$n = \frac{3\ \text{A} \times 2\ \text{s}}{96.485\ \text{C/mol}} \cong \frac{3 \times 2}{10^5} \cong 6 \times 10^{-5}\ \text{mol}$$

Match: (A) is correct.

35. A

Stop: Answer choices are numbers packed closely together. Exact calculation is needed.

Think: This question asks for the mass of the daughter of U-238 after a single alpha decay. Alpha decay is the release of an alpha particle, which is 2 protons plus 2 neutrons.

Predict: The atomic number will be lowered by 2, and the mass number will be lowered by 4. 238 – 4 = 234.

Match: (A) is correct.

36. B

Stop: Answer choices describe types of radioactive decay.

Think: The difference between plutonium-241 and americium-241 is an atomic number increase of 1 with no change in mass number.

Predict: Beta minus decay increases atomic number by 1 without changing mass number:

$$^{241}_{94}\text{Pu} \rightarrow {}^{241}_{95}\text{Am} + {}^{0}_{-1}\beta$$

Match: (B) is correct.

37. C

Stop: Answer choices are time in days.

Think: The question states how much of a sample has decayed in 82 days and then asks for the length of one half-life. Find the number of half-lives. Then, divide 82 by that number to get the length of the half-life.

Predict: The amount of a sample remaining is given by the following, where n = the number of half-lives that have passed:

$$\text{Fraction of sample decayed} = 1 - \frac{1}{2^n}$$

$$\frac{15}{16} = 1 - \frac{1}{2^n}$$

$$\frac{1}{2^n} = 1 - \frac{15}{16} = \frac{16}{16} - \frac{15}{16} = \frac{1}{16}$$

$$2^n = 16$$

$$n = 4$$

If there are 4 half-lives completed in 82 days, then the length of a given half-life is

$$\frac{82\ \text{days}}{4\ \text{half lives}} \cong \frac{80}{4} \cong 20\frac{\text{days}}{\text{half life}}$$

Match: (C) is correct.

Organic Chemistry 2

1. D	14. D	27. D
2. C	15. B	28. B
3. B	16. B	29. B
4. C	17. D	30. A
5. E	18. D	31. C
6. D	19. E	32. C
7. A	20. E	33. C
8. C	21. A	34. E
9. E	22. C	35. D
10. C	23. B	36. E
11. E	24. B	37. B
12. B	25. D	38. C
13. C	26. A	

1. D

Stop: Answer choices are small whole numbers.

Think: The question asks for the number of sigma bonds. A sigma bond is a stronger, end–to–end overlap of two hybridized orbitals to form a single bond. Pi bonds can be added to a single bond to form double or triple bonds.

Predict: Each single, double, or triple bond will contain one sigma bond. This molecule has eight single bonds, one double bond, and one triple bond. Each will contribute one sigma bond for a total of 10.

Match: (D) matches the prediction.

2. C

Stop: Answer choices are small whole numbers.

Think: The question asks for the number of pi bonds. Pi bonds can be added to a single bond to form double or triple bonds.

Predict: Disregard the single bonds. This molecule has one double bond and one triple bond. The double bond has one pi bond, and the triple bond has two, so there are three pi bonds.

Match: (C) matches the prediction.

3. B

Stop: Answer choices are angle measures.

Think: The question asks for the angle between two hydrogens in ammonia. The molecular geometry and bond angles depend on the number of electron pairs attached to the central atom, which is nitrogen.

Predict: Nitrogen has three bonding pairs of electrons and one nonbonding pair. Therefore, it has a trigonal pyramidal molecular geometry and a bond angle of 107 degrees, slightly less than the tetrahedral bond angle of 109.5 degrees since nonbonding electron pairs occupy more space than bonding pairs.

Match: (B) matches the prediction.

4. C

Stop: Answer choices are hybridizations.

Think: The question asks for the hybridization of the carbons in ethene. Hybrid orbitals are required so that each attached group (atom or lone pair) can have a sigma bond with s character. The sum of the exponents on s and p shows how many hybrid orbitals are formed.

Predict: Each carbon in ethene is double bonded to one atom (the other carbon) and single bonded to two atoms (the hydrogens). A total of three groups are bound, so the hybridization will be sp^2.

Match: (C) is correct.

5. E

Stop: Answer choices are either yes or no and why a compound would or would not be aromatic.

Think: Aromatic compounds are a special class of compounds made especially stable by delocalization. They are planar, cyclic, conjugated, and follow Hückel's rule. To follow Hückel's rule the molecule must have $(4n + 2)$ pi electrons (where n is zero or a positive integer). A simple way to remember Hückel's rule is to remember a list of numbers of pi electrons that indicate aromaticity: 2, 6, 10, 14, etc.

Predict: This compound is cyclic and conjugated but has seven pi electrons, so it does not follow Hückel's rule. In fact, it has a very reactive unpaired electron, also known as a free radical. It is not aromatic because of the single electron.

Match: (E) is correct.

6. D

Stop: This is a Roman numeral question with cyclic structures in the statements.

Think: The question asks which of the three are aromatic. To be aromatic, the compound must be planar, cyclic, conjugated, and have $(4n + 2)$ pi electrons when n equals zero or a positive integer.

Predict: Compound (I) is conjugated and cyclic. Although one carbon has a positive charge on it, there are two pi electrons, which fulfills Hückel's rule of $(4n + 2)$ when n is equal to zero. The compound is aromatic, so eliminate any choices that don't include (I).

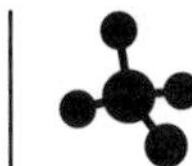

Match: Finding that the compound in statement I is aromatic eliminates every choice except (D), which is the correct answer. It isn't necessary to evaluate II and III to answer the question, but they are both aromatic with six pi electrons.

7. A

Stop: Answer choices describe the addition of reactants in different orders.

Think: The product has two substituents that are *meta* to each other.

Predict: The group that was added first must have been *meta* directing, and NO_2 is a *meta* director, so it was added first.

Match: (A) is correct.

8. C

Stop: Answer choices are aromatic structures with bromine and nitro group substituents.

Think: The question asks what the product(s) will be when reacting bromobenzene with HNO_3/H_2SO_4. All of the products have the same substituents, so focus on their placement. The substituent already on the ring—bromine—will direct the addition of other groups.

Predict: Bromine an *ortho*/*para* director. Therefore, the nitro group will be in either the *ortho* or *para* position; both products are possible. The question doesn't ask for the major product, so expect both products to be in the answer.

Match: (C) is correct.

9. E

Stop: Answer choices are functional groups.

Think: The question asks which group is not electron-donating. Predict what groups are, and then eliminate.

Predict: Electron donating groups include: $-NH_2$, $-OH$, $-OR$, $-R$, $-Ph$, $-NHCOR$, $-OCOR$, $-NR_2$, and $-H$. Eliminate any of these.

Match: (E) is correct. Chlorine is electron-withdrawing.

10. C

Stop: Answer choices are names of molecules, most of which are based on propane and all of which include bromine.

Think: The question asks for the products after the addition of two equivalents of hydrogen halide to an ether. The first hydrogen halide reacts with the ether to produce an alkyl halide and an alcohol. The second hydrogen halide reacts with the alcohol to produce a second alkyl halide.

Predict: The products will be two identical three carbon alkyl halides and water. The bromine will be attached to the second carbon.

Match: (C) is correct. Note that the number 2 does not indicate that there are two molecules but instead that the bromine is attached to carbon 2.

11. E

Stop: Answer choices describe adding or removing components of a reaction.

Think: The question asks how to improve the yield of ethanol, the product. According to Le Châtelier's principle, a system will shift in the direction that counteracts any imposed change.

Predict: To improve the yield of the reaction, the product ethanol should be removed from the reaction mixture.

Match: (E) is correct. Some of the other choices sound more complex, but don't assume that the most complicated answer is right. Instead, use STPM to avoid being tempted by distracting choices.

12. B

Stop: Answer choices are sentences comparing ethers and alcohols.

Think: The question asks why alcohols have higher boiling points. When estimating a boiling point, first consider intermolecular forces and then molecular weight. The higher the intermolecular forces and larger the molecular weight, the higher the boiling point.

Predict: When comparing the intermolecular forces and molecular weights of alcohols and ethers, the most striking intermolecular force difference is that the alcohol group (R–OH) can hydrogen bond with itself, while the ether group (R–O–R) cannot. You cannot make a prediction about molecular weight since ethers and alcohols include molecules of varying molecular weights.

Match: (B) is correct. Note that ethers can form hydrogen bonds with other molecules but not with themselves. (C) would explain a higher boiling point for alcohols, but it would depend on the specific ethers and alcohols, and the question asks about them generally.

13. C

Stop: Answer choices are molecular structures.

Think: The question asks for the product. The carbonyl carbon of 2-butanone is an electrophile, and cyanide is a good nucleophile. This is a nucleophilic addition reaction. The cyanide attacks the carbonyl carbon, breaking the pi bond between the carbon and oxygen and forming a sigma bond with the carbon. The next step is protonating the oxygen.

Predict: The double bond is broken; the cyanide attaches to the carbon on one side, and a hydroxyl group is on the other.

Match: (C) is correct.

14. D

Stop: Answer choices are reactants.

Think: The question asks which reactants produce an aldol. In aldol addition reactions, a base abstracts the alpha hydrogen of one carbonyl, forming an enolate ion, which in turn attacks the carbonyl carbon of an aldehyde, breaking the enolate pi bond and forming a carbonyl. The oxygen is later protonated to create the hydroxyl on carbon 3 in the product.

Predict: The reactants are two carbonyls. Reversing the reaction by breaking the bond between carbon 2 and carbon 3 and replacing the hydroxyl on carbon 3 with a carbonyl, you are left with two propanals as reactants.

Match: (D) is correct. Notice that (B) and (E) can be eliminated quickly because they contain the wrong number of total carbons.

15. B

Stop: Answer choices are hydrogens on an aldehyde.

Think: The question asks which is most acidic. Alpha hydrogens on an aldehyde are the most acidic because their conjugate base, the enolate, is stabilized by resonance. Alpha hydrogens are attached to the alpha carbon, which is the first carbon attached to a functional group.

Predict: Hydrogen (b) is an alpha hydrogen, so it's the most acidic.

Match: (B) is correct.

16. B

Stop: Answer choices are types of reactions.

Think: The question shows the addition of water to triacylglyceride, resulting in a fatty acid and a diacylglyceride.

Predict: The addition of water resulting in the cleavage of a bond is called hydrolysis.

Match: (B) is correct. Hydration (A) is the addition of water across a double bond. Hydrogenation (C) is the addition of hydrogen, not water. Dehydration (D) is the removal of water, making water a product rather than a reactant. Esterification (E) is a dehydration reaction.

17. D

Stop: Answer choices are structures, each containing a phenyl ring.

Think: The question asks which will most rapidly undergo ester hydrolysis. In ester hydrolysis water is used to convert an ester to a carboxylate ion and an alcohol: $RCOOR' \rightarrow RCOO^- + R'OH$.

Predict: Anything that can stabilize the negative charge on the $RCOO^-$ will help the reaction move faster. The substituent on the ring that is most deactivating—to prevent side electrophilic aromatic substitution reactions—and electron withdrawing—to stabilize the negative charge—will best stabilize the $RCOO^-$ product.

Match: (D) is correct because the nitro group is a strong electron–withdrawing and deactivating group. The bromine in (B) is electron–withdrawing but not nearly as strongly so as the nitro group.

18. D

Stop: Answer choices are sentences describing water.

Think: The question asks why water will not help ester formation. Esterification is a dehydration reaction.

Predict: In dehydration reactions, including esterification, water is a product. The production of ester and water will continue until equilibrium is reached. If this reaction were to be carried out in water, there would be an extreme excess of product, and, according to Le Châtelier's principle, the reverse reaction, hydrolysis, will be favored until the system is back in equilibrium.

Match: (D) is correct.

19. E

Stop: Answer choices are alcohols.

Think: The question asks for the product when $Ph–COCH_3$ is reacted with a Grignard reagent (R–MgBr) followed by a reaction with water.

Predict: Reacting the carbonyl with a Grignard reagent followed by water will break the pi bond between the carbon and the oxygen, add the R group from the Grignard reagent in the opposite position, and protonate the oxygen to create a hydroxyl group. Given the initial compound and the addition of the three carbon chain from the Grignard R group, the product will have a five–carbon chain (one carbon from the methyl group on the original compound, the original carbonyl carbon, and three carbons from the addition). The phenyl and a hydroxyl will be on the second carbon. So, 2–phenyl–2–pentanol.

Match: (E) is correct.

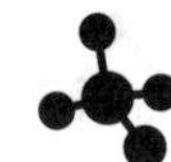

20. E

Stop: Answer choices are long sentences involving *cis–trans* isomers.

Think: The question asks why Diels–Alder requires a diene to be able to take on *cis* conformation.

Predict: Since both double bonds react with the alkene or alkyne, they should be on the same side in a stable *cis* conformation. Angle strain prevents the *trans* alkene from forming a ring, preventing the reaction for occurring.

Match: (E) is correct.

21. A

Stop: Answer choices are steps in a reaction.

Think: The question asks for the mechanism of the Wittig reaction. The Wittig reaction converts aldehydes and ketones to alkenes.

Predict: The first step of the reaction is the ylide (the nucleophile) attacking the carbonyl carbon (the electrophile). The oxaphosphetane intermediate that forms later decomposes leaving an alkene product.

Match: (A) is correct. The anionic carbon is the nucleophile and not the electrophile, making (B) incorrect.

22. C

Stop: Answer choices are molecules that are either carboxylic acids (–oic acid) or aldehydes (–al).

Think: The question asks for the product. $KMnO_4$ is a strong oxidizing agent, and $(CH_3)_2CHCH_2OH$ is a primary alcohol.

Predict: $KMnO_4$ will turn a primary alcohol into a carboxylic acid. Therefore, $(CH_3)_2CHCH_2OH$ will become $(CH_3)_2CHCOOH$.

Match: (C) is correct. (A), (B), and (D) can be eliminated once you know that the product is a carboxylic acid. Then, be careful with nomenclature. Butanoic acid (E) would have four unbranched carbons ($CH_3CH_2CH_2COOH$).

23. B

Stop: Answer choices are alkenes.

Think: The question asks for the original alkene. Ozonolysis is the cleavage of an alkene or alkyne with O_3 such that the double or triple carbon–carbon bond(s) are replaced by carbonyls.

Predict: To find the starting material, take the CO bonds in the resulting compounds and put them together to make a double bond. The two compounds will combine to form $CH_3CH_2CHC(CH_3)_2$. The longest chain has five carbons (pent–), and the methyl group is on the second carbon.

Match: (B) is correct.

24. B

Stop: Answer choices are molecules.

Think: The question asks which molecule would not react with $NaBH_4$. $NaBH_4$ is a reducing agent, though not as strong of a reducing agent as $LiAlH_4$.

Predict: $NaHB_4$ can reduce an aldehyde or a ketone but not an ester or a carboxylic acid. The correct answer will be either an ester (–oate) or carboxylic acid (–oic acid).

Match: (B) is correct.

25. D

Stop: Answer choices are rankings.

Think: The question asks you to rank the molecules from least basic to most basic. A more basic molecule will be able to stabilize a positive charge by donating electron density. Conversely, a more acidic (less basic) molecule will stabilize a negative charge by withdrawing electron density.

Predict: When approaching ranking problems, start with the extreme values. To find the most basic, look for electron–donating groups. All of the compounds start with Ph–NH_2. The NH_2 is strongly electron–donating. The CH_3 on compound (II) is also electron–donating, making it more basic, while the Cl on compound (III) is electron–withdrawing, making it less basic.

Match: (D) is correct. Notice that this is the only choice that ranks compound (II) as the most basic, so the question can be answered without evaluating the difference between compounds (I) and (III). However, (D) also ranks (III) as the least basic, which is correct due to the chloride.

26. A

Stop: Answer choices are rankings.

Think: The question asks you to rank the compounds from least acidic to most acidic. A more acidic molecule will be able to stabilize negative charge by having electron–withdrawing groups remove some of the electron density from the oxygen.

Predict: When approaching ranking problems, start with the extremes. To find the most acidic, look for electron–withdrawing groups. Compound (IV) has three electron–withdrawing groups (–COOH and two –Br), making it the most acidic. Compound (I) has an electron–donating group (CH_3), so it will be the least acidic.

Match: (A) is correct. This is the only list that ranks compound (IV) as the most acidic and compound (I) as the least acidic. Compound (III) has one more electron–withdrawing group than compound (II). That is not necessary for answering the question, but it confirms the order to be I > II > III > IV.

27. D

Stop: Answer choices are molecules.

Think: The question stem gives IR data and asks you to identify the compound. When reading IR graphs, look for a sharp peak at 1700, which would indicate the presence of a carbonyl (CO) and a broad peak at about 3300, which would indicate the presence of a hydroxyl (–OH).

Predict: With a broad peak at 3300, expect an –OH group, and; with no sharp peak at 1700, rule out any answer choice with a carbonyl.

Match: (D), the alcohol, is the only choice with a hydroxide group, so it is correct.

28. B

Stop: Answer choices involve reasoning based on different IR peaks.

Think: The question is asks for IR proof of a conversion from an alcohol (sec–butanol) to a ketone (2–butanone).

Predict: The conversion will involve the loss of a hydroxyl group (loss of broad peak at 3300) and the gain of carbonyl group (gain of sharp peak at 1700).

Match: (B) is correct.

29. B

Stop: Answer choices are molecules.

Think: The question presents an ^{1}H NMR spectrum that contains four peaks: three peaks in the alkane range, and one peak in the aldehyde range.

Predict: Look for an aldehyde with four distinct hydrogen families.

Match: (B) ($CH_3CH_2CH_2CHO$) is correct. (A) and (E) would have five peaks. (C) would have a tall phenyl peak. (D) would have two peaks since it has four hydrogen atoms, not four distinct hydrogen families.

30. A

Stop: Answer choices are different molecules.

Think: The question stem presents an ^{1}H NMR spectrum with only one peak, which is in the aromatic range.

Predict: Look for an aromatic molecule where all of the hydrogen atoms are equivalent.

Match: (A) is correct. (B) is the only other choice containing an aromatic ring, but it has two families of hydrogen because of the carboxylic acid group.

31. C

Stop: Answer choices are numbers.

Think: The question asks for the number of distinct ^{13}C NMR peaks in toluene. Toluene is an aromatic compound with one methyl substituent.

Predict: Toluene has seven carbons. However, the two carbons *ortho* to the methyl group are equivalent and thus produce the same peak. The same goes for the two carbons *meta* to the methyl group. Therefore, the total number of peaks is five.

Match: (C) is correct.

32. C

Stop: The answer choices are NMR absorption peaks, and the range indicates ^{13}C NMR.

Think: The question asks for the peaks seen in alanine. Alanine has only three carbons. Look for notable functional groups. Carbon 1 is in a carboxyl group; carbon 2 has a methyl group; carbon 3 has an amine.

Predict: Carboxyls have an absorption peak of around 170–185 ppm. Carbons 2 and 3 should have considerably lower absorption peaks.

Match: (C) is correct. Notice that (A), (D), and (E) can be eliminated based solely on the number of peaks.

33. C

Stop: Answer choices are functional groups.

Think: The question asks which will show a broad IR peak at 3,400. A broad peak around 3,300 indicates the presence of a hydroxyl (–OH).

Predict: The answer will contain a hydroxyl group.

Match: (C) is correct.

34. E

Stop: Answer choices are small whole numbers.

Think: The question asks for the number of ^{1}H NMR peaks, or distinct families of hydrogen atoms, on $CH_3CHC(OH)CH_3$.

Predict: There are four distinct families of hydrogen atoms.

Match: (E) is correct.

35. D

Stop: Answer choices are types of splitting.

Think: Splitting of hydrogen atoms can occur up to three bonds away, and there will be one more peak than there are hydrogen atoms within three bonds of the original hydrogen.

Predict: A methyl group will have three hydrogen atoms, which will cause splitting of the hydrogen in question into four peaks.

Match: (D) is correct.

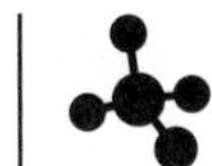

36. E

Stop: Answer choices are comparing properties of liquids.

Think: The question asks what must be true if distillation and recrystallization purify a mixture of two liquids. Distillation is used to separate liquids with different boiling points, and recrystallization is used to remove impurities from a crystal.

Predict: The liquids must have different boiling points.

Match: (E) is correct.

37. B

Stop: The answer choices are long sentences, and the question stem is very long. On Test Day, you might consider triaging and returning later, but the answer choices are parallel to each other, so it may not be as time-consuming as it looks.

Think: The question asks why extraction would be more effective with $NaHCO_3$ than with NaOH. Extraction is a purification technique used to separate compounds based on their solubilities or acid–base properties. In the experiment, cresol needs to be extracted from benzoic acid.

Predict: Consider the effect of adding each base to the mixture. Benzoic acid (a carboxylic acid) is much more acidic than cresol (an alcohol). NaOH (a strong base) will deprotonate both, causing both to end up in the aqueous layer. $NaHCO_3$ (a weak base) can only deprotonate benzoic acid, separating it into the aqueous layer while leaving cresol in the organic layer.

Match: (B) is correct. If you had trouble making the prediction, though, notice that (A), (C), (D), and (E) all claim that at least one of the bases protonates rather than deprotonates. Look for choices that make scientific errors like this whenever you need to eliminate. (D) and (E) also incorrectly identify $NaHCO_3$ as a strong base. Knowing acids and bases is very valuable on Test Day.

38. C

Stop: Answer choices list separation methods.

Think: The question asks how to separate a mixture of ethanol and water, which have the same boiling point. An azeotropic mixture has the same boiling point for both compounds at a specific combination of the two components at a specific pressure.

Predict: The answer cannot be simple or fractional distillation. However, changing the pressure above the liquid will change the boiling point of each component differently and allow distillation at a different temperature.

Match: (C) is correct. (E) is Extreme.

Reading Comprehension 2

1. b	19. B	37. B
2 .e	20. –	38. D
3. a	21. A	39. E
4. g	22. A	40. C
5. c	23. C	41. D
6. d	24. E	42. E
7. f	25. A	43. E
8. A	26. E	44. C
9. B	27. B	45. E
10. D	28. E	46. A
11. C	29. B	47. C
12. D	30. A	48. A
13. E	31. E	49. C
14. E	32. D	50. B
15. C	33. D	51. B
16. E	34. D	52. D
17. –	35. E	53. E
18. D	36. E	

Question Types Exercise

1. b

This is a Detail question because the it asks you to identify information that was stated in the passage. "According to the passage" is classic Detail language.

2. e

This is a Function question because it asks you to identify why the author does something in the passage. The phrase "in order to" indicates Function.

3. a

This is a Global question because it asks about the passage as a whole.

4. g

This is a Strengthen/Weaken question because you are required to examine new information and determine whether or not it weakens a hypothesis presented in the passage.

5. c

This is a Detail EXCEPT question for which you need to find the detail that is not included in the passage. "Each of the following is listed . . . EXCEPT" tells you that four choices will be stated in the passage but that the answer will not be.

6. d

This is a Tone question. These are perhaps the most straightforward questions to identify because they almost always include the word "tone."

7. f

This is an Inference question. You must deduce what the researchers believe based on the information in the passage. Of course, recognizing the word "inferred" is a great way to identify this question type. Another way to recognize an Inference question is to determine that it is asking for something that is not stated in the passage but nonetheless must be true based on the information provided in the passage.

Passage 1—Heart Disease

Roadmap

Paragraph 1: heart disease standard model

Paragraph 2: another risk factor = lipoprotein(a)

Paragraph 3: LDL, HDL, apolipoprotein

Paragraph 4: how does it work? fibrin? growth factors?

Purpose: explain how lipoprotein(a) might cause heart disease

Questions

8. A

Stop: This is a Global question because it asks what the passage as a whole is primarily about.

Think: Refer to the overall purpose of the passage in your Roadmap.

Predict: The purpose of the passage is to explain how lipoprotein(a) might cause heart disease.

Match: (A) is correct. (B) is Opposite as the passage does not refute the standard model and in fact states that the standard model accounts for approximately three-quarters of heart disease cases. (C) is a Distortion from paragraph 4. The theories do not necessarily oppose each other, and even if they did, this only covers paragraph 4, so it is too narrow to be the answer to our primary purpose question. (D) is a Faulty Use of Detail: true based on paragraph 3 but not the answer to a Global question. Answer choice (E) is Opposite; paragraph 2 states that lipoprotein(a) likely plays a role only in "a sizeable minority" of cases, and the passage is primarily concerned with lipoprotein(a).

9. B

Stop: This is an Inference question.

Think: The author's views on the research done on lipoprotein(a) are located in paragraph 2, where the author first introduces research on lipoprotein(a)'s role in the development of heart disease, and in paragraph 4, where the author indicates that a theory that fully explains how lipoprotein(a) works has yet to be developed.

Predict: The author is interested in lipoprotein(a) but thinks that more research is needed.

Match: Answer choice (B) matches. Answer choice (A) is Opposite of paragraph 2, which explains Lawn's recent research on the role of lipoprotein(a) in heart attacks. Answer choice (C) is Out of Scope because technical problems are never discussed. Answer choice (D) is Opposite of paragraph 2, which clearly states that lipoprotein(a) is the likely contributor to about one quarter of cases of heart attack in males under the age of 60. Answer choice (E) is Out of Scope as the author does not evaluate the validity of Lawn's research.

10. D

Stop: This is a Detail question. "According to the passage" is your clue.

Think: Use your passage map. Lipoprotein(a) and LDL are discussed in paragraph 3. Refer to the actual passage to determine the difference between lipoprotein(a) and LDL.

Predict: One possible answer is that lipoprotein(a) has a surface protein—apolipoprotein(a)—while LDL does not. However, the answer could be any difference discussed in paragraph 3.

Match: This time, the exact fact that you might have predicted regarding apolipoprotein(a) is not in the answer choices, so you need to evaluate the answers to determine what is true. Start with (A). The second part of the answer, that LDL causes damage to the arteries, is true. However, lipoprotein(a) is not mentioned in relation to the liver, so that part of the answer is Out of Scope. It may have been tempting because HDL is mentioned with the liver, but HDL serves a positive function. Move on to (B). This answer choice is Extreme in that it talks about having "only" positive or "only" negative function. The passage doesn't say this and in fact is discussing the role of lipoprotein(a) in causing heart disease. Answer choice (C) is Opposite of the passage. Lipoprotein(a) is not accounted for in the standard model of heart disease that is outlined in paragraph 1. Look at answer choice (D) next. The passage suggests in paragraph 4 that lipoprotein(a) most likely contributes to plaque formation by triggering the release of growth factors. In paragraph 3, it is stated that LDL does put cholesterol in the bloodstream. Therefore, (D) is the correct answer. Answer choice (E) is a Distortion; paragraph 3 states that lipoprotein(a) does not dissolve fibrin and that HDL (not LDL) carries cholesterol to the liver.

11. C

Stop: This is an Inference question. The term "suggests" indicates that the answer is based on the passage rather than being explicitly stated in the passage as the answer to a Detail question would be.

Think: The question stem directs you to paragraph 1 and requires you to find out what the passage implies about the standard model of heart disease. Check the passage to predict.

Predict: At first look, this may seem hard to predict because the first paragraph only gives background information on the standard model. So what is implied? Check the shift in paragraph 2. The standard model seems to not account for a pretty sizeable number of cases. In fact, about one quarter of cases may be due to lipoprotein(a). Use this as the prediction. If this prediction is not apparent, you can also evaluate each answer choice against the passage.

Match: Answer choice (C) matches with the first line of paragraph 2 and is the correct answer. Answer choice (A) is Opposite: the passage indicates that the standard model does account for the majority of heart disease cases. Answer choice (B) is a Distortion. Lipoprotein(a) research has not undermined the standard model; it simply helps explain the cases that the standard model could not. Answer choice (D) is also Opposite as the standard model is still credible today. Answer choice (E) is a Distortion. Paragraph 2 states that "Excessive levels of lipoprotein(a) are associated with strokes," but strokes are never mentioned in relation to the standard model of the causes of heart disease.

12. D

Stop: This is a Detail question. Note the phrase "according to the passage."

Think: This question is about lipoprotein(a), but the answer could come from paragraphs 2, 3, or 4 as the question stem does not provide any further clues.

Predict: You cannot formulate a solid prediction on this question. Instead, evaluate each answer choices individually and look for proof in the passage (especially paragraphs 2, 3, and 4).

Match: Evaluate each answer choice. Answer choice (A) is a Faulty Use of Detail. It is apolipoprotein(a) that resembles plasminogen. Eliminate and move to (B). Answer choice (B) is Opposite. In paragraphs 3 and 4, we learn a lot of information about how lipoprotein(a) and LDL are different. Answer choice (C) is Opposite. Lipoprotein(a) is thought

to cause heart disease in a significant number of cases according to paragraph 2. Answer choice (D) is correct. In paragraph 3, it is said that "lipoprotein(a) has almost the same complex structure as LDL." Even though they are not exactly the same, this fits the bill for the answer choice, which simply requires that lipoprotein(a) and LDL resemble each other in structure. Answer choice (E) is Out of Scope. The first sentence of paragraph 3 states that "Lipoprotein(a) is closely related to low-density lipoprotein (LDL), a major contributor to atherosclerosis," but it does not imply at any point that lipoprotein(a) attacks the liver.

13. E

Stop: This is an Inference question. Note the phrase "the passage implies."

Think: The correct answer must be true based on the passage. Paragraph 2 contains information on the statistics related to heart attacks in males under the age of 60. Refer back to it.

Predict: According to the passage, "males with high lipoprotein(a) levels account for about one quarter of male heart attack victims under the age of 60." So what accounts for the other three quarters? You don't know for sure and cannot assume that it is the standard model. The only thing that must be true is that these three quarters are not accounted for by lipoprotein(a).

Match: Answer choice (E) matches. Answer choice (A) is Opposite as the passage indicates that only one quarter of cases are due to high lipoprotein(a) levels. Answer choices (B) and (C) are Out of Scope as the passage does not connect heart attack cases to LDL or HDL. Answer choice (D) is a Faulty Use of Detail and a Distortion. The inability to dissolve fibrin is associated with high lipoprotein(a) levels, which you already know only accounts for one quarter of heart attacks in males under the age of 60.

14. E

Stop: This is a Strengthen/Weaken question because it requires you to evaluate new information and determine which data would strengthen the theory discussed in the passage.

Think: The question stem provides a clue: the new information must strengthen the theory that lipoprotein(a) contributes to heart disease.

Predict: The new information will be found in the answer choices, so evaluating them will be necessary. However, the correct answer will be the one that contains new information making it more likely that lipoprotein(a) is a cause of heart disease.

Match: Evaluate each answer choice, looking for the answer that makes it more likely that lipoprotein(a) contributes to heart disease. Find proof for your answer in the passage. Answer choice (A) is Opposite. If lipoprotein(a) interfered with clot formation in the coronary arteries, it would decrease the risk for heart disease by reducing clots that could block blood flow. Answer choice (B) is also Opposite. According to paragraph 2, HDL is protective, while LDL contributes to plaque formation. If lipoprotein(a) were more like HDL, it would be less likely to contribute to heart disease. Answer choice (C) is also Opposite. This is a function of HDL mentioned in paragraph 3, so for the same reason answer choice (B) is ruled out, so too is answer (C). Answer choice (D) is another Opposite choice. Paragraph 3 states that lipoproteins transport fatty substances, and it is in performing this role that lipoprotein(a) can lead to heart attacks. On to answer choice (E), which research into the passage reveals is the correct choice. The proof can be found in paragraph 4. Up to this point, there has been only speculation that lipoprotein(a) prompts the release of growth factors that thicken artery walls. But if a true causal relationship were identified, then the case for lipoprotein(a) being a contributor to heart disease would be strengthened. Thus, (E) is the right choice.

15. C

Stop: This is a Function question. Note the phrase "in order to" in the question stem.

Think: As in most Function questions, this stem directs you to a specific place in the passage. Head to the paragraph 4 and find where the passage discusses lipoprotein(a)'s competition with plasminogen. Use context and keywords to determine why the author includes this detail.

Predict: According to the passage, the competition between lipoprotein(a) and plasminogen is for fibrin. Fibrin is associated with clots. Plasminogen dissolves fibrin clots. Because lipoprotein(a) cannot dissolve fibrin, there is an increased risk for arterial blockage. The author must provide all of these details to explain a way that lipoprotein(a) may function and contribute to the development of heart disease.

Match: Answer choice (C) matches. Answer choice (A) is Opposite because paragraph 4 is intended to provide evidence for the lipoprotein(a) theory, which is the alternative to the standard model. Answer choice (B) is a Faulty Use of Detail. Though growth factors are mentioned in paragraph 4, they are not related to the competition between lipoprotein(a) and plasminogen. Answer choice (D) is a Distortion. Fibrin is associated with clots, not dissolving lipoprotein(a) or plasminogen. The answer mixes up key ideas from the passage since plasminogen is described as being able to dissolve fibrin whereas lipoprotein(a) cannot. Answer choice (E) is another Faulty Use of Detail. This information is mentioned in paragraph 4, but it is

used to describe a second way in which lipoprotein(a) can potentially lead to heart attacks in addition to competing with plasminogen for access to fibrin.

Running Out of Time Exercise—Risk Assessment

Note: These answers and explanations are given within the context of the Running Out of Time exercise, which does not have sufficient information to answer all the questions or identify wrong answer pathologies.

Roadmap

Paragraph 1: environmental law, intro risk assessment

Paragraph 2: before risk assessment

Paragraph 3: risk assessments not neutral

Paragraph 4: risk assessment decisions = ethical choices

Purpose: to explain development of risk assessment and recommend it be viewed as an ethical choice

Questions

16. E

Stop: The phrase "main point" indicates this is a Global question. This question should be tackled right away on Test Day.

Think: Refer to the purpose of the passage.

Predict: The purpose is to explain the development of risk assessment and argue that it should be viewed as an ethical choice when applied to environmental law.

Match: Answer choice (E) matches the purpose that we were able to identify using our brief, selected reading. Stating that it is not "a value-free process" indicates that it has an ethical component.

17. –

Stop: This is a Detail EXCEPT question, which is likely to take a while. If you only have ten minutes, you should not attempt this question on Test Day. Instead, choose an answer, mark the question, and move on.

18. D

Stop: This is a Function question. It provides a clue of where to go, so this question could be done even when running out of time.

Think: Refer to paragraph 3 and find "confidence levels." Read for context. You can also try to tackle this one solely with the passage map.

Predict: The purpose of paragraph 3 is to show that the risk assessment process is not really neutral after all.

Match: Answer choice (D) is the only one that touches on the process not being neutral, so it must be the match.

19. B

Stop: This is an Inference question. This could be time-consuming, but the clue in the stem about the method that "predated" risk assessment may be enough, so try it.

Think: What came before risk assessment is found in paragraph 2, but you may be able to predict without going there.

Predict: Risk assessment seems to have come about to address problems with whatever came before it. See if an answer matches that.

Match: Answer choice (B) is the correct answer. Answer choice (A) is too Extreme with "completely ineffective." Risk assessment is the method that is associated with a scientific approach, so answer choice (C) doesn't seem to make sense. Conclusions like the one in answer choice (D) would show up in paragraph 4. Answer choice (E) seems as though it would be Opposite from the passage because a process that is more effective and less expensive likely wouldn't need to be replaced with an alternative. So, only (B) fits here.

20. –

Stop: This is a Function question. Although the question tells you where to go and what to look for, this question is long and has long answer choices, so it is best to skip it on Test Day if running out of time.

21. A

Stop: This is a Global question. It should be tackled right away on Test Day.

Think: Refer to the purpose of the passage.

Predict: The purpose is to explain the development of risk assessment and argue that it should be viewed as an ethical choice when applied to environmental law.

Match: Answer choice (A) matches the purpose from the brief, selected reading.

Passage 2—The Corpus Callosum

Roadmap

Paragraph 1: evol. of brain, corpus callosum

Paragraph 2: division of labor

Paragraph 3: hemispheres react diff.; left dominant?

Paragraph 4: counter-evidence: Wigan autopsy

Paragraph 5: more evidence

Paragraph 6: left- vs. right-brained

Paragraph 7: severing corpus callosum=no negative effects

Paragraph 8: Sperry's; "split-brain"

Paragraph 9: contralateral wiring

Paragraph 10: visual field

Paragraph 11: visual experiment

Paragraph 12: touch

Paragraph 13: role of corpus callosum

Paragraph 14: more questions, lateralization

Purpose: explain role of corpus callosum and supporting research

Questions

22. A

Stop: This is a Detail EXCEPT question, so the correct answer will be the only one that does not appear in the passage.

Think: Division of labor is the topic of paragraph 2.

Predict: You will need to compare each answer choice to the information in paragraph 2 and find the one that is not discussed.

Match: Answer choice (A) is the only division of labor that is not mentioned in paragraph 2, so it is the correct answer. For reference: Commissures are mentioned in paragraph 1, and they are networks of neurons that connect the right and left hemispheres. The divisions of labor mentioned in answer choices (B), (C), (D), and (E) are specifically mentioned in paragraph 2, so these choices are all incorrect.

23. C

Stop: The language "According to the passage" in the question-stem tells you that this is a Detail question.

Think: People who suffer from epilepsy were discussed in paragraphs 7 and 8 and then again in paragraphs 10 through 12. The correct answer will come from one of these paragraphs.

Predict: Paragraph 7 states that "severing the corpus callosum significantly retarded the severity of, or even halted altogether the occurrence of, seizures in certain epileptic patients." Look for an answer choice that gives you the same information.

Match: Answer choice (C) matches the prediction perfectly. Answer choices (A) and (B) are both Distortions; the passage mentions in paragraph 4 fully-functioning individuals who only had half of a brain, but removing part of either hemisphere was not discussed in relation to seizure patients. Answer choice (D) is a Distortion as well. Paragraph 11 discusses certain aspects of Sperry's experiments in which he limited the visual material presented to each hemisphere, but this research was performed on subjects whose corpus callosa had already been severed and was not performed in an effort to treat epilepsy. Answer choice (E) is Out of Scope since drug therapy is never discussed.

24. E

Stop: You're being asked to find the goal of the entire passage, so this is a Global question.

Think: Use the "purpose" note in your roadmap as your prediction.

Predict: The correct answer choice will be similar to your roadmap note: "explain role of corpus callosum in brain function and supporting research."

Match: Answer choice (E) matches this prediction extremely well and is the correct answer. Answer choice (A) is a Faulty Use of Detail; the passage discusses Sperry's research, but this is not the overall purpose. Answer choice (B) is Out of Scope. The passage uses the results of Sperry's study to support its main point but does not evaluate effectiveness. Similarly, answer choice (C) is Out of Scope as the author does not make any recommendations about the type or level of treatment that split-brain patients receive. Answer choice (D) is also Out of Scope. The passage details one set of studies, but this is not its entire goal.

25. A

Stop: The phrase "is most likely" indicates that this is an Inference question. You will need to use information from the passage to determine what type of brain damage potentially caused this patient's symptoms.

Think: How brain damage in different areas manifests itself is discussed in paragraphs 3 through 5. Use the information in these passages to match the symptoms to the type of damage.

Predict: Paragraph 5 describes the effects of damage to the right hemisphere: A person with damage in this area may "fail to recognize familiar surroundings and people," but the damage may "leave speech unimpaired."

Match: Answer choice (A) matches your prediction. Answer choice (B) is a Distortion. Paragraph 3 discusses the effects of damage to the left hemisphere, and these effects do not match the symptoms described. Answer choice (C) is Out of Scope; the passage does not discuss at all the results of damage to both hemispheres. Answer choice (D) is another Distortion; while severing the corpus callosum could be considered brain damage, this is only mentioned in the context of treating epileptics. Since you were able to determine that answer choice (A) is correct, you can thus eliminate answer choice (E).

26. E

Stop: You are looking for the characteristics that a person with left hemisphere brain damage will display. This information was discussed in the passage, so this is a Detail question.

Think: The effects of damage to the left hemisphere appear in paragraphs 3 and 4. Refer back to these paragraphs to formulate your prediction.

Predict: While paragraph 3 lists the commonly held views about the left hemisphere, paragraph 4 states that "if the damage to one hemisphere occurs early enough in infant development, the other hemisphere may eventually adapt and take over the tasks usually carried out by its now-damaged counterpart." So there are no characteristics that someone with damage to the left hemisphere will definitely have, and you need an answer choice that indicates that.

Match: Answer choice (E) matches the cited information from paragraph 4 and is correct. Answer choice (A) is a tempting Distortion, but paragraph 4 establishes that damage to the left hemisphere does not always lead to speech impairment, and the effect on writing ability is not discussed. Answer choice (B) is the Opposite of information presented in paragraph 5, which says that the right brain controls musical ability. Answer choice (C) is another Distortion; split-brain patients are mentioned in paragraph 8 as those who have had their corpus callosa severed. Answer choice (D) is Out of Scope. Damaging one hemisphere under controlled conditions is not discussed at any point.

27. B

Stop: You need to find the reason that the author does not cite to support a given principle, so this is a Detail EXCEPT question.

Think: Information about the vertebrate brain and the cerebrum is in paragraph 1.

Predict: You will need to evaluate every answer choice until you find the one that is not mentioned in paragraph 1.

Match: Answer choice (A) is a Faulty Use of Detail. The fact that the mammalian cerebrum has grown so large as to have two hemispheres is discussed in paragraph 1, so this answer choice is incorrect. The complexity of cerebrums is not mentioned at all, though, so answer choice (B) is the correct answer. To confirm your answer, take a quick glance at the remaining choices. Answer choices (C), (D), and (E) are all discussed in paragraph 1, so they are all Faulty Uses of Detail and are incorrect.

28. E

Stop: You are asked to describe the author's tone when he describes Sperry's research. This is a Tone question.

Think: Information about Sperry's research appears in 8, 10, and 11. The author uses positive language to describe the experiments and how they contributed to understanding the corpus callosum—paragraph 10 begins by describing "the most striking" of Sperry's discoveries.

Predict: The correct answer will use a positive adjective to describe how Sperry's research helped science understand the corpus callosum.

Match: Answer choice (E) matches your prediction well. Answer choice (A) is a Distortion. Paragraph 14 mentions that some scientists "speculate as to the evolutionary reasons behind such lateralization," but since this is just speculation, Sperry's research could not have confirmed anything. Answer choice (B) is a Distortion. Wigan and Sperry both studied the effects of brain damage, but Wigan's autopsies were on people who had lost half of their brain, while Sperry performed experiments on epileptics. Answer choice (C) is Opposite of the information in the passage. The author uses Sperry's findings to support his thesis; he is not cynical about Sperry's results. Answer choice (D) is Out of Scope. The author's overall focus is on what role the corpus callosum plays in brain function; he is not interested in the treatment of epileptic patients.

29. B

Stop: This question asks for specific information from the passage, so it is a Detail question.

Think: The author first references hemispheres in paragraph 1, so this is a good place to begin researching the correct answer.

Predict: Paragraph 1 states that "The mammal cerebrum has grown so large that it folds in on itself to form a right and left hemisphere." So the two hemispheres that the passage discusses are part of the cerebrum.

Match: Answer choice (B) is the correct answer. Answer choices (A), (C), and (D) are all Faulty Uses of Detail. All of these things are discussed at multiple points in the passage, but none was described as having two hemispheres. Answer choice (E) is Out of Scope; the cerebellum is not mentioned at any point.

30. A

Stop: You need to paraphrase "the riddle of the corpus callosum." Information about the corpus callosum that makes it intriguing to scientists is an important topic in the passage, but it is not the entire purpose, so this is a Detail question.

Think: You can use your roadmap to recall that the first several paragraphs of the passage discuss parts of the brain and the effects of damage to one hemisphere. The primary discussion about the role of the corpus callosum does not begin until paragraph 7, so start your research there.

Predict: Paragraph 7 begins by saying that a subject "of much interest" is what happens when the corpus callosum is severed. According to the research presented, severing it had seemingly no negative consequences for seizure patients. This will serve as your prediction.

Match: Answer choice (A) is just a bit less specific than the prediction, but it matches and is the correct answer. Answer choice (B) is a Distortion. Split-brain patients are described in paragraph 8, and the term has nothing to do with their personalities. Answer choice (C) is Out of Scope; the corpus callosum is the only type of commissure that the passage discusses (outside of a passing reference in paragraph 1 to less dense neural networks). Answer choice (D) is Opposite of the correct answer and of paragraph 7, which states that patients whose corpus callosa were severed had almost no ill effects. Answer choice (E) is Out of Scope. Paragraph 1 mentions the mammalian brain but does not differentiate between that of a human and those of other mammals.

31. E

Stop: This is a Weaken question. You will need to evaluate each choice to see which one makes the conclusions of Sperry's research less likely to be true.

Think: Paragraph 13 sums up Sperry's findings well: They "strongly suggest a very sharp and intricate division of labor between the two hemispheres of the brain and also answer... the riddle of the corpus callosum: its function, or at least one of its functions, is to integrate all of the different roles performed by the two hemispheres of the brain."

Predict: The correct answer will weaken these conclusions that the corpus callosum integrates the jobs of the right and left hemispheres.

Match: Answer choice (E) is the only choice that describes a patient who has a severed corpus callosum but does not have impaired functions. If true, this would certainly make the conclusion that the corpus callosum bridges the two hemispheres less convincing. (E) is the correct answer. Answer choice (A) is Out of Scope. The descriptions of Sperry's experiments only describe the inability to draw or describe images presented to the right and left visual fields, respectively. Retrieving objects is never discussed, so you do not know how an instance of hands working against each other would affect his conclusions. Answer choices (B) and (C) are both Opposites since these exact scenarios are described as occurring in Sperry's experiments in paragraphs 12 and 11, respectively. They both therefore strengthen his results. Answer choice (D) is Out of Scope as patients with intact corpus callosa were not involved in Sperry's research.

32. D

Stop: The phrase "in order to" indicates that this is a Function question.

Think: Refer to your Roadmap for the paragraph referenced in the question, paragraph 9. Then refer back to the actual paragraph if necessary. Contralateral wiring means that the right hemisphere controls the left hand and processes information from the left visual field, and vice versa.

Predict: The author is explaining certain aspects of how the brain normally functions so that, in later paragraphs, the reader will better understand what makes Sperry's experiments so significant.

Match: Answer choice (D) is a match. Answer choice (A) is a Distortion; split-brain patients are not discussed in paragraph 9. Answer choice (B) is Out of Scope, as the passage never compares the brains of vertebrates to those of mammals. Answer choice (C) is Out of Scope as well. The author never evaluates Sperry's methods of research, he merely describes the experiments and their findings. Answer choice (E) is Extreme. While knowing the term "contralateral" could be considered useful, it is by no means critical to understanding the subject matter at hand.

33. D

Stop: You can tell from the phrase "the passage suggests" that this is an Inference question.

Think: Vertebrate brains are discussed in the first paragraph of the passage. The second sentence says that "The brainstems of all vertebrates, no matter their complexity, are roughly the same size, but this is not so for their cerebrums."

Predict: You can infer from this sentence that the size of a vertebrate's cerebrum will vary depending upon how complex it is.

Match: Answer choice (D) is the only one that mentions a cerebrum, so it is correct. Answer choices (A), (C), and (E) are all Faulty Uses of Detail, as none of them is discussed in relation to a vertebrate's complexity. Answer choice (B) is Opposite from the sentence cited above, which states that brainstem size is consistent no matter the complexity.

34. D

Stop: This is another Inference question. The correct answer will be implied by, but not explicitly stated in, the passage.

Think: The author discusses the relationship between the two hemispheres in paragraphs 3 through 6. The support for the correct answer will be in one of these paragraphs.

Predict: You will likely not be able to form a specific prediction, so instead focus on evaluating choices one by

one and eliminating answer choices that are not supported by the information in paragraphs 3 through 6.

Match: Answer choice (A) can be eliminated because it is Opposite of the passage. While paragraph 3 says that the right brain has traditionally been seen as minor, paragraph 5 states that this is actually not the case. Answer choice (B) is a Distortion; while paragraph 5 describes the right hemisphere as "far from passive," this does not imply that it is dominant over the left hemisphere. Answer choice (C) is another Opposite choice as the passage describes in many places that the hemispheres are responsible for different functions. Answer choice (D) is consistent with the information in paragraphs 3 through 6, and is the correct answer. The two hemispheres have different roles, but neither is dominant over the other. Answer choice (E) is a Distortion. Handedness is briefly mentioned in paragraph 4, but it cannot be inferred that handedness determines which hemisphere is dominant.

35. E

Stop: While it may not be immediately apparent which question-type this is, a quick glance at the answer choices reveals that they are details from the passage. So this is a Detail question, and you need to choose the answer choice that illustrates lateralization.

Think: Lateralization is mentioned in the final paragraph. It is defined as "specialization between hemispheres."

Predict: The correct answer choice will be an example of each hemisphere performing a unique function.

Match: Answer choice (E) is a prime example of lateralization since it describes each hemisphere as being responsible for a specific ability. Answer choice (A) is a Faulty Use of Detail. This is an example of contralateral wiring, which is mentioned in paragraph 9. Answer choice (B) is another Faulty Use of Detail. One hemisphere compensating for the other is discussed in paragraph 4, but it does not illustrate hemispheres performing separate functions. Answer choice (C) is a third Faulty Use of Detail choice; this choice defines one role of the corpus callosum instead of giving an example of hemisphere specialization. Answer choice (D) is another Faulty Use of Detail and also comes from paragraph 4. The fact that a certain percentage of left-handed people have speech centers in their right hemispheres does not help the reader understand that the left hemisphere is responsible for other functions.

36. E

Stop: You can tell that this is an Inference question by the phrase "is most likely to be experienced".

Think: Patients with severed corpus callosa are first discussed in paragraph 7.

Predict: Use your Roadmap for paragraph 7 to predict: The Roadmap indicates that patients with severed corpus callosa did not experience negative symptoms as a result of the procedure.

Match: Answer choice (E) matches the prediction. Answer choice (A) is a Faulty Use of Detail; it is mentioned in paragraph 5 as a possible symptom of damage to the right hemisphere. Answer choice (B) is Out of Scope because headaches are not mentioned anywhere in the passage. Answer choice (C) is a Faulty Use of Detail as well. Paragraph 7 anecdotally refers to one patient with a severed corpus callosum who had a wry sense of humor, but this was not a symptom of the procedure. Answer choice (D) is a third Faulty Use of Detail choice; paragraphs 3 and 4 state that impaired speech is a potential symptom of damage to either hemisphere.

37. B

Stop: This is a Function question that asks you to identify the role that a specific paragraph plays.

Think: Use your roadmap to determine the purpose of paragraph 4.

Predict: According to the roadmap, paragraph 4 provides counterevidence to the commonly held theory discussed in paragraph 3 that the right hemisphere of the brain is less important than the left hemisphere.

Match: Answer choice (B) matches this prediction. Answer choice (A) is a Distortion. Wigan and Sperry both studied the brain, but Wigan's research is not presented as being the precedent for Sperry's. Answer choice (C) is Out of Scope; no specific examples of infant anomaly are discussed. Answer choice (D) is a Faulty Use of Detail. This fact is mentioned in paragraph 4, but it is used to support the overall point that the left hemisphere is not dominant—it is not the overall topic of the paragraph. Answer choice (E) can be eliminated for the same reason. This information is mentioned in paragraph 4, but it is used as evidence to prove the author's point and is not the paragraph's main purpose.

Passage 3—Health Benefits of Eye Exams

Roadmap

Paragraph 1: eye exams' importance

Paragraph 2: eye tracking, Alzheimer's

Paragraph 3: pupil dilation

Paragraph 4: retinopathy

Paragraph 5: Gardner syndrome

Paragraph 6: eye-related symptoms, cataracts

Paragraph 7: vitamin A deficiency

Paragraph 8: ex. yellowing sclerae—jaundice, liver

Paragraph 9: more ex.

Paragraph 10: recommend regular eye exams

Purpose: explain benefits of eye exams for monitoring overall health

Questions

38. D

Stop: This Detail question asks about the Retinal Amyloid Index study, which was mentioned in paragraph 2.

Think: The study demonstrated that Alzheimer's patients make more mistakes on eye-tracking tests than patients without the disease do. The final sentence of paragraph 2 concludes that "Healthcare professionals are excited about the possibility that this simple test can help diagnose Alzheimer's because early diagnosis is essential to successful management of the disease."

Predict: Since this is a Detail question, the correct answer will be a paraphrase of the statement. They are excited about the potential for early diagnosis and better management of Alzheimer's.

Match: (D) is correct. Answer choice (A) is a Faulty Use of Detail. This was the study's finding, but healthcare professionals are not excited about patients making mistakes. (B) is a Distortion. These tests can help diagnose the disease but cannot prevent it. (C) is Out of Scope because no previous tests were discussed. (E) is another Faulty Use of Detail. The paragraph's first sentence does say that the test is common, but the common nature of the test is not why the professionals are excited.

39. E

Stop: This is a Detail EXCEPT question, so all four incorrect choices will be in the passage. These questions often take time, so they are good candidates for triaging until late in the section.

Think: The question asks which test is not mentioned as a common part of an eye exam. Components of an eye exam are mentioned throughout the passage, but you can use your Roadmap to find some of them. The Roadmap shows that paragraphs 1–3 focused heavily the tests performed in eye exams.

Predict: You cannot Predict information that doesn't appear in the passage, so eliminate choices as you find them in the Roadmap or the passage.

Match: Eye tracking (A) and pupil dilation (C) are in the Roadmap for paragraphs 2 and 3, so eliminate them. Decreased night vision is in the Roadmap, and a quick scan of paragraph 7 confirms that the low-light ocular test (B) is performed, so eliminate (B) as well. Paragraph 1 is where eye exams were introduced, and scanning for (D) and (E) shows that the iris (D) is examined. (E) is not mentioned in the passage and is, therefore, correct.

40. C

Stop: This Detail question asks about patients with diabetes.

Think: The question asks which eye-related disease diabetics are at risk for developing. Refer back to your Roadmap. The need for preventative care for diabetics is discussed in paragraph 4. Find what this is intended to prevent.

Predict: Glaucoma, cataracts, and vision changes are indicated.

Match: (C) is correct. All other choices are Faulty Uses of Detail.

41. D

Stop: This is another Detail EXCEPT question.

Think: The question asks which condition is not discussed in relation to eye-related symptoms. Use the Roadmap to eliminate choices and to find which paragraphs to review. The Roadmap contains several conditions and a note that paragraph 9 contains more examples.

Predict: You can't Predict the answer to an EXCEPT question, so eliminate choices that are contained in the passage.

Match: Gardner syndrome (A) and retinopathy (E) are in the Roadmap, so eliminate them. The Roadmap mentions a deficiency in paragraph 7. Check to see if vitamin A deficiency is related to (C) rhodopsin deficiency. It is, so eliminate (C). Scan paragraph 9 for the other conditions. Myasthenia gravis (B) appears there, leaving drug intoxication (D) as the correct answer. Notice how using the Roadmap as a guide can help you answer Detail EXCEPT questions efficiently.

42. E

Stop: The language in this question stem tells you that it is a Tone question.

Think: The purpose in the Roadmap says that the author sought to demonstrate the benefits of eye exams by explaining how they can be used to identify a variety of health problems. The author uses the last paragraph to emphasize the need for eye exams.

Predict: The tone is very positive.

Match: (E) is correct. (D) is Opposite; the author was unrestrained in his advocacy for eye exams.

43. E

Stop: The language "most accurately depicts" indicates that this is an Inference question, and the question gives a specific clue, so it can be researched in the passage much like a Detail question could be.

Think: Use your Roadmap to recall that the Retinal Amyloid Index was described in paragraph 2.

Predict: While you generally cannot predict the precise text of the correct answer to an Inference question, you can predict that the answer must be in line with the information presented in paragraph 2: Alzheimer's patients do worse on the eye tracking test, so the test might help with early diagnosis.

Match: (E) is correct. (A) is a Distortion. The passage does not imply that one study followed the other. (B) is also a Distortion: the participants in the study were either already diagnosed with a disease or "healthy" and not diagnosed at all. (C) is Opposite since "participants with Alzheimer's were up to ten times more likely to make mistakes." (D) is Out of Scope: no comparisons were made among healthy patients of different ages.

44. C

Stop: The phrase "the passage implies" tells you that this is another Inference question. This one is specifically about having trouble seeing in low light.

Think: The question asks what must be true about any patient having trouble seeing at night. As seen in the Roadmap for paragraph 7, difficulty seeing in low light, or decreased night vision, can be caused by either cataracts or vitamin A deficiency. Going back to the passage, paragraph 7 states that, if there is a vitamin A deficiency, rhodopsin, which is critical for night vision, will not be made and that untreated vitamin A deficiency may lead to corneal ulcers and irreversible blindness. But, this does not apply to *all* patients who have trouble seeing in low light. Some of them cannot see well in low light due to cataracts. So, refer to the previous paragraph, which describes cataracts as "reversible clouding of the vision due to deposits on the lens of the eye." But, as with vitamin A deficiency, not *all* patients with poor low-light vision will have this problem.

Predict: It is impossible to know exactly what the answer will say, but it *must* be true for *any* patient who has trouble seeing in low light. Some patients will have the vitamin A deficiency problem, while some will have the cataracts problem.

Match: (C) is correct. Based on the passage, it must be true that, if the problem is caused by vitamin A deficiency, the patients would at greater risk for irreversible blindness than they would be if the problem were caused by cataracts. The passage establishes in paragraph 7 that irreversible blindness can result from vitamin A deficiency, while it says in paragraph 6 that having cataracts is a reversible condition affecting vision. (A) and (D) are Distortions. These choices assume that vitamin A deficiency and its consequences are more likely than cataracts, but this is not supported by the passage. (B) and (E) are Faulty Uses of Detail. (B) is true of those whose problem is caused by vitamin A deficiency, but that is not what the question asks. Likewise, (E) is true of those whose problem is caused by cataracts, but that also is not what was asked. The question asks what would be true for "any patient" having trouble seeing in low light.

45. E

Stop: The language "primarily concerned with" indicates that this is a Global question.

Think: To answer any Global question, refer back to the purpose your Roadmap.

Predict: The passage is primarily concerned with the benefits of eye exams and how they can be used to identify a variety of health problems.

Match: (E) is correct. (A) is a Faulty Use of Detail. The typical components of an eye test are mentioned in paragraph 1, but discussing them is not the primary concern in the passage. (B) is also a Faulty Use of Detail. The recommended schedule of visits is discussed only in the final paragraph, so it is too narrow to be the answer. (C) is a Distortion. The symptoms of several diseases are discussed, but the purpose of that is to highlight the benefits of eye exams rather than to describe the diseases. Finally, comparing optometrists to primary care physicians (D) is Out of Scope.

46. A

Stop: This is another Detail EXCEPT question that will require the process of elimination.

Think: The question asks which choice is not mentioned as a sign of retinopathy. According to the Roadmap, retinopathy is discussed in paragraph 4.

Predict: Since the question is specific to paragraph 4, Predict what would constitute an incorrect choice. Signs include bleeding, oozing, blood vessel narrowing, and damage to the macula or optic nerve. Eliminate the choices that contain any of these signs.

Match: (B), (C), (D), and (E) are incorrect as predicted. (A) is correct. Retinal lesions are mentioned in paragraph 5 as a

sign of Gardner syndrome but not in paragraph 4 as a sign of retinopathy.

47. C

Stop: The phrase "the optometrist can be confident that" is evidence that this is an Inference question.

Think: Once again, begin by checking your Roadmap. Yellowing sclera are discussed in paragraph 8. Return to the passage to predict what must be true.

Predict: Yellowing of the sclerae is a symptom of jaundice, which is caused by excess bilirubin, which is in turn a product of red blood cell destruction. This can be a sign of a number of different conditions involving any of several organs.

Match: (C) is the only answer that must be true, so it is correct. An obstructed bile duct (A), liver failure (C), and chemotherapy (E) are all possible, but not definite, causes of the sign, so these choices are Faulty Uses of Detail or Extreme. (B) is a Distortion. The passage establishes that this could be a sign of pancreatic cancer, not a sign that someone is at risk for developing the cancer. The choice would also be Extreme if it claimed that the optometrist could be confident that the patient has pancreatic cancer because this is merely possible.

48. A

Stop: You can determine that this is an Inference question by the phrase "Which of the following best aligns."

Think: The Roadmap shows that the author provides recommendations about the frequency of eye exams for different types of patients in the final paragraph.

Predict: You cannot predict exactly what the correct answer will say, but you know that it must be in line with the recommendations in paragraph 10: At risk patients, such as diabetics, and older adults should be examined every year. Healthy adults under age 60 without eye problems should be examined every two years.

Match: (A) is correct because it describes a healthy patient under 60 years old visiting her optometrist every two years. (B), (C), and (D) are Opposite because those with diabetes (b) or Grave's disease (C) and adults aged over 60 (D) should be examined every year rather than every other year. (E) is a Distortion: this patient should be examined every two, not three, years.

49. C

Stop: The language in this stem tells you that it is a Strengthen/Weaken question asking you to strengthen the author's argument.

Think: The author's basic argument about the benefits of eye exams is summarized in the first sentence of the passage: "While eye exams are commonly used to measure and correct vision, they serve an important preventative function as well."

Predict: The correct answer will make the author's stance that eye exams have an important role in preventative medicine more likely to be true. The answer will present supporting evidence that detection of disease through eye exams helps with disease prevention or treatment.

Match: (C) is correct because it provides evidence for a benefit of the early treatment of colorectal polyposis, which paragraph 5 states can be detected by an eye exam. Immunizations (A) and whether or not insurance covers the exams (B) are Out of Scope because there is no connection in the passage to these things and the health benefits of eye exams. In other words, they do not relate to the author's argument, so they cannot strengthen it. That vitamin A deficiency is no longer a problem (D) or that high bilirubin levels are common and usually benign (E) would weaken the author's argument because the author cites these potential medical problems as reasons to get eye exams. If they are not problematic, then an eye exam would not help. These choices are Opposite.

50. B

Stop: This question presents a symptom and asks for the condition of which it may be a symptom. You'll match the symptom to the condition discussed, so it is a Detail question.

Think: Eyelid droops come up in paragraph 9.

Predict: "Chronic drooping eyelids can be caused by the autoimmune disease myasthenia gravis, whereas an acute eyelid droop could potentially be a symptom of a brain aneurysm".

Match: (B) is correct. Hypothyroidism (A) and macular degeneration (E) are Out of Scope because they were not mentioned in the passage. (C) is a Distortion: myasthenia gravis often present with chronic, not acute, drooping eyelids. Diabetes (D) is also a Distortion; diabetes is mentioned elsewhere in the passage connected to other eye-related issues.

51. B

Stop: The phrase "in order to" tells you that this is an Function question. Function questions ask why the author did something.

Think: Review the Roadmap for paragraph 6: eye-related symptoms can indicate both local and systemic problems. Now, go into paragraph 6 to determine how cataracts fit into this context: Cataracts are an eye-related condition that would cause vision problems that might prompt someone to visit her optometrist.

Predict: Cataracts are used as an example to support the idea that patients often go to optometrists for eye-related reasons.

Match: (B) is correct. (A) is a Faulty Use of Detail. The author does discuss the symptoms of both cataracts and vitamin A deficiency, but he does not discuss cataracts for the sole purpose of contrasting symptoms. Remember that Function questions ask *why* the author said something, not *what* he said. (C) is a Distortion; the author says that some people will make appointments because of symptoms, but he does not make a recommendation that they do so, so this cannot be his intent. Similarly, (D) is a Distortion. The passage states that experiencing symptoms could cause someone to visit the optometrist, but the author does not focus on how the optometrist would study the lens to support a diagnosis. (E) is another Distortion. The author does is not focused on the dangers of cataracts.

52. D

Stop: "According to the passage" means that this is another Detail question.

Think: Review your Roadmap: Pupil dilation is the topic of paragraph 3.

Predict: Paragraph 3 states that "When the pupil is dilated, the optometrist can effectively examine the retina and other structures behind the eye." This is your prediction.

Match: (D) is correct. (A) and (C) are Distortions; pupil dilation is not related to these things in the passage. (B) is another Distortion; paragraph 3 begins by stating "Pupil dilation is also commonly used as part of an eye exam," so pupil dilation can be used in addition to, rather than instead of, eye tracking. (E) is Opposite since the test is described as being used for more than *only* vascular damage.

53. E

Stop: The phrase "most likely to" clues you into the fact that this is another Inference question.

Think: The author only mentions gastroenterologists in one place: paragraph 5. Research this paragraph to make your prediction.

Predict: The paragraph states that an optometrist may refer a patient to a gastroenterologist "when these lesions (on the retina) are accompanied by scarring without a known reason."

Match: (E) is correct. (A) is Out of Scope, as sudden vision changes in healthy patients is not discussed. (B) and (C) are both Faulty Uses of Detail; these symptoms are discussed in paragraphs 7 and 8, respectively, but are not related to anything gastroenterological. Finally, (D) is both Extreme and a Faulty Use of Detail. There is no connection made between patients with diabetes and gastroenterological issues, and *drastic* changes in vision are not mentioned at all.